Calculus
with Trigonometry and Analytic Geometry

Calculus
with Trigonometry and Analytic Geometry

John Saxon   **Frank Wang**

with

Diana Harvey

SAXON PUBLISHERS, INC.

Calculus with Trigonometry and Analytic Geometry

Copyright © 1997 by Saxon Publishers, Inc.

No part of this publication may be reproduced, stored in a retrieval system, or transmitted in any form or by any means, electronic, mechanical, photocopying, recording, or otherwise, without the prior written permission of the publisher.

Printed in the United States of America

ISBN: 0-939798-34-4

Editor and production supervisor: Nancy Warren
Computer-generated line art: Kennebec Laser
Compositor: Black Dot Graphics

Ninth printing: May 1999

Printed on recycled paper

┌─── *Reaching us via the Internet* ───┐
WWW: http://www.saxonpub.com
E-mail: info@saxonpub.com
└──────────────────────────────────────┘

Saxon Publishers, Inc.
2450 John Saxon Blvd.
Norman, OK 73071

Contents

Preface

This book is designed for prospective mathematics majors as well as for students whose primary interests are in engineering, physics, business, or the life sciences. This book contains an intensive review of the topics from algebra, trigonometry, and analytic geometry that are necessary for success in calculus and contains an in-depth coverage of all the topics normally taught in the first two semesters of a three-semester calculus sequence. The book is divided into 117 lessons and is designed to be taught in two semesters with four classes a week or in three quarters with four classes a week.

The authors accept the fact that an understanding of the abstractions of calculus does not occur on an initial encounter, no matter how brilliant the presentation. Thus the book uses an incremental development. An increment of a topic is presented, but the homework problem set contains only one or two problems on the new topic. The rest of the problems in the set are review problems. The emphasis on review in the problem sets permits long-term practice with beginning calculus skills and concepts and also permits long-term practice with higher-level concepts that are often neglected. The first increment of an abstraction is practiced for a number of days before the next increment of the same abstraction is presented. The understanding achieved through practice with the first increment permits understanding of the next increment. This development permits the students to grasp the abstractions of calculus to a degree that has never before been possible. For example, the first lesson on limits is Lesson 16, and at least one carefully designed problem on limits appears in every homework problem set for the next 111 lessons. The first lesson on derivatives is Lesson 27, and one or more problems on derivatives appears in every problem set for next 90 lessons.

There are 30 lessons on limits, continuity, the derivative, differentiability, and related topics. By the end of the book students will have the understanding of the fundamentals of calculus that is necessary for success in upper-division mathematics courses. Bright students attain a level of understanding that is remarkable. Students of every ability level see that calculus is really easy and have no reason to avoid upper-division mathematics courses or mathematically based disciplines.

Since the book is designed to teach and to provide for long-term retention, it differs from other calculus books in major ways. Difficult developments of fundamental theorems are sometimes postponed until the students have used the rules long enough to understand that which they are trying to prove. For example, the rules for finding the derivatives of e^x, $\ln |x|$, $\sin x$, and $\cos x$ are presented in Lesson 37 and are not proved until much later. The product rule for derivatives comes in Lesson 42, so that practice with derivatives of transcendental functions can begin early. The review of trigonometry and the early consideration of the derivatives of transcendental functions allow students to work with transcendental functions for most of the year instead of only in the second semester, when these topics are customarily presented. The differential and the notation of Leibniz are used extensively because of the understanding this approach permits. Functional notation is also given heavy emphasis, and students are encouraged to use both functional notation and the notation of Leibniz interchangeably. Differentiation of composite functions is introduced by using u substitution, and the chain rule is presented later. The techniques of integration are discussed separately in 16 lessons that are spread between Lesson 46 and Lesson 115. Once a particular technique of integration has been introduced, problems requiring the use of this technique appear regularly in the homework problem sets.

The graphical interpretation of the derivative is emphasized, and the definite integral is associated with the sum of the algebraic areas above the x axis and the negative of the areas below the x axis. Applied problems that use the derivative appear regularly in the problem sets from Lesson 56 to Lesson 117, and applied problems that use the definite integral appear in the problem sets from Lesson 57 to Lesson 117.

These are only a few of the major differences between this book and other calculus books. The development of the book is based on the premise that mathematics is learned by doing and that the understanding of abstractions comes from the long-term use of the abstractions. Understanding comes slowly as the concepts are used again and again over a long period of time. Test results from students who have used the manuscript of this book over a two-year period have lead the authors to believe that this type of development in a calculus book will lead to a considerable increase in the number of students who succeed. Students whose preparation is not adequate for success in this book should consider using the book *Geometry–Trigonometry–Algebra III,* or *GTA,* which precedes this book in the Saxon Publishers math series. The *GTA* book was designed as a precalculus book for use in high schools, but the content of the book is at the college level. Advanced topics in trigonometry and algebra are the same whether they are taught in high school or in college.

We thank Dr. Arthur Bernhart, professor emeritus of mathematics of the University of Oklahoma, for his help in the early stages of the development of this book. We thank Dr. Roger Greider of Rose State College for his keen eye and his suggestions as the book progressed from manuscript to final form. We thank Walter Hoffman for his suggestions and his encouragement. We thank Allison Barnes, Dale Fenn, Ben Funk, Dale Norman, Stig Peterson, Gaurav Sharma, and John Young for their help with the many menial tasks that are so important. We thank Bret Crock, Al Ferenz, Barbary Keith, LaWanna McMurrian, Al O'Brian, Elsio Paloni, George Padavick, Franc Rowe, Harry Smith, Charlie Spiegel, and Tom Williamson for using the book in manuscript form and pointing out errors and making suggestions. We thank Diana Harvey for providing a wealth of classroom-tested innovations that work. Foremost among these are the use of u substitution for teaching the derivatives of composite functions and the use of the differential in implicit differentiation. We thank Linda Durington, our able typist, for her typing of the original manuscript and her patience throughout the typing of its many revisions.

John Saxon and Frank Wang
Norman, Oklahoma
June 1988

The real numbers · Fundamental concept review

**A.A
The real
numbers**

The numbers that we naturally use to count make up the set called the *natural numbers,* or the *counting numbers,* or the *positive integers.* We use the symbol $\mathbb{N}$ to represent this set.

$$\mathbb{N} = \{1, 2, 3, \cdots\}$$

The negatives of these numbers are called the *negative integers.* If we include the number zero with the positive and the negative integers, we can designate the set of integers. The symbol $\mathbb{Z}$ is often used to represent this set. This symbol comes from the first letter in the German word *zahlen,* which means "integer."

$$\mathbb{Z} = \{\cdots, -3, -2, -1, 0, 1, 2, 3, \cdots\}$$

Any number that can be written as a quotient (fraction) of integers (division by zero excluded) is called a *rational number.* We use the symbol $\mathbb{Q}$ for quotient to designate this set. The following numbers are rational numbers.

$$0 \quad 4 \quad 35 \quad \frac{-7}{23} \quad \frac{45}{14} \quad \frac{43}{6} \quad \frac{19}{73}$$

Any number that cannot be written as a quotient of integers is called an *irrational number.* We do not have a symbol for this set. Examples of irrational numbers are

$$\sqrt{2} \quad \pi \quad e \quad \sqrt[3]{13} \quad \sqrt[5]{41}$$

The set of *real numbers* includes all members of the set of rational numbers and all members of the set of irrational numbers. We use the symbol $\mathbb{R}$ to represent the set of real numbers. Every natural number is an integer. Every integer is a rational number, and every rational number is a real number. If we use $\subset$ to mean "a subset of," we can write

$$\mathbb{N} \subset \mathbb{Z} \subset \mathbb{Q} \subset \mathbb{R}$$

The real numbers make up an ordered set, for the members of the set of real numbers can be arranged in order, which we indicate when we draw a real number line.

Each point on the number line is associated with a unique number called the *coordinate* of the point. When we graph a number, we place a dot on the number line to indicate the position of the point that has this number as its coordinate. On the number line above we have graphed $\frac{1}{2}$, $1 + \sqrt{2}$, and $-2\frac{1}{2}$.

The order properties of real numbers are listed in the following box.

ORDER PROPERTIES

If x, y, and z represent real numbers, then

1. **Trichotomy.**   Exactly one of the following is true:

$$x < y \qquad \text{or} \qquad x = y \qquad \text{or} \qquad x > y$$

2. **Transitivity.**   If $x < y$ and $y < z$, then $x < z$.
3. **Addition.**   If $x < y$, then $x + z < y + z$.
4. **Multiplication.**   If z is positive and $x < y$, then $xz < yz$.
   If z is negative and $x < y$, then $xz > yz$.

The set of real numbers is closed under the operations of addition and multiplication, since the sum of any two real numbers is a real number and the product of any two real numbers is a real number. The real numbers constitute a *field.* The properties of a field are shown in the following box.

THE FIELD PROPERTIES

If x, y, and z represent real numbers, then

1. **Commutative laws.** $x + y = y + x$ and $xy = yx$.
2. **Associative laws.** $x + (y + z) = (x + y) + z$ and $x(yz) = (xy)z$.
3. **Distributive law.** $x(y + z) = xy + xz$.
4. **Identity elements.**   There are two distinct numbers 0 and 1 satisfying $x + 0 = x$ and $x \cdot 1 = x$.
5. **Inverses.**   Each number x has an additive inverse (also called a *negative*), $-x$, satisfying $x + (-x) = 0$. Also, each number x except 0 has a multiplicative inverse (also called a *reciprocal*), x^{-1}, satisfying $x \cdot x^{-1} = 1$.

A.B
Fundamental concept review

Now we will review some of the fundamental concepts from algebra whose use is required in the calculus problems in this book. Rather than use an expository review, we will review by working problems whose solutions require the applications of the concepts. We assume in each step that no denominator equals zero.

Example A.1   Solve $y = v\left(\dfrac{a}{x} + \dfrac{b}{mc}\right)$ for c.

Solution   We will (1) eliminate parentheses, (2) multiply by the least common multiple of the denominators and simplify, (3) put all terms containing c on one side of the equals sign, and (4) factor c and then divide.

$$y = \frac{va}{x} + \frac{vb}{mc} \qquad \text{eliminated parentheses}$$

$$xmc \cdot y = xmc \cdot \frac{va}{x} + xmc \cdot \frac{vb}{mc} \qquad \text{multiplied by LCM of denominators}$$

$$xmcy = mcva + xvb \qquad \text{simplified}$$

$$xmcy - mcva = xvb \qquad \text{rearranged}$$

$$c(xmy - mva) = xvb \qquad \text{factored}$$

$$c = \frac{xvb}{xmy - mva} \qquad \text{divided}$$

Example A.2   Simplify: (a) $\dfrac{x}{a + \dfrac{m}{1 + \dfrac{c}{d}}}$ (b) $\dfrac{\dfrac{a}{x^2} + \dfrac{b}{x}}{\dfrac{m}{x^2} + \dfrac{k}{xc}}$

Solution   (a)   When there is no equals sign, the denominators cannot be eliminated, but we can write this expression as a simple fraction. We (1) add, (2) simplify, (3) add, and (4) simplify.

(1) $\qquad\qquad\qquad\qquad \dfrac{x}{a + \dfrac{m}{\dfrac{d + c}{d}}}$ added

(2) $\qquad\qquad \longrightarrow \quad \dfrac{x}{a + \dfrac{md}{d + c}}$ simplified

(3) $\qquad\qquad \longrightarrow \quad \dfrac{x}{\dfrac{a(d + c) + md}{d + c}}$ added

(4) $\qquad\qquad \longrightarrow \quad \dfrac{x(d + c)}{a(d + c) + md}$ simplified

(b)   There is no equals sign in this expression, so the denominators cannot be eliminated. We (1) add above and below and (2) simplify.

(1) $\qquad\qquad\qquad \dfrac{\dfrac{a + bx}{x^2}}{\dfrac{mc + kx}{x^2c}}$ added above and below

(2) $\qquad\qquad \longrightarrow \quad \dfrac{c(a + bx)}{mc + kx}$ simplified

Example A.3   Simplify: $\dfrac{4 + \sqrt{2}}{3 - 2\sqrt{2}}$

Solution   We multiply above and below by $3 + 2\sqrt{2}$ and simplify.

$$\frac{4 + \sqrt{2}}{3 - 2\sqrt{2}} \cdot \frac{3 + 2\sqrt{2}}{3 + 2\sqrt{2}} \quad \longrightarrow \quad \frac{16 + 11\sqrt{2}}{9 - 8} = \mathbf{16 + 11\sqrt{2}}$$

Example A.4   Simplify: $3\sqrt{\dfrac{3}{2}} - 4\sqrt{\dfrac{2}{3}} - \sqrt{24}$

Solution   First we use two steps to rationalize the denominator.

$$3\frac{\sqrt{3}}{\sqrt{2}} \cdot \frac{\sqrt{2}}{\sqrt{2}} - 4\frac{\sqrt{2}}{\sqrt{3}} \cdot \frac{\sqrt{3}}{\sqrt{3}} - 2\sqrt{6} \quad \longrightarrow \quad \frac{3\sqrt{6}}{2} - \frac{4\sqrt{6}}{3} - 2\sqrt{6}$$

We finish by adding these three terms, using 6 as a common denominator.

$$\frac{9\sqrt{6}}{6} - \frac{8\sqrt{6}}{6} - \frac{12\sqrt{6}}{6} = \frac{-11\sqrt{6}}{6}$$

Example A.5   Simplify: $2\sqrt{-2}\sqrt{2} + 3i\sqrt{2} - \sqrt{-2}\sqrt{-2}$

Solution   We will use three steps to simplify.

$$2\sqrt{2}i\sqrt{2} + 3i\sqrt{2} - \sqrt{2}i\sqrt{2}i \quad \longrightarrow \quad 4i + 3\sqrt{2}i + 2 \quad \longrightarrow \quad \mathbf{2 + (4 + 3\sqrt{2})i}$$

Example A.6   Simplify: $\dfrac{2i^2 - 3i + 4}{i^2 + 2i - 1}$

Solution   First we simplify above and below. Then we multiply above and below by the conjugate of the denominator.

$$\frac{2 - 3i}{-2 + 2i} = \frac{2 - 3i}{-2 + 2i} \cdot \frac{-2 - 2i}{-2 - 2i} = \frac{-10 + 2i}{8} = \mathbf{\frac{-5}{4} + \frac{1}{4}i}$$

Example A.7   Simplify: (a) $\dfrac{y^{x+3}y^{x/2-1}z^a}{y^{(x-a)/2}z^{(x-a)/3}}$ (b) $x^{3/4}\sqrt{xy}\,x^{1/2}\sqrt[3]{x^4}$

Solution   (a)   First we rearrange and then we add exponents of like bases.

$$y^{x+3+x/2-1-x/2+a/2}z^{a-x/3+a/3} = \mathbf{y^{x+2+a/2}z^{4a/3-x/3}}$$

(b)   Next we replace the radicals with fractional exponents and then add the exponents of like bases.

$$x^{3/4}x^{1/2}y^{1/2}x^{1/2}x^{4/3} \quad \longrightarrow \quad \mathbf{x^{37/12}y^{1/2}}$$

Example A.8   Factor: $4a^{3m+2} - 16a^{3m}$

Solution   If each term is written in factored form, the common factor $4a^{3m}$ can be determined by inspection. Then we factor out the common factor and finish by factoring $a^2 - 4$.

$$(4)a^{3m}a^2 - (4)(4)a^{3m} = 4a^{3m}(a^2 - 4) \qquad \text{common factor}$$

$$= \mathbf{4a^{3m}(a + 2)(a - 2)} \qquad \text{factored } a^2 - 4$$

Example A.9   Factor: (a) $8a^3 - b^3c^6$ (b) $m^3 + x^3y^6$

Solution   (a)   We know that the difference of two cubes $F^3 - S^3$ can be factored as $(F - S)(F^2 + FS + S^2)$, where F is the first term and S is the second term. We note that expression (a) can be written as the difference of the two cubes. Then the factored form can be written by using the factored form of $F^3 - S^3$ as a guide.

$$(2a)^3 - (bc^2)^3 = \mathbf{(2a - bc^2)(4a^2 + 2abc^2 + b^2c^4)}$$

(b)   The sum of two cubes $(F^3 + S^3)$ has $(F + S)$ as one factor. The other factor has F^2 as the first term and S^2 as the third term. The middle term is $-FS$.

$$F^3 + S^3 = (F + S)(F^2 - FS + S^2)$$

The expression $m^3 + x^3y^6$ can be written as the sum of two cubes. We can then write the factored form by inspection by comparing it to the factored form of $F^3 + S^3$.

$$(m)^3 + (xy^2)^3 = \mathbf{(m + xy^2)(m^2 - mxy^2 + x^2y^4)}$$

Example A.10 Evaluate: (a) $\dfrac{14!}{6!11!}$ (b) $\displaystyle\sum_{j=0}^{3} \dfrac{2^j}{j+1}$ (c) $\displaystyle\sum_{i=1}^{4} 3$

Solution (a) $\dfrac{\overset{7}{\cancel{14}} \cdot 13 \cdot \cancel{12} \cdot \cancel{11!}}{6 \cdot 5 \cdot \cancel{4} \cdot \cancel{3} \cdot \cancel{2} \cdot 1 \cdot \cancel{11!}} = \dfrac{7 \cdot 13}{30} = \dfrac{91}{30}$

(b) $\dfrac{2^0}{0+1} + \dfrac{2^1}{1+1} + \dfrac{2^2}{2+1} + \dfrac{2^3}{3+1} = 1 + 1 + \dfrac{4}{3} + 2 = \dfrac{16}{3}$

(c) $3 + 3 + 3 + 3 = \mathbf{12}$

Problem set A Problem sets in this book will end with two or three concept review questions.

Problems that compare the values of quantities come in many forms and can be used to provide practice in mathematical reasoning. In these problems, a statement will be made about two quantities A and B. The correct answer is A if quantity A is greater and is B if quantity B is greater. The correct answer is C if the quantities are equal and is D if insufficient information is provided to determine which quantity is greater.

1. Compare: A. $7\dfrac{1}{5}$ ft^2 B. 0.8 yd^2

2. If $x = t$, compare: A. $7(2t - 2x)$ B. $-6(3t - 3x)$

3. If $4 < x < 9$ and $2 < y < 14$, compare: A. x B. y

4. If a is the average of 3 and 6, compare: A. $3a$ B. $a + 6$

5. Solve for R_1: $\dfrac{m}{x} = y\left(\dfrac{1}{R_1} + \dfrac{a}{R_2}\right)$

Simplify:

6. $a + \dfrac{1}{a + \dfrac{1}{a}}$

7. $\dfrac{1}{a + \dfrac{1}{x + \dfrac{1}{m}}}$

8. $\dfrac{x^2 y}{1 + m^2} + \dfrac{x}{y}$

9. $\dfrac{4 - 3\sqrt{2}}{8 - \sqrt{2}}$

10. $3\sqrt{-4} + 2\sqrt{4} - \sqrt{-9}$

11. $-i^2 - 4i^3 + 2\sqrt{-2}\sqrt{-2}$

12. $\dfrac{3 + 2i}{4 - i}$

13. $\dfrac{x^a y^{a+b}}{x^{-a/2} y^{b-1}}$

14. $\dfrac{m^{x+2} b^{x-2}}{m^{2x/3} b^{-3x/2}}$

15. $\sqrt{xy}\, x^{2/3} y^{-3/2}$

16. Solve: $\begin{cases} 2x + 3y = -4 \\ x - 2z = -3 \\ 2y - z = -6 \end{cases}$

Factor:

17. $16a^{4m+3} - 8a^{2m+3}$

18. $a^2 b^{2x+2} - ab^{2x+1}$

19. $a^6 - 27b^3 c^3$

20. $x^3 y^6 + 8m^{12}$

Evaluate:

21. $\dfrac{12!}{8!4!}$ **22.** $\displaystyle\sum_{i=1}^{3} 4$ **23.** $\displaystyle\sum_{m=0}^{3} \dfrac{3^m}{m+1}$

REVIEW LESSON B *More concept review · Geometry review*

B.A
More concept review

We continue our review of fundamental concepts.

Example B.1   Find the coordinates of the point halfway between $(-4, 7)$ and $(13, 5)$.

Solution   The x coordinate of the midpoint is the average of the x coordinates and the y coordinate of the midpoint is the average of the y coordinates.

$$x_m = \frac{-4 + 13}{2} = \frac{9}{2} \qquad y_m = \frac{7 + 5}{2} = 6$$

Example B.2   Find the distance between $(4, 3)$ and $(-2, -1)$.

Solution   First we graph the points. The distance between the points is found by using the distance formula, which is a statement of the Pythagorean theorem.

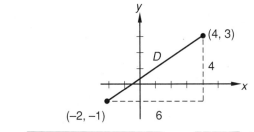

$$D = \sqrt{(x_1 - x_2)^2 + (y_1 - y_2)^2} = \sqrt{6^2 + 4^2} = \sqrt{52} = 2\sqrt{13}$$

Example B.3   Write the slope-intercept form of the equation of the line through $(-4, 2)$ that is perpendicular to $-2x + 3y + 1 = 0$.

Solution   First we find the slope of the given line. The slope of a line in general form, or $ax + by + c = 0$, is $-a/b$, or 2/3. Another way to find the slope is to rewrite the equation in slope-intercept form in which the coefficient of x is the slope.

$$y = \frac{2}{3}x - \frac{1}{3}$$

The line perpendicular to this line has a slope of $-\frac{3}{2}$. If we use $-\frac{3}{2}$ as the slope and use -4 and 2 for x and y, we can solve for b.

$$2 = -\frac{3}{2}(-4) + b \quad \longrightarrow \quad b = -4$$

Thus, we have
$$y = -\frac{3}{2}x - 4$$

Example B.4   Use the point-slope form of the equation of a line to write the slope-intercept form of the equation of the line which passes through $(-2, 4)$ and has a slope of $-\frac{2}{3}$.

Solution   We begin with the point-slope form and substitute.

$$(y - y_1) = m(x - x_1) \quad \longrightarrow \quad y - (4) = -\frac{2}{3}[x - (-2)] \qquad \text{substituted}$$

$$3y - 12 = -2x - 4 \quad \longrightarrow \quad y = -\frac{2}{3}x + \frac{8}{3} \qquad \text{rearranged}$$

Example B.5   Write the equation $y = \frac{2}{3}x - \frac{1}{4}$ in double-intercept form.

Solution   The double-intercept form is

$$\frac{x}{a} + \frac{y}{b} = 1$$

We will rearrange the equation and divide by the constant term.

$$\frac{2}{3}x - y = \frac{1}{4} \qquad \text{rearranged}$$

$$\frac{\frac{2}{3}x}{\frac{1}{4}} + \frac{y}{-\frac{1}{4}} = 1 \qquad \text{divided by constant}$$

We simplify to get

$$\frac{x}{\frac{3}{8}} + \frac{y}{-\frac{1}{4}} = 1$$

From this we see that when $y = 0$, then $x = \frac{3}{8}$, so the x intercept is $\frac{3}{8}$. When $x = 0$, $y = -\frac{1}{4}$, so the y intercept is $-\frac{1}{4}$.

Example B.6   Solve $-2x^2 + 2x - 7 = 0$ by completing the square.

Solution   We will use five steps.

(1) $\qquad -2(x^2 - x \quad\;\;) = 7 \qquad\qquad$ factored

(2) $\qquad -2\left(x^2 - x + \frac{1}{4}\right) = 7 - \frac{1}{2} \qquad$ completed the square

(3) $\qquad \left(x - \frac{1}{2}\right)^2 = \frac{-13}{4} \qquad\qquad$ simplified

(4) $\qquad x - \frac{1}{2} = \pm\sqrt{\frac{-13}{4}} \qquad\qquad$ square root

(5) $\qquad x = \frac{1}{2} \pm \frac{\sqrt{13}}{2}i \qquad\qquad$ solved

Example B.7   Solve $-2x^2 + 3x - 7 = 0$ by using the quadratic formula.

Solution $x = \dfrac{-b \pm \sqrt{b^2 - 4ac}}{2a} \quad \longrightarrow \quad x = \dfrac{-3 \pm \sqrt{9 - (4)(-2)(-7)}}{-4}$

$$= \frac{3}{4} \pm \frac{1}{4} \sqrt{47}i$$

Example B.8   Divide $x^3 - y^3$ by $x - y$.

Solution

$$
\begin{array}{r}
x^2 + xy\ + y^2 \\
x - y \overline{\smash{\big)}\ x^3 \qquad\qquad - y^3} \\
\underline{x^3 - x^2y } \\
x^2y \\
\underline{x^2y - xy^2 } \\
xy^2 - y^3 \\
\underline{xy^2 - y^3}
\end{array}
$$

Example B.9   Solve: $\begin{cases} x^2 + y^2 = 9 \\ y - x = 1 \end{cases}$

Solution   We will (1) solve the bottom equation for y, (2) square both sides, and (3) substitute for y^2 in the top equation.

(1) $y = x + 1$ solved bottom equation for y

(2) $y^2 = x^2 + 2x + 1$ squared both sides

(3) $x^2 + (x^2 + 2x + 1) = 9$ substituted for y^2 in top equation

Now we (4) simplify and (5) use the quadratic formula to solve for x.

(4) $x^2 + x - 4 = 0$ simplified

$$x = \frac{-1 \pm \sqrt{1 - 4(1)(-4)}}{2}$$

(5) $x = -\dfrac{1}{2} \pm \dfrac{\sqrt{17}}{2}$ solved by using quadratic formula

We finish by using each of the values of x to find the corresponding values of y by substituting for x in the equation $y = x + 1$.

$$y = \left(\frac{-1}{2} + \frac{\sqrt{17}}{2}\right) + 1 \qquad y = \left(\frac{-1}{2} - \frac{\sqrt{17}}{2}\right) + 1 \qquad \text{substituted}$$

$$y = \frac{1}{2} + \frac{\sqrt{17}}{2} \qquad\qquad y = \frac{1}{2} - \frac{\sqrt{17}}{2} \qquad\qquad \text{simplified}$$

Thus, the ordered pairs of x and y that satisfy the given system are

$$\left(\frac{-1}{2} + \frac{\sqrt{17}}{2}, \frac{1}{2} + \frac{\sqrt{17}}{2}\right) \quad \text{and} \quad \left(\frac{-1}{2} - \frac{\sqrt{17}}{2}, \frac{1}{2} - \frac{\sqrt{17}}{2}\right)$$

B.B
Geometry review

We tend to forget some of the fundamentals of geometry because we do not use them often enough. We will review some of these concepts in this lesson because the fundamental concepts of geometry are important in calculus. Practice of the concepts will be provided by the concept review problems at the end of each problem set.

If two parallel lines are cut by a transversal, eight angles are formed. If the transversal is perpendicular to the parallel lines, all eight angles are equal (have equal measures). If the transversal is not perpendicular to the lines, the four small angles are equal and the four large angles are equal, as we show below on the left. In this book, we will use arrowheads to indicate that lines are parallel, as we show in the following figure. Vertical angles are equal, as we show in the right-hand figure.

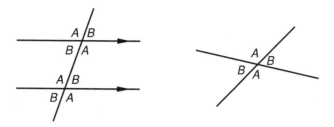

The sum of the angles in a triangle equals 180°, and an exterior angle of a triangle equals the sum of the remote interior angles, as shown in the following figure.

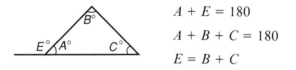

$$A + E = 180$$
$$A + B + C = 180$$
$$E = B + C$$

We define the measure of an arc of a circle to be equal to the measure of the central angle. Thus, in the circle on the left, the measure of the arc is x and the measure of the central angle is also x.

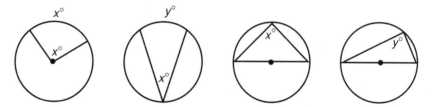

The measure of an angle inscribed in a circle is half the measure of the intercepted arc. Thus, in the second figure, x equals $\frac{1}{2}y$, and in the two figures on the right, x and y are both right angles because they both intercept an arc of 180°.

Intersecting chords in a circle have interesting properties. The product of the lengths of the two segments of one chord equals the product of the lengths of the two segments of the other chord, as we show below in the figure on the left. Can you prove that this is true? It's a simple proof.

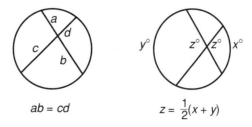

$$ab = cd \qquad\qquad z = \frac{1}{2}(x + y)$$

In the figure on the right, the measure of each of the vertical angles, z, formed by the intersecting chords equals half the sum of the intercepted arcs y and x.

A tangent to a circle is a straight line that touches the circle in exactly one point. As we show on the left below, tangents to a circle are perpendicular to the radius at the point of tangency. Also, the distances from a point outside the circle to two points of tangency are equal.

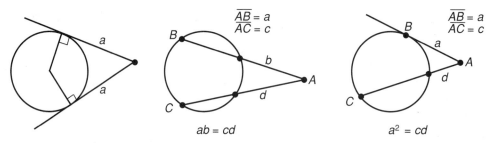

A secant to a circle is a line that intersects the circle at two points. If two secants are drawn to a circle from a point outside the circle as shown in the center figure, the product of the length of one entire secant segment times the length of its external part equals the product of the length of the other entire secant segment times the length of its external part. In the figure on the right above, the product of the length of the entire secant segment and the external secant segment equals the square of the length of the tangent segment.

When two tangents, two secants, or a secant and a tangent are drawn from a point outside the circle, the angle at the external point equals half the difference in the intercepted arcs.

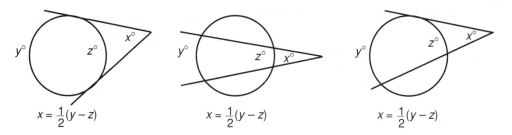

B.C
Distance between a point and a line

To find the distance between a point and a line, we can use a three-step procedure or we can develop a formula whose use will yield the desired numerical result. To review the three-step procedure, we will find the distance between $y = \frac{1}{2}x + 1$ and the point $(-3, 5)$. The first step is to find the equation of the line perpendicular to $y = \frac{1}{2}x + 1$ that passes through $(-3, 5)$. The slope of the line is -2, and we can use -3 for x, use 5 for y, and solve for b.

$$y = mx + b \quad \longrightarrow \quad 5 = -2(-3) + b \quad \longrightarrow \quad b = -1$$

Thus the equation of the perpendicular line is

$$y = -2x - 1$$

The second step is to use substitution to find the point of intersection of the lines.

$$y = \frac{1}{2}x + 1 \qquad \text{original equation}$$

$$-2x - 1 = \frac{1}{2}x + 1 \qquad \text{substituted}$$

$$x = -\frac{4}{5} = -0.8 \qquad \text{solved}$$

Now we have the x coordinate of the point of intersection. We use $-\frac{4}{5}$ for x in the original equation and solve for the y coordinate of the point of intersection.

$$y = \frac{1}{2}\left(-\frac{4}{5}\right) + 1 = \frac{3}{5} = 0.6$$

Next we use the distance formula to find the distance between $(-3, 5)$ and $(-0.8, 0.6)$. We use the decimal form of the numbers so we can use a calculator.

$$D = \sqrt{[-3 - (-0.8)]^2 + (5 - 0.6)^2}$$
$$= \sqrt{(-2.2)^2 + (4.4)^2}$$
$$= 4.92$$

Later lessons include an in-depth review of topics from trigonometry. Developing the formula for the distance from a point to a line requires only that we remember the definitions of $\sin\theta$ and $\tan\theta$ and that we remember that the slope of a line equals the tangent of the angle that the line makes with the horizontal. We will do the development in four steps. The first step is to develop an expression for D, the vertical distance from a point on the line $Ax + By + C = 0$ to a point (x_1, y_1) not on the line.

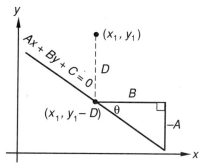

The slope of the line is $-A/B$ and is the tangent of the angle θ in the triangle shown. The x coordinate of the point on the line is x_1, and the y coordinate is $y_1 - D$. The coordinates of this point must satisfy the equation of the line. If we substitute x_1 for x and $y_1 - D$ for y and solve for D, we get

$$A(x_1) + B(y_1 - D) + C = 0 \qquad\qquad \text{substituted}$$
$$Ax_1 + By_1 - DB + C = 0 \qquad\qquad \text{multiplied}$$
(a) $$D = \frac{Ax_1 + By_1 + C}{B} \qquad\qquad \text{solved}$$

Now on the same figure we draw a perpendicular segment from (x_1, y_1) to the line. The length of this segment is d, the distance we wish to find. The second step is to define d in terms of D and $\sin\alpha$.

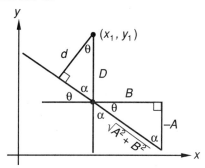

We know that the length of the hypotenuse in the lower triangle is $\sqrt{A^2 + B^2}$. Thus in the lower triangle we can solve for $\sin\alpha$ and get

(b) $\sin \alpha = \dfrac{B}{\sqrt{A^2 + B^2}}$

In the upper triangle we can solve for d and get

(c) $\sin \alpha = \dfrac{d}{D} \quad \longrightarrow \quad d = D \sin \alpha$

Finally we use equation (a) to substitute for D and equation (b) to substitute for $\sin \alpha$ in equation (c), and we get

$$d = \frac{Ax_1 + By_1 + C}{B} \cdot \frac{B}{\sqrt{A^2 + B^2}} = \frac{Ax_1 + By_1 + C}{\sqrt{A^2 + B^2}}$$

For this development we assumed that point (x_1, y_1) was above the line. If (x_1, y_1) is below the line, this formula will give us a negative answer. Since $\sqrt{A^2 + B^2}$ is always positive, we can ensure a positive result for d by using absolute value notation in the numerator. Thus we have finally

$$d = \frac{|Ax_1 + By_1 + C|}{\sqrt{A^2 + B^2}}$$

Example B.10   Find the distance between the point $(1, 4)$ and the line $y = \frac{2}{3}x - 5$.

Solution   To use the formula for the distance between a point and a line, the equation of the line must be written in general form $Ax + By + C = 0$. We do this and get

GENERAL FORM   FORMULA

$$2x - 3y - 15 = 0 \qquad d = \frac{|Ax_1 + By_1 + C|}{\sqrt{A^2 + B^2}}$$

We see that in our equation $A = 2$ and $B = -3$. The values of x_1 and y_1 are 1 and 4, respectively, so we have

$$\frac{|2(1) + (-3)(4) - 15|}{\sqrt{2^2 + (-3)^2}} = \frac{|-25|}{\sqrt{13}} = \frac{25}{\sqrt{13}}$$

Problem set B   1.   Find the distance from the midpoint of the segment joining $(4, 2)$ and $(10, -2)$ to the point $(6, 8)$.

2.   Find y.

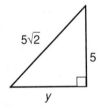

3.   Find the equation of the line that is perpendicular to the line $4y + 3x - 2 = 0$ and that passes through the point $(1, -1)$.

4.   Write the double-intercept form of the linear equation whose general form is $2x - 3y + 2 = 0$.

Solve by completing the square:

5. $x^2 - 3x + 4 = 7$ 6. $2x^2 = x + 3$

7.   Solve $3x^2 - x + 7 = 0$ by using the quadratic formula.

8.   Divide $2x^3 - 3x + 5$ by $x - 3$.   9.   Solve: $\begin{cases} xy = -4 \\ y = -x - 2 \end{cases}$

10. Solve for x: $k^2 = \dfrac{1}{bc}\left(\dfrac{x}{3} - \dfrac{6y}{d}\right)$

Simplify:

11. $\dfrac{ax}{b + \dfrac{c}{d + \dfrac{m}{t}}}$

12. $\dfrac{3 + 2i^2 - 2i}{2 - i^4 - 3i}$

13. $3\sqrt{\dfrac{2}{5}} - 4\sqrt{\dfrac{5}{2}} + 3\sqrt{40}$

14. $\dfrac{y^{a-2}z^{4a}}{y^{-2a-1}z^{a/3+2}}$

15. $\sqrt{x^3 y^3}\, y^{1/3} x^{2/3}$

16.   Solve: $\begin{cases} x + y + z = 4 \\ 2x - y - z = -1 \\ x - y + z = 0 \end{cases}$

Factor:

17. $14x^{4b-2} - 7x^{2b}$

18. $x^3 y^6 - 8x^6 y^{12}$

Evaluate:

19. $\dfrac{8!}{5!2!}$

20. $\displaystyle\sum_{n=1}^{3} (n^2 - 2)$

21. $\displaystyle\sum_{j=-2}^{1} \dfrac{2j - 3}{3}$

CONCEPT REVIEW   **22.**   If $x^2 = y^2$, then compare: *A.* x *B.* y

Find x in each of the following figures.

23.

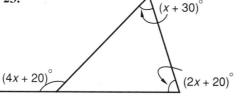

$(x + 30)^\circ$

$(4x + 20)^\circ$

$(2x + 20)^\circ$

24.

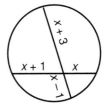

$x + 3$

$x + 1$ x

$x - 1$

25. $m\overset{\frown}{AB} = (3x + 5)^\circ$
     $m\overset{\frown}{CD} = (2x - 20)^\circ$

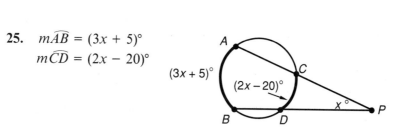

$(3x + 5)^\circ$

$(2x - 20)^\circ$

x°

LESSON 1 *Deductive reasoning · The contrapositive · Converse and inverse*

1.A
Deductive reasoning

Inductive reasoning is the process of determining or formulating a general rule by extrapolating from a number of individual observations or by just guessing. This most imprecise process produces rules that may or may not be true. A child who goes fishing in a pond and catches only fish that have scales might induce that all the fish in that pond have scales. This would be a guess at best because the child has not seen every fish in the pond and some might be catfish, a fish that does not have scales. **Deductive reasoning** is quite different. Deductive reasoning is the process of applying a given rule logically so that a mistake is not made in the application of the rule. Deductive reasoning does not consider the truth or falsity of the rule being applied.

The ancient Greeks formalized the study of logic with their use of **syllogisms** in their investigation of deductive reasoning. A *syllogism* is a formal reasoning process in which a conclusion is inferred from two statements called *premises.* We will look at syllogisms in which the premises are called *categorical propositions* because they place things in categories. We will concentrate on premises called *universal affirmatives.* These premises affirm that all members of a certain set possess a certain property. Such a premise is often called the *major premise.* The other premise is often called the *minor premise* and identifies a member of this set. The conclusion follows that this member has the property possessed by all the members of the set. We demonstrate by using one of the oldest syllogisms known.

All men are mortal.   (Major premise)

This statement establishes mortality as a property possessed by every member of the set of all men.

Aristotle is a man.   (Minor premise)

This statement identifies Aristotle as a member of the set of all men.

Aristotle is mortal.   (Conclusion)

This conclusion is a logical consequence because if Aristotle is a member of the set of all men, then he possesses the properties possessed by every member of this set.

We use this type of reasoning in geometric proofs. Observe:

The sum of the exterior angles of a convex polygon is 360°.

Triangle *ABC* is a convex polygon.

The sum of the exterior angles of triangle *ABC* is 360°.

The major premise identifies a property of every member of the set of convex polygons. The minor premise identifies triangle *ABC* as a member of the set of convex polygons. Thus, triangle *ABC* has all the properties possessed by every member of the set of convex polygons. The entire three-step process is called an **argument. In our investigation of syllogistic reasoning we will concentrate on the argument and will not consider the truth or falsity of the major premise.** Consider the following syllogism:

All frogs are green.   (Major premise)

Henry is a frog.   (Minor premise)

Henry is green.   (Conclusion)

The argument is a valid argument because the major premise states a property possessed by all frogs (they are green), and the minor premise identifies Henry as a member of the set of all frogs. The major premise is false because some frogs are not green and thus Henry might be brown or red or some other color. However, because the argument is a valid argument, we will say that the conclusion is a valid conclusion. **This does not mean that the conclusion is true. It means only that the argument is valid.**

The conclusion in the following syllogism is invalid because the argument is faulty, as the minor premise does not identify a member of the set defined by the major premise.

If it rains, I will go to town.   (Major premise)

It did not rain.   (Minor premise)

I did not go to town.   (Conclusion)

The major premise identifies an action I will take on each member of the set of days on which rain occurs. It makes no statement about what I will do on days on which there is no rain. Thus, any conclusion about what happens on dry days would be invalid. The day in question is not a member of the set of rainy days and may or may not possess the property in question.

Example 1.1   Is the following argument a valid argument?

All normal dogs have four legs.

That dog has four legs.

That dog is a normal dog.

Solution   **The argument is invalid.** The set described is the set of normal dogs. For a valid argument, the minor premise should have stated that a particular dog was a normal dog.

Example 1.2   Is the following argument valid?

All boys are good.

That child is a good child.

That child is a boy.

Solution   **Invalid.** The major premise makes a statement about the set of all boys. The minor premise talks about a member of the set of good children. To be a valid argument, the minor premise would have to identify a member of the set of all boys.

Example 1.3   Is the following argument a valid argument?

All chickens have three legs.

Henny Penny is a chicken.

Henny Penny has three legs.

Solution   **Valid.** All chickens do not have three legs, but we still say that the argument is a valid argument. This does not mean that the conclusion is true. It means that the argument is valid because the major premise identifies a property of the set of all chickens and the minor premise identifies Henny Penny as a member of the set of all chickens.

1.B
The contrapositive

The major premise either uses or implies an if-then statement that has two parts called the **hypothesis** and the **conclusion.** The hypothesis begins with the word *if* and the conclusion begins with the word *then*. When the words *if* and *then* are not written, the premise can be rewritten so that these words are used. For example, the major premise "Rabbits are fast runners" can be written as an if-then statement by writing: If an animal is a rabbit, then the animal is a fast runner.

HYPOTHESIS	CONCLUSION
If an animal is a rabbit,	then the animal is a fast runner

We can make exactly the same statement another way by turning the statement around and using negatives. We call this alternate statement of the same premise the *contrapositive.* Two steps are necessary to form the contrapositive of a premise. The first step is to replace the *if statement* with the negative of the *then statement*. The second step is to replace the *then statement* with the negative of the *if statement*. Thus, the contrapositive of this premise is:

If an animal is not a fast runner, then the animal is not a rabbit.

If a premise is true, its contrapositive is also true. If a premise is false, its contrapositive is also false. This is easy to see if we use a Venn diagram for this example.

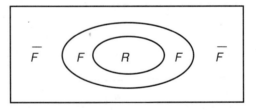

We place all rabbits (R) inside the smaller curve and all fast animals (F) inside the larger curve. This puts all animals who are not fast ($\overline{F}$) outside the larger curve. From this we can see that if an animal is a rabbit, it is also inside the F curve and is a fast runner. Also, we see that if an animal is not a fast runner, it is outside the larger curve and thus cannot be a rabbit.

Example 1.4   Is the following argument valid?

All nonathletes are vegetarians.	(Major premise)
Jim is a nonvegetarian.	(Minor premise)
Jim is an athlete.	(Conclusion)

Solution   If we write the contrapositive of the major premise, we get:

> All nonvegetarians are athletes.   (Major premise)
>
> Jim is a nonvegetarian.   (Minor premise)
>
> Jim is an athlete.   (Conclusion)

This is a **valid argument,** so the original argument is also valid. The conclusion is not necessarily true, but the argument is valid.

1.C
Converse and inverse

We will call the initial statement of a premise the ***conditional.*** If we turn the conditional around and use negatives, we form the **contrapositive,** which allows us to make the conditional statement another way. If we turn the conditional statement around and do not use negatives, we do not make the same statement. This new statement is called the ***converse.*** If we wish, we can turn the converse around and use negatives to make the converse statement another way. We call this form the ***inverse.***

The confusion that results from these four forms has delighted logicians since the time of the ancient Greeks. There are two ways in which the statements in the hypothesis and the conclusion can be written, and each of these statements can be made in an alternative form. We note that the truth or falsity of the converse does not depend on the truth or falsity of the conditional.

> Conditional: If an animal is a rabbit, then the animal is a fast runner. *True.*
>
> Converse: If an animal is a fast runner, then the animal is a rabbit. *False.*

The conditional is true, but the converse is false. If the conditional is true, its partner, the contrapositive, will be true. If the converse is false, its partner, the inverse, will be false. It is helpful to think of these equivalent statements in pairs, as we show in the accompanying table.

	if	*then*	*if-then*
Conditional Contrapositive	rabbit not fast	fast not rabbit	$P \longrightarrow Q$ $\overline{Q} \longrightarrow \overline{P}$
Converse Inverse	fast not rabbit	rabbit not fast	$Q \longrightarrow P$ $\overline{P} \longrightarrow \overline{Q}$

On the right we use P and Q to represent the original hypothesis and conclusion. We indicate the negation of P, or "not P," by writing $\overline{P}$, and we write "not Q" as $\overline{Q}$. The paired statements in the above table use different words to say the same thing. If one statement is true, the other is true. If one statement is false, the other is false. We note that the converse is a simple reversal of P and Q and that the inverse is the converse stated using negations.

The converse and inverse are important in mathematics because sometimes they are true and sometimes they are not true. For example, consider the statements about polygons listed in the following table.

	if	*then*	*if-then*	
Conditional Contrapositive	a square not a quadrilateral	a quadrilateral not a square	$P \longrightarrow Q$ $\overline{Q} \longrightarrow \overline{P}$	true true
Converse Inverse	a quadrilateral not a square	a square not a quadrilateral	$Q \longrightarrow P$ $\overline{P} \longrightarrow \overline{Q}$	false false

In the example above the converse and inverse are false.

Now consider these statements about the lengths of sides and the measures of the angles opposite these sides in a triangle.

	if	*then*	*if-then*	
Conditional Contrapositive	Sides have equal lengths Angles do not have equal measures	Angles have equal measures Sides do not have equal lengths	$P \longrightarrow Q$ $\overline{Q} \longrightarrow \overline{P}$	true true
Converse Inverse	Angles have equal measures Sides do not have equal lengths	Sides have equal length Angles do not have equal measures	$Q \longrightarrow P$ $\overline{P} \longrightarrow \overline{Q}$	true true

Mathematical statements in which all four forms are true are called **if and only if statements,** and the abbreviation **iff** is often used to mean *if and only if.* When we use the words *if and only if,* we are making two statements that symbolically have arrowheads going in both directions.

iff means both $P \longleftrightarrow Q$ and $\overline{P} \longleftrightarrow \overline{Q}$

Problem set 1   Are following arguments valid or invalid?

1. All gurus are Asian.
   Frank is a guru.

   Therefore, Frank is Asian.

2. All gurus are Asian.
   Alfred is Asian.

   Therefore, Alfred is a guru.

3. State the contrapositive of the following conditional statement: If the light is on, then the switch is on.

4. Johnny was told that p leads to q. He walked down the hall and saw "not q." Did the presence of "not q" imply p or "not p" or imply nothing at all? Explain.

5. Find the distance from the point (6, 2) to the midpoint of the line segment whose endpoints are (7, 2) and (−3, 8).

6. Write the slope-intercept form of the equation of the line which passes through the point (2, 2) and which is perpendicular to the line $2y - x - 1 = 0$.

7. Write the double-intercept form of the equation of the line which passes through the points (1, 3) and (−1, 7).

8. Complete the square to rewrite $x^2 = -6x - 13$ in the form $(x + a)^2 + b = 0$, where a and b are constants.

9. Use the quadratic formula to find all the values of x which make $x^2 - 3x + 7$ equal to zero.

10. Solve: $\begin{cases} 2y^2 - x^2 = 1 \\ y + 1 = x \end{cases}$

11. Divide $x^3 - 13x^2 + 10x - 8$ by $x - 1$.

12. Solve for R_1: $\dfrac{m + b}{c} = \dfrac{1}{k}\left(\dfrac{a}{R_1} + \dfrac{b}{R_2}\right)$

Simplify:

13. $\dfrac{4 - 2\sqrt{3}}{2 - \sqrt{3}}$

14. $\dfrac{3i^2 + 2i + 4}{3i - 7 + 2i}$

15. $5\sqrt{\dfrac{3}{7}} - 2\sqrt{\dfrac{7}{3}} + \sqrt{84}$

16. $\sqrt{x^3 y^5}\; y^{1/4} x^{3/2}$

17. $\dfrac{1}{1 + \dfrac{1}{1 + \dfrac{1}{1 + \frac{1}{2}}}}$

18. $\dfrac{m}{x + \dfrac{p}{1 - \frac{y}{m}}}$

Factor:

19. $a^3 b^3 - 8x^6 y^9$

20. $2x^3 + 3x^2 - 2x$

21. Simplify: $\dfrac{a^2 - b^2}{a + b}$

22. Evaluate: $\displaystyle\sum_{j=1}^{4} (j^2 - 2j)$

23. Evaluate: $\dfrac{41!}{38!\,3!}$

CONCEPT REVIEW **24.** If $x > y$, then compare: $A.\ \dfrac{1}{x}$ $B.\ \dfrac{1}{y}$

Find the value of x in each of the following figures:

25.

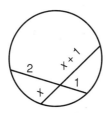

26.

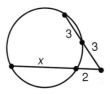

27. Solve for x and y.

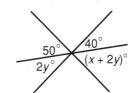

LESSON 2 *Radian measure of angles · Trigonometric ratios · Four quadrant signs · Simplifying trigonometric expressions*

2.A
Radian measure of angles

If an arc of a circle has the same length as a radius of the circle, the central angle is said to measure 1 radian.

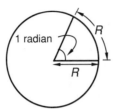  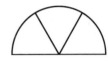

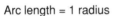

Arc length = 1 radius   Grandmother's pie   A mathematical π

The circumference of a circle measures 2π radians. Thus half a circle measures only π radians, or 180°, as we show above in the figure on the right. Therefore, the unit multipliers for radian to degree conversions are

$$\frac{\pi \text{ radians}}{180 \text{ degrees}} \quad \text{and} \quad \frac{180 \text{ degrees}}{\pi \text{ radians}}$$

Example 2.1   The little wheel rolled merrily down the hill at 400 rpm (revolutions per minute). If the radius of the wheel was 6 centimeters, what was the linear velocity of the wheel in yards per second?

Solution   The linear velocity of the wheel equals the radius of the wheel times the angular velocity of the wheel in radians per unit time, or $v = r\omega$. We will use unit multipliers to convert revolutions to radians, minutes to seconds, and centimeters to inches.

$$v = r\omega$$

$$v = (6 \text{ cm})\left(400 \ \frac{\text{rev}}{\text{min}}\right)\left(\frac{1 \text{ in}}{2.54 \text{ cm}}\right)\left(\frac{1 \text{ yd}}{36 \text{ in}}\right)\left(\frac{2\pi \text{ rad}}{1 \text{ rev}}\right)\left(\frac{1 \text{ min}}{60 \text{ sec}}\right)$$

$$v = \frac{6(400)(2\pi) \text{ yd}}{2.54(36)(60) \text{ sec}}$$

A calculator may be used to evaluate this expression if a numerical answer is desired. Note that radians are dimensionless units and the notation can be dropped where its use is not helpful.

2.B
Trigonometric ratios

Most people find a mnemonic helpful in remembering the definitions of the trigonometric ratios that we call the *sine, cosine,* and *tangent*. The letters which make up the pseudo Native American word **Soh Cah Toa** or the first letters in the sentence **O**scar **H**ad **A** **H**old **O**n **A**rthur can be used to help us remember the definitions shown here.

$$\text{Sine} = \frac{\text{Opposite}}{\text{Hypotenuse}} \qquad \text{Cosine} = \frac{\text{Adjacent}}{\text{Hypotenuse}} \qquad \text{Tangent} = \frac{\text{Opposite}}{\text{Adjacent}}$$

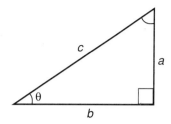

$$\sin \theta = \frac{a}{c} \qquad \cos \theta = \frac{b}{c} \qquad \tan \theta = \frac{a}{b}$$

We recall that the tangent of an angle can be expressed in terms of the sine of the angle and the cosine of the angle.

$$\tan \theta = \frac{\sin \theta}{\cos \theta}$$

The reciprocal functions of the sine, cosine, and tangent are the cosecant, secant, and cotangent, respectively, as we show here:

$$\csc \theta = \frac{1}{\sin \theta} \qquad \sec \theta = \frac{1}{\cos \theta} \qquad \cot \theta = \frac{1}{\tan \theta}$$

Mathematics books use the trigonometric functions of $\pi/3$, $\pi/4$, and $\pi/6$ (60°, 45°, and 30°, respectively) for practice problems because the exact values of the functions of these angles can be determined quickly by using the two triangles shown here.

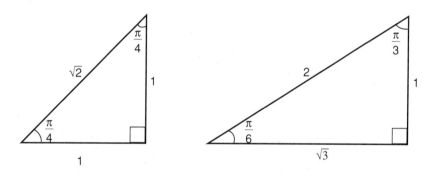

Example 2.2   Evaluate: $\sin^2 \frac{\pi}{3} - \tan \frac{\pi}{4} + \cos \frac{\pi}{6}$

Solution   We use the triangles to find $\sin \frac{\pi}{3}$, $\tan \frac{\pi}{4}$, and $\cos \frac{\pi}{6}$.

$$\sin^2 \frac{\pi}{3} - \tan \frac{\pi}{4} + \cos \frac{\pi}{6} = \left(\frac{\sqrt{3}}{2} \right)^2 - 1 + \frac{\sqrt{3}}{2} \qquad \text{substituted}$$

$$= \frac{3}{4} - 1 + \frac{\sqrt{3}}{2} \qquad \text{squared}$$

$$= -\frac{1}{4} + \frac{\sqrt{3}}{2} \qquad \text{simplified}$$

$$= \frac{-1 + 2\sqrt{3}}{4} \qquad \text{added}$$

Example 2.3   Evaluate: $\sec 30° + \csc \dfrac{\pi}{6}$

Solution   We begin by rewriting $\sec 30°$ and $\csc \dfrac{\pi}{6}$ in terms of sine and cosine.

$$\sec 30° = \frac{1}{\cos 30°} \qquad \csc \frac{\pi}{6} = \frac{1}{\sin \dfrac{\pi}{6}} \qquad \text{definition}$$

$$\sec 30° + \csc \frac{\pi}{6} = \frac{1}{\dfrac{\sqrt{3}}{2}} + \frac{1}{\dfrac{1}{2}} \qquad \text{substituted}$$

$$= \frac{2}{\sqrt{3}} + 2 \qquad \text{simplified}$$

$$= \frac{2\sqrt{3} + 6}{3} \qquad \text{added}$$

2.C
Four quadrant signs

The signs of the trigonometric functions of an angle in the first quadrant are all positive. The signs of these functions in the other four quadrants can be determined by drawing triangles in each of the quadrants as we show here. The hypotenuse is always positive.

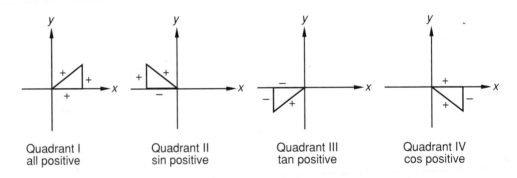

Quadrant I   Quadrant II   Quadrant III   Quadrant IV
all positive   sin positive   tan positive   cos positive

The three basic trigonometric functions are positive in the first quadrant, and only one of these functions is positive in each of the other three quadrants. The first letters of the sentence

All Students Take Calculus

can be used to help us remember that **A**ll three functions are positive in the first quadrant, the **S**ine is positive in the second quadrant, the **T**angent is positive in the third quadrant, and the **C**osine is positive in the fourth quadrant. Functions of angles greater than 360° or 2π radians can be reduced to functions of angles less than 360° or 2π radians by subtracting multiples of 360° or 2π from the angle. Thus

$$\sin 750° = \sin [750 - 2(360)°] = \sin 30°$$

$$\tan \frac{13\pi}{6} = \tan \left(\frac{13\pi}{6} - 2\pi \right) = \tan \frac{\pi}{6}$$

Example 2.4   Evaluate: $2 \sin \dfrac{7\pi}{6} + 3 \sin \left(-\dfrac{4\pi}{3} \right)$

Solution   We begin by drawing two diagrams.

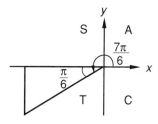   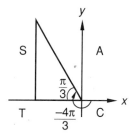

The sine is negative in the third quadrant, and, thus, sin $(7\pi/6)$ equals $-\sin(\pi/6)$, which is $-\sin 30°$. The sine is positive in the second quadrant; so sin $(-4\pi/3)$ equals sin $(\pi/3)$, or sin $60°$. Thus, we have

$$2\left(-\sin\frac{\pi}{6}\right) + 3\sin\frac{\pi}{3} = 2\left(-\frac{1}{2}\right) + 3\left(\frac{\sqrt{3}}{2}\right)$$

$$= -1 + \frac{3\sqrt{3}}{2}$$

Example 2.5   Evaluate: $4\tan\left(-\frac{11\pi}{6}\right) + 2\sec\left(-\frac{\pi}{4}\right)$

Solution   We begin by drawing the necessary diagrams.

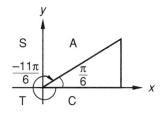   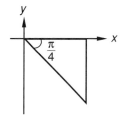

The tangent is positive in the first quadrant, and, thus, tan $(-11\pi/6)$ equals tan $(\pi/6)$, or tan $30°$. The cosine is positive in the fourth quadrant, so the secant is also positive. Thus, sec $(-\pi/4)$ equals sec $(\pi/4)$. So we have

$$4\left(\tan\frac{\pi}{6}\right) + \frac{2}{\cos\frac{\pi}{4}} = 4\left(\frac{1}{\sqrt{3}}\right) + \frac{2}{\frac{1}{\sqrt{2}}} = \frac{4\sqrt{3}}{3} + 2\sqrt{2}$$

2.D
Simplifying trigonometric expressions

Many trigonometric expressions can be simplified if we remember that tan θ is the ratio of sin θ to cos θ and that cot θ, sec θ, and csc θ are the reciprocals of tan θ, cos θ, and sin θ, respectively.

Example 2.6   Simplify: $(\cos^2\theta)(\sec\theta)(\tan\theta)$

Solution   We remember that $\cos^2\theta$ means $(\cos\theta)^2$ and does not mean cos $(\theta)^2$. Sec θ is the reciprocal of cos θ, and tan θ equals sin θ divided by cos θ. Thus, we substitute and get

$$(\cos^2\theta)\left(\frac{1}{\cos\theta}\right)\left(\frac{\sin\theta}{\cos\theta}\right) = \sin\theta$$

Example 2.7   Simplify: $\dfrac{\cot\theta\,\cos\theta}{\csc\theta}$

Solution   We substitute equivalent expressions for $\cot\theta$ and $\csc\theta$ and get $\cos^2\theta$ as our simplified answer.

$$\frac{\left(\dfrac{\cos\theta}{\sin\theta}\right)\left(\dfrac{\cos\theta}{1}\right)}{\dfrac{1}{\sin\theta}} = \cos^2\theta$$

Problem set 2

1. The wheel on Esme's unicycle revolved 20 times every minute as she rode down the straight path. If the radius of the wheel of her unicycle was 3 feet, how fast was Esme's unicycle traveling along the path?

2. Stacy pulled the tumbril down the straight path at a speed of 100 feet per minute. If the radius of the wheels of the tumbril was 1 foot, how many revolutions were the wheels making per minute?

Evaluate:

3. $\cos^2\dfrac{\pi}{3} - \cot\dfrac{\pi}{4} + \sin\dfrac{\pi}{6}$

4. $\sec 60° + \csc^2\dfrac{\pi}{3}$

5. $3\cos\dfrac{7\pi}{6} + 2\cos\left(-\dfrac{5\pi}{3}\right)$

6. $4\tan\left(-\dfrac{3\pi}{4}\right) + \sin\left(-\dfrac{\pi}{4}\right)$

Simplify:

7. $(\sin^2\theta)(\csc\theta)(\cot\theta)$

8. $\dfrac{\tan\theta\,\sin\theta}{\sec\theta}$

9. Write the contrapositive of the following statement: A fangle is a widgit if two of its marks are not equal.

10. Is the following argument valid or invalid?

    If a fangle's marks are equal, then it is a gotby.
    Susan's fangle is not a gotby.

    Therefore, Susan's fangle's marks are not equal.

11. Write the point-slope form of the equation of the line which passes through the point $(-9, -3)$ and is parallel to the line $\frac{x}{3} + 2 = -3y$. Then write the general form of the equation.

12. Factor to find the values of x which satisfy the equation $-2x^2 = 7x - 15$.

13. Solve $x^2 + x = -1$ by using the quadratic formula.

14. Multiply $3x^2 - 4x + 5$ by $2x - 1$.

15. Find the ordered pairs (x, y) which satisfy both the equation $x^2 + y^2 = 8$ and the equation $x + y = 0$.

16. Solve for r: $\dfrac{1}{r} = v\left(\dfrac{1}{r_1} + \dfrac{1}{r_2}\right)$

Simplify:

17. $\dfrac{1}{1 + \dfrac{1}{1 + \dfrac{1}{3}}}$

18. $5\sqrt{\dfrac{1}{5}} - 3\sqrt{5} + \sqrt{50}$

19. $\dfrac{2i^3 - 3i + 2}{2i + 7 + 3i^2}$

20. $\dfrac{x^3 - y^3}{x^2 + xy + y^2}$

21. Evaluate: $\displaystyle\sum_{i=-1}^{1} (2^i + i)$

CONCEPT REVIEW   Find x in each of the following figures:

22. $m\,\widehat{AB} = (60 - x)^\circ$
$m\,\widehat{BC} = (2x)^\circ$
$m\angle APB = (x + 5)^\circ$

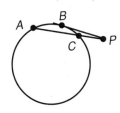

23.

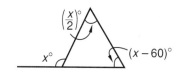

24. If $x^2 = 36$ and $y^2 = 49$, compare: *A.   x   B.   y*

LESSON 3   *Word problem review*

The standard word problems that we have encountered before have allowed us to practice the use of concepts and skills that are useful in the solution of the word problems encountered in calculus and in advanced mathematics. We will review some of the basic types of word problems in this lesson.

Example 3.1   Diana could do 4 jobs in 7 hours and Frank could do 7 jobs in 5 hours. How many hours would it take them working together to do 10 jobs?

Solution   We assume that their rates when they work together are the same as their rates when they work independently. Diana's rate is $\frac{4}{7}$ job per hour and Frank's rate is $\frac{7}{5}$ jobs per hour. They will both work t hours. Thus, we write

$$\frac{4}{7}t + \frac{7}{5}t = 10 \qquad \text{equation}$$

$$20t + 49t = 350 \qquad \text{multiplied by 35}$$

$$t = \frac{350}{69} \text{ hours} \qquad \text{solved}$$

Example 3.2 Patricia could do 5 jobs in 10 hours with 3 machines. At the same rate how long would it take her to do 4 jobs with 12 machines?

Solution In this problem Patricia's rate is in jobs per machine-hour, and the equation is rate times the number of machines times time equals the number of jobs. The rate is $\frac{1}{6}$ job per machine-hour.

Here is the basic equation:

$$\text{Rate} \times \text{machines} \times \text{time} = \text{jobs} \qquad \text{or} \qquad rmt = j$$

$$\text{Rate} = \frac{5 \text{ jobs}}{(3 \text{ machines})(10 \text{ hours})} = \frac{1}{6} \frac{\text{job}}{\text{machine-hour}}$$

Now, if we use this rate in the basic equation and use 4 for jobs and 12 for machines, we can solve for time t.

$$\left(\frac{1}{6}\right)(12)(t) = 4 \qquad \text{substituted}$$

$$t = \textbf{2 hours} \qquad \text{solved}$$

Thus, she could do 4 jobs in 2 hours if she used 12 machines.

Example 3.3 Walter and John found that the cost varied directly as the number who worked and inversely as the Sabercat index. The cost was $400 when 5 men worked and the index was 8. What was the cost when 13 men worked and the index was 2?

Solution This nonsense problem allows us practice with the fact that a direct variation equation contains variables and a constant of proportionality k. We will let M represent the number of men and let S represent the Sabercat index and write

$$\text{Cost} = \frac{kM}{S}$$

The problem is a three-step problem. The first step is to substitute to find k.

$$400 = \frac{k5}{8} \quad \longrightarrow \quad k = 640 \qquad \text{solved for } k$$

The second step is to substitute for k in the equation.

$$\text{Cost} = \frac{640M}{S} \qquad \text{substituted}$$

The last step is to substitute for M and S.

$$\text{Cost} = \frac{(640)(13)}{2} = \textbf{\$4160}$$

Example 3.4 The cost varied linearly with the number of men who worked. When 10 men worked, the cost was $70. When 20 men worked, the cost was $120. What was the cost when only 2 men worked?

Solution The words *varied linearly* tell us that the equation is a linear equation.

$$\text{Cost} = mM + b$$

We have two unknowns, so we need two equations. We get one equation by using 70 for cost and 10 for M and can get another equation by using 120 for cost and 20 for M. Then we solve this system of two equations.

$$70 = m(10) + b \quad \longrightarrow \quad (2) \quad \longrightarrow \quad 140 = 20m + 2b$$
$$120 = m(20) + b \quad \longrightarrow \quad (-1) \quad \longrightarrow \quad \underline{-120 = -20m - b}$$
$$20 = b \quad \text{solved for } b$$

Now we let $b = 20$ in the first equation to solve for m.

$$70 = m10 + 20$$
$$m = 5$$

Finally we have the linear equation.

$$\text{Cost} = 5M + 20$$

By substituting, we find that when 2 men worked the cost was $30.

$$\text{Cost} = 5(2) + 20 = \mathbf{\$30}$$

Example 3.5 When Louwan saw the bad men, it was high noon. When she caught them, the hands on the clock made a 90° angle. What time was it when she caught them?

Solution The big hand moves at 1 space per minute. The little hand moves at $\frac{1}{12}$ space per minute. The big hand will be 15 spaces ahead of the little hand when the angle equals 90°.

Spaces big hand moves $= 1t$ \qquad Spaces little hand moves $= \frac{1}{12}t$

The difference equals 15 spaces.

$$1t - \frac{1}{12}t = 15 \text{ spaces} \qquad \text{equation}$$

$$12t - t = 180 \qquad \text{multiplied}$$

$$t = \frac{180}{11} \text{ min} \qquad \text{solved}$$

Thus the time was: \qquad **12:16$\frac{4}{11}$ p.m.** \qquad $16\frac{4}{11}$ minutes later

Problem set 3

1. Dale could draw 5 graphs every 4 hours. Norman could draw 3 graphs every 2 hours. How many hours would it take Dale and Norman working together to draw 11 graphs?

2. Nancy could typeset 6 pages in 5 days with 2 computers. If Nancy continues to typeset at this rate, how many days would it take her to typeset 72 pages with 3 computers?

3. The time necessary to complete the project varied inversely with the number of engineers who worked on the project and directly with the amount of money invested. When 2 engineers work and $1000 is invested, the project takes 5 days. How many days would it take to complete the project if 3 engineers work and $3000 is invested?

4. The cost of a Jimmy Built building varies linearly with the number of floors the building has. If a 10-story Jimmy Built building costs $12 million and a 4-story Jimmy Built building costs $6 million, how much would a 7-story Jimmy Built building cost?

5. At noon, Linda began to wait for Misty. If Misty and Linda were to meet the first time the hands of the clock were pointing in opposite directions, at what time were Misty and Linda scheduled to meet?

6. A wheel 2 feet in diameter rolls straight down the hill, revolving once every second. Find the linear velocity of the wheel in feet per minute.

Evaluate:

7. $2 \cos \left(-\dfrac{5\pi}{4}\right) - \sec \dfrac{\pi}{4}$

8. $\tan^2 \dfrac{\pi}{3} - \cot^2 \dfrac{\pi}{3}$

9. $\sin^2 \left(-\dfrac{2\pi}{3}\right) - \csc \left(-\dfrac{\pi}{2}\right)$

Simplify the following expressions:

10. $(\sin^2 x)(\csc x)(\cos x)$

11. $\dfrac{\cos \alpha \, \sec \alpha}{\csc \alpha}$

12. Is the following argument valid or invalid?

All pugilists are truculent.
Adam is not truculent.

Therefore, Adam is not a pugilist.

13. Use the quadratic formula to find the values of x for which the value of the polynomial $2x^2 - 3x + 1$ is zero.

14. Write the general form of the equation of the line which is parallel to the y axis and which passes through the point (2, 3).

15. Solve: $\begin{cases} y = x^2 + 1 \\ y - 2x = 0 \end{cases}$

16. If $x^2 = \sqrt{y + 1}$, solve for y in terms of x.

Simplify:

17. $\dfrac{x^3 - a^3}{x - a}$

18. $\dfrac{\sqrt{3} + \sqrt{2}}{\sqrt{3} - \sqrt{2}}$

19. $\dfrac{2i^2 + 3}{1 - 2i}$

20. $\dfrac{4}{m + \dfrac{a}{x - 1}}$

21. Evaluate: $\dfrac{18!}{16!2!}$

CONCEPT REVIEW 22. If x and y are both less than zero and $x < y$, then compare:
    A. $-x$ B. $-y$

Solve for x in each of the following figures:

23.
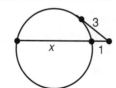

24. $m\widehat{AC} = (x + 5)°$
    $m\widehat{BD} = (2x + 7)°$
    $m\angle BED = (x + 30)°$

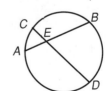

LESSON 4 *Functions: Their equations and graphs · Functional notation · Domain and range*

**4.A
Functions:
Their
equations
and graphs**

The expression $2x + 3$ has exactly one value for each value of x selected. When x equals 1, this expression has a value of 5. When x equals -6, this expression has a value of -9.

EXPRESSION	WHEN $x = 1$	WHEN $x = -3$
$2x + 3$	$2(1) + 3 = 5$	$2(-3) + 3 = -9$

Since the single value of $2x + 3$ is determined by the value of x selected, we say that $2x + 3$ is *single-valued.* If we use y as the dependent variable, we can use $2x + 3$ to write the right-hand side of an equation that has exactly one value of y for any value of x selected.

$$y = 2x + 3$$

We use the word **function** to identify the single-valued relationships specified by **single-valued equations** by saying that y is a function of x. The word **relation** is an umbrella term used to identify relationships specified by equations that have **at least one answer** for y for every value of x. In the equation

$$y^2 = x$$

y is not a function of x because if x is 4, y could be either 2 or -2. We call this equation a **double-valued equation.** Multivalued equations are useful, and we use them extensively in mathematics, but we must be careful to remember that such equations do not describe functional relationships.

Modern mathematicians have found that the process which produces exactly one answer for each value chosen for the input is extremely useful, and they use the word *function* to describe any process that does this. Thus, an equation is not necessary. All that is needed is a rule that tells: (1) what numbers can be used and (2) how to find the answer for each number. The rule allows us to match each member of a specified set, called the *domain* (the input values of x), with exactly one member of a second set (the answers), called the *range.* The individual members of the range are called the *images.* We say that the function *maps* each member of the domain to exactly one member of the range.

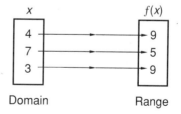

The diagram shows that if x is 4, the image (answer) is 9. If x is 7, the image is 5, and if x is 3, the image is 9. Since we have exactly one image for each value of x, we have a function. The image for both 4 and 3 is 9, but since 4 has only one image and 3 has only one image, the requirement that each member of the domain have exactly one image is satisfied. In this example, we used a diagram rather than an equation to specify the images. The only values of x that can be used are 4, 7, and 3 because in this example it was arbitrarily decided that the domain would contain only these three numbers.

The rule for a function may also be stated by a list of ordered pairs such that every first member is paired with exactly one second member. Thus, the following set of ordered pairs defines a *relation* but does not define a function

$$(4, 3), \quad (5, 7), \quad (9, 3), \quad (4, -5), \quad (8, 14), \quad (6, -3)$$

because the first and the fourth pairs have different answers (images) for 4. The following set of ordered pairs *does* define a function.

$$(4, 3), \quad (5, 7), \quad (9, 3), \quad (4, 3), \quad (8, 14), \quad (6, -3)$$

In this book we will concentrate almost exclusively on functions whose rules can be written as equations. We note that the function is defined by the equation and that the function is not the equation itself. Many authors use a letter to name the function and a colon and an arrow to indicate the pairing or mapping.

$$f(x) = x^2 + 4 \qquad\qquad f{:}x \rightarrow x^2 + 4$$
$$g(x) = x^3 - 2x + 1 \qquad g{:}x \rightarrow x^3 - 2x + 1$$

The f function rule is $x^2 + 4$ and the g function rule is $x^3 - 2x + 1$. We read the notations on the right as "f maps x to $x^2 + 4$" and "g maps x to $x^3 - 2x + 1$."

Thus, we see that the word *function* is used to describe the idea of a particular kind of mapping or pairing and that this idea has different aspects. One aspect is algebraic, another aspect is arithmetic, and a third aspect is geometric.

We use the word *function* to describe a mapping from each member of the input set, which is called the *domain*, to exactly one member of the output set, which is called the *range*. Thus, the word function brings to mind the following:

1. The numbers that are acceptable as inputs and the algebraic rule (if one exists) that can be used to find the unique output that is paired with each input.
2. A table of ordered pairs of inputs and outputs where each input member is paired with exactly one output and all equal inputs have the same outputs.
3. The graph of the geometric points whose coordinates are the ordered pairs just described.

What functions are and how they interrelate can be explained by using a box called a *function machine*. The function machine uses a rule to produce exactly one output for every input. Suppose we consider as examples two functions which we will call the f function and the g function and define them as follows:

$$f(x) = 4x \qquad g(x) = x^2 + 2$$

The f rule is to multiply any input by 4, and the g rule is to square any input and then add 2. This may be easier to understand if we use an empty set of parentheses instead of x and call the parentheses "whatever." Thus, the f function multiplies whatever is in the parentheses by 4, and the g function squares whatever is in the parentheses and then adds 2.

$$f(\ ) = 4(\ ) \qquad\qquad g(\ ) = (\ )^2 + 2$$
$$f(x) = 4x \qquad\qquad g(x) = x^2 + 2$$

$$
\begin{array}{l}
x \longrightarrow \\
3 \longrightarrow \\
5 \longrightarrow
\end{array}
\boxed{\quad f \quad}
\begin{array}{l}
\longrightarrow 4x \\
\longrightarrow 12 \\
\longrightarrow 20
\end{array}
\qquad
\begin{array}{l}
x \longrightarrow \\
3 \longrightarrow \\
5 \longrightarrow
\end{array}
\boxed{\quad g \quad}
\begin{array}{l}
\longrightarrow x^2 + 2 \\
\longrightarrow 11 \\
\longrightarrow 27
\end{array}
$$

Example 4.1   Given $f(x) = x^2 + 5$, find (a) $f(-2)$, (b) $f(x + 2)$, (c) $f(x + \Delta x)$.

Solution   We use the function machine thought process:

$$f(\ ) = (\ )^2 + 5$$

$$(\ ) \longrightarrow \boxed{\qquad f \qquad} \longrightarrow$$

This function machine will square whatever we put in and then add 5.

(a)   Insert (-2) and get out $(-2)^2 + 5 = $ **9.**
(b)   Insert $(x + 2)$ and get out $(x + 2)^2 + 5 = $ **$x^2 + 4x + 9$.**
(c)   Insert $(x + \Delta x)$ and get out $(x + \Delta x)^2 + 5 = $ **$x^2 + 2x(\Delta x) + (\Delta x)^2 + 5$.**

4.B
Functional notation

Functional notation is useful because it indicates that the relationship is single-valued and also because it can be used with letters of our choice to name or identify particular single-valued relationships. To name the equations

$$y = 2x + 3 \qquad y = e^t \qquad y = \ln u \qquad y = \sin(2s + 2)$$

we could use the letters f, θ, g, and h to write

$$f(x) = 2x + 3 \qquad \theta(t) = e^t \qquad g(u) = \ln u \qquad h(s) = \sin(2s + 2)$$

We read $f(x)$ as "f of x," $\theta(t)$ as "theta of t," and $g(u)$ and $h(s)$ as "g of u" and "h of s," respectively.

From this we see that $f(x)$, $\theta(t)$, $g(u)$, and $h(s)$ mean the same thing that y means. We also see that these notations allow us to identify the single-valued f equation in x, the single-valued θ equation in t, the single-valued g equation in u, and the single-valued h equation in s. Functional notation is also helpful because it allows us to identify the value of x used to get a particular answer.

$$y = 11 \qquad f(4) = 11$$

On the left we use the old notation that tells us that the answer is 11. On the right, the functional notation tells us that if we use the f equation and let x equal 4, the answer is 11. The additional information provided by functional notation explains why it is used so widely.

Functional notation is also useful on a graph. If we have a graph of the f equation in x, we use the single letter f to identify the graph. We will use $f(x)$ to represent the y value of the f equation when x equals some unspecified value. We will use $f(a)$ to designate the y value of the f equation when x equals the constant a. For example, we will use $f(4)$ to designate the y value of the equation when x equals

4. On the graph, $f(4)$ represents the directed vertical distance from the x axis to the graph when x equals 4. The input value of any point on the graph is represented by its distance to the right or left of the y axis. The output value for the same point is represented by its distance above or below the x axis.

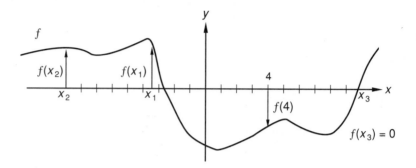

We will use the x, y notation and functional notation interchangeably in this lesson and in the rest of the book as is convenient. We will even use both notations in the same problem to emphasize this interchangeability. Note that the vertical axis in the diagram above is labeled y instead of $f(x)$.

We know how to use ordered pairs of x and y written as (x, y). Now we see that we can designate the same ordered pairs of x, the input, and $f(x)$, the output, by writing

$$(x, f(x))$$

The graph of the function is the graph of the ordered pairs of inputs x and outputs $f(x)$.

Example 4.2   Which of the following are not graphs of functions?

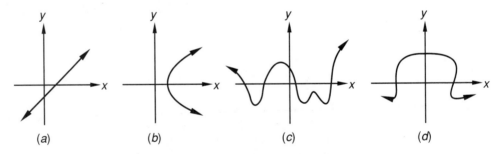

Solution   Since a function is single-valued, there can be only one y value for any value of x. **If, at any value of x, we can draw a vertical line that touches the graph more than once, then the graph is not the graph of a function.** This means the graph cannot loop back anywhere and cannot be vertical anywhere. Let's use vertical lines on these graphs.

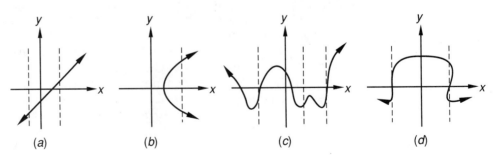

Figures (*a*) and (*c*) show graphs of functions because we see that no vertical line we can draw will touch the graph in more than one place. Figure (*b*) is not the graph of a function, for we have found a value of *x* at which a vertical line will touch the graph in two places. The graph in figure (*d*) fails the vertical line test to the left of the origin where the graph is vertical and fails the test again to the right of the origin where the graph loops back.

Example 4.3   Which of the following sets of points could lie on the graph of a function?
(*a*) {(1, 2), (2, 3), (3, 4), (4, 5)}   (*b*) {(1, 2), (2, 3), (1, 3), (4, 5)}
(*c*) {(4, 3), (2, 2), (4, 3), (3, 3)}   (*d*) {(1, −1), (4, −1), (−1, −1), (3, −2)}

Solution   A set of ordered pairs in which every first number is paired with a unique second number is a function. So we look for first numbers that are the same. In set (*a*), all the first numbers are different and each first number has a second number, so **set (*a*) describes a function.** Set (*b*) is not a function because two ordered pairs have 1 as a first number, but the second numbers are different. **Set (*c*) is a function** because this set has two ordered pairs in which 4 is the first number, but both of these ordered pairs have 3 as the second number. In set (*d*) three of the second numbers are −1, but **set (*d*) is a function** because all the first numbers are different.

Example 4.4   Determine whether the following statement is true or false and justify your answer: The mapping $f{:}x \rightarrow x^4 + x^2$ is not a function because it maps both +1 and −1 to +1.

Solution   **False. The mapping is a function.** A function is a mapping in which every value of *x* is mapped to exactly one value of *y*. Two different values of *x* can be mapped to the same value of *y*.

Example 4.5   Determine whether the following statement is true or false and explain your answer: The equation $y = x^2 + 2$ is not the equation of a function because there is a vertical line that intersects the graph of this equation at more than one point.

Solution   **False.** Any number used for *x* will result in just one answer for *y*. Thus, any vertical line will intersect the graph at only one point.

4.C
Domain and range

The definition of a function has two parts. One part is a rule which tells how to find the output value $f(x)$ for each value of the input *x*. **The other part is the description of the set of input values that may be used for *x*. This set is the domain for the function.** The domain for a function may be determined by the person who makes up the function. Here we show the rules and the domains for functions made up by Selby and Bruce.

SELBY'S FUNCTION	BRUCE'S FUNCTION
$f(x) = 2x + 3$	$g(x) = 2x + 3$
$D = \{\text{reals}\}$	$D = \{\text{integers}\}$

The algebraic part of the rule for each of these functions is the same, but the functions are different functions because the domains are different. We don't know why Selby and Bruce decided on the domains that they did. We must accept the domains they have specified because the person who makes up the algebraic part of the rule also gets to choose the domain.

In mathematics books, if the author does not specify the domain for a particular function, it is reasonable for the reader to assume that he or she is allowed to specify the domain, because a domain is necessary. Domains do not appear by magic. Someone must specify them.

Whenever we encounter a problem, we must determine the algebraic rule for the function implied by the statement of the problem. We must also determine an acceptable domain for the function. Sometimes the problem is stated in such a way that we cannot use certain numbers as values of the input variable. If boxes cost $25 each, we could use the following function machine to find the cost of x boxes.

$$\text{Cost} = 25(\ )$$

or

$$\text{Cost} = 25x$$

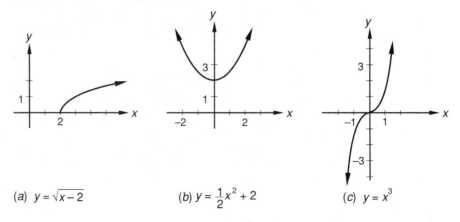

We see that 4 boxes cost $100 and 7 boxes cost $175. We would not try to use this equation to find the cost of $7\frac{1}{2}$ boxes or $4 + 2i$ boxes because we assume that only whole numbers of boxes can be purchased. Trying to buy $7\frac{1}{2}$ boxes or $4 + 2i$ boxes does not make sense. No statement about the domain was made, but it seems that the set of whole numbers is implied as the domain for this problem. We can buy no boxes, one box, two boxes, etc.

$$\text{Domain} = \{0, 1, 2, 3, \ldots\}$$

If the equation being considered is not the result of a real problem such as this one, we still need to determine the domain. We will use the following rule.

> **In this book we will deal with functions of real numbers. The domains of the functions, unless otherwise specified, are understood to be the set of real numbers that will produce images that are also real numbers.**

The **range** of a function is the set of all images that we get when all values of the domain have been used as inputs for the function machine. Thus we do not specify the range when we have an algebraic expression for the function. We mentally insert all members of the domain and investigate the set of outputs that result.

One way to determine the domain and range of a function is to look at the graph of the function. The x coordinates of the points on the graph constitute the domain and the y coordinates of the points on the graph constitute the range. Consider the following figures.

(a) $y = \sqrt{x - 2}$ (b) $y = \frac{1}{2}x^2 + 2$ (c) $y = x^3$

In figure (*a*) the *x* values on the graph begin at 2 and increase without bound, so the domain is all real numbers greater than or equal to 2. The *y* values on the graph begin at zero and increase without bound, so the range is all real numbers equal to or greater than zero. In figure (*b*) the *x* values on the graph go from negative infinity to positive infinity, so the domain is the set of real numbers. The *y* values begin at +2 and increase without bound, so the range is all real numbers greater than or equal to 2. In figure (*c*) the values of *x* include all real numbers and the values of *y* include all real numbers. Thus for this function the set of real numbers is the domain and the set of real numbers is the range.

Example 4.6   Find the domain and range of the function $f(x) = \sqrt{x + 5}$.

Solution   We will not use values of *x* that will cause $\sqrt{x + 5}$ to be an imaginary number. Thus, −8 is not an acceptable value of *x*.

$$f(-8) = \sqrt{-8 + 5} = \sqrt{-3} = \sqrt{3}\, i \quad \textbf{NO! NO!}$$

Thus we see that the domain of $\sqrt{x + 5}$ consists of the real numbers that are equal to or greater than −5. To designate domains, we can use set notation, use { } to designate the set, use the symbol ∈ to mean an element of, and use the symbol ℝ to represent the real numbers. We use a vertical line to mean *such that*. Thus we may write

$$\text{Domain of } \sqrt{x + 5} = \{x \in \mathbb{R} \mid x \geq -5\}$$

We can read this as follows: "The domain of $\sqrt{x + 5}$ is the set of all real numbers *x* such that *x* is equal to or greater than −5."

On the graph we see that there are no negative values of *y*, so the range consists of all real numbers equal to or greater than zero.

$$\text{Range of } \sqrt{x + 5} = \{y \in \mathbb{R} \mid y \geq 0\}$$

Example 4.7   Find the domain and range of $f(x) = \dfrac{\sqrt{x}}{x - 2}$.

Solution   From the numerator of the function we see that *x* cannot be a negative number because the square root of a negative number is an imaginary number. From the denominator of the function we see that *x* cannot equal 2 because this would make the denominator equal zero. Thus

$$\text{Domain} = \{x \in \mathbb{R} \mid x \geq 0, x \neq 2\}$$

Finding the range of some functions is easier if we graph the functions. We will discuss graphing techniques in later lessons. The graph of this function shows that the values of *y* include zero and all positive and negative real numbers.

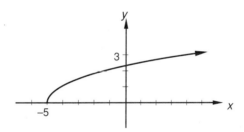

$$\text{Range} = \{y \in \mathbb{R}\}$$

Problem set 4

1. Sue could consume 9 scoops of ice cream in 3 minutes, whereas Cody required 6 minutes to consume 1 scoop of ice cream. Michael scooped 40 scoops for Sue and Cody. If Cody ate for 12 minutes and then was joined by Sue, how much time would it require Sue and Cody eating together to eat the remaining ice cream?

2. The ratio of the number of sophists to the number of pundits was 3 to 1 and the ratio of the number of pundits to the number of charlatans was 4 to 1. If there were 34 sophists, pundits, and charlatans in all, how many of each were there?

3. Five years ago, Sharon was 3 times as old as Travis. Now Sharon is 18 years older than Travis. How old are Sharon and Travis now?

4. Now it is 6 o'clock. In how many minutes will the little hand and the big hand be pointing in the same direction?

5. Express 130° per minute in terms of radians per hour.

6. Listed are sets of ordered pairs of numbers where each ordered pair represents a point on the coordinate plane. Which of the following sets lists the coordinates of points which lie on the graph of a function?
   (a) $\{(2, -2), (-3, 2), (2, -3), (3, 3)\}$
   (b) $\{(1, 2), (2, 2), (3, 2), (4, 2)\}$
   (c) $\{(1, 2), (1, 3), (6, 7), (-1, 13)\}$
   (d) $\{(-1, 2), (2, -1), (-1, 4), (5, 8)\}$

7. Shown is the graph of a function ψ.

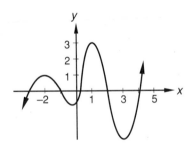

   Estimate the value of the following:
   (a) $\psi(1)$ (b) $\psi(-1)$ (c) $\psi(-2)$

8. Shown is a function machine f where only a few input and output values are given.

   $$
   \begin{array}{ccc}
   1 \rightarrow & & \rightarrow 2 \\
   2 \rightarrow & f & \rightarrow 5 \\
   -2 \rightarrow & & \rightarrow 5
   \end{array}
   $$

   Which of the following could be the equation for f?
   (a) $f(x) = 2x + 1$ (c) $f(x) = 2x^2 - 2$
   (b) $f(x) = x^2 + 1$ (d) $f(x) = 2x$

9. If $f(x) = 2x^2 - 1$, find $f(x + \Delta x)$.

10. Find the domain and range of the function $y = \sqrt{x - 1}$.

11. Find the domain of the function $y = \dfrac{\sqrt{x + 1}}{x}$.

Evaluate:

12. $2 \cos^2 \left(-\dfrac{5\pi}{4} \right) - \sec^2 \dfrac{\pi}{4}$

13. $\cot \dfrac{\pi}{6} + \sin \left(-\dfrac{\pi}{3} \right)$

14. $\sin \dfrac{\pi}{6} \cos \left(-\dfrac{\pi}{3} \right)$

Simplify the following expressions:

15. $(\cot^2 x)(\sec^2 x)(\sin x)$

16. $\dfrac{(\cot \theta)(\sec \theta)}{(\csc \theta)}$

17. Is the following argument valid or invalid?

All epicureans are hedonists.
Coach Keller is not a hedonist.
_____

Therefore, Coach Keller is not an epicurean.

18. Suppose that $y = mx + b$ and $y = nx + c$ are the equations of two lines which are perpendicular. What is the numerical value of mn?

19. Solve for s: $\sqrt{s} - \sqrt{s - 8} = 2$

20. Compute: $\displaystyle\sum_{i=-1}^{1} 3^i$

21. Simplify: $\dfrac{\sqrt{3} - \sqrt{2}}{\sqrt{3} + \sqrt{2}}$

CONCEPT REVIEW **22.** If x, y, and z are lengths as shown, compare:
A. $x + y$ B. z

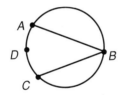

Solve for x:

23. $m\angle ABC = (5x - 10)^\circ$
$m\widehat{ADC} = (x^2 - 20)^\circ$

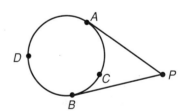

24. $\overline{PA}$ and $\overline{PB}$ are tangents to the circle shown.
$m\widehat{ACB} = (2x)^\circ$
$m\widehat{ADB} = (3x + 60)^\circ$
$m\angle P = x^\circ$

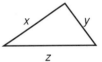

LESSON 5 *The unit circle · Graphing sinusoids*

5.A

The unit circle

In a right triangle, the sine of an acute angle θ is the ratio of the length of the side opposite angle θ to the length of the hypotenuse. Thus, if we draw a triangle whose hypotenuse is 1 unit long, the sine of angle θ will be the length of the side opposite this angle divided by 1. A circle whose radius is 1 is called a *unit circle.* If we center a unit circle at the origin, as we show here, and measure the central angles counterclockwise from the positive x axis, the y coordinate of any point on the unit circle equals the sine of the central angle because y is the length of the side opposite angle θ in the triangle. On the right we graph $y = \sin \theta$ and note that the horizontal axis is the θ axis.

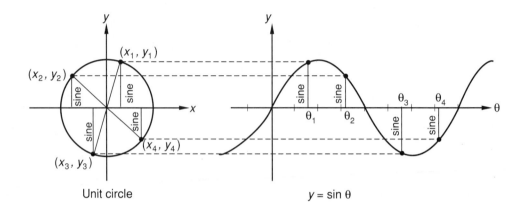

Unit circle $y = \sin \theta$

The sines of θ_1, θ_2, θ_3, and θ_4 equal the **directed lengths** of the vertical sides of the triangles since the length of every hypotenuse equals 1. This agrees with the graph of $y = \sin \theta$ on the right, where the vertical distance from the θ axis to the graph also equals $\sin \theta$. When the graph is above the θ axis, the sine is positive, and when the graph is below the θ axis, the sine is negative. Note that when θ equals zero, the sine is zero, and as θ increases from 0 to 360°, or 2π radians, the value of the sine goes from 0 to 1 to 0 to -1 and back to 0. In this discussion we have used θ to represent the independent variable to emphasize that θ represents an angle. In mathematics, the variable x is most often used as the independent variable and is also used to represent angles. In this graph of the sine curve, the horizontal axis is the θ axis. Sometimes we use θ and sometimes we use x.

From this discussion, we see that the y coordinate of any point on a unit circle equals the sine of the central angle measured counterclockwise from the positive x axis.

$$y = \sin \theta$$

The same unit circle can be used to discuss the values of the cosine because the value of $\cos x$ equals the length of the adjacent side over the length of the hypotenuse. Thus, if the length of the hypotenuse equals 1, the **directed length** of a **horizontal** side of a triangle in this unit circle equals the cosine of the angle. Thus, the x coordinate of any point on the unit circle equals the cosine of the central angle measured counterclockwise from the positive x axis. In order to show the projection of the cosine function from the unit circle it is necessary to rotate the unit circle 90° counterclockwise, as we have done in the following figure.

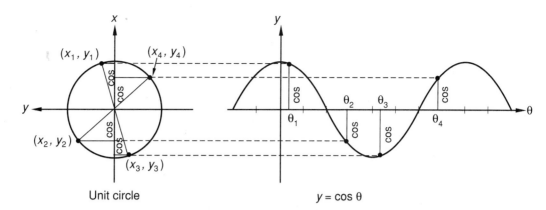

Unit circle $y = \cos \theta$

On the graph of $y = \cos \theta$, the values of $\cos \theta$ are the directed vertical distances from the x axis to the curve. These vertical distances correlate with the directed lengths of the vertical sides of the triangle in the left-hand figure. Note that the value of $\cos 0°$ is 1, and as θ goes from $0°$ to $360°$, the value of the cosine goes from 1 to 0 to -1 to 0 and back to 1.

Both the sine and cosine are periodic functions whose period is $360°$ since the values of $\sin \theta$ and $\cos \theta$ repeat in regular patterns as θ increases or decreases through multiples of $360°$, or 2π radians.

5.B
Graphing sinusoids

The Greek suffix *-oid* means "having the shape of." Thus something that has the shape of a crystal is crystalloid. Because the graph of the cosine function looks very much like the graph of the sine function, we call both of these functions *sinusoids*. The equations of a sine function and a cosine function whose period is 2π have the following forms.

$$y = A + B \sin (\theta - D) \qquad y = A + B \cos (\theta - D)$$

The constant A is the y value of the horizontal centerline of the graph, and the constant B denotes the amplitude, which is the value of the maximum deviation of the graph from the centerline. We will discuss the period of a sinusoid in Lesson 18.

In the left-hand figure below, the centerline is the θ axis and the graph goes 4 units above and 4 units below the centerline. In the equation below the figure we note that $A = 0$ and $B = 4$. In the right-hand figure the centerline is the line $y = +2$, as indicated by the $+2$ value of A in the equation. Since B is 4, this curve also goes 4 units above and below its centerline. Note that the arrowhead denoting the positive θ direction is not on the centerline because the centerline is not the θ axis.

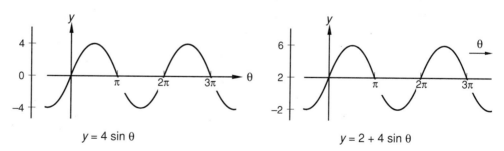

$y = 4 \sin \theta$ $y = 2 + 4 \sin \theta$

The constant D denotes the phase angle. The phase angle for a sine function is the value of θ at any point where the graph crosses the centerline on the way up as the curve is traced from left to right. It is customary to use the crossing point nearest the origin as the phase angle.

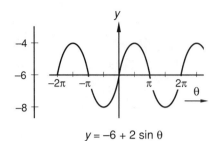

$y = -6 + 2 \sin \theta$

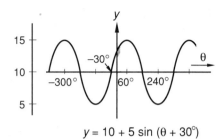

$y = 10 + 5 \sin (\theta + 30°)$

In the left-hand figure, the centerline is $y = -6$ and the amplitude is 2. Since the curve crosses the centerline on the way up where θ equals zero, the phase angle is 0. In the right-hand figure, the centerline is 10, the amplitude is 5, and the phase angle is $-30°$. **Note that the negative of the phase angle appears in the argument.**

The equations for the cosine functions for the same curves are the same except that the phase angle for the cosine function is a value of θ at which the graph is at its highest point.

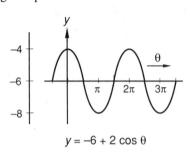

$y = -6 + 2 \cos \theta$

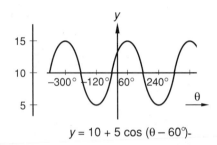

$y = 10 + 5 \cos (\theta - 60°)\text{-}$

Again we note that the negative of the phase angle appears in the argument.

We can write the equation of the curve on the right above as a negative sine function and as a negative cosine function. If we make the coefficient B a negative number, the phase angle for the sine function is a value of θ where the graph crosses its centerline on the way down, and the phase angle for the cosine function is a value of θ where the graph is at its lowest point.

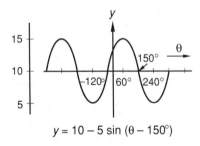

$y = 10 - 5 \sin (\theta - 150°)$

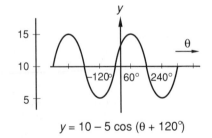

$y = 10 - 5 \cos (\theta + 120°)$

The angle in the argument is always the negative of the phase angle.

Example 5.1   Graph $y = -3 + 5 \cos (\theta - 45°)$.

Solution   The easiest way to graph a sinusoid is to draw the graph first as we do on the left.

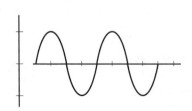

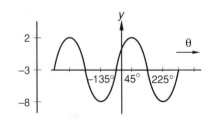

Then, on the right, we mark the centerline as −3. Since the graph goes up 5 and down 5, the peak values are +2 and −8. The argument is (x − 45°), so the phase angle is +45° and is a value of x when the graph has a maximum point. The graph crosses the x axis every 180°, and this information can be used to locate other points on the axis, as we have shown.

Example 5.2 Graph $y = -3 - 4 \sin (x + 45°)$.

Solution We draw the curve on the left, and then we put the labels on in the figure on the right. The centerline is $y = -3$ and the amplitude is 4, so the curve goes up to +1 and down to −7.

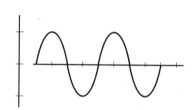
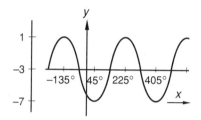

The phase angle is −45° and is a value of x where the graph of a negative sine function crosses its centerline on the way down.

Example 5.3 Graph $y = 2 - 3 \cos (\theta - 30°)$.

Solution Again we draw the curve and then put the labels on. This time the centerline is $y = 2$, and the curve goes up 3 to 5 and down 3 to −1.

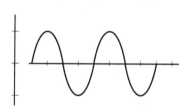
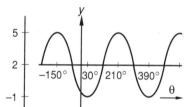

The phase angle is +30° and is a value of θ where the graph of a negative cosine function reaches a minimum point.

Problem set 5

1. The accomplishment number varies directly with the effort index and inversely with the time squandered. If the accomplishment number is 5 when the effort index is 20 and the time squandered is 8 hours, what is the accomplishment number when the effort index is 12 and the time squandered is 6 hours?

2. The number of wombats varied linearly with the number of fangles. If there were 170 wombats when there were 10 fangles, and 95 wombats when there were 5 fangles, then how many fangles were there when there were 50 wombats?

3. It was calculated that 60 Tamils working together could build the proposed gazebo in 20 days. How many more days would it take 40 Tamils to build the same gazebo?

4. The average speed for the bicyclist for the first 45 miles was 15 miles per hour (mph) and his average speed for the next 50 miles was 25 mph. What should

his average speed be for the next 85 miles if his overall average speed is to be 18 mph?

5. The wheels on the toy car had a diameter of 1 centimeter, but were revolving at 40 radians per second. What was the velocity of the car in meters per second?

Shown is a unit circle centered at the origin of the coordinate plane.

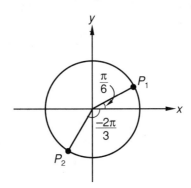

Find the coordinates of the following points:

6. P_1 7. P_2

8. Graph $y = -3 + 5 \sin (x - 45°)$.

9. Write the equation of the following sinusoid in terms of the cosine function.

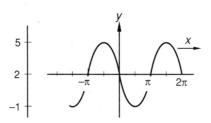

10. Determine whether the following statement is true or false and then explain why: The equation $y = x^2 + 1$ cannot be the equation of a function of x because $x = -8$ and $x = 8$ both map to the same value of y.

11. If $f(x) = x^2 - x$, find $f(x + h)$.

12. Find the domain and range of the function $y = \sin x$.

Evaluate:

13. $\sin^2 \left(-\dfrac{\pi}{4}\right) \cos^2 \dfrac{3\pi}{4}$

14. $\tan \left(-\dfrac{2\pi}{3}\right) + 2 \sin \dfrac{\pi}{3}$

Simplify the following expressions:

15. $\dfrac{\cos \theta \sin \theta}{\tan \theta}$

16. $(\cot \theta)(\sin \theta) - \cos \theta$

For Problems 17 and 18, suppose θ is an angle such that $\tan \theta = \dfrac{7}{3}$.

17. In which quadrants could θ lie?

18. Compute $\tan (-\theta)$.

19. Is the following argument valid or invalid?

    All fastidious persons are obdurate.
    Mahal is not fastidious.

    Therefore, Mahal is not obdurate.

20. Find the values of y which satisfy the equation $x^2 + y^2 = 9$ when $x = 1$.

21. Simplify: $\dfrac{\dfrac{1}{x+h} - \dfrac{1}{x}}{h}$ 22. Multiply: $(1 - 2i)(4i - 3)$

CONCEPT REVIEW 23. If x, y, and z are angles as shown, compare:
    A. $x + y$ B. z

24. Find x for the figure and the listed conditions.
    $m\widehat{AB} = (4x)°$
    $m\widehat{CD} = (2x + 20)°$
    $\angle AEB = (4x - 10)°$

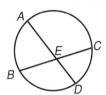

LESSON 6 *Similar triangles · Functions of $-\theta$*

6.A
Similar triangles

Two polygons are similar if the corresponding angles have equal measures and if the lengths of the corresponding sides are proportional. Triangles are the only rigid polygons, and we can prove that the angles in one triangle equal the angles in another triangle if and only if (iff) the corresponding sides are proportional. We remember that iff statements are represented by two double-headed arrows that make all four statements at the same time.

$$P \longleftrightarrow Q \qquad \overline{P} \longleftrightarrow \overline{Q}$$

P leads to Q. Q leads to P. Not P leads to not Q. Not Q leads to not P. Thus, the iff statement above contains all the following information:

$P \longrightarrow Q$	angles equal $\longrightarrow$ corresponding sides proportional	
$\overline{P} \longrightarrow \overline{Q}$	angles not equal $\longrightarrow$ corresponding sides not proportional	
$Q \longrightarrow P$	corresponding sides proportional $\longrightarrow$ angles equal	
$\overline{Q} \longrightarrow \overline{P}$	corresponding sides not proportional $\longrightarrow$ angles not equal	

This iff relationship between angles and sides in similar triangles makes similar triangles especially useful.

Example 6.1   Find b.

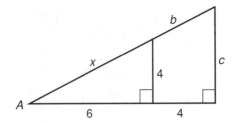

Solution   The big triangle and the little triangle are similar because the corresponding angles are equal. First we use the Pythagorean theorem to find x.

$$6^2 + 4^2 = x^2 \longrightarrow x = 2\sqrt{13}$$

Now we use the long legs and the hypotenuses to write a proportion, substitute $2\sqrt{13}$ for x, and solve for b.

$$\frac{x + b}{x} = \frac{6 + 4}{6} \longrightarrow \frac{2\sqrt{13} + b}{2\sqrt{13}} = \frac{10}{6} \longrightarrow b = \frac{4\sqrt{13}}{3}$$

Example 6.2   Solve for p.

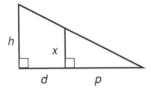

Solution   We will use the vertical and horizontal sides to write a proportion. Then we cross multiply.

$$\frac{x}{p} = \frac{h}{d + p} \longrightarrow ph = xd + xp$$

Now we solve for p.

$$ph - xp = xd \longrightarrow p(h - x) = xd \longrightarrow p = \frac{xd}{h - x}$$

Example 6.3   Solve for y.

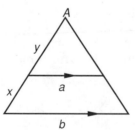

Solution   The big triangle and the little triangle are similar because both contain angle A, and since corresponding angles are equal when parallel lines are cut by a transversal, the other corresponding angles are equal. We write the proportion and cross multiply.

$$\frac{y}{a} = \frac{y + x}{b} \longrightarrow yb = ay + ax$$

Now we solve for y.

$$yb - ay = ax \longrightarrow y(b - a) = ax \longrightarrow y = \frac{ax}{b - a}$$

Example 6.4   Find x, y, and z.

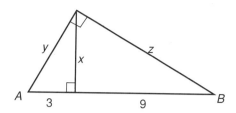

Solution   There are three triangles in the figure. They are similar triangles because all of them contain a right angle and all of them contain an angle that has the same measure as angle A. The sides opposite equal angles are proportional. We can write the proportions easily if we can remember which sides to use. A sure way is to redraw the figure as three separate triangles and label the angles that are not right angles as having the measure of angle A or angle B. The top angle in the center triangle and the top angle in the triangle on the right are not B and A, as shown, but have the same measures as angles B and A.

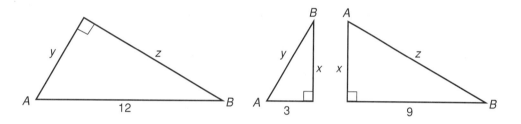

Now we can write the ratios of the lengths of the sides. In the ratios on the left, we have the sides opposite the angles A on top and the hypotenuses below. In the center we have the sides opposite the angles B on top and the hypotenuses below. On the right we have the sides opposite the angles A on top and the sides opposite the angles B below.

$$\frac{z}{12} = \frac{x}{y} = \frac{9}{z} \qquad \frac{y}{12} = \frac{3}{y} = \frac{x}{z} \qquad \frac{z}{y} = \frac{x}{3} = \frac{9}{x}$$

Now we try to find a way to use these proportions to get the answers we need. We can use two ratios from each group and write:

$$\frac{z}{12} = \frac{9}{z} \qquad \qquad \frac{y}{12} = \frac{3}{y} \qquad \qquad \frac{x}{3} = \frac{9}{x}$$

$$z^2 = 108 \qquad \qquad y^2 = 36 \qquad \qquad x^2 = 27$$

$$\mathbf{z = 6\sqrt{3}} \qquad \qquad \mathbf{y = 6} \qquad \qquad \mathbf{x = 3\sqrt{3}}$$

6.B
Functions of $-\theta$

It is often necessary to use one of the following identities:

$$\sin(-\theta) = -\sin\theta \qquad \csc(-\theta) = -\csc\theta$$

$$\cos(-\theta) = \cos\theta \qquad \sec(-\theta) = \sec\theta$$

$$\tan(-\theta) = -\tan\theta \qquad \cot(-\theta) = -\cot\theta$$

These relationships hold true for all values of θ. We need a way to recall them quickly and accurately. We can do this if we visualize the following unit circle with angles θ and $-\theta$.

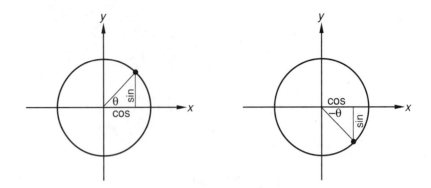

The sine of $-\theta$ and the sine of $+\theta$ are represented by the vertical sides of the triangles. We see that these vertical lengths are equal but on opposite sides of the x axis. So sin $(-\theta)$ has the same magnitude as sin θ, but the sign is different. The cosecant of an angle is the reciprocal of the sine of the angle, and this also gives us the sign relationship between csc $(-\theta)$ and csc θ.

$$\sin (-\theta) = -\sin \theta \quad \longrightarrow \quad \csc (-\theta) = -\csc \theta$$

The cosine of $-\theta$ and the cosine of θ are represented by the horizontal sides of the triangles, which are identical in length and in direction. Thus the cosines of θ and $-\theta$ are equal. The secant is the reciprocal of the cosine, so this also gives us the sign relationship between sec $(-\theta)$ and sec θ.

$$\cos (-\theta) = \cos \theta \quad \longrightarrow \quad \sec (-\theta) = \sec \theta$$

The tangent relationship can be deduced from the fact that the tangent of an angle is defined to be the ratio of the side opposite the angle to the side adjacent to the angle, which is the slope of the hypotenuse of the triangle in a unit circle. Since the slope of one hypotenuse is the negative of the slope of the other hypotenuse, we can write

$$\tan (-\theta) = -\tan \theta \quad \longrightarrow \quad \cot (-\theta) = -\cot \theta$$

For the preceding explanation, we assumed θ to be a first-quadrant angle. The same procedure can be used to show that these relationships are also true for values of θ that fall in the other three quadrants.

Example 6.5   Simplify: $\dfrac{\sin (-\theta) \cos (-\theta)}{\tan (-\theta)}$

Solution   We remember that the vertical sides of the triangles are the same length but in opposite directions. Thus, we replace sin $(-\theta)$ with $-\sin \theta$.

$$\frac{(-\sin \theta)[\cos (-\theta)]}{\tan (-\theta)}$$

Now we remember that the horizontal sides are equal and replace cos $(-\theta)$ with cos θ. We remember that the slopes are different and replace tan $(-\theta)$ with $-\tan \theta$.

$$\frac{-\sin \theta \,(\cos \theta)}{-\tan \theta} \quad \longrightarrow \quad \frac{\sin \theta \cos \theta}{\dfrac{\sin \theta}{\cos \theta}} \quad \longrightarrow \quad (\cos \theta)^2 \quad \longrightarrow \quad \mathbf{\cos^2 \theta}$$

Example 6.6   Show that $[\tan (-\theta)][\cos (-\theta)] - \sin (-\theta) = 0$.

Solution   First we substitute as necessary to get functions of θ rather than functions of $-\theta$.

$$(-\tan \theta)(\cos \theta) - (-\sin \theta) = 0$$

Now we replace tan θ with sin θ over cos θ. Then we simplify.

$$-\left(\frac{\sin \theta}{\cos \theta}\right)(\cos \theta) + \sin \theta = 0 \qquad \text{substituted}$$

$$-\sin \theta + \sin \theta = 0 \qquad \text{simplified}$$

Problem set 6

1. The ratio of the number of savants to the number of ignoramuses was 50 to 2. However, 10 times the number of ignoramuses was merely 30 fewer than the number of savants. How many savants and ignoramuses were there?

2. Two pipes are used to fill a large tank. When used alone, pipes A and B take 2 hours and 3 hours, respectively, to fill the tank. How many hours would it take to fill the tank if two pipes are used simultaneously?

3. Ten years from now, Carol will be 3 times as old as she was 6 years ago. How old is she now?

4. If a wheel rotates at a rate of 3 revolutions per second, find the number of radians through which the wheel rotates every minute.

5. Line L cuts two sides of a triangle and is parallel to the base of the triangle as shown. Find b in terms of a, c, and d.

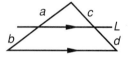

6. Solve for x in terms of L.

7. Solve for x, y, and z.

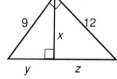

8. Shown is a unit circle centered at the origin of the coordinate plane. Find the coordinates of P.

9. Graph $y = -3 + 2 \cos \left(x - \frac{\pi}{4}\right)$.

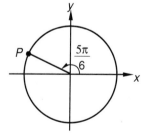

10. Write the equation of the following sinusoid in terms of the sine function.

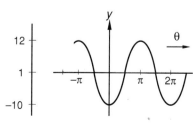

11. Shown is a function machine f where only a few input values with their corresponding output values are given.

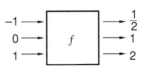

Which of the following could be the equation of f?
(a) $f(x) = 2x$ (b) $f(x) = x + \frac{3}{2}$
(c) $f(x) = 2^x$ (d) $f(x) = x^2 + 1$

12. Find the domain and range of the function $y = 1 + \sqrt{x}$.

Simplify the following expressions:

13. $\dfrac{\sec(-x)\csc(-x)}{\cot(-x)}$

14. $-\sin(-x)\csc x + 1$

Evaluate:

15. $3\tan^2 \dfrac{\pi}{6} + 2\sin^2\left(-\dfrac{\pi}{4}\right)$

16. $\cos\left(-\dfrac{13\pi}{3}\right)\sin^2\dfrac{\pi}{4}$

17. Divide $x^5 + 2x^4 + x^3 + x^2 + 2x + 1$ by $x^3 + 1$.

18. Complete the square to find the roots of $x^2 + x - 1 = 0$.

19. Solve the following equation for x: $\dfrac{1}{r^2} = \left(\dfrac{1}{x+y} - \dfrac{p}{m}\right)$

20. Find the coordinates of the midpoint of the line segment joining the points $(1, 2)$ and $(5, -7)$.

21. Find all values of x which satisfy the equation $\sqrt{2x + 3} = x$. Check to see if the answers actually satisfy the original equation.

CONCEPT REVIEW   22. If x and y are positive real numbers, then compare:
A. x percent of y B. y percent of x

Solve for y:

23. $AE = y$; $EB = y$; $CE = y - 1$; $ED = 2y$

24. O is the center of the circle shown; $m\angle ACB = (y)°$; $m\angle ABC = \left(\frac{1}{2}y\right)°$

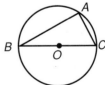

LESSON 7 *Quadratic equations*

The expression on the left below is a quadratic polynomial. The values of x that cause this quadratic polynomial to have a value of zero are called the **zeros** of the polynomial.

QUADRATIC POLYNOMIAL	QUADRATIC POLYNOMIAL EQUATION	QUADRATIC POLYNOMIAL FUNCTION
$x^2 + 2x - 3$	$x^2 + 2x - 3 = 0$	$y = x^2 + 2x - 3$
$(x + 3)(x - 1)$	$(x + 3)(x - 1) = 0$	$y = (x + 3)(x - 1)$
zeros are $-3, +1$	**roots** are $-3, +1$	**x intercepts** are $-3, +1$

In the center we have a quadratic polynomial equation. The values of x that cause the polynomial to equal zero are solutions of the equation and are called **roots** of the equation. Thus, the **zeros** of the polynomial are also the **roots** of the polynomial equation. On the right we have a quadratic polynomial function. The graph of this function will cross the x axis at x values where the function has a value of zero. Thus, zeros of the polynomial and the roots of the polynomial equation are also **zeros** of the function and are the **x-axis intercepts** of the graph of the function. The graph of a quadratic polynomial function is called a **parabola.**

Every quadratic polynomial can be written as a product of two factors. The two roots of a real polynomial equation will be complex conjugates, equal real numbers, or unequal real numbers. If the roots are complex conjugates, the graph of the parabola will not touch the x axis. If the roots are real and equal, the graph will touch the x axis at one point. If the roots are real and unequal, the graph will cross the x axis at two points. The axis of symmetry is a vertical line. The coefficients of the first two terms of a quadratic polynomial function determine the shape of the graph of the function. The constant term determines the vertical position of the graph because the y intercept of the graph equals the constant term in the polynomial. Changing the constant term will shift the graph up or down and can change the roots from a single real number to a pair of unequal real numbers or to a pair of complex conjugates. If the function is written in the form $f(x) = a(x - h)^2 + k$, the axis of symmetry is $x = h$ and the coordinates of the vertex are (h, k). We graph several of these functions below. On the next page, we show two other forms of the equations shown below.

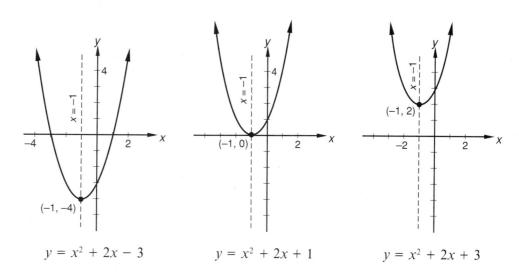

$$y = x^2 + 2x - 3 \qquad\qquad y = x^2 + 2x + 1 \qquad\qquad y = x^2 + 2x + 3$$

$$y = x^2 + 2x - 3 \qquad y = x^2 + 2x + 1 \qquad y = x^2 + 2x + 3$$
$$= (x + 3)(x - 1) \qquad = (x + 1)(x + 1) \qquad = (x + 1 - \sqrt{2}i)(x + 1 + \sqrt{2}i)$$
$$= (x + 1)^2 - 4 \qquad = (x + 1)^2 + 0 \qquad = (x + 1)^2 + 2$$

The constant term in the function on the left is -3, so the graph crosses the y axis when $y = -3$. The factored form shows that the x-axis crossing points are at x values of -3 and $+1$. The form we get when we complete the square shows that the graph of the left-hand function has an axis of symmetry of $x = -1$ and a vertex of $(-1, -4)$. In the function in the center we added 4 to the function so the constant is changed from -3 to $+1$. This graph has the same shape as the graph of the function on the left, but is shifted up 4 units, and the y intercept is now $+1$. In the function on the right, we added 2 more to the constant to get $+3$. This moved the graph up 2 more units. The graph does not cross or touch the x axis and the y intercept is now $+3$. When the graph of a real quadratic function does not touch the x axis, the zeros of the polynomial are complex conjugates, and, conversely, if the zeros are complex conjugates, the graph does not touch the x axis. We can make both statements by using **iff** and saying **the graph does not touch the x axis iff the zeros of the polynomial are complex conjugates.**

Example 7.1   Factor $2x^2 + 3x + 2$ over the set of complex numbers.

Solution   The words "over the set of complex numbers" tell us that the factors can contain complex numbers. Factors with real numbers are also acceptable, as every real number is a complex number whose imaginary part is zero. We will form a polynomial equation and use the quadratic formula to find the roots of the equation.

$$2x^2 + 3x + 2 = 0 \qquad \text{equation}$$
$$x = \frac{-3 \pm \sqrt{(3)^2 - 4(2)(2)}}{4} = -\frac{3}{4} \pm \frac{\sqrt{7}}{4}i$$

We will use the negatives of the roots when we write the factors.

$$2x^2 + 3x + 2 = 2\left[x - \left(-\frac{3}{4} + \frac{\sqrt{7}}{4}i\right)\right]\left[x - \left(-\frac{3}{4} - \frac{\sqrt{7}}{4}i\right)\right]$$

Example 7.2   Graph the parabola $f(x) = -2x^2 - 8x - 5$.

Solution   The negative coefficient (-2) of x^2 tells us that the graph opens down, and the constant -5 gives us the value of the y intercept. Next we change the form of the equation by completing the square. We begin by placing parentheses around the nonconstant terms.

$$f(x) = (-2x^2 - 8x \quad) - 5 \qquad \text{used parentheses}$$
$$f(x) = -2(x^2 + 4x \quad) - 5 \qquad \text{factored}$$
$$f(x) = -2(x^2 + 4x + 4) - 5 + 8 \qquad \text{completed the square}$$
$$f(x) = -2(x + 2)^2 + 3 \qquad \text{simplified}$$

The negative coefficient (-2) again tells us that the graph opens down. The $(x + 2)$ tells us that the axis of symmetry is $x = -2$, and the $+3$ gives us the y value of the vertex. Knowing this and knowing that the y intercept is -5 permits us to make a quick sketch of the parabola.

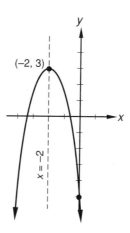

Example 7.3   Find the quadratic function whose zeros are -3 and $+2$ and whose y intercept is $+3$. Then graph the function.

Solution   Since the zeros are -3 and $+2$, we know that two of the factors of the polynomial are $(x + 3)$ and $(x - 2)$, but we do not know the value of the constant factor k.

$$y = k(x + 3)(x - 2) \quad \longrightarrow \quad y = kx^2 + kx - 6k$$

We can substitute the coordinates of any point on the curve for x and y and solve for k. The point $(0, 3)$ is on the curve because the y intercept is $+3$. When we use these coordinates for x and y, we find that $+3 = -6k$ because the x terms have a value of zero after we substitute.

$$3 = k(0)^2 + k(0) - 6k \quad \longrightarrow \quad k = -\frac{1}{2}$$

Since k is a negative number, we know that the parabola opens down. Now we have

$$y = -\frac{1}{2}(x + 3)(x - 2)$$

or
$$\boldsymbol{y = -\frac{1}{2}x^2 - \frac{1}{2}x + 3} \qquad \text{polynomial equation}$$

If we complete the square, we can find the coordinates of the vertex. We begin by using parentheses.

$$y = \left(-\frac{1}{2}x^2 - \frac{1}{2}x \qquad\right) + 3 \qquad\qquad \text{parentheses}$$

$$y = -\frac{1}{2}(x^2 + x \qquad) + 3 \qquad\qquad \text{factored}$$

$$y = -\frac{1}{2}\left(x^2 + x + \frac{1}{4}\right) + 3 + \frac{1}{8} \qquad \text{completed the square}$$

$$y = -\frac{1}{2}\left(x + \frac{1}{2}\right)^2 + 3\frac{1}{8} \qquad\qquad \text{simplified}$$

The coefficient $-\frac{1}{2}$ tells us again that the parabola opens down. We also see that the axis of symmetry is $x = -\frac{1}{2}$ and that the coordinates of the vertex are $\left(-\frac{1}{2}, \frac{25}{8}\right)$. The axis of symmetry is always halfway between the roots.

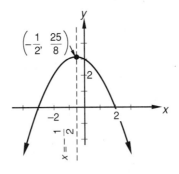

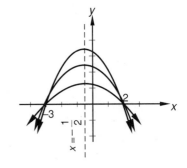

$$y = -\frac{1}{2}(x + 3)(x - 2) \qquad\qquad y = k(x + 3)(x - 2)$$

As we see in the figure on the right, there are an infinite number of parabolas whose graphs open down and cross the x axis at -3 and $+2$. All of them can be written with factors of $(x + 3)$ and $(x - 2)$, and the graph can be changed in shape by using different negative numbers as the constant factor k.

Problem set 7

1. The clock chimed once; it was 1 o'clock. In how many minutes would the hands of the clock be pointing in the same direction?

2. On the 36-mile trip to the magic fountain, Alice's pony trotted a brisk pace. On the way back, Alice's pony doubled the pace. If the total trip took 6 hours, how fast did Alice travel on the trip to the magic fountain and on the trip back?

3. Working alone, Mike can accomplish the entire task in 20 hours. Mike begins work on the task and Mary Beth joins him 3 hours later. Working together, they are able to finish the task in 4 hours. How long would it have taken Mary Beth working alone to complete the task?

4. The little red car went by at a speed of 40 kilometers per hour. What was the angular velocity of its wheels in radians per minute if the diameter of each of its wheels was 1 meter?

5. Factor $2x^2 - x + 3$ over the set of complex numbers.

6. Graph the quadratic function $f(x) = 2x^2 - 8x + 8$.

7. Find the quadratic function whose graph has x intercepts at $x = 2$ and $x = -1$, and whose y intercept is -4.

8. Find x in terms of h.

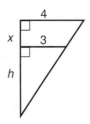

9. $\overline{AB}$ and $\overline{DE}$ are parallel as shown. Find the length of $\overline{AB}$ if the lengths of $\overline{BC}$, $\overline{CE}$, and $\overline{ED}$ are 4, 8, and 12, respectively.

10. Find the coordinates of point P on this unit circle.

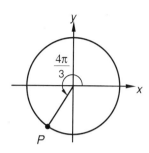

11. Graph $y = 2 - \sin x$.

12. Determine whether the following statement is true or false and explain why: The equation $y^2 = t$ cannot be the equation of a function of the independent variable t since $t = 4$ leads to two values for y, 2 and -2.

13. If $f(x) = (2x - 1)^2$, write the expression for $f(x + \Delta x)$.

Simplify the following expressions:

14. $\cot (-x) \cot x \tan^2 (-x)$

15. $\cos (-x) \sec x + 2$

Evaluate (do not use a calculator):

16. $\sin^2 14° \csc^2 14°$

17. $\sin^2 \left(-\dfrac{\pi}{6} \right) + \cos^2 \left(-\dfrac{\pi}{6} \right)$

18. Is the following argument valid or invalid?

All satyrs are immortal.
The beast is mortal.

Therefore, the beast is not a satyr.

19. Compute: $\displaystyle\sum_{i=-1}^{1} (2^i + 1)$

20. Simplify: $\dfrac{3i^3 - 4i^2}{2 - i}$

21. Write the following expression with no radicals in the denominator:

$$\frac{1}{\sqrt{x} - \sqrt{h}}$$

CONCEPT REVIEW **22.** Given x, y, z, and t as in the drawing shown, compare:
A. $z + t + y$ B. $x + y$

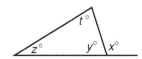

23. If L_1 and L_2 are parallel as shown, solve for x and y.

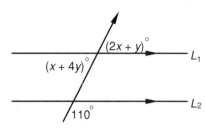

24. $\overline{AB}$ is tangent to circle O at A. If circle O has a radius of 3 and the distance from point O to point B is 5, find the length of $\overline{AB}$.

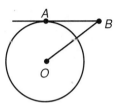

LESSON 8 *Pythagorean identities · Trigonometric identities · Cofunctions*

8.A
Pythagorean identities

We can use the triangle on the left below to prove the basic Pythagorean trigonometric identity shown on the right.

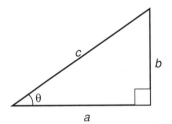

$$\sin^2 \theta + \cos^2 \theta = 1$$

We remember that $\sin^2 \theta$ means $(\sin \theta)^2$ and does not mean $\sin (\theta)^2$. First we substitute for $\sin \theta$ and $\cos \theta$.

$$\left(\frac{b}{c}\right)^2 + \left(\frac{a}{c}\right)^2$$

Next we add the fractions and get

$$\frac{b^2 + a^2}{c^2}$$

But the Pythagorean theorem tells us that the sum of the squares of the legs, $b^2 + a^2$, equals the square of the hypotenuse, which is c^2. Thus we can substitute c^2 for $b^2 + a^2$. If we show all of these steps on one line, we get

$$\sin^2 \theta + \cos^2 \theta = \left(\frac{b}{c}\right)^2 + \left(\frac{a}{c}\right)^2 = \frac{b^2 + a^2}{c^2} = \frac{c^2}{c^2} = 1$$

We could use the same triangle to prove the other two forms of the Pythagorean identity, which are

$$1 + \cot^2 \theta = \csc^2 \theta \qquad \text{and} \qquad \tan^2 \theta + 1 = \sec^2 \theta$$

Instead, we remember that the other two forms can be developed easily and accurately from $\sin^2 \theta + \cos^2 \theta = 1$ by dividing every term by $\sin^2 \theta$ or by dividing every term by $\cos^2 \theta$, as we show here.

$$\sin^2 \theta + \cos^2 \theta = 1 \qquad\qquad \sin^2 \theta + \cos^2 \theta = 1$$

$$\frac{\sin^2 \theta}{\sin^2 \theta} + \frac{\cos^2 \theta}{\sin^2 \theta} = \frac{1}{\sin^2 \theta} \qquad\qquad \frac{\sin^2 \theta}{\cos^2 \theta} + \frac{\cos^2 \theta}{\cos^2 \theta} = \frac{1}{\cos^2 \theta}$$

$$1 + \cot^2 \theta = \csc^2 \theta \qquad\qquad \tan^2 \theta + 1 = \sec^2 \theta$$

The three identities discussed are called ***Pythagorean identities*** and are frequently used in calculus problems that involve trigonometry.

PYTHAGOREAN IDENTITIES

$$\sin^2 \theta + \cos^2 \theta = 1$$

$$\tan^2 \theta + 1 = \sec^2 \theta$$

$$\cot^2 \theta + 1 = \csc^2 \theta$$

Example 8.1 Compute $\sin^2 17° + \cos^2 17°$.

Solution We remember that the Pythagorean identity

$$\sin^2 \theta + \cos^2 \theta = 1$$

is true for any value of θ. Thus, it is also true when $\theta = 17°$.

$$\sin^2 17° + \cos^2 17° = \mathbf{1}$$

8.B
Trigonometric identities

In calculus it is often helpful to change trigonometric expressions from one form to an equivalent form that is easier to work with. An equation that equates two equal trigonometric expressions is called a ***trigonometric identity.*** Problems designed to permit practice in changing trigonometric expressions from one form to another consist of two expressions connected by an equals sign. Our job is to work with one of the expressions and change it to the form of the other expression. Although an equals sign is present, we do not use the rules for equations by adding the same quantity to both sides or by multiplying both sides by the same quantity. We will restrict ourselves to three procedures. We may:

1. Substitute an equivalent expression for all or any part of a given expression.
2. Multiply the numerator and denominator of any expression or the numerator and denominator of a part of any expression by the same nonzero quantity.
3. Combine terms that have equal denominators.

There is no one "correct way" to show that two expressions are equivalent. We try one thing, and if that does not work we try something else. After much practice these transformations will become familiar and not at all troublesome. In this lesson we will consider expressions that can be simplified by using one of the Pythagorean identities. In these expressions we will learn to look for terms such as $\sin^2 x + \cos^2 x$, $1 - \sin^2 x$, $1 - \cos^2 x$, $1 + \cot^2 x$, $\csc^2 x - 1$, $\tan^2 x + 1$, and $\sec^2 x - 1$.

Example 8.2   Show that: $\dfrac{\cos^2 x + 4 + \sin^2 x}{5 \sec^2 (-x)} = \cos^2 x$

Solution   If we look carefully at the numerator of the left-hand side, we can find $\sin^2 x + \cos^2 x$ hiding there, and we recall that $\sin^2 x + \cos^2 x = 1$. So we decide to work with the left-hand side. We rearrange the numerator, and in the denominator we replace $\sec^2 (-x)$ with $\sec^2 x$.

$$\frac{(\sin^2 x + \cos^2 x) + 4}{5 \sec^2 x} \qquad \text{rearranged}$$

$$= \frac{5}{5 \sec^2 x} \qquad \sin^2 x + \cos^2 x = 1$$

$$= \mathbf{\cos^2 x} \qquad \frac{1}{\sec^2 x} = \cos^2 x$$

Example 8.3   Show that: $\dfrac{\sec^4 x + \sec^4 x \tan^2 x}{\cos^4 (-x)} = \sec^{10} x$

Solution   Let us work with the left-hand side. First we replace $\cos^4 (-x)$ with $\cos^4 x$. Nothing else is obvious, so we try factoring the numerator and get

$$\frac{(\sec^4 x)(1 + \tan^2 x)}{\cos^4 x} \qquad \text{factored left-hand side}$$

Now we are in luck because $1 + \tan^2 x$ equals $\sec^2 x$.

$$\frac{(\sec^4 x)(\sec^2 x)}{\cos^4 x}$$

But the reciprocal of $\cos^4 x$ is $\sec^4 x$, so finally we have

$$\mathbf{(\sec^4 x)(\sec^2 x)(\sec^4 x) = \sec^{10} x}$$

Example 8.4   Show that: $\cos^2 x \sec^2 x - \cos^2 x = \sin^2 x$

Solution   Again we begin by factoring the expression on the left.

$$(\cos^2 x)(\sec^2 x - 1) \qquad \text{factored}$$

$$= (\cos^2 x)(\tan^2 x) \qquad \sec^2 x - 1 = \tan^2 x$$

$$= (\cos^2 x)\left(\frac{\sin^2 x}{\cos^2 x}\right) \qquad \text{substituted}$$

$$= \mathbf{\sin^2 x} \qquad \text{simplified}$$

8.C
Cofunctions

The sum of the angles in any triangle is $180°$, or π radians. If a triangle is a right triangle, the right angle has a measure of $90°$, or $\pi/2$ radians. If one acute angle is θ, **the other acute angle** must be $90° - \theta$, or $\pi/2 - \theta$. When we write $90° - \theta$, we indicate that θ is measured in degrees, and when we write $\pi/2 - \theta$, we indicate that θ is measured in radians. If the sum of two angles is $90°$, or $\pi/2$, the angles are called **complementary angles.** Thus $90° - \theta$ and $\pi/2 - \theta$ are angles that are complements of angle θ.

In the following discussion we choose to use degree measure. In examples and problems, we will use both degree measure and radian measure.

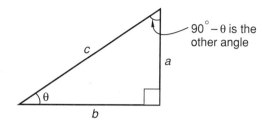

In the right triangle shown here, the sine of θ equals a over c and the cosine of the other acute angle also equals a over c.

$$\sin \theta = \frac{a}{c} \qquad \cos (90° - \theta) = \frac{a}{c}$$

The cosine of θ equals b over c, and the sine of the other acute angle equals b over c.

$$\cos \theta = \frac{b}{c} \qquad \sin (90° - \theta) = \frac{b}{c}$$

The tangent and cotangent have similar relationships.

$$\tan \theta = \frac{a}{b} \qquad \cot (90° - \theta) = \frac{a}{b}$$

$$\cot \theta = \frac{b}{a} \qquad \tan (90° - \theta) = \frac{b}{a}$$

The secant and cosecant also have similar relationships.

$$\sec \theta = \frac{c}{b} \qquad \csc (90° - \theta) = \frac{c}{b}$$

$$\csc \theta = \frac{c}{a} \qquad \sec (90° - \theta) = \frac{c}{a}$$

Thus every trigonometric function of θ has the same value as the trigonometric cofunction of $(90° - \theta)$. We can remember this if we always think of $(90° - \theta)$ as the *other angle*.

$$(90° - \theta)\ \textbf{is the other angle}$$

It is interesting to note that the words *cosine, cotangent,* and *cosecant* are abbreviations for the sine of the complementary angle (the other angle), the tangent of the complementary angle (the other angle), and the secant of the complementary angle (the other angle). Thus,

cosine	**means**	**the sine of the other angle**
cotangent	**means**	**the tangent of the other angle**
cosecant	**means**	**the secant of the other angle**

Now we have four procedures that we can use to simplify trigonometric expressions.

1. Replace functions of $(-\theta)$ with functions of $+\theta$.
2. Replace functions of $(90° - \theta)$, or $(\frac{\pi}{2} - \theta)$, with their cofunctions.
3. Look for forms of the Pythagorean identity that can be replaced.
4. Replace $\tan x$, $\cot x$, $\sec x$, and $\csc x$ with equivalent expressions that use $\sin x$ and $\cos x$.

Example 8.5   Show that: $(\cos \theta)[\cos (-\theta)](1 + \tan^2 \theta)\left[\cos \left(\dfrac{\pi}{2} - \theta\right)\right] = \sin \theta$

Solution   This problem was designed to require the use of all four steps listed above. We begin on the left-hand side by substituting to eliminate $(-\theta)$ and $(\pi/2 - \theta)$ and we get

$$(\cos \theta)(\cos \theta)(1 + \tan^2 \theta)(\sin \theta)$$

Next we replace $1 + \tan^2 \theta$ with $\sec^2 \theta$.

$$(\cos^2 \theta)(\sec^2 \theta)(\sin \theta)$$

As the last step we replace $\sec^2 \theta$ with $1/\cos^2 \theta$ and simplify.

$$(\cos^2 \theta)\left(\dfrac{1}{\cos^2 \theta}\right)(\sin \theta) = \mathbf{\sin\,\theta}$$

Example 8.6   Show that: $[\sin^2 (-\theta)](\csc^2 \theta - 1)\left[\cot \left(\dfrac{\pi}{2} - \theta\right)\right] = \sin \theta \cos \theta$

Solution   **We must be careful when we substitute for a function that is raised to a power.** Since $\sin (-\theta) = -\sin \theta$, we might be tempted to write

$$\sin^2 (-\theta) = -\sin^2 \theta \qquad \textbf{NO! NO!}$$

We remember that $\sin^2 (-\theta)$ means $[\sin (-\theta)][\sin (-\theta)]$, and since $\sin (-\theta) = -\sin \theta$, we have

$$\sin^2 (-\theta) = [\sin (-\theta)][\sin (-\theta)] = (-\sin \theta)(-\sin \theta) = \sin^2 \theta$$

Now we substitute $\sin^2 \theta$ for $\sin^2 (-\theta)$ and get

$$(\sin^2 \theta)(\csc^2 \theta - 1)(\tan \theta)$$

The middle factor looks like it may be a part of a Pythagorean identity. Let's see if it is. To investigate we begin with the basic Pythagorean identity and write

$$\sin^2 \theta + \cos^2 \theta = 1$$

If we divide by $\sin^2 \theta$, we get

$$1 + \cot^2 \theta = \csc^2 \theta$$

Aha! Now we see that $\csc^2 \theta - 1 = \cot^2 \theta$. We make this replacement and then replace $\cot^2 \theta$ with $\cos^2 \theta$ over $\sin^2 \theta$ and replace $\tan \theta$ with $\sin \theta$ over $\cos \theta$.

$$(\sin^2 \theta)(\cot^2 \theta)(\tan \theta) \quad \longrightarrow \quad (\sin^2 \theta)\left(\dfrac{\cos^2 \theta}{\sin^2 \theta}\right)\left(\dfrac{\sin \theta}{\cos \theta}\right) = \mathbf{\sin\,\theta\,\cos\,\theta}$$

Problem set 8

1. The density of a 10-foot rod, oriented horizontally, varies linearly with the distance x from the left end of the rod. If the density is 5 at the left end and 17 at the right end of the rod, what is the density of the rod 4 feet from the rod's left end?

2. The sum of the digits of a three-digit number is 9. When the order of the digits is reversed, the newly formed number is 396 greater than the original number. If the leftmost digit is one-third of the middle digit, what is the number?

3. Stacy thought that 30 workers could do 6 jobs in 4 days. How many days did she think it would it take 10 workers to do 4 jobs?

4. A motorcycle whose wheels have a radius of 60 centimeters is traveling at 30 kilometers per hour. What is the angular velocity of each of the wheels in radians per minute?

5. The basic Pythagorean identity is $\sin^2 \theta + \cos^2 \theta = 1$. Divide by $\sin^2 \theta$ and $\cos^2 \theta$ as required to develop the other two Pythagorean identities.

Evaluate the following trigonometric expressions, using Pythagorean identities as necessary.

6. $\sin^2 \dfrac{\pi}{17} + \cos^2 \dfrac{\pi}{17}$

7. $\sec^2 \dfrac{5\pi}{4} + 2\tan\left(-\dfrac{\pi}{4}\right)$

For Problems 8–10, assume that θ is an angle such that $\sin \theta = -\frac{4}{5}$. Compute:

8. $\sin(-\theta)$

9. $\cos\left(\dfrac{\pi}{2} - \theta\right)$

10. $\sec\left(\dfrac{\pi}{2} - \theta\right)$

11. Show that: $\dfrac{\sin^2 x + 2 + \cos^2 x}{3\csc^2(-x)} = \sin^2 x$

12. Show that: $\left[\sec\left(\dfrac{\pi}{2} - x\right)\right][\sin(-x)] = -1$

13. Show that: $(\sin x)\left[\cos\left(\dfrac{\pi}{2} - x\right)\right] + \cos(-x)\cos x = 1$

14. Find the zeros of the quadratic polynomial $2x^2 - 3x + 2$.

15. Use x as the independent variable to write the equation of the quadratic function f whose zeros are -3 and -2 and whose leading coefficient is 2.

16. Solve for h in terms of x.

17. Solve for x, y, and z.

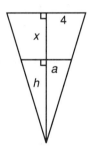

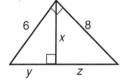

18. Find the coordinates of the point P, where P is the point on a unit circle centered at the origin as shown.

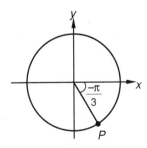

19. Write the equation of the sinusoid shown in terms of the sine function.

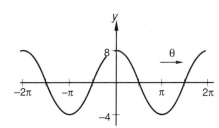

20. Which of the following sets lists the coordinates of points which lie on the graph of a function?
    (*a*) $\{(1, 5), (6, 2), (4, 3), (6, -3)\}$
    (*b*) $\{(2, 4), (1, 5), (3, 1), (6, 3)\}$
    (*c*) $\{(1, -1), (-1, 1), (1, 3), (4, \pi)\}$
    (*d*) $\{(14, 12), (-1, -7), (8, 12), (14, -3)\}$

Simplify:

21. $\sqrt{-2}\sqrt{-3}\sqrt{-6} + 14i^3$ 22. $\dfrac{(a + b)^2 - a^2}{b}$

CONCEPT REVIEW   23. If x, y, and z are real numbers and $xy > zy$, compare: A. x B. z

24. If $a + b = 10$ and $ab = 5$, compute the value of $a^2 + b^2$. (*Hint*: Begin by squaring both sides of the first equation and then make use of the second equation.)

25. Find x.

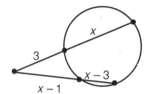

LESSON 9   *Abstract word problems*

Mathematics is a symbolic language that can be used to write many of our thoughts in ways that permit these thoughts to be investigated analytically. We find that these thoughts involve concepts that can be treated individually or in combinations. Over the years, teachers of mathematics have discovered that certain carefully contrived word problems can be used advantageously to teach particular concepts. The uniform motion problems in textbooks are never encountered in the real world, but these problems are most useful in teaching the concept of rate and in teaching the use of multiple equations in problem solving.

Chemical mixture problems, on the other hand, are encountered in the study of chemistry, but we also find that the concepts taught through the use of this kind of problem are encountered in other real-world problems. In this book we will continue to study the standard contrived textbook-type problems with the aim of increasing our mastery over the concepts that can be taught by using these problems.

The word problems in this series of books were carefully designed to build in each student a reservoir of concepts that can be recognized and the skills that permit these concepts to be applied to new problems. The study of higher mathematics, physics, and engineering requires generalizations about particular problems rather than answers that are real numbers. We find that abstract word problems in which letters are used instead of real numbers are ideal for preparing students to cope with the reality of advanced courses in mathematics and mathematically based disciplines. In this book we will devote attention to abstract word problems. In this lesson we will review a few of the basic types of word problems.

Example 9.1   Linda drove m miles at p kilometers per hour, but got to the flower market 2 hours late. How fast should she have driven to have arrived on time?

Solution   This problem requires the abstract use of the concept that rate times time equals distance. First we look at the rate, time, and distance of the first trip. The distance and the rate are given, and we find the time by dividing the distance by the rate.

$$\text{Distance} = m \qquad \text{Rate} = p \qquad \text{Time} = \frac{m}{p}$$

If the distance remains the same and the time is reduced by 2, the rate must change.

$$\text{Distance} = m \qquad \text{Time} = \frac{m}{p} - 2 \qquad \text{Rate} = \frac{m}{\frac{m}{p} - 2}$$

If we simplify the expression for rate, we get

$$\text{Rate} = \frac{mp}{m - 2p} \frac{\text{km}}{\text{hr}}$$

Example 9.2   Jill could do 3 jobs in J hours, and Sharon could do S jobs in 5 hours. How long would it take them to do w^2 jobs if they worked together?

Solution   This problem allows us to work with the idea that rate times time does not have to equal distance. Rate times time can also equal a part of a job, and parts of a job can be added to find a whole job or multiples of a whole job. The problem states that Jill's rate is 3 over J jobs per hour and that Sharon's rate is S over 5 jobs per hour.

$$R_J = \frac{3}{J} \frac{\text{jobs}}{\text{hr}} \qquad R_S = \frac{S}{5} \frac{\text{jobs}}{\text{hr}}$$

Jill and Sharon will work the same time t, and the total number of jobs to be completed is w^2. Thus, we use T_J and T_S for the times and write

$$R_J T_J + R_S T_S = w^2$$

Since the time of both workers is the same, we can write

$$\frac{3}{J}t + \frac{S}{5}t = w^2$$

We clear the denominators and solve for t.

$$(5J)\frac{3}{J}t + (5J)\frac{S}{5}t = 5Jw^2 \qquad\qquad \text{multiplied by } 5J$$

$$15t + JSt = 5Jw^2 \qquad\qquad \text{canceled}$$

$$t(15 + JS) = 5Jw^2 \qquad\qquad \text{factored}$$

$$t = \frac{5Jw^2}{15 + JS} \text{ hours} \qquad \text{solved}$$

Example 9.3   Ryan and Stephen saw that the number of cookies varied directly as the amount of sugar used. If 5 pounds of sugar was used, D cookies were produced. How many cookies would be produced if $10E$ pounds of sugar were used?

Solution   The equation is

$$N_c = kA_s$$

where N_c is the number of cookies, k is the proportionality constant, and A_s is the amount of sugar. To find k, we use D for cookies and 5 for A_s.

$$D = k(5) \longrightarrow k = \frac{D}{5}\frac{\text{cookies}}{\text{pound}}$$

Next we replace k in the first equation with $\frac{D}{5}$.

$$N_c = \frac{D}{5}A_s$$

To finish, we use $10E$ in place of A_s.

$$N_c = \frac{D}{5}(10E) = \textbf{2DE cookies}$$

Example 9.4   Ryan and Stephen's little sister found that she could buy y items for $D + 6$ dollars. How many items could she buy for \$42?

Solution   First we find the number of items per dollar.

$$\frac{y \text{ items}}{D + 6 \text{ dollars}} \longrightarrow \frac{y}{D + 6}\frac{\text{items}}{\text{dollar}}$$

If we multiply this rate by 42 dollars, the dollars will cancel and we get

$$\left(\frac{y}{D + 6}\frac{\text{items}}{\text{dollar}}\right)(42 \text{ dollars}) = \frac{\textbf{42y}}{\textbf{D + 6}}\textbf{ items}$$

Example 9.5   This year Steve is twice as old as Tom. In x years Steve will be $\frac{5}{3}$ as old as Tom will be then. Find the present age of Steve in terms of x.

Solution   We will use S_n for Steve's age now and T_n for Tom's age now. The statement of the problem gives us two equations.

$$S_n = 2T_n \qquad S_n + x = \frac{5}{3}(T_n + x)$$

We will replace T_n in the right-hand equation with $\frac{1}{2}S_n$ and solve for S_n.

$$S_n + x = \frac{5}{3}\left(\frac{S_n}{2} + x\right) \qquad \text{substituted}$$

$$S_n + x = \frac{5}{6}S_n + \frac{5}{3}x \qquad \text{multiplied}$$

$$6S_n + 6x = 5S_n + 10x \qquad \text{multiplied by 6}$$

$$\textbf{S}_n = \textbf{4x} \qquad \text{solved}$$

Example 9.6   Gary had g gallons of a 60% antifreeze solution. Ed added e gallons of a 30% antifreeze solution. If the final solution is 40% antifreeze, write an expression in terms of g that represents the number of gallons Ed added.

Solution   We begin by writing the equation for amount of antifreeze present.

Gary's antifreeze + Ed's antifreeze = total antifreeze

Gary's antifreeze equals 0.6 of his g gallons, or $0.6g$. Ed's antifreeze equals 0.3 of his e gallons, or $0.3e$. The total antifreeze equals 0.4 of $(g + e)$ gallons. Thus we substitute in the equation above and solve.

$$0.60g + 0.30e = 0.40(g + e) \qquad \text{equation}$$
$$60g + 30e = 40g + 40e \qquad \text{multiplied by 100 and expanded}$$
$$20g = 10e \qquad \text{combined like terms}$$
$$2g = e \qquad \text{divided}$$

Thus Ed added twice as much as Gary, or **2g gallons.**

Problem set 9

1. The train traveled n miles at r miles per hour and still got there 1 hour late. How fast should the train have traveled to have arrived on time?

2. Larry could do L jobs in 3 hours and Fred could do 4 jobs in F hours. If both work together, how long would it take to complete $2J$ jobs?

3. At present, Terri is twice as old as Dave. In x years, Terri will be $1\frac{1}{3}$ times as old as Dave. Find the present age of Terri in terms of x.

4. Marsha found that she could purchase S squash balls for D dollars. If she had C cents, how many squash balls could she buy, assuming she had exactly enough cents to purchase an integer number of balls?

5. The 14-inch-radius tires on Jaimie's car revolved r times every minute. If the car travels along a straight path, what is its speed in feet per hour?

6. Use a Pythagorean identity to compute the numerical value of the following:

$$\tan^2 \frac{\pi}{15} - \sec^2 \frac{\pi}{15}$$

For Problems 7–9, assume that α is an angle such that $\cos \alpha = -\frac{3}{4}$.

7. List the quadrants in which α could lie.

8. $\sec(-\alpha) = ?$ 9. $\sin\left(\frac{\pi}{2} - \alpha\right) = ?$

10. Write the basic Pythagorean identity and use it to develop the other two forms of the identity.

Prove the following identities:

11. $\dfrac{1 - \sin^2 x}{\sin\left(\frac{\pi}{2} - x\right)} = \cos x$ 12. $\left[\cos\left(\frac{\pi}{2} - x\right)\right]^2 [1 + \cot^2(-x)] = 1$

13. Find the equation of the quadratic function whose graph has x intercepts at $x = -1$ and $x = 2$ and the y intercept at $y = -4$.

14. Factor the quadratic polynomial equation $3x^2 + x + 1$ over the set of complex numbers.

15. Solve for x in the figure shown.

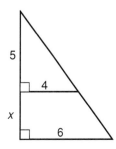

16. Graph $y = -1 + 2 \cos \left(x - \dfrac{\pi}{2} \right)$.

17. Sketch a unit circle centered at the origin O. Locate on the unit circle the point P so that $\overline{OP}$ forms an angle of $120°$ with the positive x axis. Determine the coordinates of P.

18. Find the domain and range of $y = \dfrac{1}{\sqrt{x}}$.

19. Which of the following graphs cannot be the graph of a function?

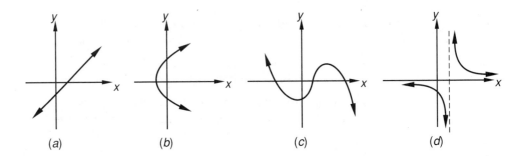

(a)   (b)   (c)   (d)

Simplify:

20. $\dfrac{2}{\sqrt{3}} - \sqrt{3} + \dfrac{\sqrt{27}}{2}$ 21. $\dfrac{a^3 b^3 - c^3}{ab - c}$

22. Begin with the point-slope form of the equation of a line to develop the general form of the equation of the line which has a slope of 3 and which passes through the point $(1, 2)$.

CONCEPT REVIEW   23. If x, y, and z are real numbers and $x > y$, then compare:
   A. xz B. yz

24. Point P lies outside a circle O and is 5 centimeters away from the center of circle O. The tangent line from P to circle O has a length of 4 centimeters. Find the radius of the circle.

LESSON 10 *Important numbers · Exponential functions*

10.A

Important numbers

Possibly the most important numbers in mathematics are the numbers 0, 1, π, and e. Zero is important because it is the additive identity. The sum of any number and 0 is identically the number itself. The number 1 is the multiplicative identity because the product of any number and 1 is identically the number itself. This property of the number 1 allows us to change the symbolic representation of a number without changing the value of the expression. For example, if *c* represents some number and we multiply *c* by *m* over *m*, we get

$$c \cdot \frac{m}{m} = \frac{cm}{m}$$

If *m* does not equal zero, the expression *cm* over *m* represents the same number that *c* does because *m* over *m* equals 1; so we have just multiplied *c* by 1.

The number π is an irrational number because it cannot be written as a fraction of integers. Thus, it cannot be written as a nonrepeating decimal numeral with a finite number of digits. The representation of π to 20 digits is

$$\pi = 3.1415926535897932384 \cdots$$

This is merely a 20-digit approximation because the digits go on and on and do not repeat in a pattern. Irrational numbers made the ancients most uncomfortable, and for centuries many insisted that these numbers were not real numbers. But π is the number that represents the number of times the diameter of a circle will divide into the circumference.

$$\frac{\text{Circumference}}{\text{Diameter}} = \pi$$

The number π *is* a real number, and we have to live with it even though it made the ancients uncomfortable.

The number *e* is also an irrational real number. The three-digit approximation of *e* is 2.72, but as with any irrational number, the decimal approximation of *e* consists of an infinite number of digits that do not repeat in a pattern.

$$e = 2.7182818 \cdots$$

In calculus the number *e* is the preferred base for logarithms and exponentials because its use makes many operations much easier.

10.B
Exponential functions

An exponential function has the form

$$y = b^x$$

The base can be any positive number except 1. We do not use 1 as a base because if we do, *y* is always equal to 1 because 1 raised to any power is 1.

$$y = 1^x \qquad \text{means} \qquad y = 1 \qquad \text{for all } x \in \mathbb{R}$$

We want all values of *x* and *y* to be real numbers, so the base cannot be a negative number because this will lead to imaginary values for *y* for some values of *x*. For example, if we use -2 as the base and let *x* equal $\frac{3}{2}$, we get a *y* value of $2\sqrt{2}\, i$, which is unacceptable.

$$y = (-2)^{3/2} \qquad \text{base is } -2$$
$$y = [(-2)^3]^{1/2} \qquad \text{equivalent expression}$$
$$y = \sqrt{-8} \qquad \text{simplified}$$
$$y = 2\sqrt{2}\, i \qquad \text{simplified}$$

If the base is a number between 0 and 1, the graph of the equation will be a continuous curve similar to the curves shown on the left on the next page. If the base is a number greater than 1, the graph of the equation will be a continuous curve similar to the curves shown on the right.

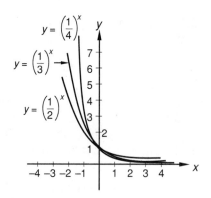 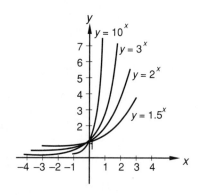

Note that all the graphs cross the y axis 1 unit above the origin at (1, 0). Graphing exponential functions is easy because these graphs have one of the two basic shapes shown here.

Example 10.1   Sketch the graph of: (a) $y = 1.3^x$ (b) $y = 4^x$

Solution   We can get three quick points on the graph of $y = 1.3^x$ by letting x equal 0, 1, and -1.

$$y = (1.3)^0 \qquad y = (1.3)^1 \qquad y = (1.3)^{-1}$$

$$= 1 \qquad\qquad = 1.3 \qquad\qquad = \frac{1}{1.3}$$

Thus the coordinates of these three points on the graph are (0, 1), (1, 1.3) and $(-1, \frac{1}{1.3})$. **This delightful result shows us that in any exponential function $y = b^x$, if we let x equal 0, 1, and -1, the y values are 1, the value of the base, and 1 over the value of the base.** This means that three points on the graph of $y = 4^x$ have coordinates (0, 1), (1, 4), and $(-1, \frac{1}{4})$. When we look at the sketches, there is a slight difference

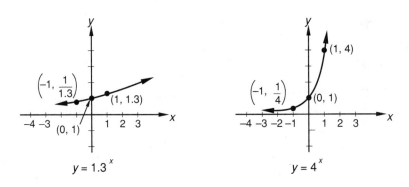

to the left of the y axis, but a great difference to the right of the y axis because the graph of $y = 4^x$ must rise rather abruptly to reach a y value of 4 when $x = 1$. The graph of $y = 40^x$ would be even steeper because a y value of 40 must be reached when $x = 1$.

Example 10.2   Sketch the graphs of: (a) $y = -e^x$ (b) $y = e^{-x}$

Solution   A negative sign can be placed in only two places in this equation. It can be placed before the e or before the x. One placement will cause the graph of $y = e^x$ to be reflected in the x axis (flipped about the x axis) and the other will cause the graph of $y = e^x$ to be reflected in the y axis. We will get three quick points on each graph by letting x equal 0, 1, and -1 and then discuss the results. First we work with $y = -e^x$.

EQUATION	WHEN $x = 0$	WHEN $x = 1$	WHEN $x = -1$
$y = -e^x$	$-e^0 = -1$	$-e^1 = -e$	$-e^{-1} = -\dfrac{1}{e}$
Coordinates	$(0, -1)$	$(1, -e)$	$\left(1, -\dfrac{1}{e}\right)$

The minus sign in $-e^x$ changes the sign of each y value in $y = e^x$ from plus to minus and causes the graph of $y = -e^x$ to be a reflection of the graph of $y = e^x$ in the x axis (flipped about the x axis). The resulting graph is shown in the center figure below. Now we will find three points on the graph of $y = e^{-x}$.

EQUATION	WHEN $x = 0$	WHEN $x = 1$	WHEN $x = -1$
$y = e^{-x}$	$e^{-(0)} = 1$	$e^{-(1)} = \dfrac{1}{e}$	$e^{-(-1)} = e$
Coordinates	$(0, 1)$	$\left(1, \dfrac{1}{e}\right)$	$(-1, e)$

The minus sign in e^{-x} changed the sign of each x and caused the graph of $y = e^x$ to be reflected in the y axis (flipped about the y axis) as we show in the graph on the right.

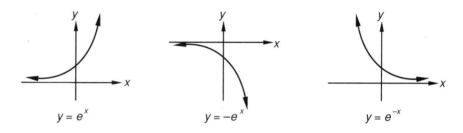

$$y = e^x \qquad y = -e^x \qquad y = e^{-x}$$

Since $y = e^{-x}$ makes the same statement as $y = (1/e)^x$, the minus sign has the effect of changing the base from e to $1/e$. In the first two graphs of this section we noted that graphs of exponential functions whose bases are reciprocals are reflections of each other in the y axis.

Example 10.3 Sketch the graph of $y = -e^{-x}$.

Solution This equation has both minus signs, so the graph will be reflected in one axis and then in the other axis. This can be a little confusing, and we can always fall back on the expedient of finding three quick points.

EQUATION	WHEN $x = 0$	WHEN $x = 1$	WHEN $x = -1$
$y = -e^{-x}$	$y = -e^{-(0)} = -1$	$y = -e^{-(1)} = -\dfrac{1}{e}$	$y = -e^{-(-1)} = -e$
Coordinates	$(0, -1)$	$\left(1, -\dfrac{1}{e}\right)$	$(-1, -e)$

We show the graph of $y = e^x$ on the left and $y = -e^{-x}$ on the right.

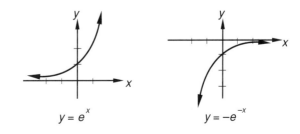

$$y = e^x \qquad y = -e^{-x}$$

Problem set 10

1. Jenny drove x miles per hour for the first 2 hours and then drove at y miles per hour for the next 3 hours. What was Jenny's average speed in miles per hour for the entire 5-hour trip?

2. Two pipes can be used to fill the tank. When used alone, the large pipe can fill the tank in 3 hours and the small pipe can fill the tank in 4 hours. If the pipes are used together, how long would it take to fill the entire tank?

3. A solution is made by mixing V quarts of vinegar with W quarts of spring water. Write an expression whose value is the percent of the solution that is vinegar.

4. The number of people listening attentively varied inversely as the indifference index. If P people listened attentively when the indifference index was I, how many people would have been listening attentively if the indifference index had been J?

5. Which of the following assertions is true for both the numbers e and π?
   (a) Both numbers are rational numbers.
   (b) Neither number can be expressed as the ratio of two whole numbers.
   (c) Both numbers can be expressed as the ratio of two whole numbers.
   (d) Both numbers are greater than 3.

Sketch the graphs of the following equations:

6. $y = e^x$ 7. $y = e^{-x}$ 8. $y = -e^{-x}$

9. Write the basic form of the Pythagorean identity, and develop two other forms of this identity by dividing once by $\sin^2 \theta$ and then by $\cos^2 \theta$.

Simplify the following expressions:

10. $\sin\left(\dfrac{\pi}{2} - \theta\right) \tan \theta \left[\sin(-\theta)\right]$ 11. $\dfrac{1 - \sin^2 \theta}{\cos^2\left(\dfrac{\pi}{2} - \theta\right)}$

12. Show that $-\sin\left(\dfrac{\pi}{2} - x\right) \cos(-x) + 1 = \sin^2 x$.

13. Find the equation for the quadratic function f, where $f(-1) = f(2) = 0$ and $f(0) = -4$. (This problem is the same as Problem 13 in Problem set 9, but is worded differently.)

14. Sketch the graph of $y = (x - 2)^2$.

15. For the triangles shown, express y in terms of a, b, and x.

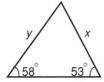

16. Write the equation of the sinusoid shown in terms of the sine function.

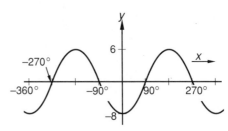

17. Could this machine be a function machine? Justify your answer.

$$
\begin{array}{ccc}
1 \longrightarrow & & \longrightarrow 2 \\
3 \longrightarrow & \boxed{h} & \longrightarrow 4 \\
1 \longrightarrow & & \longrightarrow 6
\end{array}
$$

18. Given $f(x) = x^2$, evaluate $f(x + h) - f(x)$.

19. Find the length of a diagonal of a rectangle whose length is 12 and whose width is 5.

20. Evaluate: $\displaystyle\sum_{i=-1}^{1} -\left(\frac{1}{2}\right)^i$

21. Multiply $(\sqrt{x + h} - \sqrt{x})$ by $(\sqrt{x + h} + \sqrt{x})$ and simplify the result.

CONCEPT REVIEW 22. If $0 < y < 1$, compare: *A.* $\dfrac{1}{y^2}$ *B.* $\dfrac{1}{y^3}$

23. Find x in the figure shown, where the center of the circle is O and $m\widehat{AB} = 80°$.

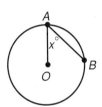

LESSON 11 *Polar coordinates (vectors) · Polar coordinates (complex numbers)*

11.A
Polar coordinates (vectors)

The location of a point in the real coordinate plane can be designated by using vector notation and either rectangular or polar coordinates. To designate a point whose x coordinate is -3 and whose y coordinate is $+2$, we can use an ordered pair $(-3, 2)$ or we can use the letters i and j and write $-3i + 2j$. The letter i designates the x direction and the letter j designates the y direction. There is only one rectangular form of a vector, but there are four ways the polar form of the same vector can be written since we can use both positive and negative angles and magnitudes.

Example 11.1 Convert $-3i + 2j$ to polar coordinates. Write the four forms of the polar coordinates of this point.

Solution On the left we graph the point and draw the triangle. Note that one side of the triangle is perpendicular to the x axis.

$$R^2 = 2^2 + 3^2 = 13$$

$$R = \sqrt{13}$$

$$\tan \theta = \frac{2}{3} = 0.6667$$

so $\theta = 33.69°$

On the right on the preceding page, we find that the length of R is $\sqrt{13}$ and that the small angle is 33.69°. If we measure counterclockwise from the x axis, the polar angle is 146.31°; and if we measure clockwise from the positive x axis, the polar angle is −213.69°. If we use negative magnitudes as shown in the right-hand figures, we find that the corresponding polar angles are fourth-quadrant angles.

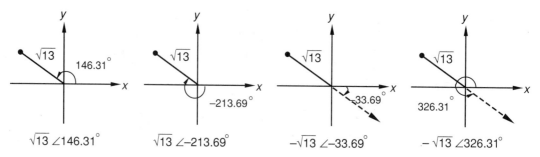

$$\sqrt{13}\angle146.31° \qquad \sqrt{13}\angle{-213.69°} \qquad -\sqrt{13}\angle{-33.69°} \qquad -\sqrt{13}\angle326.31°$$

Example 11.2 Add: $-4\angle-150° + 8\angle300°$

Solution We break each vector into horizontal and vertical components and add like components. We use a calculator to do the computations.

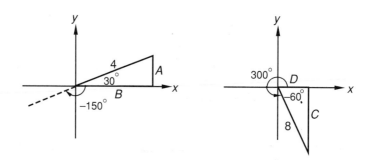

$$A = 4 \sin 30° = 2 \qquad\qquad C = 8 \sin(-60°) = -6.93$$

$$B = 4 \cos 30° = 3.46 \qquad\qquad D = 8 \cos(-60°) = 4$$

$$\text{Sum} = (3.46 + 4)i + (2 - 6.93)j = \mathbf{7.46}\boldsymbol{i} + \mathbf{-4.93}\boldsymbol{j}$$

Of course, this vector can also be written in four different polar forms.

11.B
Polar coordinates (complex numbers)

Complex numbers can also be written in either rectangular form or polar form. The real number part of the graph of a complex number is measured in the horizontal direction, and the imaginary part is measured in the vertical direction.

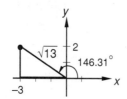

Rectangular form: $-3 + 2i$

Polar form: $\sqrt{13}(\cos 146.31 + i \sin 146.31)$

The polar form of the complex number shown on the right is used in many textbooks. This form is most unhandy, and if we use the letters "cis" to mean cos + **i** sin, we can use a polar form that is almost identical to the polar form of a real number vector.

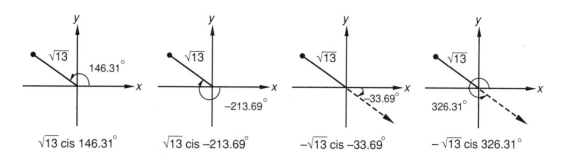

$\sqrt{13}$ cis 146.31° $\sqrt{13}$ cis −213.69° $-\sqrt{13}$ cis −33.69° $-\sqrt{13}$ cis 326.31°

While all four forms can be used, we will usually use the form on the left, which has a positive angle and a positive magnitude. While complex numbers can be added only in rectangular form, they can be multiplied in either rectangular form or polar form. We will demonstrate by squaring $\sqrt{3} + i$ and by squaring 2 cis 30°. These are two forms of the same complex number.

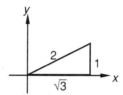

Rectangular form: $\sqrt{3} + i$

Polar form: 2 cis 30°

First we will multiply $(\sqrt{3} + i)(\sqrt{3} + i)$ and write the result in polar form.

$$\begin{array}{r} \sqrt{3} + i \\ \sqrt{3} + i \\ \hline 3 + \sqrt{3}\,i \\ + \sqrt{3}\,i + i^2 \\ \hline 2 + 2\sqrt{3}\,i \end{array}$$

$2 + 2\sqrt{3}\,i = 4$ cis 60°

To get the same result from multiplying the polar forms of the same number, we must multiply the magnitudes and add the angles.

$$(2 \text{ cis } 30°)(2 \text{ cis } 30°) = 4 \text{ cis } 60°$$

Example 11.3   Write the decimal approximation of $(6 \text{ cis } 20°)(\tfrac{1}{2} \text{ cis } 10°) + 7 \text{ cis } (-300°)$ as a complex number in standard form.

Solution   As the first step we simplify both terms and get

$$3 \text{ cis } 30° + 7 \text{ cis } 60°$$

Now we find the horizontal and vertical components of each vector.

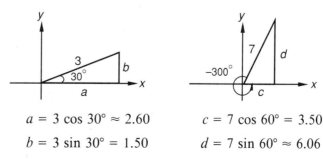

$a = 3 \cos 30° \approx 2.60$ $c = 7 \cos 60° = 3.50$

$b = 3 \sin 30° = 1.50$ $d = 7 \sin 60° \approx 6.06$

Then we find the sum by adding the real parts and adding the imaginary parts.

$$(a + c) + (b + d)i \approx (2.60 + 3.50) + (1.50 + 6.06)i = \mathbf{6.10 + 7.56}i$$

Problem set 11

1. Shelley drove at 40 mph for t hours but arrived at the Moose Lodge 14 hours late. How fast should she have driven to have arrived on time?

2. At present, Olive is two-thirds as old as Fred. Y years ago, Olive was half as old as Fred. Find Olive's present age in terms of Y.

3. Suppose $z = 4y/x$. What happens to the value of z if the value of x is doubled and the value of y is tripled?

4. The wheel was rolling merrily down the hill, revolving 20 times every minute. If the diameter of the wheel was 1 meter, how fast was the wheel rolling down the hill in kilometers per hour?

5. Write the polar form of the vector $-3i + 4j$.

6. Write the polar form of the complex number $3 + 4i$.

7. Write the polar form of the product of $2 \text{ cis } \frac{\pi}{7}$ and $3 \text{ cis } \frac{\pi}{5}$.

8. Write the rectangular form of the following product. Do not use decimal approximations.

$$\left(2 \text{ cis } \frac{\pi}{6}\right)\left[3 \text{ cis } \left(-\frac{\pi}{3}\right)\right]$$

9. Graph $y = \left(\frac{1}{2}\right)^x$ and $y = -\left(\frac{1}{2}\right)^x$ on the same coordinate plane.

For Problems 10–12, suppose β is an angle such that $\cos \beta = -\frac{1}{7}$.

10. Determine in which quadrants β could lie.

Simplify:

11. $2 \sin \left(\frac{\pi}{2} - \beta\right)(1 + \cot^2 \beta)$

12. $[\cos^2 (-\beta)](1 + \tan^2 \beta)$

13. Show that: $\cos^2 x - \cos^2 x \sin^2 x = \cos^4 x$

14. Show that: $-\cot \left(\frac{\pi}{2} - \theta\right) \tan (-\theta) + 1 = \sec^2 (-\theta)$

15. Evaluate: $2 \sec^2 \left(-\frac{9\pi}{4}\right)$

16. Find the equation of the quadratic function whose leading term has a coefficient of 1, whose graph has $x = 3$ as the axis of symmetry and whose vertex is the point (3, 1).

17. Solve for L in terms of x for the figure shown.

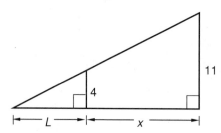

18. If $f(x) = \dfrac{1}{x}$, simplify $\dfrac{f(x + \Delta x) - f(x)}{\Delta x}$.

19. Find the coordinates of the midpoint of the line segment joining the points $(a, 2a)$ and $(-a, 4a)$.

20. Evaluate: $\dfrac{17!}{15!2!}$

21. Simplify: $\dfrac{3i^3 + 4i - \sqrt{-16}}{4i^4 + i^3}$

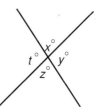

CONCEPT REVIEW 22. Given x, y, z, and t in the figure as shown. Compare:
A. $(x + y + z)°$ B. $(180 - t)°$

23. Find x, given the figure shown.
$m \angle APC = (2x)°$
$m\widehat{AEB} = (x^2 - 10)°$
$m\widehat{ADC} = (12x)°$

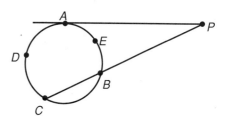

LESSON 12   *Absolute value as a distance · The line as a locus · The circle as a locus*

12.A
Absolute value as a distance

A real number has two qualities. One quality is the quality of positiveness or negativeness. The number zero is neutral in this quality, as it is neither positive nor negative. Every other real number is either a positive number or a negative number. The second quality of a real number is called the ***absolute value*** of the number. Some people think of the absolute value of a number as describing the "bigness" of the number. We can think of $+3$ and -3 as both having the same degree of bigness, which is $+3$.

$$|+3| = +3 \qquad |-3| = +3$$

Using the word *bigness* to describe the other quality of a number is not a good idea because a number does not have a physical size. But numbers can be arranged in order, and we can use the position of the graph of a number on the number line to describe the absolute value of the number. Thus we decide to think of the absolute value of a number as the positive number that defines the distance on the number line from the graph of the number to the origin. If we look at this number line,

we see that $+3$ and -3 are both the same distance from the origin and, thus, they have the same absolute value. If x equals zero or is a number greater than zero, the absolute value of x is x.

$$\text{If } x \geq 0 \qquad \text{then} \qquad |x| = x$$

If x is a negative number, the absolute value of x is a positive number that is the opposite of x, or $-x$.

$$\text{If } x < 0 \qquad \text{then} \qquad |x| = -x$$

This does not say that the absolute value of x is a negative number. The notation is confusing, because if x is already negative, then $-x$ is positive. For example,

$$\text{If } x = -4 \qquad \text{then} \qquad |x| = -(-4) = +4$$

If we write that the absolute value of x is less than zero, the statement makes no sense and has no solution because all absolute values that are not zero are positive numbers and are greater than zero.

$$|x| < -4 \qquad \text{has no solution}$$

However, if we write that the absolute value of x is less than 4, we are describing all numbers whose graphs are less than 4 units from the origin. If we write that the absolute value of x is greater than 4, we are describing all numbers whose graphs are more than 4 units from the origin.

$$|x| < 4 \qquad\qquad\qquad\qquad |x| > 4$$

Inequalities such as those shown here

$$|x - 7| > 3 \qquad |x + 4| < 3 \qquad |x - 5| < 3$$

are satisfied by numbers whose graphs lie in certain regions on the number line, and it is helpful to have a way to visualize the solution sets of these inequalities without "reinventing the absolute value wheel" every time. We will remember that the numbers that satisfy the inequality on the left below are the numbers whose graphs are within 5 units of the graph of a on the number line,

$$|x - a| < 5 \qquad |x - a| > 5$$

and that the numbers that satisfy the inequality on the right are the numbers whose graphs are farther than 5 units from the graph of a on the number line.

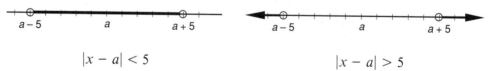

$$|x - a| < 5 \qquad\qquad\qquad\qquad |x - a| > 5$$

If $a = 0$, we have $|x - 0|$ or $|x|$, which denotes the distance from the origin.

Example 12.1   Graph $\{x \in \mathbb{R} \mid |x - 5| < 2\}$ on a number line.

Solution   We are asked to indicate all real numbers that satisfy this inequality. The solution set consists of the numbers less than 2 units from $+5$ on the number line.

$$|x - 5| < 2$$

Example 12.2   Graph $\{x \in \mathbb{Z} \mid |3x - 1| > 2\}$ on a number line.

Solution   We are asked to indicate all integers that satisfy this inequality. We begin by factoring to write the inequality so that the x has a coefficient of 1. Then we multiply both sides by $\frac{1}{3}$.

$$3\left|x - \frac{1}{3}\right| > 2 \qquad \text{factored}$$

$$\left|x - \frac{1}{3}\right| > \frac{2}{3} \qquad \text{multiplied by } \frac{1}{3}$$

$$\left|x - \left(\frac{1}{3}\right)\right| > \frac{2}{3} \qquad \text{desired form}$$

The graph of every integer except zero and $+1$ is more than $\frac{2}{3}$ unit from $\frac{1}{3}$. Thus, our graph indicates all integers except 0 and $+1$.

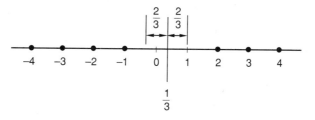

12.B

The line as a locus   A straight line is the locus of all points in a plane that are equidistant from two designated points.

Example 12.3   Find the equation of the line on which all points are equidistant from $(-2, -2)$ and $(4, 3)$.

Solution   **We always draw a diagram when we can.** The distances D_1 and D_2 in the diagram are equal, so we use the distance formula twice.

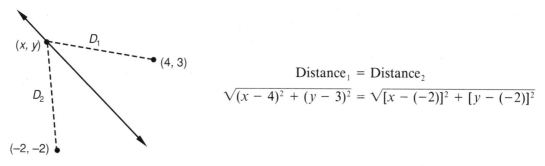

$$\text{Distance}_1 = \text{Distance}_2$$
$$\sqrt{(x - 4)^2 + (y - 3)^2} = \sqrt{[x - (-2)]^2 + [y - (-2)]^2}$$

If we square both sides, we get rid of the radicals and get

$$(x - 4)^2 + (y - 3)^2 = [x - (-2)]^2 + [y - (-2)]^2$$

Next we raise to the powers as indicated.

$$x^2 - 8x + 16 + y^2 - 6y + 9 = x^2 + 4x + 4 + y^2 + 4y + 4$$

The x^2 terms and the y^2 terms cancel. If we collect the rest of the terms and rearrange, we get the equation of the line on which all points are equidistant from $(-2, 2)$ and $(4, 3)$.

$$12x + 10y - 17 = 0$$

12.C
The circle as a locus

A circle is the locus of all points in a plane that are equidistant from a point called the center of the circle.

Example 12.4   Write the standard form and the general form of the equation of a circle whose center is $(4, -6)$ and whose radius is 5.

Solution   We begin by drawing a diagram. The distance from the center of the circle to a point (x, y) on the circle is equal to the radius.

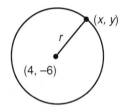

Distance from the center to (x, y) = the radius
$$\sqrt{(x - 4)^2 + [y - (-6)]^2} = r$$

For this circle, the radius is 5, so we replace r with 5.
$$\sqrt{(x - 4)^2 + [y - (-6)]^2} = 5$$

If we square both sides and simplify, we can write the equation of this circle in **standard form**.

$$(x - 4)^2 + (y + 6)^2 = 25 \qquad \textbf{standard form}$$

If we multiply as indicated and collect like terms, we can write the equation in **general form**.

$$x^2 - 8x + 16 + y^2 + 12y + 36 = 25 \qquad \text{multiplied}$$

$$x^2 + y^2 - 8x + 12y + 27 = 0 \qquad \textbf{general form}$$

Example 12.5   Write the standard form of the equation of a circle whose diameter is $4\sqrt{3}$ and whose center is $(-4, 2)$.

Solution   The standard form of the equation of a circle is

$$(x - h)^2 + (y - k)^2 = r^2$$

where the coordinates of the center are (h, k). Since the diameter of this circle is $4\sqrt{3}$, the radius is $2\sqrt{3}$, and the radius squared is 12. Since h is -4, $-h$ is 4; and since k is 2, $-k$ is -2. Thus, the standard form of the equation of our circle is

$$(x + 4)^2 + (y - 2)^2 = 12$$

Example 12.6   Describe the circle whose equation is

$$x^2 + y^2 - 8x + 4y + 17 = 0$$

Solution   If we complete the square on the x terms and on the y terms, we can write the equation in standard form. First we use parentheses and rewrite the equation as

$$(x^2 - 8x \quad) + (y^2 + 4y \quad) = -17$$

Now we add 16 and 4 to make the expressions in x and y perfect squares.

$$(x^2 - 8x + 16) + (y^2 + 4y + 4) = -17 + 16 + 4$$

Now we simplify.

$$(x - 4)^2 + (y + 2)^2 = 3$$

Since $r^2 = 3$, $r = \sqrt{3}$. **This is the equation of a circle of radius $\sqrt{3}$ whose center is (4, −2).**

Example 12.7   Find the equation of the circle whose center is $(1, -2)$ and which is tangent to the line $5x - 4y + 4 = 0$.

Solution   We have the coordinates of the center, so we write

$$(x - 1)^2 + (y + 2)^2 = r^2$$

To find the radius r, we need to find the distance between the point $(1, -2)$ and the line $5x - 4y + 4 = 0$.

First we write the formula and then we substitute.

$$\frac{|Ax_0 + By_0 + C|}{\sqrt{A^2 + B^2}} \longrightarrow \frac{|5(1) + (-4)(-2) + 4|}{\sqrt{25 + 16}} = \frac{17}{\sqrt{41}}$$

Now we can write the standard form of the equation as

$$(x - 1)^2 + (y + 2)^2 = \frac{289}{41}$$

Problem set 12

1. On the assembly line, w workers worked h hours to produce x items. If y workers quit, how many hours would it take the remaining workers to produce the same number of items?

2. The ratio of scallops to crayfish was 3 to 1 and the ratio of crayfish to prawns was 2 to 1. If there were 18 scallops, crayfish, and prawns in all, how many of each were there?

3. Evelyn and Jeannie each had containers which held mixtures of alcohol and disinfectant. Evelyn's container was 40% disinfectant and Jeannie's container was 80% disinfectant. If Derek wants 600 milliliters of a solution that is $p\%$ disinfectant, how much solution should he use from Evelyn's container and how much from Jeannie's container?

4. Graph the set $\{x \in \mathbb{R} \mid |x - 3| < 4\}$ on the number line.

5. Graph the set of all integers such that $|2x - 1| > 6$.

6. Write the general form of the equation of the straight line whose points are equidistant from the points $(1, -3)$ and $(-1, 2)$.

7. Write the standard form and the general form of the equation of the circle whose center is the point $(-1, 3)$ and whose radius is 3.

8. Describe the circle whose equation is given by

$$x^2 + y^2 + 6x - 6y + 2 = 0$$

9. Represent the real vector $-i + \sqrt{3}\, j$ in polar coordinates.

10. Compute the value of $(2 \operatorname{cis} 20°)(3 \operatorname{cis} 25°)$ and write the answer in rectangular form. (All numbers must be exact.)

11. Sketch the graph of $y = e^{-x}$.

12. Divide by $\sin^2 x$ and $\cos^2 x$ to develop two other forms of the identity $\sin^2 x + \cos^2 x = 1$.

13. Simplify: $\sin(-\theta)\sec(-\theta)\cos^2\theta\csc\left(\dfrac{\pi}{2} - \theta\right)$

14. Show that: $(\csc^2\theta - 1)\sin^2\theta\sec(-\theta) = \cos\theta$

15. Find the value of $\cos\left(\dfrac{\pi}{2} - \beta\right)\sin(-\beta)$ if $\sin\beta = \dfrac{1}{3}$.

16. Find the equation of the axis of symmetry and the coordinates of the vertex of the graph of the quadratic function $y = 2x^2 + 2x - 3$.

17. Solve for b in terms of x and y in the figure shown.

18. Sketch the sinusoid $y = -2 + 3\sin\left(x + \dfrac{\pi}{2}\right)$.

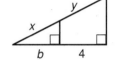

19. Find the domain and range of $y = x^2 - 1$.

20. If $f(x) = x^2$, evaluate: $\displaystyle\sum_{i=1}^{3} f(i)$

21. State the contrapositive of the following statement: If the light is on, then the switch is on.

CONCEPT REVIEW   22. If $x < 0$, compare: A. x B. x^2

23. If $\overline{AD}$ is the angle bisector of $\angle A$ of $\triangle ABC$ as shown, and if $\overline{AB}, \overline{AC}, \overline{BD}$, and $\overline{DC}$ have lengths x, y, x^2, and z, respectively, then solve for x in terms of y and z.

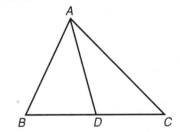

LESSON 13 *Special functions*

In later lessons we will discuss the fact that a curve does not have a defined slope at a point if the curve makes a sudden change in direction at that point. Graphs of many absolute value functions come to one or more points called *cusps* where the graph changes direction suddenly. These graphs are ideal for discussing graphs of functions that do not have a defined slope at some point. The graph of the absolute value of a function is easy to draw if we use two steps. The first step is to graph the function defined with the absolute value notation removed. The second step is to draw the graph of the absolute value function by plotting above the x axis the reflection of all points plotted below the x axis in the first graph. The graph of the opposite of the absolute value of a function is the mirror image in the x axis of the graph of the absolute value, as we show in the following figures.

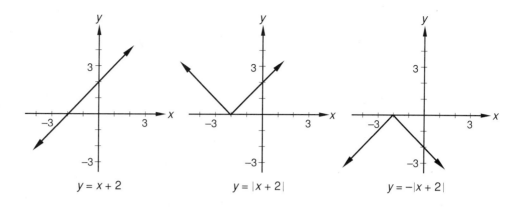

$$y = x + 2$$ $$y = |x + 2|$$ $$y = -|x + 2|$$

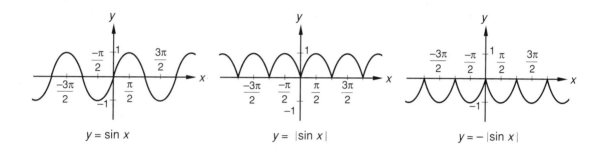

$$y = \sin x$$ $$y = |\sin x|$$ $$y = -|\sin x|$$

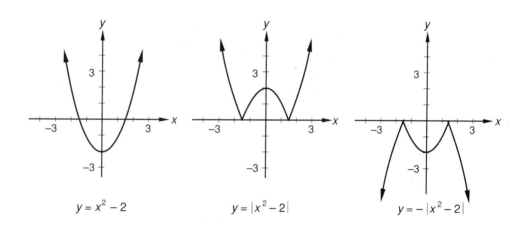

$$y = x^2 - 2$$ $$y = |x^2 - 2|$$ $$y = -|x^2 - 2|$$

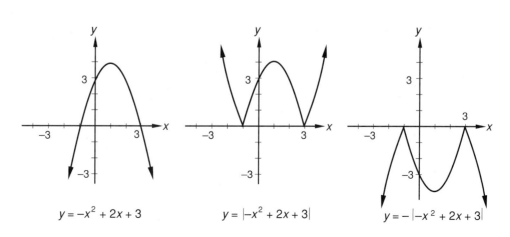

$$y = -x^2 + 2x + 3$$ $$y = |-x^2 + 2x + 3|$$ $$y = -|-x^2 + 2x + 3|$$

Example 13.1   Graph $y = |{-\sin x}|$.

Solution   On the left we show the graph of $y = -\sin x$, and on the right we make every negative value of y positive.

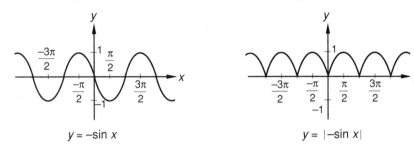

$$y = -\sin x \qquad\qquad y = |{-\sin x}|$$

We note that this is the same as the graph of $y = |\sin x|$ on page 79.

Example 13.2   Graph: (a) $y = \sqrt{x}$ (b) $y = \sqrt[3]{x}$ (c) $y = \sqrt[3]{x^2}$

Solution   These functions can be written with fractional exponents as follows:

$$(a)\quad y = x^{1/2} \qquad (b)\quad y = x^{1/3} \qquad (c)\quad y = x^{2/3}$$

The square root of x is a function whose graph terminates abruptly. Negative values of x are not in the domain of $\sqrt{x}$ because negative numbers do not have real square roots. All real numbers have cube roots, so the graph of $y = x^{1/3}$ exists for all real values of x. We can turn the graph of $y = x^{1/3}$ into a graph that has a cusp by squaring the function and getting $y = (x^{1/3})^2$, which is the same as $y = x^{2/3}$.

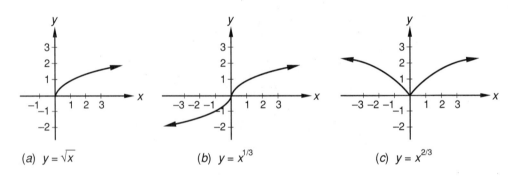

(a) $y = \sqrt{x}$ (b) $y = x^{1/3}$ (c) $y = x^{2/3}$

Example 13.3   Graph $y = [x]$.

Solution   The symbol $[x]$ stands for the **greatest integer function of x.** The value of $[x]$ is the greatest integer less than or equal to x. Note that the graph jumps to a new value as each greater integer is reached as we move from left to right.

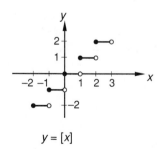

$$y = [x]$$

Example 13.4   Write the equation of the function whose graph is shown.

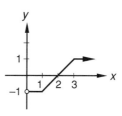

Solution   Sometimes we construct a function by stringing together "pieces" of several functions. This graph is in three pieces. For the left-hand piece $y = -1$ when x is between 0 and 1. For the middle piece $y = x - 2$ when x is between 1 and 3. For the right-hand piece $y = 1$ when x is greater than 3. To describe the function, we write the equation for each piece of the graph.

$$y = \begin{cases} -1 & \text{if } 0 < x \leq 1 \\ x - 2 & \text{if } 1 < x \leq 3 \\ 1 & \text{if } x > 3 \end{cases}$$

We call this function a *piecewise function*. **We often make up piecewise functions when we can't find another function whose graph does what we want it to do.**

Problem set 13

1. Kristin, Kathy, Beth, and Steve watched Walter open the valve so the pool could fill with water. If, after 1 hour, x/g of the pool filled with water, how many more hours would it take for the pool to become entirely filled?

2. Winston drove at 60 miles per hour for h hours, but arrived L hours late. How fast should Winston have driven to have arrived on time?

3. The number of people who patronized the café varied directly with the quality of the food served. If 200 people came when the food quality was x, how many people would come if the food quality were increased to 20?

4. Graph the following equations:
   (a) $y = |x|$ (b) $y = [x]$ (c) $y = |\sin x|$ (d) $y = -|x^2 - 3x|$

5. Graph $y = |x^2 + x - 2|$.

6. Graph the function f, where
$$f(x) = \begin{cases} \sqrt{x} & \text{when } x > 0 \\ -\sqrt{-x} & \text{when } x < 0 \end{cases}$$

7. Write the piecewise definition of the function f whose graph is shown.

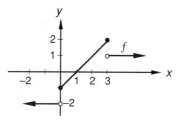

8. Graph the function $y = -2 + 2 \sin\left(x + \dfrac{3\pi}{2}\right)$.

9. Graph on the number line: $\{x \mid |2x - 3| < 4\}$

10. Write the general form of the equation of the line whose points are equidistant from (1, 2) and (−2, 3).

11. Write the standard form of the equation of the circle whose diameter is $2\sqrt{2}$ and whose center is (−2, 3).

12. Write the polar form of $\sqrt{3} + 2i$.

13. Write the rectangular form of the following product of complex numbers (all numbers must be exact):

$$\left(3 \operatorname{cis} \frac{\pi}{2}\right)\left(2 \operatorname{cis} \frac{-\pi}{6}\right)$$

14. Sketch the graphs of $y = e^{-x}$ and $y = -e^{-x}$ on the same coordinate plane.

15. Write the three forms of the Pythagorean identity for practice and then simplify:

$$\tan(-\theta)\cos(-\theta)\sec\left(\frac{\pi}{2} - \theta\right)$$

16. Show that: $\dfrac{1 - \sec^2 x}{\sin^2(-x)} = -\sec^2 x$

17. The roots of a quadratic function $y = f(x)$ are $x = 2$ and $x = -1$. If $f(3) = 8$, write the equation for f.

18. Suppose $AB = AC = BC = 3$ in the figure shown. Solve for x in terms of h. (Use the fact that $\triangle ABC$ is an equilateral triangle.)

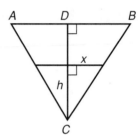

19. If $f(x) = x^2$, then write the simplified expression for $\dfrac{f(x + \Delta x) - f(x)}{\Delta x}$.

20. Simplify: $\dfrac{(2 + 3i)^3}{2 + 3i^3}$

CONCEPT REVIEW 21. If x and y are real numbers, compare: A. $(x + y)^2$ B. $x^2 + y^2$

22. O is the center of the circle shown. The radius of the circle is 5. If $AB = x$ and $BC = y$, find an equation which relates x and y.

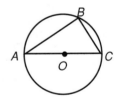

LESSON 14   *The logarithmic form of the exponential · Base 10 and base e · Simple logarithm problems*

14.A
The logarithmic form of the exponential

We remember that any positive number can be written as a positive base raised to either a positive or a negative power. We will use the letter N to represent the number and will use the letter b to represent the base. We will use the letter L to represent the logarithm, which is the exponent.

$$N = b^L$$

We read this by saying that N equals b to the L. We could also read this by saying that the logarithm for b to yield N is L.

$$\text{Logarithm for } b \text{ to yield } N \text{ is } L$$

We abbreviate the word *logarithm* with *log*, and we write this sentence in compact form by writing

$$\log_b N = L$$

We read this as the logarithm of N to the base b equals L. Thus we see that

$$N = b^L \qquad \text{and} \qquad \log_b N = L$$

are two ways to write the same thing. Since these equations make the same statement and since N is always positive in the exponential form, it must also be positive in the logarithmic form. This is the reason that a negative number cannot have a logarithm.

Example 14.1   Write $4 = 3^y$ in logarithmic form.

Solution   We remember that a logarithm is the exponent, and here the exponent is y. Therefore, we begin by writing

$$\log = y$$

Next we indicate the base, which in this case is 3.

$$\log_3 = y$$

Now the only thing left is the number 4. We insert it and have

$$\log_3 4 = y$$

14.B
Base 10 and base e

We see that exponential equations and logarithmic equations are different ways to designate the same ordered pairs. Logarithms that use 10 as a base are called **common logarithms.** Before slide rules and calculators were invented, most scientific calculations were made by using tables of common logarithms. Common logarithms are still used, a base of 2 is sometimes used in information theory, and other bases are used for special purposes. The most important base in higher mathematics is the base e. Logarithms with a base of e are called **natural logarithms.**

It is customary to designate that the base is 10 by writing *log* with no subscript, and it is customary to designate that the base is e by using the letters *ln* with no subscript. Thus

$$\log 42 \qquad \text{means} \qquad \log_{10} 42$$

$$\ln 42 \qquad \text{means} \qquad \log_e 42$$

Tables of logarithms give common logarithms and natural logarithms to four or five places, and calculators are accurate to seven or eight places. When accuracy is desired, logarithms can be obtained from these sources, but since beginners often tend to get lost in the arithmetic of logarithm problems, we will sometimes round off logarithms to two decimal places and concentrate on understanding rather than on arithmetic accuracy.

Example 14.2   Write 2.4 as a power with a base of (*a*) 10, (*b*) *e*.

Solution   A calculator or a table of logarithms will give us the logarithms (exponents) that allow us to write numbers as powers. We round off the values to two places.

$$(a) \quad 2.4 = \mathbf{10^{0.38}} \qquad (b) \quad 2.4 = \boldsymbol{e^{0.88}}$$

Example 14.3   Find: (*a*)   log 2.4   (*b*)   ln 2.4

Solution   Log means base 10 and ln means base *e*, so from the preceding example, we have

$$2.4 = 10^{0.38} \quad \text{and} \quad 2.4 = e^{0.88}$$

So we can write

$$(a) \quad \log 2.4 = \mathbf{0.38} \qquad (b) \quad \ln 2.4 = \mathbf{0.88}$$

14.C
Simple logarithm problems

The ability to change from the logarithmic form of the equation to the exponential form is most useful. We can solve some logarithmic equations if we first rewrite them as exponential equations.

Example 14.4   Solve $\log_b 9 = -\dfrac{1}{2}$.

Solution   We rewrite the equation in exponential form and solve by raising both sides to the appropriate power.

$$b^{-1/2} = 9 \qquad \text{exponential form}$$

$$(b^{-1/2})^{-2} = 9^{-2} \qquad \text{raised both sides to } -2 \text{ power}$$

$$\boldsymbol{b = \frac{1}{81}} \qquad \text{simplified}$$

Example 14.5   Solve: $\log_3 \dfrac{1}{27} = 2m + 1$

Solution   We rewrite the equation in exponential form and then solve.

$$3^{2m+1} = \frac{1}{27} \qquad \text{exponential form}$$

$$3^{2m+1} = 3^{-3} \qquad \text{changed form}$$

$$2m + 1 = -3 \qquad \text{bases equal} \rightarrow \text{exponents equal}$$

$$\boldsymbol{m = -2} \qquad \text{solved}$$

Example 14.6   Solve $\log_{1/3} P = 2$.

Solution   We rewrite the equation in exponential form and then solve.

$$\left(\frac{1}{3}\right)^2 = P \qquad \text{exponential form}$$

$$\frac{1}{9} = P \qquad \text{simplified and solved}$$

Example 14.7   Solve $\log_x (6x - 9) = 2$ where $x > 0$.

Solution   We rewrite the equation in exponential form and then solve.

$$x^2 = 6x - 9 \qquad \text{exponential form}$$
$$x^2 - 6x + 9 = 0 \qquad \text{rearranged}$$
$$(x - 3)^2 = 0 \qquad \text{factored}$$
$$\boldsymbol{x = 3} \qquad \text{solved}$$

Since the argument of a logarithm can never be negative, we check to see if using 3 for x makes $6x - 9$ nonnegative.

$$6(3) - 9 = 9 \qquad \text{check}$$

Thus, 3 is an acceptable value for x.

Problem set 14

1. The area of a rectangle is 500 square centimeters. If the difference between the length and width of the rectangle is 5 cm, find the dimensions of the rectangle.

2. It was 10 a.m. and Lori and Trent waited for the moment the hands of the clock would be pointing in opposite directions. How many minutes did they have to wait?

3. The wheels on the car had a 30-centimeter radius and the car was traveling at 60 kilometers per hour. What was the angular velocity of the wheels in radians per minute?

4. Find x, where: (*a*) $10^x = 3$ (*b*) $e^x = 5$

5. Solve $\log_3 27 = 2b + 1$ for b.   6. Solve $\log_x (3x - 2) = 2$ for x.

7. Graph f where $f(x) = [x]$ and evaluate: (*a*) $f(1.2)$ (*b*) $f(-1.2)$

8. Graph $y = |\cos x|$.

9. Graph g, where: $g(x) = \begin{cases} x^2 & \text{when } x < 1 \\ 2x & \text{when } x \geq 1 \end{cases}$

10. Write the equation of this sinusoid as a cosine function.

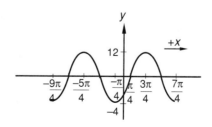

11. Describe the circle whose equation is $x^2 + y^2 - 2y = 0$.

12. Find the equation of the graph of all points which are equidistant from the points $(-1, 2)$ and $(-2, -1)$.

13. Describe the set of all real values of x such that $|x - 3| < 0.001$.

14. Add the vectors $-4 \angle 150°$ and $8 \angle -30°$ and express the answer in rectangular form.

15. Graph $y = 2^x$ and $y = 2^{-x}$ on the same coordinate plane.

16. Simplify: $\tan(-x) \sec^2\left(\dfrac{\pi}{2} - x\right) \sin(-x)$

17. Show that $\sin^4 x - \cos^4 x = \sin^2 x - \cos^2 x$.

18. The roots of a quadratic function g are 2 and -3. If $g(1) = -8$, then find an equation for g.

19. Find L in terms of x in the figure shown.

20. Find the y coordinates of P_1, P_2, and P_3 if P_1, P_2, and P_3 are points on the unit circle centered at the origin as shown.

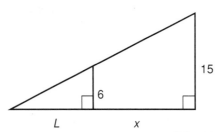

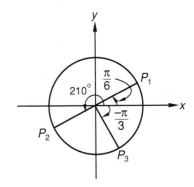

21. Determine whether or not the mapping $f: x \to \pm\sqrt{x}$ is a function of a real variable x and explain your answer.

22. Evaluate: $\dfrac{\displaystyle\sum_{i=1}^{10} i}{10}$

CONCEPT REVIEW 23. Given the figure shown, compare:
   A.   sum of areas of squares A and B
   B.   area of square C

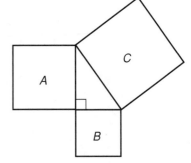

24. Solve for x.
   $m\widehat{ACB} = x°$
   $m\widehat{ADB} = (3x + 60)°$
   $m\angle APB = (x + 30)°$

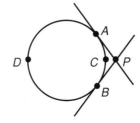

LESSON 15   *Evaluating polynomials*

15.A
The remainder theorem

To evaluate polynomials, we can make use of the remainder theorem.

> **THE REMAINDER THEOREM**
> If a constant c is a zero of a polynomial and if we divide the polynomial by $x - c$, the remainder will be zero. If the remainder is not zero, the remainder equals the value of the polynomial when x equals c.

To look at a specific example, we will manufacture a cubic polynomial by multiplying the factors $x + 1$, $x - 2$, and $x + 3$, as we show on the left below. Since one of the factors of the polynomial is $x - 2$, then $x - 2$ will divide the polynomial evenly and will have no remainder, as we show on the right.

$$f(x) = (x + 1)(x - 2)(x + 3)$$
$$f(x) = x^3 + 2x^2 - 5x - 6$$

$$
\begin{array}{r}
x^2 + 4x\ + 3 \\
x - 2\overline{\smash{)}\,x^3 + 2x^2 - 5x - 6} \\
\underline{x^3 - 2x^2} \\
4x^2 - 5x \\
\underline{4x^2 - 8x} \\
3x - 6 \\
\underline{3x - 6} \\
0
\end{array}
$$

The value of a polynomial is zero if x is replaced by a number that is a zero of the polynomial. The factored form and the unfactored form of the f polynomial of this example are equivalent expressions, and both will equal zero if x is replaced by 2.

$$f(2) = (2 + 1)(2 - 2)(2 + 3) \qquad f(2) = (2)^3 + 2(2)^2 - 5(2) - 6$$
$$= (3)(0)(5) \qquad\qquad\qquad = 8 + 8 - 10 - 6$$
$$= 0 \qquad\qquad\qquad\qquad = 0$$

Now, if we add 10 to the f polynomial, we get a new polynomial that we call the g polynomial. The g polynomial does not have $x - 2$ as a factor. When we divide the g polynomial by $x - 2$, we get a remainder of 10.

$$g(x) = (x + 1)(x - 2)(x + 3) + 10$$
$$g(x) = x^3 + 2x^2 - 5x + 4$$

$$
\begin{array}{r}
x^2 + 4x\ + 3 \\
x - 2\overline{\smash{)}\,x^3 + 2x^2 - 5x + 4} \\
\underline{x^3 - 2x^2} \\
4x^2 - 5x \\
\underline{4x^2 - 8x} \\
3x + 4 \\
\underline{3x - 6} \\
10
\end{array}
$$

Both the factored and unfactored forms of the g equation have a value of 10 when x is replaced with 2.

$$g(2) = (2 + 1)(2 - 2)(2 + 3) + 10 \qquad g(2) = (2)^3 + 2(2)^2 - 5(2) + 4$$
$$= (3)(0)(5) + 10 \qquad\qquad\qquad = 8 + 8 - 10 + 4$$
$$= 10 \qquad\qquad\qquad\qquad\quad = 10$$

Thus, if we have a polynomial and divide by $x - 11$, we can find out one of two things by looking at the remainder. If the remainder is zero, then 11 is a zero of the polynomial. If the remainder is not zero, the remainder equals the value of the polynomial when $x = 11$.

15.B
Synthetic division

Because dividing a polynomial by $x - c$ gives us such useful information, synthetic division was invented to permit this type of division to be done quickly. Synthetic division can be used to divide a polynomial by $x - 4$ or $x + 3$, but cannot be easily used to divide by forms such as $2x + 4$ or $x^2 - 5$. Both the coefficient and the exponent of x in the divisor must be 1 for this version of synthetic division to be used. To evaluate a polynomial when $x = c$, the division is a process of bringing down the lead coefficient, multiplying, adding, multiplying, adding, etc.

Example 15.1 Use synthetic division to divide $2x^3 + 3x^2 - 4x - 7$ by $x + 1$.

Solution To divide by $x + 1$, we use -1 as a divisor and write down only the constants in the dividend. The first step is to bring down the first constant, which is 2.

$$\begin{array}{r|rrrr} -1 & 2 & 3 & -4 & -7 \\ & \downarrow & & & \\ \hline & 2 & & & \end{array}$$

The next step is to multiply 2 by the divisor, -1, for a product of -2, which we record under the 3.

$$\begin{array}{r|rrrr} -1 & 2 & 3 & -4 & -7 \\ & \downarrow & -2 & & \\ \hline & 2 & & & \end{array}$$

Then we add 3 and -2 to get 1. We multiply 1 by the divisor, -1, and record the product under the -4. Then we add, multiply, record, and add again.

$$\begin{array}{r|rrrr} -1 & 2 & 3 & -4 & -7 \\ & \downarrow & -2 & -1 & 5 \\ \hline & 2 & 1 & -5 & -2 \end{array}$$

The first three numbers below the line are the coefficients of the reduced polynomial, and the remainder is -2. The greatest exponent of the reduced polynomial is always 1 less than the greatest exponent of the dividend. Thus we may write

$$2x^3 + 3x^2 - 4x - 7 = (x + 1)(2x^2 + x - 5) - 2$$

The remainder -2 is the value of the polynomial if $x = -1$. We can see this because the first factor, $(x + 1)$, of the factored form equals zero if x *equals* -1.

Example 15.2 Use synthetic division to evaluate $3x^3 - 4x - 2$ when $x = 2$.

Solution We enter the coefficients and remember to write a zero coefficient for x^2.

$$\begin{array}{r|rrrr} 2 & 3 & 0 & -4 & -2 \\ & \downarrow & 6 & 12 & 16 \\ \hline & 3 & 6 & 8 & 14 \end{array}$$

The numbers 3, 6, and 8 are the coefficients of the reduced polynomial and 14 is the remainder. Thus, the value of $3x^3 - 4x - 2$ when $x = 2$ is 14; so 2 is not a zero of the polynomial.

$$3x^3 - 4x - 2 = (3x^2 + 6x + 8)(x - 2) + 14$$

15.C
Rational zero (root) theorem

If a number is a zero of a polynomial, the number is also a root of the polynomial equation formed by setting the polynomial equal to zero. We know that we can find rational and irrational zeros of quadratic polynomials by completing the square or by using the quadratic formula. We remember that the rational zero theorem allows us to list the possible rational zeros of any polynomial, but does not tell which, if any, of these possible zeros really is a zero. There is no comparable theorem for irrational zeros. This is unfortunate because most of the polynomial equations encountered in real-world problems have irrational roots. Before computers were invented, much time was spent laboriously finding rational roots and estimating irrational roots. To prevent this waste of time, most of the polynomials encountered in this book will be contrived to have integral zeros of ± 1, ± 2, or ± 3. The rational zero theorem is useful in helping us decide which of these roots to investigate.

We remember that the rational zero (root) theorem tells us that if a polynomial whose coefficients are integers has a rational zero, then this number is a fraction whose numerator is some integral factor of the constant term and whose denominator is some integral factor of the lead coefficient. Thus, the possible rational zeros of $4x^{14} + 3x^8 + 7x + 3$ can be found by forming a fraction by using one of the integer factors of 3 above the line as a numerator

$$\frac{\text{Factors of } 3}{\text{Factors of } 4} = \frac{1, -1, 3, -3}{1, -1, 2, -2, 4, -4}$$

and one of the integer factors of 4 below the line as a denominator. If we do this, we can list the possible rational zeros as

$$1, -1, \frac{1}{2}, -\frac{1}{2}, \frac{3}{4}, -\frac{3}{4}, \frac{1}{4}, -\frac{1}{4}, \frac{3}{2}, -\frac{3}{2}, 3, -3$$

Example 15.3 Find the zeros of the function $f(x) = x^3 + 2x^2 - 2x - 4$.

Solution We could use a computer to estimate the zeros, but since this is a problem in a beginning calculus book, we hope the author put at least one rational zero in the polynomial. If so, the rational root can be found from the following list

$$\frac{+1, -1, +2, -2, +4, -4}{+1, -1} \longrightarrow 1, -1, 2, -2, 4, -4$$

We will use synthetic division to see which, if any, of these numbers are zeros.

$$\begin{array}{r|rrrr} 1 & 1 & 2 & -2 & -4 \\ & & 1 & 3 & 1 \\ \hline & 1 & 3 & 1 & -3 \end{array} \qquad \begin{array}{r|rrrr} -1 & 1 & 2 & -2 & -4 \\ & & -1 & -1 & 3 \\ \hline & 1 & 1 & -3 & -1 \end{array}$$

$$\begin{array}{r|rrrr} 2 & 1 & 2 & -2 & -4 \\ & & 2 & 8 & 12 \\ \hline & 1 & 4 & 6 & 8 \end{array} \qquad \begin{array}{r|rrrr} -2 & 1 & 2 & -2 & -4 \\ & & -2 & 0 & 4 \\ \hline & 1 & 0 & -2 & 0 \end{array}$$

The last remainder is zero; so -2 is a zero of the polynomial function and $x + 2$ is a factor of the polynomial. Now we have

$$x^3 + 2x^2 - 2x - 4 = (x + 2)(x^2 - 2)$$

We will find the roots of the equation $x^2 - 2 = 0$. These numbers are the zeros of the polynomial $x^2 - 2$.

$$x^2 - 2 = 0 \longrightarrow x^2 = 2 \longrightarrow x = \pm\sqrt{2}$$

Thus, the factors of the original polynomial are $(x + 2)$, $(x - \sqrt{2})$, and $(x + \sqrt{2})$, and the zeros are $-2, \sqrt{2}, -\sqrt{2}$.

Example 15.4   Find the roots of $x^3 - 7x - 6 = 0$.

Solution   First we list the possible rational roots.

$$+1, -1, +2, -2, +3, -3, +6, -6$$

Now we divide. Note that we write a zero for the coefficient of the x^2 term in the dividend.

$$
\begin{array}{r|rrrr}
1 & 1 & 0 & -7 & -6 \\
  &   & 1 & 1 & -6 \\
\hline
  & 1 & 1 & -6 & -12
\end{array}
\qquad
\begin{array}{r|rrrr}
-1 & 1 & 0 & -7 & -6 \\
   &   & -1 & 1 & 6 \\
\hline
   & 1 & -1 & -6 & 0
\end{array}
$$

Zero is the remainder when we divide by -1, so -1 is a zero of the polynomial. The reduced polynomial is $x^2 - x - 6$, and we can use the quadratic formula to find the zeros of this polynomial.

$$x = \frac{1 \pm \sqrt{1 - (4)(1)(-6)}}{2} = \frac{1 \pm \sqrt{25}}{2} = -2, 3$$

Thus the roots of the polynomial equation are $-2, -1,$ and 3.

Problem set 15

1. The little red airplane could fly at 6 times the speed of the wind. Flying at this rate, it could fly 700 miles downwind in 1 hour less than it took to fly 600 miles upwind. What was the speed of the little red airplane and what was the speed of the wind?

2. The cook had p pounds of food in the storehouse; this would feed w workers for d days. If 50 more workers arrived unexpectedly, how many days would the cook's food last if each person consumed food at the same rate as before?

3. Find the standard form of the equation of a circle whose center is $(-2, 3)$ and which passes through $(-2, -1)$.

4. If f is a function whose equation is given by $f(x) = x^4 - 2x^2 + 2x + 1$, use synthetic division to evaluate:
    (a) $f(-1)$ (b) $f(1)$ (c) $f(3)$

5. Use the rational zero theorem to list the possible rational zeros of the function $f(x) = x^3 - x^2 - 4x + 4$.

6. Use the information of Problem 5 to determine all the rational zeros of f, where f is the function defined in Problem 5.

7. Find x, where: (a) $10^x = 4$ (b) $e^x = 4$

8. Solve $\ln b^3 = 2$ for b.   9. Solve $\log_{1/3} 9 = 2x + 1$ for x.

10. Write the general equation of the sinusoid shown in terms of the sine function.

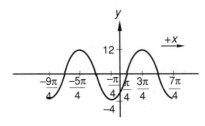

11. Sketch the graph of $y = x^{2/3}$.

12. Write the equation of the graph of the points which are a distance of 5 units from the point (1, 2) on the coordinate plane.

13. Graph the set $\{x \in \mathbb{Z} \mid |2x - 3| < 4\}$.

14. Express (2 cis 10°)[3 cis (−40°)] in rectangular form. (All numbers must be exact.)

15. Graph $y = \left(\frac{1}{2}\right)^x$ and $y = 2^x$ on the same coordinate plane.

16. Given the figure shown, find an expression for sec α in terms of a and b.

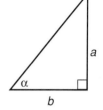

17. Show that: $\dfrac{\sin^2 (-\theta) + \cos^2 (-\theta) + 2}{3 \tan (-\theta)} = -\cot \theta$

18. Show that: $\sin x - \sin x \cos^2 x = \sin^3 x$

19. If f is a quadratic function such that $f(2) = f(-3) = 0$ and $f(3) = 6$, then find the equation for f.

20. If $f(x) = \dfrac{1}{x}$, write the simplified expression for the following:

$$\frac{f(x + \Delta x) - f(x)}{\Delta x}$$

CONCEPT REVIEW 21. Each of the base angles of an isosceles triangle has twice the measure of the vertex angle of the triangle. Find the measure of the vertex angle.

22. Solve for x in the figure shown.
$m \angle CAB = (5x - 40)°$
$m \angle ABC = (3x)°$
$m \angle ACD = (4x + 60)°$

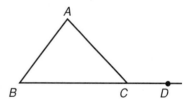

LESSON 16 *Continuity · Left-hand and right-hand limits*

16.A
Continuity

We begin our discussion of **continuity** with an intuitive definition that can be interpreted graphically. A function is a continuous function on an interval between x values of a and b if the function is defined for all values of x between a and b and if a small change in x does not produce a sudden jump in the value of y. If a function is not continuous at a value of x, we say that the function has a ***discontinuity*** at that value of x. The graphs of the continuous functions considered in this book can be drawn on an interval on which the function is defined without lifting the pencil from the paper. Calculus will let us do wonderful things with continuous functions such as polynomial functions and exponential functions, but these functions do not exhibit the aberrant behavior necessary for a discussion of some of the fundamental concepts of calculus. Thus, we will invent the necessary functions. Usually we will just draw the graph of the function we need for our discussion and will not bother with trying to find the algebraic expression for the function. The following are examples of the graphs of functions that have the types of discontinuities we would like to consider.

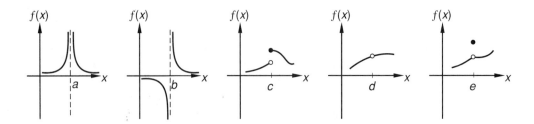

The functions whose graphs are shown here are not continuous at a, b, c, d, and e. A *vertical asymptote* is a vertical line approached but never touched by the graph of a function. The two graphs on the left have vertical asymptotes at a and b, and so the functions are not defined for these values of x. Therefore, $f(x)$ is not continuous at a and b. The function is defined at c, but the graph shows that a small change in x produces a "jump" in the value of $f(x)$ and so the function is not continuous at c. There is a hole in the graph at d; so the function is not defined at d. Therefore, the function is not continuous at d. In the rightmost graph the function is defined at e, but there is a sudden jump in the value of $f(x)$ at e and so the function is not continuous at e. Graphs such as the three graphs on the right are useful for explanations of continuity and limits but are almost never encountered again unless the author needs the graph of a function whose behavior is somewhat pathological.

16.B
Left-hand and right-hand limits

The study of calculus is based on a concept called the *limit of a function.* The limit of a function is the number the value of the function gets close to as x gets very close to some designated number. Two of the most important limits concern the values of the following expressions as the value of x gets closer and closer to zero.

$$(1 + x)^{1/x} \quad \text{and} \quad \frac{\sin x}{x}$$

If we replace x with zero in these two expressions, we get results that cannot be evaluated.

$$(1 + 0)^{1/0} \quad \text{and} \quad \frac{\sin 0}{0} = \frac{0}{0}$$

But if we let x get very, very close to zero, we will find that the value of $(1 + x)^{1/x}$ gets very, very close to the number e, and if x is in radians, the value of $\sin x$ divided by x gets very, very close to 1. We will investigate these expressions in a later lesson.

To discuss limits, it is helpful to think of x as a dot on the x axis that we can move right or left as we choose. We will move vertically from any selected position of the x dot to the graph of the function and then move horizontally to read the output value of $f(x)$ on the y axis. We show this in the left-hand figure on the following page. In the right-hand figure, we show the graph of a function that has no value when $x = 5$.

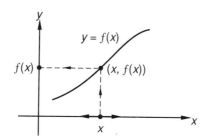 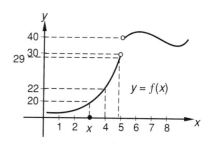

In the figure on the right, when the x dot is at 3, the output value of $f(x)$ is 20. When the x dot moves from 3 to 4, the output value of $f(x)$ increases from 20 to 22. When the x dot moves from 4 to 4.9, the output value of $f(x)$ increases from 22 to 29. We say that as the x dot moves closer to 5, x is **approaching** 5 from the left, and we see that the closer the x dot gets to 5, the closer the value of $f(x)$ gets to 30. We use the notation 5^- to show that x is approaching 5 from the left end of the number line where the negative numbers live, and we write

$$\lim_{x \to 5^-} f(x) = 30$$

We say that 30 is the left-hand limit of $f(x)$ as x approaches 5. If we let the x dot move along the x axis and approach 5 from the right-hand side, we can see that $f(x)$ will get closer and closer to 40 as x approaches 5. We use the notation 5^+ to show that x is approaching 5 from the right end of the number line where the positive numbers live, and we write

$$\lim_{x \to 5^+} f(x) = 40$$

We say that the right-hand limit of $f(x)$ as x approaches 5 is 40.

   The limit of $f(x)$ as x approaches some number a from the right or the left is the number that $f(x)$ gets closer and closer to as x gets closer and closer to a. When we discuss limits, we do not even consider the value of $f(a)$, which is the value of the function when $x = a$.

Example 16.1   Given this graph of $f(x)$, estimate:
(a) $\lim f(x)$ as $x \to 3^+$
(b) $\lim f(x)$ as $x \to 1^-$
(c) $\lim f(x)$ as $x \to 3^-$
(d) $\lim f(x)$ as $x \to 1^+$

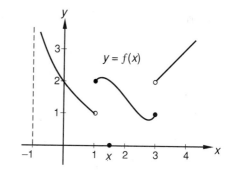

Solution   (a)   As the x dot approaches 3 from the + end of the number line, the value of $f(x)$ gets closer to 2, so the right-hand limit of $f(x)$ as x approaches 3 is **2.**
      (b)   As the x dot approaches 1 from the − end of the number line, the value of $f(x)$ gets closer to 1, so the left-hand limit of $f(x)$ as x approaches 1 is **1.**
      (c)   As the x dot approaches 3 from the − end of the number line, the value of $f(x)$ approaches 1, so the left-hand limit of $f(x)$ as x approaches 3 is **1.**
      (d)   As the x dot approaches 1 from the + end of the number line, the value of $f(x)$ gets closer and closer to 2, so the right-hand limit of $f(x)$ as x approaches 1 is **2.**

Example 16.2   Estimate: (a) $\lim\limits_{x \to 3^+} f(x)$ (b) $\lim\limits_{x \to 3^-} f(x)$

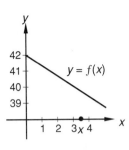

Solution   The value of $f(x)$ as x approaches 3 from the right or from the left appears to be about 40. Thus we estimate that the right-hand limit and left-hand limit are both about 40.

$$(a)   \lim\limits_{x \to 3^+} f(x) \approx \mathbf{40}   (b)   \lim\limits_{x \to 3^-} f(x) \approx \mathbf{40}$$

The fact that the value of $f(3)$ also appears to be 40 is of no concern to us, as we are only interested in values of x very, very close to 3.

Example 16.3   Given that

$$f(x) = \begin{cases} 1 & \text{if } x \geq 0 \\ -1 & \text{if } x < 0 \end{cases}$$

sketch the graph of $f(x)$ and find:

(a) $\lim\limits_{x \to 0^+} f(x)$ (b) $\lim\limits_{x \to 0^-} f(x)$

Solution   (a)   On the graph we see that as x approaches zero from the right the value of $f(x)$ is 1 and continues to be 1. Thus the right-hand limit of $f(x)$ as x approaches zero is **1**.
        (b)   The left-hand limit as x approaches zero is **−1** because x is 1 and continues to be 1 as x approaches zero from the left.

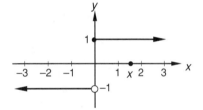

Problem set 16   1.   The number of sophists varied inversely as the square of the number of xenophobes present. If there were 8 sophists when there were 5 xenophobes present, how many sophists would there be if there were 2 xenophobes present?

2.   Find the length in inches of the shadow cast by a L-foot-tall flagpole if a R-inch ruler casts a 1-foot shadow.

3.   Given the graph of a function f, evaluate the following limits:
(a) $\lim\limits_{x \to 0^+} f(x)$ (b) $\lim\limits_{x \to 0^-} f(x)$
(c) $\lim\limits_{x \to 1^-} f(x)$ (d) $\lim\limits_{x \to 1^+} f(x)$

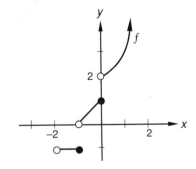

4. Graph the function g where $g(x) = [x] + 1$. Then evaluate the following limits.
   (a) $\lim_{x \to 1^+} g(x)$ (b) $\lim_{x \to 1^-} g(x)$

5. If f is a function whose equation is given by

$$f(x) = 2x^5 - 4x^4 + 3x^3 - 2x^2 + x - 1$$

   evaluate the following expressions by using synthetic division.
   (a) $f(-1)$ (b) $f(2)$ (c) $f(-2)$

6. Use the rational zero theorem to list the possible rational zeros of the equation $h(x) = 6x^3 - 19x^2 + 2x + 3$.

7. Use the information of Problem 6 to determine all the zeros of h where h is as defined in Problem 6.

8. Solve for x: $\log_x (2x - 7) = 1$

9. Find x if $e^x = 10$.   10.   Graph $y = -|\sin x|$.

11. Write the standard form of the equation of the circle whose center is $(1, 2)$ and which contains the point $(-2, 6)$.

12. Find the range of $y = x^2$ when $|x| < 2$.

13. Express $[3 \operatorname{cis} (-20°)](\operatorname{cis} 80°)$ in rectangular form. (All numbers must be exact.)

14. Sketch the graphs of $y = e^x$ and $y = -e^x$ on the same coordinate plane.

15. Show that: $-\sin (-x) \sec x \cot \left(\dfrac{\pi}{2} - x\right) + 1 = \sec^2 x$

16. Simplify: $\dfrac{\sin x - \sin x \cos^2 x}{\sec^2 x - 1}$

17. Find the coordinates of the vertex of the graph of the following quadratic function: $y = x^2 - 2x + 4$.

18. Solve for L in terms of x and H for this figure.

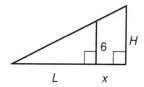

19. Sketch the graph of $y = -1 + 2 \sin \left(x - \dfrac{\pi}{2}\right)$.

20. Describe the domain and range of $y = \sqrt{x^2 - 1}$.

CONCEPT REVIEW 21. Find the area of a triangle whose three sides have lengths 5, 6, and 7, respectively. *Note*: Heron's formula states that the area A of a triangle whose sides have lengths a, b, and c is

$$A = \sqrt{s(s - a)(s - b)(s - c)} \qquad \text{where} \qquad s = \frac{1}{2}(a + b + c)$$

22. If x, y, and z are lengths of the sides of a triangle of area 10, compare:
    A. x B. $y + z$

LESSON 17   *Sum and difference identities for trigonometric functions · Double-angle identities for sine and cosine*

17.A
Sum and difference identities for trigonometric functions

If we use a calculator to find approximations for the sine of 10°, the sine of 20°, and the sine of 30°, we get this result.

$$\sin 10° \approx 0.174 \qquad \sin 30° = 0.500$$
$$\sin 20° \approx \underline{0.342}$$
$$0.516$$

We note, to our dismay, that the sine of 10° plus the sine of 20° does not equal the sine of 30°. To find the trigonometric functions of the sums and differences of two angles, we must use the appropriate trigonometric identities.

There are about 18 trigonometric identities that are used in calculus, and they are difficult to memorize because many of them are similar. The two identities

$$\tan \theta = \frac{\sin \theta}{\cos \theta} \qquad \text{and} \qquad \sin^2 \theta + \cos^2 \theta = 1$$

are reasonably easy to remember. If, in addition to these, one can memorize the identities for the sines and cosines of the sums and differences of two angles, the other identities can be developed quickly whenever one of them is required. First we remember the identities for $\sin (A + B)$ and $\cos (A + B)$ and write:

$$\sin (A + B) = \sin A \cos B + \cos A \sin B$$
$$\sin (A - B) =$$
$$\cos (A + B) = \cos A \cos B - \sin A \sin B$$
$$\cos (A - B) =$$

To help us memorize these identities, we note that the letter pattern in both cases from left to right is AB, AB, AB, and that A always comes first. We also note that if sin comes first on the left, then sin comes first on the right and that if cos comes first on the left, then cos comes first on the right. Next we write the expressions for $\sin (A - B)$ and $\cos (A - B)$. These are exactly the same as those for the sine and the cosine of $(A + B)$ except that the signs are changed.

KEY IDENTITIES

$$\sin (A + B) = \sin A \cos B + \cos A \sin B \qquad \sin^2 \theta + \cos^2 \theta = 1$$
$$\sin (A - B) = \sin A \cos B - \cos A \sin B$$
$$\cos (A + B) = \cos A \cos B - \sin A \sin B \qquad \tan \theta = \frac{\sin \theta}{\cos \theta}$$
$$\cos (A - B) = \cos A \cos B + \sin A \sin B$$

Students should practice writing this list of key identities several times a day until the key identities can be reproduced in less than 30 seconds. Writing these identities is also a suggested first step for taking any examination, because these identities can be used to develop other identities accurately and quickly.

Example 17.1   Simplify: $\sin \left(\theta + \dfrac{\pi}{4} \right)$

Solution   This is the sine of a sum and requires the use of the identity for sin $(A + B)$.

$$\sin (A + B) = \sin A \cos B + \cos A \sin B$$

Now we replace A with θ and replace B with $\frac{\pi}{4}$.

$$\sin \left(\theta + \frac{\pi}{4} \right) = \sin \theta \cos \frac{\pi}{4} + \cos \theta \sin \frac{\pi}{4}$$

Both the sine and the cosine of $\frac{\pi}{4}$ equal $\frac{\sqrt{2}}{2}$, so we get

$$\sin \left(\theta + \frac{\pi}{4} \right) = (\sin \theta)\left(\frac{\sqrt{2}}{2}\right) + (\cos \theta)\left(\frac{\sqrt{2}}{2}\right)$$

$$= \frac{\sqrt{2}}{2} \sin \theta + \frac{\sqrt{2}}{2} \cos \theta$$

Example 17.2   Find the exact value of cos 15° by using a trigonometric identity and the fact that 60° − 45° = 15°.

Solution   This problem is designed to provide practice in the use of the identity for cos $(A - B)$ and not for pointing out a better way to calculate cos 15°. First we write the identity for cos $(A - B)$.

$$\cos (A - B) = \cos A \cos B + \sin A \sin B$$

Now we replace A with 60° and B with 45°.

$$\cos (60° - 45°) = \cos 60° \cos 45° + \sin 60° \sin 45°$$

$$\cos 15° = \left(\frac{1}{2}\right)\left(\frac{\sqrt{2}}{2}\right) + \left(\frac{\sqrt{3}}{2}\right)\left(\frac{\sqrt{2}}{2}\right)$$

$$= \frac{\sqrt{2}}{4} + \frac{\sqrt{6}}{4} = \frac{\sqrt{2} + \sqrt{6}}{4}$$

17.B
Double-angle identities for the sine and cosine

We can use the sum and difference identities for the sine and the cosine to develop all the other identities quickly and accurately. To develop the identity for sin 2A, we use the identity for sin $(A + B)$ and everywhere replace B with A.

$$\sin (A + A) = \sin A \cos A + \cos A \sin A$$

$$\sin 2A = 2 \sin A \cos A$$

To develop the identity for cos 2A, we use the identity for cos $(A + B)$ and everywhere replace B with A.

$$\cos (A + A) = \cos A \cos A - \sin A \sin A$$

$$\cos 2A = \cos^2 A - \sin^2 A$$

With just a little practice it is possible to look at the identities for sin $(A + B)$ and cos $(A + B)$ and write the identities for sin 2A and cos 2A by inspection. We look at

$$\sin (A + B) = \sin A \cos B + \cos A \sin B$$

and mentally replace B with A. Then by inspection we write

$$\sin 2A = 2 \sin A \cos A$$

In the same manner we look at

$$\cos (A + B) = \cos A \cos B - \sin A \sin B$$

and mentally replace B with A. Then by inspection we write

$$\cos 2A = \cos^2 A - \sin^2 A$$

We can get two other identities for $\cos 2A$ by using the basic Pythagorean identity $\sin^2 A + \cos^2 A = 1$ and substituting. We can solve the identity above for $\cos^2 A$ as we show on the left and for $\sin^2 A$ as we show on the right.

$$\cos^2 A = 1 - \sin^2 A \qquad \sin^2 A = 1 - \cos^2 A$$

Now, in the identity for $\cos 2A$, on the left we substitute for $\cos^2 A$ and on the right we substitute for $\sin^2 A$.

$$\cos 2A = \cos^2 A - \sin^2 A$$

$$\cos 2A = (1 - \sin^2 A) - \sin^2 A \qquad \cos 2A = \cos^2 A - (1 - \cos^2 A)$$

$$\cos 2A = 1 - 2\sin^2 A \qquad\qquad \cos 2A = 2\cos^2 A - 1$$

In calculus we often encounter expressions that contain $\sin x$ and $\sin 2x$ or contain $\cos x$ and $\cos 2x$. The double-angle identities enable us to simplify those expressions by replacing $\cos 2x$ or $\sin 2x$ with expressions that contain $\cos x$ or $\sin x$.

$$\sin 2A = 2 \sin A \cos A$$
$$\cos 2A = \cos^2 A - \sin^2 A$$
$$\cos 2A = 2 \cos^2 A - 1$$
$$\cos 2A = 1 - 2 \sin^2 A$$

Thus we see that we have developed one form of an identity for $\sin 2A$ and three forms of identities for $\cos 2A$. One form contains both $\cos^2 A$ and $\sin^2 A$, and the other two forms contain either $\sin^2 A$ or $\cos^2 A$. These two forms can be rearranged into other forms that are important. If we solve the last two identities for $\cos^2 A$ and $\sin^2 A$, we get

$$\sin^2 A = \frac{1}{2} - \frac{1}{2} \cos 2A \qquad \cos^2 A = \frac{1}{2} + \frac{1}{2} \cos 2A$$

If we replace A with $\frac{x}{2}$ and take the square root of both sides, we get two half-angle identities.

$$\sin^2 \frac{x}{2} = \frac{1}{2} - \frac{1}{2} \cos 2\left(\frac{x}{2}\right) \qquad \cos^2 \frac{x}{2} = \frac{1}{2} + \frac{1}{2} \cos 2\left(\frac{x}{2}\right)$$

$$\sin \frac{x}{2} = \pm\sqrt{\frac{1}{2} - \frac{\cos x}{2}} \qquad \cos \frac{x}{2} = \pm\sqrt{\frac{1}{2} + \frac{\cos x}{2}}$$

It is important to remember that these half-angle identities are rearranged forms of the identities for $\cos 2A$ with A replaced by $\frac{x}{2}$.

Example 17.3   Draw a graph of $y = \sin^2 \theta$.

Solution   On the left we show the graph of $y = \sin \theta$ and on the right the graph of $y = \sin^2 \theta$.

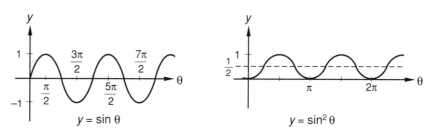

$y = \sin \theta$ $y = \sin^2 \theta$

The maximum value of $\sin \theta$ is 1, and since $(1)^2$ is also 1, the maximum value of $\sin^2 \theta$ is 1. Since all values of $\sin^2 \theta$ are positive or 0, the graph of $\sin^2 \theta$ is above or touches the x axis when the graph of $\sin \theta$ is below or touches the x axis. The $\sin^2$ curve is rounded because the square of any number less than 1 is less than that number. In Lesson 18 we will understand why this graph can be used as a visual mnemonic for remembering that

$$\sin^2 \theta = \frac{1}{2} - \frac{1}{2} \cos 2\theta$$

Example 17.4   Develop three identities for $\cos 2A$.

Solution   We look at the identity for $\cos (A + B)$

$$\cos (A + B) = \cos A \cos B - \sin A \sin B$$

and write the first identity for $\cos 2A$ by inspection.

$$\cos 2A = \cos^2 A - \sin^2 A$$

Now we do two parallel developments. On the left below we substitute $1 - \sin^2 A$ for $\cos^2 A$, and on the right we substitute $1 - \cos^2 A$ for $\sin^2 A$.

$$\cos 2A = (1 - \sin^2 A) - \sin^2 A \qquad \cos 2A = \cos^2 A - (1 - \cos^2 A)$$

We are careful with the $(-)$ signs when we simplify to get

$$\cos 2A = 1 - 2 \sin^2 A \qquad \cos 2A = 2 \cos^2 A - 1$$

Example 17.5   Show that: $\dfrac{\sin x}{\sin 2x} = \dfrac{\sec x}{2}$

Solution   Whenever we see a trigonometric function of $2x$, we get a strong hint to use a double-angle identity. We will work with the left-hand side and substitute for $\sin 2x$.

$$\frac{\sin x}{2 \sin x \cos x} \qquad \text{substituted}$$

$$\frac{1}{2 \cos x} \qquad \text{simplified}$$

$$\frac{\sec x}{2} \qquad \text{identity}$$

Problem set 17   1.   The area of a rectangle is 8 times the area of a square, and the width of the rectangle is twice the length of a side of the square. If the perimeter of the rectangle is 16 units greater than the perimeter of the square, find the dimensions of the rectangle and the square.

2. A 10-foot ladder leans against a vertical wall. If the base of the ladder is x feet away from the base of the wall, find an expression whose value equals the height of the top of the ladder above the ground.

3. Write the key trigonometric identities and develop one identity for sin $2A$ and three identities for cos $2A$.

4. If $\cos \alpha = \frac{1}{5}$, use a double-angle identity to find the value of $\cos 2\alpha$.

5. Show that $(\sin x + \cos x)^2 = 1 + \sin 2x$.

6. Graph f, where $f(x) = \begin{cases} x + 1 & \text{when } x \neq 1 \\ 3 & \text{when } x = 1 \end{cases}$

7. Evaluate the following limits if f is defined as in Problem 6.
   (a) $\lim\limits_{x \to 1^+} f(x)$ (b) $\lim\limits_{x \to 1^-} f(x)$

8. Use the rational zero theorem to list the possible rational zeros of the equation $y = 2x^3 - 7x^2 - 5x + 4$.

9. Use the information from Problem 8 to determine all the rational zeros of the function of Problem 8.

10. Solve for x: $\log_4 (3x + 1) = \frac{1}{2}$

11. Sketch the graph of $y = x^{1/3}$.

12. Find the radius of the circle whose center is $(1, -1)$ and which is tangent to the line $3x - 4y - 2 = 0$.

13. Sketch the graphs of $y = 2^x$ and $y = 2^{-x}$ on the same coordinate plane.

14. Simplify: $\sin \left(\frac{\pi}{2} - x \right) \csc (-x) \sin x \cos (-x)$

15. Find the equation of the quadratic function whose graph has x intercepts at $x = -1$ and $x = 2$ and a y intercept at $y = -2$.

16. Solve for y in terms of x for the figure shown.

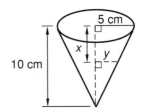

17. Graph $y = 2 + 3 \sin \left(x - \frac{\pi}{4} \right)$.

18. If $f(x) = 2x^2$, evaluate and simplify the following expression:

$$\frac{f(x + h) - f(x)}{h}$$

19. Find the real values of x for which $\sqrt{1 - x}$ is a real number.

20. Use the identities from Problem 3 to develop identities for $\sin \frac{x}{2}$ and $\cos \frac{x}{2}$.

21. State the contrapositive of the following statement: If two angles of a triangle have equal measures, then the sides opposite them have equal lengths.

22. Find x, y, and z in the figure shown.

$$m\widehat{AC} = x°$$
$$m\widehat{AB} = y°$$
$$m\widehat{BC} = z°$$

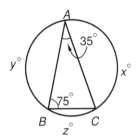

23. One base of a trapezoid is the same length as the height of the trapezoid and the other base of the trapezoid is twice the height. If the area of the trapezoid is 12, find the height of the trapezoid.

LESSON 18 *Graphs of logarithmic functions · Period of a function*

18.A
Graphs of logarithmic functions

We know that 10 raised to the power 2 equals 100. We can say this in the language of logarithms if we call the exponent a logarithm and say that the logarithm to the base 10 of 100 equals 2.

$$100 = 10^2 \quad \overset{\text{means}}{\longleftrightarrow} \quad \log_{10} 100 = 2$$

If we use b for the base, N for the number, and L for the logarithm, we can write

$$N = b^L \qquad \text{or} \qquad L = \log_b N$$

On the left we graph an exponential function whose base is greater than 1. On the right we show the graph of the logarithmic function that has the same base.

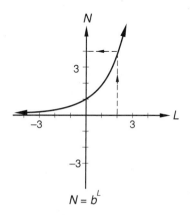

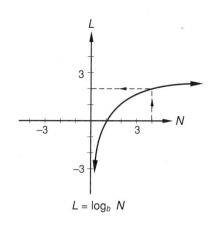

To reduce confusion in mathematics, we always use the horizontal axis for the independent variable and the vertical axis for the dependent variable (the answer). Thus, as shown in the left-hand figure and equation, we would normally begin with a value of L and find the answer which would be the corresponding value of N. In the right-hand figure and equation, we would normally begin with a value of N and the answer would be the corresponding value of L. It is customary to use x for the independent variable in both equations. If we do this, we can graph both functions on the same set of coordinate axes and find that they are mirror images of each other about the line $y = x$.

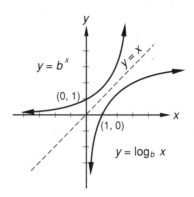

However, we must be careful to remember that in one equation y is the logarithm and in the other equation x is the logarithm.

It is most important to note that negative numbers do not have logarithms. If a positive number is raised to any real power, the result is a positive number. To illustrate, we let the base be 3 and use 2, -2, and 0 as exponents.

$$3^2 = 9 \qquad 3^{-2} = \frac{1}{9} \qquad 3^0 = 1$$

We note that all three answers are positive numbers. Thus, if we try to find the value of y in

$$y = \log_3 (-14)$$

we are doomed to failure because we are asking for the power of 3 that causes 3^y to equal -14. **From this discussion we see that 3 to any real number power is a positive number. Thus, negative numbers do not have logarithms.**

We can change the shape of the graph of a logarithmic equation by inserting negative signs, as we show in the next three examples.

Example 18.1   Sketch the graph of $y = \log_4 x$.

Solution   We do not have a table of logarithms to the base 4, but we do know how to get three quick points on the graph of an exponential function by using 0, 1, and -1 for x. To get three quick points on the graph of $y = \log_4 x$, we rewrite the equation in exponential form and use 0, 1, and -1 for y so we can find the paired values of x. Then we use these points to graph the logarithmic function.

$$y = \log_4 x \quad \longrightarrow \quad 4^y = x$$

y	1	0	-1
x	4	1	$\frac{1}{4}$

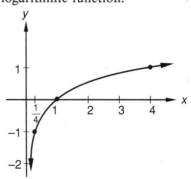

$y = \log_4 x$

Example 18.2   Sketch $y = -\log_4 x$.

Solution   First we move the $(-)$ sign across the equals sign. Then we write the equation in exponential form and use 1, 0, and -1 for y and solve for x.

$$-y = \log_4 x \quad \longrightarrow \quad 4^{-y} = x$$

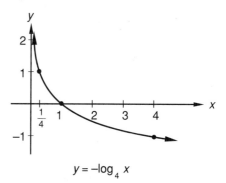

y	1	0	-1
x	$\frac{1}{4}$	1	4

$y = -\log_4 x$

We note that this graph of $y = -\log_4 x$ is the mirror image in the x axis of the graph of $y = \log_4 x$ in Example 18.1. Every value of y in this graph is the negative of the value of y in the graph in Example 18.1.

Example 18.3   If b is greater than 1, graph the following:

(a) $y = \log_b x$ (b) $y = -\log_b x$ (c) $y = \log_b(-x)$ (d) $y = -\log_b(-x)$

Solution   **The logarithmic function is one of the most important functions in all mathematics, and it is important to be able to make a quick sketch of the graph without resorting to point-by-point plotting.** We must memorize the shape of the graph of $y = \log_b x$ if b is greater than 1, which we show on the left below. This graph can be altered two ways by the presence of a minus sign in the equation. **The graph of (b) $y = -\log_b x$ is the first graph reflected in the x axis (flipped about the x axis) because every value of y is the negative of its value in $y = \log_b x$. The graph of (c) $y = \log_b(-x)$ is the first graph reflected in the y axis because every value of x is the negative of its value in $y = \log_b x$. In (d) both minus signs are present, so both reflections have taken place.**

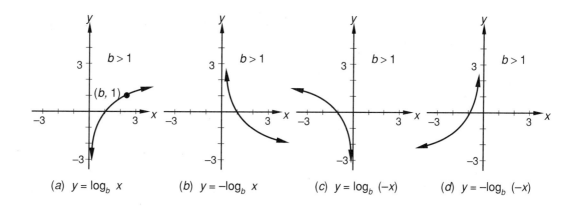

(a) $y = \log_b x$ (b) $y = -\log_b x$ (c) $y = \log_b(-x)$ (d) $y = -\log_b(-x)$

Example 18.4   Graph $y = \ln |x|$.

Solution   As we note in figure (a) above, the graph of the equation $y = \log_b x$ lies to the right of the y axis because $\log_b x$ is defined only for positive values of x. In figure (c), the graph of $y = \log_b(-x)$ lies to the left of the y axis because the function $y = \log_b(-x)$

is defined only for negative values of x. The graphs of $y = \ln x$ and $y = \ln(-x)$ exhibit the same behavior since the base e is greater than 1. The graph of $y = \ln|x|$ is a composite of the graphs of $y = \ln x$ and $y = \ln(-x)$ because this function is defined for all values of x except zero.

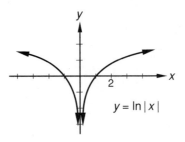

$y = \ln|x|$

Example 18.5   Sketch the graph of $y = -\log_{1/4} x$.

Solution   First we move the minus $(-)$ sign across the equals sign and write $-y = \log_{1/4} x$. Next we write the exponential form of this equation and use 1, 0, and -1 for y and solve for x.

$$\left(\frac{1}{4}\right)^{-y} = x$$

y	1	0	-1
x	4	1	$\frac{1}{4}$

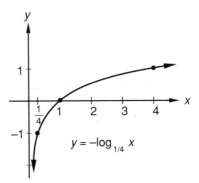

$y = -\log_{1/4} x$

The graph is exactly the same as the graph in Example 18.1 because $4^y = \left(\frac{1}{4}\right)^{-y}$.

Example 18.6   Sketch the graph of $y = \log_2(-x)$.

Solution   We write the exponential form of this equation and use 1, 0, and -1 for y to find three points on the graph.

$$2^y = -x \quad \longrightarrow \quad -2^y = x$$

y	1	0	-1
x	-2	-1	$-\frac{1}{2}$

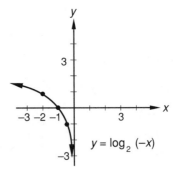

$y = \log_2(-x)$

18.B
Period of a function

The values of $\sin 30°$, $\sin(30° + 360°)$, and $\sin(30° + 720°)$ are all $\frac{1}{2}$. The sine of $30°$ is $\frac{1}{2}$, and since $30° + 360°$ equals once around plus $30°$ more, the sine of $30° + 360°$ is the same as the sine of 30°. The angle 30° + 720° means twice around and 30° more, so the sine of this angle is also the same as the sine of 30°. We can go around as many times as we please, and 30° more, and the sine of all of these angles is $\frac{1}{2}$. If n is a counting number, we can write

$$\sin(\theta + n360°) = \sin\theta$$

We say that the *period* of sin θ is 360° because the values repeat every 360°. If three different functions repeat their values every 360°, 180°, or 90°, we say that the periods of the functions are 360°, 180°, or 90°, respectively. If we use p for the period and n for a counting number, we say that a function is a periodic function if for any θ

$$f(\theta) = f(\theta + np)$$

We can see that the function $y = \sin\theta$ and $y = \sin 2\theta$ are periodic functions because the graphs of both functions repeat the same patterns again and again as θ increases.

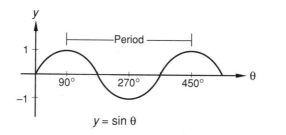

$y = \sin\theta$

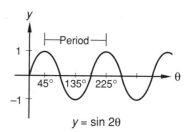

$y = \sin 2\theta$

The graph of $y = \sin 2\theta$ repeats the pattern twice as often as does the graph of $y = \sin\theta$, so we say that the period of sin 2θ is one-half the period of sin θ. The period of a function is the horizontal distance on the graph between any two corresponding points. Thus the θ distance between two successive peak values can be used to determine the period. In the graph on the left we see that the period is 450° − 90°, or 360°. In the graph on the right the period is 225° − 45°, or 180°. Thus the period for $y = \sin\theta$ is 360°, or 2π radians. In the graph of $y = \sin 2\theta$, the pattern repeats twice as often and the period is 180°, or π radians. If we draw the graph of $y = \sin 3\theta$, we will find that the pattern repeats 3 times as often and the period is 120°, or $2\pi/3$ radians. If we graph $y = \sin\frac{1}{3}\theta$, we will find that the pattern repeats one-third as often and the period is $360°/\frac{1}{3} = 1080°$, or $2\pi/\frac{1}{3} = 6\pi$ radians. From this observation we see that the constant C in $y = \sin C\theta$ equals 360° divided by the period in degrees, or 2π radians divided by the period in radians.

$$\text{Constant } C = \frac{2\pi}{\text{period}} \qquad \text{Constant } C = \frac{360°}{\text{period}}$$

Thus the general equations of a sine function and a cosine function are

$$y = A + B \sin C(\theta - D) \qquad y = A + B \cos C(\theta - D)$$

where A is the y value of the centerline, B is the amplitude, C equals 360° or 2π divided by the period, and D is the phase angle.

Example 18.7 Graph the function $y = -10 + 4\cos(3\theta - 135°)$.

Solution **The first step is to factor the argument so that the coefficient of θ is 1. If we do this, the phase angle can be read directly.** We factor and get

$$y = -10 + 4\cos 3(\theta - 45°)$$

Next we draw the sinusoid on the left.

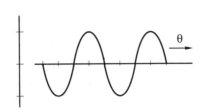 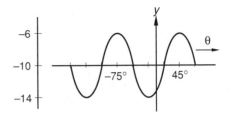

On the right we show that the y coordinate of the centerline is -10 and that the amplitude is 4. The phase angle is $+45°$, so one peak value of the graph occurs when $\theta = +45°$. The constant C is 3, so the period is $360°$ divided by 3, or $120°$. Thus we move to the left from $+45°$ a distance of $120°$ and mark the θ value below the next peak as $45° - 120°$, or $-75°$. Now, if we wish, we can locate other points of interest on the θ axis by noting that each loop of the graph spans half a period, or $60°$.

Problem set 18

1. Two boats leave the buoy at the same time. One of the boats travels north at a rate of N miles per hour, and the other boat travels east at a rate of $4N$ miles per hour. What is the distance between the boats 30 minutes after both boats leave the buoy?

2. Find the number of radians through which a wheel rotates every 5 seconds if it revolves 20 times every minute.

3. Sketch the graphs of $y = 2^x$ and $y = \log_2 x$ on the same coordinate plane.

4. Sketch the graphs of $y = \log_2 x$ and $y = \log_2 (-x)$ on the same coordinate plane.

5. Determine the amplitude, phase angle, and period of the sinusoidal function $y = 3 + 2 \sin (3x - 45°)$.

6. Graph the function f where $f(x) = -1 + 2 \sin \left(2x - \dfrac{\pi}{2} \right)$.

7. Write the key identities and develop an identity for $\sin 2x$ and three identities for $\cos 2x$.

8. Show that $(\sin x - \cos x)^2 = 1 - \sin 2x$.

9. Graph f where $f(x) = \begin{cases} \sqrt{x} & \text{when } x > 0 \\ -\sqrt{-x} & \text{when } x < 0 \end{cases}$

10. If f is as defined in Problem 9, evaluate the following limits:

    (a) $\lim\limits_{x \to 0^+} f(x)$ (b) $\lim\limits_{x \to 0^-} f(x)$

11. Use synthetic division to evaluate the following, where

    $$f(x) = 2x^4 - x^3 + 2x^2 - x + 3$$

    (a) $f(2)$ (b) $f(-2)$ (c) $f(3)$

Use a calculator as necessary to find x:

12. $e^x = 21$

13. $\log_x 4x = 2$

14. Graph $y = |x^2 - 2x - 3|$.

15. Find the standard form of the equation of a circle whose center is $(1, -2)$ and whose area is 4π.

16. Find those values of x for which $|2x - 3| < 0.01$.

17. Find the exact value of the rectangular form of the following product:
(2 cis 20°)(2 cis 20°)(2 cis 20°)

18. If $\sin A = \dfrac{1}{3}$, find the value of $\sin (-A) \cos \left(\dfrac{\pi}{2} - A\right)$.

19. Determine the domain and range of $y = 2 - \sin (3x - \pi)$.

20. If $f(x) = \dfrac{2}{x}$, simplify: $\dfrac{f(x + \Delta x) - f(x)}{\Delta x}$

CONCEPT REVIEW   **21.** If $a^3 + b^3 = 10$ and $a + b = 5$, then what is the value of $a^2 - ab + b^2$?

22. Solve for x in terms of y, z, and t.

$AE = x + y$
$EB = y$
$ED = t$
$EC = z$

LESSON 19 *Limit of a function*

A function has a limit at a particular value of x if it has both a right-hand limit and a left-hand limit at that value of x and if the limits are equal.
The limit of a continuous function as x approaches a is the value of the function when $x = a$. Thus, the values of the following functions when x approaches 3 are the values of the functions when $x = 3$.

$$\lim_{x \to 3} (x + 6) = 9 \qquad \lim_{x \to 3} (x^2 + 3) = 12$$

The limit of the sum, product, or difference of functions when x approaches a is the sum, product, or difference of the individual limits. The limit of the quotient of two functions is the quotient of the limits if the limit of the function in the denominator is not zero.

$$\lim_{x \to 3} [(x + 6) + (x^2 + 3)] = 9 + 12 \qquad \lim_{x \to 3} (x + 6)(x^2 + 3) = (9)(12)$$
$$= 21 \qquad\qquad\qquad = 108$$

$$\lim_{x \to 3} [(x + 6) - (x^2 + 3)] = 9 - 12 \qquad \lim_{x \to 3} \frac{x + 6}{x^2 + 3} = \frac{9}{12} = \frac{3}{4}$$
$$= -3$$

These examples are not good examples to teach the idea of a limit because the limit as x approaches 3 is the value of the function when $x = 3$. A better example would be a function that has a limit as x approaches 3, but that has no defined value when the value of $x = 3$. Useful functions that exhibit such behavior are not plentiful, so authors of calculus books make them up. The ploy used most often is to take a continuous function and modify it so that its graph has a hole in it when $x = 3$. We can do that to the function $x + 2$ by multiplying it by $x - 3$ over $x - 3$ as we show here.

$$y = x + 2 \qquad y = \frac{(x + 2)(x - 3)}{x - 3} \qquad y = \frac{x^2 - x - 6}{x - 3}$$

On the left we show the graph of the line $y = x + 2$, and on the right we show the graph of the same line with a hole in it.

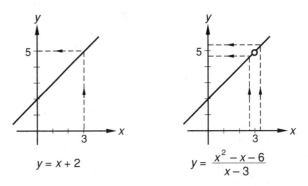

$$y = x + 2 \qquad\qquad y = \frac{x^2 - x - 6}{x - 3}$$

The new function has no value when x equals 3 because the denominator equals zero when $x = 3$. **But the new function has the same values as does $x + 2$ for all other values of x.** So we have manufactured a function whose value approaches 5 as x approaches 3 from the left and whose value also approaches 5 as x approaches 3 from the right, but has no value when $x = 3$. Thus, the right-hand limit is 5 and the left-hand limit is also 5. **We have a function that has a limit as x approaches 3 because both the left-hand and right-hand limits exist and the limits are equal.**

Example 19.1 Find $\lim\limits_{x \to 2} \dfrac{x^2 - 4}{x - 2}$.

Solution When $x = 2$, this function has no value because the denominator equals zero. If we factor the numerator, we get

$$\lim_{x \to 2} \frac{(x - 2)(x + 2)}{(x - 2)}$$

For any value of x other than 2, the $x - 2$ above and the $x - 2$ below will cancel, and we get

$$\lim_{x \to 2} (x + 2) = 4$$

Example 19.2 Find $\lim\limits_{x \to 3} \dfrac{x^2 + 2x}{x + 1}$.

Solution This problem is trivial because the limit of a quotient of continuous functions as x approaches 3 is the quotient of the limit of the two functions as long as an x value of 3 does not cause the denominator to equal zero.

$$\lim_{x \to 3} \frac{x^2 + 2x}{x + 1} = \frac{9 + 6}{3 + 1} = \frac{15}{4}$$

Example 19.3 Find $\lim\limits_{x \to 3} \dfrac{x^2 + 6x}{x - 3}$.

Solution This function has no limit as x approaches 3 because the denominator approaches zero; and although the numerator can be factored, $x - 3$ is not one of the factors.

$$\lim_{x \to 3} \frac{x(x + 6)}{x - 3} \;[\neq]\; \frac{27}{0} \qquad \textbf{Thus, the limit does not exist.}$$

We use the symbol $[\neq]$ because we do not wish to indicate that $\frac{27}{0}$ is the limit.

Example 19.4   Find $\lim\limits_{t \to 2} \dfrac{t - 2}{t^2 + 4}$.

Solution   In this problem the independent variable is t instead of x. As t approaches 2, the numerator approaches zero and the denominator approaches 8.

$$\lim_{t \to 2} \frac{t - 2}{t^2 + 4} = \frac{0}{8} = 0$$

Thus, the limit is 0 over 8, which equals 0.

Example 19.5   Find $\lim\limits_{s \to -1} \dfrac{2s^2 + 5s + 3}{s + 1}$.

Solution   When $s = -1$, the denominator equals 0, and we have a problem. Let's hope the numerator has a factor of $s + 1$. It does.

$$\lim_{s \to -1} \frac{(2s + 3)(s + 1)}{(s + 1)}$$

For all values of s except -1 the value of this function equals the value of $2s + 3$. We don't care about the value when $s = -1$, so we have

$$\lim_{s \to -1} (2s + 3) = 2(-1) + 3 = 1$$

Example 19.6   Find $\lim\limits_{x \to 2} \dfrac{x^3 - 8}{x - 2}$.

Solution   The denominator equals zero when $x = 2$. Thus we hope that $x - 2$ is a factor of the numerator. Let's see.

$$\lim_{x \to 2} \frac{(x - 2)(x^2 + 2x + 4)}{x - 2} \qquad \text{factored}$$
$$= 2^2 + 2(2) + 4 \qquad \text{substituted}$$
$$= 12 \qquad \text{simplified}$$

Example 19.7   Find $\lim\limits_{x \to 0} \dfrac{(3 + x)^2 - 3^2}{x}$.

Solution   We will expand the numerator and hope that each term in the expansion has a factor of x so we can cancel the x in the denominator.

$$\lim_{x \to 0} \frac{\cancel{9} + 6x + x^2 - \cancel{9}}{x} \quad \longrightarrow \quad \lim_{x \to 0} 6 + x = 6$$

Problem set 19
1. Two pipes can be used to fill the swimming pool. If the large pipe is used alone, the pool can be filled in k hours. If the small pipe is used alone, the pool can be filled in s hours. If the two pipes are used together, how long will it take for the swimming pool to be $\frac{7}{8}$ filled?

2. Stig traveled for h hours at m miles per hour, but arrived at the fjord 2 hours late. How fast should Stig have traveled to have arrived on time?

3. Graph $y = \dfrac{x^2 - 1}{x - 1}$.

Evaluate the following limits:

4. $\lim\limits_{x \to 1} \dfrac{x^2 - 1}{x - 1}$

5. $\lim\limits_{x \to -1} \dfrac{x^2 + 1}{x - 1}$

6. $\lim\limits_{x \to 0} \dfrac{(1 + x)^2 - (1)^2}{x}$

7. $\lim\limits_{x \to -1} \dfrac{2x^2 + x - 1}{x + 1}$

8. Graph f where $f(x) = \begin{cases} 2x - 1 & \text{when } x > 1 \\ 3 & \text{when } x = 1 \\ x^2 & \text{when } x < 1 \end{cases}$

9. If f is as defined in Problem 8, evaluate:

   (a) $\lim\limits_{x \to 1^+} f(x)$　　(b) $\lim\limits_{x \to 1^-} f(x)$　　(c) $\lim\limits_{x \to 1} f(x)$

10. Determine the amplitude, the period, and the equation of the centerline of the sinusoid whose equation is $y = 4 - 2 \sin 3x$.

11. Sketch $y = e^x$ and $y = \ln x$ on the same coordinate plane.

12. Sketch $y = \ln x$ and $y = \ln (-x)$ on the same coordinate plane.

13. Write the key identities and develop a double-angle identity to express $\cos^2 x$ in terms of $\cos 2x$.

14. Use the identity for $\sin (A + B)$ to simplify the following expression:

$$\sin \left(\frac{\pi}{2} + x \right)$$

15. Use the rational zero theorem as an aid to finding all the rational zeros of the equation $y = 6x^3 + x^2 - 4x + 1$.

16. If $y - 1 = \ln x$, what does x equal?　　　17. Sketch $y = -|x^2 - 3x - 4|$.

18. The center of circle O is $(1, 3)$ and a point on circle O is $(-2, 2)$. Write the equation of circle O in standard form.

19. Find the distance from the point $(1, 4)$ to the line whose equation is as follows: $2x = 3y + 4$.

20. Add $-4 \angle -150° + 4 \angle 30°$ and write the answer in rectangular form.

21. Write the key trigonometric identities for practice. Then show that:

$$\sec (-x) \sin \left(\frac{\pi}{2} - x \right) + \sin (-x) \cos \left(\frac{\pi}{2} - x \right) = \cos^2 x$$

22. Which of the following equations can be the equation of a function y of the independent variable x?

    (a) $x^2 + y^2 = 9$　　(b) $x^2 = y$
    (c) $x = y^2$　　　　　(d) $y = \pm\sqrt{x}$

23. Multiply and express the answer so that numerator of the final expression is the number 1:

$$\left(\frac{\sqrt{x + h} - \sqrt{x}}{h} \right) \left(\frac{\sqrt{x + h} + \sqrt{x}}{\sqrt{x + h} + \sqrt{x}} \right)$$

24. Evaluate: $\sum\limits_{x=1}^{3} \dfrac{1}{x}$

CONCEPT REVIEW   **25.** Solve for x in terms of m, y, and s.

$AB = x + y$
$BC = y$
$DC = m + s$
$ED = s$

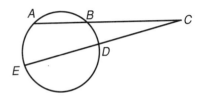

26. If x is a real number, compare: *A.* $\sqrt{x^2}$ *B.* $|x|$

LESSON 20   *The parabola as a locus · Translated parabolas*

20.A
The parabola as a locus   We remember that we can get the information necessary to make a quick sketch of a quadratic function if we complete the square on the x terms and write the equation in a different form, as we show on the left.

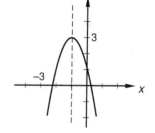

$y = -2x^2 - 4x + 1$ function

$y = -2(x + 1)^2 + 3$ completed the square

The graph of a quadratic function is a parabola. By looking at the completed-square form, we can see that the parabola opens down, that the axis of symmetry is $x = -1$, and that the y coordinate of the vertex is $+3$.

It is sometimes helpful to consider the parabola as a *locus* and to use a different form of the equation. If we solve the above equation for the $(x + 1)^2$ term, we get

$$(x + 1)^2 = -\frac{1}{2}(y - 3)$$

By using this form of the equation, it is possible to determine that this is the equation of a parabola whose vertex is $(-1, +3)$ and that every point on the parabola is equidistant from the point $\left(-1, 2\frac{7}{8}\right)$ and the line $y = 3\frac{1}{8}$. Let's see why this is true.

We remember that a line is the locus of all points in a plane that are equidistant from two given points. A circle is the locus of all points in a plane that are equidistant from a point called the *center* of the circle. The parabola also has a locus definition.

> A *parabola* is the locus of all points in a plane that are equidistant from a given line and a given point. The line is called the *directrix* and the point is called the *focus*.

The development of the equation of a parabola from this definition is very straightforward. We draw a parabola below with the vertex at the origin. The vertex is equidistant from both the focus and the directrix, and we call this distance p. Because the vertex is at the origin, the focus is at $(0, p)$ and the directrix is the line $y = -p$. The number p can be either positive or negative. The sign of p determines which way the parabola opens.

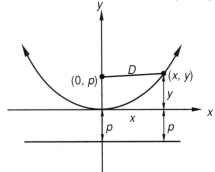

Distance from (x, y) to focus = distance from (x, y) to directrix

$$\sqrt{(x - 0)^2 + (y - p)^2} = y + p$$

$$x^2 + y^2 - 2py + p^2 = y^2 + 2py + p^2$$

$$x^2 = 4py$$

On the right we used the distance formula to represent the distance from any point (x, y) on the parabola to the focus. The distance from (x, y) to the directrix is measured vertically and is $y + p$. When we squared both sides, expanded, and simplified, we finished with the equation

$$x^2 = 4py$$

If $4p$ is positive, the parabola opens up. If $4p$ is negative, the parabola opens down. If x and y are interchanged, the parabola will open left or right as determined by the sign of $4p$, which is now the coefficient of y.

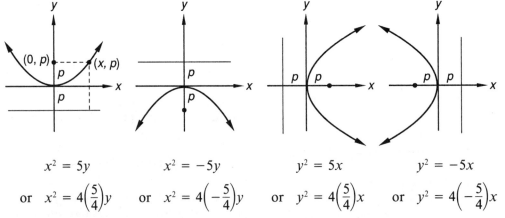

| $x^2 = 5y$ | $x^2 = -5y$ | $y^2 = 5x$ | $y^2 = -5x$ |
| or $x^2 = 4\left(\frac{5}{4}\right)y$ | or $x^2 = 4\left(-\frac{5}{4}\right)y$ | or $y^2 = 4\left(\frac{5}{4}\right)x$ | or $y^2 = 4\left(-\frac{5}{4}\right)x$ |

It is interesting to note that the width of the parabola at the focus is the absolute value of $4p$. This distance is called the *latus rectum*. From the graph of the parabola on the far left above we see the point (x, p) is a distance of $2p$ from the directrix; therefore, it must also be a distance of $2p$ from the focus. Thus, the parabola is $|4p|$ units wide at the focus. Similar arguments can be given to show that the remaining three parabolas above are $|4p|$ units wide at the focus. Some problems that use the locus definition can be unraveled by finding p and knowing that every parabola is $|4p|$ units wide at the focus.

Example 20.1   The equation of a parabola is $y^2 = -8x$. Sketch the parabola and give the coordinates of the focus, the equation of the directrix, and the length of the latus rectum.

Solution   **All we have to do is find *p* and |4*p*|.** The general equation of a parabola whose vertex is at (0, 0) is shown on the left, and the equation of our parabola is on the right.

$$y^2 = 4px \qquad y^2 = -8x$$

Thus $4p = -8$ and p must equal -2. The negative sign tells us that the parabola opens in the $-x$ direction, and the 2 tells us that

1. The distance from the vertex to the focus is 2.
2. The distance from the vertex to the directrix is 2.
3. The width of the parabola at the focus is 4(2), or 8.

This is all the information we need to sketch the parabola.

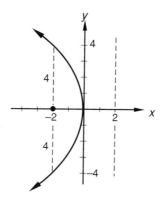

The focus is at $(-2, 0)$, the equation of the directrix is $x = 2$, and the length of the latus rectum is 8.

20.B
Translated parabolas

The basic equation of a parabola is the equation of a parabola whose vertex is the origin. To write the equation of a parabola whose vertex is $(-4, 3)$, we replace x with $(x + 4)$ and replace y with $y - 3$.

	VERTEX AT THE ORIGIN	VERTEX AT $(-4, 3)$
PARABOLA	$y^2 = 4px$	$(y - 3)^2 = 4p(x + 4)$
	$x^2 = 4py$	$(x + 4)^2 = 4p(y - 3)$

Example 20.2   Sketch the parabola $x^2 - 4x - 8y - 12 = 0$ and show the focus, the directrix, and the latus rectum.

Solution   All we have to do is find p and $|4p|$. Since x is the squared variable, we put all x terms on one side and complete the square.

$$(x^2 - 4x \qquad) = 8y + 12 \qquad \text{rearranged}$$
$$(x^2 - 4x + 4) = 8y + 12 + 4 \qquad \text{added } +4$$
$$(x - 2)^2 = 8(y + 2) \qquad \text{simplified}$$

The basic form of this equation is $x^2 = 4py$ shifted so that the vertex is at $(2, -2)$. The value of $|4p|$ is 8, so $p = 2$. This is all the information we need.

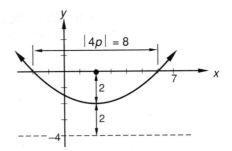

Example 20.3   Find the equation of the parabola whose directrix is $x = -4$ and whose focus is at (2, 1).

Solution   If we make a sketch, we can find p and write the equation.

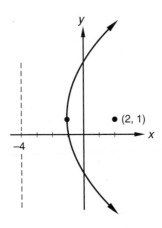

The vertex is always halfway from the focus to the directrix. This tells us that $p = 3$ and the vertex is at $(-1, 1)$. This is all we need to know. The equation opens in the $+x$ direction, so $4p$ is a positive number.

$$y^2 = 4px \qquad\qquad \text{basic form}$$

$$(y - 1)^2 = 4(3)(x + 1) \qquad (-1, 1) \text{ with } p = +3$$

$$\mathbf{(y - 1)^2 = 12(x + 1)} \qquad \text{equation}$$

Problem set 20

1. Two boats leave the buoy at the same time. One of the boats travels south at a rate of $3a$ miles per hour, and the other boat travels west at a rate of $4a$ miles per hour. What is the distance between the two boats 3 hours after they leave the buoy?

2. At present, Chris is twice as old as Todd. In x years, Chris will be $1\frac{1}{2}$ times Todd's age then. Find the present age of Todd in terms of x.

3. Sketch the graph of the parabola whose equation is $-3y^2 = -12x$ and determine the coordinates of the focus, the equation of the directrix, and the length of the latus rectum.

4. Find the equation of the locus of all points which are equidistant from the line $x = -2$ and the point (1, 3).

Evaluate the following limits:

5. $\lim\limits_{x\to 2} \dfrac{x^2 + 2x}{x + 2}$

6. $\lim\limits_{x\to 2} \dfrac{x^2 + x - 6}{x - 2}$

7. $\lim\limits_{x\to a} \dfrac{x^2 - a^2}{x - a}$

8. $\lim\limits_{x\to 0} \dfrac{(2 + x)^2 - 2^2}{x}$

9. Sketch the graph of f where $f(x) = \begin{cases} x^2 & \text{when } |x| < 3 \\ 2 & \text{when } |x| \geq 3 \end{cases}$

10. If f is as defined in Problem 9, evaluate:

   (a) $\lim\limits_{x\to 3^+} f(x)$ (b) $\lim\limits_{x\to 3^-} f(x)$ (c) $\lim\limits_{x\to 3} f(x)$

11. Sketch the graphs of $y = 3^x$ and $y = \log_3 x$ on the same coordinate plane.

12. Sketch the graphs of $y = \log_3 x$ and $y = \log_3 (-x)$ on the same coordinate plane.

13. Find the equation of the sinusoid shown in terms of the sine function.

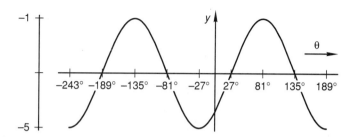

14. If $\cos A = \dfrac{2}{3}$, find the value of $\sin^2 A$.

15. Use the identity for $\sin (A + B)$ to show that:

$$\frac{\sin (x + \Delta x) - \sin x}{\Delta x} = \sin x \left(\frac{\cos \Delta x - 1}{\Delta x}\right) + \cos x \left(\frac{\sin \Delta x}{\Delta x}\right)$$

16. Determine all values of x for which $x^3 - x^2 - 2x + 2$ equals zero.

17. Write the key identities for practice, and then develop the identities for $\sin \frac{x}{2}$ and $\cos \frac{x}{2}$.

18. Find the domain and range of the function $y = |\sin x|$.

19. Find the coordinates of the points of intersection of the graphs of $y = x^2$ and $y = x$.

20. Begin with the point-slope form, and manipulate it as necessary to write the slope-intercept form of the equation of the line which passes through $(1, \pi)$ and has a slope of 1.

CONCEPT REVIEW **21.** Shown is a circle with center O. Find the measure of $\angle OAB$ if $m\widehat{AB} = 140°$.

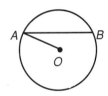

22. If x and y are real numbers and $x > y$, then compare: $A.$ $\dfrac{1}{x}$ $B.$ $\dfrac{1}{y}$

LESSON 21 *Inverse trigonometric functions ·*
Trigonometric equations

21.A

Inverse trigonometric functions

If we specify an angle, we specify the sine of the angle at the same time because the sine of each angle has only one value. If we write

$$\sin 30° = ?$$

the answer is $\frac{1}{2}$. We can turn things around and ask for the angle whose sine is $\frac{1}{2}$ three different ways.

$$\sin^{-1} \frac{1}{2} = ? \qquad \arcsin \frac{1}{2} = ? \qquad \text{The angle whose sine is } \frac{1}{2} = ?$$

All three of these statements refer to the **inverse sine** of $\frac{1}{2}$. The notations arcsin $\frac{1}{2}$, $\sin^{-1} \frac{1}{2}$, and inverse sine $\frac{1}{2}$ all mean the same thing. There is an infinite number of angles whose sine equals $\frac{1}{2}$. The sine of 30° is $\frac{1}{2}$, the sine of $(30° + 360°)$ is $\frac{1}{2}$, the sine of $[30° + 2(360°)]$ is $\frac{1}{2}$, the sine of $[30° + n(360°)]$ is $\frac{1}{2}$, etc. Also, the sine of 150° is $\frac{1}{2}$, the sine of $(150° + 360°)$ is $\frac{1}{2}$, and the sine of $[150° + n(360°)]$ is $\frac{1}{2}$ as long as n is an integer.

When we ask for the inverse sine or the inverse cosine or the inverse tangent of an angle, we would like to have only one answer so that these inverses will be functions. This will be true if we restrict ourselves to portions of the graphs of sin θ, cos θ, and tan θ where the function is always decreasing or always increasing and all values of the function are included. If we look at the graph of sin θ, we see that this is true for many portions of the graph.

Mathematicians choose the portion between $-90°$ and $+90°$ to define the range of the inverse sine because this portion is closest to the origin. Between these values of θ, the graph is always ascending and all values of sin θ between -1 and $+1$ are encountered.

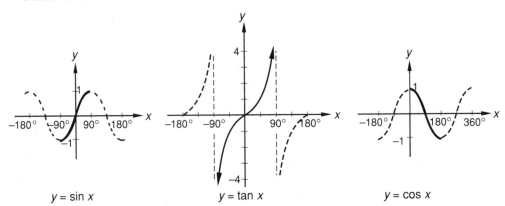

$y = \sin x$ $y = \tan x$ $y = \cos x$

In the center we see that the portion of the graph of $y = \tan \theta$ closest to the origin is everywhere ascending and that this portion includes all values of tan θ between $-\infty$ and ∞. This is the portion between $-90°$ and $+90°$, so we restrict the inverse tangent to this range of values of θ. To choose the portion to be used to define the inverse cosine, we note that the portion between $-180°$ and 0° is everywhere ascending and the portion between 0° and $+180°$ is everywhere descending, and both portions are the same distance from the origin. We assume that the portion between 0° and 180° was chosen to define the inverse cosine because this range of values of θ includes the first-quadrant angles, which are the angles used most often.

The points on the graphs of the inverse sine, inverse cosine, and inverse tangent have the same coordinates as the sine, cosine, and tangent but in reverse order. For example, the point (90°, 1) is on the graph of $y = \sin x$ on the previous page and the point (1, 90°) is on the graph of $y = \sin^{-1} x$ below.

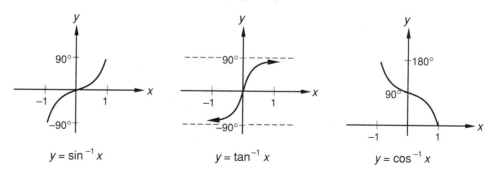

$$y = \sin^{-1} x \qquad\qquad y = \tan^{-1} x \qquad\qquad y = \cos^{-1} x$$

We note that the graphs of the inverse sine and the inverse cosine terminate abruptly because these functions are defined for only 180°, or π radians.

Example 21.1   Evaluate: $\sin^{-1} \dfrac{\sqrt{2}}{2}$

Solution   If we picture the graph of $y = \sin \theta$ and select a portion of the graph near the origin that is everywhere increasing in which all values of $\sin \theta$ are encountered, we see that the portion is between θ values of $-90°$ and $+90°$ where the graph is everywhere increasing. Thus, we are asked to specify the angle between $+90°$ and $-90°$ whose sine equals $\frac{\sqrt{2}}{2}$. The sine of $+45°$ equals $\frac{1}{\sqrt{2}}$, which equals $\frac{\sqrt{2}}{2}$. Thus our answer is 45°, or $\frac{\pi}{4}$.

$$\sin^{-1} \frac{\sqrt{2}}{2} = \frac{\pi}{4}$$

Example 21.2   Evaluate: $\cos^{-1} \left(-\dfrac{\sqrt{3}}{2}\right)$

Solution   We are asked to find the angle between 0° and 180° whose cosine is $-\frac{\sqrt{3}}{2}$. The cosine is negative between 90° and 180°, so we need a second-quadrant angle.

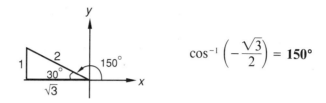

$$\cos^{-1} \left(-\frac{\sqrt{3}}{2}\right) = \mathbf{150°}$$

21.B
Trigonometric equations

Since there is an infinite number of angles whose sine equals $\frac{1}{2}$, the equation

$$\sin x = \frac{1}{2}$$

has an infinite number of solutions. We can indicate that we are only interested in values of x between 0° and 360° if we follow the equation with the following notation: $0° \le x < 360°$.

Example 21.3 Find x, given that: $\sec x = -2$ $(0° \le x < 360°)$

Solution The task is to find all values of x between $0°$ and $360°$ whose secant is -2. The secant is the reciprocal of the cosine, so we can write

$$\sec x = -2 \quad \text{but} \quad \cos x = \frac{1}{\sec x} \quad \text{so} \quad \cos x = -\frac{1}{2}$$

There are two angles between $0°$ and $360°$ whose cosine equals $-\frac{1}{2}$. They are **120°** and **240°**, as we see in these figures.

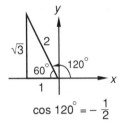
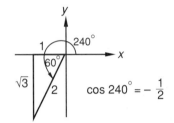

Example 21.4 Solve: $\sin^2 x = 1$ $(0 \le x < 2\pi)$

Solution The task is to find the radian measures of x between 0 and 2π which satisfy the given equation. If we move the 1 to the left side, we get an expression that can be factored. Then we set each of the factors equal to zero and solve.

$$\sin^2 x - 1 = 0 \qquad \text{added } -1 \text{ to both sides}$$
$$(\sin x - 1)(\sin x + 1) = 0 \qquad \text{factored}$$
$$\sin x = 1 \quad \text{or} \quad \sin x = -1 \qquad \text{zero factor theorem}$$
$$\boldsymbol{x = \frac{\pi}{2}} \qquad\qquad \boldsymbol{x = \frac{3\pi}{2}} \qquad \text{solved}$$

Example 21.5 Solve: $\tan^2 x = 3$ $(0° \le x < 360°)$

Solution We rearrange, factor, and solve.

$$\tan^2 x - 3 = 0 \qquad \text{rearranged}$$
$$(\tan x - \sqrt{3})(\tan x + \sqrt{3}) = 0 \qquad \text{factored}$$
$$\tan x = \sqrt{3} \qquad \tan x = -\sqrt{3} \qquad \text{solved}$$

The tangent is positive in the first and third quadrants. The angles in these quadrants whose tangent is $\sqrt{3}$ are $60°$ and $240°$. The tangent is negative in the second and fourth quadrants. The tangents of both $120°$ and $300°$ are $-\sqrt{3}$. Thus we have four answers:

$$x = 60°, 240°, 120°, 300°$$

Example 21.6 Solve: $\cos^2 x + 2 \sin x - 2 = 0$ $(0° \le x < 360°)$

Solution The trick here is to replace $\cos^2 x$ with $1 - \sin^2 x$. The resulting equation in $\sin x$ can be factored.

$$(1 - \sin^2 x) + 2 \sin x - 2 = 0 \qquad \text{subtracted}$$
$$\sin^2 x - 2 \sin x + 1 = 0 \qquad \text{simplified}$$
$$(\sin x - 1)(\sin x - 1) = 0 \qquad \text{factored}$$

$$\sin x = 1 \qquad \text{zero factor theorem}$$

$$\boldsymbol{x = 90°} \qquad \text{solved}$$

Example 21.7   Solve: $2 \sin^2 \theta = 3 + 3 \cos \theta$ $(0° \leq \theta < 360°)$

Solution   Problems like these in mathematics books are carefully contrived so that the answers are reasonable. We must learn to recognize that substitutions can be made and the result factored. We will rearrange this equation, substitute $(1 - \cos^2 \theta)$ for $\sin^2 \theta$, factor, and solve.

$$2 \sin^2 \theta - 3 \cos \theta - 3 = 0 \qquad \text{rearranged}$$

$$2(1 - \cos^2 \theta) - 3 \cos \theta - 3 = 0 \qquad \text{substituted}$$

$$-2 \cos^2 \theta - 3 \cos \theta - 1 = 0 \qquad \text{simplified}$$

$$2 \cos^2 \theta + 3 \cos \theta + 1 = 0 \qquad \text{changed signs}$$

Now this expression is of the form $2x^2 + 3x + 1$, which can be factored as follows: $(2x + 1)(x + 1)$. Thus our equation can be written in similar factored form as

$$(2 \cos \theta + 1)(\cos \theta + 1) \qquad \text{factored}$$

$$\cos \theta = -\frac{1}{2} \qquad \cos \theta = -1 \qquad \text{solved}$$

The only angle whose cosine is -1 is $180°$, but the cosines of both $120°$ and $240°$ are $-\frac{1}{2}$. Thus we have three answers.

$$\boldsymbol{\theta = 180°, 120°, 240°}$$

Problem set 21   **1.**   The strength of a beam with a rectangular cross section varies jointly with the square of the depth of its cross section and with the width of its cross section.

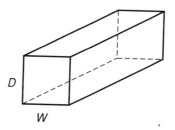

If the strength is 40 when the width is P inches and the depth is M cm, what is the strength when the width is A inches and the depth is 3 cm?

2.   Four times the first number plus 6 times the second number equals M. The first number reduced by twice the second number equals K. Express the first number in terms of M and K.

Evaluate the following trigonometric expressions:

3. $\sin^{-1} \left(-\dfrac{\sqrt{2}}{2} \right)$ **4.** $\cos^{-1} \dfrac{\sqrt{3}}{2}$

Solve for x:

5. $\csc x = -2$ $(0° \leq x < 360°)$ **6.** $\cos^2 x = 1$ $(0 \leq x < 2\pi)$

7. $\cos^2 x + 2 \sin x - 2 = 0$ $(0 \leq x < 2\pi)$

8. Write the equation of the parabola, each of whose points is equidistant from the line $x = -2$ and the point $(2, 4)$.

9. Find the coordinates of the focus, the equation of the directrix, and the length of the latus rectum of the parabola whose equation is $x^2 - 4x - 4y - 4 = 0$.

Evaluate the following limits:

10. $\lim\limits_{x \to 2} \dfrac{x - 2}{x^2 - 4}$

11. $\lim\limits_{\Delta x \to 0} \dfrac{(3 + \Delta x)^2 - 3^2}{\Delta x}$

12. Simplify the expression and find the limit: $\lim\limits_{x \to 0} \dfrac{\dfrac{1}{2 + x} - \dfrac{1}{2}}{x}$

13. Sketch the graphs of $y = \sin x$ and $y = \sin 2x$ on the same coordinate plane.

14. Sketch the graphs of $y = \ln x$, $y = -\ln x$, and $y = \ln (-x)$ on the same coordinate plane.

15. Show that:

$$\frac{\cos (x + \Delta x) - \cos x}{\Delta x} = \cos x \frac{\cos \Delta x - 1}{\Delta x} - \sin x \frac{\sin \Delta x}{\Delta x}$$

16. Determine all the zeros of the function $p(x) = x^3 - x^2 - x + 1$.

17. If $a = 16$ and $a = e^x$, use a calculator to find x.

18. Determine the domain of the function $y = \dfrac{\sqrt{x - 2}}{x}$.

19. $\triangle ABC$ is an equilateral triangle. If $AB = 3$ and DE is parallel to AB, find the length of DE in terms of h.

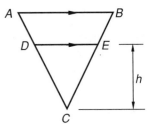

20. If $f(x) = x^2$, compute: $\dfrac{1}{4} \sum\limits_{n=1}^{4} f(1)$

21. Write the key identities and develop three identities for $\cos 2A$.

CONCEPT REVIEW 22. Given $\triangle ABC$ where $m \angle A > m \angle B$, compare: A. CB B. AC

23. If $x^2 + y^2 = 3$ and $x^2 - y^2 = 4$, find the value of $x^4 - y^4$.

LESSON 22 *Interval notation · Products of linear factors · Tangents · Increasing and decreasing functions*

22.A
Interval notation

The graph on the left below designates the real numbers between -3 and 2 but does not include the endpoints -3 and 2. The second graph designates the same numbers but includes -3 and 2. The other two graphs include one endpoint but exclude the other endpoint.

$$-3 < x < 2 \qquad -3 \le x \le 2 \qquad -3 < x \le 2 \qquad -3 \le x < 2$$

The notation below each graph designates the same set of values of x as does the graph. **We say that each of the notations designates an *interval* on the set of real numbers.** In calculus it is often necessary to designate such intervals, and we use *interval notation* for this purpose because it is more compact than the above notation. We will write the endpoint numbers separated with a comma and use a parenthesis if an endpoint number is not included in the interval and use a bracket if the endpoint number is included. We repeat the notations above, and below each one we use interval notation to make the same statement.

OPEN INTERVAL	CLOSED INTERVAL	PARTIALLY CLOSED INTERVALS	
$-3 < x < 2$	$-3 \le x \le 2$	$-3 < x \le 2$	$-3 \le x < 2$
$(-3, 2)$	$[-3, 2]$	$(-3, 2]$	$[-3, 2)$

We remark that the notation for an open interval $(-3, 2)$ is exactly the same notation we use to designate the ordered pair of x and y, $(-3, 2)$. Whether the notation designates an open interval or an ordered pair is a decision that must be made by the reader on the basis of the context in which the notation is used. The bracket is used to designate a closed end of an interval. Its meaning is easy to remember if we use the fact that the dashes on the top and bottom of the symbols] and [can remind us of equals signs. Thus, the following notations from left to right

$$(-\infty, 4) \qquad (-\infty, 4] \qquad (4, \infty) \qquad [4, \infty)$$

designate the numbers less than 4, the numbers less than or equal to 4, the numbers greater than 4, and the numbers greater than or equal to 4. The symbols ∞ and $-\infty$ are the symbols for positive infinity and negative infinity. *Infinity* is not a number but is the word we use to designate a quantity that is increasing without bound. If the symbol $+\infty$ or $-\infty$ is used in interval notation, it is always preceded or followed by a parenthesis as we see in the notations above.

Example 22.1   Designate the following intervals by using interval notation:
(*a*) $4 < x \le 30$ (*b*) $x \ge 22$ (*c*) $x < -42$

Solution   We remember to use the bracket to designate *or equal to*.

(*a*) **(4, 30]**   (*b*) **[22, ∞)**   (*c*) **(−∞, −42)**

Example 22.2   On which intervals is this function positive?

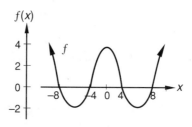

Solution   The function has a positive value whenever the graph of the function is above the x axis. Thus this function is positive (greater than zero) on these intervals.

$$f > 0 \qquad \text{on the intervals} \qquad (-\infty, -8), (-4, +4), \text{ and } (8, \infty)$$

22.B
Products of linear factors

Consider the expression

$$x - 2$$

If x equals 2, this expression equals zero. If x is less than 2, this expression represents a negative number. If x is greater than 2, this expression represents a positive number. These seemingly trivial statements are of considerable importance in determining the signs of functions on designated intervals. If a function is defined as a product of nonrepeating linear factors such as

$$f(x) = x(x + 3)(x + 6)(x - 2)(x - 5)$$

the function has a value of zero iff one of the factors equals zero. Thus, this function will equal zero iff x equals 0, -3, -6, $+2$, or $+5$. **The value of the function changes sign at each of these zeros and cannot change sign between two consecutive zeros.**

Example 22.3   Use (*a*) a number line and (*b*) interval notation to show the intervals on which the f function

$$f(x) = x(x + 3)(x + 6)(x - 2)(x - 5)$$

is positive and when the function is negative.

Solution   (*a*) First we sketch a number line and graph the zeros of the function.

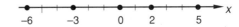

Now we must determine the sign of the function at some x value that is not a zero of the function. We decide to use $+1$ for this value of x.

$$f(1) = 1(1 + 3)(1 + 6)(1 - 2)(1 - 5) = (+)(+)(+)(-)(-) = +$$

Thus the sign of the function is positive when $x = +1$. From the graph we see that it must be positive for all x values between 0 and 2. For products of nonrepeating linear factors, the sign changes at every zero, as we show here.

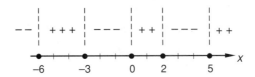

(*b*)   We can use interval notation to give the same information by saying that the function has a **positive value on the intervals (−6, −3), (0, 2), and (5, ∞) and has a negative value on the intervals (−∞, −6), (−3, 0), and (2, 5).**

22.C
Tangents

The word ***tangent*** comes from the Latin word *tangere*, which means "to touch." A tangent to a curve is a straight line that "touches" the curve. An accurate informal definition of a tangent is difficult to devise. A formal definition will be given in a later lesson. We will introduce the tangent by considering the following figure.

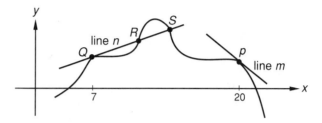

Line *m* is tangent to the curve at *p*. Line *n* is tangent to the curve at *Q* and intersects but is not tangent to the curve at two other points *R* and *S*. **The slope of a curve at a point is the slope of the tangent line to the curve at that point.** We customarily designate points of tangency by giving the *x* coordinate of the point. The points of tangency for the given lines and this curve are at *x* = 7 and *x* = 20.

Example 22.4   For what values of *x* does this curve have a slope of zero?

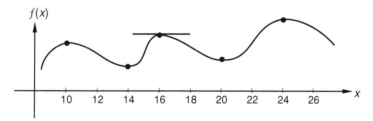

Solution   The slope of a curve is zero when the tangent is horizontal. We estimate that the point of tangency of the horizontal tangent shown in the figure has an *x* value of **16.** The other places where it seems that horizontal tangents may be drawn are at *x* values of **10, 14, 20, and 24.**

22.D
Increasing and decreasing functions

A function is an increasing function on an interval [*a*, *b*] if every greater input value of *x* on this interval produces a greater output *f*(*x*). A function is a decreasing function on an interval [*a*, *b*] if every greater input value of *x* on this interval produces a lesser output *f*(*x*). The mathematician tends to think of a function machine to represent this, but beginners find it helpful to think of the graph of the function instead.

   If the graph is everywhere ascending as *x* increases from *a* to *b*, the function is an increasing function on the interval [*a*, *b*]. If the graph is everywhere descending as *x* increases from *a* to *b*, the function is a decreasing function on the interval [*a*, *b*]. The function graphed on the left at the top of the following page is increasing on the interval [*a*, *b*] and decreasing on the interval [*b*, *c*].

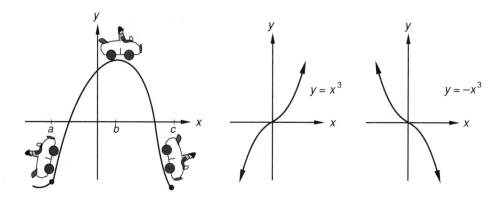

Saying that a graph is ascending on an interval [a, b] means *almost* the same thing as saying that the graph has a positive slope between x values of a and b. The difference is that an ascending graph can have a slope of zero at an isolated point (or points) if the slope is positive on both sides of the point. A descending graph can have a slope of zero at an isolated point (or points) if the slope is negative on both sides of the point. As examples, we show the graphs of the increasing function $y = x^3$ and the decreasing function $y = -x^3$. The slope of $y = x^3$ is positive everywhere except that the slope is zero when $x = 0$. The slope of $y = -x^3$ is negative everywhere except that the slope is zero when $x = 0$. The slope of the line tangent to the curve in the center figure is zero when $x = 0$, but only for this value of x. The graph is everywhere ascending and the function is an increasing function. The slope of the curve on the right is zero when $x = 0$, but only for this value of x. The graph is everywhere descending and the function is a decreasing function.

Example 22.5   On which intervals does the function graphed here appear to be a decreasing function?

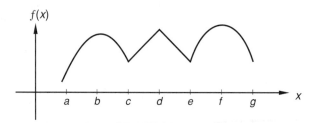

Solution   The graph appears to be descending on the intervals **[b, c], [d, e], and [f, g]**. Thus the function appears to be a decreasing function on these intervals.

Problem set 22

1. The master painter can paint an entire house in m days, and his apprentice can paint the house in A days. How long would it take the master painter and his apprentice to paint 7 entire houses of equal size if they work together?

2. The sum of two numbers is 40. If L is the larger number, express the product of the two numbers in terms of L.

3. Shown is the graph of the function f.

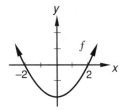

(*a*) Use interval notation to describe those intervals on which f is positive.

(*b*) Use interval notation to describe those intervals on which f is negative.

4. If f is as defined in Problem 3, determine those intervals on which f is increasing and those intervals on which f is decreasing.

5. If $f(x) = x(x - 2)(x + 3)$, show on a number line those intervals on which f is positive, those intervals on which f is negative, and indicate the values of x for which f is zero.

6. Sketch as accurately as possible the graph of $y = x^2$ where $x > 0$. Draw a tangent line to the graph at $x = 1$ and estimate its slope.

Solve the following equations for x, where $0 \le x < 2\pi$:

7. $\tan^2 x = 1$ 8. $\sin^2 x - \sin x + \dfrac{1}{4} = 0$

9. If $y = \arcsin x$, solve for x in terms of y.

10. Sketch the parabola whose equation is $x^2 - 8y - 4x + 20 = 0$. Determine the coordinates of the focus, the equation of the directrix, and the length of the latus rectum of the parabola.

Evaluate the following limits:

11. $\displaystyle\lim_{t \to 1} \frac{t^2 - 2t + 1}{t - 1}$ 12. $\displaystyle\lim_{s \to 1} \frac{s - 1}{s^2 + 1}$

13. Simplify: $\dfrac{[2(x + \Delta x) + 3] - (2x + 3)}{\Delta x}$

14. Find the value of k for which $y = \dfrac{1}{k} \sin kx$ has a period of 4π.

15. Write the key identities and develop an expression for $\sin 2x$.

16. Graph $y = e^x$, $y = -e^x$, $y = e^{-x}$, and $y = \ln x$ on the same coordinate plane.

17. If $\sin^2 A = \frac{1}{7}$, determine the value of $\cos 2A$ by using a double-angle identity.

18. Solve $\log_2 \dfrac{x - 1}{x + 1} = 3$ for x.

19. If (x, y) is a point on a unit circle centered at the origin, then what is the value of $x^2 + y^2$?

20. Find the values of y for which $|y - 3| < 0.01$.

CONCEPT REVIEW 21. Find the next term of this sequence: 1, 4, 9, 16, . . .

22. Determine the sum $x + y + z + t + s + v$ in the figure shown.

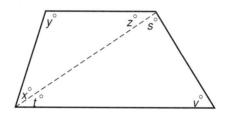

LESSON 23 *Logarithms of products and quotients ·*
Logarithms of powers · Exponential equations

23.A
Logarithms of products and quotients

We remember that we multiply powers of the same base by adding the exponents as we show on the left. We divide powers of the same base by subtracting the lower exponent from the upper exponent as we show on the right.

$$10^5 \cdot 10^2 = 10^{5+2} = 10^7 \qquad \frac{10^5}{10^2} = 10^{5-2} = 10^3$$

Since the logarithm of 10^5 is 5 and the logarithm of 10^2 is 2, we can use logarithmic notation and write

$$\log (10^5 \cdot 10^2) = \log 10^5 + \log 10^2 \qquad \log \frac{10^5}{10^2} = \log 10^5 - \log 10^2$$
$$= 5 + 2 = 7 \qquad\qquad\qquad\qquad = 5 - 2 = 3$$

Thus, the logarithm of a product equals the sum of the logarithms, and the logarithm of a quotient equals the difference of the logarithms.

$$\log_b MN = \log_b M + \log_b N \qquad \frac{\log_b M}{\log_b N} = \log_b M - \log_b N$$

This means that when we see that logarithms that have the same base are to be added, we know that the numbers were multiplied, and that when we see that logarithms that have the same base are to be subtracted, we know that the numbers were divided.

Example 23.1 Solve: $\log_4 (x + 2) + \log_4 5 = 2$

Solution The bases are the same and the logs are added, so we know that $(x + 2)$ and 5 are to be multiplied. Thus, we write

$$\log_4 5(x + 2) = 2$$

Now we write this equation in exponential form and solve.

$$5(x + 2) = 4^2 \qquad \text{exponential form}$$
$$5x + 10 = 16 \qquad \text{simplified}$$
$$x = \tfrac{6}{5} \qquad\quad \text{solved}$$

As the last step we must check to see that replacing x with $\frac{6}{5}$ does not cause $x + 2$ to be negative because negative numbers do not have logarithms.

We note that $\frac{6}{5} + 2$ is a positive number. Check.

Example 23.2 Solve: $\ln (x - 1) - \ln (x + 2) = \ln 14$

Solution On the left we note that the bases are the same and the logs are subtracted. This means that the arguments are to be divided. So we have

$$\ln \frac{x - 1}{x + 2} = \ln 14$$

If the bases are the same and the logarithms are equal, we know that the arguments are equal. Thus,

$$\frac{x-1}{x+2} = 14 \qquad \text{equal arguments}$$

$$x - 1 = 14x + 28 \qquad \text{multiplied}$$

$$-13x = 29 \qquad \text{simplified}$$

$$x = -\frac{29}{13} \qquad \text{solved, but we must check}$$

If we use $-29/13$ for x in the argument $x - 1$, the result will be a negative number. Since negative numbers do not have logarithms, this value of x is unacceptable. **Thus, the problem has no solution.**

23.B
Logarithms of powers

The third rule for logarithms is useful and for some is the most difficult to remember.

We note that the logarithm of 10^2 to the base 10 is 2 so that 3 times this logarithm equals 6.

$$\log_{10} 10^2 = 2 \qquad \text{so} \qquad 3(\log_{10} 10^2) = 3(2) = 6$$

But this last result is the same as the logarithm of $(10^2)^3$.

$$\log_{10} (10^2)^3 \qquad \text{equals} \qquad \log_{10} 10^6 = 6$$

From this we see that the logarithm of a power of a number is the same as the exponent times the logarithm of the number. **This means that the use of logarithms permits us to change an exponent to a coefficient. Also, the reverse is true because a coefficient can be changed to an exponent.**

Example 23.3 Solve: $2 \log_8 x + \log_8 4 = 1$

Solution **In the first term we change the coefficient to an exponent** and write

$$\log_8 x^2 + \log_8 4 = 1$$

The logs are added, so the arguments are multiplied.

$$\log_8 4x^2 = 1$$

We finish by rewriting the equation in exponential form and solving.

$$4x^2 = 8^1 \qquad \text{exponential form}$$

$$x^2 = 2 \qquad \text{divided}$$

$$x = \pm\sqrt{2} \qquad \text{solved}$$

However, $-\sqrt{2}$ is not an acceptable value because the argument of a logarithm can never be negative. Thus, $\sqrt{2}$ is the answer.

Example 23.4 Solve: $-2 \ln 3 - \ln (x - 1) = -\ln \frac{1}{4}$

Solution We begin by using the power rule to rewrite $-2 \ln 3$ as $\ln 3^{-2}$ or $\ln \frac{1}{9}$, and $-\ln \frac{1}{4}$ as $\ln \left(\frac{1}{4}\right)^{-1}$ or $\ln 4$.

$$\ln \frac{1}{9} - \ln (x - 1) = \ln 4 \qquad \text{used power rule}$$

$$\ln \dfrac{\frac{1}{9}}{x-1} = \ln 4 \qquad \text{quotient rule}$$

$$\dfrac{\frac{1}{9}}{x-1} = 4 \qquad \text{equal arguments}$$

$$\frac{1}{9} = 4x - 4 \qquad \text{simplified}$$

$$\frac{37}{36} = x \qquad \text{solved}$$

This value of x is acceptable since it does not make any argument negative.

23.C
Exponential equations

Exponential equations are intimidating because the variable is in the exponent. **To find the solution, it is necessary to find a way to get the variable out of the exponent.** One way to do this is to write both sides of the equation as powers of the same base. If powers of the same base are equal, the exponents must be equal.

Example 23.5   Solve $8^{3x+2} = 16$ without using logarithms.

Solution   This problem was carefully contrived so that it can be solved without using logarithms. Problems of this type appear on standardized tests because a correct solution will show that the student understands logarithms (exponents) and a calculator is not necessary. The trick is to write everything as a power of the same base. In this example the base is 2.

$$(2^3)^{3x+2} = 2^4 \qquad \text{same base}$$

$$2^{9x+6} = 2^4 \qquad \text{simplified}$$

Now, since the expressions are equal and the bases are equal, the exponents must be equal.

$$9x + 6 = 4 \qquad \text{exponents equal}$$

$$x = -\frac{2}{9} \qquad \text{solved}$$

Example 23.6   Solve: $10^{-2x+2} = 8$

Solution   This problem looks exactly like the preceding one, but is very different because 8 and 10 cannot be written as powers of the same base unless we use logarithms. One way to use logarithms would be to use a calculator and find that the logarithm (exponent) of 8 to the base 10 is 0.90309. Then we could write

$$10^{-2x+2} = 10^{0.90309}$$

and equate the exponents as we did in Example 23.5. But since we're going to have to use logarithms, why not use a standard procedure and take the logarithms of both sides? We normally use base 10 or base e because logarithms to these bases can be obtained from calculators. Since one base is already 10, we decide to use base 10, which we designate by using log with no subscript.

$$\log 10^{-2x+2} = \log 8 \qquad \text{log of both sides}$$

On the left-hand side we will use the power rule for logarithms, and on the right-hand side we will use a calculator (or a table) to find the log of 8.

$$(-2x + 2) \log 10 = 0.90309$$

But log 10 is 1, so we end up with a simple algebraic equation, which we solve.

$$-2x + 2 = 0.90309 \qquad \text{equation}$$
$$-2x = -1.09691 \qquad \text{added } -2 \text{ to both sides}$$
$$x = 0.5485 \qquad \text{divided}$$

Example 23.7   Solve: $e^{-2x+3} = 5$

Solution   Again we have variables in the exponent, and the bases cannot be written as powers of the same variable without using logarithms. Since one base is already e, we decide to take the natural logarithms of both sides. We do this by writing ln in front of both expressions.

$$\ln e^{-2x+3} = \ln 5 \qquad \text{ln of both sides}$$

Now we will use the power rule for logarithms on the left-hand side and use a calculator on the right-hand side to find the natural log of 5.

$$(-2x + 3) \ln e = 1.6094379$$

We remember that the natural logarithm of e is 1. This is the reason that we used base e instead of base 10 in this problem. Thus, we get

$$-2x + 3 = 1.6094379 \qquad \text{simplified}$$
$$-2x = -1.3905621 \qquad \text{added } -3$$
$$x = 0.695281 \qquad \text{divided}$$

Example 23.8   Solve: $5^{2x-1} = 6^{x-2}$

Solution   Again we find the variables in the exponents. We can get the variables out of the exponents by taking the logarithms of both sides. Since neither of the bases is e or 10, there is no special reason to choose either base. We decide to take the common logarithms of both sides.

$$\log 5^{2x-1} = \log 6^{x-2}$$

Next we use the power rule on both sides.

$$(2x - 1) \log 5 = (x - 2) \log 6$$

Now we use a calculator to find log 5 and log 6 and use these values.

$$(2x - 1)(0.69897) = (x - 2)(0.7781513)$$

Since exactness is not required, we will round off the logarithms before we solve.

$$(2x - 1)(0.70) = (x - 2)(0.78)$$

Now we multiply and complete the solution.

$$1.40x - 0.70 = 0.78x - 1.56 \qquad \text{multiplied}$$
$$0.62x = -0.86 \qquad \text{simplified}$$
$$x = -1.39 \qquad \text{divided}$$

Problem set 23   1.   The number of vehicles Ronk actually sells varies linearly with the number of vehicles which he shows to potential buyers. If showing 100 cars results in his selling 25 of them and if showing 120 cars results in his selling 29 of them, how many cars must he show to sell 30 cars?

2.   If the perimeter of a rectangle is p and its width is w, find the area of the rectangle in terms of p and w.

Solve the following equations for x.

3. $\ln (x + 2) - \ln (x - 1) = \ln 5$ 4. $2 \log_3 x - \log_3 4 = 2$

5. $27^{2x+1} = 9$ (Do not use logarithms.)

Find decimal approximations for x. In future problem sets decimal approximations for problems like these will be acceptable.

6. $10^{x+1} = e^{2x}$ 7. $3^{-x+1} = 4^{x+2}$

For Problems 8–10, $f(x) = |x^2 - 1|$.

8.   Graph f.

9.   On which intervals is f increasing and on which intervals is f decreasing?

10.   For which values of x does the graph of f have a zero slope?

11.   If $g(x) = x(x - 1)(x + 2)(x - 3)$, show on a graph of the x axis where $g > 0$ and where $g < 0$.

12.   Solve: $4 \sin^2 x - 3 = 0$ $(0 \le x < 2\pi)$

13.   Write the equation of the locus of all points which are equidistant from the point $(-1, 2)$ and the line $y = 3$.

14.   If $f(x) = 2x$, substitute and then simplify the following expression:

$$\frac{f(x + \Delta x) - f(x)}{\Delta x}$$

15.   If $f(x) = x^2$, substitute and then simplify:

$$\lim_{\Delta x \to 0} \frac{f(x + \Delta x) - f(x)}{\Delta x}$$

16.   Evaluate: $\lim_{x \to 0} (e^x + 1)$

17.   Write the equation of the sinusoid shown in terms of the sine function.

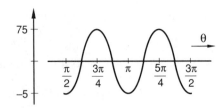

18.   Graph $y = \ln x$ and $y = \ln (-x)$ on the same coordinate plane.

19.   Describe the domain and range of $y = \ln (-x)$.

20.   Perform the indicated multiplication and write the answer in rectangular form:

$$(2 \text{ cis } 10°)(2 \text{ cis } 10°)(2 \text{ cis } 10°)$$

CONCEPT REVIEW   21.   If $x > 0$, then compare: $A. \ \dfrac{1}{\sqrt[3]{x^2}}$ $B. \ \sqrt[3]{x^{-2}}$

22. Find $x + y + z + t$.

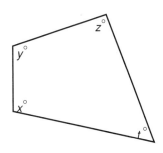

LESSON 24 *Infinity as a limit · Undefined limits*

24.A
Infinity
as a limit

We use the word *infinity* to describe a quantity whose value is increasing without bound. If x represents a positive number that is getting smaller and smaller and is approaching zero from the positive side, the value of 1 over x is a positive number that is getting larger and larger. We use the symbol ∞ to indicate that the value of 1 over x is increasing positively without bound. If x represents a negative number that is getting smaller and smaller and approaching zero from the negative side, the value of 1 over x is a negative number that is getting larger negatively. We use the symbol $-\infty$ to indicate that the value of 1 over x is increasing negatively without bound. In mathematics, when we speak of the limit of a function, we usually mean a numerical limit. However, it is sometimes convenient to be able to use $+\infty$ or $-\infty$ when discussing limits. If we use limit notation, we can make the above statement by writing

$$\lim_{x \to 0^+} \frac{1}{x} = \infty \qquad \lim_{x \to 0^-} \frac{1}{x} = -\infty$$

x	0.1	0.01	0.001	0.0001	-0.1	-0.01	-0.001	-0.0001
$\frac{1}{x}$	10	100	1000	10,000	-10	-100	-1000	$-10,000$

It is very important to remember that infinity is not a real number, because every real number has a fixed position on the number line. *Infinity* is a word we use to help us describe a quantity whose value is increasing without bound.

Example 24.1 Evaluate: $\displaystyle\lim_{x \to \infty} \frac{4x^2 + x + 6}{3x^2 + 1}$

Solution A good procedure for evaluating a quotient of polynomials as x approaches infinity is to divide every term in the numerator and in the denominator by the highest power of x in the denominator. If we divide every term by x^2 and simplify, we get

$$\lim_{x \to \infty} \frac{4 + \dfrac{1}{x} + \dfrac{6}{x^2}}{3 + \dfrac{1}{x^2}} = \frac{4}{3}$$

As x gets larger and larger, the value of each term with a power of x in the denominator gets smaller and smaller, and the value of these terms is zero in the limit.

Example 24.2 Evaluate: $\displaystyle\lim_{x \to -\infty} \frac{x^3 + 6x}{8x^2 + 5x}$

Solution In this example, we will divide every term by x^2. If we do this, we get

$$\lim_{x \to -\infty} = \frac{x + \dfrac{6}{x}}{8 + \dfrac{5}{x}} = -\infty$$

The fractional terms approach zero as x gets large, and we are left with x over 8, whose limit as x approaches negative infinity is **negative infinity.** Some authors do not use infinity as a limit and say that the limit of this expression as x approaches infinity is not defined or does not exist.

24.B
Undefined limits

If the left-hand limit and the right-hand limit as x approaches a certain value are both $-\infty$ or both $+\infty$, we can say that the limit is $-\infty$ or $+\infty$, as with the function graphed on the left, even though neither $-\infty$ or $+\infty$ qualify as a limit if we use the definition that says a limit must be a number.

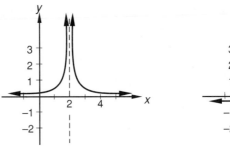

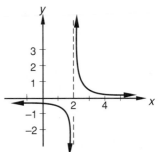

$$\lim_{x \to 2} \frac{1}{(x - 2)^2} = +\infty \qquad\qquad \lim_{x \to 2} \frac{1}{x - 2} \text{ is undefined}$$

The expression $(x - 2)^2$ does approach zero as x approaches 2, but it is squared so its value is always positive. Thus, the left-hand limit and the right-hand limit are both $+\infty$. In the graph on the right the expression $x - 2$ is positive when x approaches 2 from the right and is greater than 2, and the expression $x - 2$ is negative when x approaches 2 from the left and is less than 2. Thus, the left-hand limit is $-\infty$ and the right-hand limit is $+\infty$. Since these limits are different, we say that the limit of the function graphed on the right does not exist.

Example 24.3 Find the limit of $\dfrac{-1}{(x + 3)^2}$ as x approaches -3.

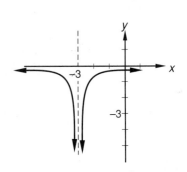

Solution
$$\lim_{x \to -3^-} \frac{-1}{(x + 3)^2} = -\infty$$

Also
$$\lim_{x \to -3^+} \frac{-1}{(x + 3)^2} = -\infty$$

Therefore
$$\lim_{x \to -3} \frac{-1}{(x + 3)^2} = -\infty$$

We say that this limit is $-\infty$ in spite of the fact that we have defined a limit to be a real number. We make this exception because using the symbols $+\infty$ and $-\infty$ is convenient.

Problem set 24

1. Mike drove the car at an average speed of 40 mph for M hours and Mary Beth drove the car at an average speed of 60 mph for the next B hours. What was the average speed of the car for the entire trip?

2. A 400-square-foot rectangular garden is enclosed by fencing. If the width of the garden is w, express the perimeter of the garden in terms of w.

Evaluate the following limits:

3. $\displaystyle\lim_{x\to\infty} \frac{3x^3 - 2x + 4}{1 - 2x^3}$

4. $\displaystyle\lim_{x\to-\infty} \frac{x^3 - 6x}{5x + x^2}$

5. $\displaystyle\lim_{x\to a} \frac{x^2 - a^2}{x - a}$

6. $\displaystyle\lim_{x\to a} \frac{x - a}{x^2 + a^2}$

For Problems 7–11 f is a function whose graph is shown.

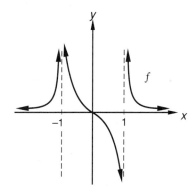

Evaluate:

7. $\displaystyle\lim_{x\to-1} f(x)$

8. $\displaystyle\lim_{x\to 1^-} f(x)$

9. $\displaystyle\lim_{x\to 1^+} f(x)$

10. $\displaystyle\lim_{x\to 1} f(x)$

11. On which intervals is f increasing and on which intervals is f decreasing?

12. Solve: $\sin^2 x + 2 \cos x - 2 = 0 \qquad (0 \le x < 2\pi)$

Solve the following equations for x.

13. $2 \ln x = \ln (x - 1) + \ln (x - 2)$

14. $4^{2x} = 16^{1-x}$ (Do not use logarithms.)

15. If $y = \arcsin x$, what does x equal?

16. Determine the amplitude, period, and the equation of the centerline of the graph of $y = -2 + 3 \sin 4x$.

17. Write the key identities and develop an expression that gives $\cos^2 A$ as a function of $\cos 2A$.

18. Show that: $2 \sin \left(\dfrac{\pi}{2} - x\right) \dfrac{1}{\sec (-x)} - 1 = \cos 2x$

19. Solve for x in terms of a, b, c, and d in the figure shown.

$AB = x + a$
$CD = x + c$
$ED = b$
$AE = d$
$BE = c$

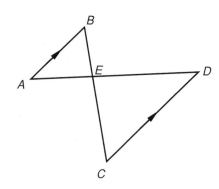

20. Find the distance between the point $(1, -1)$ and the line $2y - x + 3 = 6$.

21. Solve for p: $4^{2p-5} = 7^{3p+2}$

CONCEPT REVIEW 22. If x, y, z, a, and b are as shown, compare:
    A. $x + y + z$ B. $y + a + b$

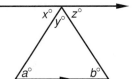

23. If A is a point outside circle O and B and C are points on circle O so that $\overline{AB}$ and $\overline{AC}$ are tangents to circle O, compare:
    A. AB B. AC

LESSON 25 *Sums, products, and quotients of functions · Composition of functions*

25.A
Sums, products, and quotients of functions

Two functions can be either added, subtracted, multiplied, or divided to find new functions whose images are the sums, differences, products, or quotients, respectively, of the original functions. The domains of the new functions are all numbers that were in the domains of both the original functions. Of course, any number that would cause the denominator of a quotient function to be zero is excluded from the domain of a quotient function.

Example 25.1   Given $f(x) = x^2$ and $g(x) = \sqrt{x}$. Find the following, including the domain of each:

(a) $(f + g)(x)$ (b) $(f - g)x$ (c) $(fg)(x)$ (d) $\left(\dfrac{f}{g}\right)(x)$

Solution   (a) $(f + g)(x)$ means the same thing as $f(x) + g(x)$. Thus

$$(f + g)(x) = x^2 + \sqrt{x}$$

(b) $(f - g)(x)$ means the same thing as $f(x) - g(x)$. Thus

$$(f - g)(x) = x^2 - \sqrt{x}$$

(c) $(fg)(x)$ means the same thing as $f(x) \cdot g(x)$. Thus

$$(fg)(x) = (x^2)(x^{1/2}) = x^{5/2}$$

(d) $\left(\dfrac{f}{g}\right)(x)$ means the same thing as $\dfrac{f(x)}{g(x)}$. Thus

$$\left(\frac{f}{g}\right)(x) = \frac{x^2}{\sqrt{x}} = x^{3/2}$$

Since negative numbers are not members of the domain of $f(x) = \sqrt{x}$, negative numbers are not members of the domains of $(f + g)(x)$, $(f - g)(x)$, and $(fg)(x)$. The domains for these functions consist of the set of real numbers equal to or greater than zero.

$$\text{Domain of } (f \pm g)(x) \text{ and } (fg)(x) = \{x \in \mathbb{R} \mid x \geq 0\}$$

Since the denominator of f/g can never be zero, we must exclude zero from the domain of this function.

$$\text{Domain of } \left(\frac{f}{g}\right)(x) = \{x \in \mathbb{R} \mid x > 0\}$$

25.B
Composition of functions

We can also form new functions by a process called *composition.* To **compose** a function we use the output of one function machine as the input of another function machine. Here we use the output of the f machine as the input of the g machine.

A composite function machine can do the work of both of these machines. It will first multiply the input by 5 and then take the square root of the product.

The composite function is denoted by $(g \circ f)(x)$, which is read "g circle f of x," or $g(f(x))$, which is read "g of f of x." Note that the g comes first in both notations to indicate that we put the output $f(x)$ of the f machine into the g machine. If we were to use -3 as an input of the f machine above, we would get an output of -15. This is unacceptable as the input for the g machine, because the g machine takes the square root of any input. Thus neither -3 nor any other negative number can be used as an input of the composite machine. From this we see that the domain for the composite machine is all real numbers equal to or greater than zero.

$$\text{Domain of } (g \circ f) = \{x \in \mathbb{R} \mid x \geq 0\}$$

The range is also the set of real numbers equal to or greater than zero.

$$\text{Range of } (g \circ f) = \{y \in \mathbb{R} \mid y \geq 0\}$$

The domain of a composite function consists of all real numbers that will produce outputs of the first machine that are acceptable as inputs for the second machine.

The following functions are not composite functions

$$e^x \qquad \sqrt{x} \qquad \sin x \qquad \cos x \qquad x + 3 \qquad \ln x \qquad \log_2 x \qquad x^3 - 4x$$

because each of the arguments is x all by itself. All of the following functions are composite functions because the arguments of these functions are not x but some function x.

$$e^{3x+2} \qquad \sqrt{2x} \qquad \sin (x + 4) \qquad \cos x^2 \qquad \sqrt{x + 3} \qquad \ln (x^2 + 2) \qquad \log_2 x^2$$

A few examples that use function machines will make this clearer.

Example 25.2   Use the functions $f(x) = x^2 + 2$ and $g(x) = 3x + 5$ to form the composite function $(f \circ g)(x)$.

Solution   **We have to use the g function first.** If we put x into the g machine, we get out $3x + 5$.

$$3(\ ) + 5 \qquad\qquad\qquad f(\ ) = (\ )^2 + 2$$

$$x \longrightarrow \boxed{\ g\ } \longrightarrow (3x + 5) \longrightarrow \boxed{\ f\ } \longrightarrow (3x + 5)^2 + 2$$

Then we put $3x + 5$ into the f machine. The f machine squares any input and then adds 2. The result of using both machines in turn is the composite function f circle g. We did g first, and $f \circ g$ says to apply "f to the output of the g machine."

$$(f \circ g)(x) = (3x + 5)^2 + 2$$

The g machine will accept any real number as an input, and all of its real number outputs are acceptable to the f machine. **Thus, the domain of f circle g consists of the set of all real numbers.**

Example 25.3   Use the functions

$$f(x) = 2 + \sin x \qquad \text{and} \qquad g(x) = x - \frac{\pi}{2}$$

to find $f(g(x))$ and state the domain and range.

Solution   The notation $f(g(x))$ says to put $g(x)$ into the f machine, so we will draw the g machine first.

$$g(\ ) = (\ ) - \frac{\pi}{2}$$

$$x \longrightarrow \boxed{\ g\ } \longrightarrow x - \frac{\pi}{2}$$

Now we put $x - \frac{\pi}{2}$ into the f machine.

$$f(\ ) = 2 + \sin (\ )$$

$$\left(x - \frac{\pi}{2}\right) \longrightarrow \boxed{\ f\ } \longrightarrow 2 + \sin \left(x - \frac{\pi}{2}\right)$$

$$f(g(x)) = 2 + \sin \left(x - \frac{\pi}{2}\right)$$

We note that x can be any real number, and since the value of the sine of any number is always between -1 and $+1$, $f(g(x))$ can be any number between 2 ± 1, or between 1 and 3. Thus

Domain of $f(g(x)) = \{x \in \mathbb{R}\}$ **Range of $f(g(x)) = \{y \in \mathbb{R} \mid 1 \le y \le 3\}$**

Example 25.4   The function e^{-2x+1} is a composite function. Use two function machines to show how it could be composed.

Solution   The first function machine multiplies any input by -2 and then adds 1. The second function machine takes the output of the first machine and uses it as an exponent for e.

Example 25.5   The function e^{-2x+1} is a composite function. Use three function machines to show how it could be composed.

Solution   Two machines are really all that is necessary, but we can use three if we wish. The first machine will multiply by -2, the second machine will add 1, and the third machine will use any input as an exponent for e.

We could have used four machines by breaking up the $-2(\ )$ machine into a machine that multiplies by 2 and another machine that multiplies by -1. **In this book we will almost always consider that composite functions are the outputs of a two-machine composition.**

Example 25.6   The function $\sin(2x + 3)$ is a composite function. Use two function machines to show how it could be composed.

Solution   We see that the input of the sine machine is $2x + 3$. Thus,

The domain of this function is the set of real numbers. The graph of $y = \sin(2x + 3)$ has the x axis as the centerline, and it deviates vertically ± 1 from the centerline. Thus the domain is all real numbers and the range is

$$\{y \mid -1 \le y \le 1\}$$

Example 25.7   If $f(x) = \sqrt{x}$ and $g(x) = 2x + 3$, find the domain and range of $f \circ g$ and the domain and range of $g \circ f$.

Solution   Let's look at $f \circ g$ first.

The g machine will accept any real number and produce a real number at the output. The f machine will only accept numbers that are not negative, so $g(x)$ must be equal to or greater than zero.

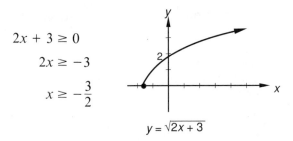

$$2x + 3 \geq 0$$
$$2x \geq -3$$
$$x \geq -\frac{3}{2}$$

$$y = \sqrt{2x + 3}$$

Thus, the domain for $f \circ g$ contains all values of x equal to or greater than $-\frac{3}{2}$. Since the value of $\sqrt{2x + 3}$ is never negative, the range consists of all real numbers greater than or equal to zero. Now let's look at $g \circ f$.

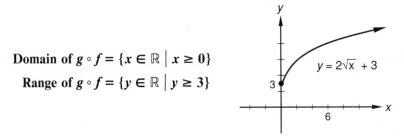

$$f(\ ) = \sqrt{(\ )} \qquad\qquad g(\ ) = 2(\ ) + 3$$

$$x \longrightarrow \boxed{\quad f \quad} \xrightarrow{\sqrt{x}} \boxed{\quad g \quad} \longrightarrow 2\sqrt{x} + 3$$

Again the difficulty is with the f machine because it will accept only nonnegative numbers. But the square root of any real number that is not negative is acceptable to the g machine. Thus, the domain of $g \circ f$ consists of zero and all of the positive real numbers.

Domain of $g \circ f = \{x \in \mathbb{R} \mid x \geq 0\}$

Range of $g \circ f = \{y \in \mathbb{R} \mid y \geq 3\}$

$$y = 2\sqrt{x} + 3$$

Example 25.8   Determine whether the following statement is true or false and explain why:

$$\text{If } f(x) = x^2 \qquad \text{and} \qquad g(x) = \sqrt{x}$$

then the domains of $f \circ g$ and $g \circ f$ are equal.

Solution   This tricky question often appears on tests, standardized and otherwise, in another form. It involves a statement which appears to be true for all real numbers but turns out to be false for any negative number.

$$\sqrt{x^2} = x \qquad \textbf{False}$$

The statement is false because if x equals -1, $\sqrt{(-1)^2} = +1$ and does not equal x, which is -1. For this problem the f machine will accept any real number and square it. The resulting nonnegative numbers are acceptable to the g machine. Thus all real numbers are acceptable to $g \circ f$. But since the g machine takes square roots, it will not accept negative numbers. Thus the domain of $f \circ g$ is the set of nonnegative real numbers.

$$\text{Domain } (f \circ g) = \{x \in \mathbb{R} \mid x \geq 0\}$$

$$\text{Domain of } (g \circ f) = \{x \in \mathbb{R}\}$$

Problem set 25   **1.**   When used alone, pipes A, B, and C can fill one tank in A, B, and C hours, respectively. How long would all three pipes have to be used together to fill M tanks?

2. Farmer Jones wants to make a rectangular pasture and wants to use an existing stone wall as one side of the rectangle. The pasture is to have an area of 20,000 square meters. If the segment of the fence parallel to the wall is P, find the total length of fencing required.

For Problems 3–9, assume that $f(x) = x^2 + 1$, $g(x) = \sqrt{x - 1}$, and $h(x) = -1$.

3. Write the equation of $f + g$ and evaluate $(f + g)(5)$.

4. Write the equation of fg and evaluate $(fg)(5)$.

5. Write the equation of $\dfrac{f}{g}$ and evaluate $\left(\dfrac{f}{g}\right)(5)$.

6. Describe the domain of $\dfrac{f}{g}$.

7. Write the equation of $f \circ g$ and evaluate $(f \circ g)(3)$.

8. Describe the domain and range of $f \circ g$.

9. Write the equation of $g \circ f$ and describe the domain and range of $g \circ f$.

Evaluate the following limits:

10. $\displaystyle\lim_{x \to \infty} \dfrac{1 - x^2}{3x^2 + 2x - 4}$

11. $\displaystyle\lim_{x \to \infty} \dfrac{3x^2}{x^3 - 4x + 1}$

12. If the graph of f is as shown, evaluate:

    (*a*) $\displaystyle\lim_{x \to -2} f(x)$ (*b*) $\displaystyle\lim_{x \to 1} f(x)$

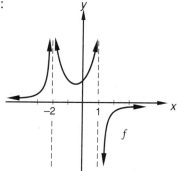

Solve the following equations for x (all answers must be exact):

13. $\dfrac{\pi}{2} = \arcsin x$

14. $\ln x - \ln (x + 1) = \ln 2$

15. If $g(x) = x(x - 2)(x + 3)$, use interval notation to designate the intervals on which the graph of g lies above the x axis and those intervals on which the graph of g lies below the x axis.

16. Graph: $y = -2 + \sin 2\left(x - \dfrac{\pi}{4}\right)$ $(0 \le x < 2\pi)$

17. On which intervals is the function of Problem 16 increasing?

18. Find the equation of the locus of all points whose distance from the point (h, k) is r.

19. Use the rational zero theorem to aid in finding all the zeros of the polynomial function $y = x^3 - x^2 - 3x + 3$.

20. Is the following argument valid or invalid?

All irrational numbers are real numbers.

A is not a real number.

Therefore, A is not an irrational number.

21. Show that: $\dfrac{(\sec^2 x - 1)[\cos(-x)]}{(1 - \cos^2 x)(\tan^2 x + 1)} = \cos x$

22. Solve for x: $7^{3x-2} = 13^{x+1}$

CONCEPT REVIEW 23. Find the area of $\triangle ABC$ in terms of x if $\angle ABC = x$ and $\triangle ABC$ is inscribed in circle O whose radius is 1. (*Hint*: Use trigonometric functions.)

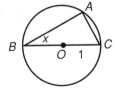

24. Find the next term of the following sequence: 1, 1, 2, 4, 7, 11, . . .

LESSON 26 *Locus development · Equation of the ellipse · Foci*

26.A
Locus development

An *ellipse* is the locus of all points in a plane such that the sum of the distances from any of these points to two fixed points called the *foci* is a constant.

To find the equation of a particular ellipse, we must use the distance formula twice. We use a diagram that shows a point (x, y) on the ellipse, and we sum the distances from this point to the two foci. To find the equation of the ellipse whose foci are $(-3, 0)$ and $(3, 0)$ and for which the sum of the distances is 10, we begin with a sketch.

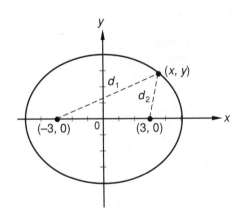

The sum of the distances d_1 and d_2 equals 10. Thus, we must use the distance formula twice

$$\sqrt{[x - (-3)]^2 + (y - 0)^2} + \sqrt{[x - (3)]^2 + (y - 0)^2} = 10$$

which we simplify and write as

$$\sqrt{(x + 3)^2 + y^2} + \sqrt{(x - 3)^2 + y^2} = 10 \qquad \text{two-focus form}$$

The algebraic simplification of this equation is straightforward but laborious. The result of this simplification is the equation

$$\frac{x^2}{25} + \frac{y^2}{16} = 1$$

26.B
The equation of an ellipse

An ellipse has two axes. The axis that passes through the foci is always the longer axis and is called the *major axis*. The shorter axis is called the *minor axis*. It is customary to use the letter a to represent half the length of the major axis and the letter b to represent half the length of the minor axis. **Thus the value of a is always greater than the value of b.** The standard equation of an ellipse whose center is the origin and whose major axis is horizontal is shown on the left. The standard equation of an ellipse whose center is the origin and whose major axis is vertical is shown on the right.

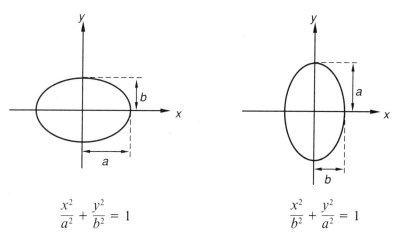

$$\frac{x^2}{a^2} + \frac{y^2}{b^2} = 1 \qquad\qquad\qquad \frac{x^2}{b^2} + \frac{y^2}{a^2} = 1$$

All we have to do is remember that if the number below x^2 is greater, the major axis lies on the x axis, and if the number below y^2 is greater, the major axis lies on the y axis.

Example 26.1 Graph the ellipse $9x^2 + 25y^2 = 225$.

Solution When the ellipse is in standard form, the constant on the right is 1. To change 225 to 1, we divide every term by 225 and get the equation on the left, which we write in more meaningful form on the right.

$$\frac{x^2}{25} + \frac{y^2}{9} = 1 \quad \longrightarrow \quad \frac{x^2}{5^2} + \frac{y^2}{3^2} = 1$$

This is the equation of an ellipse whose major axis goes 5 units to the left and right of the origin and whose minor axis goes 3 units above and below the origin.

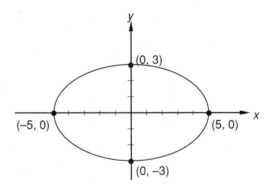

Example 26.2   Write the equation of the ellipse whose center is $(7, -3)$, whose major axis is vertical and 8 units long, and whose minor axis is 3 units long.

Solution   If this ellipse were centered at the origin, the equation would be the one on the left. The number below y^2 is the square of half the length of the vertical axis. The number below x^2 is the square of half the length of the horizontal axis.

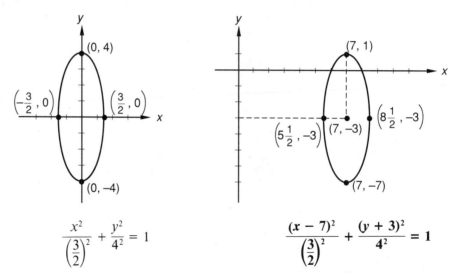

$$\frac{x^2}{\left(\frac{3}{2}\right)^2} + \frac{y^2}{4^2} = 1$$

$$\frac{(x - 7)^2}{\left(\frac{3}{2}\right)^2} + \frac{(y + 3)^2}{4^2} = 1$$

On the right we move the center of the ellipse to $(7, -3)$ by replacing x^2 with $(x - 7)^2$ and y^2 with $(y + 3)^2$.

Example 26.3   Describe the ellipse $3x^2 + 2y^2 - 6x + 8y + 5 = 0$.

Solution   This equation is in what we call the general form. To rewrite the equation in the more meaningful standard form, we must complete the square on the x terms and on the y terms. We begin by rearranging the equation and using parentheses.

$$(3x^2 - 6x \quad) + (2y^2 + 8y \quad) = -5$$

Next we factor out a 3 from the first set of parentheses and a 2 from the second set of parentheses.

$$3(x^2 - 2x \quad) + 2(y^2 + 4y \quad) = -5$$

Now we complete the squares by inserting a 1 in the first set of parentheses and a 4 in the second set of parentheses.

$$3(x^2 - 2x + 1) + 2(y^2 + 4y + 4) = ?$$

Because of the coefficients 3 and 2, we have really added 3 and 8 to the left side of the equation, so we must add 3 and 8 to the right side of the equation.

$$3(x^2 - 2x + 1) + 2(y^2 + 4y + 4) = -5 + 3 + 8$$

We simplify this expression and get

$$3(x - 1)^2 + 2(y + 2)^2 = 6$$

We need 1 on the right side of the equals sign instead of 6. Thus, we divide every term by 6 and get

$$\frac{(x - 1)^2}{2} + \frac{(y + 2)^2}{3} = 1$$

As the last step we rewrite the denominators and get

$$\frac{(x - 1)^2}{(\sqrt{2})^2} + \frac{(y + 2)^2}{(\sqrt{3})^2} = 1$$

This is the equation of an ellipse whose center is $(1, -2)$. The y term has the larger denominator, so the major axis is vertical and measures $2\sqrt{3}$. The minor axis is horizontal and measures $2\sqrt{2}$.

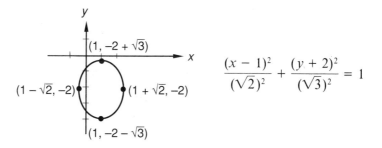

$$\frac{(x - 1)^2}{(\sqrt{2})^2} + \frac{(y + 2)^2}{(\sqrt{3})^2} = 1$$

26.C
Foci

We remember that the sum of the distances from any point on an ellipse to the two foci is a constant. With the aid of the imaginary piece of string used to draw an ellipse, we can reason that the value of the constant is $2a$, which equals the length of the string and also equals the length of the major axis of the ellipse.

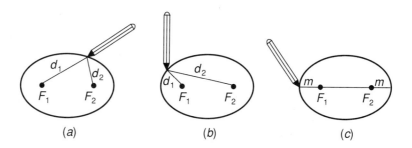

(a)   (b)   (c)

We begin at (a) and trace the ellipse by moving the pencil counterclockwise (b) until we get to the vertex in (c). Now the string goes from F_2 to the pencil and back through distance m to F_1. The string covers the distance m twice. If we mentally remove a piece of string m units long, we can use it to cover the distance m on the right. Thus, our piece of string stretches from vertex to vertex and has a length of $2a$. Now if we move the pencil to the end of the minor axis, we have the following figure.

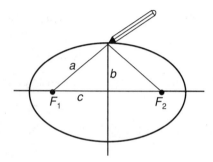

The length of the string is $2a$, so half its length is a. We have formed a right triangle whose hypotenuse is a and whose legs are b and c, as shown.

The length of one leg, c, is the distance from the origin to the focus, and the length of the other leg, b, equals half the length of the minor axis. The **eccentricity** of an ellipse is the ratio of the distance from the center to the focus to the distance from the center to the end of the major axis. This is the ratio of c to a and is a number between 0 and 1. An ellipse with an eccentricity close to 0 is "fat" or more circular, while an ellipse with an eccentricity close to 1 looks "skinny" and is less circular. We can use the Pythagorean theorem and write

$$a^2 = c^2 + b^2$$

We can use this relationship and the standard form of the equation of an ellipse to solve some interesting problems. In the next example, we are given values for c and a and must solve for b.

Example 26.4   Write the standard form of the equation of the ellipse with vertices at $(0, \pm 6)$ and foci at $(0, \pm 5)$.

Solution   **We always begin with a diagram.** We remember that the foci are always on the major axis. From the triangle, we get

$$6^2 = 5^2 + b^2 \qquad \text{equation}$$
$$36 = 25 + b^2 \qquad \text{squared}$$
$$\sqrt{11} = b \qquad \text{solved}$$

Thus the entire length of the minor axis is $2\sqrt{11}$. This time the major axis lies along the y axis, so the equation is

$$\frac{x^2}{b^2} + \frac{y^2}{a^2} = 1$$

Since $a = 6$ and $b = \sqrt{11}$, the equation of the ellipse in standard form is

$$\frac{x^2}{11} + \frac{y^2}{36} = 1$$

Example 26.5 Write the standard form of the equation of the horizontal ellipse whose center is at the origin. The length of the major axis is 10, and the length of the minor axis is 4. What are the coordinates of the foci?

Solution **Again we begin with a diagram.** From our diagram, we get

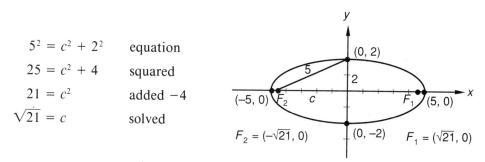

$$5^2 = c^2 + 2^2 \qquad \text{equation}$$
$$25 = c^2 + 4 \qquad \text{squared}$$
$$21 = c^2 \qquad \text{added } -4$$
$$\sqrt{21} = c \qquad \text{solved}$$

Thus, the coordinates of the foci are $(\sqrt{21}, 0)$ and $(-\sqrt{21}, 0)$, and the equation is

$$\frac{x^2}{25} + \frac{y^2}{4} = 1$$

Problem set 26

1. Each of the 26-inch tires on the bicycle revolved r times every minute. If the bicycle was pedaled along a straight path, how fast was it traveling in miles per hour?

2. The intensity of a light source measured at a point P varies inversely as the square of the distance from P to the light source. If the intensity measured at a point 5 meters from the light source is N, what would be the intensity measured at a point M meters from the light source?

3. Describe the ellipse whose equation is $4x^2 - 8x + 9y^2 + 18y - 23 = 0$.

4. Write the standard form of the equation of an ellipse whose foci are $(3, 0)$ and $(-3, 0)$ and whose vertices are $(5, 0)$ and $(-5, 0)$.

For Problems 5–7, assume that $f(x) = x^2 - 1$ and $g(x) = \ln x$.

5. Write the equation for $\left(\dfrac{f}{g}\right)(x)$ and evaluate $\left(\dfrac{f}{g}\right)(e)$.

6. Describe the domain of $\dfrac{f}{g}$.

7. Describe the domain and range of $g \circ f$ and write the equation of $f \circ g$.

Evaluate the following limits:

8. $\lim\limits_{x \to 0} \dfrac{(5 + x)^2 - (5)^2}{x}$

9. $\lim\limits_{x \to \infty} \dfrac{1 + 2x}{3 - x^2}$

10. $\lim\limits_{x \to \infty} \dfrac{3 - x^2 + 4x}{14 - x}$

11. $\lim\limits_{x \to -\infty} \dfrac{4 - x^3}{2x^2 + 4x^3}$

Solve for x:

12. $y = \ln (x + 1)$

13. $y = e^{x+1}$

14. $y = \arcsin (x + 1)$

15. Graph f where $f(x) = \begin{cases} \sqrt{x} & \text{when } x > 0 \\ \sqrt{-x} & \text{when } x \le 0 \end{cases}$

16. If f is as defined in Problem 15, describe the intervals on which f is increasing.

17. Use interval notation to describe those intervals on which the function $f > 0$, where $f(x) = (x + 1)(x + 2)(3 - x)$.

18. Find the coordinates of the focus and the equation of the directrix of the parabola which crosses the x axis at $x = -1$ and $x = 3$ and which crosses the y axis at $y = -12$. [*Hint*: First find the equation of the parabola and then write it in the form $(x - h)^2 = 4p(y - k)$.]

19. Find the exact rectangular form of $(2 \text{ cis } 20°)^3$.

20. Show that: $\dfrac{\sin^4 x - \cos^4 x}{\sin^2 x - \cos^2 x} = 1$

21. Find the equation of f if f is a linear function whose graph has a slope of 2 and if $f(1) = 2$.

22. Write the key identities and develop an identity for $\cos \dfrac{x}{2}$.

23. Solve for x: $12^{x-2} = e^{3x+2}$

CONCEPT REVIEW   24. Find the area of a square which can be inscribed in a circle whose radius is 10.

25. Find the thirteenth term of the arithmetic sequence whose first three terms are -1, 5, and 11.

LESSON 27   *The derivative*

The value of a nonconstant function may change every time x changes. The *derivative* of a function is another function that equals the ratio of the change in the value of the function to the change in x when x is changed a very, very small amount. **Thus the derivative of a function equals the rate of change of the function, and the value of the derivative for any value of x is the value of the slope of the tangent line to the graph of the function at that value of x.** To find an expression for the derivative of a function, we will begin by drawing a line through two points on the graph of the function. The line is a secant, and we will label the points P_1 and P_2 as we show in the figure on the left.

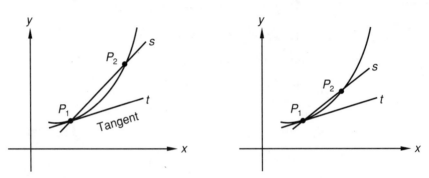

We want to find the slope of the tangent t to the curve at P_1. If we let P_2 move down the curve and get closer and closer to P_1 as we show in the figure on the right, the slope of the secant s gets closer and closer to the slope of the tangent t. **We define the**

slope of the tangent at P_1 to be the *limit* of the slope of the secant as P_2 gets closer and closer to P_1.

To find a general expression for the derivative, we let the x value of P_1 be x and let the x distance between P_1 and P_2 be Δx. Thus, the x coordinate of P_2 is $x + \Delta x$. The slope of the secant is the rise over the run, as we show in the figure on the left. The run is Δx, and the rise Δy is the difference in the y values of the function at x and at $x + \Delta x$.

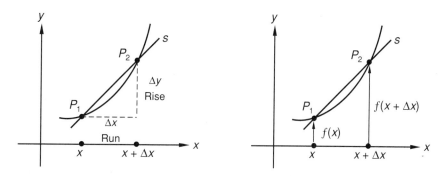

The y value of the function at x is $f(x)$ and the y value of the function at $x + \Delta x$ is $f(x + \Delta x)$, as we show in the figure on the right.

$$\text{Slope of secant} = \frac{\text{rise}}{\text{run}} = \frac{\Delta y}{\Delta x} = \frac{f(x + \Delta x) - f(x)}{\Delta x}$$

If we let P_1 move down the curve toward P_2, the triangle gets smaller and smaller, the value of Δx gets smaller and smaller, and the slope of the secant gets closer and closer to the slope of the tangent at P_1. **Thus we define the derivative of a function to be the limit of the above expression as Δx approaches zero, if this limit exists.**

$$\text{Derivative of a function} = \lim_{\Delta x \to 0} \frac{f(x + \Delta x) - f(x)}{\Delta x}$$

To find the derivative of a particular function, we write the difference of the values of y at x and at $x + \Delta x$ in the numerator and write Δx in the denominator. **The rest of the process is an algebraic game of trying to find an equivalent expression that does not have Δx as a factor of the denominator so we can let Δx approach zero.**

We use the notations

$$\frac{d}{dx} \quad \text{and} \quad D_x$$

as operation indicators to indicate the operation of taking a derivative. If the f function is $f(x) = x^2$, we can indicate the operation of taking the derivative of the f function by using d/dx or D_x and writing either

$$\frac{d}{dx} f(x) \quad \text{or} \quad D_x f(x)$$

We read both of these by saying "the derivative with respect to x of f of x." Since $f(x)$ equals x^2 in this example, we can also designate the same derivative by writing

$$\frac{d}{dx} x^2 \quad \text{or} \quad D_x x^2$$

If the function is described by using y instead of $f(x)$ and writing $y = x^2$, we could designate the derivative by writing

$$\frac{d}{dx} y \quad \text{or} \quad \frac{dy}{dx} \quad \text{or} \quad D_x y$$

We read each of these by saying "the derivative of y with respect to x" or by saying "dee y dee x."

Example 27.1   If $y = x^2$, find $\dfrac{dy}{dx}$.

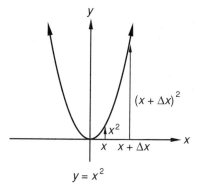

$y = x^2$

Solution   The derivative is the limit as Δx approaches zero of the difference in the y coordinates of the graph of $y = x^2$ at $x + \Delta x$ and at x, divided by Δx. The y coordinate of $y = x^2$ at x is x^2 and at $x + \Delta x$ is $(x + \Delta x)^2$. Thus we write

$$\frac{dy}{dx} = \lim_{\Delta x \to 0} \frac{(x + \Delta x)^2 - x^2}{\Delta x}$$

Next we expand the expression in the numerator and are pleased to find that the first and last terms in the resulting expression are x^2 and $-x^2$, which sum to zero.

$$\lim_{\Delta x \to 0} \frac{\boxed{x^2} + 2x\,\Delta x + \Delta x^2 \boxed{- x^2}}{\Delta x} = \lim_{\Delta x \to 0} \frac{2x\,\Delta x + \Delta x^2}{\Delta x}$$

Now since Δx does not equal zero, we can divide both terms in the numerator by Δx and get

$$\frac{dy}{dx} = \lim_{\Delta x \to 0} 2x + \Delta x$$

This new expression does not have a Δx as a factor of the denominator, and we can let Δx approach zero to get

$$\frac{dy}{dx} = 2x$$

This tells us that if x is 3, the slope of the graph of $y = x^2$ is 2 times 3, or 6. If x is 10, the slope of the graph of $y = x^2$ is 2 times 10, or 20; and if x is -30, the slope of the graph is 2 times -30, or -60. **Thus we have found a function whose value equals the slope of the graph of $y = x^2$ for any value of x.**

Example 27.2   If $y = 4x$, find $D_x y$.

Solution   This tells us that $f(x) = 4x$, and we are to find the derivative of the function. We already know that the slope of $y = 4x$ is 4 everywhere, so we already know the answer. But let's use the definition to get the same result.

$$\frac{d}{dx} f(x) = \lim_{\Delta x \to 0} \frac{f(x + \Delta x) - f(x)}{\Delta x}$$

Next we will replace $f(x)$ with $4x$ and replace $f(x + \Delta x)$ with $4(x + \Delta x)$.

$$\frac{d}{dx} 4x = \lim_{\Delta x \to 0} \frac{4(x + \Delta x) - 4x}{\Delta x}$$

Now if we expand the numerator, we are again pleased to find that the first and last terms sum to zero, and we get

$$\frac{d}{dx} 4x = \lim_{\Delta x \to 0} \frac{\boxed{4x} + 4\,\Delta x \boxed{- 4x}}{\Delta x} = \lim_{\Delta x \to 0} 4$$

Now 4 is 4 no matter what value Δx has, so we have

$$\frac{d}{dx} 4x = \lim_{\Delta x \to 0} 4 = \mathbf{4}$$

Example 27.3 Use the definition of the derivative to show that the derivative of a constant function is zero.

Solution The equations

$$y = 4 \qquad y = -17 \qquad y = 42$$

are equations of constant functions whose graphs are straight lines parallel to the x axis and thus have zero slopes. Proving this by using the definition of a derivative might seem useless until the proof is required on a test. Then the proof becomes important. We repeat the definition of the derivative here.

$$\frac{d}{dx} y = \lim_{\Delta x \to 0} \frac{f(x + \Delta x) - f(x)}{\Delta x}$$

The y value of $y = c$ is always c regardless of the values of x. So $f(x)$ equals c and $f(x + \Delta x)$ also equals c. Thus the difference is zero.

$$\frac{d}{dx} c = \lim_{\Delta x \to 0} \frac{c - c}{\Delta x} = \lim_{\Delta x \to 0} \frac{0}{\Delta x} = \lim_{\Delta x \to 0} 0 = \mathbf{0}$$

Example 27.4 If $f(x) = \frac{1}{x}$, find $\frac{dy}{dx}$.

Solution The definition of the derivative of a function is

$$\frac{dy}{dx} = \lim_{\Delta x \to 0} \frac{f(x + \Delta x) - f(x)}{\Delta x}$$

The numerator is the difference of the value of the function when x equals $x + \Delta x$, which is 1 over $x + \Delta x$, and the value of the function when x equals x, which is 1 over x.

$$\frac{dy}{dx} = \lim_{\Delta x \to 0} \frac{\dfrac{1}{x + \Delta x} - \dfrac{1}{x}}{\Delta x}$$

The value of this expression cannot be determined when $\Delta x = 0$, so we use the rules of algebra to find an equivalent expression that does not have Δx as a factor of the denominator. First we add the expressions in the numerator and get

$$\frac{\dfrac{x - (x + \Delta x)}{x(x + \Delta x)}}{\Delta x} = \frac{\dfrac{\not{x} - \not{x} - \Delta x}{x(x + \Delta x)}}{\Delta x} = \frac{-1}{x(x + \Delta x)} = \frac{-1}{x^2 + x \Delta x}$$

Now we have

$$\frac{dy}{dx} = \lim_{\Delta x \to 0} \frac{-1}{x^2 + x \Delta x}$$

In this expression Δx is not a factor of the entire denominator. As Δx approaches zero, the denominator approaches x^2, so we have

$$\boldsymbol{\frac{dy}{dx} = -\frac{1}{x^2}}$$

Problem set 27

1. The units digit of a two-digit counting number is 1 less than the tens digit. If the number is increased by 8 and then divided by the sum of the digits, the quotient is 8. What is the number?

2. Use the definition of a derivative to calculate $\dfrac{d}{dx} f(x)$ if $f(x) = -x^2$.

3. Use the definition of a derivative to calculate $\dfrac{dy}{dx}$ if $y = \dfrac{2}{x}$.

4. Use the definition of a derivative to calculate $\dfrac{d}{dx} f(x)$ if $f(x) = 3x + 2$.

5. Graph the ellipse $4x^2 + 9y^2 = 36$.

6. Write the equation of the ellipse whose center is $(2, -4)$, whose major axis is horizontal and 10 units long, and whose minor axis is 6 units long.

7. If $f(x) = \ln x$ and $g(x) = \dfrac{1}{x}$, write the equation for $f \circ g$.

8. If f and g are as defined in Problem 7, describe the domain and range of $f \circ g$.

Evaluate the following limits.

9. $\displaystyle\lim_{x \to -\infty} \dfrac{2x - 15x^3}{14x^2 - 13x}$

10. $\displaystyle\lim_{x \to -\infty} \dfrac{3 - 14x^5 + 2x^3}{x^4 - x^5 + 1}$

If the graph of f is as shown, evaluate the following limits:

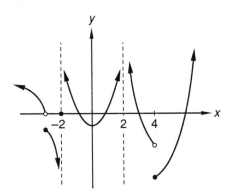

11. $\displaystyle\lim_{x \to 2} f(x)$

12. $\displaystyle\lim_{x \to -2} f(x)$

13. For the graph above use interval notation to describe the intervals on which f is increasing.

14. Find x if: $e^{-x+5} = 13^{2x+3}$

Solve the following equations for x:

15. $\log_2 x + \log_2 (x - 2) = \log_2 3$

16. $\sin x = \cos x \qquad (0 \le x < 2\pi)$

17. In the figure shown, find the area of $\triangle ABC$ in terms of x.

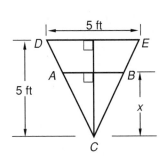

18. Describe those values of x for which $|x - 4| < \varepsilon$ if ε represents an unspecified positive small number.

19. If $\sin A = \frac{3}{5}$, $\cos A = \frac{4}{5}$, $\sin B = \frac{12}{13}$, and $\cos B = \frac{5}{13}$, find the value of $\sin (A + B)$.

20. Use the rational zero theorem to aid in locating all values of x which make the polynomial $x^3 + x^2 - 5x - 5$ equal zero.

21. Write the key trigonometric identities for practice, and then develop an expression which gives $\sin^2 x$ as a function of $\cos 2x$.

CONCEPT REVIEW 22. Find the length of the side of a square which can be circumscribed by a circle of radius 3.

23. If A, B, and C are three distinct points on the coordinate plane, then compare: *A.* AC *B.* $AB + BC$

LESSON 28 *Change of base · Logarithmic inequalities*

28.A
Change of base

If we know the logarithm of a number to some base, we can find the logarithm to any other base by dividing the known logarithm by the appropriate constant. Because tables and calculators can be used to find values of $\ln x$ and $\log x$ for any x, we usually use either $\ln x$ or $\log x$ as a starting point to find logarithms to other bases. We can change a table of base 10 logarithms to a table of base 5 logarithms by dividing every entry by $\log 5$, which is approximately 0.69897. We can change a table of base e logarithms to a table of base 5 logarithms by dividing every entry by $\ln 5$, which is approximately 1.609. We will change the bases of logarithms often in this book, and it is helpful to have a procedure we can use automatically. To demonstrate, we will show how to change the logarithm of 15 to the base 4 to another base b. First we write

$$y = \log_4 15$$

Now we rewrite this equation in exponential form and take the logarithm to the base b of both sides. Then we solve for y.

$$4^y = 15 \qquad \text{exponential form}$$

$$y \log_b 4 = \log_b 15 \qquad \log_b \text{ of both sides}$$

$$y = \frac{\log_b 15}{\log_b 4} \qquad \text{solved by } y$$

But $y = \log_4 15$, so we can write

$$\log_4 15 = \frac{\log_b 15}{\log_b 4} \qquad \text{substituted}$$

Let's look carefully at the last step. The number 4 was the old base and b is the new base. **All we have to do to change to the new base is use the new base to write the log of the argument on top and to write the log of the old base on the bottom.**

$$\log_4 15 = \frac{\log_b 15}{\log_b 4}$$

We will devise practice problems to permit us to practice keeping the argument on top and the old base on the bottom.

Example 28.1   Find $\log_4 x$.

Solution   We will always use either 10 or e as the new base because these logarithms are available from a calculator. Let's use base 10. We will keep the x on top and keep the 4 below.

$$\log_4 x = \frac{\log_{10} x}{\log_{10} 4} \approx \frac{\log_{10} x}{0.602}$$

This means that the logarithm of any number to the base 4 is the common logarithm of the number divided by 0.602, which is a three-digit approximation of $\log_{10} 4$.

Example 28.2   Find $\log_{13} y$.

Solution   This time we will use e as the new base. We keep the y on top and the 13 below.

$$\log_{13} y = \frac{\ln y}{\ln 13} \approx \frac{\ln y}{2.56}$$

Thus the logarithm of any number to the base 13 is the natural logarithm of the number divided by 2.56.

Example 28.3   Use the calculator to evaluate

$$4 \log_{15} 6 + 5 \log_4 7$$

Solution   First we find the values of $\log_{15} 6$ and $\log_4 7$. We will use base 10 logarithms as the vehicle.

$$\log_{15} 6 = \frac{\log_{10} 6}{\log_{10} 15} \approx \frac{0.778}{1.176} = 0.662$$

$$\log_4 7 = \frac{\log_{10} 7}{\log_{10} 4} \approx \frac{0.845}{0.602} = 1.404$$

Now we finish the solution.

$$4 \log_{15} 6 + 5 \log_4 7 \approx 4(0.662) + 5(1.404) = \mathbf{9.668}$$

Example 28.4   If $\log_b 47 = 17$, find b.

Solution   This problem requires the use of the INV y^x key on the calculator and does not require a change of base. First we rewrite the expression in exponential form.

$$b^{17} = 47 \qquad \text{exponential form}$$
$$\sqrt[17]{b^{17}} = \sqrt[17]{47} \qquad \text{root of both sides}$$
$$b = \mathbf{1.254} \qquad \text{used INV } y^x \text{ key}$$

28.B
Logarithmic inequalities

To begin our discussion of logarithmic inequalities, we will look at logarithms whose bases are greater than 1. We will use 5 as a base to demonstrate.

$$5^2 = 25 \qquad 5^3 = 125 \qquad 5^4 = 625$$

When the logarithm is 3, the number is 5^3, which is 125. When the logarithm is less than 3, the number is less than 5^3. When the logarithm is greater than 3, the number is greater than 5^3. If we are given the inequality

$$\log_5 N < 3$$

we must read the expression carefully. Since $\log_5 N$ is an exponent, the inequality tells us that

$$\text{The exponent} < 3$$

Now we consider the value of N when the exponent equals 3.

$$\log_5 N = 3 \quad \text{which says} \quad 5^3 = N$$

The inequality under consideration is $\log_5 N < 3$, which tells us that the logarithm (exponent) is less than 3. If the exponent is less than 3, then certainly N will be less than 5^3. N must also be greater than zero.

$$0 < N < 5^3$$

Care must be taken with the greater-than symbol, for, of course, it would be incorrect to write

$$5^3 < N \quad \text{incorrect}$$

To investigate exponentials whose bases are less than 1, we look at three expressions whose bases are $\frac{1}{2}$.

$$\left(\frac{1}{2}\right)^2 = \frac{1}{4} \qquad \left(\frac{1}{2}\right)^3 = \frac{1}{8} \qquad \left(\frac{1}{2}\right)^4 = \frac{1}{16}$$

In the center we see that when the logarithm (exponent) is 3, the number is $\frac{1}{8}$. On the left we see that when the logarithm (exponent) is less than 3, the number is greater than $\frac{1}{8}$. On the right we see that when the logarithm (exponent) is greater than 3, the number is less than $\frac{1}{8}$. Thus, if we look at the inequality

$$\log_{1/2} N < 3$$

we know that if the logarithm is less than 3, the number must be greater than $\left(\frac{1}{2}\right)^3$.

$$N > \left(\frac{1}{2}\right)^3$$

Example 28.5　Solve for x:　$\log_4 (x - 2) < 3$

Solution　If the logarithm (exponent) of $x - 2$ is less than 3, then $x - 2$ must be less than 4^3.

$$x - 2 < 4^3 \quad \text{inequality}$$
$$x < 66 \quad \text{simplified}$$

But the argument of a logarithm must be a positive number, so $x - 2$ must be greater than zero. This means x must be greater than 2. Thus, the final solution is

$$x > 2 \quad \text{and} \quad x < 66$$

which we can express in one compound statement by writing

$$2 < x < 66$$

Example 28.6　Solve:　$\log_{1/3} (x - 6) > 4$

Solution　If the log of $x - 6$ is greater than 4, then $x - 6$ must be less than $\left(\frac{1}{3}\right)^4$.

$$x - 6 < \left(\frac{1}{3}\right)^4 \qquad \text{equation}$$

$$x - 6 < \frac{1}{81} \qquad \text{expanded}$$

$$x < 6 + \frac{1}{81} \qquad \text{solved}$$

From this we see that x must be less than $6\frac{1}{81}$. Also we remember that the argument of any logarithm must be a positive number. So $x - 6$ must be greater than 0, and thus x must be greater than 6:

$$6 < x < 6\frac{1}{81}$$

Problem set 28

1. It was precisely noon and the verdict was to be rendered when the hands of the clock pointed in opposite directions. How many minutes past noon would the verdict be rendered?

2. Express $\log_{10} x$ in terms of the natural logarithm.

3. Use a calculator to approximate the value of $\log_4 15$.

Solve the following equations for x:

4. $\log_2 (x - 3) < 2$ \qquad\qquad\qquad 5. $\ln (2x - 3) > 1$

6. Use the definition of a derivative to calculate $\dfrac{d}{dx} f(x)$ where $f(x) = 5x - 3$.

7. Use the definition of a derivative to calculate $\dfrac{d}{dx} y$ where $y = 3x^2$.

8. Use the definition of a derivative to calculate $D_x f$ where $f(x) = \dfrac{-1}{x}$.

9. Find the coordinates of the foci of the ellipse whose equation is $\dfrac{x^2}{9} + \dfrac{y^2}{16} = 1$.

10. If $f(x) = \ln x$ and $g(x) = e^x$ write the equation of $f \circ g$.

11. If $f(x) = \sin x$ and $g(x) = 2x - \dfrac{\pi}{2}$, write the equation of $f \circ g$.

12. Graph $f \circ g$ where f and g are as defined in Problem 11.

Evaluate the following limits:

13. $\displaystyle\lim_{x \to 2} \dfrac{2 - \dfrac{2}{x}}{4 - x^2}$ \qquad 14. $\displaystyle\lim_{x \to 3} \dfrac{2x^2 - 2x - 12}{x - 3}$ \qquad 15. $\displaystyle\lim_{x \to \infty} \dfrac{x^2 + 3x}{x^3}$

16. Describe the intervals on the x axis for which the graph of f lies above the x axis if $f(x) = x(x - 2)(x + 4)$.

Solve the following equations for x:

17. $y = \arcsin \dfrac{x}{2}$ \qquad\qquad\qquad 18. $\sin^2 x - 1 = 0 \qquad (0 \le x < 2\pi)$

19. Use synthetic division to aid in finding the value of k for which $x = -1$ is a zero of $x^3 + 2x^2 + 3x + k$.

20. Show that: $[\sec(-x) - 1](\sec x + 1) = \tan^2 x$

21. Write $\dfrac{1 + \sqrt{3}}{2 - \sqrt{3}}$ with a rational denominator.

22. Write the key trigonometric identities and develop an identity for $\cos \frac{1}{2}x$.

CONCEPT REVIEW   **23.** Given rectangle $ABCD$ and triangle AEB where E is arbitrarily chosen on $\overline{DC}$, compare:

     A.   Area of $\triangle AEB$ *B.*   Area of $\triangle ACB$

24. Find the sixth term of the geometric sequence whose first three terms are 1, 2, and 4.

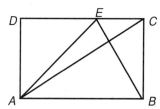

LESSON 29   *Translations of functions · Rational functions I*

29.A
Translations of functions

If we add a constant to a function, the graph of the function is translated (shifted) vertically. If we add $+2$, the graph is shifted up 2 units. If we add -2, the graph is shifted down 2 units.

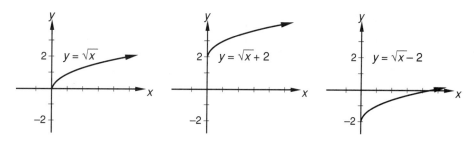

If we replace x with the sum of x and a constant, the graph of the function is shifted horizontally. If we replace x with $x + 2$, the graph of the function is shifted 2 units to the left. If we replace x with $x - 2$, the graph is shifted 2 units to the right.

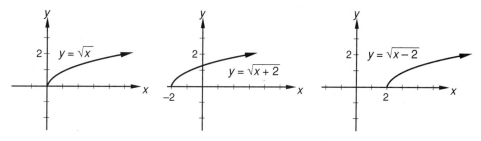

Sometimes one forgets whether replacing x with $x + 2$ moves the graph to the left or the right. It's easy to check. In the left-hand equation $y = 0$ when $x = 0$. In the center equation $y = 0$ when $x = -2$. Thus, replacing x with $x + 2$ has caused a 2-unit shift of the graph to the left.

Example 29.1   Graph the function $y = |x|$. Then change the equation to shift the graph 3 units to the left and 2 units down. Then graph the new function.

   Solution   To shift the graph 3 units to the left, we add $+3$ to the argument. To shift the graph 2 units down, we add -2 to the function.

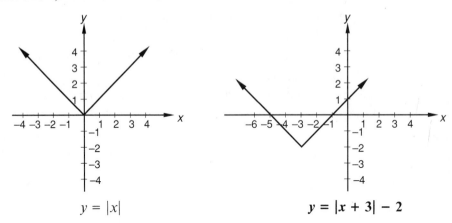

$$y = |x| \qquad\qquad y = |x + 3| - 2$$

Example 29.2   Graph the function $y = \frac{1}{2}x^2$. Then change the equation to shift the curve 3 units to the right and 2 units up. Then graph the new function.

   Solution   To get a quick sketch, we select x values of 0, 3, and -3 and find corresponding y values of 0, 4.5, and 4.5. To shift the graph 3 units to the right, we replace x with $x - 3$, and we add $+2$ to the function to shift the graph 2 units up.

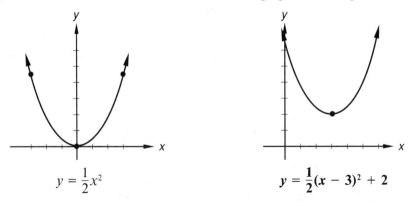

$$y = \frac{1}{2}x^2 \qquad\qquad y = \frac{1}{2}(x - 3)^2 + 2$$

Example 29.3   Graph the function $y = \frac{1}{2}x$. Then change the equation to shift the graph 2 units to the left and 1 unit down.

   Solution   On the left we show the graph of $y = \frac{1}{2}x$. In the center figure, we show the graph of $y = \frac{1}{2}(x + 2)$, which is the original graph shifted 2 units to the left. In the right-hand figure, we add -1 to the function to shift the center graph down 1 unit.

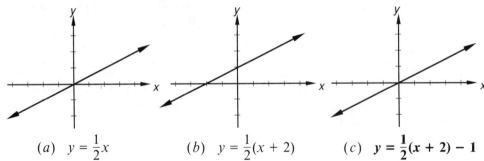

$$(a) \quad y = \frac{1}{2}x \qquad (b) \quad y = \frac{1}{2}(x + 2) \qquad (c) \quad y = \frac{1}{2}(x + 2) - 1$$

This example illustrates a peculiarity of linear functions in that a shift left or right can have the same effect as a vertical shift. We note that in (*b*), a shift 2 units to the left could be considered to be a vertical shift of +1 unit. Thus, (*c*) is the same graph as (*a*).

Example 29.4   Given $y = |4 \sin x|$, change the function so that the graph will be shifted down 2 units and $\pi/2$ units to the right.

Solution   To get the required transformation, we add $-\frac{\pi}{2}$ to the argument of the function and add -2 to the function.

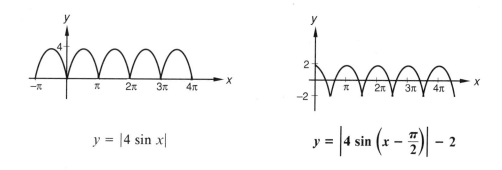

$$y = |4 \sin x| \qquad\qquad y = \left|4 \sin\left(x - \frac{\pi}{2}\right)\right| - 2$$

29.B
Rational functions I

Some algebraic expressions consist of variables whose exponents are whole numbers and whose coefficients are real numbers. We call these expressions ***polynomials.*** The following expressions are polynomials in one variable.

$$5x^2 \qquad -3x^4 \qquad 7 \qquad \sqrt{2}\,x^3$$

All of these expressions have a real number coefficient and an exponent that is a whole number. The number 7 is a polynomial because it can be written as $7x^0$ and 0 is a whole number. We can think "simplenomial" when we see the word *polynomial* because polynomials are the simplest algebraic expressions that we have. The polynomials above are also called ***monomials*** because they have only one term. The indicated sum of two or more polynomials is also called a polynomial. Thus, all three of these expressions are polynomials.

$$5x^2 + 2x \qquad 3x + 5 \qquad 2x^2 + 2x + 3$$

Polynomials of two terms are called ***binomials,*** and polynomials of three terms are called ***trinomials.*** Thus the first two expressions are binomials, and the third expression is a trinomial. If a fraction has a polynomial for both the numerator and the denominator, we say that the fraction is a ***rational polynomial expression.*** Rational polynomial functions are called ***rational functions*** and appear often in the study of calculus. Thus, the graphs of these functions are important.

Example 29.5   Graph $y = \dfrac{1}{x}$.

Solution   As we noted in Lesson 24, when x is a large positive number, $\frac{1}{x}$ is a small positive number. When x is a large negative number, $\frac{1}{x}$ is a small negative number. We indicate this with the points on the graph on the left pictured at the top of the following page.

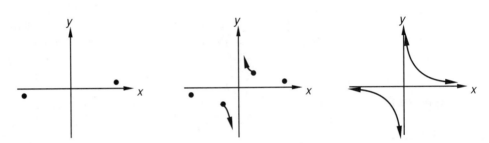

When x is 1, y is 1, and as x gets smaller, y increases positively. When x is -1, y is -1, and as $|x|$ gets smaller, y increases negatively. We show this in the center graph.

This is enough information to complete the sketch on the right. In this example the y axis is a vertical asymptote, which is a line that the graph approaches but never touches. The function has no value when $x = 0$ because we cannot divide by zero. It is important to note that the graph goes up on one side of the asymptote and reappears from the down direction on the other side of the asymptote. **This always happens when the expression in the denominator is a linear expression.** We remember that the exponent of x in a linear expression is 1.

Example 29.6   Graph $y = \dfrac{1}{x - 3} + 2$.

Solution   The x in the preceding example has been replaced with $x - 3$, so the whole graph is shifted 3 units to the right. The $+2$ shifts the graph up 2 units.

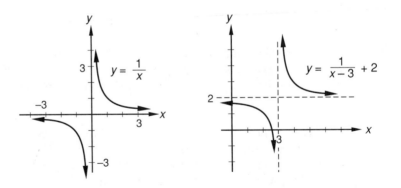

When we shift the graph 3 units to the right, the vertical asymptote is $x = 3$. We do not waste time on these graphs by trying to make them too accurate. All we need is a sketch of the function. **Again we note that the denominator is a linear expression (the exponent of x is 1) and that the graph goes off the page in opposite directions on either side of the asymptote.**

Example 29.7   Graph: (a) $y = -\dfrac{1}{x}$ (b) $y = \dfrac{1}{3 - x}$ (c) $y = \dfrac{1}{x^2}$

Solution   (a)   The graph of $y = -\dfrac{1}{x}$ is the "upside down" version of the graph of $y = \dfrac{1}{x}$. When x is $+2$, $\dfrac{1}{x}$ equals $+\frac{1}{2}$ and $-\dfrac{1}{x}$ equals $-\frac{1}{2}$. When x is -2, $\dfrac{1}{x}$ equals $-\frac{1}{2}$ and $-\dfrac{1}{x}$ equals $+\frac{1}{2}$, etc. We show the graph of $y = \dfrac{1}{x}$ on the left and the graph of $y = -\dfrac{1}{x}$ on the right. Each of these graphs is said to be a "reflection in the x axis" of the other graph.

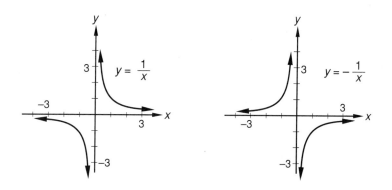

(*b*)   This graph is easy to sketch if we rewrite the expression so that the sign of x is positive and get

$$y = -\frac{1}{x-3}$$

We see that this graph will be the graph of $y = \frac{1}{x}$ shifted 3 units to the right and then flipped upside down about the x axis. On the left below, we graph $y = \frac{1}{x}$. In the center figure, we shift the graph of $y = \frac{1}{x}$ three units to the right to get the graph of $y = \frac{1}{x-3}$. **We do this by simply changing the label on the vertical asymptote from the y axis to $x = 3$.** On the right, we graph $y = -\frac{1}{x-3}$ as the mirror image of the center graph in the x axis.

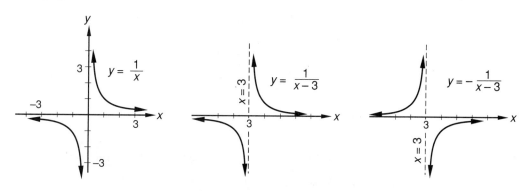

(*c*)   Every value of x is squared so every value of y is positive. The graph looks like a "volcano," as we see on the left. The graph of the negative of the function is shown on the right; it looks like an "upside down volcano."

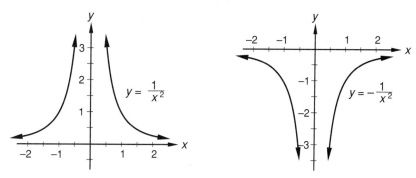

Problem set 29   1. Alan wanted to use 100 meters of fence to enclose a rectangular region which borders a river. If the length of the side of the region parallel to the river is L, find the area of the region in terms of L.

2. Graph the function $y = |x|$ and then change the equation to shift the graph to the left 2 units and down 1 unit.

3. Graph $y = \sqrt{x}$, $y = \sqrt{x} + 2$, and $y = \sqrt{x} - 2$ on the same coordinate plane.

4. Suppose $f(x) = \dfrac{1}{x}$. Let g be the function whose graph is the graph of f shifted 3 units to the left. Graph g and write the equation for g.

Express the following logarithmic expressions entirely in terms of the natural logarithm.

5. $\log_{10} x$ 6. $\log_3 x$

7. Find all real values of x for which $\log_2 (x - 3) < 2$.

8. If $y = -x^2$, find $\dfrac{dy}{dx}$.   9. If $f(x) = x^2 + 2x$, find $\dfrac{d}{dx} f(x)$.

10. Write the standard form of the equation of the ellipse whose general equation is $9x^2 + y^2 - 18x + 2y + 1 = 0$.

11. Determine the coordinates of the center, the lengths of the major and minor axes, and the coordinates of the foci of the ellipse whose equation is given in Problem 10. Finally, sketch the graph of the ellipse.

12. If $f(x) = x^2$ and $g(x) = e^x$, write the equation of $g \circ f$.

13. If f and g are as given in Problem 12, determine the domain and range of f and g and then determine the domain and range of $g \circ f$.

Evaluate the following limits:

14. $\displaystyle\lim_{x \to 0} -\dfrac{1}{x}$ 15. $\displaystyle\lim_{x \to 0} \dfrac{1}{x^2}$

16. $\displaystyle\lim_{x \to \infty} \dfrac{3x^3 - 14x^2 + 5}{1 - 2x^3}$

17. Find all values of x which satisfy the equation $10^{-2x} = 5$.

18. Graph the function $f(x) = |x^2 - 3x + 2|$ and use interval notation to describe those values of x on which the graph of f is increasing.

19. Show that $\sin x - \sin x \cos^2 x = \sin^3 x$.

20. Write the product $(\text{cis } 60°)(\text{cis } 60°)(\text{cis } 60°)$ as a complex number in standard form.

21. Write the key identities for practice, and then develop an expression that gives $\cos^2 x$ as a function of $\cos 2x$.

CONCEPT REVIEW   22. Find the fourth term in the sequence whose first three terms are 1, 8, and 27.

23. Find the perimeter of a square which can be inscribed in a circle of radius $\sqrt{2}$.

LESSON 30 *The hyperbola*

We remember that an ellipse is the locus of all points (x, y) in a plane such that the sum of the distances to two fixed points, called the *foci*, is a constant. The hyperbola is the locus of all points such that the absolute value of the difference of the distances to two fixed points is a constant.

> A *hyperbola* is the locus of all points (x, y) in a plane such that the absolute value of the difference of the distances to two fixed points, called the *foci*, is a constant.

Example 30.1 Using the definition of hyperbola, write the equation for the hyperbola whose foci are $(-5, 0)$ and $(5, 0)$ and for which the difference of the distances to the foci is 6.

Solution We begin by making a sketch.

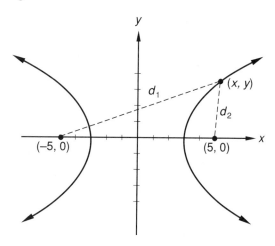

The figure has the point (x, y) on the right branch and shows that $d_1 - d_2$ will be positive. If (x, y) is on the left branch, $d_1 - d_2$ will be negative. In order to cover both cases, we will use the distance formula to write the equation that says that $d_1 - d_2 = \pm 6$.

$$\sqrt{[x - (-5)]^2 + [y - (0)]^2} - \sqrt{[x - (5)]^2 + [y - (0)]^2} = \pm 6$$

The algebraic simplification of this equation is straightforward but laborious. The result of this simplification is the equation on the left.

$$\frac{x^2}{9} - \frac{y^2}{16} = 1 \qquad \text{standard form} \qquad \frac{x^2}{a^2} - \frac{y^2}{b^2} = 1$$

We remember that the two terms in the equation of an ellipse are connected with a plus sign. This is the equation of a hyperbola, and we note that the two terms are connected with a minus sign. **We will use a^2 to identify the axis on which the foci lie and note that the minus sign always precedes the term whose denominator is b^2.**

If x^2 is over a^2, the foci lie on the x axis.

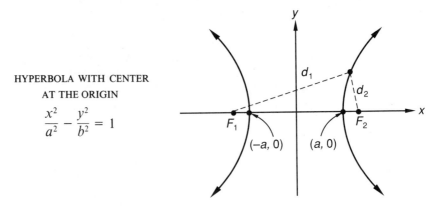

HYPERBOLA WITH CENTER
AT THE ORIGIN

$$\frac{x^2}{a^2} - \frac{y^2}{b^2} = 1$$

If y^2 is over a^2, the foci lie on the y axis.

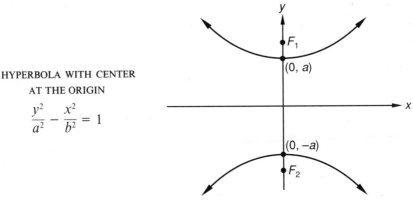

HYPERBOLA WITH CENTER
AT THE ORIGIN

$$\frac{y^2}{a^2} - \frac{x^2}{b^2} = 1$$

The distance from the origin to a focus is c, where

$$c^2 = a^2 + b^2$$

The *eccentricity* of a hyperbola is the ratio of the distance from the center to the focus to the distance from the center to the vertex and thus equals c over a. Because c is always greater than a, the eccentricity of a hyperbola will always be greater than 1. Thus the eccentricity of a hyperbola is a measure of how quickly the graph "bends" away from the directrix. The greater the eccentricity, the greater the "bend" of the hyperbola.

Example 30.2　Graph the hyperbola $4x^2 - 9y^2 - 36 = 0$.

Solution　The standard form of the equation of a hyperbola has the number 1 all by itself to the right of the equals sign. To get this equation into standard form, we add 36 to both sides to get the equation on the left and then divide every term by 36 to get the standard form shown on the right.

$$4x^2 - 9y^2 = 36 \qquad\qquad \frac{x^2}{9} - \frac{y^2}{4} = 1$$

The x^2 term is positive, so the foci lie on the x axis. On the left on page 163 we let y equal zero and solve for x. On the right we let x equal zero and solve for y.

WHEN $y = 0$ WHEN $x = 0$

$$\frac{x^2}{9} - \frac{0}{4} = 1 \qquad\qquad \frac{0}{9} - \frac{y^2}{4} = 1$$

$$x^2 = 9 \qquad\qquad y^2 = -4$$

$$x = \pm 3 \qquad\qquad y = \pm 2i$$

When $y = 0$, we find that $x = \pm 3$; so the curve passes through the points $(3, 0)$ and $(-3, 0)$. When $x = 0$, we get y values of $\pm 2i$. The points $(0, 2i)$ and $(0, -2i)$ cannot be graphed on a real coordinate system. Yet it can be shown that the points $(0, 2)$ and $(0, -2)$ and the points $(3, 0)$ and $(-3, 0)$ can be used to form a rectangle whose diagonals are the asymptotes of the hyperbola.

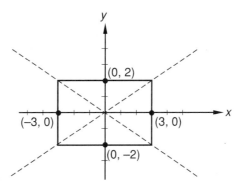

Now we can sketch the hyperbola. The graph goes through the points $(-3, 0)$ and $(3, 0)$ and gets closer and closer to the asymptotes as we get farther and farther from the center of the figure.

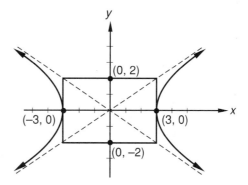

The coordinates of the upper right-hand corner of the rectangle are $(3, 2)$, and the asymptote that passes through this point also passes through the origin. We can use this information to write the equation of this asymptote as $y = \frac{2}{3}x$. The other asymptote passes through the origin and the point $(-3, 2)$. This information allows us to find that the equation of that asymptote is $y = -\frac{2}{3}x$. It is important to note that we can look at the standard form of the equation of a hyperbola and write the slope of the equation of the asymptotes by inspection. The slope is Δy over Δx and is always $\pm$ the square root of the number under y^2 divided by the square root of the number under x^2.

STANDARD FORM	CORNERS OF THE RECTANGLE	EQUATION OF ASYMPTOTES

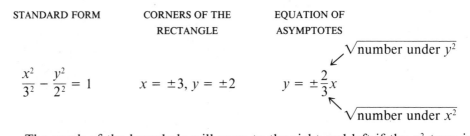

$$\frac{x^2}{3^2} - \frac{y^2}{2^2} = 1 \qquad x = \pm 3, \, y = \pm 2 \qquad y = \pm \frac{2}{3}x$$

The graph of the hyperbola will open to the right and left if the x^2 term is positive and will open up and down if the y^2 term is positive. An easy way to remember this is to let the variable with the negative sign equal zero and solve for the real values of the other variable to find the coordinates of two points on the graph. The corners of the rectangle for both of these equations

$$\frac{x^2}{3^2} - \frac{y^2}{2^2} = 1 \qquad\qquad \frac{y^2}{2^2} - \frac{x^2}{3^2} = 1$$

are $x = \pm 3$ and $y = \pm 2$. If we let y equal zero in the left-hand equation, we find that two real values of x are ± 3, so the curve passes through $(3, 0)$ and $(-3, 0)$. For the right-hand equation the negative sign goes with the x term, so we let x equal zero and find that two real values of y are ± 2. Thus the curve passes through $(0, 2)$ and $(0, -2)$.

Example 30.3 Sketch the hyperbola $9x^2 - 4y^2 + 18x - 16y - 43 = 0$ and write the equations of the asymptotes.

Solution First we rearrange the equation and use parentheses.

$$(9x^2 + 18x \quad) + (-4y^2 - 16y \quad) = 43$$

Now we factor out a 9 from the first set of parentheses and a -4 from the second set of parentheses.

$$9(x^2 + 2x \quad) - 4(y^2 + 4y \quad) = 43$$

Next we complete the square inside each set of parentheses and add $+9$ and -16 to the right-hand side of the equation.

$$9(x^2 + 2x + 1) - 4(y^2 + 4y + 4) = 43 + 9 - 16$$

Now we simplify the expressions.

$$9(x + 1)^2 - 4(y + 2)^2 = 36$$

Since the right-hand side must equal 1, we divide every term by 36 and get the following.

EQUATION	SISTER EQUATION
$\dfrac{(x + 1)^2}{4} - \dfrac{(y + 2)^2}{9} = 1$	$\dfrac{x^2}{4} - \dfrac{y^2}{9} = 1$

We will graph this equation by first graphing the sister equation. The corners of the rectangle for the sister graph are $x = \pm 2$ and $y = \pm 3$. Since the negative sign is with the y term, we mentally set y equal to zero and find that two real values of x are ± 2. Thus the sister curve passes through $(-2, 0)$ and $(2, 0)$.

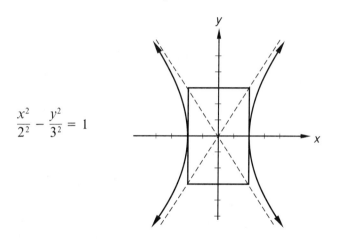

$$\frac{x^2}{2^2} - \frac{y^2}{3^2} = 1$$

The graph that we need is exactly the same except that its center is $(-1, -2)$ instead of the origin. We merely have to relabel the horizontal and vertical axes and note the coordinates of two corners of the rectangle.

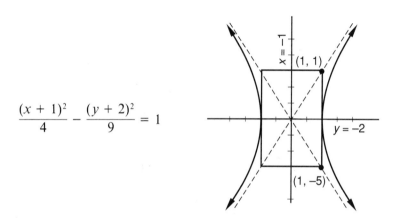

$$\frac{(x + 1)^2}{4} - \frac{(y + 2)^2}{9} = 1$$

We can look at the numbers under $(y + 2)^2$ and under $(x + 1)^2$ and see that the slopes of the asymptotes are $\pm\frac{3}{2}$. Both asymptotes pass through the center of the hyperbola, which is $(-1, -2)$. We use this point to find the intercepts of the asymptotes.

$y = \frac{3}{2}x + b$	slope $\frac{3}{2}$	$y = -\frac{3}{2}x + b$	slope $-\frac{3}{2}$
$-2 = \frac{3}{2}(-1) + b$	used $(-1, -2)$	$-2 = -\frac{3}{2}(-1) + b$	used $(-1, -2)$
$-\frac{1}{2} = b$	solved	$-\frac{7}{2} = b$	solved
$y = \frac{3}{2}x - \frac{1}{2}$	asymptote	$y = -\frac{3}{2}x - \frac{7}{2}$	asymptote

Problem set 30

1. On the outbound leg of 32 miles, Annika sauntered at a leisurely pace. On the way back, she had to double her rate to complete the entire trip in 12 hours. How fast and how long did Annika travel on each leg of the trip?

2. Write the standard form of the equation of the hyperbola whose general equation is $9y^2 - 4x^2 + 18y - 16x - 43 = 0$.

3. Determine the coordinates of the center, the coordinates of the vertices, the coordinates of the foci, and the equations of the asymptotes of the hyperbola whose equation is given in Problem 2. Graph the hyperbola.

4. Graph the function $y = x^2$. Then sketch the graph of $y = x^2$ shifted to the right 2 units and down 3 units. Write the equation of this new graph.

5. Graph the function

$$f(x) = -\frac{1}{x}$$

Then sketch the graph of f shifted 2 units up and 1 unit to the left. Write the equation of g, where g is the equation of the shifted graph of f.

6. Approximate the numerical value of x where $x = \log_4 10$.

7. Find all values of x for which $\log_2 3x > 1$.

8. If $y = -\dfrac{1}{x}$, use the definition of the derivative to find $D_x y$.

9. If $f(x) = ax^2$ where a is some constant, use the definition of the derivative to find $\dfrac{d}{dx} f(x)$.

10. If $f(x) = x^2$ and $g(x) = \ln x$, write the equation of $g \circ f$.

11. Determine the domain and range of f, g, and $g \circ f$ for the functions given in Problem 10.

Evaluate the following limits. (Use the symbols $+\infty$ and $-\infty$ when their meanings are entirely unambiguous.)

12. $\displaystyle\lim_{x \to -1} \frac{1}{1 - x}$

13. $\displaystyle\lim_{x \to -\infty} \frac{-2x - 14x^5}{x^5 + 2x^2}$

14. $\displaystyle\lim_{x \to a} \frac{x^2 - a^2}{x - a}$

Solve the following equations for x:

15. $9^{2x+1} = 27^{x-2}$

16. $\left(\sin x - \dfrac{1}{2}\right)(\sin x + 1) = 0$ $\qquad (0 \le x < 2\pi)$

17. Factor $x^3 - 3x + 2$ into linear factors. (Use the rational zero theorem as an aid.)

18. Determine the distance between the focus and the vertex of a parabola whose equation is $y^2 = -4x$.

19. For which value of k does the following function have a period of 4π?

$$f(x) = 2k \sin k\left(x - \frac{\pi}{2}\right)$$

20. Find the value of $\sin 2\theta$ if $\sin \theta = \dfrac{3}{5}$ and $\cos \theta$ is positive.

21. Simplify: $\dfrac{\sin(-\theta) \cos\left(\dfrac{\pi}{2} - \theta\right)}{1 - \cos^2 \theta}$

CONCEPT REVIEW　**22.** Four circles, each of which has a diameter of 2 meters, touch as shown. Find the area of the shaded portion.

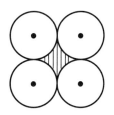

23. Find the value of x in terms of a and b in this figure.

$\angle P = x - a$
$m\widehat{BD} = x + b$
$m\widehat{AC} = ab - x$

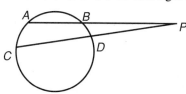

LESSON 31 *Binomial expansion · Recognizing the equations of conic sections*

31.A
Binomial expansion

The binomial theorem gives us a pattern that we can use to find the terms of the expansion of a binomial raised to a positive-integer power.

> If n is a positive integer and k is a positive integer less than or equal to $n + 1$, the kth term of $(F + S)^n$ is
>
> $$\frac{n!}{(n - k + 1)!(k - 1)!} F^{n-k+1} S^{k-1}$$

We will use F for the first term of the binomial and S for the second term and define $0!$ to equal 1. We can see the pattern of the exponents if we look at the exponents in the expansions of $(F + S)^n$. We will let n equal 6 for one example and let n equal 10 for another example. We will not consider the coefficients of the interior terms yet. We represent these coefficients with empty boxes.

$$\boxed{1}\quad\boxed{2}\quad\boxed{3}\quad\boxed{4}\quad\boxed{n+1}$$

$(F + S)^6 = F^6 + \square F^5 S + \square F^4 S^2 + \square F^3 S^3 + \cdots + S^6$

$(F + S)^{10} = F^{10} + \square F^9 S + \square F^8 S^2 + \square F^7 S^3 + \cdots + S^{10}$

We see that the first term of both expansions is F^n. The second term is $\square F^{n-1} S^1$. In each succeeding term, the exponent of F decreases by 1 and the exponent of S increases by 1. **The sum of the exponents in each term is n.** The last term is S^n. Note that the coefficients of both the first and last terms are 1.

The coefficients for the second and succeeding terms have n factorial in the numerator and the exponents factorial in the denominator, as we show below.

$$\boxed{1}\qquad\boxed{2}\qquad\boxed{3}\qquad\boxed{4}\qquad\boxed{n+1}$$

$$(F + S)^6 = F^6 + \frac{6!}{5!1!}F^5S + \frac{6!}{4!2!}F^4S^2 + \frac{6!}{3!3!}F^3S^3 + \cdots + S^6$$

$$(F + S)^{10} = F^{10} + \frac{10!}{9!1!}F^9S + \frac{10!}{8!2!}F^8S^2 + \frac{10!}{7!3!}F^7S^3 + \cdots + S^{10}$$

Example 31.1 Write the first four terms of the expansion of $(x + \Delta x)^7$.

Solution First we write the exponents and leave a space to insert the coefficients.

$$(x + \Delta x)^7 = x^7 + \Box x^6\,\Delta x + \Box x^5\,(\Delta x)^2 + \Box x^4\,(\Delta x)^3 + \cdots + (\Delta x)^7$$

The coefficient of the first term and the last term is always 1. The coefficient of every other term has 7! on top and the product of the exponents factorial below.

$$(x + \Delta x)^7 = x^7 + \frac{7!}{6!1!}x^6\,\Delta x + \frac{7!}{5!2!}x^5\,(\Delta x)^2 + \frac{7!}{4!3!}x^4\,(\Delta x)^3 + \cdots$$

Example 31.2 Find the eighth term of the expansion of $(F + S)^{12}$.

Solution An easy way is to begin is with the exponents of S. In the first term, the exponent of S is 0, then 1, etc.

TERM:	$\boxed{1}$	$\boxed{2}$	$\boxed{3}$	$\boxed{4}$	$\boxed{5}$	$\boxed{6}$
EXPONENT OF S:	S^0	S^1	S^2	S^3	S^4	$\cdots$

Thus we see that the exponent of S in the eighth term will be 7. We know that the exponent of F must add to 7 to make 12, so the exponent of F must be 5. Thus, the variables are

$$F^5S^7$$

Now the numerator of the coefficient is $(5 + 7)!$, which is 12!, and the denominator of the coefficient is $5!7!$. Using this information we can write the eighth term of the expansion of $(F + S)^{12}$ as follows:

$$\frac{12!}{5!7!}F^5S^7 = \mathbf{792}F^5S^7$$

Example 31.3 Find the tenth term of the expansion of $(2x^3 - y)^{15}$.

Solution We will begin by finding the tenth term of the expansion of $(F + S)^{15}$. Then we will replace F with $2x^3$ and replace S with $-y$. The exponent of the variable S in the tenth term is 9, so the exponent of F must be 6 because the exponents must sum to 15.

$$F^6S^9$$

Now we remember the pattern and write the coefficient

$$\text{Tenth term} = \frac{15!}{6!9!}F^6S^9 = 5005F^6S^9$$

We finish by replacing F with $2x^3$ and replacing S with $-y$; then we simplify.

$$5005(2x^3)^6(-y)^9 = 5005[64x^{18}(-y^9)] = \mathbf{-320,320}x^{18}y^9$$

31.B
Recognizing the equations of conic sections

The general equation of all conic sections is the equation

$$ax^2 + bxy + cy^2 + dx + ey + f = 0$$

If the coefficients a, b, and c are zero and the coefficients d and e are not both zero, then the result is an equation such as

STRAIGHT LINE $4x + 2y + 5 = 0$

which is the equation of a straight line. If the coefficients b and c are zero and the coefficients a and e are not zero, then the result is an equation such as

PARABOLA $x^2 + 4x - y + 1 = 0$

which is the equation of a parabola. We can change the form of this equation by completing the square and can write the equation in standard form as

PARABOLA $y = (x + 2)^2 - 3$

We can also get the equation of a parabola if a and b equal zero and if d and e do not equal zero.

If $b = 0$ and the coefficients a and c are equal, we get an equation such as

CIRCLE $x^2 + y^2 - 8x - 4y + 11 = 0$

This is the equation of a circle and can be rewritten in standard form. The standard form of this equation is

CIRCLE $(x - 4)^2 + (y - 2)^2 = 9$

If $b = 0$, a and c are both positive or both negative, and a is not equal to c, the equation is the equation of an ellipse. The standard form can be determined by completing the square on the x terms and y terms.

	GENERAL FORM	STANDARD FORM
ELLIPSE	$4x^2 + 3y^2 + 4x - 2y = 0$	$\dfrac{(x + \frac{1}{2})^2}{\frac{1}{3}} + \dfrac{(y - \frac{1}{3})^2}{\frac{4}{9}} = 1$

If $b = 0$, and a and c have opposite signs, the equation is the equation of a hyperbola. In the following equation, the coefficients 4 and -3 have opposite signs, so this equation is the equation of a hyperbola which could be rewritten in standard form.

	GENERAL FORM	STANDARD FORM
HYPERBOLA	$4x^2 - 3y^2 + 8x - 2y + 7 = 0$	$\dfrac{(y + \frac{1}{3})^2}{\frac{10}{9}} - \dfrac{(x + 1)^2}{\frac{5}{6}} = 1$

If b is not zero, the equation will have an xy term. If a conic equation contains an xy term, the axes of the graph of the function are inclined to the x and y axes, which is the same as saying that the axes of the function have been rotated. Thus the general forms of the equations of these rotated figures would contain an xy term.

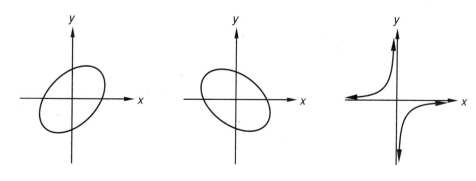

Example 31.4   Indicate whether each equation is the equation of an ellipse, a hyperbola, a circle, or a parabola.
  (a) $4x^2 + 36y^2 + 40x - 288y + 532 = 0$
  (b) $9x^2 - 54x - 16y - 79 - 4y^2 = 0$
  (c) $x - y^2 + 4y - 3 = 0$
  (d) $x^2 + y^2 - 8x + 6y - 56 = 0$
  (e) $x^2 + 36y^2 + 40 - 288y + 532 = 0$

Solution   (a)   **Ellipse.** The coefficients of x^2 and y^2 have the same sign but are not equal.
  (b)   **Hyperbola.** The coefficients of x^2 and y^2 have different signs.
  (c)   **Parabola.** The equation has an x term, a y^2 term, and no x^2 term.
  (d)   **Circle.** The coefficients of x^2 and y^2 are equal.
  (e)   **Ellipse.** The coefficients of x^2 and y^2 have the same sign but are not equal.

Problem set 31

1. Square corners of equal size are cut out of a 10 by 12 inch sheet as shown. The resulting flaps are folded up and a box with no top is formed. If the length of a side of each of the squares cut from the sheet is x, find the volume of the box in terms of x.

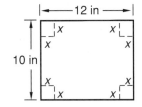

2. Use the binomial theorem to find the fourth term of the expansion of the expression $(2x^3y - 3x^5)^6$.

3. Use the binomial theorem to expand $(x + \Delta x)^6$.

4. Indicate whether each of the following is the equation of an ellipse, a hyperbola, a circle, or a parabola.
  (a) $x^2 + 2y + 3x + 5 = 0$
  (b) $2x^2 + 3x - 2y + 2y^2 + 3 = 0$
  (c) $2x^2 - 3y^2 + 7x + 4y + 5 = 0$
  (d) $9x^2 + 4y^2 + 36x - 24y + 36 = 0$

5. Identify the conic section whose equation is $x^2 - 2x - y^2 = 0$ and write the equation of the conic section in standard form.

6. Describe as fully as possible the characteristics of the conic section of Problem 5. Graph the function.

7. Graph the function f where $f(x) = |x^2 - 1|$, and then graph the function g where the equation of g is $g(x) = f(x - 1)$.

8. Write the equations of both of the asymptotes of the graph of $y = \dfrac{1}{x - 3}$.

9. Write $\log_3 x$ entirely in terms of natural logarithms.

10. Find all the values of x which satisfy the inequality $\log_2 \dfrac{x}{2} > 1$.

Use the definition of a derivative to work Problems 11 and 12.

11. If $f(x) = 3x + 5$, find $\dfrac{d}{dx} f(x)$.   12. If $y = -\dfrac{2}{x}$, find $\dfrac{dy}{dx}$.

13. If $f(x) = \ln x$ and $g(x) = x$, what domains are implied for f and g?

14. If f and g are as defined in Problem 13, determine the domain of f/g.

Evaluate:

15. $\displaystyle\lim_{x\to\infty} \dfrac{3 - 2x + x^3}{2 + 14x^3}$ 16. $\sin^{-1}[\sin(270°)]$

17. Find the values of x for which: $\sec x = -2$ $(180° \leq x < 360°)$

18. If $\triangle ABC$ is an equilateral triangle, and $\overline{ED}$ is parallel to $\overline{AB}$, then solve for x in terms of h.

19. Describe the set of all the values of x for which $|2x - 3| < \varepsilon$, where ε stands for some unspecified small positive number.

20. Write each of the following products as a complex number in standard form:
    (a) (2 cis 30°)(2 cis 30°)(2 cis 30°)
    (b) (2 cis 150°)(2 cis 150°)(2 cis 150°)
    (c) (2 cis 270°)(2 cis 270°)(2 cis 270°)

CONCEPT REVIEW   21. Find the sum of all the interior angles of the polygon shown.

22. If x is a real number, compare:
    A. x^2 B. x^3

LESSON 32   *Roots of complex numbers · Trigonometric functions of $n\theta$*

32.A
Roots of complex numbers

Taking a root is defined to be the inverse operation of raising to a power.

$$\text{If} \quad 2^3 = 8 \quad \text{then} \quad \sqrt[3]{8} = 2$$

The same definition applies to roots of complex numbers. If we raise 2 cis 12° to the third power, we get

$$(2 \text{ cis } 12)^3 = (2 \text{ cis } 12°)(2 \text{ cis } 12°)(2 \text{ cis } 12°) = 8 \text{ cis } 36°$$

Now to undo what we have done, we take the cube root of 8 cis 36°.

$$\sqrt[3]{8 \text{ cis } 36°} = 2 \text{ cis } 12°$$

But every complex number has three cube roots. The other two roots are

$$2 \text{ cis } \left(12° + \frac{360°}{3}\right) \quad \text{and} \quad 2 \text{ cis } \left[12° + 2\left(\frac{360°}{3}\right)\right]$$

or   2 cis 132°   and   2 cis 252°

We can check these last two answers by multiplying.

$$(2 \text{ cis } 132°)(2 \text{ cis } 132°)(2 \text{ cis } 132°) = 8 \text{ cis } 396° = 8 \text{ cis } 36°$$

$$(2 \text{ cis } 252°)(2 \text{ cis } 252°)(2 \text{ cis } 252°) = 8 \text{ cis } 756° = 8 \text{ cis } 36°$$

Every complex number has two square roots, three cube roots, four fourth roots, five fifth roots, and, in general, n nth roots. The angles of the cube roots differ by

360°/3, or 120°. The angles of the fourth roots differ by 360°/4, or 90°. The angles of the fifth roots differ by 360°/5, or 72°; etc. Thus, the angles of the nth roots differ by 360°/n.

Example 32.1   Find four fourth roots of i.

Solution   **To find the roots of a complex number, we begin by writing the number in polar form with a positive magnitude.**

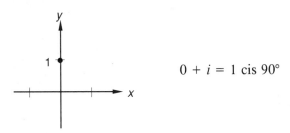

$$0 + i = 1 \text{ cis } 90°$$

The fourth root of 1 is 1, so we get

$$\sqrt[4]{1 \text{ cis } 90°} = 1^{1/4} \text{ cis } \frac{90°}{4} = \textbf{1 cis 22.5°}$$

The other three roots differ by 360°/4, or 90°. They are

1 cis 112.5°, 1 cis 202.5°, and 1 cis 292.5°

Example 32.2   Use a calculator and decimal numbers to estimate $\sqrt[5]{-17 - 14i}$.

Solution   The first step is to write the complex number in polar form.

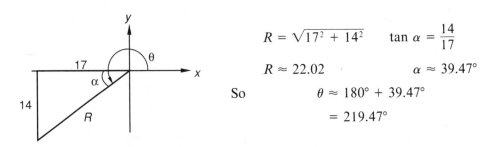

$$R = \sqrt{17^2 + 14^2} \qquad \tan \alpha = \frac{14}{17}$$

$$R \approx 22.02 \qquad\qquad \alpha \approx 39.47°$$

So $\qquad\qquad \theta \approx 180° + 39.47°$

$$= 219.47°$$

Now we restate the problem as

$$\sqrt[5]{22.02 \text{ cis } 219.47°} = 22.02^{1/5} \text{ cis } \frac{219.47°}{5} \approx \textbf{1.86 cis 43.89°}$$

There are four more roots, which we get by adding $n(360°)/5$ to 43.89° ($n = 1, 2, 3, 4$). Thus, the five fifth roots are

1.86 cis 43.89°, 1.86 cis 115.89°, 1.86 cis 187.89°,
1.86 cis 259.89°, and 1.86 cis 331.89°

32.B
Trigonometric functions of nθ

There are two angles between 0° and 360° whose sine is $\frac{1}{2}$. The sine is positive in the first and second quadrants, and the angles are 30° and 150°. Thus, the equation

$$\sin \theta = \frac{1}{2} \qquad (0° \le \theta < 360°)$$

has both 30° and 150° as solutions. The problem is more complex for functions of $n\theta$.

Example 32.3   Solve: $\sin 3\theta = \dfrac{1}{2}$ $(0° \le \theta < 360°)$

Solution   In this example the argument is 3θ, but since θ can be any angle between 0° and 360°, 3θ can be any angle between 0° and 3(360°), or 1080°. Thus 3θ can be 30° plus 360° (once around) or 390° and 30° plus 720° (twice around) or 750°.

$$3\theta = 30° \qquad 3\theta = 390° \qquad 3\theta = 750°$$
$$\boldsymbol{\theta = 10°} \qquad \boldsymbol{\theta = 130°} \qquad \boldsymbol{\theta = 250°}$$

Also, since 3θ can equal 150°, 3θ can equal 150° plus 360°, or 510°, and 3θ can equal 150° plus 720°, or 870°.

$$3\theta = 150° \qquad 3\theta = 510° \qquad 3\theta = 870°$$
$$\boldsymbol{\theta = 50°} \qquad \boldsymbol{\theta = 170°} \qquad \boldsymbol{\theta = 290°}$$

Thus we see that if $\sin \theta = k$ has two solutions, $\sin 3\theta = k$ will have six solutions, $\sin 4\theta = k$ will have eight solutions, and $\sin n\theta = k$ will have $2n$ solutions.

Example 32.4   Solve: $\tan 4\theta - \dfrac{\sqrt{3}}{3} = 0$ $(0° \le \theta < 360°)$

Solution   The equation is given and the notation following the equation indicates that angles between 0° and 360° are acceptable. First we solve for $\tan 4\theta$ by adding $\dfrac{\sqrt{3}}{3}$ to both sides.

$$\tan 4\theta = \frac{\sqrt{3}}{3} \qquad \text{or} \qquad \frac{1}{\sqrt{3}}$$

There are two angles between 0° and 360° whose tangent is $\dfrac{\sqrt{3}}{3}$. These angles are 30° and 210°. Thus,

$$4\theta = 30° \qquad \text{and} \qquad 4\theta = 210°$$

Since θ must be between 0° and 360°, 4θ must be between 0° and 4(360°), or 1440°.
   Thus, 30° and 210° can be increased by 360° for one full period, by 720° for two full periods, and by 1080° for three full periods. Thus, for 30° we have

$$4\theta = 30° \qquad 4\theta = 390° \qquad 4\theta = 750° \qquad 4\theta = 1110°$$
$$\boldsymbol{\theta = 7.5°} \qquad \boldsymbol{\theta = 97.5°} \qquad \boldsymbol{\theta = 187.5°} \qquad \boldsymbol{\theta = 277.5°}$$

and for 210° we have

$$4\theta = 210° \qquad 4\theta = 570° \qquad 4\theta = 930° \qquad 4\theta = 1290°$$
$$\boldsymbol{\theta = 52.5°} \qquad \boldsymbol{\theta = 142.5°} \qquad \boldsymbol{\theta = 232.5°} \qquad \boldsymbol{\theta = 322.5°}$$

Problem set 32

1. The circumference of a circle is equal to the perimeter of a square. Which has the greater area, the circle or the square, and by what percent?

2. Write the polar forms of the five fifth roots of i.

3. Write the rectangular forms of the four fourth roots of 1.

Solve the following equations for x $\qquad (0 \le x < 2\pi)$

4. $\sin 3x = -\dfrac{1}{2}$

5. $\tan 4x + \dfrac{\sqrt{3}}{3} = 0$

6. Identify the conic section whose equation is $x^2 + 4y^2 - 16y + 12 = 0$ and write the equation in standard form.

7. Describe as completely as possible the conic section whose equation is given in Problem 6.

8. Use the binomial theorem to expand $(x + \Delta x)^7$. (The coefficient of each term may be left in factorial form.)

9. If $f(x) = \sin x$, graph the function g where $g(x) = 2 + 3f\left(x - \dfrac{\pi}{2}\right)$.

10. Write the equation of the function whose graph is the graph of $y = \dfrac{1}{x}$ shifted 2 units to the left and 3 units up.

11. Find an expression for the exact value of x where $4^x = 17$.

12. Use the definition of a derivative to compute $D_x y$ where $y = x^3$.

13. Use the definition of a derivative to compute $\dfrac{d}{dx} f(x)$ where $f(x) = -4x + 5$.

14. Suppose f and g are functions whose equations are given by $f(x) = \sin x$ and $g(x) = x^2$. Find the domains of f and g.

15. If f and g are as defined in Problem 14, write the equation of $f \circ g$.

16. Evaluate: $\displaystyle\lim_{x \to 1} \dfrac{x^2 + x - 2}{x^2 - 1}$

17. On which intervals is the function $y = x^2 + x - 2$ increasing?

18. Sketch the graphs of $y = \ln x$, $y = \ln (-x)$, and $y = \ln |x|$.

19. Show that: $(\cot^2 x + 1)[\sin^2 (-x)] + \cos\left(\dfrac{\pi}{2} - x\right) \sin (-x) = \cos^2 x$

20. Use synthetic division to aid in finding k so that $x = 1$ is a zero of the polynomial $x^3 - 3x^2 + 4x + k$.

21. Write the key trigonometric identities and develop an expression that gives $\cos^2 x$ as a function of $\cos 2x$.

CONCEPT REVIEW   22. Find the length of a side of an equilateral triangle which can be inscribed in a circle of radius 4.

23. Find x given the figure and information shown.

PA is tangent to circle O at A
$AO = x$
$PA = 12$
$PO = 13$

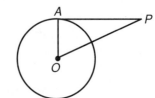

LESSON 33 *The derivative of x^n · Notations for the derivative*

33.A
The derivative of x^n

We remember the definition of the derivative of a function by remembering the geometrical interpretation. The slope of the secant through P_1 and P_2 in the figure on the left is the rise divided by the run. In the figure on the right we see that the y value of P_2 is $f(x + \Delta x)$ and the y value of P_1 is $f(x)$.

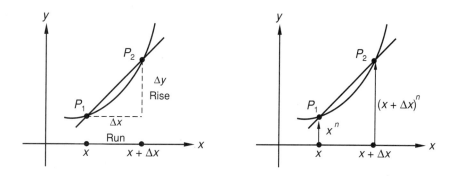

The value of the rise Δy is the difference of these two expressions. The run is Δx, so we can write the rise over the run as

$$\frac{\text{Rise}}{\text{Run}} = \frac{\Delta y}{\Delta x} = \frac{f(x + \Delta x) - f(x)}{\Delta x}$$

The derivative is the limit of this expression as Δx approaches zero. We remember that the trick is to rearrange the expression algebraically so that Δx is not a factor of the denominator when Δx approaches zero. If the function whose derivative we seek is x^3, we would proceed as follows.

$$\frac{d}{dx} x^3 = \lim_{\Delta x \to 0} \frac{(x + \Delta x)^3 - x^3}{\Delta x}$$

When we expand $(x + \Delta x)^3$ by using the binomial formula, in the numerator we get x^3 as the first term and $-x^3$ as the last term.

$$\frac{d}{dx} x^3 = \lim_{\Delta x \to 0} \frac{x^3 + 3x^2 \, \Delta x + 3x \, (\Delta x)^2 + (\Delta x)^3 - x^3}{\Delta x}$$

The first term and the last term in the numerator add to zero. Furthermore, we note that the second term has Δx as a factor and every other term has $(\Delta x)^2$ as a factor. If we divide by Δx, we no longer have a Δx in the denominator.

$$\frac{d}{dx} x^3 = \lim_{\Delta x \to 0} 3x^2 + (3x \, \Delta x + (\Delta x)^2)$$

In this expression all of the terms after the first term have Δx as a factor. If we let Δx approach zero, then the value of all of these terms approaches zero. Thus,

$$\frac{d}{dx} x^3 = 3x^2$$

This same pattern occurred when we found the derivative of x^2 and will occur when we find the derivative of x^n, where n is 4, 5, 6, or any greater counting number. This will permit us to do a general development for the derivative of x^n where n is any counting number.

Example 33.1 Find the derivative of x^n where n is a counting number $\{1, 2, 3, 4, \ldots\}$.

Solution We use the same diagrams to remember that the definition of the derivative is an algebraic expression of the limit of the rise over the run as the run approaches zero.

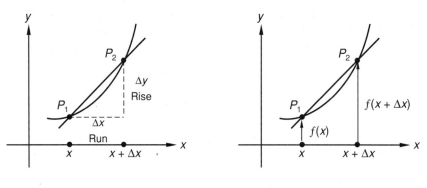

$$\frac{d}{dx} x^n = \lim_{\Delta x \to 0} \frac{(x + \Delta x)^n - x^n}{\Delta x}$$

When we expand the numerator, we get $x^n + nx^{n-1}\,\Delta x$ plus other terms whose coefficients we will represent by empty boxes since their value is of no interest. The last term in the numerator is the last term in the numerator above.

$$= \lim_{\Delta x \to 0} \frac{x^n + nx^{n-1}\,\Delta x + \square x^{n-2}\,(\Delta x)^2 + \square x^{n-3}\,(\Delta x)^3 + \cdots + (\Delta x)^n - x^n}{\Delta x}$$

We note that every term except the first two terms and the last term has $(\Delta x)^2$ as a factor.

$$= \lim_{\Delta x \to 0} \frac{x^n + nx^{n-1}\,\Delta x + [\text{terms that have } (\Delta x)^2 \text{ as a factor}] - x^n}{\Delta x}$$

Now we note that the sum of the first term and the last term in the numerator is zero. If we divide the rest by Δx, the Δx in the second term is eliminated, and every term in the parentheses still has Δx as a factor.

$$\frac{d}{dx} x^n = \lim_{\Delta x \to 0} nx^{n-1} + (\text{terms that have } \Delta x \text{ as a factor})$$

When Δx approaches zero, the values of all of the terms in the parentheses approach zero, and we have finally

$$\frac{d}{dx} x^n = nx^{n-1}$$

In this proof we used the binomial expansion of $(x + \Delta x)^n$ to show that the derivative of x^n is nx^{n-1} if n is a positive integer. This proof is not valid if n is a rational number such as $\frac{2}{3}$ or an irrational number such as π because the binomial expansion cannot be used to expand expressions such as $(x + \Delta x)^{2/3}$ or $(x + \Delta x)^\pi$. **The nx^{n-1} result is valid, however, for any real number value of n, and we will use this fact even though the proof will not be presented in this book.** This rule is called the **power rule**. The proof can be presented in five steps. The first is to extend the proof to the case where $n = 0$. Then the proof is extended in steps to cover the cases where n is a positive rational number, then a negative rational number, and finally to the case where n is an irrational number.

33.B
Notations for the derivative

We have used the notations

$$\frac{d}{dx}y \qquad \frac{dy}{dx} \qquad \frac{d}{dx}f(x) \qquad D_x f(x) \qquad \text{and} \qquad D_x y$$

to indicate the derivative of a function. Three other notations are often used.

$$y' \qquad f'(x) \qquad \text{and} \qquad f'$$

These are read as "y prime," "function prime of x," and "function prime," respectively.

Example 33.2 Find y' if: (a) $y = x^4$ (b) $y = x^\pi$

Solution The derivative of x^n for any real number value of n is nx^{n-1}. This tells us to write the exponent in front and let the new exponent be the old exponent reduced by 1.

$$(a) \quad y' = \frac{d}{dx}x^4 = \mathbf{4x^3} \qquad (b) \quad y' = \frac{d}{dx}x^\pi = \boldsymbol{\pi x^{\pi-1}}$$

Example 33.3 Find $f'(x)$ and $g'(x)$ if: (a) $f(x) = x^{-7}$ (b) $g(x) = \dfrac{1}{x^{15}}$

Solution The derivative of (a) is a little tricky because -7 reduced by 1 is -8. To find the derivative of (b), we first rewrite the expression to get x^{15} out of the denominator.

$$(a) \quad f'(x) = \frac{d}{dx}x^{-7} = \mathbf{-7x^{-8}}$$

$$(b) \quad g'(x) = \frac{d}{dx}\frac{1}{x^{15}} = \frac{d}{dx}x^{-15} = \mathbf{-15x^{-16}}$$

Example 33.4 If the f equation is $y = x^{-2/5}$, find f'.

Solution We write the exponent in front and let the new exponent be the old exponent reduced by 1.

$$f'(x) = -\frac{2}{5}x^{-7/5}$$

Example 33.5 If $s(t) = t^{3/5}$ and if $s = t^{3/5}$, find $s'(t)$, s', and $\dfrac{ds}{dt}$.

Solution The functions are the same function, and $s'(t)$, s', and $\dfrac{ds}{dt}$ are all notations for the derivative of this function.

$$s' = s'(t) = \frac{ds}{dt} = \frac{3}{5}t^{-2/5}$$

Problem set 33

1. A rectangular sheet of metal measuring 1 meter by 20 meters is to be made into a gutter by bending up its two sides at right angles to the base.

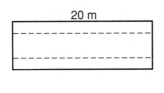 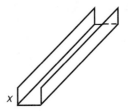

20 m

x

If both vertical sides of the gutter have the same height x, what is the capacity of the gutter in terms of x? We define the capacity of the gutter as the maximum amount of water it can hold if it were closed at both ends.

Use the power rule to compute derivatives in Problems 2–6.

2. Find $\dfrac{dy}{dx}$ if $y = x^3$.

3. Find $f'(x)$ if $f(x) = \sqrt[3]{x}$.

4. Find $\dfrac{ds}{dt}$ if $s = \dfrac{1}{t^3}$.

5. Find $D_x y$ if $y = \sqrt[4]{x^3}$.

6. Find $\dfrac{dy}{dx}$ if $y = \dfrac{1}{x^2}$.

7. Write the three cube roots of $\dfrac{1}{2} + \dfrac{\sqrt{3}}{2} i$ in polar form.

8. Solve: $\cos 3\theta = -\dfrac{1}{2}$ $(0 \le \theta < 2\pi)$

9. Describe the conic section whose equation is $4y^2 + 8y - x + 5 = 0$.

10. Find the coefficient of $x^4 y^3$ in the expansion of $(x - 2y)^7$.

11. If $f(x) = e^x$ and $g(x) = f(-x)$, then graph f and g on the same coordinate plane.

12. If $f(x) = \cos x$ and $h(x) = 1 + f\left(x - \dfrac{\pi}{4}\right)$, then graph f and h on the same coordinate plane.

13. Sketch the graph of $y = \dfrac{1}{x^2}$.

14. Rewrite the following equation so that it makes use of only natural logarithms:
$$y = \log x$$

15. Use the definition of derivative to calculate $f'(x)$ where $f(x) = 2x^2$.

16. If f and g are two functions whose equations are given by $f(x) = x^2$ and $g(x) = \sqrt{x - 4}$, write the equations of $f \circ g$ and $g \circ f$.

17. Find the domain and range of f, g, and $g \circ f$ where f and g are as defined in Problem 16.

18. Evaluate: $\displaystyle\lim_{x \to \infty} \dfrac{2x^3 - x^4}{2x^2 - 1}$

19. Find the equation of the line consisting of points which are equidistant from the points $(2, -1)$ and $(4, 2)$.

20. If L represents a constant, use interval notation to describe the values of y for which $|y - L| < 0.001$.

21. Show that: $(1 - \cos^2 x)\csc^2 x + \tan^2 x = \sec^2 x$

22. If $m \angle ABC$ in the figure shown is 40°, then what is the measure of angle ADC? Why?

23. $(1 + i)^{100}$ equals which of the following quantities?
(a) 2^{100} $\quad$ (b) -2^{50} $\quad$ (c) 2^{50} $\quad$ (d) $1 - 2^{100}$

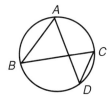

LESSON 34 *Identities for the tangent function ·*
Area and volume

34.A
Identities for the tangent function

We have used the sum and difference identities for the sine and cosine to develop double-angle and half-angle identities for these functions. Now we will see that we can also use the same identities to develop identities for the tangent function. We repeat the sum and difference identities here. We also repeat the sine-cosine definition of the tangent function as well as the basic Pythagorean identity.

KEY IDENTITIES

(a) $\quad \sin (A + B) = \sin A \cos B + \cos A \sin B$

(b) $\quad \sin (A - B) = \sin A \cos B - \cos A \sin B$

(c) $\quad \cos (A + B) = \cos A \cos B - \sin A \sin B$

(d) $\quad \cos (A - B) = \cos A \cos B + \sin A \sin B$

(e) $\quad \tan A = \dfrac{\sin A}{\cos A}$

(f) $\quad \sin^2 A + \cos^2 A = 1$

Example 34.1 Develop an identity for $\tan (A + B)$.

Solution We know that $\tan (A + B)$ equals $\sin (A + B)$ divided by $\cos (A + B)$.

$$\tan (A + B) = \frac{\sin (A + B)}{\cos (A + B)} = \frac{\sin A \cos B + \cos A \sin B}{\cos A \cos B - \sin A \sin B}$$

There are many forms of tangent identities. We will concentrate on forms in which the first entry in the denominator is the number 1. To change $\cos A \cos B$ to 1, we must divide it by itself. If we do this, we must also divide every other term in the whole expression by $\cos A \cos B$ so that the value of the expression will be unchanged.

$$\tan (A + B) = \frac{\dfrac{\sin A \, \cancel{\cos B}}{\cos A \, \cancel{\cos B}} + \dfrac{\cancel{\cos A} \sin B}{\cancel{\cos A} \cos B}}{\dfrac{\cancel{\cos A \cos B}}{\cancel{\cos A \cos B}} - \dfrac{\sin A \sin B}{\cos A \cos B}}$$

We cancel as shown and end up with

$$\tan (A + B) = \frac{\tan A + \tan B}{1 - \tan A \tan B}$$

Example 34.2   Develop an identity for $\tan (A - B)$.

Solution   The procedure is the same except we use the identities for $(A - B)$ instead of for $(A + B)$.

$$\tan (A - B) = \frac{\dfrac{\sin A \cos B}{\cos A \cos B} - \dfrac{\cos A \sin B}{\cos A \cos B}}{\dfrac{\cos A \cos B}{\cos A \cos B} + \dfrac{\sin A \sin B}{\cos A \cos B}}$$

We cancel as shown and end up with

$$\tan (A - B) = \frac{\tan A - \tan B}{1 + \tan A \tan B}$$

We will find that this identity is useful in calculus because it will give us the tangent of the angle of intersection of two lines. The two lines (1) and (2) shown on the left below form angles A and B with a horizontal line. Since the slope of a line is the tangent of the angle the line makes with a horizontal line, we can replace $\tan A$ with m_1 and $\tan B$ with m_2 and write the expression for $\tan \phi$ shown on the right.

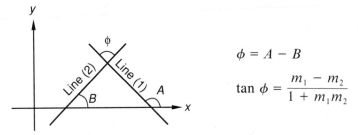

$$\phi = A - B$$

$$\tan \phi = \frac{m_1 - m_2}{1 + m_1 m_2}$$

Example 34.3   Develop the identity for $\tan (A + B)$ and use it to write an equivalent expression for $\tan (\theta + 45°)$.

Solution   **Don't skip the development,** as practice with this development will make access to the identity for $\tan (A + B)$ very easy.

$$\tan (A + B) = \frac{\sin (A + B)}{\cos (A + B)} = \frac{\sin A \cos B + \cos A \sin B}{\cos A \cos B - \sin A \sin B}$$

Now we mentally divide every term by $\cos A \cos B$ and get

$$\tan (A + B) = \frac{\tan A + \tan B}{1 - \tan A \tan B}$$

Now we replace A with θ and B with 45° and remember that the tangent of 45° is 1.

$$\tan (\theta + 45°) = \frac{\tan \theta + \tan 45°}{1 - (\tan \theta)(\tan 45°)} = \frac{\tan \theta + 1}{1 - \tan \theta}$$

Example 34.4   Use the identity for $\tan (A + B)$ developed in Example 34.3 to write the identity for $\tan 2A$.

Solution   The procedure is the same as we used for finding $\sin 2A$ and $\cos 2A$. We just replace B with A and write

$$\tan(A + A) = \frac{\tan A + \tan A}{1 - \tan A \tan A}$$

$$\tan 2A = \frac{2\tan A}{1 - \tan^2 A}$$

34.B
Area and volume

In future lessons we will explore the use of calculus in problems that involve the areas and volumes of basic geometric figures. We will review a few of the formulas here. The area of a circle is πr^2, and since π is the ratio of the circumference to the diameter ($2r$), the circumference equals $2\pi r$.

$$\frac{\text{Circumference}}{\text{Diameter}} = \pi$$

Circumference $= \pi d = 2\pi r$ Area $= \pi r^2$ Area $= \dfrac{\theta}{2\pi}(\pi r^2) = \dfrac{1}{2}r^2\theta$

On the right we show that the area of a sector of a circle can be calculated by multiplying the area of the whole circle by the measure of the central angle in radians divided by 2π.

The volume of a solid whose sides are perpendicular to the base is the area of the base times the height, as we show in these figures.

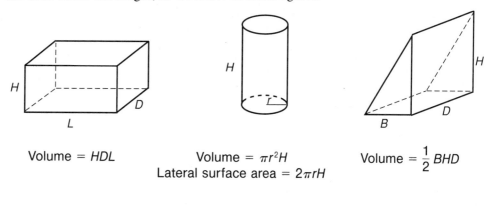

Volume $= HDL$ Volume $= \pi r^2 H$ Volume $= \dfrac{1}{2}BHD$
Lateral surface area $= 2\pi rH$

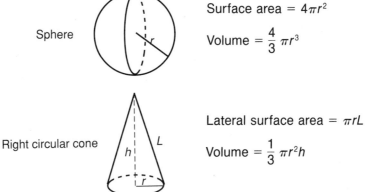

Sphere   Surface area $= 4\pi r^2$

Volume $= \dfrac{4}{3}\pi r^3$

Right circular cone   Lateral surface area $= \pi rL$

Volume $= \dfrac{1}{3}\pi r^2 h$

In the bottom figure we note that the slant height L can be computed as the hypotenuse of a right triangle if we know h and r.

The area of an ellipse is πab. The area of a trapezoid can be computed by drawing a diagonal and summing the areas of the two triangles formed. The area of a triangle can be found if the measures of two sides and the included angle are known.

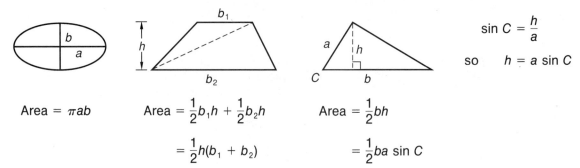

$$\text{Area} = \pi ab$$

$$\text{Area} = \frac{1}{2}b_1 h + \frac{1}{2}b_2 h$$

$$= \frac{1}{2}h(b_1 + b_2)$$

$$\text{Area} = \frac{1}{2}bh$$

$$= \frac{1}{2}ba \sin C$$

$$\sin C = \frac{h}{a}$$

$$\text{so} \quad h = a \sin C$$

Example 34.5 The radius of a right circular cone is 10 cm. If the lateral surface area of the cone is 300π cm^2, what is the height of the cone?

Solution If we draw a diagram of a cone, we can see that the slant height L equals $\sqrt{r^2 + h^2}$. Thus, since r equals 10, we can substitute as we show here.

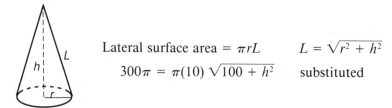

$$\text{Lateral surface area} = \pi r L \qquad L = \sqrt{r^2 + h^2}$$

$$300\pi = \pi(10)\sqrt{100 + h^2} \qquad \text{substituted}$$

Now, if we divide both sides by 10π and square the result, we can solve for h.

$$900 = 100 + h^2 \qquad \text{divided}$$

$$800 = h^2 \qquad \text{simplified}$$

$$\mathbf{20\sqrt{2}\ cm = h} \qquad \text{solved}$$

Example 34.6 A right circular cone whose diameter is 10 cm and whose height is 7 cm is partially filled with water. Find the volume when the depth of the water at the center is 4 cm.

Solution The volume of the part of the cone that contains the water is $\frac{1}{3}\pi r^2 h$. Since the depth is 4 cm, we can find r by using similar triangles, as we show here.

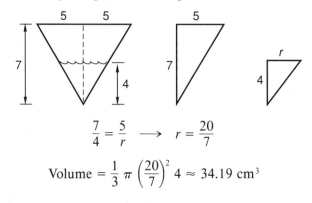

$$\frac{7}{4} = \frac{5}{r} \quad \longrightarrow \quad r = \frac{20}{7}$$

$$\text{Volume} = \frac{1}{3}\pi \left(\frac{20}{7}\right)^2 4 \approx 34.19 \text{ cm}^3$$

Problem set 34   1. The pressure of an ideal gas varies directly as the temperature and inversely as the volume. If the initial pressure, volume, and temperature were N newtons per square meter, L liters, and $K°$ kelvin, what would the pressure be if the volume were 4 liters and the temperature were 1000° kelvin?

2. Write the key identities for practice, and then develop identities for $\tan (A + B)$ and $\tan (A - B)$.

3. Use the sum identity for the tangent function to find the exact value of $\tan 75°$. [*Hint*: $\tan 75° = \tan (45° + 30°)$.]

4. Find the surface area of a sphere whose volume is $\frac{4}{3} \pi$ cubic meters.

5. Find the volume of a right circular cone whose base has an area of 4π square centimeters and whose height is 4 centimeters.

6. Find the volume of a trough 5 meters long whose ends are equilateral triangles, each of whose sides has a length of 2 meters.

Use the power rule of differentiation to differentiate.

7. Find $\dfrac{dy}{dx}$ if $y = \dfrac{1}{x^3}$.

8. Find $f'(x)$ if $f(x) = \sqrt{x^3}$.

9. Find $\dfrac{ds}{dt}$ if $s(t) = \dfrac{1}{\sqrt{t}}$.

10. Find $D_x y$ if $y = x^{14}$.

11. Express the four fourth roots of $\dfrac{1}{2} - \dfrac{\sqrt{3}}{2} i$ in polar form.

12. Find all values of x which lie between 0 and 2π which satisfy the equation $\cos 3x = \frac{1}{2}$.

13. The general equation of a conic section is $x^2 + y^2 - 2x + 4y - 4 = 0$. Write this equation in standard form and fully describe the conic section.

14. Find all integer values of x which satisfy the inequality $|x - 2| > -1$.

15. Find the coefficient of $x^3 y^2$ in the expansion of $(x - 2y)^5$.

16. If $f(x) = \sqrt{x}$ and $g(x) = f(x + 2) + 2$, graph both f and g on the same coordinate plane.

Evaluate the following limits:

17. $\displaystyle\lim_{x \to 1} \dfrac{x^2 - 1}{x^2 + 2x - 3}$

18. $\displaystyle\lim_{n \to \infty} \dfrac{(n + 1)(n - 3)}{2 - n^2}$

19. Graph $f(x) = [x]$ and evaluate $f(1.2)$, $f(-1.5)$, and $f(-2\frac{1}{2})$.

20. Find the distance between the point (2, 3) and the line $5y = 12x + 4$.

CONCEPT REVIEW   21. Find the radius of the circle if $AB = 8$ and $OD = 3$.

22. Find the sum of all the terms of the geometric sequence $\{1, \frac{1}{2}, \frac{1}{4}, \frac{1}{8}, \ldots\}$.

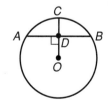

LESSON 35 *The constant-multiple rule · The derivatives of sums and differences · Alternative notation*

**The constant-
multiple rule**

If we form a new function by multiplying a given function by 5, the slope of the graph of the new function at every value of x will be 5 times as steep as the slope of the graph of the original function. If we multiply a function by $-\frac{1}{3}$, the slope of the graph of the new function at every value of x will be $-\frac{1}{3}$ as steep as the graph of the original function. If we multiply a function by any constant c, the slope of the graph of the new function at every value of x will be c times the slope of the graph of the original function. The derivative of a function of x is the rate of change of the function with respect to x and has the same value as the slope of the graph of the function.

If $y = x$ $\qquad \dfrac{d}{dx} x = 1$

If $y = 2x$ $\qquad \dfrac{d}{dx} 2x = 2$

If $y = \dfrac{1}{3}x$ $\qquad \dfrac{d}{dx}\left(\dfrac{1}{3}x\right) = \dfrac{1}{3}$

The slope of the graph of $y = x$ is 1 and the derivative of x is 1. The slope of the graph of $y = 2x$ is 2 and the derivative of $2x$ is 2, which is twice the derivative of x. The slope of the graph of $y = \frac{1}{3}x$ is $\frac{1}{3}$ and the derivative of $\frac{1}{3}x$ is $\frac{1}{3}$. This is one-third the derivative of x. This explanation uses a linear function as an example, but the rule demonstrated is valid for any function.

> **The derivative of the product of a constant and a function equals the product of the constant and the derivative of the function.**
>
> $$\frac{d}{dx} cf(x) = c \frac{d}{dx} f(x)$$

In Lesson 19 we noted that the limit of the product of two functions is the product of the individual limits. If one of the functions is a constant function, the limit of the product equals the constant times the limit of the other function. We can use this property of limits to prove the constant-multiple rule. To do this, we use $cf(x)$ in the definition of the derivative and factor out the c.

$$\frac{d}{dx} cf(x) = \lim_{\Delta x \to 0} \frac{cf(x + \Delta x) - cf(x)}{\Delta x}$$

$$= c \lim_{\Delta x \to 0} \frac{f(x + \Delta x) - f(x)}{\Delta x} = c \frac{d}{dx} f(x)$$

This means that we can always move a constant factor from the right side of the derivative operator d/dx to the left side of the derivative operator.

$$\frac{d}{dx} 20x^{15} = 20 \frac{d}{dx} x^{15} \quad \text{and} \quad \frac{d}{dx}(-13x^{-14}) = -13 \frac{d}{dx} x^{-14}$$

Example 35.1   If $f(x) = 20x^3$, find $f'(x)$.

Solution $f'(x)$ means the same thing as dy/dx. The derivative of x^3 is $3x^2$, and the derivative of 20 times x^3 is 20 times $3x^2$.

$$f'(x) = \frac{d}{dx} 20x^3 = 20 \frac{d}{dx} x^3 = 20(3x^2) = \mathbf{60x^2}$$

It is not necessary to write the two steps, as we can find this derivative in one step by mentally multiplying the coefficient 20 by the exponent 3 and reducing the exponent by 1.

$$f'(x) = \frac{d}{dx} 20x^3 = \mathbf{60x^2}$$

Example 35.2   Find $f'(x)$ and $g'(x)$ if: *(a)* $f(x) = 3x^{\sqrt{2}}$ *(b)* $g(x) = -14x^{-5}$

Solution   We will mentally multiply the exponent by the coefficient, reduce the exponent by 1, and write the answer in one step.

(a) $f'(x) = \dfrac{d}{dx} 3x^{\sqrt{2}} = \mathbf{3\sqrt{2}\ x^{\sqrt{2}-1}}$ *(b)* $g'(x) = \dfrac{d}{dx}(-14x^{-5}) = \mathbf{70x^{-6}}$

35.B
The derivatives of sums and differences

The rule for the derivative of the sum or the difference of two linear functions is applicable to all functions. We can get a feel for this rule by considering two particular linear functions. The slope of the graph of $f(x) = 2x$ is 2. The slope of the graph of $g(x) = 10x$ is 10. If we add the functions, we get the function $(f + g)(x) = 12x$. The slope of the graph of this function is 12, which equals the sum of the individual slopes. **The slope of the graph of the sum or difference of two functions is the sum or the difference of the individual slopes.** The slope of the graph of a function has the same value as the derivative of the function.

> The derivative of the sum or the difference of two functions equals the sum or the difference of the derivatives of the individual functions.
>
> $$\frac{d}{dx}(f + g)(x) = \frac{d}{dx} f(x) + \frac{d}{dx} g(x) = f'(x) + g'(x)$$
>
> $$\frac{d}{dx}(f - g)(x) = \frac{d}{dx} f(x) - \frac{d}{dx} g(x) = f'(x) - g'(x)$$

Example 35.3   Find $\dfrac{dy}{dx}$ if $y = 4x^{-3} - 2x^{\sqrt{2}} + 4$.

Solution   We take the derivative of each term and sum the derivatives. We remember that the derivative of 4 (or of any constant) is zero.

$$\frac{dy}{dx} = \mathbf{-12x^{-4} - 2\sqrt{2}\ x^{\sqrt{2}-1}}$$

Example 35.4   Find $f'(x)$ if $f(x) = \dfrac{3}{x^4} - 2x^\pi + \dfrac{2}{x^{-2}} + 4$.

Solution   The first step is to write $f(x)$ with no variables in the denominator.

$$f(x) = 3x^{-4} - 2x^\pi + 2x^2 + 4$$

The derivative of the sum equals the sum of the individual derivatives.

$$f'(x) = -12x^{-5} - 2\pi x^{\pi-1} + 4x$$

Example 35.5   If $s = -16t^2 + 42t$, find $\dfrac{ds}{dt}$.

Solution   The derivative of a sum equals the sum of the individual derivatives.

$$\frac{ds}{dt} = -32t + 42$$

35.C
Alternative notation

Many modern calculus books use the letter h instead of Δx in the definition of the derivative. Thus they use the notation on the right instead of the notation on the left.

$$\frac{d}{dx} f(x) = \lim_{\Delta x \to 0} \frac{f(x + \Delta x) - f(x)}{\Delta x} \qquad \frac{d}{dx} f(x) = \lim_{h \to 0} \frac{f(x + h) - f(x)}{h}$$

Example 35.6   Use the h notation of the definition of the derivative to find g' if $g(x) = \sqrt{x}$.

Solution   If we just wanted an answer, we could use the rule for the derivative of x^n and write $g'(x) = \frac{1}{2} x^{-1/2}$. Problems like this one are designed to teach the concept, not just to get the answer, so we are not going to take a shortcut. First we write

$$\frac{d}{dx} \sqrt{x} = \lim_{h \to 0} \frac{\sqrt{(x + h)} - \sqrt{x}}{h}$$

We must find a way to get the h out of the denominator so we can let h approach zero. Sometimes one algebraic procedure will work and sometimes another algebraic procedure will work. Usually a suitable procedure can be found but not always. Fortunately, in this case, if we multiply above and below by the conjugate of the numerator, we can get a numerator with a factor of h that will cancel the h in the denominator.

$$\frac{d}{dx} \sqrt{x} = \lim_{h \to 0} \frac{\sqrt{x + h} - \sqrt{x}}{h} \cdot \frac{\sqrt{x + h} + \sqrt{x}}{\sqrt{x + h} + \sqrt{x}} \qquad \text{conjugate}$$

$$= \lim_{h \to 0} \frac{x + h - \sqrt{x + h}\sqrt{x} + \sqrt{x + h}\sqrt{x} - x}{h(\sqrt{x + h} + \sqrt{x})} \qquad \text{multiplied}$$

Now when we simplify the numerator, we get

$$\frac{d}{dx} \sqrt{x} = \lim_{h \to 0} \frac{h}{h(\sqrt{x + h} + \sqrt{x})} = \lim_{h \to 0} \frac{1}{\sqrt{x + h} + \sqrt{x}} \qquad \text{canceled } h$$

In this expression we still have an h in the denominator, but h is not a factor of the denominator, so h can approach zero without causing the denominator to approach zero. Thus

$$\frac{d}{dx}\sqrt{x} = \lim_{h\to 0}\frac{1}{\sqrt{x+h}+\sqrt{x}} = \frac{1}{\sqrt{x}+\sqrt{x}}$$

$$= \frac{1}{2\sqrt{x}} = \frac{1}{2}x^{-1/2} \qquad \text{simplified}$$

This is the same result we could have obtained by using the rule for the derivative of x^n.

35.D
Proof of the derivative of a sum (optional)

This proof is straightforward. We will use the definition of the derivative and a few basic algebraic manipulations. We want to show that the derivative of a sum of two functions equals the sum of the individual derivatives. We want to show that

$$\frac{d}{dx}[f(x) + g(x)] = \frac{d}{dx}f(x) + \frac{d}{dx}g(x)$$

First we will use the definition of the derivative to define the sum of the derivative of $f(x)$ and the derivative of $g(x)$.

$$\frac{d}{dx}f(x) + \frac{d}{dx}g(x) = \lim_{\Delta x\to 0}\frac{f(x+\Delta x)-f(x)}{\Delta x} + \lim_{\Delta x\to 0}\frac{g(x+\Delta x)-g(x)}{\Delta x} \qquad (1)$$

Next we will write the definition of the derivative of $f(x) + g(x)$ and see if we can rearrange this expression into the form of the expression (1) above.

$$\frac{d}{dx}(f(x) + g(x)) = \lim_{\Delta x\to 0}\frac{[f(x+\Delta x)+g(x+\Delta x)]-[f(x)+g(x)]}{\Delta x}$$

Now we rearrange the numerator and write this expression as the sum of two fractions.

$$= \lim_{\Delta x\to 0}\left[\frac{f(x+\Delta x)-f(x)}{\Delta x} + \frac{g(x+\Delta x)-g(x)}{\Delta x}\right]$$

But the limit of a sum equals the sum of the individual limits, so we can write

$$= \lim_{\Delta x\to 0}\frac{f(x+\Delta x)-f(x)}{\Delta x} + \lim_{\Delta x\to 0}\frac{g(x+\Delta x)-g(x)}{\Delta x}$$

This is the same expression as equation (1) above and equals the sum of the individual derivatives. So we have our proof.

$$\frac{d}{dx}[f(x) + g(x)] = \frac{d}{dx}f(x) + \frac{d}{dx}g(x)$$

The proof of the derivative of the difference of two functions is exactly the same except that the sign between the functions is a minus sign instead of a plus sign.

Problem set 35

1. Express the distance between a point (x, y) on the graph of $y = x^2$ and the point $(3, 4)$ entirely in terms of x.

2. If $f(x) = \frac{1}{5}x^5 + 5x^{-2} + 6x^4 + 3$, find $f'(x)$.

3. If $y = \frac{4}{u^2} - 3\sqrt{u}$, find $\frac{dy}{du}$.

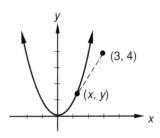

4. If $s(t) = v_0 t + \frac{1}{2} at^2$ (a and v_0 are constants), find $s'(t)$.

5. Use the definition

$$f'(x) = \lim_{h \to 0} \frac{f(x + h) - f(x)}{h}$$

   to calculate $f'(x)$ when $f(x) = \sqrt{x}$.

6. An inverted right circular cone is partially filled with liquid as shown. Find the volume of the liquid if the diameter of the base of the cone is 4 cm, the height of the cone is 6 cm, and the depth of the liquid is 2 cm.

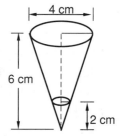

7. Find the surface area of a rectangular solid whose height is h, whose width is w, and whose length is L.

8. Write the key identities for practice, and then develop an identity for $\tan 2A$. If A is a number such that $\tan A = \frac{1}{2}$, find the value of $\tan 2A$.

9. Find the three cube roots of 1 and express each of the roots in rectangular form. (All numbers should be exact.)

10. Find the values of θ which lie between 0 and 2π for which $\cos 3\theta = -1$.

11. Write the equation $x^2 - 4x - y^2 = 0$ in standard form and fully describe this conic section.

12. Factor $x^2 - x + 4$ over the set of complex numbers.

13. Suppose $f(x) = e^x$ and $g(x) = f(x - 1)$. Graph both f and g on the same coordinate plane.

14. Determine on which intervals the function $f(x) = \dfrac{1}{x - 3} + 2$ is increasing.

15. Find all values of x for which $\log_2 (x - 3) > 1$.

16. Find all values of x for which $\ln (3x + 2) - \ln (2x - 1) = \ln 5$.

17. Show on a number line those intervals on which f is positive and on which f is negative, where

$$f(x) = x(x - 2)(x + 4)(x + 1)$$

18. Show that: $\dfrac{2 \cos x}{\sin 2x} \csc (-x) = -\csc^2 x$

19. Solve for k: $e^{9k} = 2$

CONCEPT REVIEW 20. If P lies outside circle O and $\overline{PA}$ and $\overline{PB}$ are two line segments which are tangent to points A and B on circle O, respectively, compare: *A.* length of $\overline{PA}$ *B.* length of $\overline{PB}$

21. If $\overline{BD}$ is the angle bisector of $\angle ABC$ as shown and $AB = x$, $BC = a$, $AD = c$, and $DC = a + b$, find x in terms of a, b, and c.

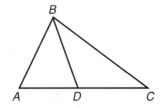

LESSON 36 *Exponential growth and decay*

Exponential equations of the form

$$A_t = A_0 e^{kt}$$

are important because exponential equations can be used to help us understand everyday problems such as the growth of bacteria in biology, the voltage on a capacitor in engineering, radioactive decay in physics, and the growth of money in banking. The independent variable is t and is plotted on the horizontal axis. The dependent variable is A_t and is plotted on the vertical axis. The letters A_0 and k are constants whose values must be determined for each problem. Real-world problems often begin when time equals zero, so negative time has no meaning in these problems. Thus, the graphs begin when t is zero.

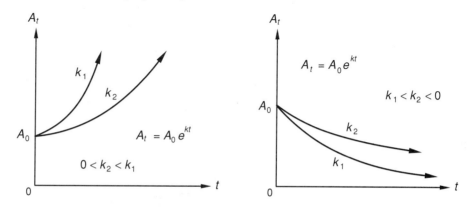

We use A_0 to designate the value of A_t when time is zero and call this value the *initial value* or the *initial amount.* In the left-hand figure, A_t equals A_0 when time is zero, and A_t increases as time increases because k is positive. In the right-hand figure, A_t equals A_0 when time is zero and decreases as time increases because k is negative. In each figure, the curves show that the change is faster for k_1 than for k_2. This is true if $|k_1|$ is greater than $|k_2|$.

We remember that direct and inverse variation problems are two-step problems and that the first step is to solve for the value of the constant of proportionality k. Exponential growth or decay problems are also two-step problems in which the first step is to solve for the value of the constant k in the exponent. We will solve for k first by taking the logarithm of both sides of the equation. Next we will replace k in the equation with the proper value.

Then we will do the second part of the solution. **If time is given and the amount is the unknown, a simple evaluation is required. If the amount is given and time is the unknown, we must again take the logarithm of both sides to find t.** The scientific calculator will enable you to find accurate solutions to these problems quickly.

Example 36.1   The number of bacteria present at noon was 400, and 9 hours later the bacteria numbered 800. Assume exponential growth and find the number of bacteria present at noon the next day.

Solution   We begin by writing the exponential equation for the number of bacteria present at some time t. We use the symbol A_t to represent this number.

$$A_t = A_0 e^{kt}$$

For this problem, time began at noon. The number of bacteria was 400 when time equaled 0 (noon), so $A_0 = 400$. Now we have

$$A_t = 400e^{kt}$$

Solving for k always requires that we take the natural logarithm of both sides of the equation. To solve for k, we use 9 for t and 800 for A_t. Next we divide both sides of the equation by 400 to isolate the exponential. Then we take the natural logarithm of both sides so we can solve for k. Then we use this value of k in the equation.

$$A_t = 400e^{kt} \qquad \text{equation}$$
$$800 = 400e^{9k} \qquad \text{substituted}$$
$$2 = e^{9k} \qquad \text{divided by 400}$$
$$\ln 2 = \ln e^{9k} \qquad \text{ln of both sides}$$
$$0.693 = 9k \qquad \text{evaluated}$$
$$0.077 = k \qquad \text{solved for } k$$
$$A_t = 400e^{0.077t} \qquad \text{replaced } k \text{ with } 0.077$$

Now that we have k, we can complete the second part of the solution. We are asked for A_{24}, which is the value of A_t when $t = 24$. All that is required is an evaluation of the exponential when t is replaced with 24.

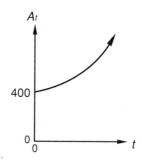

$$A_{24} = 400e^{0.077(24)} \qquad \text{substituted}$$
$$A_{24} = 400e^{1.848} \qquad \text{simplified}$$
$$\mathbf{A_{24} = 2540} \qquad \text{evaluated and rounded}$$

The sketch shown at the right is accurate enough for most purposes. It shows that time is plotted horizontally and the amount is plotted vertically. It also shows the amount when time equals zero and indicates that the amount increases exponentially as time increases.

Example 36.2 The number of bacteria present when the experiment began was 1200. After 100 hours there were 2700 bacteria present. Assume exponential growth and find the time required for the number of bacteria to increase to 30,000. Sketch the curve.

Solution First we must find the constant k for this problem and insert this number into the equation in place of k. We begin with the equation and use 1200 for A_0. Next we replace A_t with 2700 and t with 100. Then we divide to isolate the exponential and take the natural logarithm of both sides to solve for k.

$$A_t = 1200e^{kt} \qquad \text{used 1200 for } A_0$$
$$2700 = 1200e^{100k} \qquad \text{substituted}$$
$$2.25 = e^{100k} \qquad \text{divided by 1200}$$
$$\ln 2.25 = \ln e^{100k} \qquad \text{ln of both sides}$$
$$0.81093 = 100k \qquad \text{evaluated}$$

$$0.00811 = k \qquad \text{solved for } k$$

$$A_t = 1200e^{0.00811t} \qquad \text{substituted}$$

Now that we have the value for k, we can solve for the time when the amount present is 30,000. **To solve for t, we must again take the natural logarithm of both sides of the equation.**

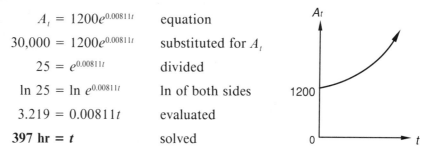

$$A_t = 1200e^{0.00811t} \qquad \text{equation}$$

$$30{,}000 = 1200e^{0.00811t} \qquad \text{substituted for } A_t$$

$$25 = e^{0.00811t} \qquad \text{divided}$$

$$\ln 25 = \ln e^{0.00811t} \qquad \text{ln of both sides}$$

$$3.219 = 0.00811t \qquad \text{evaluated}$$

$$\mathbf{397 \ hr = t} \qquad \text{solved}$$

The sketch shown is adequate. It shows the initial amount and indicates that the amount increases exponentially as time increases.

Example 36.3   The amount of substance initially present was 400 grams, and after 90 hours only 380 grams remained. Assume an exponential decrease and determine the half-life of the substance. Make a sketch of the graph.

Solution   The **half-life** is the time required for the amount to decrease to half the original amount. Thus, we are asked to find the time required for the amount present to decrease from 400 grams to 200 grams. **We begin, as always, by substituting, isolating the exponential, and then taking the natural logarithm of both sides to find k.**

$$A_t = 400e^{kt} \qquad \text{equation}$$

$$380 = 400e^{90k} \qquad \text{substituted}$$

$$0.95 = e^{90k} \qquad \text{divided}$$

$$-0.051 = 90k \qquad \text{ln of both sides}$$

$$-0.00057 = k \qquad \text{solved}$$

$$A_t = 400e^{-0.00057t} \qquad \text{substituted}$$

Now that we have a value for k, we can solve for the time required to have only 200 grams left.

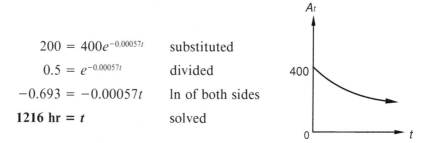

$$200 = 400e^{-0.00057t} \qquad \text{substituted}$$

$$0.5 = e^{-0.00057t} \qquad \text{divided}$$

$$-0.693 = -0.00057t \qquad \text{ln of both sides}$$

$$\mathbf{1216 \ hr = t} \qquad \text{solved}$$

The graph shows all that we want to know. It shows the amount when $t = 0$ and indicates that the amount decreases exponentially with time. The amount present always decreases with time when k is a negative number. It is helpful to remember that half-life problems are solved by first finding k. When we work a half-life problem, we will find that we always get the equation $0.5 = e^{kt}$.

Problem set 36

1. The weight of the bag grew exponentially. At noon the bag weighed 150 grams, and 1 hour later the bag weighed 200 grams. How much would the bag weigh at 3 p.m.?

2. The area of the spot decreased exponentially. At midnight the area of the spot was 1 square centimeter (cm²), and 2 hours later the area of the spot was 0.8 cm². How long after midnight would the area of the spot be 0.5 cm²?

3. If $f(t) = \dfrac{\sqrt{2}}{t^2} + 3t^{-3}$ find $f'(t)$.

4. If $y = 3x^4 - \dfrac{2}{\sqrt{x}} + 2$, find $\dfrac{dy}{dx}$.

5. If $y = 2u^2 - \dfrac{\sqrt[3]{u}}{3} + c$, find $D_u y$.

6. Use the definition

$$f'(x) = \lim_{h \to 0} \frac{f(x + h) - f(x)}{h}$$

to find $f'(x)$ if $f(x) = -\dfrac{1}{x}$.

7. Write the key identities and develop an identity for $\tan(A - B)$. Then use this identity for the tangent function to compute the exact value of $\tan 15°$. [*Hint*: $\tan 15° = \tan(60° - 45°)$.]

8. Find the surface area of a right circular cone whose volume is 12π cm³ and whose base has an area of 9π cm².

9. Write the three cube roots of -1 in rectangular form. (All numbers should be exact.)

10. Find all values of x for which $0 \le x < 2\pi$ and $\tan 3\theta = 1$.

11. Write the equation $y^2 - 4x^2 - 16 = 0$ in standard form, and fully describe this conic section.

12. Factor $2x^2 + 3x + 5$ over the set of complex numbers.

13. Express the equation $y = \log_2 x$ entirely in terms of the natural logarithm.

14. Write the equation of the ellipse whose center is $(-2, 3)$ and whose major axis is vertical and is 4 units long and whose minor axis is 2 units long.

15. Find those real values of x for which $2 \log_2 x + \log_2 9 = 1$.

16. Find the coordinates of the focus and the equation of the directrix of the parabola whose equation is $(y - 1)^2 = -16(x + 2)$.

17. Write the key identities for practice, and then develop an expression that gives $\sin^2 A$ as a function of $\cos 2A$. Then find $\sin^2 x$ if $\cos 2x = \frac{1}{3}$.

18. Sketch the graph of $y = -|\sin x|$.

19. If $f(x) = 2 + \sin x$ and $g(x) = f\left(x - \dfrac{\pi}{4}\right)$, sketch the graph of g.

20. Find the distance from the midpoint of the line segment whose endpoints are $(2, 1)$ and $(4, 5)$ to the line whose equation is $x - y + 1 = 0$.

CONCEPT REVIEW

21. Find the number of diagonals which can be drawn for a six-sided regular polygon.

22. Find the sum of the first 100 positive integers.

LESSON 37 *Derivative of e^x and ln $|x|$ · Derivative of sin x and cos x*

37.A
Derivative of e^x and ln $|x|$

The slope of the graph of $y = e^x$ is e^x. In the graph on the left, we note that when $x = 0.5$, the value of the function is $e^{0.5}$, or 1.649, and that the slope of the graph is also 1.649. This lovely relationship between the value of the function and the slope of the graph of the function (the derivative) makes e^x an easy function to use in calculus.

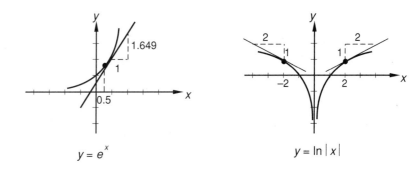

$$y = e^x$$

$$y = \ln |x|$$

The natural logarithm function is also a friendly function. We show the graph of $y = \ln |x|$ on the right. The slope of this graph at any value of x is $\frac{1}{x}$. Thus, when $x = 2$, the slope of the graph of the function is $\frac{1}{2}$, and when $x = -2$, the slope is $-\frac{1}{2}$.

The derivative of e^x is e^x.   The derivative of ln $|x|$ is $\dfrac{1}{x}$.

$$\frac{d}{dx} e^x = e^x \qquad\qquad \frac{d}{dx} \ln |x| = \frac{1}{x}$$

The derivative of ln x is $\frac{1}{x}$. The derivative of ln $(-x)$ is $\frac{1}{-x}$. The derivative of ln $|x|$ is $\frac{1}{x}$. The function $y = \ln x$ is defined only for positive values of x. The function $y = \ln (-x)$ is defined only for negative values of x. The function $y = \ln |x|$ is defined for all positive and negative values of x and is the most comprehensive form of the natural logarithm function. We do not need to discuss the derivative of $y = e^{|x|}$ because $y = e^x$ is defined for all real values of x. We will use the definition of the derivative to prove these rules in a later lesson.

Example 37.1 Find $\dfrac{dy}{dx}$ if $y = 4 \ln x - 6e^x + 2x^2$.

Solution The derivative of a sum equals the sum of the individual derivatives. Thus,

$$\frac{dy}{dx} = \frac{4}{x} - 6e^x + 4x$$

Example 37.2 Find dy/dx if $y = 4 \ln |x| - 6e^x + 2x^2$, and tell how this derivative is different from the derivative of Example 37.1.

Solution   The algebraic expression for the derivative is the same, because the derivative of 4 ln $|x|$ and the derivative of 4 ln x are both $\frac{4}{x}$.

$$\frac{dy}{dx} = \frac{4}{x} - 6e^x + 4x$$

The difference is that both the function and the derivative in this problem are defined for both positive and negative values of x, while the function and the derivative in the preceding problem were defined only for positive values of x.

37.B
Derivative of sin x and cos x

The derivatives of sin x and cos x are also easy to remember. **If x is measured in radians,** the slope of the sine function for any value of x equals the value of cos x. **If x is measured in radians,** the slope of the cosine function for any value of x equals the value of $-\sin x$.

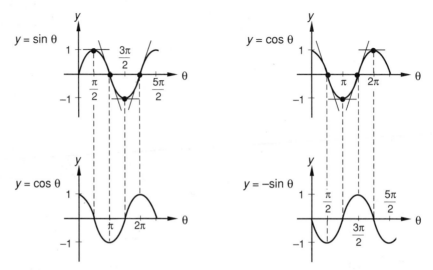

In the figures, the slope of the uppermost graph at any value of x equals the value of the function in the graph below for that same value of x. In the top graph on the left we note that the slope of sin x is zero when x equals $\pi/2$ and $3\pi/2$. In the graph just below we see that the value of cos x is zero when x equals $\pi/2$ and $3\pi/2$. The slope of the graph of $y = \sin x$ is $+1$ when x equals 0 and is -1 when x equals π. The value of cos x is $+1$ when x equals 0 and -1 when x equals π. This correspondence between the slope of the graph of $y = \sin x$ and the value of cos x occurs for every value of x if x is measured in radians.

We have drawn tangent lines at four places in the top graph on the right. The slopes of these tangents to the graph of $y = \cos x$ equal the values of $-\sin x$, as we see in the graph below. This correspondence between the slope of the graph of $y = \cos x$ and the value of $-\sin x$ occurs for every value of x.

Since the slope of the graph equals the rate of change of the function, which we call the derivative, we have the following rules.

The derivative of sin x with respect to x is cos x.	The derivative of cos x with respect to x is $-\sin x$.
$$\frac{d}{dx} \sin x = \cos x$$	$$\frac{d}{dx} \cos x = -\sin x$$

We will use the definition of the derivative to prove these rules in a later lesson.

Example 37.3 Find the derivative of $y = 3 \sin x - \cos x + 2e^x$.

Solution The derivative of a sum is the sum of the individual derivatives.

$$\frac{dy}{dx} = 3 \cos x + \sin x + 2e^x$$

Example 37.4 Find the derivative of $y = -3 \cos x + 3 \ln x - 2 \sin x$.

Solution The derivative of a sum is the sum of the individual derivatives.

$$\frac{dy}{dx} = 3 \sin x + \frac{3}{x} - 2 \cos x$$

Problem set 37

1. The volume of the balloon increased exponentially. At 1 p.m. the volume of the balloon was 100 cm³, and 2 hours later the volume of the balloon was 300 cm³. What time was it when the volume of the balloon was 400 cm³?

2. At present, Blanche is K times as old as Pearl. In 10 years, Blanche will be M times as old as Pearl will be then. State Blanche's age now in terms of K and M.

3. Find $\dfrac{dy}{du}$ if $y = \ln u - 2e^u + \sqrt{u}$.

4. Find $D_x y$ if $y = 2 \sin x + 14e^x - \dfrac{14}{x}$.

5. Find $s'(t)$ if $s(t) = x_0 + v_0 t + \frac{1}{2}at^2$ (x_0, v_0, and a are constants).

6. Find $f'(x)$ if $f(x) = 3e^x - 4 \cos x - \frac{1}{4} \ln |x|$.

7. If A and B are numbers such that $\sin A = \frac{3}{5}$ and $\sin B = \frac{4}{5}$, find $\cos A$ and $\cos B$ if both $\cos A$ and $\cos B$ are positive.

8. Write the key identities for practice, and develop an identity for $\tan(A - B)$. Then, if A and B are as defined in Problem 7, find the value of $\tan(A - B)$.

9. Find the total surface area of a right circular cylinder whose volume is 9π cm³ and whose height is 1 cm.

10. Write the equation $x^2 - y^2 - 2x - 4y - 4 = 0$ in standard form and fully describe this conic section.

11. Sketch the graph of the function $y = \sin x$. Then change the equation so that the graph would be shifted 2 units up and $\pi/4$ units to the right.

12. Use the definition of a derivative to compute $D_x y$ where $y = -3x^2$.

13. Evaluate: $\displaystyle\lim_{x \to \infty} \frac{2x - 3x^2 + 4}{2x^2 + 14}$

14. Find all values of x which satisfy the equation $\sin^2 x + 2 \cos x - 2 = 0$, where $0 \le x < 2\pi$.

15. Sketch the graphs of $y = 2^x$ and $y = \log_2 x$ on the same coordinate plane.

16. Find an expression involving only natural logarithms which expresses the exact value of x where $4 = 3^x$.

17. Sketch the graphs of $y = e^x$, $y = e^{-x}$, and $y = -e^x$ on the same coordinate plane.

18. Solve for the value of x in terms of L in the figure shown.

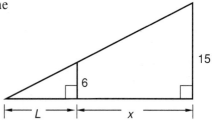

19. State the converse of the following statement: If a function f has a derivative at $x = a$, then the function is continuous at $x = a$.

CONCEPT REVIEW   20. Find the area of the triangle whose sides have lengths 5, 7, and 10. [*Note:* Heron's formula states that a triangle whose sides have lengths a, b, and c has area $\sqrt{s(s - a)(s - b)(s - c)}$, where $s = \frac{1}{2}(a + b + c)$.]

21. A parallelogram is placed on the plane so that one of its vertices is placed at the origin and one of its sides lies on the x axis. The coordinates of all four vertices are as shown. Find the midpoint of the line segment which joins (b, c) and $(a, 0)$ and find the midpoint which joins $(0, 0)$ and $(a + b, c)$. Explain the significance of your answer.

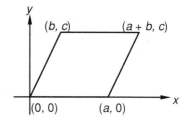

LESSON 38   *Equation of the tangent line · Higher-order derivatives*

38.A
Equation of the tangent line

The slope of the tangent to a curve at a designated value of x can be found by evaluating the derivative at that value of x.

Example 38.1   If $y = x^2 - 4x + 3$, compute $\left.\dfrac{dy}{dx}\right|_3$.

Solution   The vertical line with the small 3 next to it as shown is the notation we use to indicate that the derivative should be evaluated at an x value of 3. If we use functional notation to write the same problem, we would say "If $f(x) = x^2 - 4x + 3$, find $f'(3)$."

$$\frac{dy}{dx} = 2x - 4 \qquad \left.\frac{dy}{dx}\right|_3 = 2(3) - 4 = \mathbf{2}$$

Example 38.2   Find the equation of the line tangent to the graph of $y = x^2 - 4x + 3$ when $x = 3$.

Solution   We can find the equation of a line if we know the coordinates of a point on the line and the slope of the line. For this problem we know the tangent touches the graph when $x = 3$. We let x equal 3 and solve for y to get

$$y = (3)^2 - 4(3) + 3 = 0$$

Thus the point $(3, 0)$ is on the curve and on the line. To find the slope when $x = 3$, we find $f'(3)$.

$$f'(x) = 2x - 4$$
$$f'(3) = 2(3) - 4 = 2$$

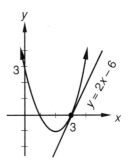

$y = 2x + b$	slope is $+ 2$
$0 = 2(3) + b$	passes through $(3, 0)$
$-6 = b$	solved for b
$y = 2x - 6$	equation of tangent

Example 38.3   Find the equation of the line that is tangent to $y = e^x$ when $x = 0.8$.

Solution   We will use a calculator on this one. When $x = 0.8$, the value of the function is $e^{0.8}$, or 2.23. The slope of this lovely function is everywhere equal to the value of the function. Thus the tangent line passes through $(0.8, 2.23)$ and has a slope of 2.23.

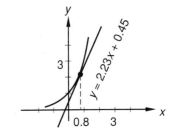

$y = 2.23x + b$	slope is 2.23
$2.23 = 2.23(0.8) + b$	substituted $(0.8, 2.23)$
$b = 0.45$	solved
$y = 2.23x + 0.45$	equation

Example 38.4   Find the equation of the line tangent to $f(x) = \sin x$ when $x = 1$.

Solution   Be sure to have the calculator set on radians for this problem. The point on the line will be $(1, f(1))$ and the slope will be $f'(1)$.

$$f(x) = \sin x \qquad f'(x) = \cos x$$
$$\sin (1) = 0.84 \qquad \cos (1) = 0.54$$

Thus the tangent has a slope of 0.54 and passes through the point $(1, 0.84)$.

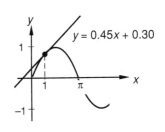

$y = 0.54x + b$	slope is 0.54
$0.84 = 0.54(1) + b$	$(1, 0.84)$
$b = 0.30$	solved
$y = 0.54x + 0.30$	equation

38.B
Higher-order derivatives

If a function is differentiable, its derivative is another function called the *first derivative.* If the first derivative is differentiable, its derivative is a function called the *second derivative.* If the second derivative is differentiable, its derivative is a function called the *third derivative,* etc.

FUNCTION	FIRST DERIVATIVE	SECOND DERIVATIVE	THIRD DERIVATIVE
$f(x)$ or y	$f'(x)$ or $\dfrac{dy}{dx}$	$f''(x)$ or $\dfrac{d^2y}{dx^2}$	$f'''(x)$ or $\dfrac{d^3y}{dx^3}$

We read the notations for the second derivative as "function double prime of x" or as "dee squared y dee x squared." We read the notations for the third derivative as "function triple prime of x" or as "dee cubed y dee x cubed."

Example 38.5   If $y = 3u^5$, find $\dfrac{d^2y}{du^2}\Big|_2$.

Solution   We find the first derivative and then find the derivative of the first derivative.

$$y = 3u^5 \longrightarrow \frac{dy}{du} = 15u^4 \longrightarrow \frac{d^2y}{du^2} = 60u^3$$

Now we evaluate $60u^3$ when $u = 2$.

$$60u^3\Big|_2 = 60(2)^3 = \mathbf{480}$$

Example 38.6   If $f(x) = \dfrac{1}{x^2}$, find $f'''(2)$.

Solution   We rewrite the function as $f(x) = x^{-2}$ and take the derivative three times.

$$f'(x) = -2x^{-3} \longrightarrow f''(x) = 6x^{-4} \longrightarrow f'''(x) = -24x^{-5}$$

If we evaluate $-24x^{-5}$ when $x = 2$, we get

$$-24x^{-5}\Big|_2 = \frac{-24}{(2)^5} = \frac{-24}{32} = -\frac{3}{4}$$

Problem set 38

1. The assets increased exponentially. After 1 year in business, the assets were worth \$1,530,000, and after 3 years in business, the assets were worth \$3 million. What was the value of the assets after 7 years in business?

Differentiate the functions of Problems 2 and 3.

2. $y = \dfrac{1}{\sqrt{x^3}} - \dfrac{1}{3}e^x + 4 \cos x$ 3. $f(x) = \dfrac{1}{x} + 2 \ln |x| - 3 \sin x$

Differentiate as many times as necessary to solve Problems 4 and 5.

4. Find $\dfrac{d^3y}{dx^3}$ if $y = 3e^x - 2x^3$.   5. Find $f''(t)$ if $f(t) = 3 \sin t + \ln t$.

6. If $f(x) = \ln |x|$, approximate $f''(-14)$ to two decimal places.

7. Approximate to two decimal places the slope of the tangent line which can be drawn to the graph of $y = 2 \sin x - \cos x$ at $x = -1$.

8. Find the equation of the tangent line which can be drawn to the graph of

$y = 2e^x$ at $x = 2$. (Use a calculator as necessary to write all numbers to two decimal places.)

9. Write the key identities for practice, and then develop an identity for tan $2A$.

10. Write the key identities and develop an expression that gives $\cos^2 \theta$ as a function of $\cos 2\theta$.

11. Express the five fifth roots of $-i$ in polar form.

12. Find all values of x, where $0° \le x < 360°$, which satisfy the following equation: $\sin 4\theta + 1 = 0$.

13. Write the equation $4y^2 - 9x^2 - 8y - 32 = 0$ in standard form and fully describe this conic section.

14. Find all real values of x for which $\log_2 (x - 2) < 2$.

15. Approximate the value of $\log_3 5$ to two decimal places.

16. Find the domain and range of f and g where $f(x) = \sqrt{x - 1}$ and $g(x) = x^2$.

17. If f and g are as defined in Problem 16, write the equation of $f \circ g$ and determine the domain and range of $f \circ g$.

18. Use interval notation to designate those intervals on which the graph of f lies above the x axis if $f(x) = (2 - x)(x + 3)(x - 1)$.

19. Graph the function $y = \dfrac{x^2 - 1}{x - 1}$ and find: $\lim\limits_{x \to 1} \dfrac{x^2 - 1}{x - 1}$

20. Use the rational zero theorem to aid in finding all the zeros of the equation $f(x) = x^3 - 2x^2 - 5x + 6$.

21. Find the equation of the quadratic function which has zeros at $x = 1$ and $x = -2$ and whose graph has a y intercept at $y = -4$.

CONCEPT REVIEW   22. Find x in the figure shown.

23. If $x - y = 4$ and $xy = 3$, find the value of $x^2 + y^2$.

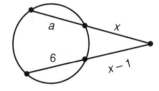

LESSON 39 *Graphs of rational functions II · A special limit*

39.A
Poles and zeros

The graph of a function touches the x axis at every value of x for which the function y or $f(x)$ equals zero. These values of x are called the *zeros* of the function. We do not know the equation for the function graphed on the left on page 200, but we see that the graph touches the x axis at x values of -2, $+2$, 6, and 8, so these numbers are zeros of this function. **The value of a function can be zero only for values of x that cause the numerator of the function to equal zero.** Thus, the function $1/(x - 2)$

graphed on the right has no zeros, and the graph of the function can never touch the x axis because the numerator of this function is 1. The number 1 always equals 1 and 1 never equals 0.

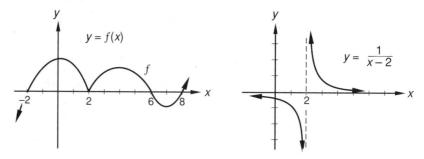

However, the denominator of the function on the right equals zero when $x = 2$, and thus the value of the function is not defined when $x = 2$. We say that 2 is a *pole* of the function because it makes the denominator of the function equal zero. There is a *vertical asymptote* at every pole on the graph of a function if the numerator does not have a zero at that value of x.

39.B
Rational functions II

A *rational function* is a fraction of polynomials such as

$$f(x) = \frac{a_1 x^3 + a_2 x^2 + a_3 x + a_4}{b_1 x^4 + b_2 x^3 + b_3 x^2 + b_4 x + b_5}$$

We remember that every polynomial of degree n can be factored into the product of a constant and exactly n linear factors of the form $(x + a)$, where a can be complex. We will restrict this discussion to polynomials whose linear factors are all real linear factors. Thus, it is possible to factor the numerator into a product of a constant k_1 and three linear factors of the form $(x + a)$. The denominator can be factored into the product of k_2 and four linear factors.

$$f(x) = \frac{k_1(x + a)(x + b)(x + c)}{k_2(x + d)(x + c)(x + f)(x + g)}$$

The zeros of the numerator are the zeros of the function, and the zeros of the denominator are the poles of the function.
We begin our investigation of the graphs of rational functions by considering the special case of functions that are factored into linear real factors that occur only once each and that have more factors in the denominator than in the numerator. This last stipulation will ensure that the x axis is the horizontal asymptote.
Since a rational function that is composed of unique nonrepeating linear factors changes signs at every zero of the numerator and the denominator, the graph must cross the x axis at every zero and must jump across the x axis at every pole.
The graphs of these functions can be sketched quickly if we begin by drawing vertical dotted lines at the poles and placing dots on the x axis at the zeros. Next we determine whether the function is positive or negative for large positive values of x. Then we work our way from right to left, crossing the x axis at the zeros and going off the paper vertically at the poles.
Suppose we have a function that has a small positive value when x is a large positive number, and the zeros and the vertical asymptotes are as shown at the top of the following page.

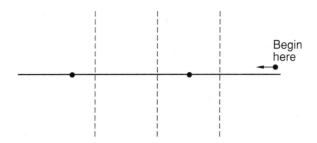

We will begin on the right at a small positive value of *y* and move to the left. The graph cannot cross the *x* axis because there is no zero, so it goes off the figure vertically at the asymptote.

The graph went off the figure in the up direction at the right asymptote. Thus, the graph must reappear from the down direction on the left side of this asymptote. It sees a crossing point, so it crosses and goes off the figure again in the up direction.

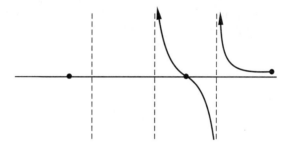

Now it must reappear from the down direction on the left side of the second asymptote. This time it sees no zero, so it must not touch the *x* axis. Thus, it turns around and goes back down. We will find ways to determine exactly where the graph turns around later in the book. For now we just guess.

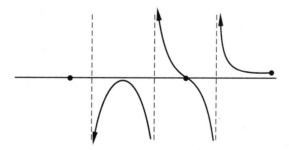

The graph must reappear on the left side of the left asymptote from above. Then it crosses at the zero and then comes back to approach the horizontal asymptote, which is the *x* axis.

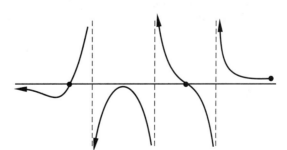

Example 39.1   Graph $f(x) = -\dfrac{x(x-7)}{(x+5)(x+2)(x-2)(x-5)}$.

Solution   First we plot the zeros and the vertical asymptotes.

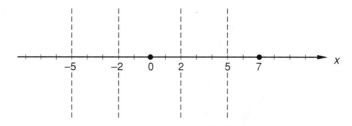

Next we must determine the starting point for the right end of the graph. The term of highest degree in a polynomial is the dominant term, because for large absolute values of x, the value of the highest-degree term will be greater than the absolute value of the sum of all the other terms in the polynomial. Thus, if x is a large positive number, we can estimate the value of a rational function whose denominator is of higher degree than the numerator by considering only the lead terms in the numerator and denominator as shown.

$$f(x) = -\frac{x^2 + \text{(other terms)}}{x^4 + \text{(other terms)}}$$

As x takes on larger and larger positive values, both x^2 and x^4 are large positive numbers, and since x^4 is in the denominator and since there is a minus sign in front, the value of the fraction is a small negative number. This gives us our starting point on the right end of the graph.

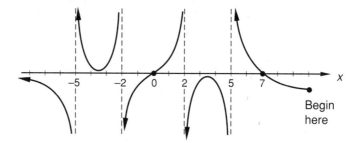

Example 39.2   Sketch $y = \dfrac{(x+5)(x-3)(x-1)}{(x-4)(x+2)(x+4)(x-1)}$.

Solution   First we simplify the expression by canceling the $x - 1$ factors above and below, and we will remember to put a hole in the graph when $x = 1$ because the function is not defined at that point. Then we plot the zeros and the vertical asymptotes. We begin our sketch on the right end by noting that when x is a large positive number, y is a small positive number because the ratio of the lead polynomial terms is $+x^2/x^3$.

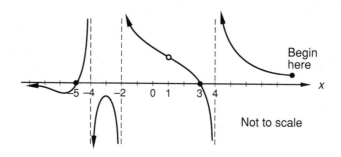

39.C
A special limit

Consider the following limits:

$$(a) \ \lim_{x \to 0} \frac{1}{x} \qquad (b) \ \lim_{x \to 0} \frac{-1}{x^2} \qquad (c) \ \lim_{x \to 0} \frac{4x + 8}{x + 2} \qquad (d) \ \lim_{x \to 3} \frac{x^2 - 9}{x - 3}$$

Limit (a) does not exist because the left-hand limit does not equal the right-hand limit. Limit (b) is $-\infty$. Limit (c) is 8 divided by 2 and equals 4. Limit (d) is 6 because the numerator is factorable. But what is the value of the following limit?

$$\lim_{h \to 0} \frac{\sin \left(\frac{\pi}{2} + h \right) - \sin \frac{\pi}{2}}{h}$$

This limit can be evaluated easily if we recognize that the expression is the definition of the derivative of $\sin x$ evaluated at $\pi/2$. The derivative of $\sin x$ can be written as follows.

$$\lim_{h \to 0} \frac{\sin (x + h) - \sin x}{h} = \cos x$$

If $x = \pi/2$, $\cos x = 0$, so this limit equals zero when $x = \pi/2$.

Authors of calculus books and people who make up standardized tests believe that students should be so familiar with the definition of the derivative that they sprinkle their work with limit problems that can be evaluated by recognition. We will do the same. The following limit problems will appear in future homework problem sets. Look for them.

$$\lim_{\Delta x \to 0} \frac{\ln (x + \Delta x) - \ln x}{\Delta x} \qquad \lim_{h \to 0} \frac{e^{x+h} - e^x}{h}$$

The limit on the left is the limit definition of the derivative of $\ln x$. The derivative of $\ln x$ is $1/x$, so the value of this limit is $1/x$. The limit on the right is the limit definition of the derivative of e^x. The derivative of e^x is e^x, so the value of this limit is e^x.

Problem set 39

1. The amount of money in the treasury was decreasing at an exponential rate. If the treasury contained $2 million on the first of the month and contained only $100 on the thirtieth of the month, during which day did the treasury contain $0.5 million?

Graph the functions of Problems 2 and 3, showing clearly all x intercepts and asymptotes. Other than these features, the graphs need not be precisely drawn.

2. $f(x) = \dfrac{(x - 2)(x + 3)}{(x - 5)(x + 2)(x - 3)}$ 3. $y = \dfrac{-x(x - 3)}{(x - 1)(x + 2)(x + 3)}$

4. Use a calculator as necessary to approximate to two decimal places the slope of the tangent line which can be drawn to the graph of $y = 2 \sin x + \cos x$ when $x = 4.2$.

5. Find the equation of the tangent line which can be drawn to the graph of the equation $y = 1/x$ at $x = 1$.

6. If $s(t) = x_0 + v_0 t + \frac{1}{2} gt^2$, find the equation of s''. The symbols x_0, v_0, and g represent constants.

Use a calculator as necessary to approximate the answers to Problems 7 and 8 to two decimal places.

7. If $y = \dfrac{1}{u}$, compute $\dfrac{d^2 y}{du^2} \bigg|_2$.

8. If $y = \frac{1}{5}e^x - 2 \cos x + 3 \ln |x|$, find $\dfrac{dy}{dx}\bigg|_2$.

9. Find the value of $\displaystyle\lim_{h \to 0} \dfrac{\sin\left(\dfrac{\pi}{2} + h\right) - \sin \dfrac{\pi}{2}}{h}$

10. Write the equation $x^2 + y^2 - 2x + 12y + 6 = 0$ in standard form and completely describe this conic section.

11. If one linear factor of $x^3 + x^2 + 2x + 2$ is $x + 1$, what are the other two linear factors?

12. Suppose f and g are functions such that $f(x) = \sqrt{x}$ and $g(x) = 1 + \sqrt{x - 2}$. Describe the graph of g in terms of the graph of f.

13. Write the standard form of the equation of the ellipse with vertices at $(0, \pm 5)$ and foci at $(0, \pm 4)$.

14. Find all real values of x for which $-2 \ln 2 + \ln (x - 2) = \ln (2x - 4)$.

15. Write the equation of the curve which is the locus of all points equidistant from the point $(2, 1)$ and the line $x = -1$.

16. Sketch the graph of f where $f(x) = \dfrac{x^2 + x - 6}{x + 3}$.

17. If f is as defined in Problem 16, compute $\displaystyle\lim_{x \to -3} f(x)$.

18. Describe the set of all integer values of x for which $|3x - 1| < 16$.

19. Show that: $\dfrac{(\sin x + \cos x)^2 - 1}{2 \sin (-x)} = -\cos x$

20. Rewrite $\dfrac{2 - \sqrt{3}}{1 - \sqrt{2}}$ so that the denominator is a rational number.

21. An arbitrarily drawn triangle is oriented on the coordinate plane so that one of its vertices lies at the origin and one of its sides lies on the x axis. The coordinates of all three vertices of the triangle are as shown. Use the midpoint formulas to find the coordinates of the midpoints shown. Write the equation of the line that passes through the midpoints. What does this imply about any line that bisects two sides of a triangle?

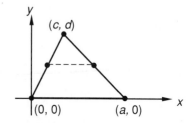

LESSON 40 *Newton and Leibniz · The differential*

40.A
Newton and Leibniz

We have defined the derivative of a function to be the limit of the ratio of the change in y to the change in x as the change in x approaches zero.

$$\frac{d}{dx} f(x) = \lim_{\Delta x \to 0} \frac{\Delta y}{\Delta x} = \lim_{\Delta x \to 0} \frac{f(x + \Delta x) - f(x)}{\Delta x}$$

Sir Isaac Newton, an Englishman, and Gottfried Wilhelm Leibniz, a German, invented calculus independently of one another in the seventeenth century. To designate the derivative of a function, Newton placed a dot over the y and wrote $\dot{y}$ (read "y dot"). Over the years the dot has changed to a prime and now we write y' (read "y prime") as Newton's designation of the derivative. The derivative as conceived by Newton and indicated by his notation $\dot{y}$ was a single entity and had no numerator or denominator.

Leibniz designated the derivative with the fractional notation $\frac{dy}{dx}$ and considered the derivative to be a fraction of very small quantities dy and dx which he called *infinitesimals* and which he moved about by using the rules of algebra. Leibniz could multiply $\frac{dy}{dx}$ by dx and get dy by canceling the dx above and the dx below as we show here.

$$\frac{dy}{d\!\!\!/x} \, d\!\!\!/x = dy$$

Many scientists prefer the notation of Leibniz because it facilitates the solution of practical problems whose solutions would be more difficult using the notation of Newton. In this book we will use both notations. We will use the notation of Leibniz often because this notation is easier for the beginner to understand. It is easy to think of $\frac{dy}{dx}$ as meaning almost the same thing as a very, very small Δy over a very, very small Δx. In the next section we will show that dy can have a meaning all by itself and dx can have a meaning all by itself; so this thought process is acceptable.

40.B
The differential

The slope of the graph of a function at a point has the same value as the derivative of the function at that point. In the figure on the left, if we begin at P_2 and move to P_1, the change in x is Δx and the change in y is Δy. We would like to show that in the limit, as P_2 moves closer to P_1, the Δy in the left-hand figure is approximately equal to the dy in the right-hand figure.

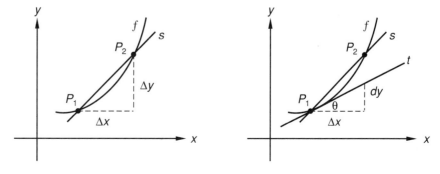

In the right-hand figure on page 205, a segment of the tangent to the curve at P_1 forms the hypotenuse of a right triangle whose vertical side is dy. If P_2 moves down the curve and gets closer to P_1, the secant s will get closer to the tangent t and the length of the segment dy in the right-hand figure will get closer to the length of the whole side which we call Δy. **We call the segment dy the *differential* of the function.** We can solve the small triangle for dy by using the definition of $\tan \theta$.

$$\frac{dy}{\Delta x} = \tan \theta \quad \longrightarrow \quad dy = \tan \theta \, \Delta x$$

But the tangent of θ, the slope of the tangent line, equals the derivative of the function f, which is $f'(x)$. If we replace $\tan \theta$ with $f'(x)$, we have

$$dy = f'(x) \, \Delta x$$

We can show that in the limit, the value of Δy equals dy, which is the differential. To do this, we show that the ratio of Δy to dy approaches 1 as Δx approaches 0.

$$\lim_{\Delta x \to 0} \frac{\Delta y}{dy} = \lim_{\Delta x \to 0} \frac{\Delta y}{f'(x) \, \Delta x} \quad \left(\frac{\Delta y}{\text{definition of } dy} \right)$$

Next we divide the numerator and the denominator by Δx. Now we have

$$\lim_{\Delta x \to 0} \frac{\dfrac{\Delta y}{\Delta x}}{f'(x)}$$

The denominator, $f'(x)$, has already been determined and is considered to be a constant and does not change as Δx changes. The limit of the numerator $\Delta y / \Delta x$ as Δx approaches zero is the derivative, which is also $f'(x)$, so we have

$$\lim_{\Delta x \to 0} \frac{\Delta y}{dy} = \frac{f'(x)}{f'(x)} = 1$$

We have shown that in the limit, dy is approximately equal to Δy because the ratio Δy over dy approaches 1. Thus, $dy \approx \Delta y$ if $dx = \Delta x$ and if Δx is "small." So we may write

$$dy = f'(x) \, dx$$

We have shown that it is reasonable to consider dy and dx as variables that represent very small quantities. If we do this, dy and dx can be multiplied and divided in the same manner as other variables. If we divide both sides of this last expression by dx, we get

$$\frac{dy}{dx} = f'(x)$$

The derivative of a function has meaning as the rate of change of the function or as the slope of the graph of the function. The differential has no similar meaning. We use the differential because its use will permit algebraic manipulations that are helpful in the solutions of problems.
We use a small letter d as an operational indicator to indicate the operation of taking a differential. If we have the functions

$$y = 5x^4 \qquad f(t) = 3 \sin t \qquad g(u) = \ln u$$

we could indicate the operation of finding the differentials of these functions by writing the following:

$$dy \qquad df \qquad dg$$

The differential of a function of x is the derivative with respect to x with dx as an additional factor. The differential of a function of t is the derivative of the function with respect to t with dt as an additional factor. The differential of a function of u is the derivative of the function with respect to u with du as an additional factor. Thus

$$dy = 20x^3\, dx \qquad df = 3 \cos t\, dt \qquad dg = \frac{1}{u}\, du = \frac{du}{u}$$

The differential of an algebraic sum of functions is the sum of the individual differentials.

Example 40.1 If $y = 3x^{-2} + 2 \cos u - 5e^t$, find dy.

Solution The differential of a sum is the sum of the differentials. Thus

$$dy = -6x^{-3}\, dx - 2 \sin u\, du - 5e^t\, dt$$

Note that we did not find the differential of y with respect to a particular variable. The variable in each of the functions was different, and the differential of y is the sum of the differentials of the individual terms.

Problem set 40

1. It was 1 o'clock when the bell in the clock tower chimed once. In how many minutes would the hands of the clock be pointing in precisely the same direction?

2. At noon, the bacteria colony covered 20 square centimeters. The area which the bacteria covered was found to increase exponentially. If at 2 p.m. the bacteria covered 50 square centimeters, how much area was covered at 5 p.m.?

Compute dy in Problems 3–5.

3. $y = \dfrac{3}{x^2} + 2 \sin u + 2e^t$

4. $y = 2 \ln |u| - \dfrac{4}{\sqrt{x}}$

5. $y = \sqrt[3]{t} + 2$

6. Sketch the graph of $y = \dfrac{(x - 3)(x + 2)}{x(x - 1)(x + 1)}$.

7. Write the equation of the line which can be drawn tangent to the graph of $y = \sqrt{x}$ at $x = 4$.

Approximate to two decimal places the answers to Problems 8 and 9.

8. Find $\left. \dfrac{d^3y}{dx^3} \right|_{3.5}$ if $y = \sin x$.

9. Find $\left. \dfrac{du}{dx} \right|_{-1.78}$ if $u = 4 \ln |x| + 2e^x - \cos x$.

10. Write the key identities for practice, and then develop an identity for $\tan 2A$. Then, if $\tan A = -\frac{1}{4}$, find the value of $\tan 2A$.

11. Find the volume of a prism whose length is L centimeters, each of whose ends are equilateral triangles, each of whose sides are E centimeters long.

12. Express the four fourth roots of $\dfrac{\sqrt{2}}{2} + \dfrac{\sqrt{2}}{2} i$ in polar form.

13. Find all values of x such that $0 \le x < 2\pi$ and $\sin 4x = -\dfrac{1}{2}$.

14. Sketch and describe as completely as possible the hyperbola whose equation is given by $4y^2 - 9x^2 - 8y + 36x - 68 = 0$.

15. Find: $\displaystyle\lim_{\Delta x \to 0} \frac{\ln(x + \Delta x) - \ln x}{\Delta x}$ **16.** Evaluate: $\displaystyle\lim_{x \to \infty} \frac{2x^3 - x^2 + 1}{1 - 5x^3}$

17. Sketch the graphs of $y = \dfrac{1}{x}$ and $y = \dfrac{1}{(x - 3)^2}$.

18. (*a*) Evaluate $\sin^{-1}\dfrac{1}{2}$, and (*b*) solve: $\sin x = \dfrac{1}{2}$ $(0 \le x < 2\pi)$

19. Write the key identities for practice, and then develop three forms of the identity for $\cos 2A$.

20. Sketch $y = x^{1/3}$ and $y = x^{2/3}$.

21. Find the domain and range of $y = 1 + 2 \sin(-x)$.

22. Approximate the value of x to two decimal places if $2^x = 5$.

CONCEPT REVIEW   **23.** An arbitrarily drawn right triangle is oriented on the Cartesian plane so that one of its legs coincides with the x axis and one of its legs coincides with the y axis. The coordinates of all three vertices are as shown.

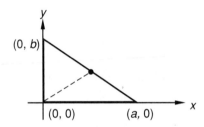

Find the length of the hypotenuse and the length of the median drawn to the hypotenuse which is shown by the dashed line. How are these two lengths related?

LESSON 41 *Graph of tan θ · Graphs of reciprocal functions*

41.A
Graph
of tan θ

As we have seen, the unit circle is an excellent visual aid for understanding the graphs of the sine function and the cosine function.

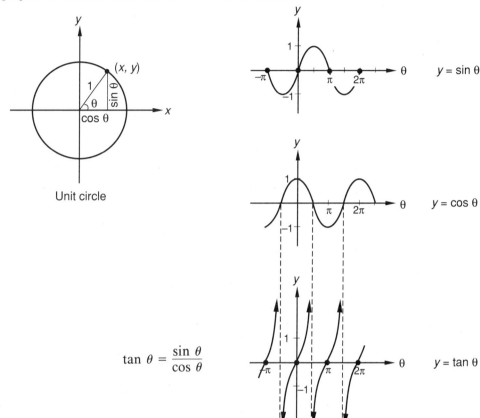

Unit circle

$$\tan \theta = \frac{\sin \theta}{\cos \theta}$$

We can look at the unit circle and see that the y coordinate of any point on the unit circle equals the value of sin θ and the x coordinate equals the value of cos θ. **The value of tan θ is the value of sin θ divided by cos θ, and this ratio equals the slope of the hypotenuse of the triangle drawn in the unit circle.** This fact is easy to remember because the slope of a line and the tangent of its angle with the horizontal have the same definition.

The graph of $y = \tan \theta$ shown above is drawn directly under the graphs of $y = \sin \theta$ and $y = \cos \theta$. **Note that the graph of $y = \tan \theta$ crosses the x axis at every point at which sin θ equals zero (marked with dots on both graphs) and has a vertical asymptote at every point at which cos θ equals zero (noted by the dotted lines).** We note that the graphs of the sine and cosine functions repeat every 2π radians (360°), so the period of both the sine and cosine functions is 2π radians (360°). **The graph of the tangent function repeats every π radians (180°), so the period of the tangent function is half the period of the sine function and half the period of the cosine function.**

41.B
Graphs
of reciprocal
functions

If we know the graph of a function $f(x)$, the graph of the reciprocal function can be sketched by inspection.

$$\text{Reciprocal function} = \frac{1}{f(x)}$$

There are three things that are especially helpful in graphing a reciprocal function.

1. The poles and zeros of the original function change places and become the zeros and poles of the reciprocal function. Thus, the graph of the reciprocal function has a vertical asymptote at every point where the graph of the function touches the x axis and will touch the x axis at every vertical asymptote of the original function.

2. The points where the y coordinate is $+1$ or -1, $(x, 1)$ and $(x, -1)$, appear on both graphs. For example, if the points $(4, 1)$ and $(7, -1)$ are on the graph of the original function, then the same points will be on the graph of the reciprocal function.

3. When the value of the original function is a large positive (negative) number, the value of the reciprocal function is a small positive (negative) number. When the value of the original function is a small positive (negative) number, then the value of the reciprocal function is a large positive (negative) number.

Example 41.1   Use the graph of $y = \sin x$ to sketch the graph of $y = \csc x$.

Solution   The cosecant function is the reciprocal of the sine function. We sketch the graph of $y = \sin x$ on the left and draw vertical asymptotes where the sine graph crosses the x axis. We put dots at the points where $\sin x = \pm 1$ because $\csc x$ will also equal ± 1 for these values of x. Then we sketch the graph of $\csc x$ on the right.

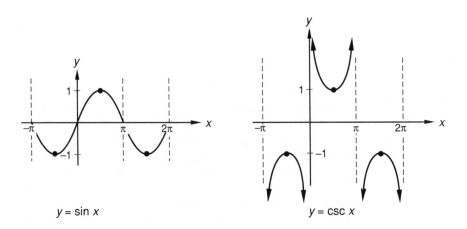

$y = \sin x$ $y = \csc x$

Example 41.2   Use the graphs of $y = \cos x$ and $y = \tan x$ to sketch the graphs of $y = \sec x$ and $y = \cot x$.

Solution   We sketch the graphs of $y = \cos x$ and $y = \tan x$ and draw vertical asymptotes where these curves cross the x axis and make dots at places where the functions have a value of ± 1.

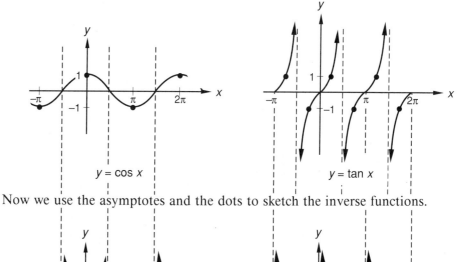

$y = \cos x$ $y = \tan x$

Now we use the asymptotes and the dots to sketch the inverse functions.

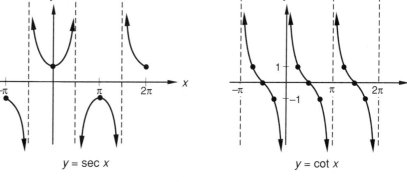

$y = \sec x$ $y = \cot x$

Example 41.3   Graph $y = \csc(\theta + 45°)$.

Solution   A quick way to graph a cosecant function is to use the graph of the corresponding sine function. On the left we graph $y = \sin(\theta + 45°)$. On the right we draw vertical asymptotes at the zeros of the sine function and place dots at the points where $\sin x$ has a value of $+1$ or -1. Then we use the asymptotes and dots to help us sketch the cosecant function.

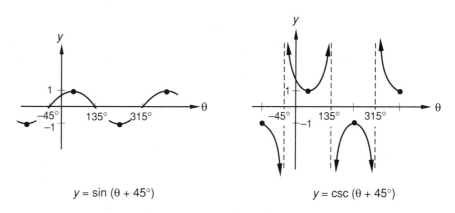

$y = \sin(\theta + 45°)$ $y = \csc(\theta + 45°)$

Constants that shift the graph vertically are ignored until the last step. For example, to sketch the graph of $y = 5 + \csc(\theta + 45°)$, we would find the graph of $y = \csc(\theta + 45°)$ as we have done and then shift this graph up 5 units by simply relabeling the centerline as $y = 5$.

Example 41.4   Graph $y = \sec(x - 20°)$.

Solution   On the left we graph $y = \cos(x - 20°)$. On the right we use asymptotes and dots to graph the secant function.

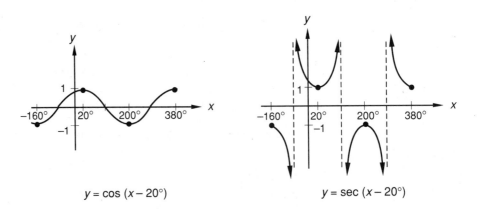

$y = \cos(x - 20°)$ $y = \sec(x - 20°)$

To sketch the graph of $y = A + \sec(x - 20°)$, we would use the graph on the right and relabel the centerline $y = A$.

Example 41.5   Sketch the reciprocal function of the function shown in the figure.

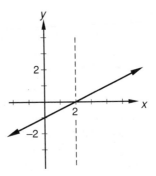

Solution   The graph of the reciprocal function will have a vertical asymptote at $x = 2$. The function graphed gets large and positive when x gets large and positive, so the reciprocal function will get small and positive. The function graphed gets large and negative when x gets large and negative, so the reciprocal function will get small and negative. We remember to place dots on the original graph at y values of ± 1 and to draw the graph of the reciprocal functions through the dots.

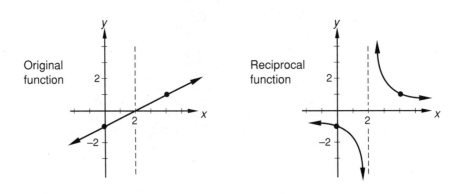

Example 41.6 The graph of f is shown. Sketch the graph of the reciprocal function $\frac{1}{f}$.

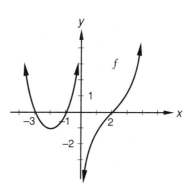

Solution We see that the reciprocal function will have vertical asymptotes when $x = -1, -3$, and $+2$. First we draw the asymptotes and place dots at y values of ± 1. The y axis is a vertical asymptote of the function, which indicates that the origin is a zero of the reciprocal function. Then we use these aids to sketch the reciprocal function.

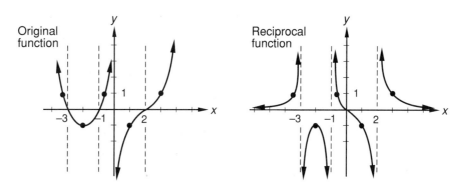

Problem set 41

1. Dee and Hudson drove at M miles per hour for H hours, but got to the shore 2 hours late. How fast should they have driven to have arrived on time?

2. Sketch the graph of $y = \tan x$, indicating clearly on the graph the location of the asymptotes.

3. Sketch f and g on the same coordinate plane, where

$$f(x) = 2x + 1 \quad \text{and} \quad g(x) = \frac{1}{f(x)}$$

4. Graph the following functions on the same coordinate plane:

$$y = \sin\left(x - \frac{\pi}{4}\right) \quad \text{and} \quad y = \csc\left(x - \frac{\pi}{4}\right)$$

5. If $y = 3 \sin u - \sqrt{2}\, e^t + \frac{1}{3} \ln x$, then write the expression for the differential dy.

6. Sketch the graph of $y = \dfrac{(x - 3)(x + 2)}{(x + 5)x(x - 2)}$.

7. Find the equation of the tangent line which can be drawn to the graph of $y = \ln x + \sin x$ when $x = 3$.

8. Approximate $\dfrac{d^5 y}{dx^5}\bigg|_2$ to two decimal places if $y = 3e^x$.

Differentiate the functions given in Problems 9 and 10.

9. $y = 14 \cos u + \dfrac{e^u}{2} - \ln u$ 10. $y = \sqrt[3]{t^2} - \dfrac{3}{t}$

11. Recall the definition of a derivative. Write by inspection the value of

$$\lim_{h \to 0} \frac{e^{(2+h)} - e^2}{h}$$

12. Write the equation $4y^2 + x^2 - 2x - 3 = 0$ in standard form and describe this conic section.

13. Find all real values of x which satisfy the following inequality:

$$\log_2 \left(\frac{1}{3} x + 2 \right) > 2$$

14. If $f(x) = \ln x$ and $g(x) = \sqrt{x + 1}$, write the equations of $f \circ g$ and $g \circ f$ and find the domain and range for both.

15. Write the key identities and develop an identity for $\cos \dfrac{x}{2}$.

16. Use interval notation to indicate the intervals on which the graph of f lies below the x axis, where

$$f(x) = x(1 - x)(x + 3)(x + 1)$$

17. If $f(x) = \ln x$ and $g(x) = e^x$, graph the functions $y = f(-x)$ and $y = g(-x)$ on the same coordinate plane.

18. Graph the function whose equation is $y = 4 + \sec (\theta - 30°)$.

19. Compute the algebraic sum of the two real vectors: $2 \angle 30° - 3 \angle 60°$. Use a calculator and give decimal approximations.

20. Shown is a unit circle centered at the origin in the coordinate plane.

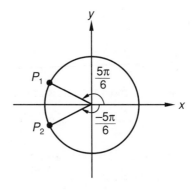

Find the coordinates of the following points: (a) P_1 (b) P_2

21. Solve for x in the figure shown.

$AP = x$
$PC = x - 1$
$BC = x - 2$

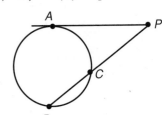

22. If x, y, and z are real numbers, compare:
    A. the average of x, y, and z B. $x + y + z$

LESSON 42 *Product rule for derivatives and differentials · Proof of the product rule*

42.A
Product rule

The slope of the graph of the sum of two functions is the sum of the slopes of the graphs of the individual functions. We know this because the derivative of a sum of two functions equals the sum of the derivatives of the individual functions.

$$f(x) = 2x + 5 \qquad g(x) = x^2 + 3x \qquad (f + g)(x) = x^2 + 5x + 5$$

$$\text{Slope} = 2 \qquad\qquad \text{Slope} = 2x + 3 \qquad\qquad \text{Slope} = 2x + 5$$

$$f'(x) = 2 \qquad\qquad g'(x) = 2x + 3 \qquad\qquad (f + g)'(x) = 2x + 5$$

Unfortunately, the derivative of the product of two functions (the slope of the graph) does not equal the product of the individual derivatives. **The derivative of a product of two functions is the first function times the derivative of the second function plus the second function times the derivative of the first function.** If we call the functions *one* and *two* and use *dee* to mean derivative, we can say that the derivative of the product of two functions equals

one dee two plus two dee one

For the functions above, if we let $f(x)$ be function one and $g(x)$ be function two, we would have

$$(fg)'(x) = f(x)g'(x) + g(x)f'(x)$$

and if we substitute the values, we get

$$(fg)'(x) = (2x + 5)(2x + 3) + (x^2 + 3x)(2) \qquad \text{substituted}$$

$$= 6x^2 + 22x + 15 \qquad\qquad\qquad \text{simplified}$$

Many calculus books use a notation that calls the functions u and v and their derivatives u' and v'. If we do this, we say

$$u = 2x + 5 \qquad\qquad v = x^2 + 3x$$

$$u' = 2 \qquad\qquad\qquad v' = 2x + 3$$

The derivative of a product $y = uv$ using this notation is

$$\frac{d}{dx}(uv) = u\frac{dv}{dx} + v\frac{du}{dx}$$

or

$$(uv)' = uv' + vu'$$

This last notation is perhaps the cleanest of all. It shows clearly that if u and v are functions of x, the derivative of the product of u and v is the sum of two quantities. Each quantity has a factor that is one of the functions, and the other factor is the derivative of the other function.

  The differential of a product of two functions is the first times the differential of the second plus the second times the differential of the first. Thus the differential of uv could be written as

$$d(uv) = u\,dv + v\,du$$

Example 42.1 If $y = x^2 \sin x$, find y'.

Solution The derivative of x^2 is $2x$ and the derivative of $\sin x$ is $\cos x$.

$$\frac{d}{dx}\, x^2 = 2x \qquad \frac{d}{dx}\, \sin x = \cos x$$

To find the derivative of the product, we will use the jingle "one dee two plus two dee one" and write

$$y' = x^2(\cos x) + (\sin x)(2x) \qquad \text{derivative}$$
$$= x^2 \cos x + 2x \sin x \qquad \text{rearranged}$$

Example 42.2 If $f(x) = x^2 e^x$ find $f'(x)$.

Solution We will write the first times the derivative of the second plus the second times the derivative of the first.

$$f'(x) = x^2 e^x + e^x(2x) \qquad \text{derivative}$$
$$= x^2 e^x + 2x e^x \qquad \text{rearranged}$$

Example 42.3 If $u = \ln x$, $v = 2e^x$, and $y = uv$, find y'.

Solution This time we remember $\dfrac{d}{dx}\, uv = uv' + vu'$.

$$y' = (\ln x)2e^x + 2e^x \frac{1}{x} \qquad \text{derivative}$$

$$= 2e^x \ln x + 2\frac{e^x}{x} \qquad \text{rearranged}$$

Example 42.4 If $f(x) = e^x \cos x$, use a calculator to evaluate $f'(1.2)$.

Solution First we find $f'(x)$.
$$f'(x) = e^x(-\sin x) + (\cos x)e^x \qquad \text{derivative}$$
$$= -e^x \sin x + e^x \cos x \qquad \text{rearranged}$$

To evaluate $e^{1.2}$, we use the inverse $\ln x$ key and remember to set the calculator to radians to evaluate $\sin 1.2$ and $\cos 1.2$.

$$f'(1.2) = -(3.32)(0.932) + (3.32)(0.362) = -1.89$$

Example 42.5 If $g(x) = e^x \sqrt{x}$, find $g'(2)$.

Solution Let $u = e^x$ and let $v = \sqrt{x}$. So $u' = e^x$ and $v' = \dfrac{1}{2\sqrt{x}}$. Then we can find $g'(x)$.

$$g'(x) = \frac{e^x}{2\sqrt{x}} + e^x \sqrt{x}$$

To evaluate $g'(x)$, we use a calculator.

$$\frac{e^2}{2\sqrt{2}} + e^2 \sqrt{2} \approx \frac{7.39}{2.83} + (7.39)(1.41) \approx 13.03$$

Example 42.6 If $s = x^2 y^3$, find ds.

Solution The differentials of x^2 and y^3 are

$$d(x^2) = 2x\, dx \qquad d(y^3) = 3y^2\, dy$$

The differential of a product is the first factor times the differential of the second factor plus the second factor times the differential of the first factor. Thus

$$ds = x^2(3y^2 \, dy) + y^3(2x \, dx) = 3x^2y^2 \, dy + 2xy^3 \, dx$$

Example 42.7   If $y = s^2 \sin t$, find dy.

Solution   The differentials of s^2 and $\sin t$ are

$$d(s^2) = 2s \, ds \qquad d \sin t = \cos t \, dt$$

Now we write the differential of y as the first times the differential of the second plus the second times the differential of the first.

$$dy = s^2(\cos t \, dt) + (\sin t)(2s \, ds)$$
$$= s^2 \cos t \, dt + 2s \sin t \, ds$$

42.B
Proof of the product rule (optional)

If we use the definition of the derivative to write an expression for $f'(x)$ and $g'(x)$, we get

$$f'(x) = \lim_{\Delta x \to 0} \frac{f(x + \Delta x) - f(x)}{\Delta x}$$

and

$$g'(x) = \lim_{\Delta x \to 0} \frac{g(x + \Delta x) - g(x)}{\Delta x}$$

We want to show that the derivative of a product of $f(x)$ and $g(x)$ is $f(x)$ times the derivative of $g(x)$ plus $g(x)$ times the derivative of $f(x)$. This means we want to show that

$$(fg)'(x) = f(x) \lim_{\Delta x \to 0} \left[\frac{g(x + \Delta x) - g(x)}{\Delta x} \right] + g(x) \lim_{\Delta x \to 0} \left[\frac{f(x + \Delta x) - f(x)}{\Delta x} \right]$$

We begin by noting the definition of $(fg)'(x)$.

$$\frac{d}{dx}(fg)(x) = \lim_{\Delta x \to 0} \frac{(fg)(x + \Delta x) - (fg)(x)}{\Delta x}$$

Now we remember that $(fg)(x)$ means $f(x)$ times $g(x)$, and thus we can write

$$\frac{d}{dx}(fg)(x) = \lim_{\Delta x \to 0} \frac{f(x + \Delta x)g(x + \Delta x) - f(x)g(x)}{\Delta x}$$

Next we use an algebraic trick and add $-f(x + \Delta x)g(x)$ and $+f(x + \Delta x)g(x)$ to the numerator and regroup the terms to get

$$= \lim_{\Delta x \to 0} \frac{f(x + \Delta x)g(x + \Delta x) - f(x + \Delta x)g(x) + f(x + \Delta x)g(x) - f(x)g(x)}{\Delta x}$$

$$= \lim_{\Delta x \to 0} f(x + \Delta x) \frac{g(x + \Delta x) - g(x)}{\Delta x} + \lim_{\Delta x \to 0} g(x) \frac{f(x + \Delta x) - f(x)}{\Delta x}$$

This is exactly what we wanted to show except that we wanted to get $f(x)$ instead of $f(x + \Delta x)$ as the first factor. But the limit of $f(x + \Delta x)$ as Δx approaches zero is $f(x)$. Thus, we have

$$\frac{d}{dx} fg(x) = f(x) \lim_{\Delta x \to 0} \frac{g(x + \Delta x) - g(x)}{\Delta x} + g(x) \lim_{\Delta x \to 0} \frac{f(x + \Delta x) - f(x)}{\Delta x}$$

This shows that the derivative of $(fg)(x)$ equals $f(x)$ times the derivative of $g(x)$ plus $g(x)$ times the derivative of $f(x)$, which completes our proof.

Problem set 42

1. Equal-sized squares are cut from the corners of a 10 by 10 inch sheet. The resulting flaps are folded up to form an open box. If the length of a side of a square is x, find the volume of the box in terms of x.

2. The volume was increasing exponentially. One minute after the big bang, the volume was 10 cubic kilometers, and three minutes after the big bang, the volume was 30 cubic kilometers. How many minutes after the big bang would the volume be 60 cubic kilometers?

Use the product rule for derivatives and differentials as indicated in Problems 3–6.

3. Find y' if $y = x^3 e^x$.

4. Find $\dfrac{dy}{dt}$ if $y = -3t \cos t$.

5. Evaluate $f'(-2)$ if $f(x) = x^2 \ln |-x|$.

6. Find ds if $s = 2x^2 y$.

Differentiate as many times as is necessary in Problems 7 and 8.

7. If $s = -\dfrac{1}{\sqrt{x}} + 2 \cos x$, find s''.

8. If $f(t) = 3 \sin t - \sqrt{2}\, e^t$, find $f'''(t)$.

9. Graph the functions f and g on the same coordinate axes, where

$$f(x) = x^2 - 1 \quad \text{and} \quad g(x) = \frac{1}{f(x)}$$

Graph the functions of Problems 10 and 11.

10. $y = \tan x$

11. $y = \dfrac{x - 1}{x(x + 2)(3 - x)}$

12. Find the equation of the tangent line which can be drawn to the graph of $y = \sqrt[3]{x^2}$ at $x = 8$.

13. Sketch the graph of $y = \sqrt[3]{x^2}$ and draw the tangent line at $x = 8$.

14. Begin with the key identities and develop an identity for $\tan (A + B)$. Then, if $\tan A = \frac{1}{2}$ and $\tan B = 4$, compute the value of $\tan (A + B)$.

15. The base of this right circular cone has a radius of 3 cm, and the height of the cone is 8 cm. Find the volume of the liquid in the cone (as shown) if its depth is 4 cm.

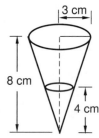

16. Find all values of x which lie between 0 and 2π for which $\sin 3x = -\sqrt{2}/2$.

17. If $f(x) = |x|$, then graph the equation $y = f(x - 1)$.

18. Write the standard form of the equation $4x^2 + y^2 - 2y - 3 = 0$ and completely describe this conic section.

19. Solve for x: $2 \ln x - \ln \left(x + \dfrac{1}{2}\right) = \ln 2$

20. Evaluate: $\lim\limits_{x \to -2} \dfrac{2x^2 + 3x - 2}{x^2 + 4}$

21. Use the rational zero theorem as an aid to find all the zeros of the following function: $y = x^3 - x^2 + 2x - 2$.

22. Write the contrapositive of this statement: If a conditional statement is true, then its contrapositive is also true.

23. Suppose P is a point that lies outside circle O, which has a radius of 3. If the distance from P to the center of circle O is 6, what is the length of $\overline{PA}$ if $\overline{PA}$ is tangent to circle O at A?

24. Find the sum of the infinite geometric series: $1 + \dfrac{1}{3} + \dfrac{1}{9} + \ldots$

LESSON 43 *An antiderivative · Integration*

43.A
An antiderivative

Multiplication and division are inverse operations because multiplication will undo division and division will undo multiplication. When we differentiate a function, we find a second function that is the derivative of the original function. The inverse operation of differentiation is the operation of going back to the original function, and we call this operation ***antidifferentiation.*** Unfortunately we cannot go back to **the** original function by finding **the** antiderivative because many functions have the same derivative and we don't know to which one we should go back. Let's look at three different functions each of whose derivatives is $2x$.

$$(a) \quad \frac{d}{dx} x^2 = 2x \qquad (b) \quad \frac{d}{dx}(x^2 + 42) = 2x \qquad (c) \quad \frac{d}{dx}(x^2 - 165) = 2x$$

Each of the original functions has a constant term on the end. The constant for (a) is zero because x^2 is the same as $x^2 + 0$. The constants on the ends of $x^2 + 42$ and $x^2 - 165$ are $+42$ and -165, respectively. Since the derivative of each of these functions is $2x$, we see that $2x$ has many antiderivatives of which we have shown only three. **There is no one function that is the antiderivative of $2x$ because there is an infinite number of functions that have $2x$ as the derivative.**

Example 43.1   If $f(x) = 2x$, find a function $F(x)$ that is an antiderivative of $f(x)$.

Solution   If we differentiate x^2, we get $2x$. We also get $2x$ as a result if we differentiate $x^2 + 157$. To make the point that any constant will work, we choose $x^2 - 463$ as our antiderivative.

$$F(x) = x^2 - 463$$

43.B
Integration

We say that ***integration*** is the process of finding the set of all antiderivatives of a given function. We call this set ***the indefinite integral.*** Thus, it is incorrect to speak of **the** antiderivative of a function because there is more than one, but it is correct to speak of **the** indefinite integral of a function. We use an elongated S to indicate the

process of finding the integral of a function, and we call this symbol an ***integral sign.***
Thus we can write the integral of $2x$ as

$$\int 2x = x^2 + \text{(any real number)}$$

We use a capital C to represent *any real number* and call C the **constant of integration.**

$$\int 2x = x^2 + C$$

There are two routes available for antidifferentiation. We remember that we can find the derivative of the original function or we can find the differential of the original function. If we begin with $y = x^2 - 32$, we can write either

$$\frac{dy}{dx} = 2x \qquad \text{or} \qquad dy = 2x \, dx$$

The original function is the same for the derivative and for the differential, so we can antidifferentiate either form.

$$\int 2x = x^2 + C \qquad \int 2x \, dx = x^2 + C$$

There are three advantages to using the differential form. The first is that the dx indicates that x is the **variable of integration** and that we are integrating with respect to x. The second is that dx can be given a geometrical meaning in some problems. The third is that the differential form will make some complicated expressions easier to integrate.

The derivative is defined as a limit approached by the value of the following expressions as Δx and h approach zero.

$$\frac{d}{dx} f(x) = \lim_{\Delta x \to 0} \frac{f(x + \Delta x) - f(x)}{\Delta x} \qquad \text{or} \qquad = \lim_{h \to 0} \frac{f(x + h) - f(x)}{h}$$

There is no corresponding definition of the indefinite integral of a function. Finding the integral of a function requires the ability to guess the answer based on experience with the derivative and the differential. Then we check our guess by finding the differential or the derivative of our guess.

Example 43.2   Find $\int \cos x$.

Solution   Although it is not necessary, we will insert the dx to get the differential form which indicates that x is the variable of integration. We remember that the differential of $\sin x$ is $\cos x \, dx$, so the integral of $\cos x \, dx$ is $\sin x + C$.

$$\int \cos x \, dx = \textbf{sin } \textbf{\textit{x}} + \textbf{\textit{C}}$$

Now we check our guess.

$$d(\sin x + C) = d \sin x + d(C) = \cos x \, dx \qquad \text{check}$$

Example 43.3   Find $\int -\sin t$.

Solution   First we insert dt to get the differential form which indicates that t is the variable of integration.

$$\int -\sin t \, dt$$

The differential of $\cos t$ is $-\sin t \, dt$. Thus the integral of $-\sin t \, dt$ is $\cos t + C$.

$$\int -\sin t \, dt = \textbf{cos } \textbf{\textit{t}} + \textbf{\textit{C}}$$

Now we check our guess.

$$d(\cos t + C) = d \cos t + d(C) = -\sin t \, dt \qquad \text{check}$$

Example 43.4   Find $\int e^x$.

Solution   We write the dx and we have

$$\int e^x \, dx$$

Next we guess the answer.

$$\int e^x \, dx = e^x + C$$

Now we check our guess.

$$d(e^x + C) = de^x + d(C) = e^x \, dx \qquad \text{check}$$

Example 43.5   If $\dfrac{dy}{dx} = \cos x$, find y.

Solution   The derivative of y with respect to x equals $\cos x$. Thus y must equal some antiderivative of $\cos x$.

$$y = \int \cos x \, dx = \sin x + C$$

Now we check our guess.

$$\frac{d}{dx}(\sin x + C) = \cos x \qquad \text{check}$$

Problem set 43   1.   Describe how the surface area of a sphere changes if its volume is doubled.

2.   Jeffrey could shovel 200 pounds of gravel in J minutes and Taylor could shovel B pounds of gravel in T minutes. How long would it take Jeffrey and Taylor shoveling together to shovel T^2 pounds of gravel?

Find an antiderivative of the expressions of Problems 3 and 4.
   3. $5x^4$ 4. $3t^2$

Integrate:

5. $\displaystyle\int \cos x \, dx$ 6. $\displaystyle\int e^t$ 7. $\displaystyle\int -\sin x$

8.   If $\dfrac{dy}{dx} = \dfrac{1}{x}$, find y.

Use the product rule for derivatives and differentials to solve Problems 9–11.
   9.   If $u = x^2 y$, find du.

10.   If $f(x) = e^x$, $g(x) = \sin x$, and $h(x) = f(x)g(x)$, find $h'(x)$.

11.   If $y = x \ln x$, evaluate: $\left.\dfrac{dy}{dx}\right|_{2.5}$

12.   If $f(x) = x^2 + x - 2$ and $g(x) = 1/f(x)$, graph f and g on the same coordinate plane.

13.   Sketch the graph of $y = \dfrac{x}{(x - 2)(x + 3)}$.

14. If $y = 2\sqrt[4]{x^3} - \dfrac{4}{x}$, find $\dfrac{dy}{dx}$.

15. Sketch and describe fully the hyperbola whose equation is $x^2 - (y - 1)^2 = 4$.

16. Write the key identities for practice, and then develop an identity for both

$$\sin \tfrac{1}{2}x \qquad \text{and} \qquad \cos \tfrac{x}{2}$$

17. Evaluate: $\displaystyle\lim_{x \to \infty} \dfrac{3x^3 - 5}{1 - x^2}$

18. Find the equation of the locus of all points equidistant from the point $(0, -1)$ and the line $y = 4$.

19. Suppose f is a function defined as follows:

$$f(x) = \begin{cases} \cos x & \text{if } x > 0 \\ \sin x & \text{if } x \le 0 \end{cases}$$

Graph f and evaluate: $\displaystyle\lim_{x \to 0^+} f(x)$ and $\displaystyle\lim_{x \to 0^-} f(x)$

20. Find those values of x for which $|x - 1| < 0.4$.

21. If A is a number such that $\sin A = \tfrac{1}{3}$ and $\cos A$ is positive, find the exact value of $\cos A$.

22. If A is as defined in Problem 21, compute the value of the following:

$$\sin(-A) \cos\left(\dfrac{\pi}{2} - A\right) \cos A$$

CONCEPT REVIEW   23. A square is oriented on the coordinate plane so that two of its sides lie on the coordinate axes. The length of each side is a, as shown in the figure. Find the slopes of the diagonals of the square. How are the slopes of the two diagonals related? What does this indicate?

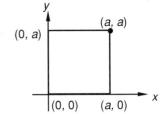

LESSON 44 *Factors of polynomial functions · Graphs of polynomial functions*

44.A
Factors of polynomial functions

In Lesson 39 we considered the graphs of rational polynomial functions. In this lesson we will do a more detailed investigation of the factors of polynomials and will look closely at the graphs of second-, third-, and fourth-degree polynomial equations.

If all the coefficients of a polynomial are real numbers, the polynomial is called a ***real polynomial.*** The degree of a polynomial is the value of the greatest exponent. The seventh-degree polynomial on the left below is not a real polynomial because one of the coefficients is a complex number. This polynomial is a ***complex polynomial,*** and complex polynomials will not be considered in this book. The sixth-degree polynomial on the right is a real polynomial because all the coefficients are real numbers.

$$3x^7 + \sqrt{-3}x^6 + 2x + 4 \qquad 5x^6 - \sqrt{6}x^4 + 0.003x^3 - 3.\overline{212}$$

The German mathematician Carl Friedrich Gauss proved that every real polynomial of degree n can be factored into exactly n linear factors.

A real polynomial can have complex linear factors if they occur in conjugate pairs. To illustrate we will form a real cubic polynomial function by multiplying two complex conjugate linear factors and one real linear factor.

$$\begin{aligned} f(x) &= (x + 2i)(x - 2i)(x - 3) &&\text{three linear factors} \\ &= (x^2 + 4)(x - 3) &&\text{multiplied the complex factors} \\ &= x^3 - 3x^2 + 4x - 12 &&\text{multiplied again} \end{aligned}$$

The quadratic factor $(x^2 + 4)$ of this polynomial is called an ***irreducible quadratic factor*** because it cannot be factored into linear real factors. **This factor can never equal zero because $x^2 + 4$ is a positive real number for any real number value of x. Thus, irreducible quadratic factors never cause a polynomial to equal zero.** If $x = 3$, the linear factor $(x - 3)$ will equal zero, and therefore 3 is a zero of the polynomial. The graph of this polynomial function crosses the x axis when $x = 3$. If we multiply this cubic polynomial by $(x - 3)$, we get a quartic polynomial.

$$g(x) = (x^2 + 4)(x - 3)(x - 3) = x^4 - 6x^3 + 13x^2 - 24x + 36$$

If we combine the $x - 3$ factors, we can write

$$g(x) = (x^2 + 4)(x - 3)^2$$

When $x = 3$, the $(x - 3)^2$ factor equals zero. Thus the graph will touch the x axis when $x = 3$ but will not cross the x axis because the value of $(x - 3)^2$ never changes sign. If this expression does not equal zero, it equals some positive number. This would also be true if the exponent of $(x - 3)$ were 4, 6, 8, or any even number.

From this we can induce that any polynomial can be written as a product of linear real factors and irreducible quadratic factors. **Only linear real factors can cause a polynomial to equal zero. The graph will cross the x axis at a linear zero if the linear real factor occurs an odd number of times and will touch but not cross the x axis if the linear real factor occurs an even number of times.**

Example 44.1   If $f(x) = (x + 4)(x + 2)^4(x^2 + 3)(x - 5)^3(x - 7)^2$, at what values of x will the graph touch the x axis and at what values of x will the graph cross the x axis?

Solution   The irreducible quadratic factor $x^2 + 3$ can never equal zero and can never cause the graph to touch the x axis. One of the linear factors equals zero when $x = -4$; one of the linear factors equals zero when $x = -2$; one of the linear factors equals zero when $x = 5$; and another equals zero when $x = 7$. Thus the graph touches the x axis at these values of x. The graph will cross the x axis at zeros caused by linear factors that have an odd exponent, so the graph will cross the x axis when $x = -4$ and $+5$. The graph will touch but will not cross the x axis when $x = 7$ and -2 because the factors $(x - 7)$ and $(x + 2)$ occur an even number of times.

Example 44.2 The graph of $y = (x - 1)^2(x + 2)^2$ could most resemble which of the following graphs?

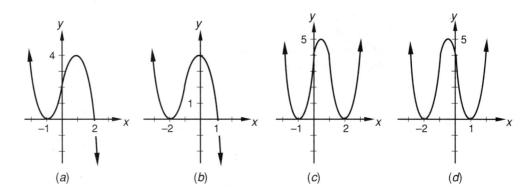

(a)   (b)   (c)   (d)

Solution The graph of the given equation must touch the x axis at the zeros of the linear real factors. Thus the graph must touch the x axis at x values of $+1$ and -2. This eliminates (*a*) and (*c*). In the equation, both linear factors are squared, so the graph does not cross the x axis at either $+1$ or -2. This eliminates (*b*). The graph (*d*) touches the x axis at $+1$ and -2 and does not cross, so this graph would most resemble the graph of the function.

44.B
Graphs of polynomial functions

The discussion of factors of polynomials gives us some insight into the behavior of graphs of polynomial functions but is not of great value in graphing higher-order polynomial functions because of the great difficulty usually encountered in trying to find the factors.

Graphs of polynomial functions are smooth continuous curves that have no holes, no breaks, and no sharp points. **The turning point theorem tells us that the graph of a polynomial function has fewer turning points than the degree of the polynomial.** Thus the graph of a third-degree polynomial function has at most two turning points; the graph of a fourth-degree polynomial function has at most three turning points; etc. Here we show the graphs of a second-degree, a third-degree, and a fourth-degree polynomial equation and note the number of turning points in each graph.

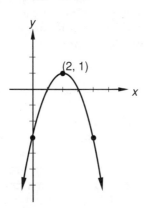

SECOND-DEGREE
$y = -x^2 + 4x - 3$
One turning point

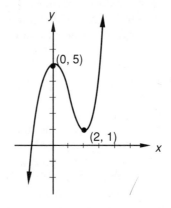

THIRD-DEGREE
$y = x^3 - 3x^2 + 5$
Two turning points

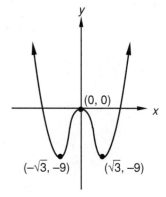

FOURTH-DEGREE
$y = x^4 - 6x^2$
Three turning points

The term of highest degree in a polynomial is the dominant term because, for large absolute values of x, the value of the highest-degree term will be greater than the absolute value of the sum of all the other terms in the equation. The greater the absolute value of x, the greater the dominance of the highest-degree term becomes. **Thus, the value of the polynomial for large absolute values of x can be determined by looking at the exponent of the highest-degree term and looking at the sign of the coefficient of this term.** In the graph on the left on page 224, the $-x^2$ term is dominant. Since $-x^2$ is negative for any real value of x, the graph will continue smoothly in the negative y direction as the absolute value of x increases. In the center graph, the dominant term is x^3. This term is negative for negative values of x and positive for positive values of x. In this graph, we see that for large positive values of x, the y values of the function are positive, and for large negative values of x, the y values of the function are negative. The graph will continue to increase and decrease smoothly as shown on the left and the right sides of this graph. The fourth-degree equation has increasingly large values of y in both directions, as we see in the graph on the right, because if x is not zero, x^4 is always positive, and the coefficient of x^4 is $+1$. If the coefficient of x^4 had been negative, then the y values would have increased negatively for large absolute values of x.

Graphs of higher-degree polynomials can be drawn by using the same procedures that we use to graph third- and fourth-degree polynomials. In this book we will not encounter problems that require the graphing of polynomial functions of degree 5 or greater. Most of the polynomial functions will be quadratic functions, some will be cubic functions, and a few will be quartic functions. When we look at the equations of one of these functions, it is nice to have some idea of what the graph of the function could look like. The general cubic equation has the form

$$f(x) = ax^3 + bx^2 + cx + d$$

The graph of a cubic function can have a flex point or can have a flex point and two turning points. If the x^3 term is preceded by a plus sign (a is a positive number), the graph will have one of the two forms shown on the left below. If the x^3 term is preceded by a minus sign (a is a negative number), the graphs are flipped upside down as shown on the right.

The shape of a graph is determined by the values of the coefficients a, b, and c. The vertical position of the graph can be changed by changing the value of d.

The general equation of a quartic function is

$$y = ax^4 + bx^3 + cx^2 + dx + e$$

The first term is the dominant term, and the value of x^4 is a positive number for any value of x. If a is a positive number, the graph will "open up," as in these graphs.

The graph of a quartic function can resemble the graph of a quadratic function, as we show on the left on page 225. It can have one turning point and one flex point as in the next two graphs. The graph can also have three turning points as shown in the three graphs on the right. The shape of the graph is determined by the values of the coefficients a, b, c, and d, and the vertical position of the graph is determined by the value of the constant e. If the coefficient a of the first term is a negative number, the graphs will be upside-down forms of the graphs on page 225, as we show here.

An in-depth study of polynomial functions will reveal several interesting but seldom discussed properties of polynomials. The general form of an nth-degree polynomial function is

$$f(x) = ax^n + bx^{n-1} + cx^{n-2} + \cdots + k$$

The sum of all real and complex roots is $-b/a$, and the product of all real and complex roots is k/a if the degree of the polynomial is even and is $-k/a$ if the degree of the polynomial is odd. The average value of all the roots is

$$\text{Average of all roots} = \bar{x} = \frac{-b}{na}$$

For a quadratic polynomial, $\bar{x}$ equals the x value of the vertex. For a cubic polynomial, $\bar{x}$ equals the x value of the flex point. For a quartic polynomial, the value of $\bar{x}$ will give us a good idea of the x value of the center of the graph.

Example 44.3 Make a very rough sketch of the graph of $y = -x^3 + 3x^2 - 2x + 3$.

Solution Every cubic polynomial has at least one real root, so the graph of every cubic polynomial function crosses the x axis somewhere. We just need a rough sketch, so we will not search for this root. The x value of the flex point is $-b/3a$, which equals $3/3$, or 1. If we let x equal 1, we can solve for y.

$$y = -(1)^3 + 3(1)^2 - 2(1) + 3 = 3$$

Thus the flex point is $(1, 3)$. The coefficient of x^3 tells us the curve goes down on the right and up on the left.

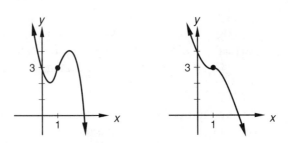

We are not sure whether the graph has one flex point or one flex point and two turning points. In a later lesson we will discuss the use of the derivative to discover which form the graph has and how to find the x values of the turning points if the graph has turning points.

Example 44.4   Make a rough sketch of the graph of $y = x^4 - 3x^3 + 2x + 5$.

Solution   First we find $\bar{x}$.

$$\bar{x} = \frac{-(-3)}{4(1)} = \frac{3}{4}$$

The value of $\bar{x}$ is 3 divided by 4, so the center of the graph is close to the origin. The lead coefficient is positive, so it "opens up." The graph could have one turning point or three turning points and could look like one of these.

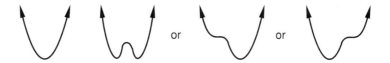

Problem set 44

1. A right triangle is inscribed in a unit circle as shown. Find the area of the triangle in terms of y.

2. The intensity of the questioning increased exponentially. If the intensity was 10 at noon and was 20 one hour later, what was the intensity of the questioning at 5 p.m.? (Do not use a calculator.)

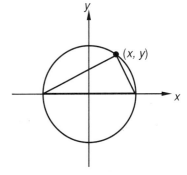

3. Sketch the graph of $y = (x - 1)(x + 1)^2$. Show clearly those places where the graph either crosses or touches the x axis.

4. Use your knowledge of polynomial sketching to make a rough sketch of the possible shapes of the graph of $y = 3x^3 + ax^2 + bx + c$, where a, b, and c are real numbers.

5. Which of the following graphs could be the graph of $y = -x(x - 2)^2$?

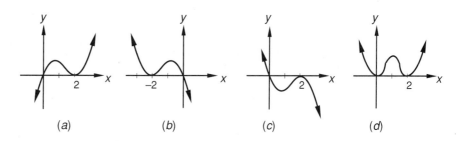

6. Find: $\int \cos u \, du$

7. Find a function y which satisfies $\dfrac{dy}{dx} = e^x$.

Use the product rule as necessary in Problems 8 and 9.

8. If $y = \sin x \cos x$, find $\dfrac{dy}{dx}$.

9. If $f(t) = 3(\cos t)e^t$, approximate $f'(6)$ to two decimal places.

10. Graph the following equations on the same coordinate plane:

$$y = \cos\left(x - \frac{\pi}{4}\right) \quad \text{and} \quad y = \sec\left(x - \frac{\pi}{4}\right)$$

11. If $y = 2e^x - \ln u + 4 \sin t$, find the differential dy.

12. Write the equation of the line which can be drawn tangent to the graph of $y = \sin x$ at $x = 16.3$.

13. If $f(x) = 2 \sin x$, find $f'(x)$, $f''(x)$, and $f'''(x)$.

14. A sector of a unit circle is shaded. If the central angle of the sector measures $\pi/6$, find the area of the sector.

15. Describe the conic section whose general equation is $9x^2 + y^2 - 4y - 5 = 0$.

16. Use a calculator to approximate to two decimal places the value of $\log_3 10$.

17. Write the key identities for practice, and then develop an identity for $\tan 2A$.

18. Solve the following equation for x: $\quad y = \arcsin x$

19. If $f(x) = 2 \sin x$ and $g(x) = |x|$, graph h where $h(x) = g(f(x))$.

20. Show that: $\quad 1 + 2 \sin(-x) \cos\left(\frac{\pi}{2} - x\right) = \cos 2x$

CONCEPT REVIEW 21. Find the number of ways 6 different colored balls can be arranged in a row.

22. A fair coin is flipped and comes up heads 8 times in a row. If it is flipped a ninth time, what are the chances it will come up tails?

LESSON 45 *Implicit differentiation*

An equation that defines y as a function of x is written in explicit form when it is in the "y equals" form with a single y on one side of the equals sign and no y's on the other side of the equals sign. Any other form of the equation is an implicit form. On the left and right below, we show implicit and explicit forms of the same equation.

IMPLICIT   EXPLICIT

$$xy + 1 = 2x - y \qquad\qquad y = \frac{2x - 1}{x + 1}$$

We can use a method called *implicit differentiation* to find dy/dx when y is defined implicitly. This procedure is useful because some equations that define y as a function of x cannot be written in explicit form. Also, some equations in x and y define more than one function. The equation $x^2 + y^2 = 25$ is the equation of a circle. This equation does not describe a function because if we exclude $+5$ and -5, there are two values of y for every value of x on the interval $[-5, 5]$. When we solve the equation for y, we see that it contains the description of two functions.

$$x^2 + y^2 = 25 \quad \longrightarrow \quad y^2 = 25 - x^2 \quad \longrightarrow \quad y = \pm\sqrt{25 - x^2}$$

We show the graph of the circle on the left and the graph of the two functions this equation describes in the center and on the right.

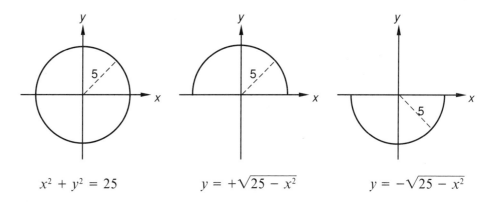

$$x^2 + y^2 = 25 \qquad\qquad y = +\sqrt{25 - x^2} \qquad\qquad y = -\sqrt{25 - x^2}$$

While the equation of the circle does not define a function, the equation of the upper portion of the circle and the equation of the lower portion of the circle do define functions because for each value of x there is only one value of y. The method of implicit differentiation will permit us to find the slope of the graph of the curve at any point on the graph. Explicit differentiation always results in an expression for the derivative that contains only constants and the variable x. The derivatives found by using implicit differentiation often contain constants and both x and y. This outcome is not unwelcome because it permits us to write expressions for the slopes of curves that are not graphs of functions. If the equation contains a description of more than one function for a portion of the domain, the expression for the slope will always contain the y variable as well as the x variable so that the slope of the graph at every point on the curve is defined. We will assume that the equations in x and y encountered in this book contain the description of at least one function.

We will use differentials to begin our investigation of the derivatives of implicitly defined functions. The first step is always the same. We find the differential of each term. Then if we want to find the derivative with respect to x, we divide each term of the differential expression by dx. If we want to find the derivative with respect to y, we divide each term by dy. Often we encounter problems in which both variables are functions of time. To find the derivatives with respect to time in these problems, we divide each term by dt.

Example 45.1   If $xy + 1 = 2x - y$, find $\dfrac{dy}{dx}$.

Solution   We will use implicit differentiation. To do this we will always use three steps. **The first step is always the same. We find the differential of every term on both sides of the equation.** We remember to use the product rule to find the differential of xy.

$$x\,dy + y\,dx + 0 = 2\,dx - dy \qquad \text{differentials}$$

Since we want to find the derivative with respect to x, the second step will be to divide every term by dx.

$$x\frac{dy}{dx} + y\frac{dx}{dx} = 2\frac{dx}{dx} - \frac{dy}{dx} \qquad \text{divided by } dx$$

We simplify this as

$$x \frac{dy}{dx} + y = 2 - \frac{dy}{dx} \qquad \text{simplified}$$

The third step is to solve algebraically for $\dfrac{dy}{dx}$.

$$x \frac{dy}{dx} + \frac{dy}{dx} = 2 - y \qquad \text{rearranged}$$

$$\frac{dy}{dx}(x + 1) = 2 - y \qquad \text{factored}$$

$$\boldsymbol{\frac{dy}{dx} = \frac{2 - y}{x + 1}} \qquad \text{divided by } x + 1$$

Example 45.2   If $y^2 - xy = \sin x$ and both x and y are functions of time, find:

(a) $\dfrac{dy}{dx}$ (b) $\dfrac{dx}{dy}$ (c) $\dfrac{dy}{dt}$

Solution   **The first step is always the same.** We find the differential of every term on both sides of the equation.

$$2y\, dy - x\, dy - y\, dx = \cos x\, dx$$

(a) To find dy/dx, we divide every term by dx and solve for dy/dx.

$$2y \frac{dy}{dx} - x \frac{dy}{dx} - y = \cos x \qquad \text{divided by } dx$$

$$\frac{dy}{dx}(2y - x) = \cos x + y \qquad \text{rearranged}$$

$$\boldsymbol{\frac{dy}{dx} = \frac{\cos x + y}{2y - x}} \qquad \text{divided}$$

(b) To find dx/dy, we divide every term by dy and solve for dx/dy.

$$2y - x - y \frac{dx}{dy} = \cos x \frac{dx}{dy} \qquad \text{divided by } dy$$

$$\frac{dx}{dy}(\cos x + y) = 2y - x \qquad \text{rearranged}$$

$$\boldsymbol{\frac{dx}{dy} = \frac{2y - x}{\cos x + y}} \qquad \text{divided}$$

We see that the expressions for dy/dx and dx/dy are reciprocals. One treats x as the independent variable and gives the rate of change of y as x is changed. The other treats y as the independent variable and gives the rate of change of x as y is changed.

(c) To find dy/dt, we divide every term by dt and solve for dy/dt.

$$2y \frac{dy}{dt} - x \frac{dy}{dt} - y \frac{dx}{dt} = \cos x \frac{dx}{dt} \qquad \text{divided by } dt$$

$$\frac{dy}{dt}(2y - x) = \frac{dx}{dt}(y + \cos x) \qquad \text{rearranged}$$

$$\boldsymbol{\frac{dy}{dt} = \frac{\frac{dx}{dt}(y + \cos x)}{2y - x}} \qquad \text{divided}$$

Example 45.3   If $x^2y - ye^x = \cos x$, find $\dfrac{dy}{dx}$.

Solution   First we find the differential of each term on both sides of the equation.

$$x^2\,dy + y(2x\,dx) - y(e^x\,dx) - e^x\,dy = -\sin x\,dx \qquad \text{differentials}$$

Next we divide each term by dx.

$$x^2\frac{dy}{dx} + 2xy - ye^x - e^x\frac{dy}{dx} = -\sin x \qquad \text{divided by } dx$$

Now we solve for $\dfrac{dy}{dx}$.

$$\frac{dy}{dx}(x^2 - e^x) = -\sin x - 2xy + ye^x \qquad \text{rearranged}$$

$$\boldsymbol{\frac{dy}{dx} = \frac{-\sin x - 2xy + ye^x}{x^2 - e^x}} \qquad \text{divided}$$

Example 45.4   Find the slope of the tangent to the graph of $x^2 + y^2 = 2$ at $(1, 1)$.

Solution   First we find the differential of every term on both sides of the equation.

$$2x\,dx + 2y\,dy = 0 \qquad \text{differentials}$$

Now we divide each term by dx and solve for dy/dx.

$$2x + 2y\frac{dy}{dx} = 0 \qquad \text{divided}$$

$$2y\frac{dy}{dx} = -2x \qquad \text{rearranged}$$

$$\frac{dy}{dx} = \frac{-x}{y} \qquad \text{divided}$$

To evaluate the slope, we substitute 1 for x and 1 for y and find that the slope of the tangent at $(1, 1)$ is -1.

$$\frac{dy}{dx} = \frac{-1}{1} = \boldsymbol{-1} \qquad \text{evaluated}$$

Example 45.5   If x and y are both functions of time and $x^2 + y^2 = 2$, find:

(*a*) $\dfrac{dx}{dt}$ (*b*) $\dfrac{dx}{dt}$ at $(1, 1)$ when $\dfrac{dy}{dt} = 7$

Solution   (*a*)   First we find the differential of every term on both sides of the equation.

$$2x\,dx + 2y\,dy = 0 \qquad \text{differentials}$$

Next we divide each term by dt and solve for dx/dt.

$$2x\frac{dx}{dt} + 2y\frac{dy}{dt} = 0 \qquad \text{divided by } dt$$

$$\boldsymbol{\frac{dx}{dt} = \frac{-y}{x}\frac{dy}{dt}} \qquad \text{solved}$$

(b)   To find dx/dt at $(1, 1)$ when $dy/dt = 7$, we substitute for x, y, and dy/dt and get

$$\frac{dx}{dt} = \frac{-1}{1}(7) = -7$$

Problem set 45

1.   It was 6 p.m. and the Grand Happening was to occur exactly when the hands of the clock were pointing in the same direction. What was the scheduled time of the Grand Happening?

Use implicit differentiation in Problems 2–4.

2.   If $y^3 - xy - 1 = x^2 + y^2$, find $\dfrac{dy}{dx}$.

3.   If x and y are both functions of time, solve for dx/dt if $y^2 - x^2 = \cos x$.

4.   Find the slope of the tangent line which can be drawn to the graph of the equation $x^2 + y^2 = 1$ at the point $(-\sqrt{2}/2, \sqrt{2}/2)$.

5.   Sketch the graph of $y = x(x - 1)^2(x + 2)^3$. (Indicate clearly where the graph touches or intersects the x axis. The graph need not be entirely accurate otherwise.)

6.   Use knowledge of graphs of polynomial functions to sketch the possible shapes of the graphs $y = -2x^3 + x^2 - 5x + 2$.

7.   If $f(x) = 3x^2$, find a function $F(x)$ such that $F'(x) = f(x)$.

Integrate:

8. $\displaystyle\int 5x^4\,dx$ 9. $\displaystyle\int e^t\,dt$ 10. $\displaystyle\int -\sin u\,du$

Use the product rule in Problems 11 and 12.

11.   If $y = x^3 \cos x$, find y'.   12.   If $s = -3u^2v$, find ds.

Differentiate as many times as necessary in Problems 13 and 14.

13.   Find $\dfrac{dy}{dx}$ if $y = 2 \ln x + 4 \sqrt[3]{x^2} - \dfrac{e^x}{3}$.

14.   Find $s''(t)$ if $s(t) = s_0 + v_0 t + \dfrac{1}{2} gt^2$, where s_0, v_0, and g are constants.

15.   Graph f and g on the same coordinate plane, where

$$f(x) = x^2 - 2x - 1 \quad\text{and}\quad g(x) = \frac{1}{f(x)}$$

16.   Sketch the graph of the following, indicating clearly all asymptotes and zeros:

$$y = \frac{(2 - x)(x + 1)}{(x - 1)(x + 3)x}$$

17.   Find the three cube roots of $8(\cos 33° + i \sin 33°)$.

18.   If $f(x) = \sin x$ and $g(x) = f(2x)$, graph g.

19. F and G are two distinct points on the coordinate plane, and C is a constant that is greater than the length FG. Describe the locus of all points P in the coordinate plane such that $PF + PG = C$.

20.   Solve for x: $y = e^x$

21. Simplify: $\sin(-x)\cos\left(\dfrac{\pi}{2} - x\right)\sec^2\left(\dfrac{\pi}{2} - x\right)$

CONCEPT REVIEW   **22.** How many different ways can 4 identical red balls and 3 identical green balls be arranged in a row?

23. If $m\widehat{AB} = x$ and $m\widehat{CD} = y$, express $m\angle D$ and $m\angle B$ in terms of x and y. Then, express $m\angle CED$ in terms of $m\angle B$ and $m\angle D$. Finally, express $m\angle CED$ in terms of x and y.

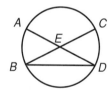

LESSON 46 *The integral of a constant · Integral of Cf(x) · Integral of x^n*

46.A
The integral of a constant

The derivative of $5x$ is 5 and the differential of $5x$ is 5 dx.

$$\text{If} \quad y = 5x \quad \text{then} \quad \frac{dy}{dx} = 5 \quad \text{and} \quad dy = 5\,dx$$

We can perform the inverse operation of integration by beginning with either the derivative or the differential.

$$\int 5 = 5x + C \qquad \int 5\,dx = 5x + C$$

The expression $\int 5$, on the left, does not have a dx to indicate that x is the variable of integration, so we have to guess that x is this variable. The expression $\int 5\,dx$, on the right, tells us quite plainly that x is the variable of integration. Thus, this form is usually preferred. Sometimes the variable of integration is t or v or u and the presence of dt or du or dv makes this clear.

$$\int dt = t + C \qquad \int 5\,dv = 5v + C \qquad \int 7\,du = 7u + C$$

46.B
Integral of Cf(x)

We remember that the derivative of a constant times a function is the constant times the derivative of a function. This means that a constant factor of a function can be moved across the operator d/dx. On the left below, we have the derivative of 4 times x^2. On the right, we have moved the 4 across the operator d/dx so that the 4 is in front.

$$\frac{d}{dx}\,4x^2 \quad \longrightarrow \quad 4\frac{d}{dx}\,x^2$$

Now we find that the derivative of x^2 is $2x$ and multiply this result by 4.

$$4\frac{d}{dx}\,x^2 = 4(2x)$$

To undo what we have done we will first insert a dx.

$$\int 4(2x)\, dx$$

The operator for antidifferentiation is the integral sign, and we can move the 4 across the integral sign and get

$$4 \int 2x\, dx =$$

Now we antidifferentiate and remember to write the C.

$$= 4(x^2 + C) = 4x^2 + 4C$$

But C is a symbol that we use to represent any number. Thus $4C$ is 4 times any number, which again equals any number, so the 4 is not necessary. Thus we do not multiply the constant of integration by 4 and just write

$$4 \int 2x\, dx = \mathbf{4x^2 + C}$$

We must be careful never to move a variable across the integral sign.

Example 46.1 Find $\int 4 \cos t$.

Solution We will insert a dt after $\cos t$ to get the differential form and move the 4 across the integral sign.

$$\int 4 \cos t\, dt = 4 \int \cos t\, dt = \mathbf{4 \sin t + C}$$

Now we check our answer by finding the differential.

$$d(4 \sin t + C) = 4 \cos t\, dt \qquad \text{check}$$

Example 46.2 Find $\int \sin u\, du$.

Solution The ability to move a constant across the integral sign will be very helpful here. We know that the derivative of $\cos u$ is $-\sin u$, but we have $+\sin u$. The trick is to multiply $\sin u$ by $(-1)(-1)$ and move one of the $-$ signs across the integral sign, as we show here.

$$\int (-1)(-1) \sin u\, du = - \int (-\sin u)\, du = -(\cos u) + C = \mathbf{-\cos u + C}$$

Now we check our answer by finding the differential.

$$d(-\cos u + C) = \sin u\, du \qquad \text{check}$$

46.C
Integral of x^n

The derivative of x^n is nx^{n-1}. Thus, the derivative of x^4 is $4x^3$. To antidifferentiate, we must get back to x^4.

$$\int 4x^3 = x^4$$

To do this we must develop a procedure to get rid of the 4 in front and to change the exponent from 3 to 4. To get rid of the 4 in front, we can divide by $3 + 1$, and we can get back to the original exponent of 4 by writing $3 + 1$ as the new exponent. Thus, we have

$$\int 4x^3 = 4\left(\frac{x^{3+1}}{3 + 1}\right) + C = x^4 + C$$

Since the derivative of $x^4 + C$ is $4x^3$, we are correct. We can generalize this example into a general rule for finding the integral of x^n. To find the integral of x^n, we change n to $n + 1$ and divide by $n + 1$.

$$\int x^n = \frac{x^{n+1}}{n+1} + C$$

This rule works for all values of the exponent n except -1, a special case which we will discuss in Lesson 49.

Example 46.3 Find $\int 5s^{-20} \, ds$.

Solution As the first step we move the 5 across the integral sign and write

$$5 \int s^{-20} \, ds$$

We must be careful with negative exponents because -20 increased by 1 is -19. We divide by $-20 + 1$ and make the new exponent $-20 + 1$, and remember to record the constant of integration C.

$$5 \int s^{-20} \, ds = 5 \left(\frac{s^{-19}}{-19} \right) = \frac{-5s^{-19}}{19} + C$$

The derivative of this expression is $5s^{-20}$, so our answer is correct.

Example 46.4 Find $\int \frac{1}{3} \sqrt[3]{t^2} \, dt$.

Solution To begin, we move the $\frac{1}{3}$ across the integral sign and rewrite $\sqrt[3]{t^2}$ with a fractional exponent.

$$\frac{1}{3} \int t^{2/3} \, dt$$

To integrate, we make the new exponent $\frac{2}{3} + 1$ and divide by $\frac{2}{3} + 1$. We remember to write the constant of integration.

$$\frac{1}{3} \int x^{2/3} \, dt = \frac{1}{3} \left(\frac{t^{2/3+1}}{\frac{2}{3} + 1} \right) = \frac{1}{5} t^{5/3} + C$$

Example 46.5 Find $\int \frac{3 \, du}{\sqrt{u}}$.

Solution We move the 3 across the integral sign and write $1/\sqrt{u}$ as $u^{-1/2}$.

$$3 \int u^{-1/2} \, du$$

Now we increase the exponent by 1 to get $-\frac{1}{2} + 1 = \frac{1}{2}$ and divide by the same number.

$$3 \int u^{-1/2} \, du = 3 \left(\frac{u^{1/2}}{\frac{1}{2}} \right) = 6u^{1/2} + C$$

Example 46.6 Find $\int 5z^\pi$.

Solution We move the 5 across the integral sign and add a dz to denote the variable of integration.

$$5 \int z^\pi \, dz$$

Now we increase π by 1 to get $\pi + 1$, and we also divide by $\pi + 1$.

$$5 \int z^\pi \, dz = \frac{5z^{\pi+1}}{\pi + 1} + C$$

Problem set 46

1. The surface area of a rectangular solid is 100 cm^2. If the length L and width w of the solid are equal, find the volume of the solid in terms of L.

2. The speed of the seraph increased exponentially. At noon, the speed of the seraph was 50 fathoms per second. If at 1 o'clock the speed of the seraph was 60 fathoms per second, what was the speed of the seraph at 6 p.m.?

Integrate:

3. $\displaystyle\int 3 \sin x \, dx$

4. $\displaystyle\int \frac{2 \, dt}{\sqrt{t}}$

5. $\displaystyle\int \frac{1}{2} \sqrt[3]{u} \, du$

6. $\displaystyle\int 3x \, dx$

Use implicit differentiation in Problems 7–9.

7. If $2x^2y + y^2 = \cos x$, find $\dfrac{dy}{dx}$.

8. If u and v are both functions of time, find $\dfrac{du}{dt}$ if $u^2 + v^2 = 2uv$.

9. Find the equation of the tangent line which can be drawn to the graph of the equation $y^2 - x^2 = 1$ at the point $(0, 1)$.

10. Which of the following graphs most resembles the graph of $y = x^3(x + 2)^2$?

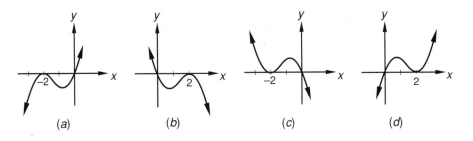

(a)   (b)   (c)   (d)

11. Make a rough sketch of the possible shapes of the graph of the following: $y = -x^4 + ax^3 + bx^2 + cx + d$ where a, b, c, and d are real numbers.

12. Approximate $s''(2)$ to two decimal places if $s(t) = \sqrt[3]{t} - 2\sqrt{t} + \dfrac{3}{t}$.

Evaluate the following limits:

13. $\displaystyle\lim_{\Delta x \to 0} \frac{e^{x+\Delta x} - e^x}{\Delta x}$

14. $\displaystyle\lim_{x \to 2} \frac{x^2 + x - 6}{x - 2}$

15. $\displaystyle\lim_{x \to \infty} \frac{x + 1}{x}$

16. Sketch the graph $f(x) = x^3 + 1$ and determine on which intervals the function f is increasing.

17. Solve for x: $8^{2x-1} = 4$. Do not use a calculator.

18. Find the value of k so that $x = -1$ is a zero of $y = 2x^3 + x + k$.

19. If $f(x) = e^x$ and $g(x) = -f(-x)$, graph f and g on the same coordinate plane.

20. Graph g if $f(x) = \sin x$ and $g(x) = -3 + 2f\left(x - \dfrac{\pi}{3}\right)$.

21. Find values of x where $0 \le x < 2\pi$ and $2 \sin^2 x - 3 \sin x + 1 = 0$.

CONCEPT REVIEW   22. Find the area of an equilateral triangle each of whose sides has a length of 5.

23. If $x = 5 + y$, find the value of $x^2 - 2xy + y^2$.

LESSON 47 *Critical numbers*

The word *point* causes some confusion in calculus because authors often use the word point to describe a location on the x axis and students tend to think of the word point as a point on the graph of the function. In this book we have been using the idea of the position of the x dot instead of using the word point to describe a value of x. We have used $f(c)$ to indicate the value of the function when $x = c$ and have used $(c, f(c))$ to indicate the point on the graph of the function when $x = c$.

We remember that a function is an input-output process and that the input is the position of the x dot on the x axis and that the output is the position of the y dot on the y axis, as we show in this graph.

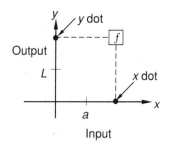

If we move the x dot left and right along the x axis, the rule of the function will move the y dot up and down along the y axis. We also remember that a function has a limit L, when $x = a$, if the y dot approaches L when the x dot approaches a both from the left and from the right. The two-limit condition cannot be satisfied at an endpoint because endpoints cannot be approached from both the left and the right. Let us consider a function that has a left endpoint E_L and a right endpoint E_R. These endpoints are the x-dot positions on either end of the interval of the domain of f. The coordinates of the points on the ends of the graph are $(E_L, f(E_L))$ and $(E_R, f(E_R))$.

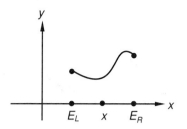

The x dot can approach the left endpoint E_L of the function defined by this graph only from the right, so only a right-hand limit exists at the left endpoint. The x dot can approach the right endpoint E_R only from the left, so this endpoint only has a left-hand limit. Since neither endpoint has both a left-hand limit and a right-hand limit, the function does not have a limit at the endpoints. Thus the derivative does not exist at the endpoints.

If the graph of a function makes a sudden change in direction at $(c, f(c))$, the left-hand limit of f' as x approaches c^- and the right-hand limit of f' as x approaches c^+ will not be equal. Thus the limit does not exist, and the function does not have a derivative at $x = c$. The absolute value function is a good example. On the following page, we show the graph of $y = |x|$ on the left and the graph of the derivative of this function on the right.

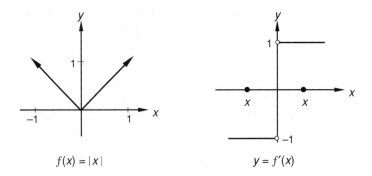

$$f(x) = |x| \qquad\qquad y = f'(x)$$

The graph on the left has two parts. One part is the line $y = x$ for values of x greater than 0. The slope of this line is $+1$, as we show in the graph of f' on the right. In the graph of f', for any position of the x dot to the right of the y axis, the value of $f'(x)$ is $+1$.

The other part of the graph of $y = |x|$ is for values of x less than 0, and the slope of this line to the left of the y axis is -1. For any position of the x dot in the graph of f' to the left of the y axis, the value of $f'(x)$ is -1. Thus, in the right-hand figure, as the x dot approaches zero from the right, the limit of $f'(x)$ is $+1$, and as the x dot approaches zero from the left, the limit of $f'(x)$ is -1. The limits are different, so the limit of $f'(x)$ as x approaches zero does not exist and the derivative f' does not exist for an x value of zero.

For the reason illustrated here, any function whose graph comes to a sharp point at $(c, f(c))$ does not have a derivative at $x = c$. This sentence is confusing because *sharp point* gives the word *point* still another meaning. Authors of some calculus textbooks resolve this difficulty by using the word *corner* or *cusp* instead of *sharp point* and say that if the graph of a function has a corner or cusp at $(c, f(c))$, the derivative does not exist at $x = c$. Some authors use the word *number* or *value* to designate points on the x axis and avoid using the word *point* to refer to points on the graph of the function.

In calculus we are often interested in values of x for which $f(x)$ is greater (or less) than other nearby values of $f(x)$. For these x-dot positions the graph of a function has a local high point or a local low point. We call these x-dot positions **critical points, critical numbers,** or **critical values.**

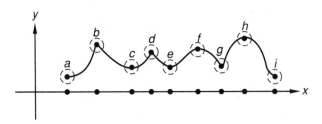

On this graph the critical points (or numbers or values) are indicated by the dots on the x axis, and the corresponding points on the graph are circled. We will call these points on the graph **local maximum points** or **local minimum points.** We see that local maximum and minimum values of the function can occur at endpoints or at corners where the derivative is not defined or can occur at other points c, e, f, and h where the graph has a slope of zero. It is customary to use the word **stationary** to name a point at which the slope of the graph is zero. Thus a stationary number or a stationary value or a stationary point is a position of the x dot for which the slope of the graph is zero, which means that $f'(x) = 0$.

> A critical number (value or point) of a function is a number (x-dot position) for which the derivative equals zero or for which the derivative does not exist.

The derivative does not exist at endpoints or at corners. In applied problems, the critical values at which the derivative does not exist are not as frequently encountered as those at which the derivative equals zero.

Example 47.1   Find the critical numbers of the function f where $f(x) = x^3 + \frac{9}{2}x^2 + 6x + 5$. Also, find where the relative maximum and minimum values of f occur.

Solution   Critical numbers are those numbers for which f' is equal to zero or does not exist. Fortunately, we seldom encounter functions whose derivatives do not exist. This is a polynomial function, and the derivatives exist for polynomial functions for every number on the interval $(-\infty, +\infty)$. Thus the critical numbers for this function are the stationary numbers, which are the numbers at which the derivative equals zero. First we find $f'(x)$.

$$f(x) = x^3 + \frac{9}{2}x^2 + 6x + 5 \qquad \text{equation}$$

$$f'(x) = 3x^2 + 9x + 6 \qquad \text{differentiated}$$

$$x^2 + 3x + 2 = 0 \qquad \text{set } f'(x) = 0$$

$$(x + 2)(x + 1) = 0 \qquad \text{factored}$$

$$x = -2, -1 \qquad \text{solved}$$

Thus f has critical numbers at $x = -2$ and $x = -1$. We use our knowledge of the graphs of cubics to sketch these three possible forms of this graph. The coefficient of the x^3 term is positive, so $f(x)$ has large positive values for large positive values of x.

The graph on the left has no critical points, for there are no corners, endpoints, or places where the slope equals zero. The graph in the center has one critical point (the slope is zero). The graph on the right has two critical points (the slope is zero). We have found that the x values of P_1 and P_2 are -2 and -1. We can use the equation of the function to find the y values if we wish.

When $x = -2$, $\qquad y = (-2)^3 + \frac{9}{2}(-2)^2 + 6(-2) + 5 = 3$

When $x = -1$, $\qquad y = (-1)^3 + \frac{9}{2}(-1)^2 + 6(-1) + 5 = 2.5$

Thus the local maximum point on the graph is $(-2, 3)$ and the local minimum point is $(-1, 2.5)$.

Example 47.2   Find the critical numbers of the function $f(x) = \frac{1}{4}x^4 - \frac{1}{3}x^3 - x^2 + 5$ and indicate where the relative maximum and minimum values occur.

Solution   This is a polynomial function that has no endpoints and no corners because polynomial functions have a derivative for all x on the interval $(-\infty, +\infty)$. Thus the critical numbers will be stationary numbers. To find the numbers, we differentiate the fourth-degree equation and get a third-degree equation. This problem was carefully contrived so that this cubic could be factored easily. We are investigating critical points, not the methods of finding the roots of cubics, and contrived problems are helpful.

$$f(x) = \frac{1}{4}x^4 - \frac{1}{3}x^3 - x^2 + 5 \qquad \text{original function}$$

$$f'(x) = x^3 - x^2 - 2x \qquad \text{differentiated}$$

$$f'(x) = x^3 - x^2 - 2x = 0 \qquad \text{set } f'(x) = 0$$

$$x(x^2 - x - 2) = 0 \qquad \text{factored}$$

$$x(x - 2)(x + 1) = 0 \qquad \text{factored again}$$

$$x = 2, 0, \text{ and } -1 \qquad \text{solved}$$

We know the graph of a fourth-degree polynomial can have one, two, or three places where the slope is zero. Because the lead coefficient is positive, the graph could have one of the following forms.

Since our function has three critical points, its graph must look like one of the three graphs on the right. The x coordinates of the critical points on the graph are **−1, 0, and 2,** and we could substitute these values into the equation of the function to find the y values of those points if we wished. Since the graph of f must resemble one of the three graphs on the right, f must attain local minimum values at $x = -1$ and $x = 2$ and a local maximum value at $x = 0$.

Problem set 47   **1.** A cone is formed by cutting a sector whose central angle has a measure of $x°$ from a circle of radius 10 cm and joining the two edges of the sector.

Find the circumference and radius of the circular base of the cone.

2. Find the critical numbers of $y = \frac{1}{3}x^3 - x$. Use a rough sketch of the graph of the function y and its equation to determine the local maximum and minimum values of y and where they occur.

3. Find the critical numbers of the function $f(x) = x^3 - \frac{9}{2}x^2 + 6x + 3$. Use a rough sketch of the function and its equation to determine the local maximum and minimum values of y and where they occur.

Integrate:

4. $\displaystyle\int \frac{\sqrt{u}}{20}\, du$ **5.** $\displaystyle\int 2\cos t\, dt$ **6.** $\displaystyle\int 3\, dx$

Use implicit differentiation to solve Problems 7–9.

7. If $y^3 + xy = e^x$, find $\dfrac{dy}{dx}$. **8.** If $x = \sin y$, find $\dfrac{dy}{dx}$.

9. If x and y are both functions of time and $2x - y^2 = \ln x$, find $\dfrac{dx}{dt}$.

10. Approximate to two decimal places the slope of the tangent line which can be drawn to the graph of f at $x = -1$ if $f(x) = x \sin x$.

11. If $y = 2x^2 + 3\sin x - 4\cos x + \ln x$, find $\dfrac{dy}{dx}$.

12. Make a rough sketch of the possible shapes of $y = 3x^3 + ax^2 + bx + c$ where a, b, and c are real numbers.

13. Sketch the basic shape of $y = x(x - 1)(x + 2)^2$, indicating clearly the behavior of the graph near the points where the graph touches or intersects the x axis.

14. Sketch the graph of $y = \tan x$, indicating all asymptotes.

15. Sketch the graph of the following equation, indicating clearly all zeros and asymptotes:

$$y = \frac{x(x - 2)}{(x - 3)(x + 1)(x - 1)}$$

16. Write the key identities for practice. Then develop an identity for $\tan(A + B)$ and an identity for $\tan 2A$.

17. Identify the conic section whose equation is $y - 4x^2 + 8x - 6 = 0$ and describe its properties.

18. Solve for b if $\log_b 27 = 3$. **19.** Evaluate: $\displaystyle\lim_{t \to \infty} \frac{2t^2 + 3}{4 - 5t^2}$

20. Graph f where

$$f(x) = \begin{cases} x^2 & \text{when } x \le 1 \\ 2x & \text{when } x > 1 \end{cases}$$

Then evaluate $\displaystyle\lim_{x \to 1^+} f(x)$ and $\displaystyle\lim_{x \to 1^-} f(x)$.

21. Express $\sqrt{3} + 2i$ in polar form.

22. State the converse of the following statement: If $f' > 0$ on the interval $[a, b]$, then f is increasing on the interval $[a, b]$.

CONCEPT REVIEW **23.** Find the radius of the circle which can be circumscribed around a square, each of whose sides has a length of 5 centimeters.

24. If $x - y > 0$, compare: *A.* $x^2 - 2xy + y^2$ *B.* $x^2 + 2xy + y^2$

LESSON 48 *Differentiation by u substitution*

One of the most powerful tools in mathematics is substitution.

SUBSTITUTION AXIOM

If two expressions *a* and *b* are of equal value, *a* = *b*, then *a* may replace *b* or *b* may replace *a* in another expression without changing the value of the expression. Also *a* may replace *b* or *b* may replace *a* in any statement without changing the truth or falsity of the statement. Also *a* may replace *b* or *b* may replace *a* in any equation or inequality without changing the solution set of the equation or inequality.

Substitution is especially useful in calculus because we can substitute a simple expression for a complicated expression. Then we work with the simple expression and make a reverse substitution as the last step. Knowing when to substitute and what to substitute comes from experience and practice. It is important to be able to look at a complicated expression and be able to recognize the basic form of the expression. This recognition will often suggest the substitution that should be used. In this lesson we will use the letter *u* to write the basic form, and we will call this substitution *u substitution.*

$$y = e^{x^2+2} \qquad \text{has the form of} \qquad y = e^u$$

$$y = (x^3 - 2x^2 + 1)^{100} \qquad \text{has the form of} \qquad y = u^{100}$$

$$y = \ln(x^2 + 42) \qquad \text{has the form of} \qquad y = \ln u$$

$$y = \sin(x^2 - 15) \qquad \text{has the form of} \qquad y = \sin u$$

$$y = (\sin x)^3 \qquad \text{has the form of} \qquad y = u^3$$

We can find the derivative of a function by using the differential and by substituting. To find the derivative of

$$y = e^{x^2+2} \qquad \text{equation}$$

we note that the basic form of this equation is

$$y = e^u \qquad \text{basic form}$$

We have already made the first substitution because we have written *u* instead of $x^2 + 2$. Next we compute the differential *du* and record both *u* and *du* in a box to be used in the second substitution.

$$\boxed{\begin{array}{l} u = x^2 + 2 \\ du = 2x\, dx \end{array}}$$

Then we find the differential of the basic form and get

$$y = e^u \quad \longrightarrow \quad dy = e^u\, du \qquad \text{differential}$$

Now we make the second substitution. We replace *u* with $x^2 + 2$ and replace *du* with $2x\, dx$. As the last step we divide by *dx*.

$$dy = (e^{x^2+2})(2x \, dx) \qquad \text{substituted}$$

$$\frac{dy}{dx} = 2xe^{x^2+2} \qquad \text{divided by } dx$$

Example 48.1   If the *f* equation is $y = (x^2 + 2x)^{10}$, find $f'(x)$.

Solution   The first step is to recognize the basic form of the equation and use *u* to write the basic form.

$$y = u^{10} \qquad \text{basic form}$$

When we do this, we have already made the first substitution. We then record the substitution we have made for *u* in a box, compute *du*, and record it in the same box. Thus the first step has two parts.

$$y = u^{10} \qquad \boxed{\begin{array}{l} u = x^2 + 2x \\ du = (2x + 2) \, dx \end{array}}$$

The second step has three parts. We find the differential *dy* of the basic *u* expression, use the information in the box to make the second substitution, and finish by dividing both sides by *dx*.

$$dy = 10u^9 \, du \qquad \text{differential}$$

$$dy = 10(x^2 + 2x)^9(2x + 2) \, dx \qquad \text{substituted}$$

$$f'(x) = \frac{dy}{dx} = 10(x^2 + 2x)^9(2x + 2) \qquad \text{divided by } dx$$

Example 48.2   If the *h* equation is $h(x) = \sqrt[3]{x^2 + 2x}$, find $h'(x)$.

Solution   **We always rewrite radical expressions as expressions with fractional exponents.** If we do this, we get $y = (x^2 + 2x)^{1/3}$, whose basic form is $y = u^{1/3}$. We have already made the substitution when we write the basic form. Next we record the substitution in a box.

$$y = u^{1/3} \qquad \boxed{\begin{array}{l} u = x^2 + 2x \\ du = (2x + 2) \, dx \end{array}}$$

Now we find the differential of *y*, make the second substitution, and then divide by *dx*.

$$dy = \frac{1}{3} u^{-2/3} \, du \qquad \text{differential}$$

$$dy = \frac{1}{3}(x^2 + 2x)^{-2/3}(2x + 2) \, dx \qquad \text{substituted}$$

$$h'(x) = \frac{dy}{dx} = \frac{1}{3}(x^2 + 2x)^{-2/3}(2x + 2) \qquad \text{divided by } dx$$

Example 48.3   If the *g* equation is $g(x) = \ln (x^2 - 42)$, find $g'(x)$.

Solution   First we use *u* to write the basic form of $\ln (x^2 + 42)$. This is the first substitution. Then we compute *du* and record *u* and *du* in a box.

$$y = \ln u \qquad \boxed{\begin{array}{l} u = x^2 - 42 \\ du = 2x\ dx \end{array}}$$

Now we find the differential of y, make the second substitution, and divide by dx.

$$dy = \frac{1}{u}\ du \quad \longrightarrow \quad dy = \frac{2x\ dx}{x^2 - 42} \qquad \text{differential and substituted}$$

$$g'(x) = \frac{dy}{dx} = \frac{2x}{x^2 - 42} \qquad \text{divided by } dx$$

Example 48.4   If the f equation is $f(t) = \sin(t^3 - 15)$, find $f'(t)$.

Solution   First we use u to write the basic form of the equation. This is the first substitution. Then we compute du and record u and du in a box.

$$y = \sin u \qquad \boxed{\begin{array}{l} u = t^3 - 15 \\ du = 3t^2\ dt \end{array}}$$

Now we find dy, make the second substitution, and then divide by dt.

$$dy = \cos u\ du \quad \longrightarrow \quad dy = [\cos(t^3 - 15)](3t^2\ dt) \qquad \text{substituted}$$

$$f'(t) = \frac{dy}{dt} = 3t^2 \cos(t^3 - 15) \qquad \text{divided by } dt$$

Example 48.5   If $y = \sin^3 x$, find $\dfrac{dy}{dx}$.

Solution   We remember that $\sin^3 x$ means $(\sin x)^3$. Now we substitute and record u and du in a box.

$$y = u^3 \qquad \boxed{\begin{array}{l} u = \sin x \\ du = \cos x\ dx \end{array}}$$

Now we find dy, make the second substitution, and divide by dx.

$$dy = 3u^2\ du \qquad \text{differential}$$

$$dy = 3(\sin x)^2(\cos x\ dx) \qquad \text{substituted}$$

$$f'(x) = \frac{dy}{dx} = 3 \cos x \sin^2 x \qquad \text{divided by } dx$$

Example 48.6   If $y = \cos e^x$, find $f'(x)$.

Solution   This time we let $u = e^x$.

$$y = \cos u \quad \longrightarrow \quad dy = -\sin u\ du \qquad \boxed{\begin{array}{l} u = e^x \\ du = e^x\ dx \end{array}}$$

Now we make the second substitution and divide by dx.

$$dy = (-\sin e^x)(e^x\ dx) \qquad \text{substituted}$$

$$f'(x) = \frac{dy}{dx} = -e^x \sin e^x \qquad \text{divided by } dx$$

Example 48.7   If $y = (e^x + 1)^{1/2}$, find y'.

Solution   This time we let $u = (e^x + 1)$.

$$y = u^{1/2} \longrightarrow dy = \frac{1}{2} u^{-1/2} \, du \qquad \boxed{\begin{array}{l} u = e^x + 1 \\ du = e^x \, dx \end{array}}$$

Now we make the second substitution and divide by dx.

$$dy = \frac{1}{2}(e^x + 1)^{-1/2} \, e^x \, dx$$

$$y' = \frac{dy}{dx} = \frac{e^x}{2(e^x + 1)^{1/2}}$$

Problem set 48

1. Four thousand liters of a $P\%$ alcohol solution was available. How many liters of alcohol had to be extracted so that the solution would be only 80% alcohol?

In Problems 2–7, use u substitution to find the derivative.

2. If $f(x) = (x^3 - 3x^2 + 1)^{20}$, find $f'(x)$.

3. If $y = \sin(t^3 + 1)$, find $\dfrac{dy}{dt}$.   4. If $g(x) = \cos^3 x$, find $g'(x)$.

5. If $y = \ln(x^2 + 1)$, find $\dfrac{dy}{dx}$.   6. If $h(x) = \sqrt[3]{x^3 + 2x - 1}$, find $h'(x)$.

7. If $y = \dfrac{1}{\sqrt{x^2 - 1}}$, find $\dfrac{dy}{dx}$.

8. Find the critical numbers of $f(x) = -3x^4 - 4x^3 + 12x^2 - 12$. Use this equation and a rough sketch of the graph of f to determine where the local maximum and local minimum of f occur and what their values are.

Integrate:

9. $\displaystyle \int \frac{3}{\sqrt{u}} \, du$ 10. $\displaystyle \int -4 \sqrt[3]{t^2} \, dt$

11. $\displaystyle \int x\sqrt{x} \, dx$ (*Hint*: Multiply first.)

Use implicit differentiation to solve Problems 12 and 13.

12. If $xy^2 - 2y = e^x$, find $\dfrac{dy}{dx}$.

13. Find the equation of the line which can be drawn perpendicular to the graph of $x^2 - 4y^2 = 0$ at the point $(4, 2)$.

14. Use the definition of a derivative to find $f'(x)$ where $f(x) = \sqrt{x}$.

15. Sketch the graph of $y = x(x - 3)^2(x + 2)^3$.

16. If $f(x) = \ln x$ and $g(x) = \sqrt{x - 1}$, find the domain and the range of f and g.

17. If f and g are as defined in Problem 16, find the equation of $f \circ g$ and determine the domain of $f \circ g$.

18. Solve for θ: $-\sqrt{3} + 3 \tan 3\theta = 0$ $(0 \le \theta < 2\pi)$

19. Find the four fourth roots of $16(\cos 40° + i \sin 40°)$ and express them in polar form.

20. Write the key identities and develop an expression that gives $\sin^2 x$ in terms of $\cos 2x$.

21. Find the equation of the quadratic function whose x intercepts are $x = -1$ and $x = 2$ and whose y intercept is $y = -2$.

22. Simplify: $\sin(-x) \csc\left(\dfrac{\pi}{2} - x\right)$

CONCEPT REVIEW   23. If $\begin{vmatrix} a & b \\ c & d \end{vmatrix} = ad - bc$, find the value of d for which $\begin{vmatrix} 2 & 3 \\ -1 & d \end{vmatrix} = 4$

24. If $x > y > 0$, compare: A. x^y B. y^x

LESSON 49   *Integral of a sum · Integral of $\dfrac{1}{x}$*

49.A
Integral of a sum

We remember that the derivative of a sum is the sum of the individual derivatives.

$$\frac{d}{dx}(x^2 + e^x + \sin x) = \frac{d}{dx}x^2 + \frac{d}{dx}e^x + \frac{d}{dx}\sin x$$

When we take these derivatives, we get the following sum.

$$2x + e^x + \cos x$$

To undo what we have done, we must undo each of these individual operations. This lets us write

$$\int (2x + e^x + \cos x) = \int 2x + \int e^x + \int \cos x$$

Each of these integrals will have a constant of integration that represents some number.

$$\int 2x + \int e^x + \int \cos x = (x^2 + C_1) + (e^x + C_2) + (\sin x + C_3)$$

Now we rearrange this expression to get

$$x^2 + e^x + \sin x + C_1 + C_2 + C_3$$

Each letter C represents some number, so their sum equals some number plus some number plus some number. This sum, of course, equals some number, which we again represent with a single letter C.

$$x^2 + e^x + \sin x + C$$

Thus we see that the constants of integration of a sum can be combined into a single constant of integration.

Example 49.1   Find: $\displaystyle\int (6s^{12} + 5s + 3e^s + 4)$

Solution   First we remember that the integral of a sum is the sum of the individual integrals.

$$= \int 6s^{12} + \int 5s + \int 3e^s + \int 4$$

Next we move the constants so that they are in front of the integral signs and put ds on the end of each integrand.

$$= 6 \int s^{12} \, ds + 5 \int s \, ds + 3 \int e^s \, ds + 4 \int ds$$

Now we integrate each term and write a single constant of integration at the end.

$$= \frac{6}{13} s^{13} + \frac{5}{2} s^2 + 3e^s + 4s + C$$

Example 49.2   Find: $\int (6 \sin u + 5u^{-5} + 3e^u - 2)$

Solution   We will use just two steps this time. First we write the sum of the integrals in differential form and put the constants in front. Note how we handled the signs in the first term so we could integrate $-\sin u$, which is the derivative of $\cos u$.

$$= -6 \int -\sin u \, du + 5 \int u^{-5} \, du + 3 \int e^u \, du - 2 \int du$$

Now we integrate and write the constant C at the end.

$$= -6 \cos u - \frac{5}{4} u^{-4} + 3e^u - 2u + C$$

49.B
Integral of 1/x

The function $y = \ln x$ is defined only for positive values of x, for only positive numbers have logarithms. The derivative of $\ln x$ is $1/x$, so the slope of the graph of $y = \ln x$ is $1/x$. When $x = 3$, the slope is $\frac{1}{3}$, as we see in the left-hand figure below. The function $y = \ln (-x)$ is defined only for negative values of x because the opposite of a negative number is a positive number.

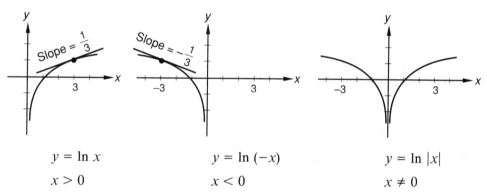

| $y = \ln x$ | $y = \ln (-x)$ | $y = \ln |x|$ |
| $x > 0$ | $x < 0$ | $x \neq 0$ |

The slope of the graph of $y = \ln (-x)$ when x is a negative number is also $1/x$, so the slope when $x = -3$ is $-\frac{1}{3}$, as we see in the center figure. The function $y = \ln |x|$ is a combination of these two functions, as we see in the graph on the right.

The derivative of $\ln x$ when x is greater than zero is $1/x$. The derivative of $\ln (-x)$ when x is less than zero is $1/x$. The derivative of $\ln |x|$ is $1/x$ for any positive or negative value of x. Although the derivatives are the same, the functions are different functions because their domains are different. One is defined for positive values of x. One is defined for negative values of x. One is defined for both positive and negative values of x. When we write

$$\int \frac{1}{x}$$

we are asking for the family of antiderivatives that is defined for all nonzero values of x. So

$$\int \frac{1}{x}\, dx = \ln |x| + C$$

If we were to write

$$\int \frac{1}{x}\, dx = \ln x + C$$

we would be designating a function that is defined only for positive values of x.

We can find the integral of $1/x^2$ by rewriting it as x^{-2} and using the method we devised to integrate x^n.

$$\int \frac{1}{x^2}\, dx = \int x^{-2}\, dx = \frac{x^{-1}}{-2+1} + C = -x^{-1} + C$$

If we try to use the same procedure to integrate $1/x$, we find ourselves dividing by zero.

$$\int \frac{1}{x}\, dx = \int \frac{dx}{x} = \int x^{-1}\, dx = \frac{x^{-1+1}}{-1+1} = \frac{x^0}{0} \qquad ?????$$

From this we see that the rule for finding the integral of x^n cannot be used if $n = -1$. The rule can be used for any value of n except -1, and -1 is a special case.

$$\int x^{-1}\, dx = \int \frac{1}{x} = \ln |x| + C$$

Example 49.3 Find: $\displaystyle\int \left(\frac{4}{t} + 3t^{-1} + 4\cos t + 3\sin t\right)$

Solution The integral of a sum is the sum of the integrals. We insert the dt's and write the constants in front of the integral signs.

$$4\int \frac{dt}{t} + 3\int \frac{dt}{t} + 4\int \cos t\, dt - 3\int -\sin t\, dt$$

We could have combined the first two terms. Note how we handled the signs in the last term. To finish, we combine the first two integrals and write

$$7 \ln |t| + 4 \sin t - 3 \cos t + C$$

49.C
Derivative of ln |whatever|

In many functions the use of the absolute value changes the function and thus changes the derivative of the function. To illustrate, we show the graphs of $y = \sin x$ and $y = \sin |x|$.

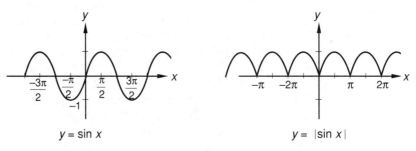

$$y = \sin x \qquad\qquad y = |\sin x|$$

The slopes of the tangent lines to the graph of the function on the left are not the same as those for the function on the right for every value of x, because the functions are different functions and have different derivatives. We will discuss absolute value functions in a later lesson.

The natural logarithm function is an exception. The derivatives of ln x, ln $(-x)$, and ln $|x|$ are all $1/x$. For the natural logarithm function, the use of the absolute value changes only the domain so that x can be any real number except zero.

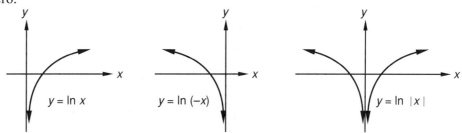

$y = \ln x$ $y = \ln(-x)$ $y = \ln|x|$

We can use u substitution to find the derivative of $y = \ln x$, $y = \ln|\sin x|$, $y = \ln|4x^2 + 2|$, or $y = \ln|\text{whatever}|$, as long as "whatever" does not equal zero.

Example 49.4   Use u substitution to find dy/dx if $y = \ln|\cos x|$.

Solution   We write the basic form and record the substitution in a box.

$$y = \ln|u| \qquad \boxed{\begin{array}{l} u = \cos x \\ du = -\sin x\, dx \end{array}}$$

Now we find the differential of the basic form, substitute again, and divide by dx as the last step.

$$dy = \frac{du}{u} \qquad\qquad \text{differential}$$

$$dy = \frac{-\sin x\, dx}{\cos x} \qquad \text{substitution}$$

$$\frac{dy}{dx} = -\tan x \qquad\qquad \text{divided}$$

Problem set 49   1.   The hole kept on getting larger. In fact, the volume of the hole increased exponentially. At midnight the volume of the hole was 10 cubic meters. Two hours later the volume of the hole was 15 cubic meters. How many minutes after midnight would the volume of the hole be 30 cubic meters?

2.   Kyle's age Y years ago was half the age he will be F years from now. How old is Kyle now in terms of Y and F?

Integrate:

3. $\displaystyle\int \left(2x^2 - \frac{3}{\sqrt{x}} + 3\right) dx$ 4. $\displaystyle\int \left(2\cos u - \frac{2}{u} + 3\sin u\right) du$

Use u substitution to solve Problems 5–8.

5.   If $y = \cos(x^3 + 2x + 1)$, find $\dfrac{dy}{dx}$.

6.   If $y = \ln|\cos x|$, find y'.

7.   If $f(x) = \dfrac{1}{\sqrt{x^2 + 1}}$, find $f'(x)$.

8. If $s(t) = 2 \ln |\sin t + 2e^t|$, find $\dfrac{ds}{dt}$.

9. If $f(x) = 3x^4 - 8x^3 - 6x^2 + 24x - 1$, find the critical numbers of f. Use the equation of f and a sketch of f to locate and determine the values of all local maxima and minima of f.

Use implicit differentiation to solve Problems 10–12.

10. Find $\dfrac{dy}{dx}$ if $xy - y^3 = \sin x$.

11. Find $f'(x)$ if $[f(x)]^2 - 2x\,f(x) = e^x$.   [*Hint*: Replace $f(x)$ with y.]

12. Find $\dfrac{dx}{dt}$ if $x^3 - y^3 = e^t$ and if x and y are functions of time t.

Sketch the graphs of the following equations:

13. $y = \cot x$ 14. $y = \sqrt{x^3}$

15. $y = \dfrac{(2 - x)(x + 1)(x - 4)}{(x - 4)(x - 3)(x - 1)(x + 2)}$

16. If $f(x) = \sin x$ and $g(x) = 1/f(x)$, sketch the graphs of f and g on the same coordinate plane.

17. Write the equation $4x^2 - y^2 + 2y - 5 = 0$ in standard form and describe this conic section fully.

18. Approximate x to two decimal places if $49^{x+1} = 7^{3x^2-6}$. Use the quadratic formula and a calculator as necessary.

19. If $f(x) = x(x + 2)(x - 3)(x + 1)$, indicate on the number line those intervals on which f is positive and those intervals on which f is negative.

20. Determine the equation of the centerline, the period, and the amplitude of the sinusoid whose equation is $y = -2 + 3 \sin (4x - 3)$.

21. Show that: $\sin x \cos \left(\dfrac{\pi}{2} - x\right) + \cos (-x) \sin \left(\dfrac{\pi}{2} - x\right) = 1$

CONCEPT REVIEW   22. Find the area of an equilateral triangle each of whose sides has length 5.

23. If $x - y = 3$, compare: *A.* $x^2 + y^2$ *B.* $9 + 2xy$

LESSON 50   *Units for the derivative · Normal lines*

50.A

Units for the derivative

For physical applications of calculus it is necessary to consider the units of the independent variable and the units of the dependent variable. When we consider these units, we find that the derivative of a function also has units. Consider the graph of $V(t)$, where V is volume in cubic centimeters and t is time in seconds.

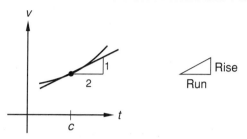

The graph shows that when $t = c$, the slope of $V(t)$ equals 1 cubic centimeter divided by 2 seconds, or

$$V'(c) = \frac{1 \text{ cm}^3}{2 \text{ sec}} = \frac{1}{2} \frac{\text{cm}^3}{\text{sec}}$$

Thus we see that the unit of the derivative of a function is the unit of the dependent variable (unit on the vertical axis) divided by the unit of the independent variable (unit on the horizontal axis).

Example 50.1   The distance s of the particle from the origin is given by the equation $s = t^2 + 3t + 7$, where s is in meters and time t is in minutes. What is the rate of change of the distance with respect to time when time equals 4 minutes?

Solution   The rate of change of s with respect to t when t equals 4 minutes is $\left.\dfrac{ds}{dt}\right|_4$.

$$s = t^2 + 3t + 7 \qquad\qquad \text{equation}$$

$$\frac{ds}{dt} = 2t + 3 \qquad\qquad \text{derivative}$$

$$\left.\frac{ds}{dt}\right|_4 = 2(4) + 3 = 11 \; \frac{\text{meters}}{\text{minute}} \qquad \text{evaluated}$$

The rate of change of distance with time is **velocity,** so the velocity when $t = 4$ is

$$\textbf{Velocity} = \left.\frac{ds}{dt}\right|_4 = 11 \; \frac{\textbf{meters}}{\textbf{minute}}$$

Example 50.2   The velocity v of the particle in meters per second is given by the quadratic equation $v = 4t^2 + 2t + 4$ if time t is in seconds. What is the acceleration when $t = 3$ seconds?

Solution   Acceleration is the rate of change of velocity with respect to time. So we want the acceleration when $t = 3$, which is $\left.\dfrac{dv}{dt}\right|_3$.

$$v = 4t^2 + 2t + 4 \;\; \frac{\text{meters}}{\text{sec}} \qquad\qquad \text{equation}$$

$$\text{Acceleration} = \frac{dv}{dt} = 8t + 2 \quad \frac{\frac{\text{meters}}{\text{sec}}}{\text{sec}} \qquad \text{derivative}$$

$$\left.\frac{dv}{dt}\right|_3 = 8(3) + 2 = 26 \quad \frac{\frac{\text{meters}}{\text{sec}}}{\text{sec}} \qquad \text{evaluated}$$

The units of velocity are meters/second, or meters per second. The units of acceleration are meters/second/second, or meters per second per second. This is often written as meters per second squared, or m/sec². Thus in this problem the rate of change of velocity is

$$26 \ \frac{\text{m}}{\text{sec}^2}$$

50.B
Normal lines

In mathematics, the word *normal* does not mean ordinary but means perpendicular. This use of the word normal began with the ancient Romans, as the Latin word for a carpenter's square is *norma*.

Example 50.3 Find the equation of the normal line to the graph of $y = e^x$ at $x = 1$.

Solution When $x = 1$, $e^x = e^1$, or e, so the point of intersection is $(1, e)$. **The slope of the normal line is the negative reciprocal of the slope of the tangent line.** The slope of the tangent line at $x = 1$ equals the value of the derivative of e^x evaluated at $x = 1$.

$$\frac{dy}{dx} = e^x \quad \longrightarrow \quad \left.\frac{dy}{dx}\right|_1 = e$$

Since the slope of the tangent line is e, the slope of the normal line is $-1/e$.

$$y = -\frac{1}{e}x + b \qquad \text{slope is } -\frac{1}{e}$$

$$e = -\frac{1}{e}(1) + b \qquad \text{passes through } (1, e)$$

$$b = e + \frac{1}{e} = \frac{e^2 + 1}{e} \qquad \text{solved for } b$$

$$y = -\frac{1}{e}(x) + \frac{e^2 + 1}{e} \qquad \text{equation of the normal line}$$

The constants in this equation are exact because we used e instead of a decimal approximation of e. A calculator may be used to change the exact answer to an approximate answer with decimal numerals if we wish.

$$y = -0.368x + 3.09$$

Example 50.4 Use a calculator as necessary to write the equation of the line normal to the graph of $y = e^{\sin x}$ when $x = 2.7$.

Solution First we will use a calculator to find the value of y when $x = 2.7$. We are careful to have the calculator set to radians.

$$y = e^{\sin 2.7} = e^{0.427} = 1.53$$

Thus the point of intersection of the normal line and the graph is $(2.7, 1.53)$.
   Next we evaluate the derivative of $y = e^{\sin x}$ at 2.7 to find the slope of the tangent. First we write the basic form and record the substitution in a box.

$$y = e^u \qquad \boxed{\begin{array}{l} u = \sin x \\ du = \cos x \, dx \end{array}}$$

Now we find the differential of the basic form, substitute, and then divide by dx.

$$dy = e^u \, du \qquad \text{differential}$$

$$dy = (e^{\sin x})(\cos x \, dx) \qquad \text{substituted}$$

$$\frac{dy}{dx} = (\cos x)e^{\sin x} \qquad \text{divided by } dx$$

Next we evaluate the derivative when $x = 2.7$.

$$\left.\frac{dy}{dx}\right|_{2.70} = (\cos 2.70)e^{\sin 2.70} \approx -0.90(1.53) = -1.38$$

The slope of the normal line is

$$-\frac{1}{-1.38} = 0.72$$

If we use 2.70 for x, 1.53 for y, and 0.72 for m, we can solve for b.

$$y = mx + b \qquad \text{equation}$$

$$1.53 = (0.72)(2.70) + b \qquad \text{substituted}$$

$$b = -0.41 \qquad \text{solved}$$

So the equation of the normal line is

$$y = 0.72x - 0.41$$

Problem set 50

1. The variable p varies jointly as the square root of m and as y^2 and varies inversely as x^2. What happens to p when y is halved, m is quadrupled, and x is tripled?

2. The volume V (in cubic centimeters) of the balloon at a given time t (in seconds) is given by the equation

$$V(t) = 20e^t$$

Find the rate of change of the volume when $t = 3$ seconds.

3. A particle is moving along the number line so that its distance from the origin at any time t (in seconds) is given by

$$s(t) = -2t^2 + t^3$$

Find the velocity of the particle when $t = 1$ second.

4. Find the equation of the normal line to the graph of $y = -3 \ln |x|$ at $x = -3$.

5. Find the critical numbers of f where $f(x) = x^3 + \frac{3}{2} x^2 - 6x + 2$. Use this equation and a rough sketch of the graph of the function to determine where the local maximum and minimum of f occur and what their values are.

Integrate:

6. $\displaystyle\int \left(2 \sin x - 4x - \frac{3}{2} \sqrt{x} - 3 \right) dx$ 7. $\displaystyle\int \left(\frac{\sqrt{2}}{t} + 3 \cos t + 1 \right) dt$

8. $\displaystyle\int \left(\frac{x + 1}{x} \right) dx$ (*Hint*: Rewrite the integrand as the sum of two terms.)

9. $\displaystyle\int \left(4e^x - \frac{1}{\sqrt{x}} + 6 \right) dx$

Use u substitution to differentiate the functions in Problems 10–12.

10. $y = \sqrt[3]{x^2 + 5}$ **11.** $s = \ln |\sin t|$ **12.** $y = -\sin^4 x$

Use implicit differentiation to solve Problems 13 and 14.

13. Find $\dfrac{dy}{dx}$ if $\sin x + \cos y = xy$.

14. Find dA/dt where $A = \frac{4}{3}\pi r^3$ and where the area A and the radius r are both functions of time t.

Differentiate as many times as necessary to solve Problems 15 and 16.

15. If $f(x) = 2 \ln |x|$, evaluate $f'''(-2)$.

16. Find $\dfrac{dy}{dx}$ if $y = e^x \ln |x|$.

17. Sketch the graph of g if $f(x) = x^2 + x - 2$ and $g(x) = 1/f(x)$.

18. Write the polar form of the five fifth roots of 1.

19. Determine $\log_3 5$ to two decimal places.

20. Evaluate: $\displaystyle\lim_{x \to \infty} \dfrac{x^3 - 4x + 5}{1 - 2x^3}$

21. Find the roots of $x^3 + 2x^2 - x - 2 = 0$.

22. A unit circle is centered at the origin. The center of the circle is the point O. If P is a point on the unit circle with coordinates $(\frac{1}{2}, \sqrt{3}/2)$, find the angle which OP makes with the positive x axis.

CONCEPT REVIEW **23.** Find the area of an equilateral triangle each of whose sides has length 6.

24. If $x = 2y$, compare: *A.* y^2 *B.* $0.25x^2$

LESSON 51 *Graphs of rational functions III · Repeated factors*

51.A
Graphs of rational functions III

To review the properties of factors of polynomials, we note that if x equals 2 or -2 the polynomial on the left below has a value of zero. No real value of x will cause the polynomial on the right to equal zero. If x equals zero, the value of the polynomial on the right is 4, and if x is any other real number, x^2 is a positive number and $x^2 + 4$ is a positive number greater than 4.

$$x^2 - 4 \qquad x^2 + 4$$

The polynomial on the left can be factored into two linear real factors. The polynomial on the right cannot be factored into linear real factors, and we remember that this polynomial is called an irreducible quadratic polynomial.

$$x^2 - 4 = (x + 2)(x - 2) \qquad (x^2 + 4) = (x + 2i)(x - 2i)$$

Since irreducible quadratic factors never equal zero for any real number value of x, the vertical asymptotes and x intercepts of rational functions are not affected by quadratic factors. Quadratic factors do cause "bends" in the graphs, but do not affect our rough sketches.

Example 51.1   Graph: $y = \dfrac{-(x^2 + 2)(x - 1)}{(x + 3)(x - 2)(x - 3)(x + 2)}$

Solution   We ignore the irreducible quadratic factor in the numerator, plot the zeros and vertical asymptotes, and graph the function. The ratio of the dominant terms in the two polynomials is

$$\frac{-x^3}{x^4}$$

so the graph will begin on the right at a small negative value of x.

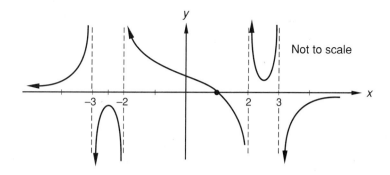

Not to scale

51.B
Repeated factors   If a linear real factor is repeated an even number of times in the numerator or in the denominator of a rational function, the graph of the function is changed. If the factor is in the numerator and is raised to an even power, the factor can equal zero, but it can never have a negative value. **Thus the graph of a rational function does not cross the x axis at a zero caused by a factor raised to an even power.** It touches the x axis at this zero and goes back in the vertical direction from whence it came. In the same way, linear zeros of the denominator are still poles and cause vertical asymptotes, but the graph does not "jump" across the x axis at the vertical asymptotes.

Example 51.2   Graph: (a) $y = \dfrac{4}{(x - 3)^2}$ (b) $y = \dfrac{-4}{(x - 3)^2}$

Solution   The number 3 is a pole for both functions, and there is a vertical asymptote at $x = 3$. However, the value of $(x - 3)^2$ is never negative, so this factor does not change sign when x goes from a value less than 3 to a value greater than 3. The graph "jumps" across the vertical asymptote, but does not jump across the x axis.

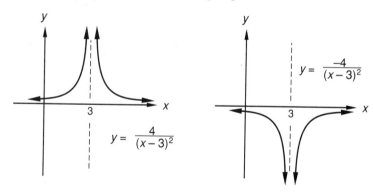

The graph on the left on page 255 resembles a volcano, and the graph on the right resembles a volcano that is upside down. Whenever we see a "volcano" in a graph of a rational function, we know that the denominator of the function contained a linear real factor raised to an even power.

Example 51.3   Graph: $y = \dfrac{(x - 1)^2(x^2 + 1)}{(x + 2)(x - 3)^2(x - 6)^2}$

Solution   We begin by ignoring the irreducible quadratic factor in the numerator. Then we locate the zeros and the vertical asymptotes. Next, we note that the ratio of the lead terms of the numerator and denominator polynomials is x^4 over x^5. This tells us that when x is a large positive number the function has a small positive value.

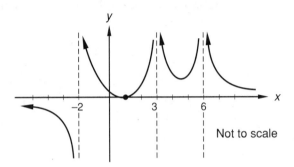

We note that the $(x - 3)^2$ and $(x - 6)^2$ in the denominator caused "volcanos" in the graph at the poles of $+3$ and $+6$ and that the $(x - 1)^2$ in the numerator caused the graph to touch but not cross the x axis at the zero of $+1$.

Problem set 51

1. The volume of liquid decreased exponentially. At midnight there was 3 liters of liquid, and 1 hour later there was only 1 liter of liquid. How much liquid would there be at 7 a.m.?

Sketch the functions whose equations are given in Problems 2 and 3, showing clearly the asymptotes and x intercepts of the graphs. Other than these features, the graphs need not be precise.

2. $y = \dfrac{(x + 1)^2(x^2 + 1)}{(x - 3)(x - 1)^2(x - 5)^2}$

3. $y = \dfrac{-(x^2 + 1)(x - 1)}{x(x + 1)^2(x - 2)}$

4. The population P at any given time t is given by the equation

$$P(t) = 20{,}000e^{4t}$$

Find the rate of change of the population when $t = 3$.

5. Find the equation for the rate of change of the area, dA/dt, if $A = \frac{4}{3}\pi r^3$ and if A and r are both functions of time t.

6. Write the equation of the line which can be drawn normal to the graph of $y = x + \ln x$ at $x = 1$.

7. Find all the critical numbers of $y = \frac{1}{4}x^4 + \frac{2}{3}x^3 - \frac{1}{2}x^2 - 2x + 5$. Use a rough sketch of the graph of the function and its equation to determine the local maximum and minimum values of y and where they occur.

Integrate:

8. $\displaystyle\int \left(2 \sin u - \frac{3}{u^3}\right) du$

9. $\displaystyle\int -\frac{3\,dt}{t}$

10. $\displaystyle\int \left(\frac{2}{\sqrt{x}} - 4\right) dx$

Use u substitution to differentiate the functions given in Problems 11–13.

11. $f(x) = \dfrac{1}{\sqrt{x^2 + 1}}$ **12.** $y = \ln |x^2 + 1|$ **13.** $y = \ln |\sin x|$

Use the product rule to differentiate the functions given in Problems 14 and 15.

14. $y = x^2 e^x$ **15.** $y = x \ln |x|$

16. If $f(x) = |x|$ and $g(x) = 1 + f(x - 3)$, sketch the graphs of f and g on the same coordinate plane.

17. If $f(x) = \ln x$ and $g(x) = 1/x$, write the equation of $fg(x)$ and determine the domain of $fg(x)$.

18. Describe both the domain and the range of the function $y = \sin^{-1} x$.

19. Evaluate: $\lim\limits_{x \to 1^-} f(x)$ and $\lim\limits_{x \to 1^+} f(x)$ where

$$f(x) = \begin{cases} x & \text{when } x \geq 1 \\ -x + 1 & \text{when } x < 1 \end{cases}$$

20. Solve for r in terms of h in the figure shown.

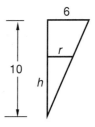

CONCEPT REVIEW **21.** Find the area of the isosceles triangle shown in terms of s.

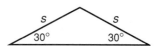

22. If $x > y$ and $y > z$, then compare: *A.* $-x$ *B.* $-z$

LESSON 52 *The derivative of a quotient · Proof of the quotient rule*

52.A
The derivative of a quotient

We remember the rule for the derivative of a product by saying

one dee two plus two dee one

The rule for the derivative of the quotient of two functions is a little more complicated. For the derivative of a quotient to exist, the derivative of each of the functions must exist, and, in addition, the derivative of the denominator function must not equal zero.

The derivative of a quotient of two functions equals the denominator times the derivative of the numerator minus the numerator times the derivative of the denominator, all divided by the square of the denominator.

A mnemonic for remembering the derivative of a quotient is

low dee high minus high dee low, over the square of what's below

Example 52.1 If $f(x) = \dfrac{\ln x}{2x + 3}$, find $f'(x)$.

Solution We remember "low dee high minus high dee low over the square of what's below" and write

$$f'(x) = \frac{\overset{\text{low}}{(2x + 3)} \overset{\overset{\text{dee}}{\text{high}}}{\left(\dfrac{1}{x}\right)} - \overset{\text{high}}{(\ln x)} \overset{\overset{\text{dee}}{\text{low}}}{(2)}}{(2x + 3)^2}$$

We rearrange this result by multiplying both top and bottom by x to get

$$f'(x) = \frac{(2x + 3) - 2x \ln x}{x(2x + 3)^2}$$

Example 52.2 Find $D_x \dfrac{x^3 - 2x + 2}{\sin x}$.

Solution We will write the denominator times the derivative of the numerator minus the numerator times the derivative of the denominator, all divided by the square of the denominator.

$$\frac{dy}{dx} = \frac{(\sin x)(3x^2 - 2) - (x^3 - 2x + 2)(\cos x)}{\sin^2 x}$$

There are many ways this derivative can be written and all are rather complicated, so we will leave it as it is.

Example 52.3 If $y = \dfrac{\cos x}{e^x + x}$ find $\dfrac{dy}{dx}$.

Solution We use the rule for the derivative of a quotient and write

$$\frac{dy}{dx} = \frac{(e^x + x)(-\sin x) - (\cos x)(e^x + 1)}{(e^x + x)^2}$$

We could leave this derivative in its present form, but we decide to rearrange the expression and write

$$\frac{(-\sin x)(e^x + x) - (\cos x)(e^x + 1)}{(e^x + x)^2}$$

Example 52.4 Find the differential of $y = \dfrac{x}{\cos x}$.

Solution   We will use low dee high, etc., but use differentials instead of derivatives.

$$dy = \frac{(\cos x)(dx) - (x)(-\sin x\, dx)}{(\cos x)^2} = \left(\frac{\cos x + x \sin x}{\cos^2 x}\right) dx$$

52.B
Proof of the quotient rule (optional)

The derivatives of two functions $f(x)$ and $g(x)$ are defined as follows.

$$f'(x) = \lim_{\Delta x \to 0} \frac{f(x + \Delta x) - f(x)}{\Delta x} \qquad g'(x) = \lim_{\Delta x \to 0} \frac{g(x + \Delta x) - g(x)}{\Delta x}$$

If we use $h(x)$ to designate the quotient of $f(x)$ and $g(x)$, to prove the quotient rule we would like to show that

$$h'(x) = \frac{g(x) \lim\limits_{\Delta x \to 0} \dfrac{f(x + \Delta x) - f(x)}{\Delta x} - f(x) \lim\limits_{\Delta x \to 0} \dfrac{g(x + \Delta x) - g(x)}{\Delta x}}{[g(x)]^2}$$

By definition, the derivative of the function $h(x)$ is

$$h'(x) = \lim_{\Delta x \to 0} \frac{h(x + \Delta x) - h(x)}{\Delta x} = \lim_{\Delta x \to 0} \frac{\dfrac{f(x + \Delta x)}{g(x + \Delta x)} - \dfrac{f(x)}{g(x)}}{\Delta x}$$

If we add the two terms in the numerator and then divide by Δx as indicated, we get

$$\lim_{\Delta x \to 0} \frac{f(x + \Delta x) \cdot g(x) - f(x) \cdot g(x + \Delta x)}{\Delta x \cdot g(x) \cdot g(x + \Delta x)}$$

To get the form we want, we use an algebraic trick. We subtract and add $f(x) \cdot g(x)$ in the numerator and get

$$h'(x) = \lim_{\Delta x \to 0} \frac{f(x + \Delta x) \cdot g(x) - \boldsymbol{f(x) \cdot g(x)} - f(x) \cdot g(x + \Delta x) + \boldsymbol{f(x) \cdot g(x)}}{\Delta x \cdot g(x) \cdot g(x + \Delta x)}$$

Because the limit of a sum or product or quotient equals the sums or products or quotients of the respective individual limits, this can be rearranged as

$$= \frac{\lim\limits_{\Delta x \to 0} g(x) \cdot \lim\limits_{\Delta x \to 0} \dfrac{f(x + \Delta x) - f(x)}{\Delta x} - \lim\limits_{\Delta x \to 0} f(x) \cdot \lim\limits_{\Delta x \to 0} \dfrac{g(x + \Delta x) - g(x)}{\Delta x}}{\lim\limits_{\Delta x \to 0} g(x) \cdot \lim\limits_{\Delta x \to 0} g(x + \Delta x)}$$

The limits of $g(x)$ and $f(x)$ as Δx approaches zero are $g(x)$ and $f(x)$, respectively, because these expressions do not contain Δx. Also, as Δx approaches zero, the value of $g(x + \Delta x)$ in the denominator approaches $g(x)$ so the denominator approaches $[g(x)]^2$. Thus, we have our proof.

Problem set 52

1. Fifty men could consume P pounds of chicken in H hours. If each of the men consumes chicken at the same rate, how long would it take half the number of men to consume k pounds of chicken?

Use the quotient rule to differentiate the functions of Problems 2 and 3.

2. $y = \dfrac{\sin x}{e^x - x}$ **3.** $f(x) = \dfrac{\sin x}{\cos x}$

4. Use the quotient rule to write the differential dy in terms of u, v, du, and dv, where $y = u/v$.

5. Sketch the graph of: $y = \dfrac{(x^2 + 3)(x - 1)}{x(x + 4)^2(x + 2)}$

6. The pressure P at any given time t is given by

$$P(t) = 16e^{-4t}$$

Find the rate of change of P at $t = 4$.

7. Use implicit differentiation to find the equation for the rate of change of volume V if $V = \frac{1}{3}\pi r^2 h$, and the radius r and the height h are both functions of time t.

8. Find the equation of the line normal to the graph of $y = \cos x$ at $x = \pi$.

9. Find the critical numbers of the function $f(x) = -\frac{1}{4}x^4 + \frac{1}{2}x^2 - 3$. Use this equation and a rough sketch of f to determine the local maximum and minimum values of f and where they occur.

Integrate:

10. $\displaystyle\int \left(2x^2 - \dfrac{1}{\sqrt{x}} + e^x + \dfrac{1}{x} - \sin x \right) dx$

11. $\displaystyle\int -\dfrac{4u}{\sqrt{u}}\, du$ (First simplify the integrand.)

12. If x and y are both functions of t, differentiate implicitly to find dx/dt where $x^2 + y^2 = 9$.

Use u substitution to differentiate the functions of Problems 13 and 14.

13. $y = \ln |x^2 + \sin x|$ 14. $y = \dfrac{1}{\sqrt{x^3 + 3}}$

Differentiate the functions of Problems 15 and 16 using the sum and product rules.

15. $s(t) = \dfrac{2}{\sqrt{t}} + \ln |t|$ 16. $y = 2u^3 e^u$

17. If $f(x) = \sin 2x$, where $0 \le x \le 2\pi$, use interval notation to describe those intervals on which the function is increasing.

18. If the base of a right circular cone has a radius of 3 cm and the height of the cone is 6 cm, find the volume of the cone.

19. Write the key identities and develop identities for $\cos \dfrac{x}{2}$ and $\sin \dfrac{x}{2}$.

20. Use interval notation to describe those values of x for which $|x - 1| < 0.01$.

21. Find a, b, and c where $f(x) = ax^2 + bx + c$ and the graph of f intersects the x axis at $x = -1$ and $x = 2$ and intersects the y axis at $y = -4$.

CONCEPT REVIEW   22. Find the area of a regular hexagon, each of whose sides has a length of 6 centimeters.

23. If (x, y) is a point which lies on a unit circle centered at the origin, compare:
    A. $x^2 + y^2$ B. $\frac{3}{2}$

LESSON 53 *Area under a curve*

In everyday life when we want to describe the size of a surface we use the word *area*, a number, and units. Thus we might say "the area of this table is 1450 square centimeters." In the applied problems in this book we will find that areas can also be used to represent velocity, acceleration, work, energy, and power. In mathematics we find it helpful to strip away the units and consider area to be a real number equal to or greater than zero that can be used to describe numerically an abstract quality associated with every closed planar geometric figure. This allows us to study the numerical aspect of area without having to consider the myriad units that could possibly cause confusion. **For our basic definition of area we define the area of a rectangle to be its length times its width.** Then we use this definition to help us define the area of a triangle. Then we use the area of a triangle to define the area of a trapezoid. We have used the formula πr^2 to find the area of a circle but have not defined exactly what we mean by an area that has a curved boundary. We will begin our investigation of areas that have curved boundaries by considering graphs of continuous functions that are everywhere increasing and are nonnegative on the interval $[a, b]$. This last restriction means that the graph of the function does not go below the x axis between a and b. We will consider the area bounded by the graph, the x axis, and the lines $x = a$ and $x = b$. **We call this area the area under the curve on the interval $[a, b]$.**

The area of the rectangle shown on the left below is 32. In the figure on the right we can see the area under the f function, above the x axis and between x values of a and b, but what is the number?

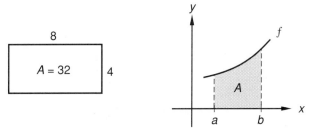

Can we prove that such a number exists? If it does exist, can we develop a method of finding it precisely? In this lesson we will concentrate on developing a definition of "the area under a curve." We will begin by finding an approximation for the area by drawing rectangles and adding the areas of the rectangles. We can do this because we have already defined the area of a rectangle to be a number and we have defined what we mean by the addition of numbers. To demonstrate the procedure of adding the areas of rectangles, we will approximate the area below the graph of $y = x^2 + 1$, above the x axis and between x values of 0 and 2. This is the area shaded in the top figure on the left on page 262. As the first step, we divide the distance between 0 and 2 into four intervals of equal length, as we show in the center figure. Since this divides the line segment between 0 and 2 into nonoverlapping parts, we say that we have **partitioned** the interval $[0, 2]$. Then, in the figure on the right, we draw vertical lines from the end of each partition to the graph of the function.

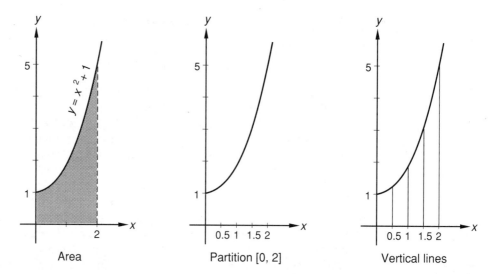

| Area | Partition [0, 2] | Vertical lines |

Now we can draw our rectangles. In the figure on the left below we use the left side of each partition as the height of each rectangle, which makes all parts of the rectangles fall below the curve. In the figure on the right we use the right side of each partition as the height of each rectangle, and some part of each rectangle extends above the curve.

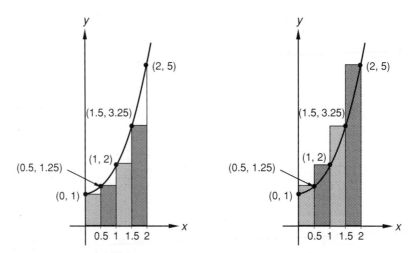

The sum of the areas of the four rectangles in the figure on the left is called a *lower sum,* because we used the least value of $f(x)$ on each interval as the height of the rectangle. We can compute this sum S_L. The width of each rectangle is 0.5, and if we use the value of $f(x)$ at the left end of each interval as the height of the rectangle, we get

$$S_L = (1)(0.5) + (1.25)(0.5) + (2)(0.5) + (3.25)(0.5) = 3.75$$

The sum of the areas of the four rectangles in the right-hand figure is called an *upper sum* because we used the greatest value of $f(x)$ on each interval as the height of the rectangle. We can compute this sum S_u. Again the width of each rectangle is 0.5, and if we use the value of $f(x)$ at the right end of each interval as the height, we get

$$S_u \doteq (1.25)(0.5) + (2)(0.5) + (3.25)(0.5) + (5)(0.5) = 5.75$$

The rectangles used in the computation of the lower sum all lie beneath the curve, so the lower sum is less than A (for area), the number we are trying to approximate. The rectangles used in the computation of the upper sum all extend above the curve, so the upper sum is greater than A, the number we are trying to approximate.

$$3.75 < A < 5.75 \quad \text{or} \quad S_L < A < S_u$$

The exact value of the number A that we are trying to approximate in this example is $4\frac{2}{3}$. The lower sum of 3.75 is less than $4\frac{2}{3}$ and the upper sum of 5.75 is greater than $4\frac{2}{3}$. Thus for our first try

$$S_L < A < S_u \quad \text{because} \quad 3.75 < 4.\overline{66} < 5.75$$

The error in our lower sum is approximately 0.92, which is the sum of the four "triangular" areas below the curve in the left-hand figure. The error in our upper sum is approximately 1.1, which is the sum of the four "triangular areas" above the curve in the right-hand figure. If we were to use eight partitions instead of four partitions, the lower sum would be approximately 4.19 and the upper sum would be approximately 5.19.

$$4.19 < 4.\overline{66} < 5.19$$

Now the error in the lower sum is approximately 0.48 and the error in the upper sum is approximately 0.52. If we increase the number of partitions on the interval, the errors will become smaller and smaller and the lower sum and the upper sum will get closer and closer to $4.\overline{66}$.

The reduction in the error of a sum as the number of subintervals is increased is pictured in the graphs below. The shaded areas indicate the errors in the lower sum of the area under the graph of $y = x + 2$, above the x axis and between the x values of 0 and 6. As the number of partitions is increased from 2 to 3 to 6, the error decreases from 9 to 6 to 3.

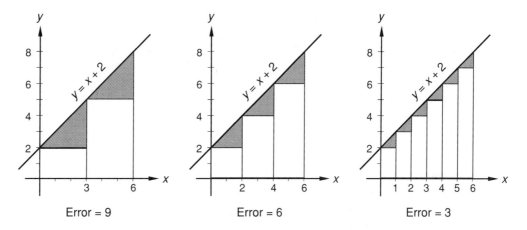

To write a general expression for the lower sum and upper sum estimates of the area under a curve on the interval $[a, b]$, we will consider that this interval is partitioned into n nonoverlapping subintervals of equal lengths Δx. We will use $f(x_{L1})$ to represent the least value of $f(x)$ in the first subinterval, so the area of the first rectangle is $f(x_{L1}) \Delta x$. The least value of $f(x)$ in the second subinterval is $f(x_{L2})$, so the area of the second rectangle is $f(x_{L2}) \Delta x$. Thus the lower sum of n rectangles can be written as

$$S_L = f(x_{L1}) \Delta x + f(x_{L2}) \Delta x + f(x_{L3}) \Delta x + \cdots + f(x_{Ln}) \Delta x$$

We can use summation notation to write this sum as

$$S_L = \sum_{i=1}^{n} f(x_{Li}) \Delta x$$

If we use $f(x_{g1})$ to represent the greatest value of $f(x)$ in the first subinterval and $f(x_{g2})$ to represent the greatest value of $f(x)$ in the second subinterval, etc., we can write a general expression for an upper sum.

$$S_u = f(x_{g1}) \, \Delta x + f(x_{g2}) \, \Delta x + f(x_{g3}) \, \Delta x + \cdots + f(x_{gn}) \, \Delta x$$

This sum can also be written in summation notation.

$$S_u = \sum_{i=1}^{n} f(x_{gi}) \, \Delta x$$

The area A is a number greater than any lower sum and less than any upper sum. Thus we may write

$$\sum_{i=1}^{n} f(x_{Li}) \, \Delta x < A < \sum_{i=1}^{n} f(x_{gi}) \, \Delta x$$

We define the area on the interval [a, b] between the curve and the x axis to be A, the number approached by both of these sums as n approaches infinity. We will assume that both of these limits exist and are equal. This is quite an assumption, and we will leave the proof of the existence and uniqueness of these limits to a later course. We denote this area between a and b by writing

$$A = \int_a^b f(x) \, dx$$

Now we must look carefully at the two-limit definition seven lines above. Note that it makes no reference to a graph or to area in the usual sense. The definition contains only the limits of the sums of products of a partitioned function. Rectangles are not mentioned. We have defined the area under the graph of f between a and b to be the limit of either of two sums and note that this definition of area has absolutely nothing to do with area as we normally think of area. **We used a graph to get started, but this definition of area stands alone without the graph!**

For this development we used a continuous function that is everywhere increasing on the interval and is nonnegative everywhere on the interval. The result is valid for continuous functions that are not everywhere increasing and will be discussed in a later lesson. The discussion of the extension of this procedure to functions that are negative on the interval will lead to the development of a limit that we call the *definite integral*.

Problem set 53

1. A window has the shape of a rectangle topped by a semicircle as shown. If the perimeter of the entire window is 20, the length of one side of the rectangle is h, and the radius of the semicircular part is r, find h in terms of r and express the area of the entire window in terms of r.

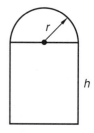

2. Sketch the graph of $y = x^2 + 1$. Partition the interval [2, 4] into four subintervals of equal length. Estimate the area under the curve between $x = 2$ and $x = 4$ by calculating a lower sum.

3. Sketch the graph of $f(x) = 1 + \sin x$. Partition the interval [0, 1.2] into six subintervals of equal length. Use a calculator as necessary to estimate the area under the curve on the interval [0, 1.2] by calculating an upper sum.

4. If f is as defined in Problem 3, use summation notation to indicate a general lower sum of $f(x)$ that uses a partition of 10 subintervals.

Use the quotient and sum rules to differentiate the functions in Problems 5 and 6.

5. $y = \dfrac{e^x + x}{\cos x}$

6. $y = \dfrac{x^2 + 3}{x^3 - 2x}$

7. Use the quotient rule to find $d\left(\dfrac{u}{v}\right)$.

8. Sketch the graph of: $y = \dfrac{(x - 1)^2(x + 2)}{(x + 1)(x + 2)(x + 3)^2(x^2 + 1)}$

9. The number of disenchanted people, N, at any given time t is given by the equation

$$N(t) = 2000e^{3t}$$

Find the rate of change of the number of disenchanted people when $t = 4$.

10. A particle moves along the number line so that its distance from the origin at any time t (measured in seconds) is given by

$$s(t) = \sin t$$

Find the velocity of the particle when $t = \pi$ seconds.

11. Find the critical numbers of $f(x) = x^3 - \frac{9}{2}x^2 + 6x + 2$. Use a rough sketch of f and its equation as necessary to determine the local maximum and minimum values of f and where they occur.

Use u substitution to differentiate the functions in Problems 12 and 13.

12. $y = \sqrt{e^x - 1}$

13. $f(x) = \dfrac{1}{\sqrt[3]{x^2 - 1}}$

Integrate:

14. $\displaystyle\int \dfrac{3}{\sqrt{u}}\, du$

15. $\displaystyle\int \left(\dfrac{3}{x} + \sqrt{2}x^{4/3} + \cos x - 4e^x\right) dx$

16. Make a rough sketch of the graph of $f(x) = (x - 1)(x + 1)(2 - x)$.

17. If f is as defined in Problem 16 and $g(x) = 1/f(x)$, sketch the graph of g.

18. Graph $f(x) = \ln |x|$.

19. If f is as defined in Problem 18, evaluate: $\displaystyle\lim_{x \to 0^+} f(x)$

20. For which values of x is $\ln (\cos x)$ defined?

    (a) $0 \le x < 2\pi$ (b) $0 \le x < \pi$

    (c) $-\dfrac{\pi}{2} \le x \le \dfrac{\pi}{2}$ (d) $-\dfrac{\pi}{2} < x < \dfrac{\pi}{2}$

CONCEPT REVIEW   21. Find the radius of the circle which can be circumscribed about the triangle whose sides have lengths 3, 4, and 5.

22. If $a - b = 2$, compare: *A.* a^2 *B.* $b^2 + 4b + 3$

LESSON 54 *The chain rule · Equivalent forms for the derivative*

54.A
The chain rule

If the first function machine shown here multiplies any input by 3 and the second function machine multiplies any input by 2, the two machines linked together will multiply any input of the first machine by 6.

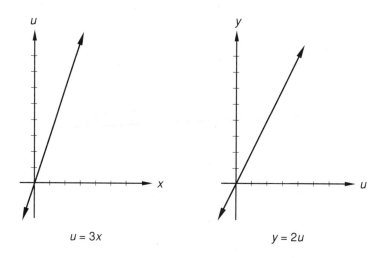

If we call the input of the first machine x, call the output of the first machine u, and call the output of the second machine y, we can write the following equations and draw the graphs.

$$u = 3x \qquad\qquad y = 2u$$

The rate of change of u with respect to x is the slope of the left-hand graph, which is 3. The rate of change of y with respect to u is the slope of the right-hand graph, which is 2. If we let x change 1 unit, u will change 3 units. But if u changes 3 units, then y will change 3 times 2, or 6 units. Thus a change of 1 unit in x will cause a change of 6 units in y, and the rate of change of y with respect to x is 6, which is the product of the two rates of change. Since the derivative of a function is the rate of change of the function, we can say that the derivative of this function of a function is the product of the individual derivatives. We used linear functions for this example, but the rule is true for any two functions if the derivatives exist for the values of x and u being considered. This rule is called the **chain rule.** The chain rule contains a nuance that is not obvious. It states that the derivative of a composite function equals the product of the slope of the second machine evaluated at u times the slope of the first machine evaluated at x.

The chain rule is easy to remember if we use the notation of Leibniz and write

$$\frac{dy}{dx} = \frac{dy}{du} \cdot \frac{du}{dx}$$

The first part of the product is the rate of change of the second function, and the second part of the product is the rate of change of the first function. This product can be extended to define the derivative of any number of functions linked together in this fashion. If x is a function of s and s is a function of t, we could extend this notation and write

$$\frac{dy}{dt} = \frac{dy}{du} \cdot \frac{du}{dx} \cdot \frac{dx}{ds} \cdot \frac{ds}{dt}$$

Each new dependence adds another link to the chain. The notation of Leibniz, which considers that dy, du, dx, ds, and dt are infinitesimals, allows us to check our expression by canceling numerators and denominators.

$$\frac{dy}{dt} = \frac{dy}{d\!\!\!/u} \cdot \frac{d\!\!\!/u}{d\!\!\!/x} \cdot \frac{d\!\!\!/x}{d\!\!\!/s} \cdot \frac{d\!\!\!/s}{dt}$$

Example 54.1   If $y = u^2 + 4u$ and $u = 5x^3$, find $\dfrac{dy}{dx}$.

Solution   First we compute the individual derivatives.

$$\frac{dy}{du} = 2u + 4 \qquad \frac{du}{dx} = 15x^2$$

Now we use the notation of Leibniz to write the chain rule. Then we substitute.

$$\frac{dy}{dx} = \frac{dy}{du} \cdot \frac{du}{dx} = (2u + 4)(15x^2)$$

But $u = 5x^3$, so we substitute $5x^3$ for u and then simplify.

$$\frac{dy}{dx} = [2(5x^3) + 4](15x^2) = (10x^3 + 4)(15x^2)$$

$$= \mathbf{150x^5 + 60x^2}$$

Example 54.2   If $y = 2 \ln v$ and $v = u^2$, find $\dfrac{dy}{du}$.

Solution   First we find the individual derivatives.

$$\frac{dy}{dv} = \frac{2}{v} \qquad \frac{dv}{du} = 2u$$

Now we write the chain rule and substitute.

$$\frac{dy}{du} = \frac{dy}{dv} \cdot \frac{dv}{du} = \left(\frac{2}{v}\right)(2u) = \frac{4u}{v}$$

But $v = u^2$, so we substitute u^2 for v and get

$$\frac{dy}{du} = \frac{4u}{(u^2)} = \frac{\mathbf{4}}{\mathbf{u}}$$

Example 54.3   If $y = \sin t$ and $t = \dfrac{1}{\sqrt{x}}$, find $\dfrac{dy}{dx}$.

Solution   First we find the individual derivatives.

$$\frac{dy}{dt} = \cos t \qquad \frac{dt}{dx} = \frac{d}{dx} x^{-1/2} = -\frac{1}{2} x^{-3/2}$$

Now we write the chain rule and substitute.

$$\frac{dy}{dx} = \frac{dy}{dt} \cdot \frac{dt}{dx} = (\cos t)\left(-\frac{1}{2}x^{-3/2}\right)$$

But $t = \dfrac{1}{\sqrt{x}}$, so we substitute $\dfrac{1}{\sqrt{x}}$ for t.

$$\frac{dy}{dx} = \left(\cos\frac{1}{\sqrt{x}}\right)\left(-\frac{1}{2}x^{-3/2}\right) = -\frac{1}{2}x^{-3/2}\cos\frac{1}{\sqrt{x}}$$

54.B
Equivalent forms for the derivative

We are familiar with the two forms of the derivative shown here. The notation on the left defines the derivative as a limit as Δx approaches zero. The definition on the right makes the same statement but uses h as the variable that approaches zero.

$$f'(x) = \lim_{\Delta x \to 0}\frac{f(x + \Delta x) - f(x)}{\Delta x} \qquad f'(x) = \lim_{h \to 0}\frac{f(x + h) - f(x)}{h}$$

An alternative notation uses the value of the function at some constant a and at x and finds the limit as x approaches a.

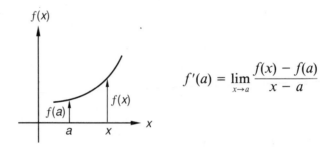

$$f'(a) = \lim_{x \to a}\frac{f(x) - f(a)}{x - a}$$

The value of $f(x) - f(a)$ equals Δy and the value of $x - a$ equals Δx, so this is a different way to make the same statement made by both notations above.

Example 54.4 Use the new form of the definition of the derivative to find $f'(x)$ if $f(x) = x^2 + 1$.

Solution We know from the rule for the derivative of x^n that the answer will be $2x$. We are doing this problem to enhance our understanding of the definition of the derivative and to acquaint ourselves with the thought processes and procedures necessary for success in mathematics. The height of the curve when $x = x$ is $f(x)$, or $x^2 + 1$. The height of the curve when $x = a$ is $f(a)$, or $a^2 + 1$. The x difference between x and a is $x - a$. Thus we write the definition for the slope when $x = a$, which is $f'(a)$.

$$f'(a) = \lim_{x \to a}\frac{(x^2 + 1) - (a^2 + 1)}{x - a} \qquad \text{definition}$$

We have $x - a$ in the denominator, and as x approaches a the denominator approaches zero. **We must find a way to get the $x - a$ out of the denominator.** If we simplify the numerator, we get $x^2 - a^2$, which can be factored into $(x + a)(x - a)$.

$$f'(a) = \lim_{x \to a}\frac{(x + a)(x - a)}{x - a} = \lim_{x \to a}(x + a)$$

We have succeeded in getting $x - a$ out of the denominator, so we can let x approach a without causing a division by zero.

$$f'(a) = \lim_{x \to a}(x + a) = 2a$$

In this discussion, x has been the variable and a has been a constant. But since a can be any value of x that we choose, we can use x instead of a and write

$$\text{If} \quad f(x) = x^2 + 1 \quad \text{then} \quad f'(x) = \mathbf{2x}$$

Example 54.5 If $f(x) = x^2$, use the new form of the definition of the derivative to find $f'(1)$.

Solution If we use the power rule, the derivative of x^2 is $2x$, and when x equals 1, $2x$ equals 2(1), which equals 2. In this problem we are playing a calculus game rather than just trying to find the answer. If we want to be successful in mathematics, we must learn to play the games that will help us understand the fundamental concepts. In this problem the constant 1 will be absorbed, and we will get a numerical answer instead of a general answer. The height of the curve when x equals x is x^2, and the height of the curve when $x = 1$ is $(1)^2$. So we have

$$f'(1) = \lim_{x \to 1} \frac{x^2 - (1)^2}{x - 1}$$

Again we have a denominator trying to go to zero. This cannot be permitted, so we work with the numerator to find a way out. Fortunately the numerator can be factored.

$$f'(1) = \lim_{x \to 1} \frac{x^2 - 1}{x - 1} = \frac{\lim (x + 1)(x - 1)}{x - 1} = \lim_{x \to 1} (x + 1)$$

$$= \lim_{x \to 1} x + 1 = \mathbf{2}$$

Example 54.6 If $f(x) = \sqrt[3]{x}$, use the new form of the definition of the derivative to find $f'(-1)$.

Solution We know that

$$f'(x) = \frac{1}{3} x^{-2/3} \quad \text{and} \quad f'(-1) = \frac{1}{3} (-1)^{-2/3} = \frac{1}{3}$$

But we have been asked to play the derivative game and so we shall.

$$f'(-1) = \lim_{x \to -1} \frac{f(x) - f(-1)}{x - (-1)} \quad \text{definition of } f'(-1)$$

$$= \lim_{x \to -1} \frac{x^{1/3} - (-1)}{x + 1} = \lim_{x \to -1} \frac{x^{1/3} + 1}{x + 1}$$

Now we have to get the $x + 1$ out of the denominator. To do this we use a trick. We consider that the denominator, $x + 1$, is the sum of two cubes $(x^{1/3})^3 + (1)^3$. Then we factor this expression and cancel as shown here.

$$\frac{x^{1/3} + 1}{x + 1} = \frac{(x^{1/3} + 1)}{(x^{1/3} + 1)[(x^{1/3})^2 - (x^{1/3})(1) + (1)^2]}$$

Now we have

$$f'(-1) = \lim_{x \to -1} \frac{1}{x^{2/3} - x^{1/3} + 1}$$

We got rid of the $x + 1$ in the denominator. If this new expression does not equal zero when $x = -1$, we are home-free. Substituting -1 for x, we get

$$\frac{1}{(-1)^{2/3} - (-1)^{1/3} + 1} = \frac{1}{\left((-1)^2\right)^{1/3} - (-1)^{1/3} + 1} = \frac{1}{1 - (-1) + 1} = \frac{1}{3}$$

Problems like this one are carefully contrived so that students can find a solution using the skills and concepts that they have studied thus far. If the function had been $g(x) = \sqrt[14]{x}$, the trick we used in this problem would not have worked.

54.C
Proof of the chain rule (optional)

The chain rule can be stated by using the notation of Leibniz, which we show on the left below. If we define $h(x)$ to be the composition $g(f(x))$, we can use functional notation to state the chain rule, as we show on the right.

$$\frac{dy}{dx} = \frac{dy}{du} \cdot \frac{du}{dx} \qquad \text{or} \qquad h'(x) = g'(f(x))f'(x)$$

$$x \;\longrightarrow\; \boxed{f} \;\longrightarrow\; f(x) \;\longrightarrow\; \boxed{g} \;\longrightarrow\; g(f(x)) \;\longrightarrow\; h(x)$$

The output of the first function machine is $f(x)$, and the derivative of this output is $f'(x)$. The output of the first machine is the input of the second machine, and the output of the second machine is $g(f(x))$, so the derivative of this output is $g'(f(x))$. When we write the chain rule, we put the derivative of the second machine first and write that the derivative of the composition machine $h'(x)$ equals the product of the derivative of the output of the second machine times the derivative of the output of the first machine. We want to prove that

$$h'(x) = \underset{\substack{\text{derivative of } g \\ \text{evaluated at } f(x)}}{g'(f(x))} \quad \text{multiplied by} \quad \underset{\substack{\text{derivative of } f \\ \text{evaluated at } x}}{f'(x)}$$

For our proof we will let a be some value of x and show that

$$h'(a) = g'(f(a))f'(a)$$

If we use the definition of the two derivatives to write this product, we see that we would like to show that

$$h'(a) = \lim_{f(x) \to f(a)} \frac{g(f(x)) - g(f(a))}{f(x) - f(a)} \cdot \lim_{x \to a} \frac{f(x) - f(a)}{x - a}$$

To do this we write the limit definition of $h'(a)$.

$$h'(a) = \lim_{x \to a} \frac{h(x) - h(a)}{x - a}$$

But $h(x)$ equals $g(f(x))$ and $h(a)$ equals $g(f(a))$, so we can write

$$h'(a) = \lim_{x \to a} \frac{g(f(x)) - g(f(a))}{x - a}$$

Now we will use a trick to get the form we want. We multiply above and below by $f(x) - f(a)$, rearrange, and get

$$h'(a) = \lim_{x \to a} \frac{g(f(x)) - g(f(a))}{f(x) - f(a)} \cdot \frac{f(x) - f(a)}{x - a}$$

The limit of a product equals the product of the individual limits, so we can write

$$h'(a) = \lim_{x \to a} \frac{g(f(x)) - g(f(a))}{f(x) - f(a)} \cdot \lim_{x \to a} \frac{f(x) - f(a)}{x - a}$$

The function f is a continuous function, so as x approaches a, $f(x)$ approaches $f(a)$. Thus we can rewrite the first limit and get

$$h'(a) = \lim_{f(x) \to f(a)} \frac{g(f(x)) - g(f(a))}{f(x) - f(a)} \cdot \lim_{x \to a} \frac{f(x) - f(a)}{x - a}$$

This is the form we were looking for, and the proof is complete. Since division by zero is not defined, it was necessary to assume in the last three steps that $f(x)$ does not equal $f(a)$ for any x in some neighborhood of a, so that $f(x) - f(a)$ does not equal zero. This is a reasonable assumption for most functions encountered in elementary calculus. Except for constant functions it is unusual for a function to have the same value at more than a finite number of points in an interval of finite length.

Problem set 54

1. The number of troubles Ben experienced increased exponentially. On the first of the month, Ben experienced 6 troubles, and on the fourth of the month Ben experienced 48 troubles. How many troubles would Ben experience on the fifteenth of the month?

2. It was noon and Jill needed to feed Kyle precisely the next time when the hands of the clock formed a right angle. At what time must Jill feed Kyle?

Use the chain rule to find $\dfrac{dy}{dx}$ in Problems 3–5.

3. $y = \sin u \qquad u = 5x^3$

4. $y = \ln |u| \qquad u = x^3 + e^x$

5. $y = \sqrt{u} \qquad u = x^3 + 2x + 1$

6. Use the definition

$$f'(a) = \lim_{x \to a} \frac{f(x) - f(a)}{x - a}$$

to find $f'(1)$ where $f(x) = x^2$.

7. Sketch the graph of $y = -x^2 + 1$ and partition the interval $[0, 1]$ into four subintervals of equal length. Estimate the area under the curve on the interval $[0, 1]$ by calculating the upper sum.

Use the quotient rule to differentiate the functions of Problems 8 and 9.

8. $f(x) = \dfrac{\sin x}{e^x + x^2}$

9. $y = \dfrac{\ln x}{\sin x + \cos x}$

10. Sketch the graph: $y = \dfrac{(x^2 + 1)(x - 1)}{(x + 2)^2 x^2}$

11. A particle moves along the number line so that its position at a time t is given by $s(t) = -2 \ln (t + 1)$. Find the velocity of the particle at $t = 2$ seconds.

12. Find the equation of the normal line which can be drawn to the graph of the function $y = \sin x$ at $x = \pi/2$.

Integrate:

13. $\displaystyle \int \left(\frac{3}{\sqrt{t}} + 4 \cos t + 6t^2 + 6 \right) dt$

14. $\displaystyle \int \left(\frac{3}{x} + 4 \sin x + 5e^x + x^{-6} \right) dx$

Use the constant, sum, and product rules as required in Problems 15–17.

15. Find $(fg)'(x)$ if $f(x) = 3e^x$ and $g(x) = 4 \sin x$.

16. Find $\dfrac{dy}{dx}$ if $y = \dfrac{2}{x} + 3x \ln |x| - 6$.

17. Find $h'(x)$ if $h(x) = \dfrac{1}{\sqrt{x^2 - 4}}$.

18. If L and x are both functions of time, find dL/dt if

$$\frac{10}{L + x} = \frac{5}{L}$$

Evaluate:

19. $\lim\limits_{t \to \infty} \dfrac{2t - t^3}{14t^3 - 4t^4}$

20. $\lim\limits_{x \to -1} \dfrac{2x + 2}{x^2 + 2x + 1}$

21. Write the polar form of the five fifth roots of $32(\cos 20° + i \sin 20°)$.

22. Find all values of x for which $\log_2 (x - 1) < 3$.

CONCEPT REVIEW   23. Solve for x in terms of y for the figure shown.

24. If $x > y > z$, compare:
     A. $x - z$ B. $y - z$

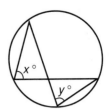

LESSON 55   *Using f' to characterize f · Using f' to define max and min*

55.A
Using f' to characterize f

We remember that when we use interval notation to designate an interval on the x axis, we can indicate whether or not the endpoints are included. If we write (a, b), the x values of a and b are not included in the interval. But if we write $[a, b]$, the x values of a and b are included in the interval. Sometimes we use a capital letter I to designate an interval and say the open interval I, or the closed interval I, or the partially closed interval I if we wish to be more specific.

We know that a function is an increasing (decreasing) function on an interval I if every greater value of x is paired with a greater (lesser) value of $f(x)$. **If $f'(x)$, the derivative of $f(x)$, is greater than zero (is positive) for every value of x on an interval I, the function is an increasing function on I.** The graph shown at the top of the next page is the graph of $f(x) = x^3 + 2x$. The equation of f' is $f'(x) = 3x^2 + 2$, and we see that for any real value of x, f' is positive because x^2 is always positive and thus $3x^2 + 2$ is always positive. Hence f is increasing on the entire interval $(-\infty, \infty)$.

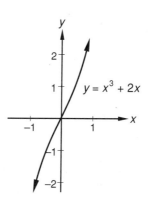

The converse of the statement in boldface on page 272 is not necessarily true. If f is increasing on an interval I, $f'(x)$ does not have to be greater than zero (positive) for all values of x in I. An example of this is the function $f(x) = x^3$. For this function, f is increasing for all real values of x; yet $f'(x)$ is not greater than 0 for every value of x because the derivative $3x^2$ equals zero when $x = 0$.

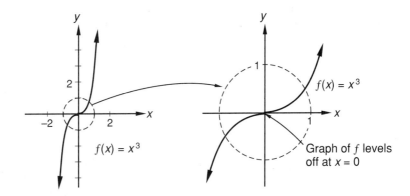

We can make similar definitions for decreasing and constant functions, as we show in the box.

If $f'(x) > 0$ for all x on an interval I, then **f is increasing on I.**

If $f'(x) < 0$ for all x on an interval I, then **f is decreasing on I.**

If $f'(x) = 0$ for all x on an interval I, then **f is constant on I.**

Example 55.1   Shown is the graph of a function f. Choose from the points labeled those points at which f' appears to be positive.

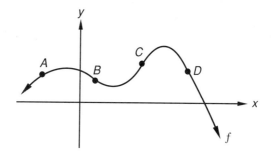

Solution   At points A and C, the slope of the graph of f is positive and hence **f' is positive at the x coordinates of A and C.**

Example 55.2   If f is a function such that $f'(x) > 0$ for all x, then describe the graph of f. Sketch how f could possibly look.

Solution   The graph of f is rising for all values of x. The graph of f could look like one of the graphs shown below.

Example 55.3   Shown is the graph of some quadratic function f. Sketch the graph of f'.

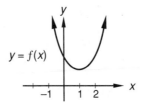

Solution   We see that the slope of the graph of f is negative for all $x < 1$ and that the slope of the graph of f is positive for all $x > 1$. At $x = 1$, the slope of the graph is 0.

   Since f is a quadratic function, f' must be a linear function. Thus the graph of f' must be a line which passes through $(1, 0)$ and lies below the x axis when $x < 1$ and above the x axis when $x > 1$.

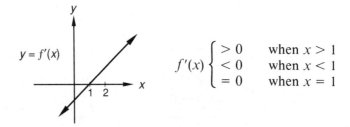

$$f'(x) \begin{cases} > 0 & \text{when } x > 1 \\ < 0 & \text{when } x < 1 \\ = 0 & \text{when } x = 1 \end{cases}$$

We are unable to determine the slope of the line since we are unable to determine the value of f at any value of x other than $x = 1$.

Example 55.4   If $f'(x)$ exists for all values of x, guess the basic shape of the graph of the function f where:

$$f'(x) \begin{cases} > 0 & \text{when } x < 1 \\ = 0 & \text{when } x = 1 \\ < 0 & \text{when } 1 < x < 2 \\ = 0 & \text{when } x = 2 \\ < 0 & \text{when } x > 2 \end{cases}$$

Solution We use that fact that the graph of *f* must be rising on intervals where $f' > 0$, falling on intervals where $f' < 0$, and horizontal at points where $f' = 0$.

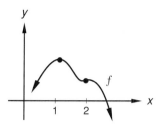

Note that we can shift the graph of *f* vertically and not change the properties of *f'*. In the next two figures we illustrate how the slope of the tangent line to the graph of a function *f* remains the same as we shift the graph vertically a distance of *c*.

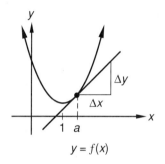

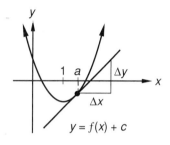

55.B
Using f'
to define
max and min

If the first derivative *f'* of a function *f* equals zero for a particular value of *x* which we call x_1, we know that the slope of the graph of *f* is zero at x_1. If the slope is positive just to the left of x_1 and negative just to the right of x_1, we know that x_1 is a local maximum. If the slope is negative just to the left of x_1 and positive just to the right of x_1, we know that x_1 is a local minimum.

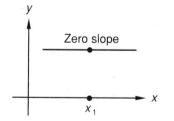

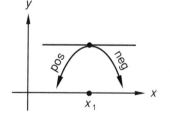

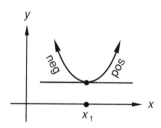

Since the slope is positive when the value of the derivative *f'* is positive and negative when the value of the derivative is negative, we can define a local maximum using the input-output concept without using a graph. First we must find some value of *x*, which we call *c*, for which the value of *f'* equals 0.

$$c \longrightarrow \boxed{f'} \longrightarrow f'(c) = 0$$

Now if the numbers c^- which are close to *c* but less than *c* have positive values of *f'* and numbers c^+ which are close to *c* but greater than *c* have negative values of *f'*, then the number *c* is a stationary number at which *f* has a local maximum value.

$$c^- \longrightarrow \boxed{\quad f' \quad} \longrightarrow \begin{array}{l} f'(c^-) > 0 \\ f'(c) = 0 \\ f'(c^+) < 0 \end{array} \qquad \text{Local maximum}$$

For f to have a local minimum value, the derivative $f'(c)$ must be zero. Also, numbers c^- that are close to c but less than c must have negative values of f' and numbers c^+ that are close to c but greater than c must have positive values of f'.

$$c^- \longrightarrow \boxed{\quad f' \quad} \longrightarrow \begin{array}{l} f'(c^-) < 0 \\ f'(c) = 0 \\ f'(c^+) > 0 \end{array} \qquad \text{Local minimum}$$

Example 55.5   Suppose f is a function where $f'(1) = 0$ and f' is positive on the interval $(-3, 1)$ and negative on the interval $(1, 4)$. Sketch the graph of f for values of x near $x = 1$ and indicate any special characteristics of the function f.

Solution   We use the information given to sketch the graph of f for values of x between -3 and 4.

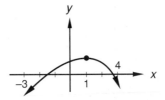

We see that the graph of f has a relative maximum point at $x = 1$, and hence the function f has a relative maximum value at $x = 1$.

Example 55.6   Use the first derivative to demonstrate that the graph of $f(x) = x^2 + 2x + 3$ has a relative minimum point at $x = -1$.

Solution
$$f(x) = x^2 + 2x + 3 \qquad \text{equation for } f$$
$$(a) \quad f'(x) = 2x + 2 \qquad \text{differentiated}$$

Setting $f'(x) = 0$, we find that
$$2x + 2 = 0$$
$$\longrightarrow \quad x = -1$$

Thus,
$$f' = 0 \quad \text{at} \quad x = -1$$

From equation (a) above we see that $f' > 0$ for all x greater than -1 and $f' < 0$ for all x less than -1. Thus, the graph of f is rising for all $x > -1$ and falling for all $x < -1$. Since the slope of the graph of f is zero precisely at $x = -1$, the graph of f must have a relative minimum point at $x = -1$.

Problem set 55   **1.**   A 10-foot-long ladder leans against a vertical wall. If the base of the ladder is x feet away from the wall, how high above the ground is the top of the ladder?

2. Shown is the graph of a function f. At which of the points A, B, C, and D is f' positive?

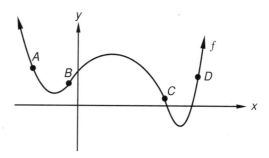

3. If $f'(x)$ exists for all real values of x, then sketch the basic shape of the graph of f where

$$f'(x) \begin{cases} < 0 & \text{when } x < 1 \\ = 0 & \text{when } x = 1 \\ > 0 & \text{when } 1 < x < 2 \\ = 0 & \text{when } x = 2 \\ < 0 & \text{when } x > 2 \end{cases}$$

4. Suppose f is a function where $f'(-1) = 0$ and f' is negative on the interval $(-3, -1)$ and positive on the interval $(-1, 2)$. Sketch the graph of f for values of x near $x = -1$. Indicate where f attains a local maximum value or a local minimum value.

Use the chain rule to compute $\dfrac{dy}{dx}$ in Problems 5–7.

5. $y = \sin t \qquad t = \sqrt{x}$

6. $y = \dfrac{1}{u} \qquad u = \sqrt{x^2 + 1}$

7. $y = \ln |u| \qquad u = 1 + e^x$

8. Use the definition

$$f'(a) = \lim_{x \to a} \frac{f(x) - f(a)}{x - a}$$

to find $f'(1)$ if $f(x) = x^3$.

9. Sketch the graph of $y = \sin x$ where $0 \le x \le \pi$. Partition the interval $[0, \pi]$ into four equal subintervals and estimate the area between the graph of $y = \sin x$ and the x axis on the interval $[0, \pi]$ by computing a lower sum.

10. If $y = \dfrac{\cos x}{\sin x}$, find y'.

11. If $f(x) = \dfrac{e^x}{1 + x^2}$, find $f'(x)$.

12. Find the critical numbers of f where $f(x) = \frac{1}{3}x^3 + \frac{3}{2}x^2 + 2x + 2$. Use this equation and a rough sketch of f to determine the local maximum and minimum values of f and where they occur.

Use the constant, sum, and product rules and u substitution as required to differentiate the functions of Problems 13–15.

13. $y = \dfrac{1}{\sqrt{x^3 + 5}}$

14. $f(x) = x - x \ln |x|$

15. $s(t) = s_0 + v_0 t + \dfrac{1}{2}gt^2 \qquad (s_0, v_0, \text{and } g \text{ are constants})$

Integrate:

16. $\displaystyle\int (\pi e^t - 2 \sin t + 1)\, dt$ **17.** $\displaystyle\int \left(\frac{4}{u} + 3u^{-15}\right) du$

18. If $f(x) = \sqrt{x}$ and $g(x) = -1 + f(x - 2)$, graph f and g on the same coordinate plane.

19. If $f(x) = \sqrt{x}$ and $g(x) = x^2 - 1$, write the equation of $f \circ g$.

20. Find the domain and range of $f \circ g$ where f and g are as defined in Problem 19.

21. Evaluate: $\displaystyle\lim_{x \to -1} \frac{x^3 + 1}{x + 1}$

22. Find the value of k such that $x = -2$ is a zero of $x^2 + kx + 4$.

CONCEPT REVIEW   **23.** Find the sum of the first twenty terms of the arithmetic sequence whose first three terms are -2, 1, and 4.

24. Find the radius of a circle which can be circumscribed about a rectangle whose length is 3 units and whose width is 4 units.

LESSON 56 *Related rate problems*

A ***related rate problem*** is a problem that presents a situation where one or more related quantities are changing and that asks for the rate at which one of the quantities is changing. The first step to solving such a problem is writing an equation that relates the variable quantities of the problem. This equation is called the ***relating equation.***

Differentiating the relating equation gives us an equation that tells us how the rates of the change of the various variable quantities relate to each other. Then we use the specific information given in the problem that can be substituted into the relating equation to solve for the desired quantities.

The following problems are classic examples of related rate problems which appear in virtually every calculus book.

Example 56.1   A 13-meter-long ladder leans against a vertical wall. The base of the ladder is pulled away from the wall at a rate of 1 meter per second. Find the rate at which the top of the ladder is falling when the base of the ladder is 5 meters away from the wall.

Solution   **The first task in a related rate problem is to find the equation that relates the variables.** We begin by drawing a diagram of the problem. We let x represent the distance from the base of the ladder to the wall and let y represent the distance from the ground to the top of the ladder. The distances x and y form the sides of a right triangle, and 13 is the hypotenuse. Thus we use the Pythagorean theorem to write the equation that relates x and y.

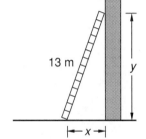

$$x^2 + y^2 = 13^2 \quad \longrightarrow \quad x^2 + y^2 = 169 \qquad \text{relating equation}$$

To find an equation which will relate dx/dt, dy/dt, x, and y, we differentiate the relating equation implicitly with respect to time t.

$$x^2 + y^2 = 169 \quad\quad \text{relating equation}$$

$$2x \, dx + 2y \, dy = 0 \quad\quad \text{differentials}$$

$$2x \frac{dx}{dt} + 2y \frac{dy}{dt} = 0 \quad\quad \text{divided by } dt$$

We want to find dy/dt, so we solve this equation for dy/dt.

$$2y \frac{dy}{dt} = -2x \frac{dx}{dt} \quad\quad \text{rearranged}$$

$$\frac{dy}{dt} = -\frac{x}{y} \frac{dx}{dt} \quad\quad \text{divided}$$

To get a numerical answer for dy/dt, we need to know values of x, y, and dx/dt. We were given that $dx/dt = 1$ and that $x = 5$. We can use the Pythagorean theorem again to find y when $x = 5$.

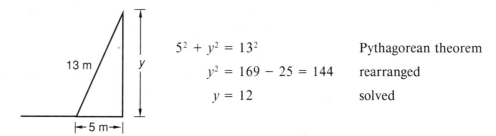

$$5^2 + y^2 = 13^2 \quad\quad \text{Pythagorean theorem}$$

$$y^2 = 169 - 25 = 144 \quad\quad \text{rearranged}$$

$$y = 12 \quad\quad \text{solved}$$

Now, we replace dx/dt with 1, x with 5, and y with 12.

$$\frac{dy}{dt} = -\frac{5}{12} (1) = -\frac{5}{12} \text{ meter per second}$$

The negative sign tells us that the value of y is decreasing as time increases.

Example 56.2   A 6-foot-tall man is walking straight away from a 15-foot-high streetlight. At what rate is his shadow lengthening when he is 20 feet away from the streetlight if he is walking away from the light at a rate of 4 feet per second?

Solution   The first task in a related rate problem is to find the equation that relates the variables. We begin by drawing a diagram of the problem. We use x to represent the distance of the man from the streetlight and L to represent the length of the shadow. Then we use properties of similar triangles to find the equation that relates x and L.

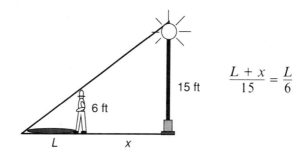

$$\frac{L + x}{15} = \frac{L}{6}$$

We rearrange the equation and find the differential of every term.

$$L + x = \frac{15}{6}L \quad \longrightarrow \quad x = \frac{3}{2}L \quad \longrightarrow \quad dx = \frac{3}{2}dL \quad \text{differential}$$

Next we divide every term by dt and solve for dL/dt.

$$\frac{dx}{dt} = \frac{3}{2}\frac{dL}{dt} \quad \text{divided by } dt$$

$$\frac{dL}{dt} = \frac{2}{3}\frac{dx}{dt} \quad \text{solved for } \frac{dL}{dt}$$

We were given that $dx/dt = 4$ feet per second, so we substitute 4 for dx/dt.

$$\frac{dL}{dt} = \frac{2}{3}(4) = \frac{8}{3} \text{ feet per second}$$

It turned out that the variables of x and L did not appear in the equation for dL/dt, so these values were not needed in the last step. Thus, the rate at which the man's shadow is lengthening is $\frac{8}{3}$ feet per second regardless of his distance from the light.

Example 56.3   A conical container has a height of 9 centimeters and a diameter of 6 centimeters as shown. It is leaking water at the rate of 1 cubic centimeter per minute. Find the rate at which the water level h is dropping when h equals 3 centimeters.

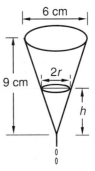

Solution   We are given that $dV/dt = -1$ and are asked to find dh/dt. Thus we need an equation that relates the volume V and the height of the water h. The formula for the volume of a cone is

$$V = \frac{1}{3}\pi r^2 h$$

In this equation we have V as a function of both r and h. Since the shape of the cone is known, we can use the similar triangles we find in a side view of the cone to write the relationship between r and h. We do this on the left below. On the right we substitute to get the desired relating equation.

$$\frac{3}{r} = \frac{9}{h} \qquad V = \frac{1}{3}\pi r^2 h \qquad \text{volume}$$

$$\longrightarrow \quad r = \frac{h}{3} \qquad V = \frac{1}{3}\pi \left(\frac{h}{3}\right)^2 h \qquad \text{substituted}$$

$$V = \frac{\pi h^3}{27} \qquad \text{substituted}$$

We take the differential of both sides, divide every term by dt, and then solve for dh/dt.

$$dV = \frac{\pi h^2}{9}\, dh \qquad \text{differentials}$$

$$\frac{dV}{dt} = \frac{\pi h^2}{9}\frac{dh}{dt} \qquad \text{divided by } dt$$

$$\frac{dh}{dt} = \frac{9\dfrac{dV}{dt}}{\pi h^2} \qquad \text{solved for } \frac{dh}{dt}$$

As the last step we use -1 for dV/dt and 3 for h.

$$\frac{dh}{dt} = \frac{9(-1)}{\pi(3)^2} = -\frac{1}{\pi} \approx -0.32 \text{ centimeter per second}$$

The negative sign means that h is decreasing as time increases.

Problem set 56

1. A 10-meter-long ladder leans against a vertical wall. The base of the ladder is pulled away from the wall at a rate of 1 meter per second. How fast is the top of the ladder falling when the base of the ladder is 4 meters away from the wall?

2. A 5-foot-tall man walks straight away from a lamppost which is 35 feet high. How fast is the length of his shadow changing when he is 12 feet away from the lamppost if he walks at a rate of 3 feet per second?

3. If $f'(x)$ exists for all real values of x, then sketch the basic shape of the graph of f where

$$f'(x) \begin{cases} > 0 & \text{when } x < 2 \\ = 0 & \text{when } x = 2 \\ > 0 & \text{when } 2 < x < 3 \\ = 0 & \text{when } x = 3 \\ < 0 & \text{when } x > 3 \end{cases}$$

4. Use the first derivative to find where the critical numbers of f occur if $f(x) = x^2 + 6x - 4$. Then use the first derivative to determine whether f attains a maximum or minimum value at some critical number.

Use the chain rule to find $\dfrac{dy}{dx}$ in Problems 5 and 6.

5. $y = \sqrt{u} \qquad u = x^2 + 1$

6. $y = e^u \qquad u = \sin x$

7. Use the fact that

$$f'(a) = \lim_{x \to a} \frac{f(x) - f(a)}{x - a}$$

to find $f'(1)$ where $f(x) = \sqrt{x}$. (*Hint*: Factor the denominator.)

8. Sketch the graph of $y = -x^2 + 4$ where $0 \le x \le 2$ and partition the interval $[0, 2]$ into four equally long subintervals. Use an upper sum to estimate the area bounded by the graph of y and the x axis on the interval $[0, 2]$.

Use u substitution and the sum, product, and quotient rules as necessary to differentiate the functions of Problems 9–12.

9. $f(x) = \dfrac{\sin x}{\cos x + \sin x}$

10. $y = 2x \ln |x| + 5$

11. $y = \sqrt{x^2 + 1}$

12. $y = e^{\sin x}$

13. Approximate to two decimal places the slope of the line which can be drawn normal to the graph of $y = \ln |x| + e^x$ at $x = -2$.

14. Find the critical numbers of $f(x) = 3x^4 + 4x^3 - 12x^2 + 5$. Then use this equation and a sketch of the graph of f to determine where f attains a local maximum or minimum.

Integrate:

15. $\int \left(3x + e^x - \dfrac{1}{\sqrt{x}} + \dfrac{1}{3} \right) dx$ 16. $\int \left(t + \dfrac{1}{t} - 3 + t^5 + t^{-5} - \sin t \right) dt$

17. Sketch the graph of $y = \tan x$.

18. If $f(x) = 2 \sin x$, approximate $f'''(2)$ to two decimal places.

19. Begin with the key identities and develop an identity for $\tan 2a$.

20. Find the coordinates of the vertices and the equations of the asymptotes of the conic whose equation is

$$\frac{(x-2)^2}{4} - \frac{(y+1)^2}{9} = 1$$

21. A chord 10 centimeters long is drawn inside a circle of radius r. The distance from the center of the circle to the midpoint of the chord is 12 centimeters. Find the radius of the circle.

22. If $a - b = 2$, then compare: A. $a^2 + b^2$ B. $4 + 2ab$

LESSON 57 *Fundamental theorem of integral calculus*

We have defined the area under a curve on the interval $[a, b]$ to be the number that is the limit of the sum of the areas of the rectangles on a partition of $[a, b]$ between the x axis and the graph of a nonnegative continuous function, as the number of rectangles increases without limit. On the left below we show the area under the graph of the function f between x values of a and b. The width of each rectangle is Δx and the height of each rectangle is the least value of $f(x)$ on each interval, so the sum of the areas of these rectangles will be a lower sum (we could have used an upper sum). On the right we use summation notation to indicate this sum whose limit we have defined to be the number that we call the area A.

$$A = \lim_{n \to \infty} \sum_{i=1}^{n} f(x_{Li}) \, \Delta x$$

$$A = \int_a^b f(x) \, dx$$

Underneath the summation notation we have written the integral notation for the same sum. We read this as "the area A equals the integral from a to b of f of x dee x."

Note that this notation reminds us that one border of the area is the graph of f and suggests that the width of each rectangle can be thought of as dx. We have been estimating the areas under curves by the rather laborious process of drawing the rectangles, finding the individual areas, and summing the areas. From now on we will use the *fundamental theorem of integral calculus* to find these areas exactly and with a minimum of effort.

This theorem is a statement of the wonderful discovery of Newton and Leibniz. In part, the theorem tells us that the area under the graph of any continuous nonnegative function between a and b equals the value of any antiderivative evaluated at a subtracted from the value of the same antiderivative evaluated at b.

This means that the area under the graph of a nonnegative function and above the x axis between x values of a and b equals the ordered difference of the distances from the x axis to the graph of any antiderivative at a and at b. It is customary to use a small f to designate a function and a capital F to designate an antiderivative of the function. Thus the derivative of $F(x)$ will be $f(x)$, and some antiderivative of $f(x)$ will be $F(x)$.

$$\frac{d}{dx} F(x) = f(x) \quad \text{and} \quad \int f(x)\,dx = F(x)$$

If we use this notation, we can designate the area under the graph of a continuous nonnegative function between x values of a and b by writing

$$A_{ab} = \int_a^b f(x)\,dx = F(b) - F(a)$$

For a specific example we will use the fundamental theorem of integral calculus to find the area under the graph of $y = 2x$ between x values of 2 and 3. In the figure on the left we show that this area equals the area of the rectangle, 4, plus the area of the triangle, 1, for a total area of 5.

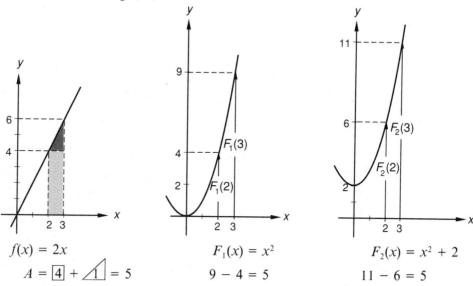

$f(x) = 2x$ $F_1(x) = x^2$ $F_2(x) = x^2 + 2$

$A = \boxed{4} + \triangle = 5$ $9 - 4 = 5$ $11 - 6 = 5$

In the center figure and in the right-hand figure we show graphs of the functions $F_1(x) = x^2$ and $F_2(x) = x^2 + 2$, both of which are antiderivatives of $f(x)$. The difference in the values of $F_1(3)$ and $F_1(2)$ is $9 - 4$, which equals 5. The difference in the values of $F_2(3)$ and $F_2(2)$ is $11 - 6$, which also equals 5. **The difference between $F(3)$ and $F(2)$ will be 5 regardless of the antiderivative chosen because the contribution of the unique constant of each antiderivative is eliminated when we subtract.**

To this point we have restricted our statement of the fundamental theorem of integral calculus to functions that are continuous and nonnegative on the interval.

Thus, until we discuss this topic further, we will be careful in the problem sets to select functions whose graphs do not go below the x axis on the interval being considered. In a later lesson we will find how this theorem can be used with any continuous function. We will also present one informal proof and two formal proofs of this theorem.

Example 57.1 Find the area under the graph of $f(x) = 4 \sin x$ between 0 and π.

Solution On the left we show the graph of the equation $f(x) = 4 \sin x$ and have shaded the area that we want to find. On the right we show the graph of $F(x) = -4 \cos x + 0$, which is the graph of an antiderivative of $4 \sin x$. We use arrows to indicate the distance from the x axis to the graph when $x = 0$ and when $x = \pi$.

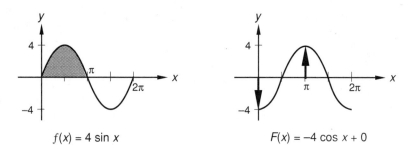

$f(x) = 4 \sin x$ $\qquad\qquad\qquad\qquad$ $F(x) = -4 \cos x + 0$

We can see that $F(0) = -4$ and $F(\pi) = 4$ and that the answer must be

$$\int_0^\pi 4 \sin x \, dx = 4 - (-4) = 8$$

Rather than drawing pictures, it is customary to proceed as follows.

$$A = \int_0^\pi 4 \sin x \, dx = 4 \left[-\cos x\right]_0^\pi = -4[\cos x]_0^\pi$$

We use the notation on the right to indicate that the value of x at the left end of the interval is zero, and we call zero the **lower limit.** The value of x at the right end of the interval is called the **upper limit** and is π in this example. We note that here the word *limit* has a different meaning from that in the phrase *limit of a function.* Here the word *limit* is used to designate the values of x at the ends of the interval $[0, \pi]$. We always evaluate the antiderivative at the upper limit first and subtract from it the value of the same antiderivative evaluated at the lower limit.

$$-4 \cos x]_0^\pi = -4(\cos \pi - \cos 0)$$
$$= -4[(-1) - (1)] = -4(-2) = \mathbf{8 \ units^2}$$

Example 57.2 Find the area under the graph of the function $y = x^2 + 2x + 5$ between x values of 1 and 3.

Solution We could take the time to draw an accurate graph but this is unnecessary. We know the function is positive for x values between 1 and 3, so we draw a general continuous curve above the x axis, call it f, and indicate the area we want to find. Then we draw another curve and label it $\int f = F$ and indicate the distance from the x axis to this curve at x values of 1 and 3. **The curves shown on the next page do not represent the graph of the function in this problem or the graph of an antiderivative but are just general curves.**

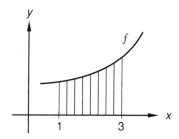 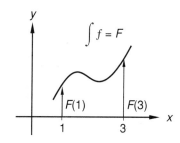

The area under f between 1 and 3 equals $F(3) - F(1)$. We begin by writing the integral of a sum as the sum of the integrals.

$$A = \int_1^3 (x^2 + 2x + 5)\, dx = \int_1^3 x^2\, dx + 2 \int_1^3 x\, dx + 5 \int_1^3 dx$$

Now we find an antiderivative and evaluate this antiderivative at the endpoints of the interval to determine the area.

$$\left[\frac{x^3}{3} + x^2 + 5x\right]_1^3 = [9 + 9 + 15] - \left[\frac{1}{3} + 1 + 5\right] = 33 - \frac{19}{3} = \frac{80}{3} \text{ units}^2$$

Example 57.3   Find the area under the graph of the function $y = 3e^x + \dfrac{2}{x} + x^2$ between x values of 1 and 2.

Solution   This time we will not bother to draw the graph but will keep the graph of the preceding example in mind as we find the area. First we write the integral of a sum as the sum of integrals

$$A = 3 \int_1^2 e^x\, dx + 2 \int_1^2 \frac{dx}{x} + \int_1^2 x^2\, dx$$

Now we find an antiderivative and evaluate it at the endpoints of the interval to find the area.

$$\left[3e^x + 2 \ln x + \frac{1}{3}x^3\right]_1^2 = \left[3e^2 + 2 \ln 2 + \frac{1}{3}(2^3)\right] - \left[3e^1 + 2 \ln 1 + \frac{1}{3}(1^3)\right]$$

$$= 3e^2 + 2 \ln 2 - 3e + \frac{7}{3} \text{ units}^2$$

Problem set 57   **1.**   A 13-meter-long ladder leans against a vertical wall. The base of the ladder is pulled away from the wall at a rate of 2 meters per second. How fast is the top of the ladder falling when the base of the ladder is 5 meters away from the wall?

2.   The volume of a spherical ball is increasing at a rate of 1 cubic centimeter per second. What is the rate at which the radius is increasing in length when the radius of the ball is 10 centimeters?

Use the fundamental theorem of integral calculus to compute the areas of the shaded regions shown in Problems 3–6.

3.
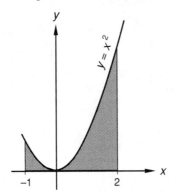

4.
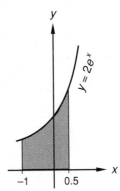

5.
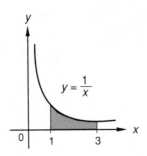

6.
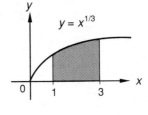

7. Find all the critical numbers of f where $f(x) = -2x^3 - 3x^2 - 4$. Use the equation and a sketch of the graph of f to find the values of x at which f attains local maximum or minimum values.

8. Use the first derivative to justify your answers to Problem 7.

Use the chain rule to find $\dfrac{dy}{dx}$ in Problems 9 and 10.

9. $y = e^u \qquad u = x + \sin x$

10. $y = \dfrac{1}{\sqrt{u}} \qquad u = e^x + 1$

11. Use the definition $f'(a) = \lim\limits_{x \to a} \dfrac{f(x) - f(a)}{x - a}$ to compute $f'(2)$ if $f(x) = x^2 + 1$.

Differentiate the functions whose equations are given in Problems 12–15.

12. $y = 3e^{x + \sin x}$

13. $y = 4t^3 \ln t$

14. $y = 6u - \dfrac{1}{\sqrt{u}}$

15. $y = \dfrac{\sin x}{x^2 + 1}$

16. Approximate the value of $f'''(3)$ to two decimal places if $f(x) = -3 \cos x$.

Sketch the equations of Problems 17 and 18, indicating clearly all x intercepts and asymptotes of the graphs.

17. $y = \dfrac{2}{(x - 2)^2}$

18. $y = x^2(x - 1)(x + 1)^2$

19. Determine the domain and range of the inverse trigonometric function $y = \arccos x$.

20. Express $\sin^2 x$ in terms of $\cos 2x$.

21. Find all real values of x for which $0 \le x < 2\pi$ and $\sin 3x = 1$.

22. Integrate: $\int \left(4e^x + 2 \cos x + x^{-5} + \dfrac{1}{x} + \sqrt{x} \right) dx$

CONCEPT REVIEW 23. Write the number $1.2727 \cdots = 1.\overline{27}$ as a fraction written in lowest terms.

24. Find the sum of all the terms of the infinite geometric sequence whose first three terms are $2, \frac{2}{3}, \frac{2}{9}$.

LESSON 58 *Derivatives of trigonometric functions · Summary of rules for derivatives and differentials*

58.A
Derivatives of trigonometric functions

When we try to use the definition of the derivative to find the derivatives of $\sin x$, $\cos x$, $\tan x$, and other trigonometric functions, we find that we encounter limits of expressions that cannot be evaluated by using elementary algebraic manipulations. There is a way to prove that the derivative of $\sin x$ is $\cos x$ if we use the limits of geometric areas as a part of the proof. We will present this proof in Lesson 116.

We are fortunate that we can use the fact that the derivative of $\sin x$ is $\cos x$ to find the derivatives of other trigonometric functions. We will begin by using this fact to find the derivative of $\cos x$. To find the derivative of $\cos x$, all we have to do is remember that $\cos x$ is the cosine of x, which means that $\cos x$ is the sine of the other angle. From the diagram we see that the other angle is $(90 - x)°$, or $\frac{\pi}{2} - x$.

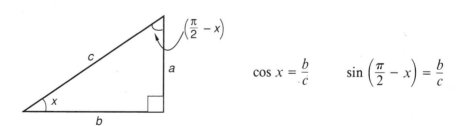

$$\cos x = \frac{b}{c} \qquad \sin\left(\frac{\pi}{2} - x\right) = \frac{b}{c}$$

Example 58.1 Use the fact that the derivative of $\sin x$ is $\cos x$ to find the derivative of $\cos x$.

Solution We know how to differentiate the sine function, so we will substitute $\sin\left(\frac{\pi}{2} - x\right)$ for $\cos x$. Then we will use u substitution to differentiate this function. We begin by writing

$$y = \cos x$$

Next we replace cos x with its cofunction, $\sin\left(\dfrac{\pi}{2} - x\right)$.

$$y = \sin\left(\frac{\pi}{2} - x\right) \qquad \text{cofunction}$$

We note that this expression has the form $y = \sin u$. We can find the differential of this form, so we write

$$dy = \cos u \, du \qquad \boxed{\begin{aligned} u &= \frac{\pi}{2} - x \\[4pt] du &= (-1)\,dx \end{aligned}}$$

Now we use the box to substitute again. We simplify the expression and divide both sides by dx to find the derivative.

$$dy = \cos\left(\frac{\pi}{2} - x\right)(-1)\,dx \qquad \text{substituted}$$

$$dy = -\cos\left(\frac{\pi}{2} - x\right) dx \qquad \text{simplified}$$

$$\frac{dy}{dx} = -\cos\left(\frac{\pi}{2} - x\right) \qquad \text{divided by } dx$$

We began by replacing cos x with its cofunction, $\sin\left(\dfrac{\pi}{2} - x\right)$. We finish by replacing $\cos\left(\dfrac{\pi}{2} - x\right)$ with its cofunction, $\sin x$.

$$\frac{dy}{dx} = -\sin x$$

Example 58.2   Use the quotient rule and the derivatives of sin x and cos x to find the derivative of tan x.

Solution   We begin by writing the derivatives of sin x and cos x.

$$\frac{d}{dx}\sin x = \cos x \qquad \frac{d}{dx}\cos x = -\sin x$$

Now we define tan x.

$$\tan x = \frac{\sin x}{\cos x}$$

Next we use the quotient rule to find the derivative.

$$\frac{d}{dx}(\tan x) = \frac{(\cos x)(\cos x) - (\sin x)(-\sin x)}{\cos^2 x}$$

$$= \frac{\cos^2 x + \sin^2 x}{\cos^2 x}$$

But $\sin^2 x + \cos^2 x = 1$, and the reciprocal of $\cos^2 x$ is $\sec^2 x$, so

$$\frac{d}{dx}(\tan x) = \frac{1}{\cos^2 x} = \sec^2 x$$

Example 58.3   Use the quotient rule and the derivatives of sin x and cos x to find the derivative of cot x.

Solution   Again we begin by writing the derivatives of sin x and cos x.

$$\frac{d}{dx}\sin x = \cos x \qquad \frac{d}{dx}\cos x = -\sin x$$

Now we define cot x.

$$\cot x = \frac{\cos x}{\sin x}$$

Now we use the quotient rule to find the derivative.

$$\frac{d}{dx}(\cot x) = \frac{(\sin x)(-\sin x) - (\cos x)(\cos x)}{\sin^2 x}$$

$$= \frac{-\sin^2 x - \cos^2 x}{\sin^2 x}$$

But $-(\sin^2 x + \cos^2 x) = -1$ and the reciprocal of $\sin^2 x$ is $\csc^2 x$, so

$$\frac{d}{dx}(\cot x) = \frac{-1}{\sin^2 x} = -\csc^2 x$$

Example 58.4   Use the fact that sec x is the reciprocal of cos x to find the derivative of sec x.

Solution   First we will rewrite sec x as a power of cos x.

$$y = \sec x = \frac{1}{\cos x} \quad \longrightarrow \quad y = (\cos x)^{-1}$$

We note that this equation has the form $y = u^{-1}$, so we use u substitution and begin by finding the differential dy.

$$y = u^{-1} \quad \longrightarrow \quad dy = (-1)u^{-2}\,du \qquad \boxed{\begin{array}{l} u = \cos x \\ du = -\sin x\,dx \end{array}}$$

Next we substitute again and get

$$dy = (-1)(\cos x)^{-2}(-\sin x)\,dx \qquad \text{substituted}$$

$$dy = \frac{\sin x}{\cos^2 x}\,dx \qquad \text{simplified}$$

$$dy = \frac{1}{\cos x}\frac{\sin x}{\cos x}\,dx \qquad \text{rearranged}$$

$$dy = \sec x \tan x\,dx \qquad \text{simplified}$$

$$\frac{d}{dx}(\sec x) = \sec x \tan x \qquad \text{derivative}$$

This shows that $$\frac{d}{dx}\sec x = \sec x \tan x$$

Example 58.5   Use the fact that csc x is the reciprocal of sin x to find the derivative of csc x.

Solution   First we will rewrite csc x as a power of sin x.

$$y = \csc x = \frac{1}{\sin x} \quad \longrightarrow \quad y = (\sin x)^{-1}$$

We note that this equation has the form $y = u^{-1}$, so we use u substitution and begin by finding the differential dy.

$$y = u^{-1} \quad \longrightarrow \quad dy = -1u^{-2} \, du \qquad \boxed{\begin{array}{l} u = \sin x \\ du = \cos x \, dx \end{array}}$$

Next we substitute again and get

$$dy = (-1)(\sin x)^{-2}(\cos x \, dx) \qquad \text{substituted}$$

$$dy = -\frac{\cos x}{\sin^2 x} \, dx \qquad \text{simplified}$$

$$dy = -\frac{1}{\sin x} \frac{\cos x}{\sin x} \, dx \qquad \text{rearranged}$$

$$dy = -\csc x \cot x \, dx \qquad \text{simplified}$$

$$\frac{dy}{dx} = -\csc x \cot x \qquad \text{divided by } dx$$

This shows that $\qquad\qquad\qquad \dfrac{d}{dx} \, \csc x = -\csc x \cot x$

The results of Examples 58.2, 58.3, 58.4, and 58.5 should be memorized.

Example 58.6   If $y = e^x(\sec x) + \sec^2 x$, find $\dfrac{dy}{dx}$.

Solution   We have to use the product rule.

$$\frac{dy}{dx} = e^x \sec x \tan x + \sec x \, e^x + 2 \sec x \sec x \tan x$$

$$= e^x \sec x \tan x + \sec x \, e^x + 2 \sec^2 x \tan x$$

Example 58.7   If $y = x^2 \tan x + \csc^2 x$, find y'.

Solution   Again we must use the product rule.

$$y' = x^2 \sec^2 x + 2x \tan x + (2 \csc x)(-\csc x \cot x)$$

$$= x^2 \sec^2 x + 2x \tan x - 2 \csc^2 x \cot x$$

Example 58.8   If $y = \ln x \csc x$, find $\dfrac{dy}{dx}$.

Solution   We use the product rule again.

$$\frac{dy}{dx} = (\ln x)(-\csc x \cot x) + \frac{1}{x} \csc x$$

$$= -\ln x \csc x \cot x + \frac{1}{x} \csc x$$

Example 58.9   If $y = \dfrac{\tan^3 x}{e^x + 1}$, find y'.

Solution   We use the quotient rule.

$$y' = \frac{(e^x + 1)(3)(\tan^2 x)(\sec^2 x) - (\tan^3 x)(e^x)}{(e^x + 1)^2}$$

$$= \frac{3(e^x + 1)(\tan^2 x)(\sec^2 x) - e^x \tan^3 x}{(e^x + 1)^2}$$

58.B
Summary of rules for derivatives and differentials

If c represents a constant and u and v are differentiable functions of x, the rules for derivatives and differentials that we have discussed to this point are as follows:

DERIVATIVES	DIFFERENTIALS
$\dfrac{d}{dx} c = 0$	$d(c) = 0$
$\dfrac{d}{dx} cu = c \dfrac{d}{dx} u \longrightarrow$	$d(cu) = c\, du$
$\dfrac{d}{dx}(u + v) = \dfrac{du}{dx} + \dfrac{dv}{dx} \longrightarrow$	$d(u + v) = du + dv$
$\dfrac{d}{dx} uv = u \dfrac{dv}{dx} + v \dfrac{du}{dx} \longrightarrow$	$d(uv) = u\, dv + v\, du$
$\dfrac{d}{dx} \dfrac{u}{v} = \dfrac{v \dfrac{du}{dx} - u \dfrac{dv}{dx}}{v^2} \longrightarrow$	$d\left(\dfrac{u}{v}\right) = \dfrac{v\, du - u\, dv}{v^2}$
$\dfrac{d}{du} u^n = nu^{n-1} \longrightarrow$	$du^n = nu^{n-1}\, du$
$\dfrac{d}{du} e^u = e^u \longrightarrow$	$de^u = e^u\, du$
$\dfrac{d}{du} \sin u = \cos u \longrightarrow$	$d \sin u = \cos u\, du$
$\dfrac{d}{du} \cos u = -\sin u \longrightarrow$	$d \cos u = -\sin u\, du$
$\dfrac{d}{du} \ln u = \dfrac{1}{u} \longrightarrow$	$d(\ln u) = \dfrac{1}{u}\, du$
$\dfrac{d}{du} \tan u = \sec^2 u \longrightarrow$	$d \tan u = \sec^2 u\, du$
$\dfrac{d}{du} \cot u = -\csc^2 u \longrightarrow$	$d \cot u = -\csc^2 u\, du$
$\dfrac{d}{du} \sec u = \sec u \tan u \longrightarrow$	$d \sec u = \sec u \tan u\, du$
$\dfrac{d}{du} \csc u = -\csc u \cot u \longrightarrow$	$d \csc u = -\csc u \cot u\, du$

Problem set 58   **1.**   The radius of the base of a right circular cone increases at a rate of 1 centimeter per second while its height remains constant at 10 centimeters. Find the rate at which the volume of the cone is increasing at the instant when the base of the cone has a 24-centimeter radius.

2. The chamber leaked noxious fumes at an exponential rate. At noon the chamber leaked fumes at a rate of 3 cm³/sec, and 3 hours later the chamber leaked fumes at a rate of 8 cm³/sec. How many hours past noon did the chamber leak fumes at a rate of 20 cm³/sec?

3. Use the fact that the derivative of sin x is cos x to find the derivative of cos x.

4. Use the quotient rule and the derivatives of sin x and cos x to find the derivative of cot x.

5. Use the fact that csc x is the reciprocal of sin x to find the derivative of csc x.

Find the derivative of each of the following functions:

6. $y = e^x \csc x$ 7. $y = x^2 \sec x$

Use the fundamental theorem of integral calculus to compute the areas of the shaded regions shown in Problems 8–11.

8.

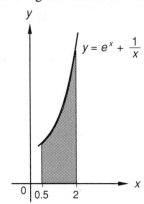

9.

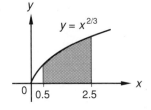

10.

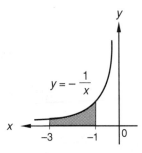

11.

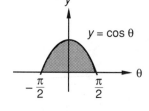

12. Suppose $f(x) = x^2 + bx + c$ where b and c are real numbers. Use the first derivative to determine where the minimum value of f occurs. Use a rough sketch of f to justify your answer.

13. If g is a function such that $g'(2) = 0$ and $g' < 0$ when x lies in the interval $(0, 2)$ and $g' > 0$ when x lies in the interval $(2, 4)$, determine whether g attains a local maximum or minimum value at $x = 2$.

Use the chain rule to find $\dfrac{dy}{dx}$ in Problems 14 and 15.

14. $y = 4 \sin u$ $u = x^2$ 15. $y = -\dfrac{1}{\sqrt{u}}$ $u = e^x - 1$

16. A particle moves along the number line so that its position at time t is given by the equation $s(t) = t^3 - t^2 - 12$. Find the velocity of the particle at $t = 3$.

Integrate:

17. $\int \left(-\dfrac{1}{\sqrt{u}} + 2u^2 - 1 + 3\sqrt{u} + 2 \sin u - \cos u + u^{-5} - 4e^u \right) du$

18. $\int \dfrac{x^2 + x + 1}{x} \, dx$ (First rewrite the integrand as a sum.)

19. Determine to two decimal places the real values of x where $\log_x 3 = 5$.

20. Rewrite $y = \log_2 x$ entirely in terms of the natural logarithm function.

21. Sketch the graph of $y = -2 + 3 \sin (2x - 90°)$.

22. Sketch the graph of $y = x^{2/3}$.

23. Suppose f is a quadratic function and that $f(0) = -4$ and $f(2) = f(-1) = 0$. Find the equation of f.

CONCEPT REVIEW   **24.** Two circles whose diameters are equal intersect at two points. The chord joining these two points is 8 centimeters long. If the distance between the centers of the two circles is 6 centimeters, find the length of the radius of each circle.

25. If $xy = 1$, compare: *A.* $-x$ *B.* $-\dfrac{1}{y}$

LESSON 59 *Concavity and inflection points · Applications of the second derivative*

59.A
Concavity and inflection points

If we can draw a tangent line to the graph of a function f at an x value of c, there are three possibilities for the behavior of the graph near the point of tangency P.

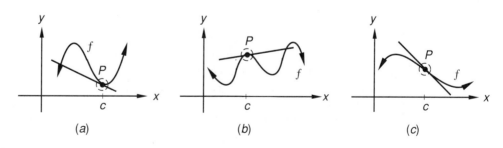

(a)   (b)   (c)

(*a*) All points on the graph near the point of tangency P lie above the tangent line. In this case the graph moves **up** and away from the tangent line on both sides of P, and we say that the graph of f is ***concave upward*** at $x = c$.

(*b*) All points on the graph near the point of tangency P lie below the tangent line. In this case the graph moves **down** and away from the tangent line on both sides of P, and we say that the graph of f is ***concave downward*** at $x = c$.

(*c*) The points on the graph near the point of tangency P are above the tangent line on one side of P and below the tangent line on the other side of P. Thus the curve moves up and away (concave upward) on one side and down and away (concave downward) on the other side. We say that the point P is an ***inflection point*** and say that f has an inflection point at $x = c$.

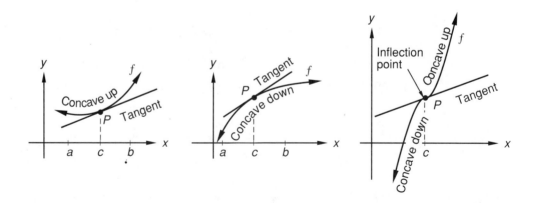

Example 59.1   Shown is the graph of f.

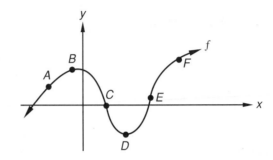

Indicate if the graph appears to have positive or negative concavity or has an inflection point at the points labeled.

Solution A: **Negative.** B: **Negative.** C: **Inflection point.** D: **Positive.** E: **Inflection point.** F: **Negative.**

Notice that the graph is concave upward on one side of both inflection points and is concave downward on the other side.

59.B
Geometric meaning of the second derivative

The derivative of a function is another function called the **first derivative** whose value equals the rate of change of the original function with respect to x. The value of the first derivative where $x = c$ equals the slope of the line tangent to the graph when $x = c$.

If we differentiate the first derivative of a function, we get another function called the **second derivative** of the function. The value of the second derivative equals the rate of change of the first derivative. Thus the value of the second derivative equals the rate of change of the slope of the graph of the original function. **If the second derivative is positive when $x = c$, the slope of the graph of the function is increasing as the x dot moves to the right and the graph will be concave upward at that point.** In the figure at the top of page 295, we show the graph of a function f that is concave upward at every value of x. If the x dot is in the position shown, we estimate the slope of the graph to be -2.

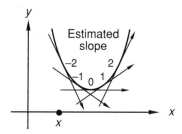

The slope of the curve increases as the x dot moves from left to right.

As the x dot moves to the right we see that the estimated slope goes from -2 to -1 to 0 to $+1$ to $+2$. Each value of the slope is greater than the value to its left, and thus the rate of change of the slope is positive.

If the second derivative is negative when $x = c$, the slope of the graph of the function is decreasing as the x dot moves to the right and the graph will be concave downward at that point. In the next figure we show the graph of a function f that is concave downward at every value of x. If the x dot is in the position shown, we estimate the slope of the graph to be $+2$.

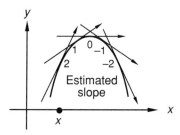

The slope of the curve decreases as the x dot moves from left to right.

In this graph of a function, as the x dot moves to the right we see that the values of the estimated slope go from $+2$ to $+1$ to 0 to -1 to -2. Each value of the slope is less than the one to its left, and thus the rate of change of the slope is negative.

We can remember the connection between positive and negative values of the second derivative and concave upward and concave downward by using these faces as a mnemonic.

f'' positive means
concave upward

f'' negative means
concave downward

The first derivative tells us whether the slope is positive, negative, or zero and tells us how steep the slope is if the slope is not zero. To illustrate, we show the graphs of

$$y = \frac{1}{3}x \qquad y = 2x \qquad y = -\frac{1}{3}x \qquad \text{and} \qquad y = -2x$$

on the following page.

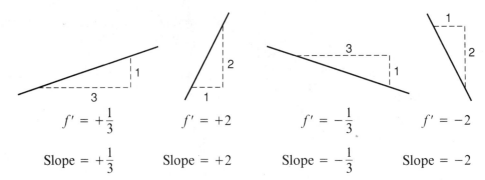

$$f' = +\frac{1}{3} \qquad f' = +2 \qquad f' = -\frac{1}{3} \qquad f' = -2$$

$$\text{Slope} = +\frac{1}{3} \qquad \text{Slope} = +2 \qquad \text{Slope} = -\frac{1}{3} \qquad \text{Slope} = -2$$

If the second derivative is not zero for some value of x, its value tells us whether the slope is increasing positively or negatively and tells us how fast the slope is increasing, which is a measure of the "bend" in the graph at that value of x.

Here we show tangent lines drawn to the graphs of four different functions. The slopes of the tangent lines are equal, so the values of the first derivatives of these functions are equal at the points of tangency.

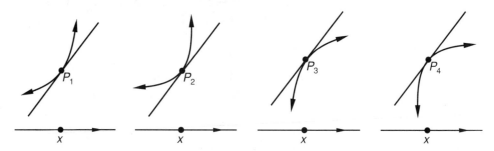

The values of the second derivatives are all different. At P_1 and P_2 the graphs are concave upward, so the slope is increasing as the x dot moves from left to right. The bend in the graph at P_2 is greater, so if the value of the second derivative at P_1 were $+2$, a value of $+4$ at P_2 would not be unreasonable. At P_3 and P_4 the graphs are concave downward, so the slope is decreasing as the x dot moves from left to right. The bend in the graph at P_4 is greater, so if the value of the second derivative at P_3 were -2, a value of -4 at P_4 would not be unreasonable.

Example 59.2 At which of the points labeled on the graph shown is $\frac{d^2y}{dx^2}$ positive?

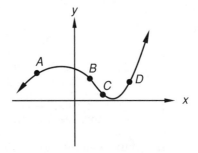

Solution The places at which the second derivative is positive are those places on the graph of the function where the graph is concave upward. Only two of the points on the graph appear to satisfy this condition; they are **C and D.**

59.C
First and second derivative tests

We remember that critical points or critical numbers are values of x for which the value of a function f could be a local maximum or a local minimum. Local maximum values and local minimum values are sometimes called ***local extrema.*** Local extrema can occur at the endpoints of the domain and also at values of x for which the graph of a function has a corner or "sharp point." Local extrema can also exist at values of x for which the first derivative equals zero (the slope of the graph of f equals zero). We remember that these critical points are called *stationary points* or *stationary numbers.* **If the function f is continuous at c and if $f'(c) = 0$, then we can use the first derivative test to see if $f(c)$ is a local maximum or a local minimum, or if the graph of f has an inflection point at $(c, f(c))$.**

FIRST DERIVATIVE TEST

If the first derivative of f equals zero when $x = c$, $f'(c) = 0$, and

1. If the derivative of f (slope of the graph of f) is positive for all values of x just to the left of c and negative for all values of x just to the right of c, then $f(c)$ is a local maximum.
2. If the derivative of f (slope of the graph of f) is negative for all values of x just to the left of c and positive for all values of x just to the right of c, then $f(c)$ is a local minimum.
3. If the derivative of f (slope of the graph of f) has the same sign for all values of x just to the left and right of c, then $(c, f(c))$ is an inflection point on the graph of f.

The three possibilities are shown here.

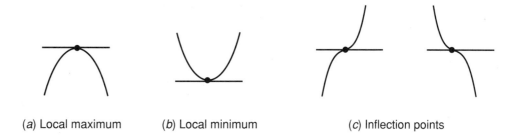

(*a*) Local maximum   (*b*) Local minimum   (*c*) Inflection points

If the value of the second derivative, $f''(x)$, is positive or negative when $x = c$, the second derivative test can be used to obviate the requirement for checking the value of the first derivative on both sides of $x = c$. If the value of the second derivative is zero, $f''(c) = 0$, the second derivative test cannot be used.

> SECOND DERIVATIVE TEST
>
> If the first derivative of f equals zero when $x = c$ [$f'(c) = 0$], and
>
> 1. If the second derivative of f is a negative number when $x = c$ [$f''(c) < 0$], then $f(c)$ is a local maximum value.
> 2. If the second derivative of f is a positive number when $x = c$ [$f''(c) > 0$], then $f(c)$ is a local minimum value.

Note: A zero value of the second derivative does not necessarily indicate an inflection point. A zero value of the second derivative [$f''(c) = 0$] tells us to go back and use the first derivative test.

Example 59.3   Suppose f is a polynomial function such that $f'(3) = 0$ and $f''(3) = 3$. Sketch the graph of f where x is close to 3 and indicate the property of the function f at $x = 3$.

Solution   With the information given, we can only guess at the shape of the graph in the vicinity of $x = 3$. This graph shows that f has a local minimum point at $x = 3$. Hence, the function f has a local minimum at $x = 3$.

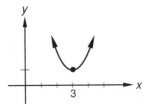

Example 59.4   Suppose f is a polynomial function such that $f'(3) = 0$ and $f''(3) = 0$. In addition f' is positive for all values of x near $x = 3$. Sketch the graph of f for x near $x = 3$ and indicate the significance of the point on the graph of f at $x = 3$.

Solution   Since $f' = 0$ and $f'' = 0$ at $x = 3$, then $f(3)$ is a local maximum or minimum value of f, or the graph of f has an inflection point at $(3, f(3))$. We cannot use the second derivative test because $f''(3) = 0$, so we go back to the first derivative test. We were told that the first derivative has the same sign on both sides of 3, so the point $(3, f(3))$ must be an inflection point.

We use this information to sketch the graph of f.

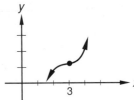

Example 59.5   Given $f(x) = x^4$, use f' and f'' to describe the graph of f near and at $x = 0$.

Solution   We begin by finding the equations of f' and f''.

$$f(x) = x^4$$
$$f'(x) = 4x^3 \quad \longrightarrow \quad f'(0) = 4(0)^3 = 0$$
$$f''(x) = 12x^2 \quad \longrightarrow \quad f''(0) = 12(0)^2 = 0$$

At $x = 0$, f' and $f'' = 0$. The fact that $f' = 0$ at $x = 0$ tells us that f has a stationary point at $f = 0$. The second derivative test cannot be used because $f''(0) = 0$. If we use the first derivative test, we see that f' is negative when x is negative and positive when x is positive. Thus $f(0)$ is a local minimum value of f.

$$f'(x) = 4x^3 \begin{cases} < 0 & \text{when } x < 0 \\ > 0 & \text{when } x > 0 \end{cases}$$

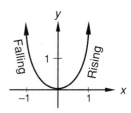

Problem set 59

1. An inverted right circular cone whose depth is 10 cm and whose base has a 5-cm radius is dripping liquid at a rate of 1 cm³/sec. How fast is the depth of the liquid changing when the depth of the liquid is 5 cm?

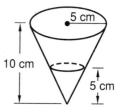

2. Sketch the basic shape of the graph of f where

$$f''(x) \begin{cases} > 0 & \text{when } x > 1 \\ = 0 & \text{when } x = 1 \\ < 0 & \text{when } x < 1 \end{cases}$$

3. Find all the critical numbers of $f(x) = x^4 - 2x^2$. Use the equation of f and its graph to determine where the extrema of f occur and what their values are.

4. Suppose f is as defined in Problem 3. Use the second derivative test to determine whether the graph of f has an extremum point or an inflection point at each of the critical numbers of f.

Use the fundamental theorem of integral calculus to compute the areas of the shaded regions shown in Problems 5–8.

5.

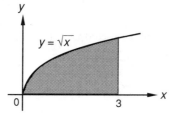

6.

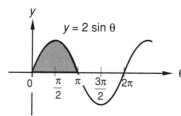

7.

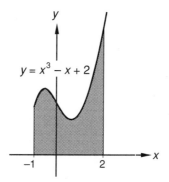

8.

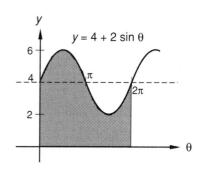

9. Shown is a line which is the graph of f'. Make a rough sketch of the shape of the graph of f.

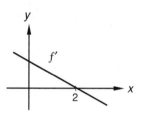

Differentiate the functions of Problems 10–12.

10. $y = 4x \csc x$ 11. $g(x) = x \ln x - x \tan x$

12. $y = 13(\sin x + \cos x)^{22}$

13. Use the chain rule to find $\dfrac{dy}{dx}$ if $y = 6u^4$ and $u = \sin x + \cos x$.

14. Evaluate $f'''(-2)$ where $f(x) = 2 \ln |x| + 3$.

Sketch the graphs of the equations given in Problems 15 and 16.

15. $y = \dfrac{(1 - x)(x^2 + 1)(x - 4)}{(x^2 + 2)(x - 2)(x - 4)x}$ 16. $y = x(x - 1)(x + 1)^3$

17. Use the fact that the derivative of $\sin x$ is $\cos x$ to prove that the derivative of $\cos x$ is $-\sin x$.

18. Find y' if $y = 2e^x - \cos x + 14 \sin x$.

19. If $f(x) = \sin x$ and $g(x) = f\left(x - \dfrac{\pi}{4}\right)$, sketch the graph of g.

Evaluate the following limits:

20. $\displaystyle\lim_{n \to \infty} \frac{3n^3 - 4n^2}{n^2 - 5n^3}$ 21. $\displaystyle\lim_{h \to 0} \frac{3xh - 4h^2}{h}$

22. Integrate: $\displaystyle\int \left(\frac{4}{\sqrt{x}} - 3\sqrt{x} - x^\pi + x^{-\pi} - 3 \sin x + \cos x - 2e^x\right) dx$

23. Use the derivatives of $\sin x$ and $\cos x$ to prove that the derivative of $\tan x$ is $\sec^2 x$.

CONCEPT REVIEW   24. Find x in terms of the other constants in the figure shown.

$AE = x$
$DE = a + b$
$CE = x + 1$
$BE = a$

25. Find the sixth term in the sequence $-2, -\sqrt{2}, -1, \ldots$.

LESSON 60 *Derivatives of composite functions · Derivatives of products and quotients*

60.A
Derivatives of composite functions

We have been using two methods to find the derivative of a composite function. First we learned to use u substitution, and then we learned to treat the equations separately and use the chain rule. The function

$$y = e^{2x}$$

is a composite function formed by composing two function machines into one as we show here.

$$2(\ ) \longrightarrow e^{2(\ )}$$

$$x \longrightarrow \boxed{u = 2x \longrightarrow y = e^{u}} \longrightarrow e^{2x}$$

The derivative of this composite function is the same whether we use u substitution or whether we use the chain rule.

$$\frac{d}{dx}\, e^{2x} = e^{2x} \frac{d}{dx}(2x) \qquad \text{so} \qquad \frac{d}{dx}\, e^{2x} = 2e^{2x}$$

We need to differentiate composite functions often, and it is helpful to realize that a shortcut can be used. We treat the argument of the composite function as if it were a single entity and multiply the derivative of this function by the derivative of the argument. Thus, if ( ) is the argument of the function,

$$\frac{d}{dx}\, c(\ ) = c\frac{d}{dx}(\ ) \qquad\qquad \frac{d}{dx}(\ )^{n} = n(\ )^{n-1}\frac{d}{dx}(\ )$$

$$\frac{d}{dx}\, e^{(\ )} = e^{(\ )}\frac{d}{dx}(\ ) \qquad\qquad \frac{d}{dx}\ln(\ ) = \frac{1}{(\ )} \cdot \frac{d}{dx}(\ )$$

$$\frac{d}{dx}\sin(\ ) = \cos(\ )\frac{d}{dx}(\ ) \qquad\qquad \frac{d}{dx}\cos(\ ) = -\sin(\ )\frac{d}{dx}(\ )$$

$$\frac{d}{dx}\tan(\ ) = \sec^{2}(\ )\frac{d}{dx}(\ ) \qquad\qquad \frac{d}{dx}\cot(\ ) = -\csc^{2}(\ )\frac{d}{dx}(\ )$$

$$\frac{d}{dx}\sec(\ ) = \sec(\ )\tan(\ )\frac{d}{dx}(\ ) \qquad\qquad \frac{d}{dx}\csc(\ ) = -\csc(\ )\cot(\ )\frac{d}{dx}(\ )$$

Example 60.1 If $f(x) = \sin(2x^{2} + 4x + 6)$, find $f'(x)$.

Solution We remember that

$$\frac{d}{dx}\sin(\ ) = \cos(\ )\frac{d}{dx}(\ )$$

Now we write $2x^{2} + 4x + 6$ in each of the parentheses.

$$\frac{d}{dx}\sin(2x^{2} + 4x + 6) = \cos(2x^{2} + 4x + 6)\frac{d}{dx}(2x^{2} + 4x + 6)$$

We finish by taking the derivative of the argument and writing either

$$[\cos(2x^{2} + 4x + 6)](4x + 4) \qquad \text{or} \qquad (4x + 4)\cos(2x^{2} + 4x + 6)$$

Example 60.2   If $g(x) = \ln \sin x$, find $g'(x)$.

Solution   We remember that

$$\frac{d}{dx} \ln (\ \ ) = \frac{1}{(\ \ )} \frac{d}{dx} (\ \ )$$

Now we write $\sin x$ in each of the parentheses.

$$\frac{d}{dx} \ln (\sin x) = \frac{1}{\sin x} \frac{d}{dx} (\sin x)$$

Next we take the derivative of the argument and simplify.

$$\frac{d}{dx} \ln (\sin x) = \frac{1}{\sin x} \cdot \cos x = \boldsymbol{\cot x}$$

Example 60.3   If $h(x) = (x^2 + 4x)^{100}$, find $h'(x)$.

Solution   We remember that

$$\frac{d}{dx} (\ \ )^{100} = 100(\ \ )^{99} \frac{d}{dx} (\ \ )$$

Now we write $x^2 + 4x$ in each set of parentheses, take the derivative of the argument, and simplify.

$$\frac{d}{dx} (x^2 + 4x)^{100} = 100(x^2 + 4x)^{99} \frac{d}{dx} (x^2 + 4x)$$

$$\longrightarrow \quad 100(x^2 + 4x)^{99} (2x + 4) = \boldsymbol{200(x + 2)(x^2 + 4x)^{99}}$$

60.B
Derivatives of products and quotients

The process of finding the derivatives of products and quotients of composite functions can be a little confusing. It is helpful to write the individual derivatives as a first step.

Example 60.4   If $f(x) = e^x(x^2 + 1)^{100}$, find $f'(x)$.

Solution   We are asked to find the derivative of a product, and one of the factors is a composite function. We will write the derivatives of both factors of the product as the first step.

$$\frac{d}{dx} e^x = e^x \qquad \frac{d}{dx}(x^2 + 1)^{100} = 100(x^2 + 1)^{99}(2x)$$

$$= [200x(x^2 + 1)^{99}]$$

The derivative of a product is the first times the derivative of the second plus the second times the derivative of the first. We have the functions and the derivatives so we can write the result.

$$f'(x) = e^x [200x(x^2 + 1)^{99}] + [(x^2 + 1)^{100}] (e^x)$$

We can simplify this expression a little, and we write

$$f'(x) = 200xe^x(x^2 + 1)^{99} + e^x(x^2 + 1)^{100}$$

This answer is totally satisfactory, but some people prefer that answers be in a fully factored form. We note that e^x is a factor of both terms, and if we look closely, we can see that $(x^2 + 1)^{100}$ can be written as $(x^2 + 1)(x^2 + 1)^{99}$. Since $(x^2 + 1)^{99}$ is a factor of both terms, we can write

$$f'(x) = e^x(x^2 + 1)^{99}(200x + x^2 + 1)$$

Example 60.5 If $f(t) = \dfrac{\sin 2t + \ln t}{(t^3 + 3t)^5}$, find $f'(t)$.

Solution We are asked to find the derivative of a quotient. We will write the derivatives of the numerator and of the denominator as the first step.

$$\frac{d}{dt}(\sin 2t + \ln t) = 2\cos 2t + \frac{1}{t}$$

$$\frac{d}{dt}(t^3 + 3t)^5 = 5(t^3 + 3t)^4(3t^2 + 3)$$

The quotient rule is the denominator times the derivative of the numerator minus the numerator times the derivative of the denominator all over the square of the denominator. We have all the components and just have to write them.

$$f'(t) = \frac{(t^3 + 3t)^5\left(2\cos 2t + \dfrac{1}{t}\right) - (\sin 2t + \ln t)5(t^3 + 3t)^4(3t^2 + 3)}{(t^3 + 3t)^{10}}$$

This expression can be simplified just a little if we note that the denominator and both terms of the numerator have $(t^3 + 3t)^4$ as a factor.

$$f'(t) = \frac{(t^3 + 3t)\left(2\cos 2t + \dfrac{1}{t}\right) - 5(\sin 2t + \ln t)(3t^2 + 3)}{(t^3 + 3t)^6}$$

Problem set 60

1. A particle is moving along a circular path that is described by the equation $x^2 + y^2 = 9$. Find the rate at which the x coordinate is changing the instant when the particle is passing through the point $(2\sqrt{2}, 1)$ if the y coordinate is decreasing at a rate of 2 units per second.

2. Sketch the basic shape of the graph of f where

$$f''(x) \begin{cases} < 0 & \text{when } x < 2 \\ = 0 & \text{when } x = 2 \\ < 0 & \text{when } x > 2 \end{cases}$$

3. Find all the critical numbers of $f(x) = -12x^4 + 4x^3 + 12x^2 - 1$. Use the equation of f and its graph to determine the extremum values of f and where they occur.

4. Suppose f is as defined in Problem 3. Find where the inflection points of the graph of f occur, and describe those intervals on which the graph of f is concave upward and those intervals on which the graph of f is concave downward.

Find the derivatives of these functions:

5. $f(x) = \tan(3x^2 - 4x + 1)$

6. $y = \ln(\sec x)$

7. $h(x) = (x^2 - 4)^{50}$

8. $y = e^x(x^2 + 4)^{50}$

9. $g(t) = \dfrac{\sin 2t}{\cos^2 t}$

Use the fundamental theorem of integral calculus to compute the areas of the shaded regions in Problems 10–12.

10.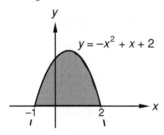

$y = -x^2 + x + 2$

11.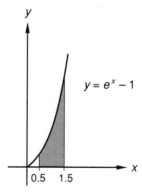

$y = e^x - 1$

0.5   1.5

12.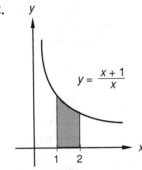

$y = \dfrac{x + 1}{x}$

1   2

Integrate:

13. $\displaystyle\int \sqrt{x}\,(x - 2)\,dx$

14. $\displaystyle\int (x - 2)^2\,dx$

15. Use implicit differentiation as required to find the equation of the tangent line which can be drawn to the graph of $x^2 + y^2 = 9$ at $(2\sqrt{2},\,1)$.

16. Approximate $\left.\dfrac{d^2y}{dx^2}\right|_2$ to two decimal places if $y = -2\cos x$.

17. Evaluate: $\displaystyle\lim_{h\to 0} \frac{e^{x+h} - e^x}{h} + \lim_{n\to\infty} \frac{1}{1 - n^2}$

18. Integrate: $\displaystyle\int \left(3\sqrt{x} - \frac{4}{\sqrt[3]{x}} + \sin x - 2x^{-4} - \frac{7}{x} - 3e^x\right) dx$

Sketch the graphs of the equations given in Problems 19 and 20.

19. $y = \dfrac{x(x - 2)}{x(x^2 + 2)(x + 1)}$

20. $y = -x(x + 1)^2(x - 1)^3$

21. If $f(g(x)) = \sin(x^2 + 1)$ and $f(x) = \sin x^2$, then find the equation of g.

CONCEPT REVIEW   **22.** Suppose x and y are real numbers such that $x + y = 5$ and $x^3 + y^3 = 2$. Determine the value of $x^2 - xy + y^2$.

23. Suppose a and b are nonequal real numbers. Compare:
A. $a^2 + b^2$ B. $2ab$

LESSON 61   *Integration by guessing*

It can be shown that every continuous function has an antiderivative, and thus the indefinite integral exists for every continuous function. Finding an explicit expression for many of these integrals is difficult, and for some it is impossible. But we know that the integrals do exist. Thus far we have concentrated on integrating carefully contrived expressions that have one of the following basic forms. An explicit expression for each of the following integrals can be written by inspection.

$$\int u^n \, du \qquad \int \frac{du}{u} \qquad \int e^u \, du \qquad \int \sin u \, du \qquad \int \cos u \, du$$

Now we will extend our investigation to finding integrals of carefully contrived expressions that are differentials of composite functions. **We remember that our basic technique for integrating is to guess the answer. Then we check our guess by finding the differential of our guess.** If the differential turns out to be the expression we are trying to integrate, we have our answer. If it is not, we guess again and check the new guess. The ability to make good guesses improves with practice.

Example 61.1   Find $\int 20x(2x^2 + 4)^4 \, dx$.

Solution   First we note the exponent 4 on the factor $(2x^2 + 4)^4$. We hope that this expression is a factor of the differential of an expression whose basic form is u^5. We guess an expression that has this basic form and check our guess by finding its differential. If our guess is correct, we will be able to write the answer by inspection. For our first try we guess that u^5 is $(2x^2 + 4)^5$. Then we find its differential.

$$d \underbrace{(2x^2 + 4)^5}_{u^n} = \underbrace{5(2x^2 + 4)^4}_{nu^{n-1}} \underbrace{(4x \, dx)}_{du} \qquad \boxed{\begin{array}{l} u = 2x^2 + 4 \\ du = 4x \, dx \end{array}}$$

The expression on the right of the equals sign is a rearranged form of the expression we wish to integrate. We have, in effect, made the substitution shown in the box. **Since the differential of the expression on the left of the equals sign is the expression on the right of the equals sign, the integral of the expression on the right is the expression on the left if we also include a constant of integration.**

$$\int 5(2x^2 + 4)^4 (4x \, dx) = (2x^2 + 4)^5 + C$$

so

$$\int 20x(2x^2 + 4)^4 \, dx = \mathbf{(2x^2 + 4)^5 + C}$$

Example 61.2   Find $\int 7 \sin^6 t \cos t \, dt$.

Solution   We note the exponent 6 in $\sin^6 t$ and hope that $\sin^6 t$ is a factor of the differential of a function whose basic form is u^7. We make a guess and check our guess by finding its differential. We guess that $u^7 = \sin^7 t$.

$$d \underbrace{\sin^7 t}_{u^n} = \underbrace{7 \sin^6 t}_{nu^{n-1}} \underbrace{\cos t \, dt}_{du} \qquad \boxed{\begin{array}{l} u = \sin t \\ du = \cos t \, dt \end{array}}$$

Our guess was a good one, and we have, in effect, made the substitution shown in the box. **Since the differential of $\sin^7 t$ is the expression on the right of the equals sign, the** integral of the expression on the right of the equals sign is $\sin^7 t$ plus a constant of integration.

$$\int 7 \sin^6 t \cos t \, dt = \sin^7 t + C$$

Example 61.3 Find $\int \dfrac{3x^2 \, dx}{2\sqrt{x^3 + 4}}$.

Solution Let's begin by rewriting the radical expression with a fractional exponent.

$$\int \frac{3}{2} x^2 (x^3 + 4)^{-1/2} \, dx$$

We note the exponent $-\frac{1}{2}$ on $(x^3 + 4)^{-1/2}$ and hope that this factor is a part of the differential of an expression whose basic form is $u^{1/2}$. We guess that $u^{1/2} = (x^3 + 4)^{1/2}$ and check our guess by finding its differential.

$$d \underbrace{(x^3 + 4)^{1/2}}_{u^n} = \underbrace{\frac{1}{2}(x^3 + 4)^{-1/2}}_{nu^{n-1}} \underbrace{(3x^2 \, dx)}_{du}$$

We made a good guess because the expression on the right of the equals sign is a rearranged form of the expression we wish to integrate. This time we will not bother to record the substitution in a box. **Since the differential of $(x^3 + 4)^{1/2}$ is the expression on the right of the equals sign, the integral of the expression on the right of the equals sign is $(x^3 + 4)^{1/2}$ plus a constant of integration.**

$$\int \frac{3x^2 \, dx}{2\sqrt{x^3 + 4}} = (x^3 + 4)^{1/2} + C$$

Example 61.4 Find $\int 8x(e^{4x^2}) \, dx$.

Solution The presence of the factor e^{4x^2} is the key for this carefully contrived problem. Let's hope this expression is a factor of a differential whose basic form is $e^u \, du$. We guess that the expression is e^{4x^2} and check our guess by finding the differential.

$$d \underbrace{e^{4x^2}}_{e^u} = \underbrace{e^{4x^2}}_{e^u} \underbrace{(8x \, dx)}_{du}$$

The differential is a rearranged form of the expression we want to integrate, so we can write the answer by inspection if we remember to include a constant of integration.

$$\int 8x(e^{4x^2}) \, dx = e^{4x^2} + C$$

Example 61.5 Find $\int \dfrac{12x^2 + 2}{4x^3 + 2x} \, dx$.

Solution We note that we do not have an expression raised to a power, such as $e^{(4x^3+2x)}$ or $(12x^2 + 2)^4$ or $\sqrt{12x^2 + 2}$. Thus we do not guess a basic form of e^u or u^n. The differential of $\ln |u|$ is du/u, so we will guess a form of $\ln |u|$ and find its differential to check our guess. This is a good first guess whenever we encounter an integrand that is a quotient of polynomials.

$$d \ln |4x^3 + 2x| = \underbrace{\frac{1}{4x^3 + 2x}}_{\frac{1}{u}} \cdot \underbrace{(12x^2 + 2) \, dx}_{du}$$

$$\underbrace{\ln |u|}$$

We made a good guess, so we can write the answer by inspection.

$$\int \frac{12x^2 + 2}{4x^3 + 2x} \, dx = \ln |4x^3 + 2x| + C$$

Example 61.6   Find $\int -4e^{4 \cos x} \sin x \, dx$.

Solution   The most striking part of this expression is $e^{4 \cos x}$. For our integral, let's guess a basic form of e^u and check by finding its differential.

$$d \underbrace{e^{4 \cos x}}_{e^u} = \underbrace{e^{4 \cos x}}_{e^u} \underbrace{(-4 \sin x) \, dx}_{du}$$

Our guess was a good one, so we can write the answer by inspection.

$$\int -4e^{4 \cos x} \sin x \, dx = e^{4 \cos x} + C$$

Example 61.7   Find $\int 2 \cos x \sin x \, dx$.

Solution   This integrand is the differential of two different forms of an expression of the form u^n. This is difficult to see because n is 2 and $n - 1$ is 1, and we don't usually write $(\sin x)^1$ or $(\cos x)^1$ but just write $\sin x$ or $\cos x$.

$$d \underbrace{(\sin x)^2}_{u^n} = \underbrace{2 \sin x}_{nu^{n-1}} \underbrace{\cos x \, dx}_{du} \qquad d \underbrace{[-(\cos x)^2]}_{-u^n} = \underbrace{-(2 \cos x)}_{-nu^{n-1}} \underbrace{(-\sin x \, dx)}_{du}$$

Since the integrand in this problem is the differential of $\sin^2 x$ or the differential of $-\cos^2 x$, the integral of $2 \cos x \sin x \, dx$ is either $\sin^2 x$ plus a constant or $-\cos^2 x$ plus a constant.

$$\int 2 \cos x \sin x \, dx = \sin^2 x + C \qquad \text{or} \qquad -\cos^2 x + C$$

Problem set 61

1. A large spherical balloon is deflated at a rate of 3 cubic centimeters per second. Find the rate at which the length of the radius of the sphere is changing when the radius is 5 centimeters long.

2. Sketch the basic shape of the graph of f, where

$$f''(x) \begin{cases} > 0 & \text{when } x > 1 \\ = 0 & \text{when } x = 1 \\ < 0 & \text{when } x < 1 \end{cases}$$

Indicate on the graph of f any points which possess special properties.

3. Find all the critical numbers of f where $f(x) = 2x^3 - 3x^2 - 12x + 1$. Use the equation of f and its graph as necessary to determine the extremum values of f and where they occur.

4. Find where all the inflection points of the graph of f in Problem 3 occur. Use interval notation to describe the intervals on which the graph of f is concave upward.

Integration by guessing requires that we recognize the basic form of the integrand. In Problems 5–10, integrate by guessing. Check each guess.

5. $\displaystyle\int 12x(x^2 + 4)^5\,dx$

6. $\displaystyle\int 6\sin^5 t\cos t\,dt$

7. $\displaystyle\int \frac{x\,dx}{\sqrt{x^2 + 4}}$

8. $\displaystyle\int 4xe^{2x^2}\,dx$

9. $\displaystyle\int \frac{6x + 1}{3x^2 + x}\,dx$

10. $\displaystyle\int 4e^{4\,\sin\,x}\cos x\,dx$

Find the derivatives of these functions:

11. $y = (x^2 + 1)^{30}$

12. $y = e^x(x^2 - 1)^{30}$

13. $f(x) = \dfrac{\sin x}{(x^2 + 1)^{10}}$

14. $g(x) = 3\ln|\cos x|$

Use the fundamental theorem of integral calculus to compute the areas of the shaded regions shown.

15.

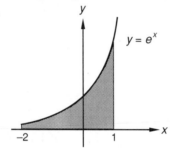

16.

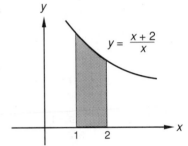

Evaluate. Use the formal definition of a derivative in Problem 18.

17. $\displaystyle\lim_{x\to 0}\frac{x + 1}{x}$

18. $\displaystyle\lim_{x\to 1}\frac{e^x - e}{x - 1}$

Sketch the graphs of the equations given in Problems 19 and 20.

19. $y = \dfrac{x + 1}{x}$

20. $y = 1 + 2\sin\left(x - \dfrac{\pi}{4}\right)$

CONCEPT REVIEW

21. Suppose $f(x_1) + f(x_2) = f(x_1 + x_2)$, where x_1 and x_2 are real numbers. Which of the following could be an equation of f?
(a) $f(x) = e^x$ (b) $f(x) = \ln x$
(c) $f(x) = 3x$ (d) $f(x) = x^2$

22. A point P lies outside a circle whose center is O. If the distance between P and O is 5 and the length of a tangent drawn from P to the circle is 4, find the length of the radius of the circle.

LESSON 62 *Maximization and minimization problems*

We remember that the critical numbers of a function of x on an interval I are the values of x for which the function may have a local maximum value or a local minimum value. Local maximum values and local minimum values are often called local extrema. Critical numbers can be (1) values of x at which the derivative equals zero. For these values of x the tangent to the graph of the function is horizontal. Critical numbers can also be (2) values of x for which the derivative does not exist. The derivative does not exist at values of x for which the graph has a corner or a sharp point or for which the tangent to the graph is vertical. Critical numbers can also be (3) the numbers at the endpoints of the domain of the function. In this lesson we will consider applied problems that require that we find the **absolute maximum (minimum)** value of a function on a designated interval. The absolute maximum (minimum) value is sometimes called the **global maximum (minimum)** value. The absolute maximum (minimum) value must also be a local maximum (minimum) value, which must be the value of $f(x)$ when x is a critical number. **So our search for an absolute maximum (minimum) value of a function on an interval begins by finding all the critical numbers of the function on the interval.** Then we find which of these numbers produce local maximum (minimum) values. Then we choose the greatest (least) value as our answer.

Unfortunately, applied maximum (minimum) value problems that would require us to use this procedure do not abound. To get the necessary practice we are forced to play games with familiar functions. Suppose we are searching for the maximum area of a function, and the area is described by the following equation.

$$\text{Area} = -3x^2 + 6x + 2$$

We already know that this is the equation of a parabola that opens downward, and we know that the x value of the vertex is $-b$ over $2a$, which equals 1.

$$\bar{x} = \frac{-(6)}{2(-3)} = 1$$

Thus, the maximum value of this function occurs when $x = 1$ and is

$$A(1) = -3(1)^2 + 6(1) + (2) = 5$$

Since the parabola opens down, any other value of x will lead to a lesser value of A, so 5 is the maximum value of the function.

We are interested in using calculus to find the maximum and minimum values of functions, so we will play a game. We pretend that we do not know that 5 is the maximum value and begin our search for the maximum value by locating the critical numbers of the function.

1. The graph of a polynomial function is a smooth curve that has no corners and no vertical tangents, so there are no critical numbers for this function that are caused by the failure of the derivative to exist.
2. No domain was specified, so we assume that the domain is the set of real numbers. The set of real numbers does not have endpoints, so there are no endpoint critical numbers.
3. The only other critical numbers are those numbers for which the first derivative equals zero. Thus we find the first derivative and set it equal to zero.

$$\frac{dA}{dx} = -6x + 6 \qquad \text{first derivative}$$

$$0 = -6x + 6 \qquad \text{equals } 0$$

$$x = 1 \qquad\qquad \text{solved}$$

Thus we find that this function has only one critical number. The value of this function when $x = 1$ is 5.

$$A(1) = -3(1)^2 + 6(1) + 2 = 5$$

Now we pretend that we do not know if 5 is a local maximum value, a local minimum value, or the y value of an inflection point. We can check x values on either side of $x = 1$ and find that these numbers produce values of $f(x)$ that are less than 5, so 5 must be a local maximum value of the function. Or, we can use the second derivative test and find that the second derivative is negative when $x = 1$, so 5 must be a local maximum value of the function

$$A''(x) = -6 \qquad \text{second derivative}$$

$$A''(1) = -6 \qquad \text{evaluated}$$

The graph of the function is a parabola that opens downward, so 5 is the absolute maximum value.

In the applied problems, we will not play the complete game because the functions will be polynomial functions. In these problems we will just determine the critical numbers for which the derivative equals zero. If the function is a familiar function, such as a second-, third-, or fourth-degree polynomial function, we will use our knowledge of the graph of the function to justify a claim for an absolute maximum or minimum value. We will also use our knowledge of the function and its graph to make a statement about endpoint values of the function. In Lesson 72 we will consider contrived problems in which the endpoint values of the function produce the absolute maximum or minimum values of $f(x)$.

Example 62.1   Mr. Wallen has 100 yards of fence. He wants to form a rectangular field enclosed on three sides by the fence and on one side by a river whose banks are straight. Find the dimensions of the field which can be enclosed by the fence that has the greatest area.

Solution   We begin by making a drawing of the problem.

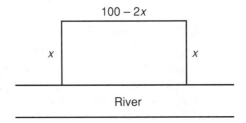

The area of the field is the length times the width.

$$A = x(100 - 2x) \quad \longrightarrow \quad A = 100x - 2x^2$$

Now we will find the values of x for which the derivative equals zero.

$$\frac{dA}{dx} = 100 - 4x \qquad \text{first derivative}$$

$$0 = 100 - 4x \qquad \text{equals } 0$$

$$x = 25 \qquad\qquad \text{solved}$$

This function has only one value of x at which A could be a maximum or a minimum. If we use the second derivative test, we find that $A''(25)$ is a negative number.

$$A''(x) = -4 \qquad \text{second derivative}$$

$$A''(25) = -4 \qquad \text{evaluated}$$

Thus $A(25)$ is a local maximum.

$$A(25) = 25[100 - 2(25)] = 1250 \text{ square yards (yd}^2)$$

The graph of the function reveals that this function has only one maximum value, so the absolute maximum value is **1250 yd^2**. We did not consider the endpoint values of 0 and 50 because if x had a value of either 0 or 50, the area enclosed would equal zero because the rectangle would have a width of zero.

Example 62.2   Find two positive numbers whose sum is 8 and whose product is a maximum.

Solution   The statement of the problem gives us two equations. We use p to represent the product and use x and y to represent the numbers.

$$p = xy \qquad x + y = 8$$

If we substitute, we can find p as a function of x.

$$p = x(8 - x) \quad \longrightarrow \quad p = 8x - x^2$$

The extreme value of p will occur when dp/dx equals zero.

$$\frac{dp}{dx} = 8 - 2x \qquad \text{derivative}$$

$$0 = 8 - 2x \qquad \frac{dp}{dx} = 0$$

$$x = 4 \qquad \text{solved}$$

An extreme value of p occurs when $x = 4$. We know that this is a maximum value because the second derivative is negative when $x = 4$.

$$f''(x) = -2 \quad \longrightarrow \quad f''(4) = -2$$

Knowing that $x = 4$, we can find y by substituting in our original equation.

$$4 + y = 8 \quad \longrightarrow \quad y = 4$$

Thus the two numbers we are looking for are both **4**.

Example 62.3   We would like to make an open cardboard box by cutting squares (x inches on a side) from each corner of a 12 by 15 inch piece of cardboard and folding up the edges. Find the value of x that will result in the largest possible volume, and find the volume of that box.

Solution   We make a drawing of the problem and label all the dimensions of the box in terms of x.

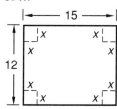 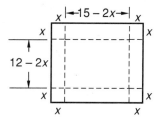 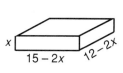

We then express the volume V as a function of x.

$$V = (15 - 2x)(12 - 2x)x$$
$$V = 180x - 54x^2 + 4x^3$$

Now we need to find the value of x which maximizes V.

$$V = 180x - 54x^2 + 4x^3 \quad \text{equation for } V$$
$$V' = 180 - 108x + 12x^2 \quad \text{differentiated}$$
$$0 = 180 - 108x + 12x^2 \quad \text{set } V = 0$$
$$0 = x^2 - 9x + 15 \quad \text{simplified and rearranged}$$
$$x = \frac{9 \pm \sqrt{81 - 4(15)}}{2} \quad \text{solved for } x$$
$$x \approx 2.21, 6.79 \quad \text{approximated numerically}$$

We can use the second derivative test to find out if x values of 2.21 and 6.79 produce local maximum values or local minimum values of V.

$$V''(x) = 24x - 108$$
$$V''(2.21) = 24(2.21) - 108 = -54.96$$
$$V''(6.79) = 24(6.79) - 108 = +54.96$$

Since $V''(2.21)$ is a negative number, $V(2.21)$ is a local maximum value of the function. Since $V''(6.79)$ is a positive number, $V(6.79)$ is a local minimum value of the function. We know that the graph of a cubic can have two turning points and that if the leading coefficient is positive the graph looks like this:

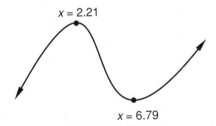

We have found the x values of the two turning points. The box is only 12 inches wide, so **x can be any number between 0 and 6.** The number 6.79 is greater than 6 and has no meaning in this problem. The endpoint values of 0 and 6 result in a volume of zero. Thus the maximum volume of the box is $V(2.21)$.

$$V(2.21) = 180(2.21) - 54(2.21)^2 + 4(2.21)^3 = \textbf{177.23 in}^3$$

Problem set 62

1. Use the first derivative and a rough sketch of f to determine the location and the values of the local maxima and minima of $f(x) = -x^3 + 3x - 2$. Use the second derivative test as necessary to justify your answer. Find the coordinates of any points of inflection.

2. Find two positive numbers whose sum is 10 and whose product is a maximum.

3. Detia wants to enclose a rectangular plot of land that adjoins a straight brick wall. If she has only 200 yards of fence, what should be the dimensions of the rectangular plot so that the area enclosed is a maximum?

4. An open box was made by cutting squares from the corners of a rectangular piece of tin and folding up the edges. Find the maximum volume of the box to two decimal places if the piece of tin measured 10 cm by 20 cm.

Integrate by guessing:

5. $\int 5 \cos x \sin^4 x \, dx$

6. $\int (2x) \left(\frac{3}{2}\right) \sqrt{x^2 + 3} \, dx$

7. $\int 2xe^{x^2} \, dx$

8. $\int \frac{2x \, dx}{x^2 - 1}$

Expand and then integrate:

9. $\int (x - 1)\sqrt{x} \, dx$

10. $\int (x^{-3} + 1)^2 \, dx$

Differentiate:

11. $y = \dfrac{\sqrt{x + 1}}{\sqrt{x - 1}}$

12. $y = (x^2 + 3)^4 \sin x$

13. $y = xe^{x^2 + 1}$

14. $y = \sec^2 x$

Use the fundamental theorem of integral calculus to compute the areas of the shaded regions shown.

15.

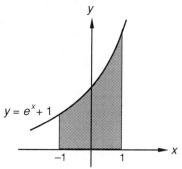

$y = e^x + 1$

16.

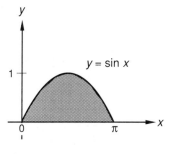

$y = \sin x$

Evaluate the following limits. Use the formal definition of a derivative when necessary.

17. $\lim\limits_{n \to \infty} \dfrac{3n^2}{n^2 + 1000n}$

18. $\lim\limits_{h \to 0} \dfrac{e^{x+h} - e^x}{h}$

19. Determine the domain of the function $f(x) = \dfrac{\sqrt{x}}{x - 1}$.

20. Find the range of f if $f(x) = \dfrac{1}{x^2 - 1}$ and if the domain is $\{x: |x| > 1\}$.

CONCEPT REVIEW 21. Suppose f is a function such that $f(x_1 x_2) = f(x_1) + f(x_2)$ for all $x_1, x_2 > 0$. Which of the following could be the equation of f?

   (a) $f(x) = \ln x$ (b) $f(x) = \dfrac{1}{x}$

   (c) $f(x) = x^2$ (d) $f(x) = \sin x$

22. Suppose g is a function such that for all real values of x and h

$$g(x + h) - g(x) = 3xh + h^2$$

   Find $g'(x)$.

LESSON 63 *Riemann sum · The definite integral*

63.A
Riemann sum

In Lesson 53 we used the limits of upper sums and lower sums to define what we mean by the phrase *the area under a curve*. During the nineteenth century the French mathematician A.-L. Cauchy and the German mathematician G. F. Riemann made major contributions to the development of a precise mathematical definition of the area under a curve, and the result is named for Riemann. **Instead of upper sums and lower sums they defined a single sum. In this sum any point in a subinterval of a partition of an interval [a, b] can be used to determine $f(x)$, the height of the rectangle drawn on the subinterval.** Thus some of the rectangles can have all portions below the curve and some of the rectangles can have portions above the curve and below the curve. The only restriction is that the top of each rectangle must touch the graph of the function at least once. **Also the widths of the subintervals can be different.** If we use $f(x_1)$ to designate the value of $f(x)$ at any chosen point in the first subinterval and Δx_1 as the length of this subinterval, the area of the first rectangle would be $f(x_1)\,\Delta x_1$. Using the same notation, the area of the second rectangle would be $f(x_2)\,\Delta x_2$, and the sum of n rectangles could be expressed as follows.

$$\text{Riemann sum} = f(x_1)\,\Delta x_1 + f(x)_2\,\Delta x_2 + f(x_3)\,\Delta x_3 + \cdots + f(x_n)\,\Delta x_n$$

On the left we show six rectangles drawn on a partition of six subintervals of [a, b]. On the right we use summation notation to indicate the sum of the areas of six rectangles drawn on a partition of six subintervals.

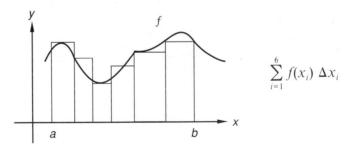

$$\sum_{i=1}^{6} f(x_i)\,\Delta x_i$$

The width of the largest subinterval, Δx_i, of a partition is called the **norm** of the partition and is designated by $\|\mathscr{P}\|$. The work of Cauchy and Riemann included a proof that if $\|\mathscr{P}\|$ approaches zero as the number of subintervals n increases without bound, then the limit of this sum exists for any continuous function and is unique. The limit of this sum is called the **Riemann integral.** We use the notation $\|\mathscr{P}\| \to 0$ to indicate that the norm of $\mathscr{P}$ approaches zero and that n increases without bound.

$$\text{Riemann integral} = \lim_{\|\mathscr{P}\|\to 0} \sum_{i=1}^{n} f(x_i)\,\Delta x_i = \int_a^b f(x)\,dx$$

If the limit of this sum exists for any function f, then that function is said to be *integrable* on [a, b] *in the sense of Riemann*, which means that $\int_a^b f(x)\,dx$ exists and is a uniquely determined real number.

There is a distinct difference in the meanings of the two notations that use the integral sign

$$\int f(x)\,dx \qquad\qquad \int_a^b f(x)\,dx$$

The notation on the left represents the family of functions that consists of all the antiderivatives of the function f. This family of functions is called the **indefinite** *integral* of the function *f*. The notation on the right at the bottom of the preceding page represents a **Riemann integral** or a **definite integral,** which is the **number** approached as the limit of a Riemann sum.

63.B
The definite integral

Our search for a precise definition of the word *area* when applied to a closed geometric figure has led us to the Riemann integral. This integral equals the area between the graph of a nonnegative continuous function and the *x* axis on the interval [*a*, *b*]. **If we look at the following integral closely,**

$$\lim_{\|\mathscr{P}\| \to 0} \sum_{i=1}^{n} f(x_i)\, \Delta x_i = \int_a^b f(x)\, dx$$

we note that it does not specifically address the geometric concept of area. Instead it describes a number that is the limit of the sum of products that involve values of a function. Thus it is also applicable to functions that are negative for some portion of an interval. For example, the integral of sin *x* from *π* to 2*π* is −2.

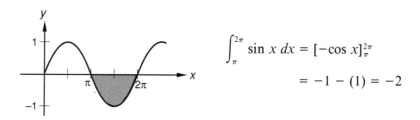

$$\int_\pi^{2\pi} \sin x\, dx = [-\cos x]_\pi^{2\pi}$$
$$= -1 - (1) = -2$$

We began by defining area as a number that tells "how much" of something a particular closed geometric figure has, and ended up with a procedure that produces negative numbers for some areas. Now we have a choice. We can say that an area can be negative. But this would require that we change our basic definition of area, which specifies that every area be equal to or greater than zero. Instead of changing the basic definition of area, mathematicians decided to call a Riemann integral **a definite integral** instead of calling it area. **Thus the definite integral of a function that is continuous on the interval [*a*, *b*] equals the sum of all areas on the interval that are above the *x* axis added to the negative of the sum of the areas that are below the *x* axis.**

Example 63.1 Evaluate: $\displaystyle\int_0^{3\pi/2} \sin x\, dx$

Solution On the left we draw the graph, and on the right we find the definite integral.

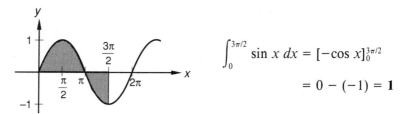

$$\int_0^{3\pi/2} \sin x\, dx = [-\cos x]_0^{3\pi/2}$$
$$= 0 - (-1) = \mathbf{1}$$

The area under one loop of the graph of *y* = sin *x* is 2. Thus our result is the area of the first loop, 2, minus half the area of the second loop! In the next figure we see that if the interval had been from −*π* to *π*/2, the answer would have been −1, which is the negative of the area of the loop below the curve plus one-half of the area of loop above the curve.

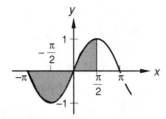

$$[-\cos x]_{-\pi}^{\pi/2} = 0 - [-(-1)] = -1$$

Example 63.2   Evaluate: $\displaystyle\int_1^2 (x^2 - e^x)\, dx$

Solution   We won't worry about a graph but will remember that the number we find is the definite integral, which is the sum of all areas above the x axis and the negative of all areas below the x axis.

$$\int_1^2 (x^2 - e^x)\, dx = \int_1^2 x^2\, dx - \int_1^2 e^x\, dx$$

$$= \left[\frac{x^3}{3} - e^x\right]_1^2 = \left(\frac{8}{3} - e^2\right) - \left(\frac{1}{3} - e\right) = \frac{7}{3} + e(-e + 1)$$

Problem set 63

1. Farmer Yu-Heng wanted to build a rectangular enclosure whose area would be 200 square yards. Find the amount of fencing required if the amount of fencing used is to be minimized.

2. Lori snipped square pieces of metal from the corners of a 6 by 6 inch sheet of metal. Then she folded up the flaps to form an open box. Find the dimensions of the box of maximum volume.

3. A square is being enlarged so that each of its sides are increasing at a rate of 2 cm/sec. How fast is the area of the square increasing when the side of the square is 6 cm? How fast is the perimeter of the square increasing at the same moment?

Evaluate:

4. $\displaystyle\int_0^{3\pi/2} \cos x\, dx$

5. $\displaystyle\int_1^3 (x^3 - e^x)\, dx$

6. Use geometric formulas to find the area of the region bounded by the graph of $y = x$ and the x axis on the interval $[0, 2]$.

7. Write a definite integral whose value equals the area of the region described in Problem 6. Evaluate this integral.

Integrate:

8. $\displaystyle\int \left(3e^x - \frac{2}{x} + \sin x - \cos x - \frac{1}{\sqrt{x}} + 2x^5\right) dx$

9. $\displaystyle\int 8\sin^7 x \cos x\, dx$

10. $\displaystyle\int (4x^3)\left(\frac{1}{2}\right)(x^4 - 3)^{-1/2}\, dx$

11. $\displaystyle\int 8xe^{4x^2}\, dx$

12. $\displaystyle\int \frac{4x^3\, dx}{x^4 - 42}$

Differentiate:

13. $y = 2x \ln (x^2 + 1) + 4 \tan x$

14. $y = -\dfrac{e^x}{\cot^2 x + x}$

15. Given the graph of f,

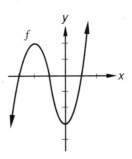

which of the following graphs most resembles the graph of f'?

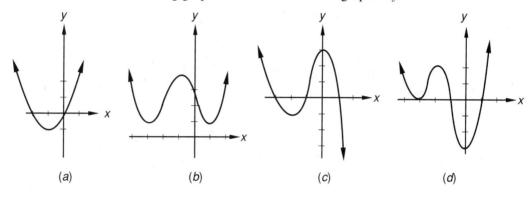

(a)   (b)   (c)   (d)

16. Sketch the graph of $y = \dfrac{(x - 2)(x + 3)(x - 1)}{x(x - 3)(x - 1)(x + 1)}$.

17. If f is a function such that

$$\lim_{x \to 1^+} f(x) = \lim_{x \to 1^-} f(x)$$

then f is continuous at $x = 1$. True or false? Why?

18. Evaluate: $\lim_{x \to 2} \dfrac{f(x) - f(2)}{x - 2}$ if $f(x) = x^2 - 2$

CONCEPT REVIEW **19.** The line joining the points which have coordinates of $(\sin 26°, 0)$ and $(0, -\cos 26°)$ has a slope of which of the following?
(a) $\tan 26°$ (b) 1   (c) $\cot 26°$ (d) $-\cot 26°$

20. Let $g(x) = f(x + 3)$. Which of the following statements is true?
(a) The graph of g is the graph of f shifted 3 units to the right.
(b) The graph of g is the graph of f shifted 3 units to the left.
(c) The graph of g is the graph of f shifted up 3 units.
(d) The graph of g is the graph of f shifted down 3 units.

LESSON 64 *Velocity and acceleration (motion I) · Motion due to gravity*

64.A
Velocity and acceleration

The instantaneous speed of an object tells how fast the position of the object is changing with time. The instantaneous velocity of an object tells how fast the position of an object is changing with time and also designates the direction the object is moving. If an object is at the origin when time equals zero and moves to the right at 6 inches per second, it would travel 6 inches in 1 second. It would travel 12 inches in 2 seconds and $6t$ inches in t seconds. Its position in relation to the origin is described by the **position function**

$$x(t) = 6t$$

The velocity is the rate of change of position, and thus the velocity function is the derivative of the position function with respect to time.

$$v(t) = x'(t) = \frac{d}{dt} 6t = 6$$

If the position function is not a linear function, the velocity is not constant as it is in this example. If the position of an object at time t is given by the equation on the left below, its velocity at any time t is designated by the velocity function. The velocity function is the derivative of the position function, as we show on the right.

$$x(t) = t^3 + t + 1 \qquad v(t) = x'(t) = 3t^2 + 1$$

The acceleration of an object tells us how fast and in what direction the velocity of the object is changing with respect to time. If time is measured in seconds, acceleration is measured in units per second per second, or units per second squared. For example, if the velocity changed 6 inches per second in 2 seconds, then the average acceleration, a, for the 2 seconds is

$$a = \frac{\Delta v}{\Delta t} = \frac{6\frac{\text{in}}{\text{sec}}}{2 \text{ sec}} = \frac{3\frac{\text{in}}{\text{sec}}}{\text{sec}} = 3\frac{\text{in}}{\text{sec}^2}$$

If the velocity function is not a linear function, the **acceleration function** is not a constant function. If the velocity function is given by the equation on the left below, the acceleration function is the derivative shown on the right.

$$v(t) = x'(t) = 3t^2 + 1 \qquad a(t) = v'(t) = x''(t) = 6t$$

Thus acceleration is the rate of change of velocity, which is the rate of change of position. From this we see that position, velocity, and acceleration are all functions of time.

A reference scale is needed to describe the position, velocity, and acceleration of an object. We have used the x axis for this purpose because this axis is convenient. But this use of the horizontal axis causes a problem because we always use the horizontal axis as the axis of the independent variable. The independent variable in this example is t. Thus, to accommodate this physical problem to the input-output function concept, we are forced to graph t on the horizontal axis and $x(t)$, $x'(t)$, and $x''(t)$ on the vertical axis (see the graphs at the top of page 319). Yet we will still consider that the object is moving left and right along the horizontal axis.

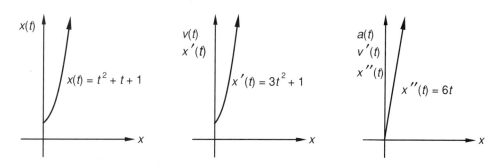

We have arbitrarily decided to define positive velocities to be velocities in the positive x direction and to call velocities in the opposite direction negative velocities. Thus, if an object is "speeding up" in the positive direction, the object is accelerating, the acceleration is positive, and the object's velocity is increasing. If an object is speeding up in the negative direction, the object is decelerating, the acceleration is negative, and the velocity is decreasing.

Example 64.1 The position of a particle moving along the x axis at any given time t in seconds is given by the equation $x(t) = -3t^2 + 4t + 2$. Find the position, velocity, and acceleration of the particle when $t = 3$.

Solution The position when $t = 3$ is $x(3)$.

$$x(3) = -3(3)^2 + 4(3) + 2 = -13$$

Thus **the position when $t = 3$ is 13 units to the left of the origin.**
The velocity function is the derivative of the position function.

$$v(t) = x'(t) = -6t + 4$$

The velocity of the particle when $t = 3$ is $v(3)$.

$$v(3) = -6(3) + 4 = -14$$

Thus **the velocity when $t = 3$ is -14 units per second in the positive x direction, which means the object is moving to the left.**
The acceleration function is the derivative of the velocity function.

$$a(t) = v'(t) = x''(t) = -6$$

This acceleration is a constant. **For $t = 3$ or any other value of t, the acceleration is -6. This means that the acceleration is 6 units/sec^2 in the negative x direction.**

Example 64.2 The position of a particle moving along the x axis at any given time t is given by the equation

$$x(t) = t^2 - 3t + 2$$

Find the times when the particle is momentarily at rest, when the particle is moving to the right, and when the particle is moving to the left. Also find the times when the particle is decelerating or accelerating.

Solution We begin by finding the equations of the velocity and acceleration functions.

$$x(t) = t^2 - 3t + 2 \qquad \text{position function}$$

$$v(t) = x'(t) = 2t - 3 \qquad \text{velocity function}$$

$$a(t) = v'(t) = x''(t) = 2 \qquad \text{acceleration function}$$

The particle is momentarily at rest when its velocity is zero.

$$v(t) = 2t - 3 \qquad \text{velocity function}$$

$$0 = 2t - 3 \qquad \text{set equal to zero}$$

$$t = \frac{3}{2} \qquad \text{solved for } t$$

The particle is moving to the right when the velocity is greater than zero and moving to the left when the velocity is less than zero.

MOVING TO THE RIGHT	MOVING TO THE LEFT
$2t - 3 > 0$	**$2t - 3 < 0$**
$t > \dfrac{3}{2}$	$t < \dfrac{3}{2}$

Thus, **the particle is moving to the right when $t > \frac{3}{2}$ and moving to the left when $t < \frac{3}{2}$.**

The particle decelerates when the acceleration is negative ($a < 0$) and accelerates when acceleration is positive ($a > 0$). In this case, $a = 2$ for all values of t so **the particle is always accelerating.**

64.B
Motion due to gravity

If we release a physical object at or near the surface of the earth, the object will accelerate toward the center of the earth at 9.8 meters per second per second (m/sec^2). This acceleration is caused by the attraction of the mass of the object to the mass of the earth and is called **acceleration due to gravity.** This tells us that a feather will have the same acceleration as a lead ball in the earth's gravitational field.

It is customary to use the surface of the earth (sea level) as a reference plane and use the up direction as the positive direction and the down direction as the negative direction. Thus, positive velocity and acceleration are in the up direction. We will learn to develop the equations of vertical motion in a later lesson. In this lesson we will investigate the use of these equations.

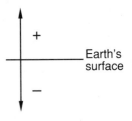

Example 64.3 A ball is thrown vertically into the air so that its height in meters at any time t in seconds is

$$h(t) = -4.9t^2 + 20t + 2$$

(*a*) Find the height of the ball and the velocity of the ball when $t = 1$.
(*b*) At what time t is the ball the greatest distance above the ground?
(*c*) How high will the ball go?
(*d*) What is the greatest value of the acceleration?

Solution We begin by writing the position function and finding the velocity function and the acceleration function.

$$h(t) = -4.9t^2 + 20t + 2$$

$$v(t) = h'(t) = -9.8t + 20$$

$$a(t) = v'(t) = h''(t) = -9.8$$

We can get all the answers from these three equations.

(*a*)   The height of the ball when $t = 1$ is $h(1)$, and the velocity of the ball when $t = 1$ is $v(1)$.

$$h(1) = -4.9(1)^2 + 20(1) + 2 = \textbf{17.1 m}$$

$$v(1) = -9.8(1) + 20 = \textbf{10.2 m/sec}$$

(*b*)   The velocity is positive on the way up. On the way down the velocity is negative. At the top, the velocity equals zero, so we set the velocity function equal to zero and solve for t.

$$-9.8t + 20 = 0 \longrightarrow t = 2.04 \text{ sec}$$

Thus, the velocity is zero at the top when **$t = 2.04$ sec.**

(*c*)   The distance to the top is $h(2.04)$.

$$h(2.04) = -4.9(2.04)^2 + 20(2.04) + 2 = 22.41 \text{ m}$$

Thus, the distance to the top is **22.41 m.**

(*d*)   The acceleration is the acceleration due to gravity and is always **−9.8 m/sec²** for any object at or near the surface of the earth.

Problem set 64

1.   What is the least amount of fencing required to enclose Emily's rectangular field if the area is to be 3600 square meters?

2.   The position of a particle moving along the x axis at any given time t in seconds is given by the equation $x(t) = -4t^2 + 2t - 1$. Find the position, velocity, and acceleration of the particle when $t = 2$.

3.   The position of a particle moving along the x axis at any given time is given by the equation

$$x(t) = t^2 + t - 2$$

Find the times when the particle is momentarily at rest and when the particle is moving to the right. Also, tell when the particle is accelerating and decelerating.

4.   Lacey's ball is thrown vertically into the air so that its height in meters above the ground at any time t in seconds is given by

$$h(t) = -4.9t^2 + 40t + 5$$

Find the time when the ball is at its greatest height above the ground. How high above the ground is the ball when it is at its greatest height?

Evaluate the following definite integrals:

5. $\displaystyle\int_0^4 \sqrt{x}\, dx$ 6. $\displaystyle\int_1^3 \frac{1}{x}\, dx$ 7. $\displaystyle\int_1^2 x^{-2}\, dx$

8.   Use basic geometry to find the area of the region between the graph of $y = x + 2$ and the x axis on the interval [2, 4]. Then express the area of the region as a definite integral. Evaluate this integral.

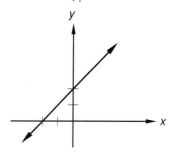

Integrate:

9. $\displaystyle\int 2x\left(\frac{3}{2}\right)\sqrt{x^2+1}\ dx$ 10. $\displaystyle\int (\cos x)e^{\sin x}\ dx$

11. $\displaystyle\int \left(\frac{1}{x}\right)(4)(\ln x)^3\ dx$ 12. $\displaystyle\int 2\tan x\sec^2 x\ dx$

13. Use implicit differentiation to find $\dfrac{dy}{dx}$ if $x^2 - x\cos y + y^3 = 0$.

14. Find $\dfrac{dy}{dx}$ if $y = \dfrac{e^{x^2}\cos^2 x}{x^2+1} + e^x\csc x$.

15. Determine the equation of the line tangent to the graph of $y = \ln\dfrac{x}{3}$ at $x = e$.

16. If $dy/dx = \sin 2x$, then y equals which of the following?

   (a) $\cos 2x + C$ (b) $\dfrac{1}{2}\cos 2x + C$ (c) $-\dfrac{1}{2}\cos 2x + C$

   (d) $\dfrac{1}{2}\sin 2x + C$ (e) $-\dfrac{1}{2}\sin 2x + C$

Evaluate:

17. $\displaystyle\lim_{n\to\infty}\frac{5n^2}{10,000n + n^3}$ 18. $\displaystyle\lim_{h\to 0}\frac{e^{e+h} - e^e}{h}$

CONCEPT REVIEW   19. Graph $y = \sqrt{1 - x^2}$, where $-1 \le x \le 1$. Use geometry to evaluate:

$$\int_{-1}^{1}\sqrt{1 - x^2}\ dx$$

20. Suppose $f(x) = k\cos\left(\frac{1}{k}x\right)$

   For which value of k does f have a period of 3?

LESSON 65   *More integration by guessing*

Each integration-by-guessing problem in the problem sets thus far was carefully designed so that the integrand was the exact differential of an expression whose basic form was u^n, e^u, $\ln u$, $\sin u$, or $\cos u$. Now we will consider integrands that would be an exact differential of one of these forms if the integrand had an additional constant factor. We can insert the needed constant factor to the right of the integral sign if we insert its reciprocal as a factor to the left of the integral sign.

Example 65.1   Find $\displaystyle\int \sin 3t\ dt$.

Solution   We guess that the answer is $-\cos 3t$ and check our guess by finding the differential.

$$d\underbrace{(-\cos 3t)}_{\cos u} = \underbrace{(\sin 3t)}_{\sin u}\underbrace{(3\ dt)}_{du}$$

This differential differs from our integrand by a factor of 3. Thus we insert a factor of 3 behind the integral sign and a factor of $\frac{1}{3}$ in front of the integral sign.

$$\int \sin 3t \, dt = \frac{1}{3} \int (\sin 3t)(3 \, dt) = -\frac{1}{3} \cos 3t + C$$

Example 65.2 Find $\int x^2(3x^3 + 4)^4 \, dx$.

Solution We note the exponent on the $(3x^3 + 4)^4$ and guess that this is a factor of the differential of an expression whose basic form is u^5. We guess that the expression is $(3x^3 + 4)^5$ and check our guess by finding its differential.

$$d \underbrace{(3x^3 + 4)^5}_{u^n} = \underbrace{5(3x^3 + 4)^4}_{nu^{n-1}} \underbrace{9x^2 \, dx}_{du}$$

The differential is the same as our integrand except for the factors 5 and 9, whose product is 45. Thus we insert a factor of 45 to the right of the integral sign and a factor of $\frac{1}{45}$ in front of the integral sign to get

$$\int x^2(3x^3 + 4)^4 \, dx = \frac{1}{45} \int (5)(x^2)(3x^3 + 4)^4(9) \, dx = \frac{1}{45}(3x^3 + 4)^5 + C$$

Example 65.3 Find $\int \dfrac{x^2 \, dx}{\sqrt{x^3 + 1}}$.

Solution We begin by rewriting the integral as

$$\int (x^3 + 1)^{-1/2}(x^2) \, dx$$

We guess that $(x^3 + 1)^{-1/2}$ is a factor of the differential of an expression whose basic form is $u^{1/2}$. We guess that the expression is $(x^3 + 1)^{1/2}$ and check our guess by finding the differential.

$$d \underbrace{(x^3 + 1)^{1/2}}_{u^n} = \underbrace{\frac{1}{2}}_{n} \underbrace{(x^3 + 1)^{-1/2}}_{u^{n-1}} \underbrace{(3x^2) \, dx}_{du}$$

The differential is the same as our integrand except for the factors of $\frac{1}{2}$ and 3. We insert these factors to the right of the integral sign and insert $\frac{2}{3}$, which is the reciprocal of their product, to the left of the integral sign.

$$\int x^2(x^3 + 1)^{-1/2} \, dx = \frac{2}{3} \int \left(\frac{1}{2}\right)(x^3 + 1)^{-1/2}(3)x^2 \, dx = \frac{2}{3}(x^3 + 1)^{1/2} + C$$

Example 65.4 Find $\int \cos^3 2t \sin 2t \, dt$.

Solution We note the exponent 3 in $\cos^3 2t$ and guess that the whole expression is the differential of a form of u^n. We guess that u^n is $(\cos 2t)^4$.

$$d \underbrace{\cos^4 2t}_{u^n} = \underbrace{(4 \cos^3 2t)}_{nu^{n-1}} \underbrace{(-\sin 2t)(2 \, dt)}_{du}$$

We find that the differential of $\cos^4 2t$ has factors of $\cos^3 2t$ and $\sin 2t \, dt$, and has 4, 2, and -1 as additional factors. The product of these factors is -8. The integrand in this problem does not have a factor of -8. We can obviate this difficulty by writing the original expression with a factor of -8 to the right of the integral sign and a factor of $-\frac{1}{8}$ to the left of the integral sign. The product of these additional factors is 1, so the value of the expression is unchanged.

$$\int \cos^3 2t \sin 2t \, dt = -\frac{1}{8} \int -8 \cos^3 2t \sin 2t \, dt$$

The integral of $-8 \cos^3 2t \sin 2t$ is $-\cos^4 2t$, so we have

$$-\frac{1}{8} \int -8 \cos^3 2t \sin 2t \, dt = -\frac{1}{8} \cos^4 2t + C$$

Example 65.5 Find $\int 4 \sec^2 3t \, dt$.

Solution First we move the 4 to the left of the integral sign and get

$$4 \int \sec^2 3t \, dt$$

This time the exponent of 2 does not indicate a form of e^u or u^n. We remember that the derivative of $\tan \theta$ is $\sec^2 \theta$, and this gives us the clue for our guess.

$$d \underbrace{(\tan 3t)}_{\tan u} = \underbrace{(\sec^2 3t)}_{\sec^2 u} \underbrace{(3 \, dt)}_{du}$$

We need an extra factor of 3 in our original expression, so we insert a factor of 3 to the right of the integral sign and a factor of $\frac{1}{3}$ to the left of the integral sign.

$$4 \left[\frac{1}{3} \int (\sec^2 3t)(3) \, dt \right] = \frac{4}{3} \tan 3t + C$$

Example 65.6 Find $\int \dfrac{e^{\sqrt{x}} \, dx}{\sqrt{x}}$.

Solution As the first step we replace the radicals with fractional exponents and write everything in the numerator.

$$\int e^{x^{1/2}} x^{-1/2} \, dx$$

Let's guess an answer of $e^{x^{1/2}}$ and check our guess.

$$d \underbrace{e^{x^{1/2}}}_{e^u} = \underbrace{(e^{x^{1/2}})}_{e^u} \underbrace{\left(\frac{1}{2} x^{-1/2} \, dx \right)}_{du}$$

The differential on the right is the same as the integrand in this problem except for the additional factor of $\frac{1}{2}$. Thus, we insert reciprocal constant factors of $\frac{1}{2}$ and 2 and complete the solution.

$$2 \int (e^{x^{1/2}}) \left(\frac{1}{2} \right) x^{-1/2} \, dx = 2e^{x^{1/2}} + C$$

Example 65.7 Find $\int \dfrac{2x^3 + x}{x^4 + x^2} \, dx$.

Solution We guess that this expression has the form du over u and is the differential of $\ln |x^4 + x^2|$.

$$d (\ln |x^4 + x^2|) = \left(\frac{1}{x^4 + x^2}\right) (4x^3 + 2x) \, dx$$

We need an additional factor of 2, which we insert to the right of the integral sign, and a factor of $\frac{1}{2}$, which we insert to the left of the integral sign.

$$\int \frac{2x^3 + x}{x^4 + x^2} \, dx = \frac{1}{2} \int \frac{2(2x^3 + x)}{x^4 + x^2} \, dx = \frac{1}{2} \ln |x^4 + x^2| + C$$

Example 65.8 Find $\displaystyle\int \frac{\cos ax \, dx}{\sqrt{b + \sin ax}}$.

Solution A good first step in any problem with a radical is to replace the radical with a fractional exponent. We begin by changing the square root radical to a fractional exponent and moving it to the numerator.

$$\int (b + \sin ax)^{-1/2} \cos ax \, dx$$

We note the fractional exponent and guess that $(b + \sin ax)^{-1/2}$ is a factor of the differential of an expression whose basic form is $u^{1/2}$. We guess that the expression is $(b + \sin ax)^{1/2}$. Then we take the differential of our guess.

$$d \underbrace{(b + \sin ax)^{1/2}}_{u^n} = \underbrace{\frac{1}{2} (b + \sin ax)^{-1/2}}_{nu^{n-1}} \underbrace{[(\cos ax)(a \, dx)]}_{du}$$

The integrand in this problem does not have a factor of $\frac{1}{2}$ or a factor of a, both of which we need. We can correct this by inserting factors of $\frac{1}{2}$ and a to the right of the integral sign and a factor of $2/a$ to the left of the integral sign. The product of these factors is 1, so the value of the expression is unchanged.

$$\frac{2}{a} \int \left(\frac{1}{2}\right) (b + \sin ax)^{-1/2} (\cos ax)(a) \, dx$$

The expression to the right of the integral sign is the differential of $(b + \sin ax)^{1/2}$, so the integral of $2/a$ times this expression is $2/a$ times $(b + \sin ax)^{1/2}$ plus a constant.

$$\frac{2}{a} \int \frac{1}{2}(b + \sin ax)^{-1/2}(\cos ax)(a \, dx) = \frac{2}{a}(b + \sin ax)^{1/2} + C$$

Problem set 65

1. Rectangular boxes shipped via Global Airlines are subject to the condition that the sum of the three dimensions of the package cannot exceed 120 cm. Find the dimensions of a package with square ends that has the greatest volume which can be shipped via Global Airlines.

2. If x is positive and increasing at a rate of 2 units/sec, at what rate is x^4 increasing when $x = 6$?

3. The position of a particle moving along the x axis at any time t is given by $x(t) = t^3 + 2t^2 - 7t + 4$. Find the times when the particle is momentarily at rest, when it is moving to the left, and when it is moving to the right.

4. A ball is thrown straight upward from the top of a 100-ft-high building. Its height in feet above the ground at t sec after it is thrown is given by

$$h(t) = -16t^2 + 40t + 100$$

Find the height of the ball above the ground when it is at its highest point.

Evaluate the following definite integrals:

5. $\displaystyle\int_{-\pi/2}^{\pi} 2 \sin x \, dx$

6. $\displaystyle\int_{1}^{4} \sqrt{x} \, dx$

Integrate:

7. $\displaystyle\int 4xe^{x^2} \, dx$

8. $\displaystyle\int \frac{1}{4} \sin^6 t \cos t \, dt$

9. $\displaystyle\int \frac{x}{2x^2 + 1} \, dx$

10. $\displaystyle\int 3x^2(x^3 - 2)^{1/2} \, dx$

11. $\displaystyle\int 4 \cos 3t \sin^2 3t \, dt$

12. $\displaystyle\int \frac{\cos ax}{\sqrt{1 + \sin ax}} \, dx$

Differentiate:

13. $y = \dfrac{\sin (2x + 1)}{x^2 + 2} + 2 \tan x$

14. $y = \ln |\sin x + x| + \csc 2x$

15. Describe the concavity of the graph of $y = x \ln x$ at $x = e^2$.

16. Find the equation of the tangent line which can be drawn to the graph of the equation $y = \ln |x^2|$ at $x = 1$.

17. Find the slope of the line which can be drawn tangent to the hyperbola

$$\frac{x^2}{9} - \frac{y^2}{4} = 1 \qquad \text{at the point} \qquad \left(\frac{9}{2}, \sqrt{5}\right)$$

(Begin by differentiating implicitly.)

18. Sketch f on the interval $-2 \le x \le 3$ if $f'(1) = 0, f'(x) < 0$ when $-2 \le x < 1$, and $f'(x) > 0$ when $1 < x \le 3$.

19. Sketch the graph of $y = \dfrac{x(x + 4)}{(x - 1)(x^2 + 2)(x + 5)}$.

CONCEPT REVIEW   **20.** Find $\displaystyle\lim_{x \to 3} f(x)$ if f is defined as follows:

$$f(x) = \begin{cases} \dfrac{x^2 - 9}{x - 3} & \text{for} \quad x \ne 3 \\ 0 & \text{when } x = 3 \end{cases}$$

21. Express $\log_3 x$ as a natural logarithm.

22. Determine the measure of an angle inscribed in a semicircle whose diameter is $\frac{3\pi}{2}$ units long.

LESSON 66   *Properties of the definite integral*

We remember that the definite integral is a number that is the limit of a Riemann sum. The definite integral of $f(x)$ from a to b in the figure at the top of the following page is -2.

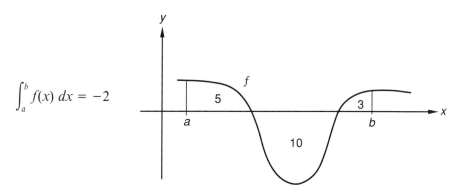

$$\int_a^b f(x)\,dx = -2$$

The definition of the definite integral of a function that is continuous on the interval [a, b] requires that a be less than b. The definite integral equals the sum of the areas between a and b that are below the graph of f and above the x axis and the negatives of the areas above the graph and below the x axis. For the figure shown, the sum of the areas above the x axis is 8 and the sum of the areas below the x axis is 10, so the value of the definite integral from a to b is −2.

We also remember that we usually evaluate a definite integral by finding the value of some antiderivative of f evaluated at b and subtracting the value of the same antiderivative of f evaluated at a.

$$\int_a^b f(x)\,dx = F(b) - F(a)$$

The definition of the definite integral and the way we evaluate the definite integral require us to make several definitions that an examination of the following figure will make clear. Here we show the graph of y = x + 2 and show an antiderivative that can be evaluated to get the definite integral from 2 to 4.

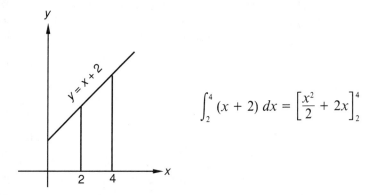

$$\int_2^4 (x + 2)\,dx = \left[\frac{x^2}{2} + 2x\right]_2^4$$

The definition of the definite integral requires that we evaluate the upper limit first. To begin, we will let 4 be the upper limit and will let 2 be the lower limit, and we will find the definite integral from 2 to 4.

$$\left[\frac{x^2}{2} + 2x\right]_2^4 = \left(\frac{16}{2} + 8\right) - \left(\frac{4}{2} + 4\right) = 16 - 6 = 10$$

Now if we interchange the limits and let 2 be the upper limit and 4 be the lower limit, we will find the definite integral from 4 to 2.

$$\left[\frac{x^2}{2} + 2x\right]_4^2 = \left(\frac{4}{2} + 4\right) - \left(\frac{16}{2} + 8\right) = 6 - 16 = -10$$

We see that interchanging the limits of integration reverses the sign of the definite integral. Thus, in this example, the integral from 4 to 2 is −10, which is the negative of the integral from 2 to 4.

$$\int_4^2 f(x)\,dx = -\int_2^4 f(x)\,dx$$

Since the definition of the definite integral comes from the Riemann sum, which requires that b be greater than a, we make the definition stated here to allow us to let the notation have meaning when a is used as the upper limit and b is used as the lower limit.

$$\int_b^a f(x)\,dx = -\int_a^b f(x)\,dx$$

Now to find the area between 0 and 2 and the area between 0 and 4, we can use these limits and evaluate.

$$\left[\frac{x^2}{2} + 2x\right]_0^2 = \left(\frac{4}{2} + 4\right) - 0 = 6 \qquad \left[\frac{x^2}{2} + 2x\right]_0^4 = \left(\frac{16}{2} + 8\right) - 0 = 16$$

Now we have

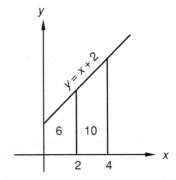

$$\int_0^2 (x+2)\,dx = 6 \qquad \int_2^4 (x+2)\,dx = 10$$

$$\int_0^4 (x+2)\,dx = 16$$

This illustrates the fact that the integral of a continuous function from 0 to 2 plus the integral from 2 to 4 equals the integral from 0 to 4. In general, if a is less than b and b is less than c, $(a < b < c)$, then

$$\int_a^b f(x) + \int_b^c f(x) = \int_a^c f(x)$$

Since each of the expressions represents a number, we can use the rules of algebra to move the expressions about and write other equivalent expressions, such as

$$\int_b^c f(x) = \int_a^c f(x) - \int_a^b f(x) \qquad \text{and} \qquad -\int_a^c f(x) + \int_a^b f(x) + \int_b^c f(x) = 0$$

Since each definite integral equals a number and the sum of a number and the opposite of the same number equals zero, we can write

$$\int_a^b f(x) - \int_a^b f(x) = 0$$

We can also make the following definition, which says that if the upper and lower limits are equal, the definite integral equals zero.

$$\int_a^a f(x)\,dx = 0$$

We can use this geometric interpretation of the definite integral to justify making several other definitions. If the graph of the function is on or above the x axis ($f(x) \geq 0$) between a and b, then the definite integral from a to b will be greater than or equal to zero.

If $f(x) \geq 0$ on $[a, b]$, then $\displaystyle\int_a^b f(x)\,dx \geq 0$

If the graph of the function is on the x axis everywhere between a and b, the definite integral from a to b will be zero.

$$\text{If } f(x) = 0 \text{ on } [a, b], \text{ then } \int_a^b f(x) = 0$$

If the graph of the function is on or below the x axis between a and b, the definite integral from a to b will be less than or equal to zero.

$$\text{If } f(x) \leq 0 \text{ on } [a, b], \text{ then } \int_a^b f(x) \leq 0$$

If the graph of g is always below the graph of f between a and b, then the definite integral of g on the interval $[a, b]$ will be less than the definite integral of f on the same interval.

$$\text{If } g(x) < f(x) \text{ on } [a, b], \text{ then } \int_a^b g(x) < \int_a^b f(x)$$

Of course, if $f(x) = g(x)$ on $[a, b]$, the integrals of f and g will be equal.

$$\text{If } f(x) = g(x) \text{ on } [a, b], \text{ then } \int_a^b g(x) = \int_a^b f(x)$$

We will make several observations about the possible maximum and minimum values of the definite integral of a function on $[a, b]$. If the maximum value of f on an interval is max f, the maximum possible value of $\int_a^b f(x)$ is $(b - a)$ times max f. If max f is greater than zero, the maximum value of the definite integral equals the area of a rectangle $(b - a)$ wide and max f high. If max f is less than zero, the maximum value of the definite integral equals the negative of the area of the rectangle shown in the figure on the right.

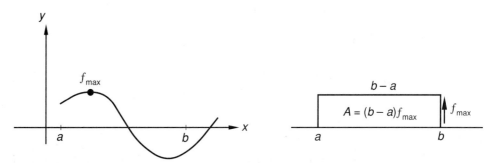

If the minimum value of f on an interval is min f, the minimum possible value of $\int_a^b f(x)$ is $(b - a)$ times min f. If min f is greater than zero, this integral equals the area of a rectangle $(b - a)$ wide and min f high. If min f is less than zero, the integral equals the negative of the area of this rectangle.

The observations that we have made in this lesson allow us to play games with the notation of the definite integral.

Example 66.1   If

$$\int_{-1}^1 f(x)\, dx = 7 \quad \text{and} \quad \int_1^4 f(x)\, dx = 2$$

find

$$\int_{-1}^4 f(x)\, dx$$

Solution   The integral from -1 to 4 equals the integral from -1 to 1 plus the integral from 1 to 4.

$$\int_{-1}^{4} f(x)\,dx = \int_{-1}^{1} f(x)\,dx + \int_{1}^{4} f(x)\,dx = 7 + 2 = \mathbf{9}$$

Example 66.2   If f and g are functions such that

$$\int_{1}^{3} f(x)\,dx = 4 \qquad \text{and} \qquad \int_{1}^{3} g(x)\,dx = -1$$

find

$$\int_{1}^{3} \left[3f(x) - \frac{1}{3}g(x) \right] dx$$

Solution   The rules for products of constants and functions are the same for definite integrals as they are for indefinite integrals, so we can move the constants across the integral signs.

$$\int_{1}^{3} 3f(x) = 3 \int_{1}^{3} f(x) \qquad \text{and} \qquad \int_{1}^{3} \frac{1}{3} g(x) = \frac{1}{3} \int_{1}^{3} g(x)$$

Now we write the given integral as the sum of two integrals.

$$\int_{1}^{3} \left[3f(x) - \frac{1}{3}g(x) \right] dx = 3 \int_{1}^{3} f(x)\,dx - \frac{1}{3} \int_{1}^{3} g(x)\,dx$$

We finish by using 4 and -1 as the values of the two integrals.

$$3(4) - \frac{1}{3}(-1) = \frac{37}{3}$$

Example 66.3   If

$$\int_{-2}^{1} f(x)\,dx = 3 \qquad \text{and} \qquad \int_{3}^{1} f(x)\,dx = 7$$

find

$$\int_{-2}^{3} f(x)\,dx$$

Solution   We know that the integral of $f(x)$ from -2 to 3 equals the integral of $f(x)$ from -2 to 1 plus the integral of $f(x)$ from 1 to 3.

$$\int_{-2}^{3} f(x)\,dx = \int_{-2}^{1} f(x)\,dx + \int_{1}^{3} f(x)\,dx$$

The value of the first integral was given as 3. We were also given that the integral of $f(x)$ from 3 to 1 is 7. This tells us that the integral of $f(x)$ from 1 to 3 is -7. So we have

$$\int_{-2}^{3} f(x)\,dx = 3 + (-7) = \mathbf{-4}$$

Problem set 66   **1.**   We are given a line joining (0, 6) and (4, 0) as shown. Find the coordinates of the point (x, y) which maximizes the area of the inscribed rectangle.

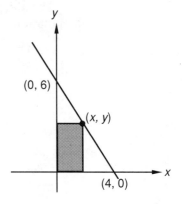

2. A particle moves in a circular orbit described by the equation $x^2 + y^2 = 25$. As it passes through (4, 3), its y coordinate is decreasing at a rate of 3 units/sec. What is the rate of change of the x coordinate the instant the particle is passing through the point (4, 3)?

3. A particle is moving along the number line so that its position at time t is given by

$$s(t) = -12t + t^3$$

Find the times when the particle is momentarily at rest.

4. If $\int_{-1}^{4} f(x)\, dx = -3$ and $\int_{4}^{5} f(x)\, dx = 2$, find $\int_{-1}^{5} f(x)\, dx$.

5. If $\int_{1}^{3} f(x)\, dx = -2$ and $\int_{1}^{3} g(x)\, dx = 4$, find $\int_{1}^{3} [-3f(x) + 2g(x)]\, dx$.

6. If f is a function which is continuous on $[-1, 3]$ and if f attains a maximum value of 4 on $[-1, 3]$, then which of the following must be true?

    (a) $\int_{-1}^{3} f(x)\, dx \le 16$ (c) $\int_{-1}^{3} f(x)\, dx = 16$

    (b) $\int_{-1}^{3} f(x)\, dx = 4$ (d) $\int_{-1}^{3} f(x)\, dx \ge 0$

Evaluate:

7. $\int_{1}^{9} \frac{1}{\sqrt{x}}\, dx$ 8. $\int_{-\pi/2}^{3\pi} \cos x\, dx$

Integrate:

9. $\int \frac{3x + 1}{3x^2 + 2x}\, dx$ 10. $\int (4x + 2)e^{x^2 + x}\, dx$

11. $\int \frac{2x + 1}{\sqrt{x^2 + x + 1}}\, dx$ 12. $\int \tan^3 x \sec^2 x\, dx$

13. Make a rough sketch of f if $f'(3) = 0$, if $f''(x) < 0$ when $x < 3$, and if $f''(x) > 0$ when $x > 3$.

14. Find the area of the region between the x axis and the graph of $y = \frac{1}{x}$ over the interval $[1, e]$.

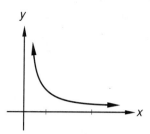

15. Given this graph of f',

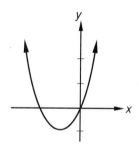

which of the graphs on the following page most resembles the graph of f?

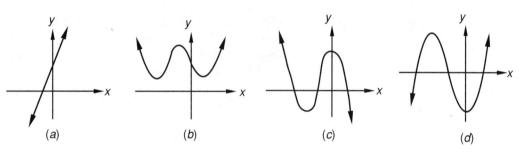

(a)   (b)   (c)   (d)

16. Find $\dfrac{dy}{dx}$ if $y = \dfrac{e^{x^2} + x}{x^2 + 2x} + \sec^3 2x + \csc^3 4x$.

17. Find the equation of the line which can be drawn normal to the graph of

$$y = \frac{\sqrt{x + 2}}{x} \qquad \text{at } x = 2$$

18. Sketch the graph of $f(x) = \dfrac{(1 - x)}{x(1 - x)}$.

CONCEPT REVIEW 19. Without using a calculator, determine the exact value of $\cos 20° \csc 70°$.

20. Evaluate

$$\int_0^1 \sqrt{1 - x^2} \, dx$$

without using calculus. (Recognize the geometric interpretation of the definite integral given.)

21. A right triangle is inscribed inside a circle. The legs of the triangle have lengths 3 and 4. Find the length of the diameter of the circle.

LESSON 67 *Explicit and implicit equations ·*
Inverse functions

67.A
Explicit and implicit equations

We customarily use x as the input of a function machine, and we call the output y or $f(x)$.

$$x \; \longrightarrow \; \boxed{f} \; \longrightarrow \; y \qquad x \; \longrightarrow \; \boxed{f} \; \longrightarrow \; f(x)$$

We remember that if an equation is written in the form "y equals" or "$f(x)$ equals," we say that the equation is written in *explicit form* and is an *explicit equation.* Thus the following equations are all explicit equations.

$$y = 2x + 6 \qquad f(x) = 2x + 6 \qquad y = e^x \qquad h = \log_b x$$

Most equations have forms other than the "y equals" form. These other forms of the equation are called *implicit forms.* Equations that are not "y equals" or "$f(x)$ equals" equations are called *implicit equations.* Three of the many implicit forms of the linear equation $y = 2x + 6$ are

$$2x - y = -6 \qquad x = \frac{1}{2}y - 3 \qquad \frac{x}{-3} + \frac{y}{6} = 1$$

The logarithmic function machine takes the number x as an input and produces the output y, which is the logarithm of the input.

$$\log_b (\ )$$
$$x \longrightarrow \boxed{f} \longrightarrow y$$

The equation of this function machine has both an explicit form and an implicit form. If we use 10 as the base, the forms are as follows.

EXPLICIT FORM	IMPLICIT FORM
$y = \log_{10} x$	$10^y = x$

It is most important to understand that these two equations are two forms of the same equation and pair the same values of x and y. The equation on the left says that y is the logarithm and x is the number. The equation on the right also says that y is the logarithm and that x is the number. If we let the exponent of 10 equal 2, the number is 100 because 10^2 equals 100. If we use 2 for y and 100 for x in the equations above, we get two numerical equations that make the same statement.

$$2 = \log_{10} 100 \qquad\qquad 10^2 = 100$$

The function machine for the exponential function takes the logarithm x as the input and produces the output y, which is the number that results when the base is raised to the x power.

$$10^{(\ )}$$
$$x \longrightarrow \boxed{} \longrightarrow y$$

The equation of this function machine also has both an explicit form and an implicit form. If we use 10 as the base, the forms are

EXPLICIT FORM	IMPLICIT FORM
$y = 10^x$	$x = \log_{10} y$

These equations seem to be the same equations as the two forms of the logarithmic function, but they are not. In these equations the input x is the logarithm and the output y is the number. If we use 2 as the value of the input x and 100 as the output y, we again get two numerical equations that make the same statement.

$$100 = 10^2 \qquad 2 = \log_{10} 100$$

The explicit forms of the basic sine, cosine, and tangent equations are

$$y = a \sin x \qquad y = a \cos x \qquad y = a \tan x$$

If we divide both sides of these equations by a, we get forms of the equations that suggest the triangles shown here:

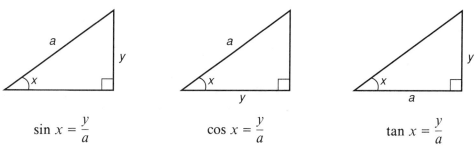

$$\sin x = \frac{y}{a} \qquad\qquad \cos x = \frac{y}{a} \qquad\qquad \tan x = \frac{y}{a}$$

We can use the Pythagorean formula to find the values of the other sides of the triangles.

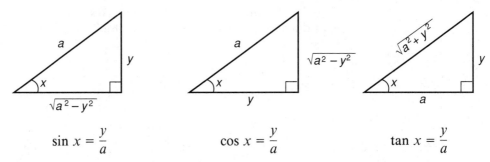

$$\sin x = \frac{y}{a} \qquad\qquad \cos x = \frac{y}{a} \qquad\qquad \tan x = \frac{y}{a}$$

These equations are implicit equations, and define y as a function of x implicitly. We will use words to write implicit forms of these equations and then use two different notations that make the same statements as the words. The notations $\sin^{-1}$, $\cos^{-1}$, and $\tan^{-1}$ are read as "the inverse sine of," "the inverse cosine of," and "the inverse tangent of." Recall that the $^{-1}$ is a special notation and is not a negative exponent. Each column below lists four ways to designate the inverse sine, the inverse cosine, and the inverse tangent, respectively, of angle x.

x is an angle whose sine is $\frac{y}{a}$	x is an angle whose cosine is $\frac{y}{a}$	x is an angle whose tangent is $\frac{y}{a}$
x is the inverse sine of $\frac{y}{a}$	x is the inverse cosine of $\frac{y}{a}$	x is the inverse tangent of $\frac{y}{a}$
$x = \arcsin \frac{y}{a}$	$x = \arccos \frac{y}{a}$	$x = \arctan \frac{y}{a}$
$x = \sin^{-1} \frac{y}{a}$	$x = \cos^{-1} \frac{y}{a}$	$x = \tan^{-1} \frac{y}{a}$

Beginners often find the implicit form of these trigonometric equations intimidating and find that drawing the triangle defined is very helpful. If we draw a triangle on the left in which one acute angle x is defined by $x = \tan^{-1} 3$, we get

$$\sin x = \frac{3}{\sqrt{10}} \qquad \cos x = \frac{1}{\sqrt{10}} \qquad \tan x = 3$$

$$\csc x = \frac{\sqrt{10}}{3} \qquad \sec x = \sqrt{10} \qquad \cot x = \frac{1}{3}$$

We see that, on the right, we can use the triangle to define all six basic trigonometric functions of x.

67.B
Inverse functions

In Lesson 21 we began our investigation of inverse trigonometric functions. In this lesson we will consider other inverse functions as well. Addition and subtraction are inverse operations because addition will "undo" subtraction and subtraction will undo addition. On the left we begin with 7 and add 3 to get 10. On the right we subtract 3 from 10 and get back to 7, where we began.

ADDITION   SUBTRACTION

$7 + (3) = 10$ $10 - (3) = 7$

Inverse function machines perform inverse operations. An inverse function machine is a function machine that will take the output of the first function machine and will produce the input of the first function machine.

If the f function machine took inputs of 4 and 5 and produced outputs of 43 and 13, the inverse function machine f^{-1} would take 43 and 13 as inputs and produce 4 and 5 as outputs. We would use g^{-1} to designate the inverse function of the g function and use h^{-1} to designate the inverse function of the h function. We read g^{-1} as "g inverse" and h^{-1} as "h inverse."

Not all functions have inverses. Consider the function machine on the left below. It produces exactly one output for each input. The inputs of 3 and 11 both have an output of 5, but this is acceptable behavior for a function machine because 3 has exactly one output and 11 has exactly one output. But when we try to define an inverse g machine, we are not successful since the machine doesn't have a way to get back to 3 and 11 because all 5's look alike to it.

Thus for a function machine to have an inverse, every different input must have only one output and all the outputs must be different. We call a function of this type a *one-to-one function.* In a one-to-one function, every value of x is paired with exactly one value of y and every value of y is paired with exactly one value of x.

Some authors say that every function has an inverse, but the inverse of a function might not be a function. They say that the inverse of a function is obtained by interchanging the x and y members of the ordered pairs. If the g function above is defined with the ordered pairs

(3, 5)   (7, 14)   and   (11, 5)

these authors would say that the inverse of this function is the relation defined by the ordered pairs

(5, 3)   (14, 7)   and   (5, 11)

This set of ordered pairs is the inverse of the first set of ordered pairs but does not define a function because 5 has two different images.

We can tell if a function is a one-to-one function by looking at the graph of the function. **If the slope of the graph of a function is always positive (with the exception of isolated points) or if the slope of the graph of a function is always negative (with the exception of isolated points), the function is a one-to-one function and has an inverse.**

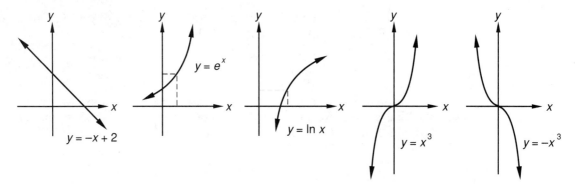

The slope of the graph of $y = -x + 2$ is always negative, and thus the function is a one-to-one function and has an inverse. The slopes of $y = e^x$ and $y = \ln x$ are everywhere positive, so these functions are one-to-one functions and have inverses. The slope of $y = x^3$ is everywhere positive except at the isolated point $(0, 0)$, where the slope is zero. Thus this function is a one-to-one function and has an inverse. The slope of $y = -x^3$ is everywhere negative except at the isolated point $(0, 0)$, where the slope is zero. Thus this function is a one-to-one function and has an inverse.

The functions shown here are not one-to-one functions

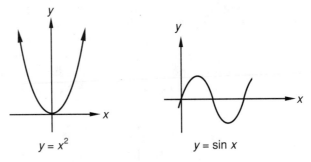

because some values of y are paired with two or more values of x. We can tell this at a glance because the slopes of these graphs are not everywhere positive or everywhere negative.

To find the inverse of an equation all we have to do is to interchange x and y in the equation. Suppose we have the equation

$$y = 2x + 4$$

and want to write the inverse equation. If we interchange x and y, we get the implicit form of the inverse equation shown on the left, which we can rearrange into the explicit form shown on the right.

IMPLICIT FORM	EXPLICIT FORM
$x = 2y + 4$	$y = \dfrac{1}{2} x - 2$

Now on the left below we show the original f function machine, and on the right we show the f^{-1} inverse function machine. If we use an input of 4 on the left, we get an output of 12. If we use an input of 12 on the right, we get an output of 4, our original input. Thus, an input of x would result in an output of x.

$$2(\ ) + 4 \qquad\qquad \frac{1}{2}(\ ) - 2$$

$$4 \rightarrow \boxed{f} \rightarrow 12 \qquad 12 \rightarrow \boxed{f^{-1}} \rightarrow 4$$

Example 67.1   If $f(x) = 2x - 3$, find $f^{-1}(4)$.

Solution   First we replace $f(x)$ with y. Then to find an implicit form of f, we simply interchange x and y, as we show in the center. On the right we rearrange this equation into its explicit form.

EQUATION	IMPLICIT INVERSE	EXPLICIT INVERSE
$y = 2x - 3$	$x = 2y - 3$	$y = \dfrac{1}{2}x + \dfrac{3}{2}$

Now to find $f^{-1}(4)$, we replace x with 4 and get

$$f^{-1}(4) = \frac{1}{2}(4) + \frac{3}{2} = \frac{7}{2}$$

Example 67.2   Find $f^{-1}(8)$ if the equation of the function is $f(x) = 4 \ln x$.

Solution   First we replace $f(x)$ with y. Then we find an implicit form of f inverse by interchanging x and y in the equation. Since $f^{-1}(8)$ is the value of y when $x = 8$, we also need the explicit form.

EQUATION	IMPLICIT INVERSE	EXPLICIT INVERSE
$y = 4 \ln x$	$x = 4 \ln y$ or $\dfrac{x}{4} = \ln y$	$y = e^{x/4}$

Now we replace x with 8 in the explicit form to get $f^{-1}(8)$.

$$f^{-1}(8) = e^{8/4} = e^2 \approx \mathbf{7.39}$$

Example 67.3   If $f(x) = 2x - 3$ and $f^{-1}(x) = \frac{1}{2}x + \frac{3}{2}$, as in Example 67.1, find $(f^{-1} \circ f)(6)$ and $(f \circ f^{-1})(6)$.

Solution   The notation $(f \circ f^{-1})(6)$ tells us to put 6 into the f^{-1} machine and put the resulting output of $\frac{9}{2}$ into the f machine. The notation $(f^{-1} \circ f)(6)$ tells us to put 6 into the f machine and put the resulting output of 9 into the f^{-1} machine.

$$(f \circ f^{-1})(6) = f[f^{-1}(6)] = f\left(\frac{9}{2}\right) = 2\left(\frac{9}{2}\right) - 3 = \mathbf{6}$$

$$(f^{-1} \circ f)(6) = f^{-1}[f(6)] = f^{-1}(9) = \frac{1}{2}(9) + \frac{3}{2} = \mathbf{6}$$

For any function of x, $(f^{-1} \circ f)(x) = (f \circ f^{-1})(x) = x$.

Example 67.4   Find $f^{-1}(9)$ if the f equation is $\dfrac{y}{3} = \cot x$.

Solution   On the left we interchange x and y to write the implicit form of f^{-1}. Then we write the explicit form on the right and let $x = 9$ to find $f^{-1}(9)$.

IMPLICIT FORM OF f^{-1}	EXPLICIT FORM OF f^{-1}	$f^{-1}(9)$
$\dfrac{x}{3} = \cot y$	$y = \cot^{-1}\dfrac{x}{3}$	$y = \cot^{-1}\dfrac{9}{3} = \cot^{-1} 3$

If y is the angle whose cotangent is 3, then the tangent of y is $\frac{1}{3}$. We set the calculator to radians and use the inverse tangent key to get a numerical answer.

$$y = \tan^{-1}\frac{1}{3} = \mathbf{0.322}$$

67.C

Graphs of inverse functions

The two functions shown here are inverse functions. The g function is the inverse of the f function and the f function is the inverse of the g function.

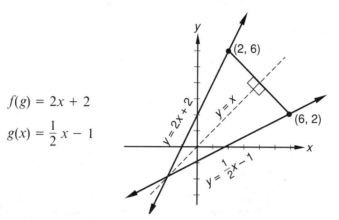

$$f(g) = 2x + 2$$

$$g(x) = \frac{1}{2}x - 1$$

The graph of any function and the graph of its inverse are reflections of each other in the line $y = x$. Because the coordinates of any point and its reflection are the same numbers but in reverse order, the perpendicular distance from a point to the line $y = x$ is the same as the perpendicular distance to the line $y = x$ from its reflection in that line. In the figure above we note that the distance from the point $(2, 6)$ to the line $y = x$ is the same as the distance from the point $(6, 2)$ to the line $y = x$.

In the graph on the left below we see that the graph of $y = \ln x$ and $y = e^x$ are reflections of each other in the line $y = x$.

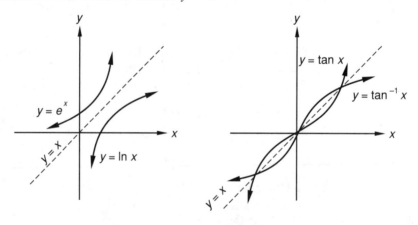

On the right we note that the graphs of $y = \tan x \left(-\frac{\pi}{2} < x < \frac{\pi}{2} \right)$ and $y = \tan^{-1} x$ are reflections of each other in the line $y = x$.

Problem set 67

1. A rectangle of width x is inscribed in a circle whose radius is 2. Write an expression for the area A of the rectangle in terms of x.

2. Find the value of x which maximizes the area of the rectangle described in Problem 1.

3. The radius of a spherical ball is expanding at a rate of 3 cm/sec. How fast is the surface area of the ball increasing when the radius of the ball is 10 cm?

4. A ball is thrown vertically upward from the top of a 100-ft-high building. Its height above the ground at time t is given by

$$h(t) = 100 + 30t - 16t^2$$

At what time is the ball falling toward the earth at 46 ft/sec?

5.   If $f(x) = 4x - 3$, write the equation of $f^{-1}(x)$. Evaluate $(f \circ f^{-1})(x)$ and $(f^{-1} \circ f)(x)$

6.   Find $f^{-1}(3)$ if $f(x) = 2 \ln x$.

7.   Write an equation which expresses the inverse of $y = \sin x \cos y$ implicitly.

8.   If $\int_{-1}^{3} f(x)\, dx = 4$ and $\int_{-1}^{3} g(x)\, dx = -2$, evaluate $\int_{-1}^{3} [3f(x) - g(x)]\, dx$.

9.   Suppose f is a continuous function on $[-1, 2]$ whose maximum value is 10 and whose minimum value is -5. Then which of the following must be true?

   (a) $-15 \le \int_{-1}^{2} f(x)\, dx \le 30$ (b) $-5 \le \int_{-1}^{2} f(x)\, dx \le 10$

   (c) $-10 \le \int_{-1}^{2} f(x)\, dx \le 20$ (d) $0 \le \int_{-1}^{2} f(x)\, dx \le 30$

10. Use implicit differentiation to find $\dfrac{dy}{dx}$ if $\sin xy = x$.

11. Use implicit differentiation as required to find the equation of the tangent line which can be drawn to the curve $x^3 + y^2 = y$ at $(0, 1)$.

12. Find the equation of the line which can be drawn normal to the graph of $y = \sqrt{2x + 1}$ where $x = 4$.

Differentiate the following functions:

13. $y = \dfrac{e^{2x} + e^{-x^2}}{x^3 + 1} - 3 \cot x$

14. $y = \dfrac{1}{\ln 2} \ln (x^2 + 3x - 1) - \dfrac{\sin x}{\cos ax}$

Integrate:

15. $\displaystyle\int \cos ax \sin^4 ax\, dx$

16. $\displaystyle\int (\cos x - 1)e^{\sin x - x}\, dx$

17. Evaluate: $\displaystyle\lim_{x \to \infty} \dfrac{x^2 - 3}{3 + x - 5x^2}$

18. For which of the following functions is $\dfrac{d^3y}{dx^3} = \dfrac{dy}{dx}$?

   (a) $y = \sin x$ (b) $y = 2e^x$ (c) $y = x^3$

CONCEPT REVIEW 19. Let $f(x) = \dfrac{1}{c} \sin cx$. For what value of c does f have a period of 5?

20. Find $\sec^2 2\theta$ for the angle θ in this triangle.

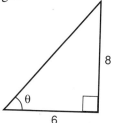

21. Use a trigonometric function to relate h, 6, and θ.

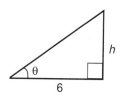

Suppose h and θ are functions of t. Differentiate the equation found implicitly with respect to t.

LESSON 68 *Computing areas*

We have found that the definite integral of a function on a closed interval $[a, b]$ equals the sum of the areas bounded by the x axis and by the graph of the function that are above the x axis and the negative of the areas with the same bounds that are below the x axis. To find the total area on an interval, it is often necessary to integrate piecewise as dictated by the graph of the function.

Example 68.1 Find the area between the graph of $y = \sin x$ and the x axis between $x = 0$ and $x = 2\pi$.

Solution If we find the definite integral of $\sin x$ between 0 and 2π, we will get an answer of zero because half of the area is above the x axis and half of the area is below the x axis. To get the total area, we must use two integrals. We will add the integral of $\sin x$ from 0 to π to the negative of the integral of $\sin x$ from π to 2π.

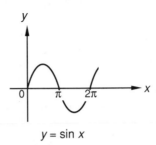

$$y = \sin x$$

$$\text{Total area} = \int_0^\pi \sin x \, dx - \int_\pi^{2\pi} \sin x \, dx = [-\cos x]_0^\pi - [-\cos x]_\pi^{2\pi}$$

$$= [1 - (-1)] - [-1 - (1)] = 2 + 2 = \textbf{4 units}^2$$

We note that the area of one loop of $y = \sin x$ equals 2. This means that the area of one loop of $y = 42 \sin x$ would be 84, because the integral of $42 \sin x$ equals 42 times the integral of $\sin x$. Thus, for future use we will remember that the area under one loop of $y = k \sin x$ is $2k$.

Example 68.2 Find the area of the region bounded by the graph of $y = x^2 - 1$ and the x axis over the interval $[-2, 2]$.

Solution From the graph we see that the area between -2 and -1 is above the x axis. The area between -1 and $+1$ is below the x axis. The area between 1 and 2 is above the x axis. To find the total area we will find the sum of three numbers. The first number is the definite integral from -2 to -1. The second number is the negative of the definite integral from -1 to $+1$, and the third number is the definite integral from 1 to 2.

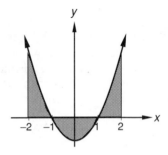

$$\text{Total area} = \int_{-2}^{-1} (x^2 - 1) \, dx - \int_{-1}^{1} (x^2 - 1) \, dx + \int_{1}^{2} (x^2 - 1) \, dx$$

$$= \left[\frac{x^3}{3} - x\right]_{-2}^{-1} - \left[\frac{x^3}{3} - x\right]_{-1}^{1} + \left[\frac{x^3}{3} - x\right]_{1}^{2}$$

We use symbols of inclusion as necessary to guard against making mistakes in signs.

$$\left[\left(-\frac{1}{3}+1\right)-\left(\frac{-8}{3}+2\right)\right]-\left[\left(\frac{1}{3}-1\right)-\left(\frac{-1}{3}+1\right)\right]+\left[\left(\frac{8}{3}-2\right)-\left(\frac{1}{3}-1\right)\right]$$

$$= -\frac{1}{3}+1+\frac{8}{3}-2-\frac{1}{3}+1-\frac{1}{3}+1+\frac{8}{3}-2-\frac{1}{3}+1 = \frac{12}{3} = \textbf{4 units}^2$$

Example 68.3   Find the area of the region completely enclosed by the graph of $y = -x^3 - x^2 + 2x$ and the x axis.

Solution   We begin by factoring so we can find the zeros of the function.

$$-x^3 - x^2 + 2x = -x(x+2)(x-1) \quad \longrightarrow \quad \text{zeros are } -2, 0, +1$$

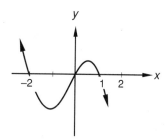

From the graph we see that we can find the total area by adding the negative of the definite integral from $x = -2$ to $x = 0$ to the definite integral from $x = 0$ to $x = 1$.

$$\text{Total area} = -\int_{-2}^{0} (-x^3 - x^2 + 2x)\, dx + \int_{0}^{1} (-x^3 - x^2 + 2x)\, dx$$

$$= -\left[\frac{-x^4}{4} - \frac{x^3}{3} + x^2\right]_{-2}^{0} + \left[\frac{-x^4}{4} - \frac{x^3}{3} + x^2\right]_{0}^{1}$$

Again we use symbols of inclusion to help prevent making mistakes in signs.

$$-\left[0 - \left(\frac{-16}{4} + \frac{8}{3} + 4\right)\right] + \left[\left(-\frac{1}{4} - \frac{1}{3} + 1\right) - 0\right]$$

$$= -\left(-\frac{32}{12}\right) + \left(\frac{5}{12}\right) = \frac{37}{12} \textbf{ units}^2$$

Problem set 68   **1.** A rectangular sheet of cardboard, 4 by 8 m, is cut as indicated and folded along the dotted lines to form a box as shown.

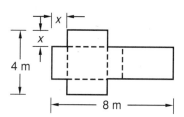

If x is the width of one of the flaps, write an expression in terms of x whose value equals the volume of the box. Then find the value of x which maximizes the volume of the box.

2. The height h of the right triangle shown is increasing at a rate of 1 unit per second. Find $d\theta/dt$ when $h = 8$.

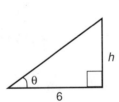

3. Find the area between the graph of $y = \cos x$ and the x axis on the interval $[0, 2\pi]$.

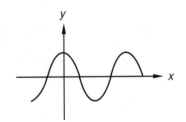

4. Express as the sum of two definite integrals the area of the region completely enclosed by the graph of

$$y = (x - 1)(x + 1)(x - 2)$$

and the x axis.

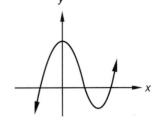

5. Find the equation of f^{-1} if $f(x) = 3x + 2$. Evaluate $f^{-1}(4)$, $(f \circ f^{-1})(x)$, and $(f^{-1} \circ f)(x)$.

6. Suppose g is the inverse function of f and $f(x) = \dfrac{1}{x}$. Find the equation of g.

7. Write the implicit form of the inverse of $y = \tan x$.

8. Suppose f is continuous on $[1, 4]$. Then which of the following statements must be true?

   (a) $\displaystyle\int_1^2 f(x)\, dx + \int_2^4 f(x)\, dx = \int_1^4 f(x)\, dx$

   (b) $\displaystyle\int_1^4 f(x)\, dx \geq 0$

   (c) $\displaystyle\int_1^2 f(x)\, dx \leq \int_2^4 f(x)\, dx$

Integrate:

9. $\displaystyle\int 2x(x^2 + 2)^3\, dx$ 10. $\displaystyle\int \frac{2x - 1\ dx}{\sqrt{x^2 - x + 1}}$ 11. $\displaystyle\int \pi \cos^2 2x \sin 2x\, dx$

12. Find the values of x for which the graph of $y = 2x^3 - 3x^2 + 12x + 1$ is concave upward.

13. Evaluate: $\displaystyle\lim_{x \to 2} \frac{e^x - e^2}{x - 2}$

14. Sketch the graph: $y = \dfrac{x(x - 2)}{x(x^2 + 1)(x + 1)}$

15. Differentiate: $y = \dfrac{\cos 3x}{x^2 + 2} + \tan 2x$

16. Use a calculator to find an equation of the line which can be drawn normal to the graph of the function

$$y = \frac{e^{\pi - x}}{2} \qquad \text{at } x = 2$$

17. Differentiate implicitly to find $\dfrac{dy}{dx}$ if $x = \sin xy$.

CONCEPT REVIEW

18. Graph $f(x) = 2^x + 1$ and $g(x) = 2^{-x} + 1$ on the same coordinate plane.

19. Graph $y = f(x)$ and $y = f(-x)$ on the same coordinate plane if $f(x) = 3^x - 1$.

20. If the graph of $y = x - 1$ for positive values of x is reflected in the y axis, what is the equation of the reflection? Write one equation that describes both portions of the graph.

LESSON 69 *Area between two curves*

We can find the area bounded by the graphs of two continuous functions on the interval $[a, b]$ by using the limit of a sum of rectangular areas to represent the area, and evaluating the sum by using the fundamental theorem of integral calculus. In the figure on the left, to find the area between the graphs of f and g on the interval $[a, b]$, we would partition the interval and draw rectangles, each of whose height is $f(x) - g(x)$ and whose width is Δx as shown. We note that f is the "high" function on the interval and that g is the "low" function.

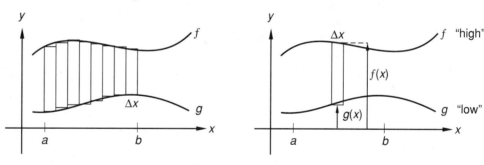

A **representative rectangle** is shown on the right. The width of the rectangle is Δx, and the height of the rectangle is $f(x) - g(x)$. The area between $x = a$ and $x = b$ can be represented by the limit of the following sum.

$$\text{Area} = \lim_{\Delta x \to 0} \sum_{i=1}^{n} (f - g)(x_i)\, \Delta x_i$$

We note that this sum is similar to a Riemann sum, and we know that we can use the fundamental theorem of integral calculus and find the limit of the sum by evaluating the integral.

$$\int_a^b (f - g)(x)\, dx \qquad \text{which is} \qquad \int_a^b (\text{high} - \text{low})\, dx$$

We will use this informal argument to justify this procedure.

When we set up this integral, we must be careful to use $(f - g)(x)$ as the height of the rectangle. If we use $(g - f)(x)$ as the height, the computed area will be the negative of the area that we want to find.

Example 69.1   Find the area of the region completely bounded by the graphs of $f(x) = x^2 + 2$ and $g(x) = -x$ between $x = 0$ and $x = 1$.

Solution   We make a rough sketch of the curves and draw a representative rectangle. The width of the rectangle is Δx and the height is $(f - g)(x)$. We use this information to set up the integral.

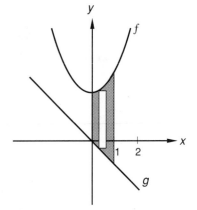

$$\text{Area} \int_0^1 (f - g)(x)\, dx$$

$$\int_0^1 [x^2 + 2 - (-x)]\, dx$$

We will evaluate the integrals by using the fundamental theorem.

$$\int_0^1 (x^2 + x + 2)\, dx = \left[\frac{x^3}{3} + \frac{x^2}{2} + 2x\right]_0^1 = \frac{1}{3} + \frac{1}{2} + 2 = \frac{17}{6}\ \textbf{units}^2$$

Example 69.2   Find the area of the region completely bounded by the graphs of $f(x) = 2 - x^2$ and $g(x) = x$.

Solution   Problems like this one in calculus books are carefully designed so that the coordinates of the points of intersection of the graphs are easy to find. The solution to this system

$$\begin{cases} y = x \\ y = 2 - x^2 \end{cases}$$

is $(1, 1)$ and $(-2, -2)$.

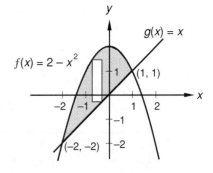

The width of the representative rectangle is Δx, and the height of the rectangle is $(f - g)(x)$, or $(2 - x^2) - (x)$. The width Δx tells us that x is the variable of integration. We will integrate from $x = -2$ to $x = +1$.

$$\text{Area} = \int_{-2}^1 (2 - x^2 - x)\, dx = \left[2x - \frac{x^3}{3} - \frac{x^2}{2}\right]_{-2}^1$$

$$= \left(2 - \frac{1}{3} - \frac{1}{2}\right) - \left(-4 + \frac{8}{3} - 2\right) = \frac{9}{2}\ \textbf{units}^2$$

Example 69.3   Find the area of the region bounded by the graphs of $f(x) = 2 - x^2$, $g(x) = x$, and $x = 2$.

Solution   The boundary functions are the same as in the preceding example, but this time the top boundary is the graph of $y = x$ and the bottom boundary is the graph of $y = 2 - x^2$.

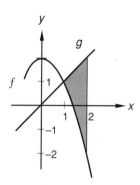

$$\text{Area} = \int_1^2 [x - (2 - x^2)]\, dx = \int_1^2 (x - 2 + x^2)\, dx$$

$$= \left[\frac{x^2}{2} - 2x + \frac{x^3}{3}\right]_1^2 = \left(\frac{4}{2} - 4 + \frac{8}{3}\right) - \left(\frac{1}{2} - 2 + \frac{1}{3}\right) = \frac{11}{6} \text{ units}^2$$

Example 69.4   Find the area of the region bounded by the graphs of $y = x^2$ and $y = 2x^2 - 4$.

Solution   On the left we factor to find the x coordinates of the points of intersection, and on the right we show the graphs of the functions and a representative rectangle.

$$x^2 = 2x^2 - 4$$

$$0 = x^2 - 4$$

$$0 = (x + 2)(x - 2)$$

The width of the representative rectangle is Δx. The height of the representative rectangle is $(x^2) - (2x^2 - 4)$, or $-x^2 + 4$, and the limits of integration are from -2 to $+2$.

$$\text{Area} = \int_{-2}^2 (-x^2 + 4)\, dx = \left[-\frac{x^3}{3} + 4x\right]_{-2}^2 = \frac{16}{3} - \left(-\frac{16}{3}\right) = \frac{32}{3} \text{ units}^2$$

Problem set 69

1.   Find the dimensions of a closed rectangular box that has a square base and a volume of 1000 cubic inches, and which uses the least amount of material to construct. (Assume the surface area of the box is a measure of the material used.)

2.   The position of a particle moving along a straight line is given by

$$s(t) = e^t \sin t$$

Approximate to two decimal places the velocity of the particle when $t = \pi$.

Integrate:

3. $\int \sin^3 2x \cos 2x \, dx$

4. $\int \dfrac{\sin x}{\sqrt{1 + \cos x}} \, dx$

5. $\int \dfrac{x + 1}{x} \, dx$

6. $\int (\sec^2 x)(\sec x \tan x) \, dx$

7. Find the area of the region completely enclosed by the graphs of $y = x^2 - 1$ and $y = -x^2 + 1$.

8. Find the area of the region bounded by the graphs of $y = e^x$, $y = x$, and the lines $x = -1$ and $x = 2$.

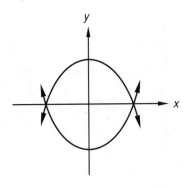

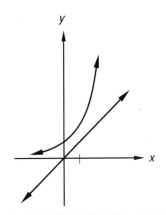

9. Find the area completely enclosed by the graph of $y = (x - 1)(x + 2)^2$ and the x axis.

10. Find $f^{-1}(2)$ if $f(x) = 2 \ln x$.

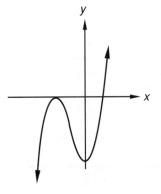

11. Write the explicit inverse equation of $y = \sin x$ where $-\dfrac{\pi}{2} \le x \le \dfrac{\pi}{2}$.

Differentiate:

12. $y = e^{(\ln 2)(x^2+1)}$

13. $y = \dfrac{\ln |\sin x|}{x^2 - 1}$

14. $y = e^{x^2+2x}(\cot x)^2$

15. Find $\dfrac{d^2y}{dx^2}$ evaluated at $x = 1$ when $y = x \ln x - x$.

16. Find the slope of the line which can be drawn tangent to the ellipse

$$\frac{x^2}{4} + \frac{y^2}{9} = 1 \qquad \text{at} \left(\sqrt{3}, \frac{3}{2}\right)$$

17. Shown is a graph of f. At which point(s) are both $\dfrac{df}{dx}$ and $\dfrac{d^2f}{dx^2}$ positive?

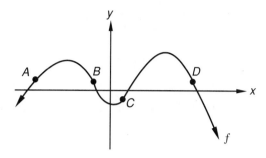

18. Suppose $f(x) = [x]$. Sketch the graph of $y = f(x - 2) + 1$.

CONCEPT REVIEW   **19.** Suppose $f(x) = \left(\frac{1}{2}\right)^x - 1$. Sketch $y = f(x)$ and $y = -f(x)$ on the same coordinate axes.

20. Evaluate, without using a calculator, $(\sin 15° + \cos 15°)^2$.

LESSON 70   *Game playing with f, f', and f"*

Problems that permit one to explore the relationships between a function and the first and second derivatives of the function are designed to enhance our understanding of these relationships and have no other purpose. These problems allow us to play games with concepts. In this lesson we will look at problems that let us consider the information we can get from the graphs and equations of f, f', and $f"$. We remember that we can determine the constants in the linear equation

$$y = mx + b$$

if we know two points on the line. If the line passes through $(1, 2)$ and $(5, 6)$, we can write

$$\begin{cases} 2 = m(1) + b \\ 6 = m(5) + b \end{cases}$$

and solve this system for m and b.

If we have the equation of a quadratic function

$$y = ax^2 + bx + c$$

we need three pieces of information because we need three independent equations to find a, b, and c. If we have a general cubic with four terms, we need four pieces of information to solve for the four constants. In general, we need as many independent pieces of information as we have coefficients in the equation. It is possible to design problems so that some of the needed information can be found from either the f, f', or $f"$ equations.

Example 70.1 If $f(x) = ax^3 + b$, find a and b if the graph passes through $(2, 25)$ and we know that $f'(3) = 81$.

Solution We get the first equation from the fact that $f(2) = 25$.

$$25 = a(2)^3 + b \quad \longrightarrow \quad 25 = 8a + b \qquad (1)$$

The second equation comes from the fact that $f'(3) = 81$.

$$f'(x) = 3ax^2 \quad \longrightarrow \quad 81 = 3a(3)^2 \quad \longrightarrow \quad a = 3 \qquad (2)$$

Now we replace a with 3 in the first equation and solve for b.

$$25 = 8(3) + b \quad \longrightarrow \quad b = 1$$

Thus the equation we want is

$$f(x) = 3x^3 + 1$$

Example 70.2 The function f is a real quadratic function whose graph passes through $(2, 9)$ and $(0, 1)$, and the slope of the graph is 6 at $x = 2$. Find the equation of f.

Solution The equation is of the form $f(x) = ax^2 + bx + c$, so we need three independent equations to solve for a, b, and c. We get the first two equations from the fact that $(2, 9)$ and $(0, 1)$ are on the graph.

$$9 = a(2)^2 + b(2) + c \quad \longrightarrow \quad 9 = 4a + 2b + c \qquad (1)$$

$$1 = (a)(0)^2 + b(0) + c \quad \longrightarrow \quad 1 = c \qquad (2)$$

The third equation comes from the fact that $f'(2) = 6$.

$$f'(x) = 2ax + b \quad \longrightarrow \quad 6 = 2a(2) + b \quad \longrightarrow \quad 6 = 4a + b \qquad (3)$$

If we combine equations (1) and (2) and copy equation (3), we get the following linear system.

$$\begin{array}{rl} (1) \text{ and } (2) & \left\{ \begin{array}{l} 8 = 4a + 2b \\ 6 = 4a + b \end{array} \right. \end{array}$$

We have already used the fact that $c = 1$. If we solve this system, we will find that $a = 1$ and $b = 2$. Thus the equation we want is

$$f(x) = x^2 + 2x + 1$$

Example 70.3 If this is the graph of the derivative f' of the function f, sketch the basic form of f.

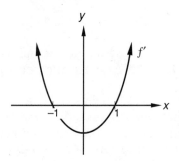

Solution We will be able to guess the basic form of the graph of f but will not be able to determine the vertical position of the graph because when we took the derivative we lost the constant on the end of the function.

The graph above is the graph of the slope of f. When this graph is above the x

axis, the slope of the graph of *f* is positive. When this graph touches the *x* axis, the slope of the graph of *f* is zero and the tangent line is horizontal. When the graph is below the *x* axis, the slope of the graph of *f* is negative. We can use the signs of the function *f'* we have determined to make the following rough sketch of the graph of *f*.

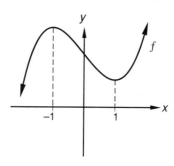

Example 70.4   If *f* is a function such that the graph of *f"* is a straight line as shown, sketch the basic shape of the graph of *f*.

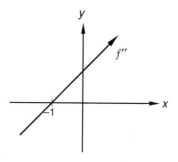

Solution   To the right of *x* = −1, the graph of *f"* is above the *x* axis, so the second derivative is positive when *x* > −1. Thus the graph of *f* will be concave up when *x* > −1. To the left of *x* = −1, the graph of *f"* is below the *x* axis, so *f"* is negative when *x* < −1. Thus the graph of *f* will be concave down when *x* < −1. Thus we have an inflection point when *x* = −1, and a reasonable guess of the shape of the graph of *f* is as follows.

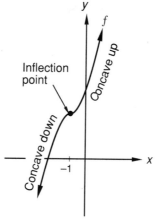

Example 70.5   If $f"(x) = 10$, $f'(0) = 2$, and $f(0) = 3$, find the equation of *f*.

Solution   The equation of $f"(x)$ is $f"(x) = 10$, which is a linear equation. We integrate *f"* to get *f'*.

$$f'(x) = \int f''(x)\, dx = \int 10\, dx = 10x + C$$

We were given the fact that $f'(0) = 2$. If we substitute, we can solve for C.

$$f'(x) = 10x + C \quad \longrightarrow \quad 2 = 10(0) + C \quad \longrightarrow \quad C = 2$$

Now we have $\qquad\qquad\qquad\qquad f'(x) = 10x + 2$

If we integrate $f'(x)$, we get $f(x)$.

$$f(x) = \int f'(x) = \int (10x + 2)\, dx = \frac{10x^2}{2} + 2x + C_2$$

We were given that $f(0) = 3$. If we substitute, we can solve for C_2.

$$f(x) = 5x^2 + 2x + C_2 \quad \longrightarrow \quad 3 = 5(0)^2 + 2(0) + C_2 \quad \longrightarrow \quad C_2 = 3$$

Now we can write the equation for f.

$$f(x) = 5x^2 + 2x + 3$$

Problem set 70

1. A hemispherical bowl has a diameter of 14 inches. If water is poured into the bowl at a rate of 1 cubic inch per second, how fast is the water rising when the water is 4 inches deep? The formula for the volume of a hemisphere of radius r filled to a depth h is

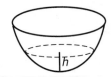

$$V = \pi r h^2 - \frac{1}{3}\pi h^3$$

2. The equation of f is $f(x) = ax^3 + b$. Find a and b if the graph of f passes through the point $(1, 5)$ and $f'(2) = 12$.

3. If f is a real quadratic function whose graph passes through the points $(1, 5)$ and $(-1, -1)$ and the slope of the graph is 5 at $x = 1$, find the equation of f.

4. Shown is the graph of f''. Sketch a graph of f.

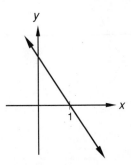

5. If $f''(x) = 6$, $f'(1) = f(1) = 4$, find the equation of f.

Integrate:

6. $\displaystyle \int \sin 3x\, dx$

7. $\displaystyle \int \frac{\cos x}{\sin^2 x}\, dx$

8. $\displaystyle \int \frac{1}{e^x}\, dx$

9. Find the area of the region in the first quadrant bounded by the axes and the graph of the equation $y = x\sqrt{9 - x^2}$.

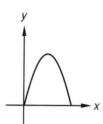

11. Find k if $\int_{-2}^{2} (4x^3 + k)\, dx = 15$.

10. Find the area in the first quadrant that is enclosed by the graphs of $y = x^3 + 3$ and $y = x + 3$.

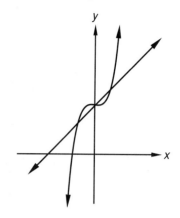

12. Find the area under one arch of the graph of $y = 2 \sin 3x$.

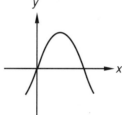

13. We are given that k is a number such that the area between $y = 1/x$ and the x axis from $x = 1$ to $x = k$ is equal to 1. Find k.

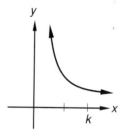

14. Suppose f is a polynomial function such that $f''(3) = 4$ and $f'(3) = 0$. Sketch f for the values of x near $x = 3$.

15. The graph of f'' is a horizontal line below the x axis. Describe the graph of f.

16. Sketch the graph of $y = -\dfrac{(x - 2)(x + 1)(x - 1)}{x(x - 3)(x - 1)(x + 2)}$.

17. Use the definition of derivative to find f' if $f(x) = \dfrac{1}{x}$.

18. Differentiate: $y = \dfrac{1}{\sqrt{x^3 + x + 1}} + e^{4x-3} \tan \pi x$

19. What is the domain of $y = \arcsin x$?

CONCEPT REVIEW 20. Suppose f is a function which is defined as being continuous on $[1, 3]$ and nowhere else. On which interval is g defined and continuous if $g(x) = f(x - 2)$?

21. Write the equation of the part of the graph of an ellipse

$$\frac{x^2}{a^2} + \frac{y^2}{b^2} = 1$$

which is contained in the first two quadrants.

LESSON 71 *Applications of the definite integral I*

In today's science books, distances are measured in meters and forces are measured in newtons. Mechanical work is defined as force times distance.

Mechanical work = force × distance

If a block that weighs 3 newtons is moved vertically upward a distance of 4 meters, 12 newton-meters of work is done.

4 newtons × 3 meters = 12 newton-meters

A newton-meter is called a ***joule.*** The work done is represented by the area of the rectangle on the left below, where F is the force in newtons and x is the distance in meters. In this figure the number 12 that is the mathematical area represents 12 joules, the work done.

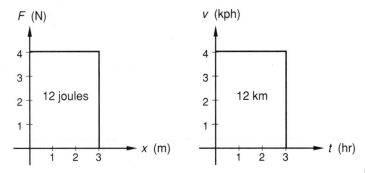

If a man walks at 4 kilometers per hour for 3 hours, he walks 12 kilometers.

$$\frac{4 \text{ km}}{\text{hr}} \times 3 \text{ hr} = 12 \text{ km}$$

This distance can be represented by the area of the rectangle on the right above, where v is velocity in kilometers per hour and t is the time in hours. In this figure the number 12 that is the mathematical area represents 12 kilometers, the distance traveled.

From this investigation we see that the units for any rectangular area equal the product of the units used for the horizontal measurement and the units used for the vertical measurement. Since we have carefully defined area beneath a curve to be the limit of a sum of rectangles, the units for any area under a curve also equal the product of the horizontal units and the vertical units. For the present we will restrict our investigation to areas that lie above the x axis.

Example 71.1 A steady force of 50 newtons (N) is applied to an object to move it 100 meters (m). What is the work done by the force?

Solution The area under the curve is the integral of the constant force times the distance.

$$\text{Work} = \int_0^{100} 50 \, dx$$

$$= [50x]_0^{100}$$

$$= \textbf{5000 joules}$$

Example 71.2   A variable force $F = \frac{1}{2}x^2$ newtons is applied to an object to move it 6 meters from $x = 0$ to $x = 6$. What is the work done by the force?

Solution   The work done equals the area under the graph of $F = \frac{1}{2}x^2$ newtons between x values of 0 and 6 meters.

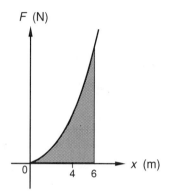

$$\text{Work} = \int_0^6 \frac{1}{2} x^2 \, dx$$

$$= \frac{1}{2} \int_0^6 x^2 \, dx = \frac{1}{2} \left[\frac{x^3}{3} \right]_0^6$$

$$= \frac{1}{2} \left(\frac{6^3}{3} - \frac{0}{3} \right) = \textbf{36 joules}$$

Example 71.3   In Example 71.2 how much work was done by the force in moving the object from the 4-meter mark to the 6-meter mark?

Solution   The work required equals the area under the curve of $F = \frac{1}{2}x^2$ newtons between x values of 4 and 6 meters.

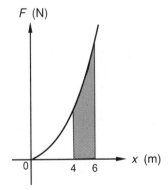

$$\text{Work} = \int_4^6 \frac{1}{2}x^2 \, dx$$

$$= \frac{1}{2} \left[\frac{x^3}{3} \right]_4^6 = \frac{1}{2} \left(\frac{6^3}{3} - \frac{4^3}{3} \right)$$

$$= \frac{1}{2} \left(72 - \frac{64}{3} \right) = \frac{76}{3} \text{ joules}$$

Example 71.4   Simon calculated that the velocity of the object would equal $\frac{1}{2}t^2 + t$ meters per second, where t is the total time elapsed in seconds. Approximately how far would the object travel between the fifth and the seventh seconds?

Solution   The distance traveled equals the area under the graph of $v = \frac{1}{2}t^2 + t$ meters per second between $t = 5$ and $t = 7$ seconds.

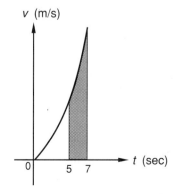

$$\text{Distance} = \int_5^7 v \, dt = \int_5^7 \left(\frac{t^2}{2} + t \right) dt$$

$$\text{Distance} = \left[\frac{t^3}{6} + \frac{t^2}{2}\right]_5^7 = \left(\frac{7^3}{6} + \frac{7^2}{2}\right) - \left(\frac{5^3}{6} + \frac{5^2}{2}\right)$$

$$\approx (57.17 + 24.5) - (20.83 + 12.5) \approx \textbf{48.34 meters}$$

We used a calculator to get an approximate answer because an exact answer is not required.

Example 71.5   Hooke's law for perfectly elastic springs tells us that the force on a spring is proportional to the displacement of the spring from the position of rest, or $F = kx$. The constant k is called the ***spring constant.*** If the spring constant for a spring is $\frac{1}{2}$ newton per meter, how much work is done in stretching the spring from 3 meters to 4 meters?

Solution   On the left we show the spring, and on the right we show the graph of the force F versus the distance x that the spring has been stretched.

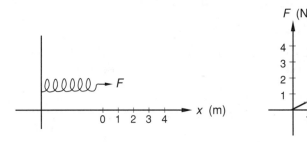

The total work done in stretching the spring from its rest position to $x = 4$ equals the area under the graph from $x = 0$ to $x = 4$. The work done between x values of 3 and 4 is the area under the graph between $x = 3$ and $x = 4$.

$$\text{Work}\Big|_3^4 = \int_3^4 \frac{1}{2}x\, dx = \left[\frac{x^2}{4}\right]_3^4 = \frac{16 - 9}{4} = \frac{7}{4} \text{ joules}$$

Problem set 71   1.   Find the area of the largest rectangle which can be inscribed in the region bounded by the x axis and the graph of $y = 12 - x^2$. (Begin by drawing the rectangle. Let x be the distance from the origin to the lower right-hand corner of the rectangle. Express the area of the rectangle in terms of x.)

2.   A steady force of 20 newtons is applied to an object to move it 30 meters. What is the work done by the force?

3.   A variable force $F(x) = \frac{1}{2}x^3 + x$ newtons is applied to an object to move it from $x = 0$ to $x = 3$ meters. Find the work done by the force.

4.   The spring constant for a spring is 3 newtons per meter. How much work is done in stretching the spring from 2 to 4 meters?

5.   Katherine and Martine estimated that the velocity of an object moving along the x axis at a time t was given by

$$v(t) = 3t + 4$$

Find the distance the object moved between $t = 1$ and $t = 4$.

6.   Suppose $f(x) = ax^3 + bx$. Find a and b if the graph of f passes through $(1, -1)$ and $f'(1) = 3$.

7.   Suppose f is a function whose slope at any point is twice its x coordinate. If the graph of f passes through $(1, 1)$, find the equation of f.

Integrate:

8. $\int \cos\left(2x - \dfrac{\pi}{2}\right) dx$

9. $\int \dfrac{x-1}{\sqrt{x}} dx$

10. $\int \cos t \sqrt{\sin t}\ dt$

11. $\int \tan^3 x \sec^2 x\ dx$

12. Find the area of the region enclosed by the graphs of $y = 2 - x^2$ and $y = -x$.

13. Find the area between the graph of $y = x(x - 2)$ and the x axis between $x = -1$ and $x = 2$.

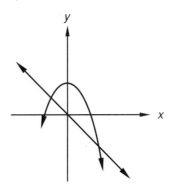

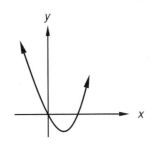

14. Suppose $y = f(x) = x^3 + x$. Write an implicit equation of f^{-1}.

15. If $f(x) = \ln x$, find $f^{-1}(1)$.

16. A ball is thrown straight up from ground level. Its height above the ground in feet at time t is given by

$$h(t) = 200t - 16t^2$$

How high will the ball go?

17. Differentiate: $y = \dfrac{e^{\sin x}}{\sqrt{2x - 1}} + \ln 2x$

18. Find $\dfrac{d^2y}{dx^2}$ if $y = 2e^{\sin x}$.

19. Evaluate: $\displaystyle\lim_{x \to 2} \dfrac{\ln x - \ln 2}{x - 2}$

20. The function $f(x) = \ln(\cos x)$ is defined for all x in which of the following intervals?

(a) $-\dfrac{\pi}{2} \le x \le \dfrac{\pi}{2}$ (b) $0 < x < \pi$ (c) $0 \le x \le \pi$

(d) $-\dfrac{\pi}{2} < x < \dfrac{\pi}{2}$

CONCEPT REVIEW   **21.** A trough 4 feet long has ends which are shaped like equilateral triangles as shown. Find the volume of water in the trough when it is h feet deep.

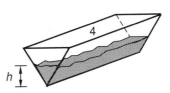

22. If $h(x) = f(g(x))$, $f(x) = \ln x$, and $h(x) = \ln \sqrt{x^2 + 1}$, then find the equation of g.

LESSON 72 *Critical number (closed interval) theorem*

The **maximum-minimum value existence theorem** tells us that a continuous function must have both a maximum value and a minimum value on any closed interval.

MAXIMUM-MINIMUM VALUE EXISTENCE THEOREM

If f is defined and continuous on a closed interval $I = [a, b]$, then f attains both a maximum value and a minimum value on I.

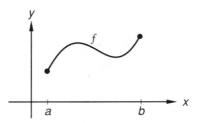

This statement is intuitively obvious, but the proof of the theorem is beyond the scope of an elementary calculus book. This theorem tells us that the maximum and minimum values of the function exist but gives us no clue as to how to find them. This clue comes from the **critical number theorem,** sometimes called the **closed interval theorem,** which we will state but will not prove. The critical number theorem tells us that the maximum value and the minimum value must occur either at an endpoint of the domain, or at a value of x for which the derivative does not exist (the graph of the function comes to a corner), or at a value of x for which the derivative (the slope of the graph) equals zero.

THE CRITICAL NUMBER (CLOSED INTERVAL) THEOREM

If f is a function which is defined and continuous on a closed interval I and if f attains a maximum or minimum value at $x = c$ where $c \in I$, then either

       1. c is an endpoint, or
       2. $f'(c)$ does not exist, or
       3. $f'(c) = 0$

In the applied problems that we have worked thus far, the maximum and minimum values have occurred at values of x for which the derivative equals zero (stationary numbers). It is difficult to find applied problems for which a maximum or minimum value occurs at an endpoint (endpoint numbers). One way to manufacture such a problem is to define a function and choose an interval arbitrarily so that the value of the function at one or both endpoints is an extreme value.

Since absolute value functions do not have a derivative at the values of x where a cusp occurs on the graph (singular points), these functions are often used as examples of functions that have critical points at which $f'(x)$ does not exist. Other continuous functions that do not have derivatives at some values of x are odd roots of even powers of x, such as $y = x^{2/3}$ and $y = x^{4/5}$. To get still more examples, we can devise piecewise functions so that they are continuous but do not have derivatives at one or more values of x.

Example 72.1   Find the maximum and minimum values of $f(x) = 2x^3 - 3x^2 - 12x + 1$ on the interval $[-2, 4]$.

Solution   The maximum-minimum value existence theorem tells us that the function f does attain a maximum value and a minimum value on any closed interval such as $[-2, 4]$. The closed interval theorem tells us these maximum and minimum values **must** occur at a critical number.

We begin by making a list of all the critical numbers. Since a polynomial function has a derivative at every value of x, there are no critical numbers at which the derivative does not exist. This function has endpoints at $x = -2$ and $x = 4$. It also has critical numbers when $f' = 0$.

$$f'(x) = 6x^2 - 6x - 12$$
$$0 = 6x^2 - 6x - 12$$
$$0 = 6(x - 2)(x + 1)$$

We see that $f'(x) = 0$ at $x = 2$ and $x = -1$. Thus, on the interval $[-2, 4]$ the critical numbers are $x = -2, 4, 2,$ and -1. **The closed interval test consists of finding the values of $f(x)$ for all critical numbers and comparing these values.**

CLOSED INTERVAL TEST

$$f(-2) = -3 \qquad f(-1) = 8 \qquad f(2) = -19 \qquad f(4) = 33$$

We see that f attains a **maximum value of 33 at $x = 4$** and a **minimum value of -19 at $x = 2$** on the closed interval $[-2, 4]$.

Example 72.2   A 10-inch-long string is cut into two pieces. One of the pieces is bent to form a square, and the other piece is formed into a circle. Find where the string should be cut so that the total area of the circle and the square is a maximum.

Solution   This problem is a classic example contrived to have a critical point that is a stationary number (where the slope of the graph is zero) and two critical points that are endpoints. The graph of the function is a parabola that opens upward and is chopped off at the endpoints. We will not show the graph, as the closed interval test does not require a graph. We begin by drawing a picture of the problem. We let x be the length of the segment used to form the circle.

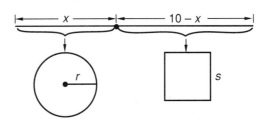

We see that $10 - x$ is the length of the segment used to form the square. Thus the perimeter of the square is $10 - x$, and the circumference of the circle is x. To find the areas, we need to solve for the radius r and the length of the side of the square, s.

$$x = 2\pi r \qquad\qquad\qquad 4s = 10 - x$$

$$r = \frac{x}{2\pi} \qquad\qquad\qquad s = \frac{10 - x}{4}$$

$$\text{Area of circle} = \pi\left(\frac{x}{2\pi}\right)^2 \qquad\qquad \text{Area of square} = \left(\frac{10 - x}{4}\right)^2$$

$$\text{Total area} = A(x) = \pi\left(\frac{x}{2\pi}\right)^2 + \left(\frac{10 - x}{4}\right)^2$$

Note that the domain of A is the closed interval [0, 10] because x must be equal to or greater than zero and less than or equal to 10.

$$\text{Domain of } A = \{x \mid 0 \le x \le 10\}$$

We now find all the critical numbers of A where $0 \le x \le 10$.

$$A(x) = \frac{1}{4\pi}x^2 + \frac{1}{16}x^2 - \frac{5}{4}x + \frac{100}{16} \qquad \text{function}$$

$$A'(x) = \left(\frac{1}{2\pi} + \frac{1}{8}\right)x - \frac{5}{4} \qquad \text{derivative}$$

$$0 = \left(\frac{1}{2\pi} + \frac{1}{8}\right)x - \frac{5}{4} \qquad \text{derivative set equal to 0}$$

$$\frac{5}{4} = \left(\frac{4 + \pi}{8\pi}\right)x \qquad \text{solved}$$

$$\left(\frac{10\pi}{4 + \pi}\right) = x \quad\longrightarrow\quad 4.40 \approx x$$

Thus the critical numbers for $A(x)$ are the endpoints 0 and 10 and the stationary number 4.4. The maximum value of the function must occur at one of these numbers.

The closed interval test consists of computing the values of $A(x)$ for all critical numbers and comparing these values. If we do this, we get the following.

CLOSED INTERVAL TEST

$$A(0) = 6.25 \qquad A(4.4) = 3.50 \qquad A(10) = 7.96$$

The value 7.96 for $A(10)$ is greater than the other values, so **A attains its maximum value at $x = 10$ and the maximum value is 7.96.**

Note that in this example the maximum value of the function occurred not at a stationary number but at an endpoint. When $x = 10$, we see that none of the string is used to form the square and the entire length of the string is used to form the circle.

Example 72.3   Find the maximum and minimum values of f on the interval $[-2, 3]$ if $f(x) = x^{2/3}$.

Solution   The maximum and minimum values must occur at a critical number. Two of the critical numbers are the endpoints of the interval $[-2, 3]$. The other critical numbers occur when $f' = 0$ or where f' does not exist. Thus we find f'.

$$f'(x) = \frac{2}{3}x^{-1/3} = \frac{2}{3x^{1/3}}$$

This derivative can never equal zero because 2 can never equal zero. Thus, there are no critical numbers caused by the derivative being equal to zero. The derivative does not exist when $x = 0$ because

$$f'(0) = \frac{2}{0} \qquad \text{not defined}$$

Thus zero is a critical number caused by the failure of f' to exist, and the critical numbers for this function are 0 and the endpoints -2 and 3. If we compute the values of f for 0, -2, and 3, we get the following.

CLOSED INTERVAL TEST

$$f(0) = 0 \qquad f(-2) = 1.59 \qquad f(3) = 2.08$$

From this we see that the **minimum value of f on $[-2, 3]$ is 0** and the **maximum value is 2.08.**

Example 72.4   A function is continuous on the closed interval $[-2, 4]$ such that $f(-2) = 2$, $f(-1) = -1$, and $f(4) = 5$. Also, the functions f' and f'' have the properties shown in the table below.

x	$-2 < x < -1$	$x = -1$	$-1 < x < 2$	$x = 2$	$2 < x < 4$
$f'(x)$	negative	fails to exist	positive	0	positive
$f''(x)$	negative	fails to exist	negative	0	positive

Find the values of x for which f attains absolute maximum and minimum values. Also, describe any other points of interest.

Solution   This function is continuous on the interval $[-2, 4]$, has endpoint critical numbers of -2 and 4, and has a singular critical number of -1. The fact that $f''(-1)$ does not exist is extraneous information. We use the rest of the information to make a rough sketch of the function.

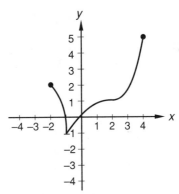

From the graph of f, we see that f **attains an absolute minimum value at $x = -1$ and an absolute maximum value at $x = 4$.**

We also see that the graph of f has an inflection point at $x = 2$. Since we are able to sketch the function, we can obtain the maximum and minimum values from the graph. We note that in this problem we were able to find the x values of the extrema even though we did not have the equation for f.

Problem set 72   **1.**   A trough 4 feet long has ends which are shaped like equilateral triangles as shown. If water is being poured into the trough at a rate of 1 ft³/min, how fast is the water rising the instant the water is about to spill over the top?

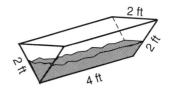

2. Find the maximum and minimum values of $f(x) = 2x^3 + 3x^2 - 12x + 1$ on the interval $[-3, 1]$.

3. Find the maximum and minimum values of $f(x) = x^{2/3}$ on the interval $[-1, 8]$. (*Note*: No calculus need be used. Begin by graphing f.)

4. Suppose f is a function which is continuous on the closed interval $[-1, 4]$, $f(-1) = 3$, and $f(4) = 6$. In addition, f, f', and f'' have the properties listed in the table below.

x	$-1 < x < 2$	$x = 2$	$2 < x < 4$
$f'(x)$	negative	undefined	positive
$f''(x)$	negative	undefined	negative

Sketch a graph of f and find where on the interval f attains its maximum and minimum values.

5. A variable force of $F(x) = 2x$ newtons is applied to an object. Find the work done in moving the object from $x = 1$ to $x = 3$ if x is measured in meters.

6. The velocity of an object moving along a number line is given by

$$v(t) = 3t^2 + 1$$

Find the distance traveled by the object from $t = 0$ to $t = 2$.

7. Suppose $f(x) = ae^x + b$. If $f'(0) = f(0) = 3$, solve for a and b.

8. For what values of x is the graph of $y = \ln x$ concave upward?

9. Evaluate: $\int_1^3 \frac{x^2 - 1}{x + 1} \, dx$ (Simplify the integrand first.)

Integrate:

10. $\int \cos 2x \, e^{\sin 2x} \, dx$ 11. $\int e^{-2x} \, dx$ 12. $\int \frac{3x^2 + 2x}{\sqrt{x^3 + x^2}} \, dx$

13. Find the area completely enclosed by the graph of $y = -x(x - 1)(x + 1)$ and the x axis.

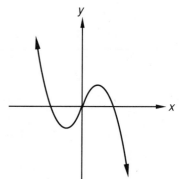

14. If $\int_a^b f(x) \, dx = -4$, find $\int_b^a 2f(x) \, dx$.

Differentiate the following functions:

15. $y = e^{2x} \tan^2 x$ 16. $y = \dfrac{\sqrt{x^2 + 1}}{x + \sin x}$

17. Which of the following statements is true about the function $f(x) = x \ln x$ for $x > 0$?
   (*a*) f is decreasing for all positive real values of x.
   (*b*) f is increasing for all positive real values of x.
   (*c*) f is increasing for all numbers x, $0 < x < e$.
   (*d*) f is increasing for all numbers greater than e.

18. Suppose $f(x) = \dfrac{1}{x-1}$. Evaluate: $\displaystyle\lim_{x \to 1^+} f(x)$ and $\displaystyle\lim_{x \to 1^-} f(x)$

CONCEPT REVIEW **19.** Express $\cos y$ in terms of x if $\cos y$ is positive and if $\dfrac{x}{a} = \sin y$.

20. Does the graph of $y = 2x\sqrt{4 - x^2}$ lie above or below the x axis on the interval $(0, 2)$?

21. Economics books often use p for price per item and Q for quantity (the number of items). In a free market, the number of items sold is price-sensitive. This means that if the price of the item is changed, the number of items sold will change. If 4000 items are sold when the price is \$16, we could write

$$Q(p) = 4000 \text{ when the price is } 16$$

If each price increase of \$1 would cause the number sold to decrease by 200, we could write

$$Q(p) = 4000 - 200(p - 16)$$

The second term equals zero if $p = \$16$. If the price is \$17 per item, the number sold would be

$$Q(17) = 4000 - 200(17 - 16) = 3800$$

The total revenue would be the number sold, $Q(p)$, times p, the price per item.

$$R(p) = pQ(p) = p[4000 - 200(p - 16)] \qquad \text{revenue}$$
$$R(p) = -200p^2 + 7200p \qquad\qquad\qquad \text{simplified}$$

We see that the total revenue $R(p)$ can be expressed as a quadratic function of p, the price per item.

Suppose that 10,000 items are sold when the price is \$20 per item. If the number of items sold decreases by 50 for each \$1 increase in unit price, write an equation that gives the money received as a function of the price per item.

LESSON 73 *Derivatives of inverse trigonometric functions · What to memorize*

73.A
Derivatives of inverse trigonometric functions

We have a definition of the derivative of a function and have rules that we can use to find the derivatives of functions. The search for antiderivatives, which we call integration, is a haphazard process at best. We have found that we can find the integrals of the three expressions shown here if we guess that the expressions are differentials of functions that have the forms of u^n, $\ln u$, and e^u, respectively.

$$\int \frac{-2x\,dx}{\sqrt{a^2 - x^2}} \qquad \int \frac{2x\,dx}{a^2 + x^2} \qquad \int e^{\sin x} \cos x\,dx$$

We cannot find the integrals of the following expressions by making one of the same guesses because none of these expressions is a differential of a function whose form is u^n, $\ln u$, or e^u.

$$\int \frac{dx}{\sqrt{a^2 - x^2}} \qquad \int \frac{dx}{a^2 + x^2} \qquad \int \frac{dx}{x\sqrt{x^2 - a^2}}$$

These integrands are differentials of inverse trigonometric functions. We will investigate the derivatives of inverse trigonometric functions, not because these derivatives are so important in themselves, but because we would like to be able to integrate expressions such as these.

The differentials in which we are interested are

$$d \sin^{-1} \frac{x}{a} = \frac{dx}{\sqrt{a^2 - x^2}} \qquad d \cos^{-1} \frac{x}{a} = \frac{-dx}{\sqrt{a^2 - x^2}}$$

$$d \tan^{-1} \frac{x}{a} = \frac{a \, dx}{a^2 + x^2} \qquad d \cot^{-1} \frac{x}{a} = \frac{-a \, dx}{a^2 + x^2}$$

$$d \sec^{-1} \frac{x}{a} = \frac{a \, dx}{x\sqrt{x^2 - a^2}} \qquad d \csc^{-1} \frac{x}{a} = \frac{-a \, dx}{x\sqrt{x^2 - a^2}}$$

It is poor practice to memorize things that can be developed quickly and accurately. The derivatives of inverse trigonometric functions fall into this category. The expressions above for which we want to find antiderivatives contain an unspecified constant a. With this in mind we will look at inverse trigonometric functions that have x/a as an argument.

Example 73.1   If $y = \arcsin \frac{x}{a}$, find y'.

Solution   We begin by writing the implicit form of this equation and drawing the triangle it defines.

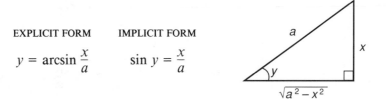

EXPLICIT FORM   IMPLICIT FORM

$$y = \arcsin \frac{x}{a} \qquad \sin y = \frac{x}{a}$$

Drawing the triangle is very helpful because it allows us to write all six trigonometric functions of y by inspection.

$$\sin y = \frac{x}{a} \qquad \cos y = \frac{\sqrt{a^2 - x^2}}{a} \qquad \tan y = \frac{x}{\sqrt{a^2 - x^2}}$$

$$\csc y = \frac{a}{x} \qquad \sec y = \frac{a}{\sqrt{a^2 - x^2}} \qquad \cot y = \frac{\sqrt{a^2 - x^2}}{x}$$

To find y', we take the differential of both sides of the implicit form, divide by dx, and solve for dy/dx.

$$y = \arcsin \frac{x}{a} \qquad \text{equation}$$

$$\sin y = \frac{x}{a} \qquad \text{implicit form}$$

$$\cos y \, dy = \frac{dx}{a} \qquad \text{differential}$$

$$\cos y \frac{dy}{dx} = \frac{1}{a} \qquad \text{divided by } dx$$

$$\frac{dy}{dx} = \frac{1}{a} \left(\frac{1}{\cos y} \right) \qquad \text{solved for } \frac{dy}{dx}$$

But from the triangle we see that

$$\cos y = \frac{\sqrt{a^2 - x^2}}{a} \qquad \text{and} \qquad \frac{1}{\cos y} = \frac{a}{\sqrt{a^2 - x^2}}$$

We substitute for $1/(\cos y)$ and get

$$\frac{dy}{dx} = \frac{1}{a}\left(\frac{a}{\sqrt{a^2 - x^2}}\right) = \frac{1}{\sqrt{a^2 - x^2}}$$

Example 73.2   If $y = \arccos \frac{x}{a}$, find y'.

Solution   We write the implicit form of the equation and draw the triangle it defines.

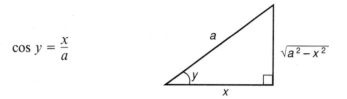

$$\cos y = \frac{x}{a}$$

Now we take the differential of both sides of the implicit form, divide by dx, solve for dy/dx, and finish by using the triangle to find the proper substitution for $-1/(\sin y)$.

$$-\sin y \, dy = \frac{dx}{a} \qquad\qquad \text{differential}$$

$$-\sin y \, \frac{dy}{dx} = \frac{1}{a} \qquad\qquad \text{divided by } dx$$

$$\frac{dy}{dx} = \frac{1}{a}\left(\frac{-1}{\sin y}\right) \qquad\qquad \text{solved}$$

$$\frac{dy}{dx} = \frac{1}{a} \cdot \frac{-a}{\sqrt{a^2 - x^2}} \qquad\qquad \text{substituted}$$

$$\frac{dy}{dx} = -\frac{1}{\sqrt{a^2 - x^2}} \qquad\qquad \text{simplified}$$

Example 73.3   If $y = \tan^{-1}\frac{x}{a}$, find y'.

Solution   We write the implicit form and draw the triangle.

$$\tan y = \frac{x}{a}$$

Now we find the differential, divide, and solve for dy/dx.

$$\sec^2 y \, dy = \frac{dx}{a} \quad \longrightarrow \quad \sec^2 y \, \frac{dy}{dx} = \frac{1}{a} \quad \longrightarrow \quad \frac{dy}{dx} = \frac{1}{a}\left(\frac{1}{\sec^2 y}\right) = \frac{1}{a}\cos^2 y$$

Now we go back to the triangle to find the value of $\cos^2 y$ and substitute.

$$\frac{dy}{dx} = \frac{1}{a}\left(\frac{a}{\sqrt{x^2 + a^2}}\right)^2 = \frac{a}{x^2 + a^2}$$

In Examples 73.1 and 73.2, we noted that the derivative of $\sin^{-1}(x/a)$ and $\cos^{-1}(x/a)$ are the negatives of each other. If we interchange the sides a and x in the triangle, we can use the same procedure to show that the derivative of the inverse cotangent of x/a is the negative of the derivative of the tangent of x/a.

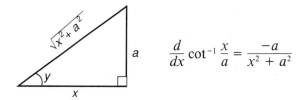

$$\frac{d}{dx}\cot^{-1}\frac{x}{a} = \frac{-a}{x^2 + a^2}$$

Example 73.4   If $y = \csc^{-1}\frac{x}{a}$ and $\frac{x}{a} > 0$, find y'.

Solution   We write the implicit form and draw the triangle.

$$\csc y = \frac{x}{a}$$

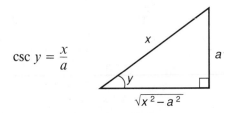

Now we find the differentials, divide, and solve for dy/dx.

$$-\csc y \cot y \, dy = \frac{dx}{a} \qquad\qquad\qquad \text{differentials}$$

$$\csc y \cot y \frac{dy}{dx} = -\frac{1}{a} \qquad\qquad\qquad \text{divided by } dx$$

$$\frac{dy}{dx} = \left(-\frac{1}{a}\right)\left(\frac{1}{\csc y \cot y}\right) = -\frac{1}{a}\sin y \tan y \qquad \text{solved}$$

Now we go back to the triangle to find values of $\sin y$ and $\tan y$.

$$\sin y = \frac{a}{x} \qquad \tan y = \frac{a}{\sqrt{x^2 - a^2}}$$

Now we make the final substitution.

$$\frac{dy}{dx} = \left(-\frac{1}{a}\right)\left(\frac{a}{x}\right)\left(\frac{a}{\sqrt{x^2 - a^2}}\right) = \frac{-a}{x\sqrt{x^2 - a^2}}$$

If the sides of the triangle a and $\sqrt{x^2 - a^2}$ are interchanged, we can use the same procedure to show that the derivative of the inverse secant of x/a is the negative of the derivative of the inverse cosecant of x/a.

$$\frac{d}{dx}\sec^{-1}\frac{x}{a} = \frac{a}{x\sqrt{x^2 - a^2}}$$

In the statement of the problem we noted that the value of x over a must be a positive number. If we did not make this restriction, the derivative of the inverse secant and the inverse cosecant would contain absolute value notations, as

$$\frac{d}{dx} \operatorname{arcsec} \frac{x}{a} = \frac{-a}{|x|\sqrt{x^2 - a^2}} \qquad \frac{d}{dx} \operatorname{arccsc} \frac{x}{a} = \frac{a}{|x|\sqrt{x^2 - a^2}}$$

The absolute value notation is awkward and could lead to an ambiguous integration formula later. The restriction that x be greater than zero is not unreasonable because applications of the inverse cosecant (or inverse secant) almost always have values of x that are positive numbers.

73.B
What to memorize

In Lesson 58, we developed the derivatives of tan x, cot x, sec x, and csc x. In the problem sets since that lesson we have found that it is convenient to have these derivatives memorized. In this lesson we have demonstrated that the derivatives of inverse trigonometric functions can be developed easily by drawing the triangles and finding the differentials of the implicit forms of the inverse functions. The derivatives of the inverse cosine, secant, cotangent, and cosecant are rarely encountered. The derivatives of the inverse sine and inverse tangent appear much more frequently, and it is a good idea to include these derivatives with the list of derivatives in Lesson 58 that should be memorized.

$$\frac{d}{dx} \sin^{-1} \frac{u}{a} = \frac{1}{\sqrt{a^2 - u^2}} \frac{du}{dx} \qquad \frac{d}{dx} \tan^{-1} \frac{u}{a} = \frac{a}{u^2 + a^2} \frac{du}{dx}$$

Example 73.5 If $y = \tan^{-1}(\cos x)$, find $\frac{dy}{dx}$.

Solution This problem requires the use of the chain rule and the fact that if ( ) is a function of x, then

$$\frac{d}{dx} \tan^{-1} \frac{(\ )}{a} = \frac{a}{(\ )^2 + a^2} \frac{d}{dx} (\ )$$

We replace ( ) with cos x and finish the problem.

$$\frac{d}{dx} \tan^{-1} \frac{\cos x}{1} = \left(\frac{1}{\cos^2 x + 1}\right)(-\sin x) = \frac{-\sin x}{\cos^2 x + 1}$$

Example 73.6 If $y = \arcsin 2x$, find y'.

Solution We have to use the chain rule and the fact that if ( ) is a function of x, then

$$\frac{d}{dx} \sin^{-1} \frac{(\ )}{a} = \frac{1}{\sqrt{a^2 - (\ )^2}} \frac{d}{dx} (\ )$$

Now we replace ( ) with $2x$ and finish the problem.

$$\frac{d}{dx} \sin^{-1} 2x = \frac{1}{\sqrt{1 - (2x)^2}} \frac{d}{dx} (2x) = \frac{2}{\sqrt{1 - 4x^2}}$$

Problem set 73

1. If the price of the tickets to the concert is \$16 each, 4000 tickets will be sold. For each \$1 increase in price, the number of tickets sold will decrease by 100. What should be the price per ticket for the revenue to be a maximum?

2. A semicircular region is bounded by the x axis and the graph of the semicircle $y = \sqrt{9 - x^2}$. Find the dimensions of the rectangle of greatest area that can be inscribed in the region.

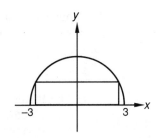

3. Use the critical number theorem to determine the maximum and minimum values of $f(x) = x^{3/2} - x$ on the interval $[0, 2]$.

4. The function f is continuous on the interval $[1, 5]$. If $f(1) = 2$ and $f(5) = 10$ and if f has the properties listed in the table below, make a rough sketch of f. Determine the maximum and minimum values of f.

x	$1 < x < 3$	$x = 3$	$3 < x < 5$
$f'(x)$	positive	0	positive
$f''(x)$	negative	0	positive

5. If $y = \arcsin \dfrac{x}{3}$, find $\dfrac{dy}{dx}$.

6. If $y = \cos^{-1} \dfrac{x}{5}$, find y'.

7. If $y = \tan^{-1} \dfrac{x}{2}$, find $\dfrac{dy}{dx}$.

8. If $y = \operatorname{arcsec} \dfrac{x}{a}, \dfrac{x}{a} > 0$, find y'.

9. A force is applied to an object so that the force at a given position along the x axis is given by

$$f(x) = 2x \text{ newtons}$$

Find the work done by the force if the object is moved from $x = 2$ to $x = 4$ meters.

10. Find a and b if $f(x) = a \sin x + b$, $f'(0) = 3$, and $f\left(\dfrac{\pi}{2}\right) = 5$.

11. Find the area between the graphs of $y = 2e^x$ and $y = 3e^x$ from $x = \ln 2$ to $x = \ln 3$.

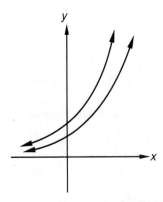

12. Find the area in the first quadrant between the x axis and the graph of $y = 2x\sqrt{4 - x^2}$.

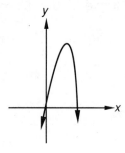

13. Evaluate $\dfrac{d^2y}{dx^2}$ at $x = 1$ if $y = \sqrt{x}$.

14. Write the equation of the line which can be drawn tangent to the graph of $y = \sin(\cos x)$ at $x = \pi/2$.

15. Differentiate: $y = \sqrt[3]{\sin 2x + x} + \dfrac{\csc 3x}{x^3 + 1}$

16. Integrate: $\displaystyle\int (3x^2 + 2x + 1)(\sqrt{x^3 + x^2 + x}) \, dx$

Evaluate:

17. $\displaystyle\lim_{x \to \infty} \dfrac{x^3 - 2x^2}{1 - x^4}$

18. $\displaystyle\lim_{\Delta x \to 0} \dfrac{\cos(\pi + \Delta x) - \cos \pi}{\Delta x}$

CONCEPT REVIEW

19. The following equation is the equation of an ellipse. Write the equation of the portion of the ellipse that lies in the first quadrant.

$$\frac{x^2}{a^2} + \frac{y^2}{b^2} = 1 \qquad (a, b > 0)$$

20. Use a definite integral to describe the first-quadrant area of the ellipse whose equation is

$$\frac{x^2}{a^2} + \frac{y^2}{b^2} = 1 \qquad (a, b > 0)$$

LESSON 74 *Falling body problems*

In Lesson 64 we began to use calculus to solve problems that concern the position, velocity, and acceleration of a physical object such as a ball, a car, or a projectile that moves in a straight line. In this lesson we will investigate the motion of bodies falling freely in a gravitational field. These problems are easy because the acceleration is a constant. In a later lesson we will consider problems in which the acceleration is a function of time.

We remember that at or near the surface of the earth the attraction between the earth and any physical object causes the object to accelerate downward at 9.8 meters per second per second. This acceleration is called the **acceleration due to gravity.** The acceleration due to gravity is the same for all objects regardless of their mass or shape, and if we neglect air resistance (that is, if we assume a vacuum), the motion of a feather and a lead ball will be the same.

If an object is released 100 feet above the surface of the earth, it will accelerate downward. If another object is released 200 feet above the surface of the earth at the same time, it will also accelerate downward, and will always be 100 feet above the first object because it was 100 feet higher when it was released.

If an object is thrown downward with an initial velocity of 40 meters per second, its downward velocity will increase with time because it will accelerate downward at 9.8 meters per second per second. If an object is thrown upward with a velocity of 40 meters per second, its upward velocity will decrease because the object will accelerate downward at 9.8 meters per second per second. Its upward velocity will decrease until the upward velocity becomes zero at the highest point. Then the steady downward acceleration of 9.8 meters per second per second will cause it to fall, and its downward velocity will increase with time. For free falling body problems we remember that often it is convenient to designate up as the positive direction and measure positive distances upward from the surface of the earth (sea level).

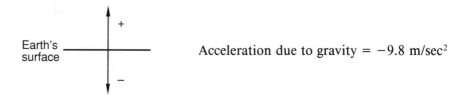

Acceleration due to gravity = -9.8 m/sec^2

If we use the earth's surface as our reference plane, positive positions are positions above the surface of the earth, and negative positions are positions below the surface of the earth. Positive velocities and positive accelerations are upward velocities and upward accelerations, and negative velocities and negative accelerations are downward velocities and downward accelerations. **Since the acceleration due to gravity is always in the downward direction, we use a minus sign and say that the acceleration due to gravity is -9.8 meters per second per second.**

The position function of a body in a free-fall near the surface of the earth is determined by its initial position, its initial velocity, and its acceleration. Since the acceleration is always -9.8 m/sec^2 for any physical object in a free-fall near the surface of the earth, the only difference in the position, velocity, and acceleration functions is caused by different values of the initial position h_0 and the initial velocity v_0. The position, velocity, and acceleration functions for any free-falling body at or near the surface of the earth are

$$h(t) = -4.9t^2 + v_0t + h_0 \qquad \text{meters}$$

$$h'(t) = v(t) = -9.8t + v_0 \qquad \text{meters/sec}$$

$$h''(t) = v'(t) = a(t) = -9.8 \qquad \text{meters/sec}^2$$

In physics we can find the answers to problems by inserting the indicated values of h_0 and v_0 in these equations. In calculus we are interested in learning to develop these equations because the same procedure will be used to find the velocity and position functions for the motion of particles whose acceleration is not -9.8 m/sec^2.

In motion problems the concept of t_{0^+} is very important. If a ball is released at $t = 0$, we consider the problem begins at t_{0^+}, which is the instant after it is released. **At t_{0^+} the ball has not moved and the ball has no velocity, but it does have a negative acceleration and its upward velocity is increasing in the negative direction at 9.8 m/sec^2. If the ball is thrown upward or downward, at t_{0^+} the ball has not moved but has an initial velocity of v_0.** Of course, its acceleration at t_{0^+} (and at any other time) is -9.8 m/sec^2. Since the ball has not moved, its position at t_{0^+} is still h_0.

We always begin by integrating the acceleration function to get the velocity function. When we do, we get a constant of integration C. To find the value of the constant of integration, we set $t = 0$, let $v(0)$ be the given value of v_0, and solve to find that $C = v_0$. Then we integrate the velocity function to get the position function, which also has a constant of integration C. Then we substitute h_0 for $h(0)$, set $t = 0$, and solve to find that $C = h_0$.

Example 74.1   An object is dropped from a height of 2000 meters. Begin with the acceleration function and develop the position function. How far above the earth will the object be 20 seconds later?

Solution   Since h_0 is 2000 and v_0 is zero, we know that the position function will be

$$h(t) = -4.9t^2 + 2000$$

But our job is to develop this equation, so we begin by integrating the acceleration function to get the velocity function.

$$a(t) = -9.8 \quad \longrightarrow \quad v(t) = \int -9.8 \, dt = -9.8t + C$$

We know that at $t = 0^+$, $v(0) = 0$ because the ball was dropped and was not thrown. So we replace t with zero and replace $v(0)$ with zero and solve for C.

$$0 = -9.8(0) + C \quad \longrightarrow \quad C = 0$$

This gives us the velocity function.

$$v(t) = -9.8t$$

Now we integrate the velocity function to get the position function.

$$h(t) = \int -9.8t \, dt \quad \longrightarrow \quad h(t) = \frac{-9.8t^2}{2} + C$$

When $t = 0^+$, $h(t) = 2000$. We substitute and solve for C.

$$2000 = -4.9(0)^2 + C \quad \longrightarrow \quad C = 2000$$

Now we have developed the position function.

$$\mathbf{h(t) = -4.9t^2 + 2000}$$

To find the position when $t = 20$ sec, we find $h(20)$.

$$h(20) = -4.9(20)^2 + 2000 = \mathbf{40 \ m}$$

Example 74.2   A ball is thrown downward with a velocity of 40 meters per second from a height of 2000 meters. Begin with the acceleration function and develop the position function for the ball. What will be the position of the ball after 8 seconds?

Solution   The equations for freely falling bodies are always the same except that the constants $h(0)$ and $v(0)$ are different. With the data given we know that the velocity function and the position function will be as follows.

$$v(t) = -9.8t - 40 \qquad \text{velocity function}$$
$$h(t) = -4.9t^2 - 40t + 2000 \qquad \text{position function}$$

But our job is to develop these equations. We will begin with the acceleration function. At or near the surface of the earth the acceleration is always -9.8 m/sec^2.

$$a(t) = -9.8$$

To find the velocity function, we integrate the acceleration function.

$$v(t) = \int a(t) \, dt = \int -9.8 \, dt = -9.8t + C$$

To solve for C, we let $t = 0$ and remember that $v(0) = -40$ because the ball was thrown downward and down is the negative direction.

$$-40 = -9.8(0) + C \quad \longrightarrow \quad C = -40 \quad \longrightarrow \quad v(t) = -9.8t - 40$$

To find the position function, we integrate the velocity function.

$$h(t) = \int (-9.8t - 40) \, dt \quad \longrightarrow \quad h(t) = \frac{-9.8}{2}t^2 - 40t + C$$

We know that when $t = 0$, $h(0) = 2000$. Thus we substitute.

$$2000 = -4.9(0)^2 - 40(0) + C \quad \longrightarrow \quad C = 2000$$

Now we have the position function $h(t)$.

$$h(t) = -4.9t^2 - 40t + 2000$$

To find the position after 8 seconds, we find $h(8)$.

$$h(8) = -4.9(8)^2 - 40(8) + 2000$$

$$= -313.6 - 320 + 2000 = \mathbf{1366.4 \text{ m}}$$

We note that the ball fell 320 m because of the initial velocity of 40 m/sec times 8 sec. The ball fell an additional 313.6 meters because of the acceleration component of the position equation.

Example 74.3 A boy stood on top of a building 40 meters high and threw a stone so that it had an initial upward velocity of 20 meters per second. Begin with the acceleration function and develop the velocity function and the position function for the stone. How high will the stone go? How long after the stone is thrown will it hit the ground?

Solution We already know that the velocity function and the position function for the stone will be

$$v(t) = -9.8t + 20 \quad \text{and} \quad h(t) = -4.9t^2 + 20t + 40$$

But our job is to develop these equations. We know that at or near the surface of the earth the acceleration function is always the same.

$$a(t) = -9.8$$

The velocity function is the integral of the acceleration function.

$$v(t) = \int -9.8 \, dt = -9.8t + C$$

When time equaled 0^+, the velocity equaled $+20$.

$$20 = -9.8(0) + C \quad \longrightarrow \quad C = 20$$

Thus the velocity function is

$$v(t) = \mathbf{-9.8t + 20}$$

The position function is the integral of the velocity function.

$$h(t) = \int (-9.8t + 20) \, dt = \frac{-9.8}{2} t^2 + 20t + C$$

When t equaled 0^+, the position was $h(0) = 40$.

$$40 = -4.9(0)^2 + 20(0) + C \quad \longrightarrow \quad C = 40$$

Thus the position function is

$$h(t) = \mathbf{-4.9t^2 + 20t + 40}$$

We can answer all the questions by using the velocity function and position function that we have developed. To find out how high the stone goes, we use the velocity function to find the time when the velocity equals zero, which is at the highest point.

$$0 = -9.8t + 20 \quad \longrightarrow \quad t = 2.04 \text{ seconds}$$

Now we use the position function to find the height at $t = 2.04$.

$$h(2.04) = -4.9(2.04)^2 + 20(2.04) + 40 = \mathbf{60.41 \text{ meters}}$$

When the stone hits the ground, the elevation will be zero. We can find the time the stone hits the ground by setting the position function equal to zero and using the quadratic formula to solve for t.

$$0 = -4.9t^2 + 20t + 40 \quad\longrightarrow\quad t = \frac{-20 \pm \sqrt{20^2 - 4(-4.9)(40)}}{-9.8} = 5.55, -1.47$$

The negative number -1.47 is a solution of the quadratic equation but has no meaning in this physical problem. Thus the time from release to impact with the ground is **5.55 seconds.**

Since the maximum altitude is 60.41 meters, we can solve the problem another way by finding the time required for the stone to free-fall from 60.41 meters and adding this result to 2.04 seconds. From Example 74.1 we see that the position function for a free-fall of 2000 meters is

$$h(t) = -4.9t^2 + 2000$$

Thus the position function for a free-fall of 60.41 meters would be

$$h(t) = -4.9t^2 + 60.41$$

Since $h(t) = 0$ when the stone hits the ground, we have

$$0 = -4.9t^2 + 60.41 \quad\longrightarrow\quad t = \sqrt{\frac{60.41}{4.9}} = 3.51$$

If we add the 3.51 seconds required to fall 60.41 meters to the 2.04 seconds required to get to the height of 60.41 meters, we get

$$2.04 + 3.51 = \textbf{5.55 seconds}$$

Problem set 74

1. An airplane is in level flight toward a reference point on the ground. The speed of the airplane is 100 meters per second and its altitude is 1000 meters. What is the rate of change of the angle of elevation, θ, when the horizontal distance from the reference point is 2000 meters? (Neglect the height of the airplane.)

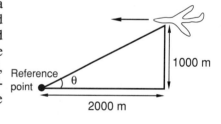

2. A ball is dropped from a height of 500 meters. Develop an equation which describes the height of the ball a time t after it is dropped. Find the elevation, velocity, and acceleration of the ball 3 seconds after it is released.

3. A ball is thrown straight up from the top of a 100-meter building with an initial velocity of 30 meters per second. Develop an equation which describes the height of the ball above the ground as a function of time t. What will be the maximum height attained by the ball?

4. Begin with the equation $f(x) = y = \cos x$. Then write the implicit equation of the inverse of f. The equation of the inverse defines a right triangle. Draw this triangle. Differentiate this equation implicitly and then use the triangle to write the expression for $d/dx\, f^{-1}(x)$. Evaluate $(f^{-1})'(0.2)$.

5. If $y = \arcsin \dfrac{x}{3}$, evaluate $\left.\dfrac{dy}{dx}\right|_2$.

6. If $y = \arctan \dfrac{x}{2}$, find $\dfrac{dy}{dx}$.

7. Apply the critical number theorem to find where the maximum and minimum of $f(x) = |x - 1|$ occur and what their values are if f is defined on the interval $[-1, 3]$. (*Note*: No calculus is needed.)

8. A function *f* is continuous on the closed interval $[-3, 2]$. In addition, $f(-3) = 4$, $f(-1) = 6$, $f(1) = 1$, $f(2) = 2$, and $f(x)$ has the properties listed on the chart shown.

x	$-3 < x < -1$	$x = -1$	$-1 < x < 1$	$x = 1$	$1 < x < 2$
$f'(x)$	positive	zero	negative	zero	positive

Sketch a possible graph of *f* and determine the maximum value of *f*.

9. The spring constant for a spring is 2 newtons per meter. How much work is required to stretch the spring from $x = 1$ meter to $x = 2$ meters?

10. Suppose $f(x) = ax^2 + b$ and $g(x) = x^2 + ax$. Find *a* and *b* if $f'(2) = g'(2)$ and if $f(1) = 5$.

Integrate:

11. $\displaystyle\int \frac{\cos 2x}{\sqrt{1 + \sin 2x}}\, dx$

12. $\displaystyle\int xe^{x^2 + \pi}\, dx$

13. Find the area completely enclosed by the graphs of $y = \sqrt{x}$ and $y = x$.

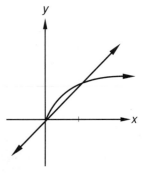

14. Suppose that $1 \le c \le 5$ and *f* is continuous on $[1, 5]$. Find

$$\int_1^c f(x)\, dx \quad \text{if} \int_1^5 f(x)\, dx = 10 \quad \text{and} \quad \int_c^5 f(x)\, dx = -2$$

15. Evaluate: $\displaystyle\int_1^e \frac{1}{x}\, dx$

16. Evaluate $\dfrac{d^4 y}{dx^4}$ at $x = \dfrac{\pi}{2}$ if $y = 2 \sin x$.

17. Differentiate: $y = \sqrt{1 - \sin x} + \dfrac{e^{2x}}{\sec x + 1} + \ln x \csc x$

18. Describe the intervals on which *f* is concave up and concave down if

$$f(x) = \frac{x(x - 1)}{(x - 2)(x + 1)(x + 2)}$$

Note: f'' need not be computed. Only the graph of *f* is required.

19. Evaluate: $\displaystyle\lim_{x \to 2} \frac{e^x - e^2}{x + 2}$

CONCEPT REVIEW 20. Determine the range of $y = \dfrac{1}{x^2 - 1}$ if the domain of *y* is $\{x: |x| > 1\}$.

21.   Suppose f is a function such that $f(xy) = f(x) + f(y)$. Which of the following could be the equation of f?
    (*a*) $f(x) = e^x$ (*b*) $f(x) = \ln x$ (*c*) $f(x) = x^2$ (*d*) $f(x) = 2x$

LESSON 75   *U substitution · Change of variable · Proof of the substitution theorem (optional)*

75.A
U substitution

There are procedures and techniques for integration, but there are few rules for integration because integration is defined to be the inverse of differentiation. Guessing the answer is our primary weapon. We have found that often it is necessary to change our first guess by inserting a constant and its reciprocal on either side of the integral sign. If we wish, we can use a mechanical procedure called ***u substitution*** that will obviate the requirement for using the constant and its reciprocal. We can also use u substitution to find some integrals that would be almost impossible to guess.

Example 75.1   Find $\displaystyle\int 40x(x^2 - 4)^5 \, dx$.

Solution   As the first step we move the constant 40 to the left of the integral sign. Then we let u equal $x^2 - 4$ and record this substitution in the box on the right.

$$40 \int x(x^2 - 4)^5 \, dx \qquad \boxed{\begin{array}{l} u = x^2 - 4 \\[4pt] du = 2x \, dx \\[4pt] \dfrac{du}{2} = x \, dx \end{array}}$$

$$\rightarrow \quad 40 \int x(u)^5 \, dx$$

We have substituted u for $x^2 - 4$, but we also want to substitute for $x \, dx$. Thus in the box we have found du and have solved this expression for $x \, dx$. Now we substitute for $x \, dx$, integrate, and remember the constant of integration.

$$40 \int u^5 \, \frac{du}{2} = 20 \int u^5 \, du = 20\left(\frac{u^6}{6}\right) = \frac{10u^6}{3} + C$$

Now we use the value of u in the box to make the second substitution and get

$$\frac{10u^6}{3} + C \quad \longrightarrow \quad \frac{10}{3}(x^2 - 4)^6 + C$$

Example 75.2   Find $\displaystyle\int \frac{20 \cos ax \, dx}{\sqrt{b + \sin ax}}$.

Solution   We write the constant in front of the integral sign and record our proposed u substitution in a box.

$$20 \int \frac{\cos ax \, dx}{\sqrt{b + \sin ax}}$$

$$
\boxed{
\begin{aligned}
u &= b + \sin ax \\
du &= (\cos ax)(a \, dx) \\
\frac{du}{a} &= \cos ax \, dx
\end{aligned}
}
$$

Since we needed to substitute for $\cos ax \, dx$, we have solved for this expression in the third entry in the box. Now we substitute and integrate.

$$20 \int \frac{\frac{du}{a}}{\sqrt{u}} = \frac{20}{a} \int u^{-1/2} \, du = \frac{20}{a} \frac{u^{1/2}}{\frac{1}{2}} + C = \frac{40}{a} u^{1/2} + C$$

Now we look in the box and find that $u = b + \sin ax$. We make this substitution and get

$$\frac{40}{a} u^{1/2} = \frac{40}{a} (b + \sin ax)^{1/2} + C$$

Example 75.3 Find $\int 7x \sqrt{x - 1} \, dx$.

Solution The derivative of $x - 1$ is 1, not x, so this integrand is not the differential of an expression whose form is $u^n \, du$. But u substitution will still work. We write the constant in front of the integral sign and record the u substitution in a box.

$$7 \int x\sqrt{x - 1} \, dx
\qquad
\boxed{
\begin{aligned}
u &= x - 1 \\
du &= dx \\
x &= u + 1
\end{aligned}
}$$

This time we had to solve the equation $u = x - 1$ for x to find the proper substitution for x.

$$7 \int x\sqrt{x - 1} \, dx \longrightarrow 7 \int (u + 1)(u^{1/2}) \, du$$

Now we multiply and integrate.

$$= 7 \left(\int u^{3/2} \, du + \int u^{1/2} \, du \right) = 7 \left(\frac{u^{5/2}}{\frac{5}{2}} + \frac{u^{3/2}}{\frac{3}{2}} \right)$$

Next we simplify and make the second substitution.

$$\frac{14}{5} u^{5/2} + \frac{14}{3} u^{3/2} \longrightarrow \frac{14}{5} (x - 1)^{5/2} + \frac{14}{3} (x - 1)^{3/2} + C$$

If we factor out $(x - 1)^{3/2}$ and simplify, we can write this derivative as

$$\frac{14}{15}(x - 1)^{3/2}(3x + 2) + C$$

75.B
Change of variable

There is a useful alternative procedure for evaluating definite integrals. It is not necessarily easier or simpler but is a procedure that is sometimes helpful. The procedure is called *changing the variable of integration.* When we change the variable of integration, it is usually necessary to change the limits of integration. Suppose we need to evaluate the following integral.

$$\int_0^2 \underbrace{(x^2 + 1)^3}_{u^3}\underbrace{(2x\ dx)}_{du} \qquad \boxed{\begin{array}{l} u = x^2 + 1 \\ du = 2x\ dx \end{array}}$$

We note that we have the form $u^3\ du$, whose integral is $u^4/4$, or $(x^2 + 1)^4/4$. Thus we have our choice of evaluating either

$$\frac{(x^2 + 1)^4}{4}\ \Big|_{x=0}^{x=2} \qquad \text{or} \qquad \frac{u^4}{4}\ \Big|_{u=1}^{u=5}$$

On the right we changed $(x^2 + 1)$ to u. We also changed the lower limit of integration from 0 to 1 because when $x = 0$ (the lower x limit), $u = 0^2 + 1 = 1$. We changed the upper limit from 2 to 5 because when $x = 2$ (the upper limit), $u = 2^2 + 1 = 5$. Now we evaluate both expressions and see that the answers are the same.

$$\frac{1}{4}[(x^2 + 1)^4]_0^2 = \frac{1}{4}(625 - 1) = \mathbf{156} \qquad \frac{1}{4}[u^4]_1^5 = \frac{1}{4}(625 - 1) = \mathbf{156}$$

Example 75.4   Use the change of variable method to evaluate $\int_0^1 x \sin \pi x^2\ dx$.

Solution   We note that the form of the integrand is $\sin u\ du$ and that we need additional factors of $1/2\pi$ and 2π.

$$\frac{1}{2\pi}\int_0^1 \underbrace{(\sin \pi x^2)}_{\sin u}\underbrace{(2\pi x\ dx)}_{du} \qquad \boxed{\begin{array}{l} u = \pi x^2 \\ du = 2\pi x\ dx \end{array}}$$

We can evaluate this integral by integrating $\sin u\ du$ if we change the lower limit to the value of u when $x = 0$ and change the upper limit to the value of u when $x = 1$.

$$u(0) = \pi(0)^2 = 0 \qquad u(1) = \pi(1)^2 = \pi$$

We make these changes and evaluate the integral.

$$\frac{1}{2\pi}\int_0^\pi \sin u\ du = \frac{1}{2\pi}[-\cos u]_0^\pi = -\frac{1}{2\pi}(\cos \pi - \cos 0) = \frac{-1 - 1}{-2\pi} = \frac{1}{\pi}$$

Example 75.5   Use the change of variable method to evaluate $\int_0^\pi e^{\sin 5x} \cos 5x\ dx$.

Solution   We note that this integral can be written as $e^u\ du$ if we insert the necessary constants.

$$\frac{1}{5}\int_0^\pi \underbrace{(e^{\sin 5x})}_{e^u}\underbrace{(5 \cos 5x\ dx)}_{du} \qquad \boxed{\begin{array}{l} u = \sin 5x \\ du = 5 \cos 5x\ dx \end{array}}$$

When $x = 0$, $u = 0$, and when $x = \pi$, $u = 0$. So we have

$$\frac{1}{5}\int_0^0 e^u\ du = 0$$

When the upper and lower limits of integration are equal, the integral is zero by definition. A graph of the original function would show equal areas above and below the x axis on the x interval $[0, \pi]$. We would get the same result if we had evaluated the original integral, as

$$\frac{1}{5}\int_0^\pi (e^{\sin 5x})(5 \cos 5x)\ dx = \frac{1}{5}[(e^{\sin 5x})]_0^\pi = \frac{1}{5}(e^0 - e^0) = \mathbf{0}$$

75.C
Proof of the substitution theorem (optional)

The justification for the use of this procedure is straightforward. First we will state the theorem.

SUBSTITUTION THEOREM FOR DEFINITE INTEGRALS

The following statement of equality is true

$$\int_a^b f(u(x))\, u'(x)\, dx = \int_{u(a)}^{u(b)} f(u)\, du$$

if the function in the integral on the left is continuous from a to b inclusive and the function in the integral on the right is continuous from $u(a)$ to $u(b)$ inclusive.

We note that the expression on the left in the box is the integral of the derivative of a composite function. For a concrete illustration we will use the example at the top of page 375, in which we used the following substitution.

$$\int_0^2 (x^2 + 1)^3(2x\, dx) = \int_1^5 u^3\, du$$

To develop our proof we will define an f function and a u function as follows.

$$f(x) = x^3 \quad \text{and} \quad u(x) = x^2 + 1 \quad \text{so} \quad u'(x) = 2x$$

If we substitute the equivalent general expression in the concrete example above, we can get the following general equality.

$$\int_{x=a}^{x=b} f(u(x))u'(x)\, dx = \int_{u(a)}^{u(b)} f(u)\, du$$

To prove that this is a true statement of equality, we will show that both the left-hand side and the right-hand side of this equality equal $F(u(b)) - F(u(a))$, where F is some antiderivative of f. The right-hand side is easier, because we just substitute $u(a)$ and $u(b)$ for the lower and upper limits of the integral in the general statement of the fundamental theorem of calculus.

FUNDAMENTAL THEOREM   SUBSTITUTED

$$\int_a^b f(x)\, dx = F(b) - F(a) \longrightarrow \int_{u(a)}^{u(b)} f(u)\, du = F(u(b)) - F(u(a))$$

To show that the left side also equals $F(u(b)) - F(u(a))$, we use the chain rule to find the derivative of $F(u(x))$.

$$\frac{d}{dx} F(u(x)) = F'(u(x))u'(x)$$

Now, since $F' = f$, we can substitute f for F' and get

$$\frac{d}{dx} F(u(x)) = f(u(x))u'(x)$$

which can be turned around to write

$$\int f(u(x))u'(x)\, dx = F(u(x)) + C$$

Now if we use the fundamental theorem of calculus to evaluate this definite integral from $x = a$ to $x = b$, we can write the following to finish our proof.

$$\int_{x=a}^{x=b} f(u(x))u'(x) \, dx = F(u(b)) - F(u(a))$$

Problem set 75

1. An object is propelled along the x axis by a force of $x^2 - 3x$ newtons. Find the work done on the object between x values of 1 meter and 5 meters.

2. A building is 160 meters high. If a ball is dropped from the top of the building, find the acceleration of the ball when it is 100 meters above the ground.

3. A ball is thrown straight up from the top of a 160-meter-tall building with a velocity of 20 meters per second. Develop an equation which expresses the height h of the ball as a function of time. Find $h(2)$, $v(2)$, and $a(2)$.

Use the change of variable method to evaluate the following integrals:

4. $\displaystyle\int_0^1 x \cos \pi x^2 \, dx$

5. $\displaystyle\int_0^\pi (\sin 5x)e^{\cos 5x} \, dx$

6. Write the equation of the inverse of $y = \csc x$ defined on $[-\pi/2, \pi/2]$. Differentiate this equation and find $(f^{-1})'$, and express $(f^{-1})'$ in terms of x, where $x > 0$.

7. Find the slope of the tangent line to the graph of

$$y = \arcsin \frac{x}{3} \qquad \text{at } x = \frac{3}{2}$$

8. Find $\dfrac{dy}{dx}$ if $y = \arctan (\sin x)$.

9. Determine the maximum and minimum values of f on the interval $[0, 2]$ if $f(x) = x^2 - 2x$.

10. Suppose f is continuous on $[1, 4]$ and has the properties listed below.

x	$x = 1$	$1 < x < 2$	$x = 2$	$2 < x < 4$	$x = 4$
$f(x)$	15	....	10	....	20
$f'(x)$	....	negative	0	positive	....
$f''(x)$	....	positive	positive	positive	....

Sketch a graph of f and determine the maximum and minimum values of f.

11. If $f(x) = a \sin x + b \cos x$, find a and b if $f'(\pi) = 2$ and $f'(\pi/2) = 4$.

12. Integrate by using u substitution: $\displaystyle\int x\sqrt{x + 1} \, dx$

Integrate:

13. $\displaystyle\int (1 + \cos x)(x + \sin x)^3 \, dx$

14. $\displaystyle\int \frac{x^2 + 1}{x} \, dx$

15. $\displaystyle\int \frac{x}{x^2 + 1} \, dx$

Differentiate:

16. $y = \dfrac{\tan (x^3 - 1)}{e^2 + e^x}$

17. $y = e^{2x} \sec \pi x$

18. Find the equation of the tangent line which can be drawn to the graph of

$$y = \frac{x}{x^2 + 1} \qquad \text{at } x = 1$$

19. Suppose $y = f(x)$ is a polynomial function of degree n. Which of the following must be true?
(a) f intersects the x axis at least n times.
(b) f intersects the x axis at least once.
(c) f is continuous for all values of x.
(d) f always has some finite maximum value.

20. In the definite integral shown, a and b are positive constants. The integral represents the area of a familiar geometric figure multiplied by b over a. Evaluate this integral by inspection and without using calculus.

$$\int_0^a \frac{b\sqrt{a^2 - x^2}}{a}\, dx$$

21. Find $\cos^2 \theta$ in terms of x if $\tan \theta = \dfrac{x}{10}$.

LESSON 76 *Functions of y*

In the area problems we have worked thus far, y has been a function of x. Thus x has been the independent variable, and we have used the horizontal axis as the x axis. For some problems it is convenient to use y as the independent variable and let x be a function of y. When we do this, we still graph x horizontally. When x is a function of y, the input axis is the y axis and the output axis is the x axis.

Example 76.1   Find the area of the region completely enclosed by the y axis and the graph of $x = 1 - y^2$.

Solution   If we solve this equation for y, we get $y = \pm\sqrt{1 - x}$. This equation describes two functions: $y = \sqrt{1 - x}$, whose graph is the upper half of the parabola, and $y = -\sqrt{1 - x}$, whose graph is the lower half of the parabola. We could use either of these functions and one of the representative rectangles shown in the left-hand figure below to find half the desired area and double this result to get the whole area.

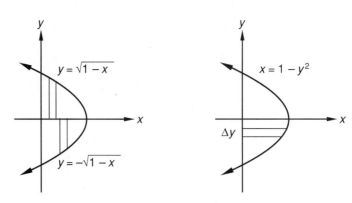

Another way to solve this problem is to let x be a function of y and use the representative rectangle shown in the figure on the right. When we do this, y will be the variable of integration and the limits of integration will be the y values of the points of intersection of the graph of $x = 1 - y^2$ and the y axis. First we find the y values of these points.

$$x = 1 - y^2 \longrightarrow 0 = (1 - y)(1 + y) \longrightarrow y = \pm 1$$

The height of the representative rectangle is $1 - y^2$, and its width is Δy. Thus the area we want is designated by the following integral.

$$\text{Area} = \int_{-1}^{1} (1 - y^2)\, dy$$

We finish by integrating and evaluating the integral.

$$\text{Area} = \left[y - \frac{y^3}{3} \right]_{-1}^{1} = \left(1 - \frac{1}{3} \right) - \left[-1 - \left(-\frac{1}{3} \right) \right] = \frac{2}{3} - \left(-\frac{2}{3} \right) = \frac{4}{3} \text{ (units)}^2$$

Example 76.2 Find the area of the region completely bounded by the graphs of $x = 3 - y^2$ and $y = x - 1$.

Solution We must be careful when we draw the representative rectangle, as we see in the figure on the left below. The left-hand representative rectangle shown looks all right because it is bounded above by the graph of $y = x - 1$ and below by the graph of $x = 3 - y^2$. Trying to use this representative rectangle to find the area leads to trouble, as we see when the rectangle is moved to the right-hand part of the figure. Here it is bounded both above and below by the graph of $x = 3 - y^2$. There are several ways this difficulty can be overcome. One way is to draw the representative rectangle horizontally and let dy be its width, as we show in the figure on the right.

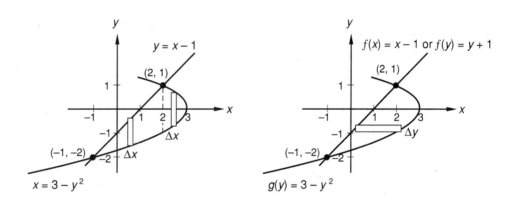

In the right-hand figure the right end of the rectangle is bounded by $g(y) = 3 - y^2$ and the left end is bounded by $f(y) = y + 1$. The width of the rectangle is dy, and the limits of integration are y values of -2 and $+1$.

$$\text{Area} = \int_{-2}^{1} (g - f)(y)\, dy = \int_{-2}^{1} [(3 - y^2) - (y + 1)]\, dy$$

We finish by evaluating the integral.

$$\int_{-2}^{1} (-y^2 - y + 2)\, dy = \left[\frac{-y^3}{3} - \frac{y^2}{2} + 2y \right]_{-2}^{1}$$

$$= \left(-\frac{1}{3} - \frac{1}{2} + 2 \right) - \left(\frac{8}{3} - 2 - 4 \right) = \frac{9}{2} \text{ (units)}^2$$

Problem set 76

1. Gaurav is standing 5 meters away from the base of a flagpole on which a flag is being raised at the rate of 1 meter per second. Find the rate of change of the angle of elevation from Gaurav to the flag at the instant the flag is 12 meters above the ground. (Assume that Gaurav's height is zero.)

2. A ball is thrown downward with a velocity of 20 meters per second from the top of a building that is 160 meters tall. Develop the velocity and position functions for the ball. How long will it take for the ball to hit the ground?

3. Find the area completely bounded by the graphs of $x = 4 - y^2$ and $x = 3y$.

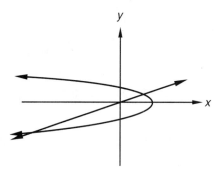

4. The area of a region is completely enclosed by the y axis and the graph of $x = 4 - y^2$. Use y as the variable of integration to write a definite integral that defines this area.

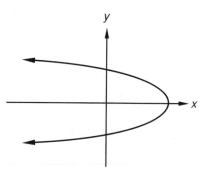

5. Use y as the variable of integration to write a definite integral whose value equals the area bounded by the coordinate axes and the graph of $y + 2x = 3$.

6. Evaluate by using the change of variable method: $\int_1^5 2x\sqrt{2x - 1}\, dx$

7. The definite integral

$$\int_0^1 x \sin \frac{\pi x^2}{2}\, dx$$

is equal to which of the following definite integrals?

(a) $\int_0^1 \frac{1}{\pi} \sin u\, du$ (b) $\int_0^{\pi/2} \frac{1}{\pi} \sin u\, du$

(c) $\int_0^{\pi/2} \sin u\, du$ (d) $\int_0^{\pi/2} \pi \sin u\, du$

8. If $f(x) = \arcsin \frac{x}{2}$, find $f'(1)$.

9. Find the slope of the line which can be drawn tangent to the graph of $y = \arctan x$ at $x = \sqrt{3}/2$.

10. An object moves along the number line so that its velocity at time t is given by

$$v(t) = t\sqrt{t^2 - 1}$$

Find the distance the object moves from $t = \sqrt{10}$ to $t = \sqrt{26}$.

Integrate:

11. $\int \sin^3 x \cos x\, dx$ 12. $\int \frac{\cos x}{\sin^2 x}\, dx$ 13. $\int \frac{1 + \cos x}{\sqrt{x + \sin x}}\, dx$

14. Find the area bounded by the x axis and the graph of $y = \cos 2x$ between $x = 0$ and $x = \pi/2$.

15. Suppose $f(x) \geq 0$ for $2 \leq x \leq 4$. Which of the following statements must be true?

   (a) $\displaystyle\int_2^4 f(x)\,dx \leq 4$ (b) $\displaystyle\int_4^2 f(x)\,dx \leq 0$

   (c) $\displaystyle\int_2^4 f(x)\,dx = \int_4^2 f(x)\,dx$ (d) $\displaystyle\int_2^4 f(x)\,dx = -\int_2^4 f(x)\,dx$

16. Find C and k if $f(x) = Ce^{kx}$, $f'(0) = 2$, and $f(0) = 4$.

17. Differentiate: $\displaystyle y = \frac{e^{-x} + e^{\cos x}}{2\sqrt{x} + 1}$

18. Evaluate: $\displaystyle \lim_{h \to 0} \frac{f(2 + h) - f(2)}{h}$ if $f(x) = \sin x$

CONCEPT REVIEW 19. A monkey cage with a square base and rectangular sides is to be constructed. The volume of the cage is to be 300 cubic feet. The cost per square foot of the top is \$8, the cost per square foot of the bottom is \$4, and the cost per square foot of each of the walls is \$15. If the height of the cage is h and the length of one side of the base is L, express h in terms of L. Express the total cost of the monkey cage in terms of L.

LESSON 77 *Even and odd functions*

Most functions are neither even functions nor odd functions. If a function is an even function, the value of $f(x)$ where x is a distance to the right of the origin equals the value of $f(-x)$ where $-x$ is the same distance but is to the left of the origin. For an even function f, if $f(x_1) = +2$, then $f(-x_1)$ must also equal $+2$. If $f(3) = -5$, then $f(-3)$ must also equal -5. **This means that the same things happen vertically to the graph of an even function at equal distances to the left and right of the origin. If a function is an odd function, the same things happen to the graph of the function at equal distances to the left and right of the origin but in opposite vertical directions.** If a function is an odd function and $f(x_1) = 5$, then $f(-x_1)$ must equal -5. In general, for an odd function, for any value of x, $f(-x)$ must equal the negative of $f(x)$. Thus, for an odd function, $f(-x) = -f(x)$.

   The graph of an even function is said to be symmetric with respect to the y axis, and the graph of an odd function is said to be symmetric with respect to the origin. The cosine function is an even function, and the sine function is an odd function.

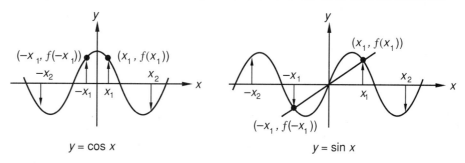

$y = \cos x$ $y = \sin x$

For the cosine function, the vertical distance and direction from the x axis to the graph is the same at x_1 and $-x_1$. The points $(x_1, f(x_1))$ and $(-x_1, f(-x_1))$ are horizontally the same distance from the y axis. For the sine function, the vertical distance from the x axis to the graph at x_1 is the same as at x_2 but in the opposite direction. The points $(x_1, f(x_1))$ and $(-x_1, f(-x_1))$ lie on a line that passes through the origin, and the points are equidistant from the origin.

To determine whether a function is odd, even, or neither, the procedure is to replace x with $-x$. If the result is the same, the function is an even function. If the magnitude is the same but the sign is different, the function is an odd function. Any other result tells us that the function is neither even nor odd.

Example 77.1   Is the function $y = x^4 + x^2 - 6$ an even function, an odd function, or neither?

Solution   We compare $f(x)$ and $f(-x)$.

$$f(x) = x^4 + x^2 - 6 \qquad f(-x) = (-x)^4 + (-x)^2 - 6 = x^4 + x^2 - 6$$

Since both $f(x)$ and $f(-x)$ equal $x^4 + x^2 - 6$, the function is an even function. **If every exponent of x in a polynomial function is even, the function is an even function.** To use this rule we must remember that the constant 6 can be written as $6x^0$. Thus, by inspection, we see that

$$y = x^4 + x^2 - 6x^0$$

is an **even function** because all exponents of x are even, and thus $f(x) = f(-x)$.

Example 77.2   Is $f(x) = x^3 - x$ an even function, an odd function, or neither?

Solution   We consider the expressions for $f(x)$ and $f(-x)$.

$$f(x) = x^3 - x \qquad f(-x) = (-x)^3 - (-x) = -x^3 + x = -(x^3 - x)$$

Since $f(x) = x^3 - x$ and $f(-x) = -(x^3 - x)$, the function is an **odd function.**

Example 77.3   Is $g(x) = x^3 - x - 4$ an even function or an odd function?

Solution   We consider the expressions for $g(x)$ and $g(-x)$.

$$g(x) = x^3 - x - 4 \qquad g(-x) = (-x)^3 - (-x) - 4 = -(x^3 - x + 4)$$

We see that $g(-x)$ is not equal to $g(x)$ nor is it equal to $-g(-x)$ because the constant 4 has the wrong sign. **Thus, the function $g(x)$ is neither even nor odd.** If we change the function by deleting the constant term and call the new function $h(x)$, we get

$$h(x) = x^3 - x \qquad h(-x) = (-x)^3 - (-x) = -x^3 + x = -(x^3 - x)$$

Thus $h(x)$ **is an odd function** because $h(x) = -h(-x)$.

From this example we see that a polynomial function is an odd function if every exponent of x is odd and there is no constant term. Thus, by inspection, we see that

$$y = x^3 - x - 4x^0$$

is neither even nor odd because both even and odd exponents are present.

Example 77.4   Is $y = -3 \tan 2\pi x$ an odd function, an even function, or neither?

Solution   Every basic trigonometric function is either an odd function or an even function. The coefficient -3 flips the graph upside down and does not affect symmetry. The 2π changes the period and does not affect symmetry. A phase shift left or right could affect symmetry, but this function does not have a phase shift. Thus we compare $f(x)$

and $f(-x)$.

$$f(x) = -3 \tan 2\pi x \qquad f(-x) = -3 \tan 2\pi(-x) = -3 \tan (-2\pi x)$$
$$= 3 \tan 2\pi x = -(-3 \tan 2\pi x)$$

In the simplification on the right we remembered that $\tan (-kx) = -\tan kx$. Since $f(x) = -3 \tan 2\pi x$ and $f(-x) = -(-3 \tan 2\pi x)$, we see that $f(-x) = -f(x)$ and that **the function is an odd function.**

Example 77.5   Are (*a*) $f(x) = e^x$ and (*b*) $g(x) = e^{-x^2}$ even functions, odd functions, or neither?

Solution   (*a*) We compare $f(x)$ and $f(-x)$.

$$f(x) = e^x \qquad f(-x) = e^{-x}$$

For $f(x)$ to be even, $f(-x)$ would have to equal e^x. For $f(x)$ to be odd, $f(-x)$ would have to equal $-e^x$. Since neither of these is true, **the function $f(x)$ is neither even nor odd.**

(*b*) Now we compare $g(x)$ and $g(-x)$.

$$g(x) = e^{-x^2} \qquad g(-x) = e^{-(-x)^2} = e^{-x^2}$$

Since $g(x) = g(-x)$, **the function $g(x)$ is an even function.**

Example 77.6   If $g(x) = \dfrac{x^2 + \cos x}{\sin x}$, is $g(x)$ an odd function, an even function, or neither?

Solution   We compare $g(x)$ and $g(-x)$.

$$g(x) = \frac{x^2 + \cos x}{\sin x} \qquad g(-x) = \frac{(-x)^2 + \cos (-x)}{\sin (-x)}$$

We remember that $\cos (-x) = \cos x$ and $\sin (-x) = -\sin x$, so on the right we have

$$g(-x) = \frac{x^2 + \cos x}{-\sin x} = -\left(\frac{x^2 + \cos x}{\sin x}\right)$$

Since

$$-\left(\frac{x^2 + \cos x}{\sin x}\right) \quad \text{is the negative of} \quad \frac{x^2 + \cos x}{\sin x}$$

the function is an odd function.

Problem set 77   1. A box-shaped building with a square base, a square top, and rectangular sides is to be constructed. The volume of the building is to be 300 cubic meters. The concrete to be used for the base costs \$8 per square meter, the concrete for the roof costs \$4 per square meter, and the concrete for the walls costs \$15 per square meter. Find the dimensions of the building which can be constructed for the lowest cost.

2. An object is dropped from a height of 400 feet. Use the fact that the acceleration due to gravity is 32 ft/sec² downward to develop an equation which expresses the height of the object as a function of the time t after the ball is dropped.

Use the definition of odd and even functions to determine whether each of the following functions is odd, even, or neither.

3. $f(x) = x^6 - x^2 + 5$ 4. $g(x) = x^3 - 2x$

5. $h(x) = e^x$ 6. $F(x) = e^{-\pi x^2}$

7. $G(x) = \dfrac{x + \sin x}{\cos x}$

8. The definite integral

$$\int_0^\pi (\sin x)e^{\cos x}\, dx$$

is equal to which of the following definite integrals?

(a) $\displaystyle\int_0^\pi e^u\, du$ (b) $\displaystyle\int_1^{-1} e^u\, du$

(c) $-\displaystyle\int_1^{-1} e^u\, du$ (d) $-\displaystyle\int_{-1}^1 e^u\, du$

Find:

9. $\dfrac{d}{dx} \dfrac{2\sqrt{x + 1}}{x^2 + \sin^3 2x}$

10. $\dfrac{d}{dx}\left(\arcsin 3x - \dfrac{1}{4}\sin^4 3x\right)$

Integrate:

11. $\displaystyle\int \cos 3x \sin^3 3x\, dx$

12. $\displaystyle\int x(x^3 + 1)\, dx$ (Multiply out first.)

13. Find the area enclosed by the graph of $x = 1 - y$ and the graph of $x = -1 + y^2$.

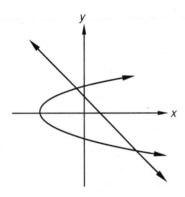

14. Use y as the variable of integration to write a definite integral whose value equals the area of the region completely enclosed by the graph of $x = 4 - y^2$ and the y axis.

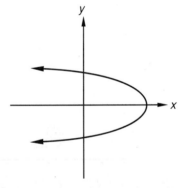

15. Approximate to two decimal places the value of x for which f attains its maximum and minimum values on the interval $[-1, 5]$ if $f(x) = x(x - 2)(x - 5)$.

16. Suppose f is continuous on $[-1, 4]$ and has the properties listed in the table below.

x	$x = -1$	$-1 < x < 2$	$x = 2$	$2 < x < 4$	$x = 4$
$f(x)$	3	....	-3	....	-6
$f'(x)$	....	negative	-1	negative	....
$f''(x)$	....	positive	0	negative	....

Sketch a graph of f and determine the maximum and minimum values of f.

17. Suppose $f(t) = Ae^t + B$, $f(0) = 5$, and $f'(0) = 10$. Find the values of A and B.

18. Suppose both f and g are functions which are continuous on [1, 4] and $f(x) > g(x)$ on [1, 4]. Express the area bounded by the graphs of f and g on [1, 4] as a definite integral.

19. If the f equation is $y = x^3 + x$, find $f^{-1}(2)$.

CONCEPT REVIEW   **20.** Suppose we are given a rectangle whose area remains 200 m² as both its width W and length L change with respect to time. Find an equation which relates W, dL/dt, and dW/dt and which does not contain L.

21. Express $y = 2^x$ as an exponential whose base is e.

LESSON 78 *Integration by parts*

Integration by parts is a procedure that will permit us to find the integrals of some products. If it worked for all products, we would call it the product rule for integration. The rule is simply a rearrangement of the results we get when we find the differential of a product. If u and v are both functions, the differential of the product uv is

$$d(uv) = u\,dv + v\,du$$

If we integrate both sides, we get

$$\int d(uv) = \int u\,dv + \int v\,du$$

Since the integral of $d(uv)$ is uv, we can write

$$uv = \int u\,dv + \int v\,du$$

Now, if we rearrange this expression, we get

$$\int u\,dv = uv - \int v\,du$$

This equation gives us an alternative method of finding the integral of $u\,dv$. We find the product of u times v and subtract from this product the integral of $v\,du$. When we use this rule, the trick is selecting u and dv. If it is possible to select u and dv so that the integral of $v\,du$ is no more difficult than the original integral, then integration by parts may be possible in one step or in several steps. In this lesson we will consider expressions that can be integrated in one step.

The u's, v's, du's, and dv's can cause confusion, and many people use a box to keep things straight. On the left at the top of the following page, we show the basic box. The original integral $u\,dv$ is on one diagonal. The equivalent expression is the product of the two boxes on top minus the integral of the product of the expressions on the other diagonal. Each time we begin by selecting u and dv as shown on the right. Then we write the differential of u below u and the integral of dv above dv.

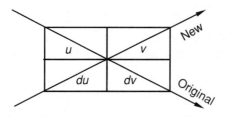

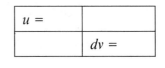

Integration by parts works especially well for expressions such as

$$\int xe^x \, dx \qquad \int xe^{2x} \, dx \qquad \int 2x \sin x \, dx$$

In these expressions the proper choice is to let x or $2x$ equal u and to let the rest of the expression equal dv.

Example 78.1   Find $\int x \sin x \, dx$.

Solution   We will use integration by parts. On the left we draw the box and let x equal u and let the rest of the expression equal dv. Then we find du and v and put them in the box, as we show on the right.

$u = x$	
	$dv = \sin x \, dx$

$u = x$	$v = -\cos x$
$du = dx$	$dv = \sin x \, dx$

Now we can use the rule for integration by parts.

$$\int u \, dv = uv - \int v \, du$$

We substitute as indicated and get

$$\int x \sin x \, dx = (x)(-\cos x) - \int -\cos x \, dx$$

$$= -x \cos x + \sin x + C$$

As always, we can check our result by differentiating.

$$\frac{d}{dx}(-x \cos x + \sin x + C) = -[x(-\sin x) + \cos x] + \cos x$$

$$= x \sin x - \cos x + \cos x = x \sin x$$

Example 78.2   Find $\int \ln x \, dx$.

Solution   The correct choice in this problem is to let $\ln x$ equal u, as we show on the left.

$u = \ln x$	
	$dv = dx$

$u = \ln x$	$v = x$
$du = \dfrac{dx}{x}$	$dv = dx$

On the right we complete the box by finding du and v. Now we write the rule for integration by parts.

$$\int u\,dv = uv - \int v\,du$$

Next we substitute as indicated and complete the solution.

$$\int \ln x\,dx = x \ln x - \int (\cancel{x})\left(\frac{dx}{\cancel{x}}\right)$$

$$= x \ln x - x + C$$

Example 78.3   Find $\int xe^{2x}\,dx$.

Solution   We let x equal u and let $e^{2x}\,dx$ equal dv.

$u = x$	
	$dv = e^{2x}\,dx$

$u = x$	$v = \dfrac{1}{2}e^{2x}$
$du = dx$	$dv = e^{2x}\,dx$

On the right we completed the box by finding du and v. Now we write the rule for integration by parts.

$$\int u\,dv = uv - \int v\,du$$

Next we substitute and complete the solution.

$$\int xe^{2x}\,dx = (x)\left(\frac{1}{2}e^{2x}\right) - \frac{1}{2}\int e^{2x}\,dx \qquad \text{substituted}$$

$$= \frac{1}{2}xe^{2x} - \frac{1}{2}\left(\frac{1}{2}\right)\int e^{2x}(2)\,dx \qquad \text{rearranged}$$

$$= \frac{1}{2}xe^{2x} - \frac{1}{4}e^{2x} + C \qquad \text{integrated}$$

Example 78.4   Find $\int 2x \sin x\,dx$.

Solution   The correct choice for u is $2x$.

$u = 2x$	
	$dv = \sin x\,dx$

$u = 2x$	$v = -\cos x$
$du = 2\,dx$	$dv = \sin x\,dx$

Now we can look at the box and use the rule for integration by parts to write

$$\int 2x \sin x\,dx = (2x)(-\cos x) - \int (-\cos x)(2\,dx) \qquad \text{expression}$$

$$= -2x \cos x + 2 \int \cos x\,dx \qquad \text{rearranged}$$

$$= -2x \cos x + 2 \sin x + C \qquad \text{integrated}$$

Problem set 78

1. A rectangle whose sides are changing in length has a constant area of 1000 square meters. Find the length of the rectangle when its width is decreasing at a rate of 1 m/sec and its length is increasing at a rate of 10 m/sec.

2. The interest was compounded continuously, so the growth of the money in the bank account was exponential. The initial deposit was $1000, and a year later $1100 was in the account. How much money would be in the account 10 years from the time of the initial deposit?

Use integration by parts to compute the following integrals:

3. $\int xe^x \, dx$

4. $\int \ln x \, dx$

5. $\int x \ln x \, dx$

6. $\int 2x \cos x \, dx$

7. $\int x \sin x \, dx$

8. Determine whether the following function is even, odd, or neither:

$$y = \frac{\sin x \cos x}{x^2}$$

9. Is the graph of $y = x^2 + \cos x$ symmetric about the y axis, the origin, or neither?

10. Find: $\dfrac{d}{dx} \dfrac{xe^{\cos 3x}}{x^3 + 1}$

11. If $y = \arcsin x^2$, find y'.

12. Integrate: $\int \dfrac{\cos x}{\sqrt{\sin x + 1}} \, dx + \int x^{-5} \, dx$

13. Evaluate by using the change of variable method: $\displaystyle\int_0^{\pi/4} (\cos 2x)(e^{\sin 2x}) \, dx$

14. Find the area of the region bounded by the graphs of $y = 1 + x$, $y = -x^2$, and the lines $x = 1$ and $x = 3$.

15. Find the area of the region completely enclosed by the graphs of $y = 2 - x^2$ and $y = x$.

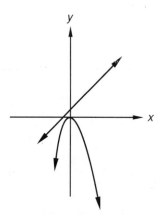

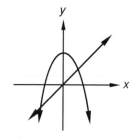

16. Write a definite integral whose value equals the area of the region in the fourth quadrant bounded by $x = y(y - 1)(y + 2)$.

17. Evaluate $f^{-1}(3)$ if $f(x) = 4x - 12$.

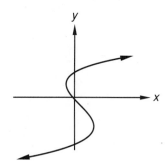

18. If $\displaystyle\int_{-1}^{5} f(x)\, dx = 7$ and $\displaystyle\int_{-1}^{3} f(x)\, dx = -3$, find $\displaystyle\int_{3}^{5} f(x)\, dx$.

CONCEPT REVIEW   19. The function $f(x) = \ln(\cos x)$ is defined for all x in which of the following intervals?

(a) $0 < x < \dfrac{\pi}{2}$ (b) $-\dfrac{\pi}{2} \le x \le \dfrac{\pi}{2}$ (c) $0 < x \le 2\pi$

(d) $-\pi \le x \le \dfrac{\pi}{2}$

20. Indicate which of the following equations describes a curve which satisfies the following property: For every point (x, y) which lies on the curve, $(-x, -y)$ also lies on the curve.

(a) $x^2 + y = x$ (b) $x^2 + y^2 = 1$ (c) $y = 2x + 1$ (d) $x^3 + y^3 = 1$

LESSON 79 *Properties of limits · Some special limits*

79.A
Properties
of limits

We remember that the limit of a function f as x approaches c is the **number** that $f(x)$ approaches as x gets closer and closer to c. We can extend what we have learned about the limits of functions to the limits of sums, products, and differences of functions. The rules for these extensions will be presented without proof. For concrete illustrations of these rules, we will use the functions f and g as defined here.

$$f(x) = x + 1 \qquad g(x) = x^2 + 3$$

The limit of f as x approaches 2 is 3, and the limit of g as x approaches 2 is 7.

$$\lim_{x \to 2} x + 1 = 3 \qquad \lim_{x \to 2} x^2 + 3 = 7$$

To make a general statement, we will let x approach c and let the limit of f be L and let the limit of g be M.

$$\lim_{x \to c} f(x) = L \qquad \lim_{x \to c} g(x) = M$$

1. **The limit of the sum of two functions equals the sum of the limits of the individual functions.**

$$\lim_{x \to 2} [(x + 1) + (x^2 + 3)] = 3 + 7 \qquad \lim_{x \to c} (f + g)(x) = L + M$$

It is important to realize that $(f + g)(x)$ is a new function that equals the sum of the original functions. In this example if we add the f function to the g function, we get $f + g$,

$$(f + g)(x) = x^2 + x + 4$$

and the limit of this new function as x approaches 2 is 10, which equals the sum of the individual limits 7 and 3.

$$\lim_{x \to 2} x^2 + x + 4 = 10$$

2. **The limit of the difference of two functions equals the difference of the limits of the individual functions.**

$$\lim_{x \to 2} [(x + 1) - (x^2 + 3)] = 3 - 7 \qquad \lim_{x \to c} (f - g)(x) = L - M$$

3. **The limit of the product of two functions equals the product of the limits of the individual functions.**

$$\lim_{x \to 2} [(x + 1)(x^2 + 3)] = 3 \cdot 7 \qquad \lim_{x \to c} (fg)(x) = LM$$

4. **The limit of the product of a constant and a function equals the product of the constant times the limit of the function.**

$$\lim_{x \to 2} 9(x + 1) = 9 \cdot 3 \qquad \lim_{x \to c} kf(x) = kL$$

5. **If the limit of the denominator does not equal zero, the limit of the quotient of two functions equals the quotient of the individual limits.**

$$\lim_{x \to 2} \frac{x + 1}{x^2 + 3} = \frac{3}{7} \qquad \lim_{x \to c} \frac{f}{g}(x) = \frac{L}{M}$$

6. **If the value of a function $g(x)$ is greater than the value of a second function $f(x)$ and less than the value of a third function $h(x)$ and if $f(x)$ and $h(x)$ both approach the same limit L as x approaches c, then $g(x)$ also approaches L as x approaches c.** This property is called the *pinching theorem* or the *sandwich theorem* because the limit of $g(x)$ is "pinched" or "sandwiched" between the limits of $f(x)$ and $h(x)$. For example, if the following inequality is true for all x in some interval,

$$f(x) \le g(x) \le h(x)$$

and $f(x)$ and $h(x)$ both approach 5 as x approaches some number c, then $g(x)$ is greater than $f(x)$ and less than $h(x)$ and is trapped between two expressions that are approaching 5. Thus $g(x)$ must also be approaching 5. Of course, the number c must be contained in the interval for which this inequality is true.

Example 79.1 If

$$\lim_{x \to 2} f(x) = 3 \quad \text{and} \quad \lim_{x \to 2} g(x) = 9$$

find

$$\lim_{x \to 2} [2f(x) + \pi g(x)]$$

Solution This problem requires that we use two rules. The first is that the limit of a sum equals the sum of the limits. Thus

$$\lim_{x \to 2} [2f(x) + \pi g(x)] = \lim_{x \to 2} 2f(x) + \lim_{x \to 2} \pi g(x)$$

The second is that the limit of the product of a constant and a function equals the product of the constant and the limit of the function. Thus the limit of $2f(x)$ is 2 times the limit of $f(x)$, or $2 \cdot 3$, and the limit of $\pi g(x)$ is π times the limit of $g(x)$, or $\pi \cdot 9$.

$$\lim_{x \to 2} 2f(x) + \lim_{x \to 2} \pi g(x) = 2 \cdot 3 + \pi \cdot 9 = \mathbf{6 + 9\pi}$$

Example 79.2 If $\lim_{x \to a} f(x) = L$, can we say that $f(a)$ exists?

Solution This problem is typical of problems that appear on standardized tests requiring calculus. In order to answer these questions, a complete understanding of the concept is required. Future problem sets will contain tricky questions like this one to enable students to develop the understanding that will allow these questions to be answered with confidence. To answer this question, we need to know that the limit of $f(x)$ as x approaches a is a statement about what happens at values of x close to a and has nothing to do with $f(a)$, which is the value of f when $x = a$. **Thus the fact that the limit exists does not imply that $f(a)$ exists.**

Example 79.3   Is the following statement true? Why?

$$\text{If} \quad \lim_{x \to 3} f(x) = L \qquad \text{then} \qquad f(3) = L$$

Solution   **The statement is false** because the value of the function when $x = 3$ does not have to equal the limit of the function as x approaches 3. Consider the following graph.

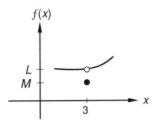

The graph shows that the limit as x approaches 3 is L and also shows that $f(3)$ equals M and does not equal L.

Example 79.4   If f is a function such that $-x^2 \le f(x) \le x^2$ for all values of x, evaluate $\lim_{x \to 0} f(x)$.

Solution   The function f is sandwiched between $-x^2$ and $+x^2$. As x approaches zero, both of these functions approach zero, so **$f(x)$ must also approach zero.**

79.B
Some special limits

We remember that the limit of a function is a **number unless the limit is $\pm\infty$.** The function $1/x$ has no limit as x approaches zero because the left-hand limit does not equal the right-hand limit.

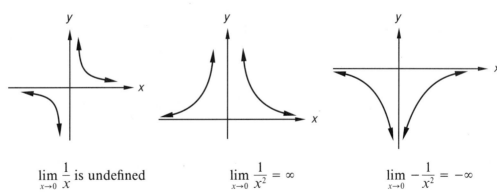

$$\lim_{x \to 0} \frac{1}{x} \text{ is undefined} \qquad \lim_{x \to 0} \frac{1}{x^2} = \infty \qquad \lim_{x \to 0} -\frac{1}{x^2} = -\infty$$

We say that the function $1/x^2$ has a limit of $+\infty$ as x approaches zero because the value of the function increases positively without bound as x approaches zero from both the left and the right. We use similar reasoning to say that the limit of $-1/x^2$ is $-\infty$ as x approaches zero.

Most of the functions that we work with are well-behaved functions. If we need a function whose behavior is somewhat aberrant, we usually design a piecewise function that has the desired behavior. But this is not always necessary since the following two functions are famous for not having limits as x approaches zero.

$$y = \frac{|x|}{x} \qquad y = \sin \frac{1}{x}$$

The graphs of the functions allow us to see why. If x is a positive number, the graph of the absolute value of x divided by x is the line $y = 1$, and if x is a negative number, the graph is the line $y = -1$. When $x = 0$, the function is not defined.

$$y = \frac{|x|}{x}$$

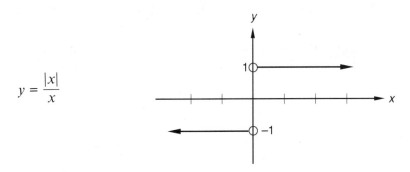

Thus, for all values of $x > 0$, $f(x) = 1$. For all values of $x < 0$, $f(x) = -1$. Since the left-hand limit and the right-hand limit are not equal, the function does not have a limit as x approaches zero.

The limit of $\sin (1/x)$ also does not exist as x approaches zero. The value of the sine function is never greater than $+1$ or less than -1. As x gets closer to zero, a small change in x produces a large change in $1/x$. Thus the closer x gets to zero the "faster" the value of $\sin (1/x)$ fluctuates between -1 and $+1$.

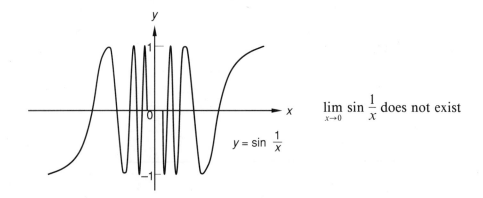

$$\lim_{x \to 0} \sin \frac{1}{x} \text{ does not exist}$$

$$y = \sin \frac{1}{x}$$

The graph of the function was terminated arbitrarily on both sides of zero, because the continuation would be impossible to draw.

Problem set 79

1. A ball is thrown straight up from the top of a building that is 100 meters tall with an initial velocity of 10 meters per second. Develop an equation which expresses the height of the ball above the ground as a function of time, $h(t)$. Find $h(3)$. How long would it take for the ball to hit the ground?

2. Use the critical number theorem to find the absolute maximum and minimum values of $y = x^{2/3}$ on the interval $[-1, 2]$. (*Note:* Only the graph of the function is needed to determine its critical numbers.)

3. Suppose f is a real quadratic function whose graph passes through $(0, 2)$, whose slope at $x = 1$ is 5, and whose slope at $x = -1$ is -1. Find the equation of f.

Evaluate the following limits if they exist. Limits of ∞ and $-\infty$ are acceptable.

4. $\lim\limits_{x \to 0} \sin \dfrac{1}{x}$

5. $\lim\limits_{x \to 0^+} \dfrac{|x|}{x}$

6. $\lim\limits_{x \to 0} \dfrac{1}{x}$

7. $\lim\limits_{x \to 0} \dfrac{1}{x^2}$

Suppose f and g are functions such that $\lim\limits_{x \to 2} f(x) = 3$, $\lim\limits_{x \to 2} g(x) = -2$, $\lim\limits_{x \to -1} f(x) = \pi$, and $\lim\limits_{x \to -1} g(x) = 5$. Evaluate the following limits.

8. $\lim\limits_{x \to 2} f(x)g(x)$

9. $\lim\limits_{x \to -1} 2[f(x)]^2$

10. $\lim\limits_{x \to 2} \dfrac{f(x) + g(x)}{f(x)\, g(x)}$

11. If f is a function such that $-x^2 + 1 \le f(x) \le x^2 + 1$ for all real values of x, evaluate $\lim\limits_{x \to 0} f(x)$.

12. Suppose that g is a function and that $\lim\limits_{x \to 2} g(x) = 4$. Does $g(2) = 4$? Explain your answer.

Integrate:

13. $\displaystyle\int 3x \sin x \, dx$

14. $\displaystyle\int 2xe^{2x} \, dx$

15. $\displaystyle\int \ln x \, dx$

16. Which of the following equations describes a curve which is symmetric about the y axis?
(a) $y = e^{x^2}$ (b) $y = x^3$ (c) $y = \sin x$ (d) $y = e^x$

17. Find the area of the region completely enclosed by the graph of $y = 1 - x^2$ and $y = x + 1$.

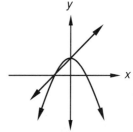

18. The value of $\displaystyle\int_1^2 x \ln (x^2 + 1) \, dx$ is equal to which of these definite integrals?
(a) $\displaystyle\int_1^2 \ln u \, du$ (b) $\dfrac{1}{2}\displaystyle\int_{\ln 5}^{\ln 2} \ln u \, du$
(c) $\dfrac{1}{2}\displaystyle\int_2^5 \ln u \, du$ (d) $\dfrac{1}{2}\displaystyle\int_{\ln 2}^{\ln 5} u \ln u \, du$

19. If $y = \dfrac{e^{\cos x} \sin x}{\ln 2x} - \arctan 2x$, find y'.

Integrate:

20. $\displaystyle\int (x + 1)e^{x^2+2x} \, dx$

21. $\displaystyle\int x \sin (x^2 + \pi) \, dx$

CONCEPT REVIEW   **22.** A rectangle of width w and height d is inscribed in a circle of radius 6. Express wd^2 entirely in terms of w.

23. Express $y = \log_3 x$ in terms of the natural logarithm.

LESSON 80 *Solids of revolution*

If we revolve a planar region about a line in the same plane, we form a figure that is called a ***solid of revolution.*** The line is called the ***axis of revolution.*** We will begin by looking at solids with circular cross sections that are formed by rotating planar regions about either the x axis or the y axis. The volume of these solids can be approximated by the sum of the volumes of n circular disks. The area of each disk is πr^2. The thickness is Δx if the x axis is the axis of revolution. The thickness is Δy if the y axis is the axis of revolution. Thus the volume of each disk is either

$$\pi r^2\, \Delta x \qquad \text{or} \qquad \pi r^2\, \Delta y$$

On the left we show a region that is bounded by the graph of f. Next we show the solid of revolution formed if the region is rotated about the x axis. The next figure shows the disk approximation of this volume.

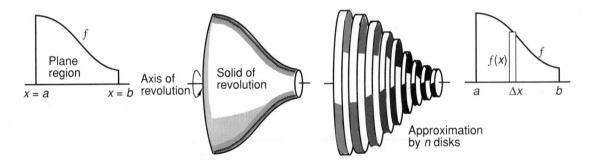

The right-hand figure shows a side view of half of a representative disk. The width of the disk is Δx, and the radius r of the disk is $f(x)$. The sum of n disks is represented in summation notation below on the left.

$$\text{Approximate volume} = \sum_{i=1}^{n} \pi(f(x_i))^2\, \Delta x \qquad \text{Exact volume} = \int_a^b \pi(f(x))^2\, dx$$

The exact volume is represented by the limit of this sum as Δx approaches zero, which is the integral shown on the right.

Example 80.1 Find the volume of the solid formed by revolving this triangular region about the x axis.

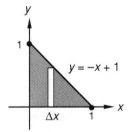

Solution The graph shows a side view of half of a representative disk. The thickness of the disk is Δx, and the radius of the disk is the height of the rectangle, which is $-x + 1$. We will mentally stack these disks from the y axis to $x = 1$, so our limits of integration will be 0 and 1.

$$\text{Volume} = \int_0^1 \pi r^2\, dx = \pi \int_0^1 (-x + 1)^2\, dx = \pi \int_0^1 (x^2 - 2x + 1)\, dx$$

Now we integrate and evaluate and get

$$\text{Volume} = \pi \left[\frac{x^3}{3} - x^2 + x\right]_0^1 = \pi \left(\frac{1}{3} - 1 + 1\right) = \frac{\pi}{3} \text{ units}^3$$

Example 80.2   Find the volume of the solid formed by rotating about the y axis the first-quadrant region bounded by the line $y = 3$ and the graph of $y = x^2$.

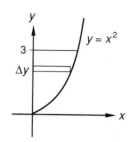

Solution   The representative disk has a thickness Δy and a radius equal to the x value of the right end of the rectangle. Since $y = x^2$, the x value of the end of the rectangle is $x = \sqrt{y}$. We will mentally stack these disks from the x axis to $y = 3$, so the limits of integration will be 0 and 3.

$$\text{Volume} = \int_0^3 \pi r^2 \, dy = \pi \int_0^3 (\sqrt{y})^2 \, dy = \pi \int_0^3 y \, dy$$

Now we integrate and evaluate to get

$$\text{Volume} = \pi \left[\frac{y^2}{2}\right]_0^3 = \frac{9\pi}{2} \text{ units}^3$$

Example 80.3   Find the volume of the solid formed by rotating about the y axis the first-quadrant region of the circle whose equation is $x^2 + y^2 = k^2$.

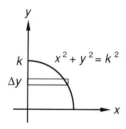

Solution   The solid will be half a sphere whose radius is k. The volume of a sphere is $\frac{4}{3}\pi k^3$, so our result should be half of this, or $\frac{2}{3}\pi k^3$. The thickness of each disk will be Δy, and we will mentally stack the disks from the x axis to $y = k$. The radius of each disk will be the x value of the end of the rectangle, which is $\sqrt{k^2 - y^2}$.

$$\text{Volume} = \int_0^k \pi r^2 \, dy = \pi \int_0^k (\sqrt{k^2 - y^2})^2 \, dy = \pi \int (k^2 - y^2) \, dy$$

Now we integrate and evaluate to get

$$\text{Volume} = \pi \left[k^2 y - \frac{y^3}{3}\right]_0^k = \pi k^3 - \frac{\pi k^3}{3} = \frac{2\pi k^3}{3} \text{ units}^3$$

Since the volume of a sphere is twice the volume of our half-sphere solid of revolution, we have used calculus to develop the formula for the volume of a sphere of radius k.

$$\text{Volume of a sphere} = 2 \left(\frac{2\pi k^3}{3}\right) = \frac{4}{3}\pi k^3 \text{ units}^3$$

Problem set 80

1. A beam of rectangular cross section is cut from a log of radius 6 as shown. The strength of the beam varies jointly with w and the square of d, where w and d are as shown. Thus $s = kwd^2$, where k is a constant. Find the value of w which maximizes the strength of the beam, assuming the log is cylindrical with circular cross section.

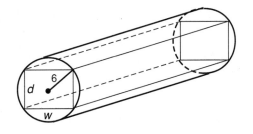

2. A variable force is applied to an object to move it along a number line. The force applied at a particular value of x is

$$F(x) = \frac{1}{2}x^2 \text{ newtons}$$

What is the work done by the force on the object to move it from $x = 1$ meter to $x = 3$ meters?

3. Find the volume of the solid formed when the triangular region shown is revolved around the x axis.

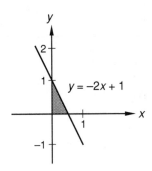

$y = -2x + 1$

4. Find the volume of the solid formed when the region shown is revolved around the y axis.

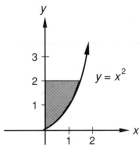

$y = x^2$

5. Suppose R is the first-quadrant region bounded by the circle $x^2 + y^2 = 4$. Use y as the variable of integration and the disk method to write an integral whose value equals the volume of the solid formed when R is revolved about the y axis.

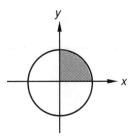

Suppose f and g are functions such that $\lim_{x \to \pi} f(x) = 2$, $\lim_{x \to \pi} g(x) = \frac{1}{3}$, $\lim_{x \to -\pi} f(x) = -2$, and $\lim_{x \to -\pi} g(x) = 2$. Evaluate the following limits.

6. $\lim_{x \to \pi} \dfrac{2f(x)}{g(x)}$

7. $\lim_{x \to -\pi} \pi[f(x)]^2$

8. $\lim_{x \to \pi} [3f(x) - g(x)]$

9. If $-|x| \le f(x) \le |x|$, evaluate $\lim_{x \to 0} f(x)$.

Integrate:

10. $\displaystyle \int xe^{2x}\, dx$

11. $\displaystyle \int 3x \sin x\, dx$

12. $\displaystyle \int 2x \ln x\, dx$

13. Let R be the area in the first quadrant bounded by the coordinate axis and the graph of a unit circle whose center is the origin. Use y as the variable of integration to write an integral whose value equals the area of R.

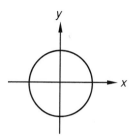

14. Suppose $f(x) = x^3$, $g(x) = x^2 + 1$, and $h(x) = f(x)g(x)$. Determine whether the graph of h is symmetric about the y axis, symmetric about the origin, or neither.

Differentiate:

15. $y = \text{arccsc}\ \dfrac{x}{4}$ $(x > 0)$ **16.** $y = \arctan e^x + \dfrac{\sqrt{2x + 1}}{\sin x - x}$

Integrate:

17. $\displaystyle\int x^2 e^{x^3}\ dx$ **18.** $\displaystyle\int (\cos x)(\sin^3 x + 1)\ dx$

19. If $f(x) = 4x - 5$, find the equation for $f^{-1}(x)$.

CONCEPT REVIEW   **20.** The real number remainder when the polynomial $f(x)$ is divided by $(x - 3)$ is which of the following?
      (a) $f(3)$ (b) $f(-3)$ (c) $f(0)$
      (d) Cannot be determined unless more information is given

21. Which of the following equations has a graph which is symmetric with respect to the origin?

     (a) $y = x^2$ (b) $y = \cos x$ (c) $y = \dfrac{x - 1}{x}$ (d) $y = 2\sin x$

LESSON 81   *Derivatives and integrals of a^x and $\log_a x$ · Derivative of $|x|$*

81.A
Derivative and integral of a^x

We remember that the derivative of e^x is e^x. If the base is some other positive number, say 42, the derivative has another factor that is the natural logarithm of the base.

$$\frac{d}{dx}\ 42^x = (\ln 42)42^x$$

To see why this additional factor is necessary, we note that e^{kx} has the form e^u, so the derivative of e^{kx} is e^{kx} times the derivative of kx.

$$\frac{d}{dx}\ e^{kx} = ke^{kx}$$

Since any positive number can be written as e raised to the appropriate power, we can write 42 as

$$42 = e^{\ln 42}$$

If we substitute $e^{\ln 42}$ for 42 in the expression 42^x, we get an expression whose form is e^{kx}.

$$42^x = (e^{\ln 42})^x = e^{(\ln 42)x}$$

Thus we find the derivative of 42^x as follows.

$$\frac{d}{dx}\, 42^x = \frac{d}{dx}\, e^{(\ln 42)x} = (\ln 42)e^{(\ln 42)x}$$

Now as the last step we remember that $e^{\ln 42} = 42$, so we write

$$\frac{d}{dx}\, 42^x = (\ln 42)42^x$$

In this illustration we used 42 as the base of an exponential function for a concrete example of the method of finding the derivative of a positive constant raised to the x power. From this development we see that if we use a instead of 42 we can write the rule for the derivative of a^x as follows.

$$\frac{d}{dx}\, a^x = (\ln a)a^x$$

Example 81.1   Find $\displaystyle\int 143^x\, dx$.

Solution   We guess that the answer is $143^x + C$. Now we check our guess.

$$\frac{d}{dx}(143^x + C) = (\ln 143)143^x$$

Thus our integral needs another factor of $\ln 143$, so we can write

$$\int 143^x\, dx = \frac{1}{\ln 143}\int (\ln 143)143^x\, dx = \frac{\mathbf{143^x}}{\mathbf{\ln 143}} + C$$

Example 81.2   If $y = 42^{(x^2 - 5x)}$, find $\dfrac{dy}{dx}$.

Solution   The derivative of 42^x is $(\ln 42)42^x$, but this derivative is in the form of 42^u, so we also need an additional factor of the derivative of $x^2 - 5x$.

$$\frac{d}{dx}\, 42^{(x^2 - 5x)} = (\ln 42)42^{(x^2 - 5x)}\, (2x - 5)$$

$$= \mathbf{(\ln 42)(2x - 5)42^{(x^2 - 5x)}}$$

Example 81.3   Find $\displaystyle\int xa^{x^2 - 2}\, dx$.

Solution   Let's guess $a^{x^2 - 2}$ and check our guess by finding its derivative.

$$\frac{d}{dx}\, a^{x^2 - 2} = (\ln a)(a^{x^2 - 2})(2x)$$

Thus we see we need additional factors of 2 and $\ln a$, which we supply.

$$\frac{1}{2 \ln a}\int (\ln a)(2)(x)a^{x^2 - 2}\, dx = \frac{1}{\mathbf{2 \ln a}}\, \mathbf{a}^{x^2 - 2} + C$$

81.B
Derivative and integral of log_a x

The logarithm of a number to any base b can be found by multiplying (dividing) the natural logarithm of the number by the appropriate constant. Before we differentiate or integrate a logarithmic function, we will change the base to e.

$$\log_b x = \frac{\ln x}{\ln b}$$

Example 81.4 If $y = \log_{42} x + \log_{10} x + \log_5 x$, find y'.

Solution First we change the base of each function.

$$y = \frac{\ln x}{\ln 42} + \frac{\ln x}{\ln 10} + \frac{\ln x}{\ln 5} = \frac{\ln x}{3.74} + \frac{\ln x}{2.30} + \frac{\ln x}{1.61}$$

Now we use the calculator to add the coefficients and get

$$y = (0.27 + 0.43 + 0.62)(\ln x) \longrightarrow y = 1.32 \ln x$$

Now we can find y'.

$$y = 1.32 \ln x \longrightarrow y' = 1.32\left(\frac{1}{x}\right) = \frac{\mathbf{1.32}}{\mathbf{x}}$$

Example 81.5 Find $\int \log_{23} x \, dx$.

Solution First we will change the base to e.

$$\int \log_{23} x \, dx = \int \frac{\ln x}{\ln 23} \, dx = \int \frac{\ln x}{3.14} \, dx = 0.32 \int \ln x \, dx$$

We remember that we use integration by parts to find the integral of the natural logarithm. We let $1 \, dx$ be dv and $\ln x$ be u.

$$0.32 \int \underbrace{\ln x}_{u} \underbrace{dx}_{dv} = 0.32 \left[\underbrace{(\ln x)}_{u}\underbrace{(x)}_{v} - \int \underbrace{x}_{v} \underbrace{\frac{dx}{x}}_{du} \right]$$

$$= \mathbf{0.32(x \ln x - x) + C}$$

81.C
Derivative of |x|

The absolute value notation changes negative quantities to positive quantities.

$$|-7| = 7 \qquad |-4.2| = 4.2 \qquad |-50| = 50$$

The absolute value notation is totally redundant if the quantities equal zero or are always positive.

$$|0| = 0 \qquad |4| = 4 \qquad |\sqrt{x^2 - 4}| = \sqrt{x^2 - 4} \qquad |4 - \sin 3x^2| = 4 - \sin 3x^2$$

The numbers 4 and 0 are unchanged by the absolute value notation. The expression $\sqrt{x^2 - 4}$ always represents the number zero or a positive number because the expression is not defined for values of x that cause $x^2 - 4$ to be negative. The value of $-\sin 3x^2$ varies between $+1$ and -1, and thus $4 - \sin 3x^2$ is always positive. The absolute value notation is most useful to define a function that would require a piecewise definition if the notation were not used. **The derivative of the absolute value of a function equals the derivative of the function on the intervals where the function is positive and equals the negative of the derivative of the function on the**

intervals where the function is negative. The derivative does not exist at an x value of c if the derivative of the absolute value function just to the left of c is not approximately equal to the value of the derivative just to the right of c.

Example 81.6   If $y = |x + 2|$ find $\dfrac{dy}{dx}$.

Solution   We redefine the function without using absolute value notation. Then we graph the function.

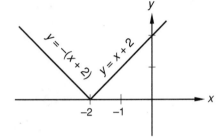

$$y = |x + 2| \text{ means } \begin{cases} y = x + 2 & \text{if } x > -2 \\ y = 0 & \text{if } x = -2 \\ y = -(x + 2) & \text{if } x < -2 \end{cases}$$

The derivative of $|x + 2|$ where x is greater than -2 is the derivative of $x + 2$, which is $+1$. The derivative of $|x + 2|$ where x is less than -2 is the negative of the derivative of $x + 2$, which is -1. The derivative does not exist at $x = -2$.

$$\frac{d}{dx}|x + 2| = 1 \qquad \text{if } x > -2$$

$$\frac{d}{dx}|x + 2| \text{ does not exist} \qquad \text{if } x = -2$$

$$\frac{d}{dx}|x + 2| = -1 \qquad \text{if } x < -2$$

Example 81.7   If $f(x) = |\sqrt{x^2 - 4}|$, find $f'(x)$.

Solution   This use of the absolute value notation is totally redundant because the expression $\sqrt{x^2 - 4}$ is never negative. This function is not defined for values of x that are between -2 and 2 and is positive for all values of x that are less than -2 or are greater than 2.

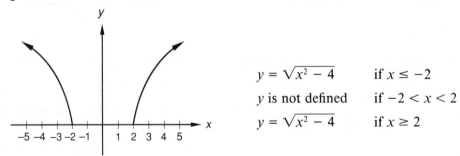

$$y = \sqrt{x^2 - 4} \qquad \text{if } x \le -2$$
$$y \text{ is not defined} \qquad \text{if } -2 < x < 2$$
$$y = \sqrt{x^2 - 4} \qquad \text{if } x \ge 2$$

$$y = \sqrt{x^2 - 4}$$

The derivative of $y = \sqrt{x^2 - 4}$ does not exist when x is between -2 and $+2$ inclusive. For other values of x the derivative is the same as the derivative of $y = \sqrt{x^2 - 4}$.

$$\frac{d}{dx}|\sqrt{x^2 - 4}| = \frac{d}{dx}(x^2 - 4)^{1/2} = \frac{1}{2}(x^2 - 4)^{-1/2}(2x) = \frac{x}{\sqrt{x^2 - 4}}$$

We note that the function is defined at $x = \pm 2$, but the derivative is not defined at $x = \pm 2$.

Example 81.8 If $g(x) = |\sin x|$, find $g'(x)$.

Solution The derivative of $|\sin x|$ is **cos x when sin x is positive.** The derivative of $|\sin x|$ is **$-\cos x$ when sin x is negative. This derivative is not defined when sin $x = 0$.**

Example 81.9 If $y = |x^2 - 4|$, find y'.

Solution A graph is always helpful.

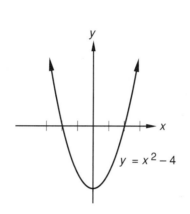

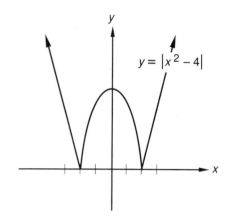

First we redefine the function on the open intervals $(-\infty, -2)$, $(-2, 2)$, and $(2, \infty)$.

On the intervals $(-\infty, -2)$ and $(2, \infty)$, $y = x^2 - 4$

On the interval $(-2, 2)$, $y = -(x^2 - 4)$

The derivatives on these intervals are as follows.

For $(-\infty, -2)$ and $(2, \infty)$, $\dfrac{d}{dx}|x^2 - 4| = \dfrac{d}{dx}(x^2 - 4) = 2x$

For $(-2, 2)$, $\dfrac{d}{dx}|x^2 - 4| = \dfrac{d}{dx}[-(x^2 - 4)] = -2x$

The derivative does not exist at $x = -2$ and $x = 2$ because the derivatives to the immediate left and right of these values of x are very different.

Problem set 81

1. The height and radius of the base of a right circular cone are each increasing at rate of 2 cm/sec. Find the rate at which the volume of the cone is increasing when the radius is 4 cm and the height of the cone is 6 cm.

2. An object is thrown straight downward from a height of 160 m with an initial velocity of 48 m/sec. Develop the velocity function $v(t)$ and the height function $h(t)$. How long does it take for the object to strike the ground?

3. Find the velocity of the object described in Problem 2 the instant before it strikes the ground.

4. Find the slope of the normal line which can be drawn to the graph of $y = \log_2 x$ at $x = 3$.

5. Use the natural logarithm function to write a definite integral whose value equals the area bounded by the x axis and the graph of $y = \log_2 x$ between $x = 2$ and $x = 8$.

6. Approximate to two decimal places the slope of the tangent line which can be drawn to the graph of $y = 3^x$ at $x = 4$. Write the equation of the tangent line.

7. Approximate to two decimal places the area of the region between the graph of $y = 2^x$ and the x axis over the interval $[1, 5]$.

8. Find $\dfrac{dy}{dx}$ if $y = 43^x + 3^x + \log_3 x - \log_{43} x$.

9. Let R be the region bounded by $y = x^3$, $y = 1$, and the y axis. Find the volume of the solid formed when R is revolved about the y axis.

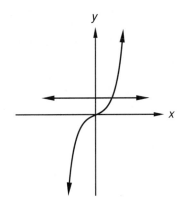

10. Let R be the region bounded by $y = -\frac{1}{2}x + 1$ in the first quadrant. Use x as the variable of integration to write a definite integral whose value equals the volume of the solid formed when R is revolved around the x axis.

11. Let R be the region completely enclosed by the graph of $y = 1 - x^2$ and the x axis. Use y as the variable of integration to write a definite integral whose value equals the volume of the solid formed when R is revolved about the y axis.

Integrate:

12. $\displaystyle\int 3xe^{3x}\, dx$

13. $\displaystyle\int \pi \sin \pi x\, dx$

14. Evaluate by using the change of variable method: $\displaystyle\int_0^3 x\sqrt{x + 1}\, dx$

15. Suppose $h(x) = f(x)g(x)$, $\displaystyle\lim_{x \to \pi} h(x) = \dfrac{1}{\pi}$, and $\displaystyle\lim_{x \to \pi} f(x) = 3$. Evaluate $\displaystyle\lim_{x \to \pi} g(x)$.

16. Suppose $f(x) = \sin x$, $g(x) = x$, and $h(x) = f(x)g(x)$. Determine whether h is an odd function, an even function, or neither.

17. Differentiate: $y = 2\cos^2 x + \arctan 2x + \dfrac{2\sqrt{2x + 1}}{x^2 + 1}$

Integrate:

18. $\displaystyle\int (x + 1)e^{-x^2 - 2x}\, dx$

19. $\displaystyle\int \dfrac{x}{x^2 + 1}\, dx$

CONCEPT REVIEW 20. Boyle's law states that for an ideal gas, if the temperature does not change, the product of the pressure and the volume is constant. The pressure of a quantity of ideal gas was 5 newtons per square meter when the volume was 1000 cubic meters. What was the volume when the pressure was increased to 15 newtons per square meter and the temperature remained constant?

LESSON 82 **Fluid force**

The weight of an object in a gravitational field equals its mass times the local acceleration of gravity, or *mg*. The unit of force in the metric system is the newton, and 1 cubic meter (m³) of water (fresh water at a temperature of 4°C) weighs 9800 newtons. The weight density of an object equals its weight divided by the volume, so the weight density of water is 9800 newtons per cubic meter. On the left we show a cubic meter of water and note that it weighs 9800 newtons.

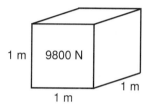   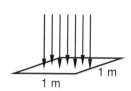

On the right we note that the weight of 9800 newtons is evenly distributed over the 1-square-meter surface at the bottom of the cube, so the average weight of the water at the bottom of the cube (the water pressure) is 9800 newtons per square meter (N/m²). If the water is 3 meters deep, the pressure at the bottom caused by the weight of the water would be 3 times 9800 N/m², or 29,400 N/m², as we show on the left.

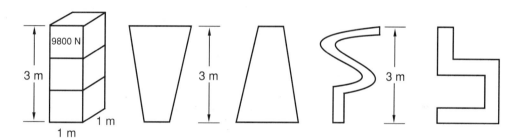

Pascal's principle is a law of physics named for Blaise Pascal (1623–1662). This law states that **the pressure exerted by a fluid at a depth *h* below the surface of the fluid is *equal in all directions.*** The application of this law leads to some rather surprising results. Even though the five containers whose cross sections are shown above have different shapes, the pressure at the bottom of all three containers is 29,400 N/m² if all are full of water, because, in each case, the bottom of the tank is 3 meters below the surface of the water.

From this we see that the pressure in a fluid at any depth *h* depends only on the depth and the weight density, *w*, of the fluid.

$$\text{Pressure at depth } h = wh$$

If the pressure is constant over a particular area, the total force exerted on the area equals the pressure times the area.

$$\text{Total force} = \frac{\text{force}}{\text{area}} \times \text{area} = \text{force}$$

Since the pressure at any depth is the same in all directions, the horizontal pressure at any depth *h* equals the vertical pressure at that depth, which is *wh*. This fact allows us to use calculus to calculate the total force exerted by a fluid on a nonhorizontal surface, such as the side of a tank, by adding up the forces on horizontal rectangular strips, each of whose height is Δy. Because the strips are very narrow, the pressure is approximately equal at every point in the strip.

Example 82.1   A rectangular tank 6 meters deep is filled with water to a depth of 5 meters as shown. Find the total force exerted by the water on the end of the tank.

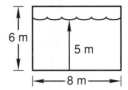

Solution   Problems like this one can be made harder or easier by the location of the coordinate system. It is often helpful to locate the x axis at the bottom of the tank, as we do here.

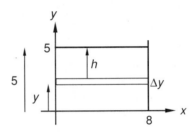

The total force on the rectangular strip equals the weight density w times the depth h times the area.

$$\text{Force} = w \times h \times \text{area}$$

The numerical value of the weight density of water is 9800. The distance from the bottom of the tank to the surface is 5, and the distance to the rectangle is y. Thus, $h = 5 - y$. The area of the rectangle is $8\,\Delta y$, so we can write

$$\text{Force} = 9800(5 - y)(8\,\Delta y)$$

To find the total force, we want to stack these rectangles from $y = 0$ to $y = 5$. Thus

$$\text{Total force} = \int_0^5 9800(5 - y)(8\,dy)$$

We finish by evaluating the integral.

$$\text{Total force} = 9800 \left(\int_0^5 40\,dy - \int_0^5 8y\,dy \right)$$

$$= 9800[40y - 4y^2]_0^5$$

$$= 9800[(200 - 100) - 0]$$

$$= \textbf{980,000 newtons}$$

Example 82.2   The figure shows the end of a tank 6 meters deep filled with liquid to a depth of 5 meters as shown. Express the total force on the end of the tank as a definite integral if the weight density of the liquid is 4000 newtons per cubic meter.

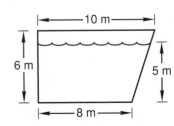

Solution   Again we place the *x* axis at the bottom of the tank.

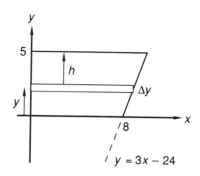

The force on the representative rectangle equals weight density times the depth *h* times the area.

$$\text{Force} = w \times h \times \text{area}$$

The depth *h* is $5 - y$, as in the preceding example, but the length of the rectangle is no longer 8 but is *x*, where *x* is determined by $y = 3x - 24$. If we solve this equation for *x*, we get $x = \frac{1}{3}y + 8$, and thus the area of the representative rectangle equals $\left(\frac{1}{3}y + 8\right) dy$. We want to stack the rectangles from $y = 0$ to $y = 5$, so the total force can be expressed as follows.

$$\text{Total force} = \int_0^5 wh(\text{area}) = \int_0^5 (4000)(5 - y)\left[\left(\frac{1}{3}y + 8\right) dy\right]$$

When we multiply, we find that we need to evaluate the following integral.

$$4000 \int_0^5 \left(-\frac{1}{3}y^2 - \frac{19}{3}y + 40\right) dy$$

This evaluation is straightforward but time-consuming. The example is a problem about an application of the definite integral; it is not designed to provide practice in evaluating integrals. Thus we will consider the solution complete.

Example 82.3   A cylindrical tank 20 meters long whose radius is 4 meters, as shown, is half filled with oil whose weight density is 3000 newtons per cubic meter. Set up an integral whose evaluation will yield the total force exerted by the oil on one end of the tank.

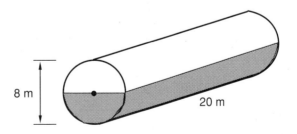

Solution   The length of the tank need not be considered since the force exerted at any point on the end of the tank is a function of only the weight density of the fluid and the vertical distance *h* from the point to the surface of the fluid. The length of the tank could be 2 meters, 20 meters, or 2000 meters. The answer would be the same. If we place the origin at the center, the equation of the circle is $x^2 + y^2 = 16$.

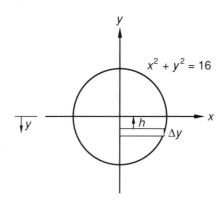

Since the end of the tank is symmetrical, we decide to find the total force on half the tank and double the result. The force on the representative rectangle again equals the weight density times the depth h times the area.

$$\text{Force} = w \times h \times \text{area}$$

The distance from the x axis to the rectangle is y, so the depth h, measured in the opposite direction, equals $-y$. The length of the rectangle is x, where x is defined by $x^2 + y^2 = 16$. Thus, the length of the rectangle is $\sqrt{16 - y^2}$, and the area is $\sqrt{16 - y^2}\, dy$. We want to stack the rectangles from $y = -4$ to $y = 0$, so the total force on the end of the tank is

$$\text{Total force} = 2 \int_{-4}^{0} 3000(-y)(\sqrt{16 - y^2}\, dy)$$

$$= -6000 \int_{-4}^{0} (16 - y^2)^{1/2} y\, dy$$

If we insert the necessary constants, we get

$$\text{Total force} = (-6000)\left(-\frac{1}{2}\right) \int_{-4}^{0} (16 - y^2)^{1/2} -(2y)\, dy$$

This integral has the form of $u^n\, du$, so we can integrate and get

$$\text{Total force} = 3000 \left[\frac{(16 - y^2)^{3/2}}{\frac{3}{2}} \right]_{-4}^{0}$$

If we do the arithmetic, we find that the total force equals 128,000 newtons. If we had placed the origin at the bottom of the tank, the equation of the circle would have been

$$x^2 + (y - 4)^2 = 16$$

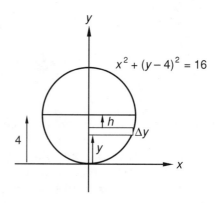

If we solve this equation for x, we get $x = \sqrt{16 - (y - 4)^2}$, so the area of the rectangle is $\sqrt{16 - (y - 4)^2}\,dy$. This time the depth h equals $4 - y$, and we want to stack the rectangles from $y = 0$ to $y = 4$. Thus the total force is given by the following integral.

$$\text{Total force} = 2\int_0^4 3000(4 - y)\sqrt{16 - (y - 4)^2}\,dy$$

If we simplify the radical, we get

$$\text{Total force} = 2\int_0^4 3000(4 - y)(-y^2 + 8y)^{1/2}\,dy$$

Placing the x axis at the bottom of the tank also gives us an integral that has the basic form of $u^n\,du$.

Problem set 82

1. Boyle's law tells us that if the temperature of a quantity of ideal gas is unchanged, the product of the pressure and the volume equals a constant k. When we have 1000 m^3 of gas at a pressure of 5 N/m^2, the pressure is increasing at a rate of 0.05 N/m^2 per second. Find the rate at which the volume is decreasing when the pressure is 10 N/m^2.

2. A variable force $F(x) = x + 2$ newtons is applied to move an object along a number line. Find the work done by the force in moving the object from $x = 1$ meter to $x = 4$ meters.

3. A tank 3 meters deep is completely filled with fluid whose weight density is 1000 N/m^3. Find the total force exerted on one end of the tank if the end of the tank is rectangular as shown in the figure.

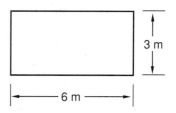

4. A container with a triangular end as shown is filled with a fluid which has a weight density of 3000 N/m^3. Find the total force exerted against the end of the container.

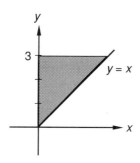

5. A container 1000 meters long has a semicircular cross section as shown below. The container is filled with a fluid whose weight density is 1000 N/m^3. Use the variable y to write a definite integral whose value equals the total force against the end of the container.

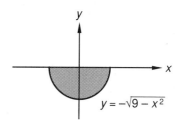

6. Let R be the region bounded by the graph of $y = (x - 1)^2$ and both coordinate axes. Find the volume of the solid formed when R is revolved about the x axis.

7. Let R be the region between the graph of $y = x^2$ and the x axis from $x = 0$ to $x = 2$. Find the volume of the solid formed when R is revolved around the x axis.

Differentiate:

8. $y = \log_5 x + 7^x + \log_8 x$

9. $y = (3.5)^x - 2 \log_3 x$

Integrate:

10. $\displaystyle\int \log_5 x \, dx$

11. $\displaystyle\int 4xe^{2x} \, dx$

12. $\displaystyle\int x \sin 2x \, dx$

13. $\displaystyle\int \sin x \sqrt{1 + 2 \cos x} \, dx$

14. $\displaystyle\int \frac{x}{\sqrt{x^2 + \pi}} \, dx$

Differentiate:

15. $y = \text{arcsec} \dfrac{x}{a} \quad a, x > 0$

16. $y = \arcsin 3x + \dfrac{\sqrt{1 - x}}{x \sin x}$

17. Which of the following limits are undefined?

(a) $\displaystyle\lim_{x \to 1} \frac{x^3 - 1}{x - 1}$ (b) $\displaystyle\lim_{x \to 0^+} \frac{|x|}{x}$ (c) $\displaystyle\lim_{x \to 0} \sin \frac{1}{x}$ (d) $\displaystyle\lim_{x \to 0^-} x \sin x$

18. Write the equation of the tangent line which can be drawn to the graph of

$$f(x) = \frac{x - 1}{x + 1} \quad \text{at } x = 1$$

CONCEPT REVIEW 19. Suppose that 1000 frankfurters can be sold every week at a food stand for $1 each. For every increase of 20 cents per frankfurter the number of frankfurters sold will decrease by 100. Write an equation which expresses the number of frankfurters sold as a function of the price p in cents. What is the total revenue received from the sale of frankfurters per week if the price of each frankfurter is p?

20. Suppose f is a function which is defined for all real numbers. Which of the following conditions guarantees that the inverse of f is also a function?
(a) f is a strictly increasing function
(b) f is an odd function
(c) f is an even function
(d) f is continuous and differentiable everywhere
(e) f is a periodic function

LESSON 83 *Continuity of functions*

The importance of some of the crucial theorems of calculus is difficult for beginners to understand because the truth of the theorems is so obvious. Two theorems about continuous functions fall into this category. They are the maximum-minimum value existence theorem, which we have already discussed, and the **intermediate**

value theorem. On the left we show an *f* function machine with input *x* and output $f(x)$. This particular machine will produce an output for any *x* input between 2 and 8 inclusive, so the domain of the function is the closed interval [2, 8]. This *f* function is a continuous function, so the graph is continuous on this interval.

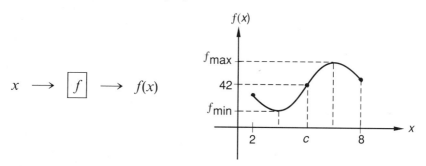

The maximum-minimum existence theorem tells us that for some *x* between 2 and 8 inclusive, the function has a maximum value, and for some *x* between 2 and 8 inclusive, the function has a minimum value. **The intermediate value theorem tells us that we can find a value of *x* between 2 and 8 inclusive that will give us any value of $f(x)$ we choose between *f* max and *f* min.** In this example, 42 is between *f* max and *f* min, so we know that we can find a number *c* between 2 and 8 for which $f(c) = 42$. The maximum-minimum value existence theorem and the intermediate value theorem are important because they are needed to prove other theorems. While these two theorems are easy to understand, a formal proof depends on a property of the real numbers called *completeness* that is usually discussed in advanced calculus textbooks. Thus the proofs are beyond the scope of this book.

MAXIMUM-MINIMUM VALUE EXISTENCE THEOREM

If *f* is continuous on the closed interval [*a*, *b*], then *f* has a maximum value *M* and a minimum value *m* on the interval [*a*, *b*].

INTERMEDIATE VALUE THEOREM

If *f* is continuous on the closed interval [*a*, *b*] and *N* is a number between *f* max and *f* min, then there is at least one number *c* between *a* and *b* inclusive for which $f(c) = N$.

Since continuous functions have such special properties, it is necessary to define *continuous functions* precisely and define them so that a graph is not necessary for the use of the definition. Here we show the graphs of three functions that are defined for every input value of *x* between *a* and *b* but not for *a* and *b*. This means that there is a value of the function for any *x* on the interval (*a*, *b*) and that the domain of each of the functions is (*a*, *b*).

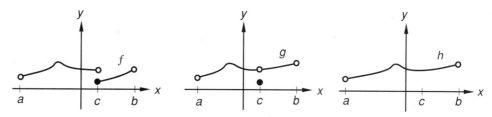

The graphs show that the functions f and g are not continuous on the interval (a, b) because there is a discontinuity at c. There is no discontinuity at any point in the graph of h between a and b, so this function is continuous on (a, b). For a definition of continuity on an open interval it is first necessary to define continuity at a point. There are three conditions that must be met for a function to be continuous at $x = c$.

1. Both a left-hand limit and a right-hand limit must exist as x approaches c.
2. The limits must be equal.
3. The value of the function at c, which is $f(c)$, must exist and must equal both the left-hand limit and the right-hand limit.

DEFINITION OF CONTINUITY AT A POINT

A function f is continuous at a point c if f exists at c and

$$\lim_{x \to c^-} f(x) = \lim_{x \to c^+} f(x) = f(c)$$

We know that for a function to have a limit as x approaches c, the function must be defined at c and both the left-hand limit and the right-hand limit must exist and they must be equal, so if f is defined at c, the notation

$$\lim_{x \to c} f(x) = f(c)$$

suffices to define continuity at a point. For a function to be continuous on an open interval (a, b) it must be continuous at every point between a and b.

DEFINITION OF OPEN-INTERVAL CONTINUITY

A function f is continuous on an open interval (a, b) if it is continuous at every point on the interval.

Sometimes we find it helpful to be able to discuss continuity on a closed interval $[a, b]$. Because the function is not defined for values of x that are less than a, it is impossible to approach a from the left, so the left-hand limit as x approaches a cannot exist. Because the function is not defined for values of x greater than b, it is impossible to approach b from the right, so the right-hand limit as x approaches b cannot exist. Thus, for a definition of continuity on a closed interval $[a, b]$, we must modify our definition of continuity on an open interval (a, b) by requiring only that the right-hand limit at a equal $f(a)$ and that the left-hand limit at b equal $f(b)$. All other points on the closed interval must be continuous, as we have defined for the open interval (a, b).

DEFINITION OF CLOSED-INTERVAL CONTINUITY

A function f is continuous on a closed interval $[a, b]$ if it is continuous at every point between a and b and if f is defined at both a and b and if

$$\lim_{x \to a^+} = f(a) \qquad \text{and} \qquad \lim_{x \to b^-} = f(b)$$

Problems about continuity are designed to help the reader understand the definitions of continuity.

Example 83.1   Given that f is defined on the interval $[1, 3]$, if $f(1) = 1$ and $f(3) = 7$, does a number c exist, $1 \leq c \leq 3$, such that $f(c) = 3$?

Solution   **Not necessarily.** The function was not defined to be continuous on $[1, 3]$, so the existence of c in $[1, 3]$ such that $f(c) = 3$ is not necessarily required.

Example 83.2   Suppose f is a function that is continuous on the closed interval $[-1, 3]$. Which of the following could be a graph of f?

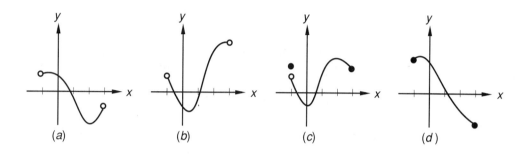

    (a)   (b)   (c)   (d)

Solution   For a function to be continuous on the closed interval $[-1, 3]$ it must be defined at the endpoints $-1, 3$ and must be continuous at every interior point. Also the one-sided limits at the endpoints of $[-1, 3]$ must equal $f(-1)$ and $f(-3)$. **Graph (d)** is the only graph that meets all the requirements.

Example 83.3   Let f be a piecewise function defined as follows.

$$f(x) = \begin{cases} |x| + 3 & \text{for } x < 1 \\ ax^2 + bx & \text{for } x \geq 1 \end{cases}$$

Find the values of a and b such that f is continuous on the interval $(-\infty, \infty)$.

Solution   We begin with a sketch of f.

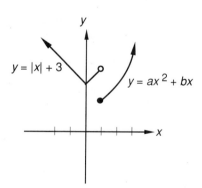

In the sketch, we see that f is continuous to the left and right of $x = 1$. The limit of $|x| + 3$ as x approaches 1 from the left is $1 + 3 = 4$. Thus if $ax^2 + bx = 4$ when $x = 1$, the function will be continuous at $x = 1$. So we let x equal 1 and y equal 4 and get

$$4 = a(1)^2 + b(1) \quad \longrightarrow \quad 4 = a + b$$

Thus any pair of values of a and b whose sum is 4 will make the function a continuous function on the interval $(-\infty, \infty)$.

Example 83.4 Let f be a piecewise function defined as follows.

$$f(x) = \begin{cases} \dfrac{x^2 - c^2}{x - c} & \text{for } x \neq c \\ 2c & \text{for } x = c \end{cases}$$

Is x continuous on the interval $(-\infty, \infty)$?

Solution When x does not equal c, the function is defined and is continuous for all x because the equation is the equation of a line.

When $x \neq c$: $\quad f(x) = \dfrac{(x + c)(x - c)}{x - c} \longrightarrow f(x) = x + c$

We were given that $f(c) = 2c$. If the limit of $f(x)$ as x approaches c is also $2c$, the limit equals $f(c)$ and the function is continuous at $x = c$.

$$\lim_{x \to c} f(x) = \lim_{x \to c} x + c = 2c$$

Since the function is continuous for all $x \neq c$ and is also continuous at $x = c$, **the function is continuous on the interval $(-\infty, \infty)$.**

Problem set 83

1. Suppose 1000 frankfurters can be sold every week if frankfurters are sold for \$1 each. For every 20-cent increase in price, sales of the frankfurters decrease by 100 per week. This means that $Q(p) = 1500 - 5p$ frankfurters would be sold if the price of each frankfurter were p (measured in cents). Find the price p for which each frankfurter should be sold to maximize the revenues received per week from the sale of frankfurters.

2. A ball is thrown straight up with an initial velocity of 10 m/sec from the top of a 200-m-high building. Develop an equation which expresses the height of the ball above the ground at a time t after the ball is thrown. How long does it take the ball to reach the ground?

3. Is the following statement true or false? Explain why. Suppose f is a function such that $f(1) = 2$ and $f(4) = 10$; then there is number c such that $1 < c < 4$ such that $f(c) = 5$.

4. Suppose f is a function which is continuous on the closed interval $[-1, 4]$. Which of the following could be a graph of f?

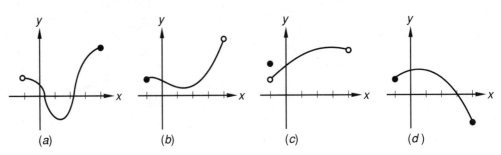

(a)   (b)   (c)   (d)

5. Let f be a piecewise function defined as follows.

$$f(x) = \begin{cases} |x| + 2 & \text{for } x < 2 \\ x^2 + bx & \text{for } x \geq 2 \end{cases}$$

Find the value(s) of b for which f is continuous for all real numbers.

6. Describe the interval(s) on which f, defined at the top of the following page, is continuous.

$$f(x) = \begin{cases} \dfrac{x^2 - c^2}{x + c} & \text{for } x \ne -c \\ 2c & \text{for } x = -c \end{cases}$$

7. A rectangular tank 4 m deep is completely filled with a fluid whose weight density is 5000 N/m³. Let F be the total force exerted on one wall, which has a width of 5 m. Use y as the variable of integration to write F as a definite integral.

8. A container with a triangular cross section as shown is filled with a fluid which has weight density 9000 N/m³. Find the total force on one end of the tank.

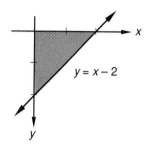

9. Find the maximum and minimum values of $f(x) = |x^2 - 2x|$ on the interval $[-2, 3]$.

10. Let R be the region bounded by the graph of $y = 4 - x^2$ and the x axis. Use y as the variable of integration to write a definite integral that equals the volume of the solid formed when R is revolved about the y axis.

11. Differentiate: $y = 5^{x^2+1} + \dfrac{2x}{\sqrt{x + 1}}$

Integrate:

12. $\displaystyle \int \left(2^x + \dfrac{1}{\sqrt{x + 1}}\right) dx$

13. $\displaystyle \int -xe^{-x}\, dx$

14. Suppose f is a function such that $-x^4 + 1 \le f(x) \le x^4 + 1$. Evaluate $\displaystyle \lim_{x \to 0} f(x)$.

15. Suppose $f(x) = x^2$ and $g(x) = e^x$. Determine whether h is odd, even, or neither if $h(x) = g(f(x))$.

16. The definite integral $\displaystyle \int_1^4 x\sqrt{x + 1}\, dx$ is equal to which of the following definite integrals?

(a) $\displaystyle \int_1^4 (u^{3/2} - u^{1/2})\, du$ (b) $\displaystyle \int_2^5 (u^{3/2} + u^{1/2})\, du$

(c) $\displaystyle \int_2^5 (u^{3/2} - u^{1/2})\, du$ (d) $\displaystyle \int_2^5 u(u + 1)\, du$

17. Write the equation of the tangent line which can be drawn to the graph of $y = \arcsin 2x$ at $x = \frac{1}{4}$.

18. Approximate to two decimal places the area of region bounded by the graph of $y = x\sqrt{1 - x^2}$ and the x axis.

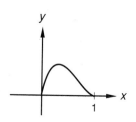

CONCEPT REVIEW   **19.** The graph of the function $y = x^9 + x^7 + x^5 + x^3$
(*a*) is always concave up
(*b*) is always concave down
(*c*) is concave down when $x > 0$ and concave up when $x < 0$
(*d*) has an inflection point at $x = 0$

20. Suppose f is defined on the closed interval $[-2, 2]$ and has the following graph.

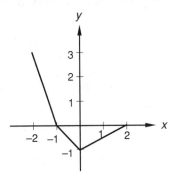

Sketch the graph of:
(*a*) $y = f(x) + 1$ (*b*) $y = f(x + 1)$ (*c*) $y = f(x - 1)$

LESSON 84   *Integration of odd powers of sin x and cos x*

The derivative of sin x is cos x, and the derivative of cos x is $-\sin x$. Also we know that sin x and cos x are related by the basic Pythagorean identity $\sin^2 x + \cos^2 x = 1$. These relationships allow us to find the integrals of $\sin^n x$ and $\cos^n x$ if n is odd and allow us to find the integrals of $\sin^n x \cos^m x$ if either n or m is odd.

Example 84.1   Find $\int \sin^3 x \, dx$.

Solution   The key to integrating odd powers of sin x is to separate a factor of (sin $x \, dx$) to be used later as du and then replace the remaining factors of $\sin^2 x$ with $(1 - \cos^2 x)$.

$$\int \sin^3 x \, dx = \int (\sin^2 x)(\sin x \, dx) \qquad\qquad \text{factored}$$

$$= \int (1 - \cos^2 x)(\sin x \, dx) \qquad\qquad \text{substituted}$$

$$= \int \sin x \, dx - \int (\cos^2 x)(\sin x \, dx) \qquad \text{multiplied}$$

The value of the first integral is $-\cos x$. The second integral would have the form $u^n \, du$ if it had a minus sign because the differential of cos x is $-\sin x \, dx$. Thus we insert the needed minus sign and change the sign in front of the integral from $-$ to $+$.

$$\int \sin x \, dx + \int \underbrace{(\cos^2 x)}_{u^n}\underbrace{(-\sin x \, dx)}_{du}$$

The integral of sin x is $-\cos x$, and the integral of $u^n \, du$ is $u^{n+1}/(n + 1)$, so we write

$$\int \sin^3 dx = -\cos x + \frac{1}{3}\cos^3 x + C$$

We could have avoided the difficulty with the minus signs if we had factored $(-\sin x \, dx)$ as the first step.

$$\int \sin^3 x = \int (-\sin^2 x)(-\sin x \, dx) \qquad \text{factored}$$

$$= \int -(1 - \cos^2 x)(-\sin x \, dx) \qquad \text{substituted}$$

$$= \int \sin x \, dx + \int (\cos^2 x)(-\sin x \, dx) \qquad \text{multiplied}$$

$$= -\cos x + \frac{1}{3}\cos^3 x + C$$

Example 84.2   Find $\int \cos^3 x \, dx$.

Solution   The key to integrating odd powers of cos x is to begin the process by separating a factor of (cos $x \, dx$) to be used later as du, and then replace the remaining factors of $\cos^2 x$ with $(1 - \sin^2 x)$. So we write

$$\int (\cos^2 x)(\cos x \, dx)$$

Now we replace $\cos^2 x$ with $(1 - \sin^2 x)$.

$$\int (1 - \sin^2 x)(\cos x \, dx) \qquad \text{substituted}$$

$$= \int \cos x \, dx - \int \underbrace{\sin^2 x}_{u^n} \underbrace{\cos x \, dx}_{du} \qquad \text{multiplied}$$

The integral of cos x is sin x, and the integral of $u^n \, du$ is $u^{n+1}/(n + 1)$, so we can write

$$\int \cos^3 x \, dx = \sin x - \frac{1}{3}\sin^3 x + C$$

Example 84.3   Find $\int \sin^4 x \cos^3 x \, dx$.

Solution   **The key step is to break up the factor that is raised to an odd power.**

$$\int (\sin^4 x)(\cos^2 x)(\cos x \, dx)$$

We know that (cos $x \, dx$) is the differential of sin x, so we want everything else to be some form of sin x. Thus we replace $\cos^2 x$ with $1 - \sin^2 x$.

$$\int (\sin^4 x)(1 - \sin^2 x)(\cos x \, dx) \qquad \text{substituted}$$

$$= \int (\sin^4 x - \sin^6 x)(\cos x \, dx) \qquad \text{multiplied}$$

$$= \int \underbrace{(\sin x)^4}_{u^4}\underbrace{(\cos x \, dx)}_{du} - \int \underbrace{(\sin x)^6}_{u^6}\underbrace{(\cos x \, dx)}_{du} \qquad \text{two integrals}$$

Since both integrals have the form $\int u^n\, du$, which equals $u^{n+1}/(n+1) + C$, we can write the answer by inspection.

$$\frac{1}{5}\sin^5 x - \frac{1}{7}\sin^7 x + C$$

Example 84.4   Find $\int \sin^3 x \cos^7 x\, dx.$

Solution   Both exponents are odd, so we have our choice. We decide to break up $\sin^3 x$ because it might be easier to handle.

$$\int (\sin^2 x)(\cos^7 x)(\sin x\, dx)$$

The derivative of $\cos x$ is $-\sin x$, so we will need a negative sign in the last set of parentheses. We decide to take care of this now and remember to write another negative sign to the left of the integral sign.

$$-\int (\sin^2 x)(\cos^7 x)(-\sin x\, dx)$$

Now we substitute $(1 - \cos^2 x)$ for $\sin^2 x$, simplify, and integrate.

$$-\int (1 - \cos^2 x)(\cos^7 x)(-\sin x\, dx) \qquad \text{substituted}$$

$$= -\left[\int (\cos^7 x)(-\sin x\, dx) - \int (\cos^9 x)(-\sin x\, dx)\right] \qquad \text{multiplied}$$

$$= -\int \underbrace{(\cos^7 x)}_{u^n}\underbrace{(-\sin x\, dx)}_{du} + \int \underbrace{(\cos^9 x)}_{u^n}\underbrace{(-\sin x\, dx)}_{du} \qquad \text{simplified}$$

$$= -\frac{1}{8}\cos^8 x + \frac{1}{10}\cos^{10} x + C \qquad \text{integrated}$$

Example 84.5   Find $\int \sin^2 x \cos^5 x\, dx.$

Solution $\sin x$ has an even exponent, so we will work with $\cos^5 x$ and write it as $\cos^4 x \cos x$.

$$\int (\sin^2 x)(\cos^4 x)(\cos x\, dx)$$

The rest of the problem is the same except that it will seem more difficult because the substitution for $\cos^4 x$ is a little more involved. First we express $\cos^4 x$ in terms of $\sin x$.

$$\cos^4 x = (\cos^2 x)^2 = (1 - \sin^2 x)^2 = 1 - 2\sin^2 x + \sin^4 x$$

Now we substitute this expression for $(\cos^4 x)$ and get

$$\int (\sin^2 x)(1 - 2\sin^2 x + \sin^4 x)(\cos x\, dx) \qquad \text{substituted}$$

$$= \int \underbrace{(\sin^2 x)}_{u^n}\underbrace{(\cos x\, dx)}_{du} - 2\int \underbrace{(\sin^4 x)}_{u^n}\underbrace{(\cos x\, dx)}_{du} + \int \underbrace{(\sin^6 x)}_{u^n}\underbrace{(\cos x\, dx)}_{du}$$

All of these have the form $u^n\, du$, and we can write the answer by inspection.

$$\int \sin^2 x \cos^5 x \, dx = \frac{1}{3} \sin^3 x - \frac{2}{5} \sin^5 x + \frac{1}{7} \sin^7 x + C$$

Problem set 84

1. The interest was compounded continuously, so the amount of money in the account increased exponentially. The initial deposit was $10,000, and after 3 years $17,000 was in the account. How much money would be in the account after 4 years?

2. The shaded area is a vertical side of a tank that is filled with 100,000 cubic centimeters of water. The measurements shown are in meters. The weight density of water is 9800 newtons per cubic meter. Use y as the variable of integration to write a definite integral whose value equals the total force against the side of the tank.

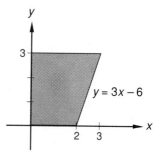

Use the appropriate Pythagorean identities as necessary to find the following integrals.

3. $\displaystyle\int \sin^3 x \, dx$

4. $\displaystyle\int \sin^2 x \cos^3 x \, dx$

5. $\displaystyle\int \sin^3 x \cos^2 x \, dx$

6. $\displaystyle\int (\sin^2 x + \cos^2 x) \, dx$

7. Let f be a piecewise function defined as follows:

$$f(x) = \begin{cases} -2x + b & \text{when } x > 0 \\ x^2 + 1 & \text{when } x \le 0 \end{cases}$$

Find b so that f is continuous for every real value of x.

8. Determine whether or not f is continuous at $x = 2$, if f is defined as follows. Justify your answer.

$$f(x) = \begin{cases} \dfrac{x^3 - 8}{x - 2} & x \ne 2 \\ 16 & x = 2 \end{cases}$$

9. Suppose f is a cubic function whose equation is

$$f(x) = x^3 + ax^2 + bx + c$$

The graph of f has an inflection point at $x = -\frac{2}{3}$ and a relative minimum point at $x = 0$. If the graph of f passes through the point $(0, 1)$, find the values of a, b, and c.

10. Find the area of the region between the graph of $y = xe^x$ and the x axis on the interval $[0, 1]$.

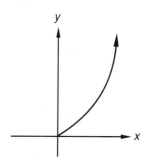

11. Use x as the variable of integration to write a definite integral whose value is the volume of the solid formed when the region enclosed by the graph of the equation $x = 1 - y^2$ and the y axis is revolved around the x axis.

12. An area A is bounded by the graph of $y = x^2$ and the x axis between x values of 0 and 4. Find the volume of the solid formed when the area is revolved about the x axis.

13. Differentiate: $y = 5^{x^2+1} + x \arctan \dfrac{x}{2} + \log_{24} x$

14. Find all the critical numbers in the interval $(0, \infty)$ of the function $y = x(\ln x)^2$.

15. Find: $\dfrac{d}{dx}(\arcsin x) + \displaystyle\int \dfrac{1}{\sqrt{1 - x^2}}\, dx$

16. Integrate: $\displaystyle\int (xe^{2x} + xe^{x^2})\, dx$

17. Find the equation of the line which can be drawn tangent to the graph of the equation $xy + y^2 = x + 1$ at $(2, 1)$.

18. Approximate to two decimal places the value of $\displaystyle\int_0^1 \cos xe^{\sin x}\, dx$.

19. Use calculus to develop a formula for the volume of a sphere. Then find the volume of a sphere whose surface area is 16π cm^2.

CONCEPT REVIEW 20. Suppose $f(x) = \dfrac{x^5 - 1}{x - 1}$. Then $f(-a)$ equals which of the following?

(a) $a^4 + a^3 + a^2 + a + 1$ (b) $a^4 - a^3 + a^2 - a + 1$
(c) $-a^5 + 1$ (d) $-a^4 + a^3 - a^2 + a - 1$

LESSON 85 *Applications of the definite integral (work II)*

We remember that mechanical work is defined as the product of force times distance.

$$\text{Mechanical work} = \text{force} \times \text{distance}$$

We know that if we move a weight of 1 kilogram vertically a distance of 1 meter, we do 1 joule of work. To find the number of joules required to pump fluid out of a tank, we sum the products of the weights of thin sheets of fluid and the distance through which this sheet is to be moved.

Example 85.1 A rectangular tank is 6 meters high, 10 meters long, and 4 meters wide. If the tank is full of water, find the work required to pump the water out of the tank.

Solution We need a coordinate system for the physical problem. There are many options, and we decide to place the origin and the axes as we show on the left at the top of the following page.

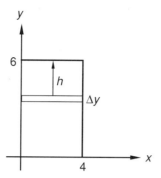 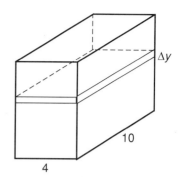

The area of the representative rectangle shown on the left is $4\,\Delta y$. The volume of the representative rectangular solid on the right is $4\,\Delta y$ times 10. The weight of the representative rectangular solid is the volume times the weight density of water, which is 9800 newtons per cubic meter.

$$\text{Weight} = \underbrace{(9800)}_{\text{density}}\underbrace{[4(10)\,\Delta y]}_{\text{volume}}$$

The distance from the x axis to the top of the tank is 6 meters, and the distance to the solid is y. Thus the distance h that the solid must be lifted is $(6 - y)$. The work done equals the distance h times the weight.

$$\text{Work} = \underbrace{(6 - y)}_{h}\underbrace{(9800)}_{\text{density}}\underbrace{[4(10)\,\Delta y]}_{\text{volume}}$$

We need to sum this work for all the rectangular solids from $y = 0$ to $y = 6$ as the thickness of these solids approaches zero. This sum can be written as an integral, as we show here.

$$\text{Total work} = 392{,}000 \int_{0}^{6} (6 - y)\,dy$$

$$= 392{,}000 \left[6y - \frac{y^2}{2}\right]_{0}^{6}$$

$$= \textbf{7,056,000 joules}$$

Example 85.2 The triangular tank shown is filled with oil to a depth of 2 meters. The dimensions of the tank are in meters. Find the work done in pumping the oil out of the tank if the weight density of the oil is 5000 newtons per cubic meter.

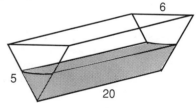

Solution We are using mathematics to solve a physical problem. There is no one way to do it. Since the tank is symmetrical, we decide to find the work required to pump the oil out of half the tank and double our answer. We place the origin as shown so the equation of the line that defines the right-hand side of the tank is a simple equation.

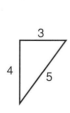 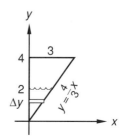

The area of the end of the representative rectangular solid is $x\,dy$, where $x = \frac{3}{4}y$. Thus the volume of the representative rectangular solid is the width $\frac{3}{4}y$ times the height Δy times the length 20. The weight of the representative rectangular solid is the weight density times the volume. The work to lift this weight a distance $h = 4 - y$ is

$$\frac{1}{2}\ \text{Total work} = \underbrace{(5000)}_{\text{density}}\ \underbrace{(4 - y)}_{h}\ \underbrace{\left(\frac{3}{4}y\ \Delta y\right)(20)}_{\text{volume}}$$

We need to sum this work for all the rectangular solids from $y = 0$ to $y = 2$. Thus the integral is

$$\frac{1}{2}\ \text{Total work} = (5000)(20)\int_0^2 (4 - y)\left(\frac{3}{4}y\right) dy$$

If we multiply, we get

$$\frac{1}{2}\ \text{Total work} = 100{,}000 \int_0^2 \left(3y - \frac{3}{4}y^2\right) dy$$

$$= 100{,}000 \left[\frac{3}{2}y^2 - \frac{y^3}{4}\right]_0^2$$

If we evaluate, we get

$$\frac{1}{2}\ \text{Total work} = 100{,}000(6 - 2) = 400{,}000 \text{ joules}$$

Thus the total work done is **800,000 joules.**

Example 85.3 The end of a tank is a semicircle whose diameter is 20 meters. The tank is filled to a depth of 4 meters with a fluid whose weight density is 6000 newtons per cubic meter. Set up an integral that could be evaluated to find the work required to pump the fluid to a point 20 meters above the top of the tank.

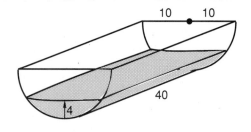

Solution We decide to place the origin as shown so the equation of the circle will be $x^2 + y^2 = 100$. We will compute the work for the right half of the tank and double this answer. The area of the end of the representative rectangular solid is $x\ \Delta y$, where $x = \sqrt{100 - y^2}$. The distance from the rectangular solid to a point 20 meters above the tank is $20 - y$ because y will always be negative. The work is the volume, $\sqrt{100 - y^2}(\Delta y)(40)$, times the weight density times the vertical distance.

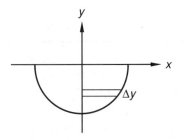

$$\frac{1}{2}\ \text{Total work} = \underbrace{(\sqrt{100 - y^2})(\Delta y)(40)}_{\text{volume}}\ \underbrace{(6000)}_{\text{density}}\ \underbrace{(20 - y)}_{h}$$

Since the x axis is at the top of the tank, we must sum the solids from $y = -10$ to $y = -6$.

$$\text{Total work} = 2 \int_{-10}^{-6} (40)(6000)\sqrt{100 - y^2}\,(20 - y)\,dy$$

The additional factor of 2 is required because the integral will give us the work required for half the tank.

Problem set 85

1. The volume of a spherical balloon is increasing at a rate of 3 cm³/sec. Find the rate at which the radius of the balloon is increasing when the surface area of the balloon is 16π cm³.

2. A rectangular tank is 5 meters deep, 10 meters long, and 4 meters wide. If the tank is full of water, find the work required to pump all the water out of the tank.

3. A trough 15 meters long whose cross section is a right isosceles triangle, as shown, is partially filled with a fluid whose weight density is 6000 newtons per cubic meter. If the depth of the fluid in the trough is 2 meters, write a definite integral that expresses the work done in pumping all the fluid out of the trough.

4. A 10 by 10 by 10 meter container is filled with water. The weight density of water is 9800 newtons per cubic meter. Find the total force against one of the sides of the container.

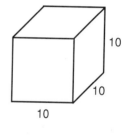

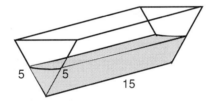

Integrate:

5. $\displaystyle\int \sin^2 x \cos^3 x \, dx$

6. $\displaystyle\int \cos^3 x \, dx$

7. Let f be a piecewise function defined as follows:

$$f(x) = \begin{cases} x^2 & \text{when } x \le 1 \\ ax + 2 & \text{when } x > 1 \end{cases}$$

Determine the value(s) of a that will make f continuous everywhere.

8. An object is thrown straight up from the top of a 100-meter-tall building with an initial velocity of 20 meters per second. Develop equations which describe the height of the object and the velocity of the object as functions of the time t after the ball is thrown.

9. Find the equation of the normal line which can be drawn to the graph of

$$y = \log_3 x \qquad \text{at } x = \frac{1}{\ln 3}$$

10. Which of the following limits are undefined?

   (a) $\displaystyle\lim_{x \to 0^+} \frac{|x|}{x}$ (b) $\displaystyle\lim_{x \to 0^+} \sin \frac{1}{x}$ (c) $\displaystyle\lim_{x \to 0} \frac{\sin x}{\cos x}$ (d) $\displaystyle\lim_{x \to 0} \frac{1}{x}$

11. If $f(x) = 3x^2$ and $g(x) = \sin x$, evaluate: $\lim\limits_{x \to \pi} (fg)(x)$

12. Suppose f and g are as defined in Problem 11. If $h(x) = f(x)/g(x)$, determine whether the graph of h is symmetric about the x axis, symmetric about the origin, or neither.

13. Find the area completely enclosed by the graphs of $y = x^3$ and $y = x^2$.

14. If f is a function which is continuous on $[1, 4]$ and attains a maximum value of 4 and a minimum value of -6 on this interval, then which of the following statements is true?

   (a) $\displaystyle\int_1^4 f(x)\, dx \geq 0$ (b) $\displaystyle\int_1^4 f(x)\, dx \leq 20$

   (c) $\displaystyle\int_1^4 f(x)\, dx = 16$ (d) $\displaystyle\int_1^4 f(x)\, dx \leq 0$

15. Differentiate: $y = \arctan 2x + \dfrac{2 \sin x}{\sqrt{\cos x + 1}} + \sec x \tan x$

Integrate:

16. $\displaystyle\int \frac{1}{1 + x^2}\, dx + \int \frac{2 \sin x}{\sqrt{\cos x + 1}}\, dx$ 17. $\displaystyle\int \frac{x^2 + 1}{x}\, dx$

18. Evaluate: $\displaystyle\lim_{h \to 0} \frac{\sin\left(\dfrac{\pi}{2} + h\right) - \sin \dfrac{\pi}{2}}{h}$

CONCEPT REVIEW   19. Suppose f and g are functions. For a number x to lie in the domain of $f \circ g$, which of the following must be true?
   (a) x is both an element of the domain of f and an element of the domain of g.
   (b) x is an element of the domain of f and $f(x)$ is an element of the domain of g.
   (c) x is an element of the domain of g and $g(x)$ is an element of the domain of f.
   (d) x is an element of the domain of f and $g(x)$ is an element of the domain of f.

20. Determine the range of $y = \sin(\arctan x)$.

LESSON 86   *Particle motion III*

We have discussed the equations of motion of bodies freely falling in a gravitational field. The acceleration function is the derivative of the velocity function, which is the derivative of the position function. If the initial conditions are known, we can begin with the acceleration function and integrate to find the velocity function and integrate again to find the position function. In freely falling body problems the acceleration is constant and is always -9.8 m/sec^2.

In calculus books it is customary to discuss position, velocity, and acceleration of a particle that moves left and right on the x axis and whose acceleration is not constant but is a function of time. Many of these problems are designed for the purpose of playing games with calculus and have acceleration functions that might never be encountered in a physical problem. Examples are $\sin 3t^2$, $e^{\cos t}$, or the function $t^3 - 5t + 3$. Since t is the independent variable and we always graph the independent variable on the horizontal axis, we will have to graph $x(t)$ vertically. This means that we are talking about horizontal motion on the x axis, but we will mentally graph this motion vertically.

Example 86.1   A particle moves along the x axis such that the acceleration function is $a(t) = 3t$. If the velocity at $t = 0$ is -10 and the position when $t = 0$ is $x(t) = 6$, find the equation which describes the position of the object as a function of time. What is the position when $t = 2$?

Solution   To get the answer, we will integrate the acceleration function to get the velocity function and integrate again to get the position function. First we integrate the acceleration function to get the velocity function.

$$v(t) = \int 3t \, dt = \frac{3t^2}{2} + C$$

When $t = 0$, $v(t) = -10$, so if we substitute we can solve for C.

$$(-10) = \frac{3(0)^2}{2} + C \quad \longrightarrow \quad C = -10$$

Thus the velocity function for this particle is

$$v(t) = \frac{3t^2}{2} - 10$$

The position function is the integral of the velocity function. Thus,

$$x(t) = \int \left(\frac{3t^2}{2} - 10 \right) dt = \frac{t^3}{2} - 10t + C$$

When $t = 0$, $x(t) = 6$, so if we substitute we can solve for C.

$$(6) = \frac{0^3}{2} - 10(0) + C \quad \longrightarrow \quad C = 6$$

Thus the position function for this particle is

$$x(t) = \frac{1}{2}t^3 - 10t + 6$$

The position when $t = 2$ is $x(2)$.

$$x(2) = \frac{1}{2}(2)^3 - 10(2) + 6 = \mathbf{-10}$$

This means that when $t = 2$, the particle is -10 units to the right of the origin, which is the same thing as 10 units to the left of the origin.

Example 86.2   A particle moves along the x axis such that the acceleration function is $a(t) = -3t$. If its position when $t = 3$ is 20 and its velocity at $t = 1$ is 5, what is its position when $t = 4$?

Solution   This problem is slightly different because we are not given initial conditions when t equals 0 but are given the position when $t = 3$ and the velocity when $t = 1$. We begin by integrating the acceleration function to get the velocity function.

$$v(t) = \int a(t) = \int -3t \, dt = \frac{-3t^2}{2} + C$$

When $t = 1$, $v(t) = 5$, so we can substitute to find C.

$$(5) = \frac{-3(1)^2}{2} + C \longrightarrow C = \frac{13}{2}$$

This gives us the velocity function.

$$v(t) = \frac{-3t^2}{2} + \frac{13}{2}$$

We integrate the velocity function to find the position function.

$$x(t) = \int \left(\frac{-3t^2}{2} + \frac{13}{2}\right) dt = \frac{-t^3}{2} + \frac{13}{2} t + C$$

When $t = 3$, $x(t) = 20$, so we can substitute to find C.

$$(20) = -\frac{(3)^3}{2} + \frac{13}{2}(3) + C \longrightarrow C = 14$$

Thus, the position function is

$$x(t) = -\frac{t^3}{2} + \frac{13}{2} t + 14$$

When $t = 4$, the position is

$$x(4) = \frac{-(4)^3}{2} + \frac{13}{2}(4) + 14 = \mathbf{8}$$

This means that when $t = 4$, the particle is 8 units to the right of the origin.

Example 86.3   A particle moves along the x axis so that its velocity at time t is given by $v(t) = \frac{1}{t}$. If the particle's position is 5 when $t = 2$, find the time when the particle is 10 units to the right of the origin.

Solution   We were given the velocity function, so we can take its derivative to get the acceleration function, or we can go the other way and integrate to find the position function. The question is about position, so we integrate to find $x(t)$.

$$x(t) = \int \frac{1}{t} dt \longrightarrow x(t) = \ln |t| + C$$

When $t = 2$, $x(t) = 5$, so we can solve for C.

$$(5) = \ln (2) + C \longrightarrow 5 = 0.69 + C \longrightarrow C = 4.31$$

Thus the position function is

$$x(t) = \ln |t| + 4.31$$

To find the time when the particle is 10 units to the right of the origin, we let $x(t)$ equal 10 and solve for t.

$$(10) = \ln t + 4.31 \longrightarrow \ln t = 5.69 \longrightarrow t = \text{inv ln } 5.69$$

We can find inv ln 5.69 by using the INV LN key or by using the e^x key to find the value of $e^{5.69}$.

$$\text{inv ln } 5.69 = e^{5.69} = \mathbf{295.90}$$

Thus, the particle is 10 units to the right of the origin when $t = 295.90$.

Problem set 86

1. Shown is the graph of $y = e^{-x^2}$ and a rectangle, two of whose corners touch the graph.

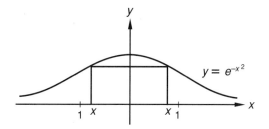

Find the value of x for which the area of the rectangle is a maximum.

2. A particle moves along the x axis so that its acceleration at time t is given by the equation $a(t) = 2t$. If the velocity of the particle at $t = 0$ is -10 and its position at $t = 0$ is 4, find the equations which express the position and the velocity of the particle as a function of t. Find the velocity and the position of the particle at $t = 2$.

3. A particle moves along the x axis so that its acceleration is given by

$$a(t) = 6t - 4$$

If its velocity at $t = 1$ is -1 and its position at $t = 0$ is $x = -4$, develop the equations which express the particle's position and velocity as functions of time.

4. A rectangular tank whose depth is 4 meters, whose width is 5 meters, and whose length is 6 meters is completely filled with a fluid whose weight density is 5000 newtons per cubic meter. Find the work done in pumping all the fluid out of the tank.

5. A 20-meter-long trough with a semi-circular cross section whose diameter is 10 meters is partially filled with a fluid whose weight density is 6000 newtons per cubic meter. If the depth of the water in the trough is 2 meters, find the work done in pumping all the fluid out of the trough.

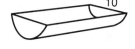

6. Use a Pythagorean identity as necessary to find $\int \sin^6 x \cos^3 x \, dx$.

7. Is the following statement true or false? Explain why.

$$\text{If } \lim_{x \to 0} f(x) = 5, \text{ then } f(0) = 5.$$

8. Approximate to two decimal places the area between the graph of $y = 3^x$ and the x axis from $x = 1$ to $x = 3$.

Integrate:

9. $\int xe^{2x} \, dx$

10. $\int \frac{x + 1}{\sqrt{x}} \, dx$

11. $\int \frac{4x}{x^2 + 1} \, dx$

12. $\int (\cos x)(\sin x + \pi)^3 \, dx$

13. Use y as the variable of integration to write a definite integral whose value equals the area of the region in the first quadrant bounded by the graphs of $y = x^2$ and $y = 4$.

14. Suppose f is a function continuous on $[0, 3]$, $f(0) = 8$, and $f(3) = 2$, and the functions f, f', and f'' have the properties shown in the table.

	$x < 1$	$x = 1$	$x > 1$
f	....	5	....
f'	negative	zero	negative
f''	positive	zero	negative

Sketch f and indicate any absolute maximum and minimum values f attains. Indicate also the coordinates of any inflection points of f.

15. Suppose $f(x) = e^x + x$. Write an equation which expresses the inverse of f implicitly.

16. Differentiate: $y = x \tan x^2 + \csc 15x + \dfrac{x}{\sin x + \cos x}$

17. Find: $\dfrac{d}{dx}(\arcsin 2x) + \displaystyle\int \dfrac{2}{\sqrt{1 - 4x^2}}\, dx$

18. Suppose that f is a function continuous on the closed interval $[-1, 1]$ and $1 \le f(x) \le 5$. The greatest possible value for $\displaystyle\int_{-1}^{1} f(x)\, dx$ is:
    (a) 0   (b) 2   (c) 10   (d) 25

19. Sketch the graph of $y = \dfrac{(x - 1)^2(x + 3)}{x(x - 3)^2(x^2 + 5)}$.

CONCEPT REVIEW   20. If we show the graph of $y = \ln x$ as the dotted curve, which solid curve could depict $y = \ln x^3$?

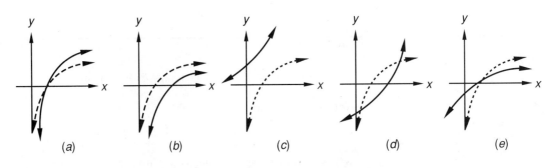

(a)   (b)   (c)   (d)   (e)

21. Suppose f is a polynomial function where $f(-1) = -2$ and $f(2) = 3$. Which of the following statements must be true?
    (a) $f(0) = 0$.
    (b) There exists a c where $-1 < c < 2$ and $f(c) = 0$.
    (c) f attains no value greater than -2 and no value less than 3 when $-1 < x < 2$.
    (d) f attains a local minimum at $x = -1$ and a local maximum at $x = 2$.

LESSON 87   *L'Hôpital's rule · Proof of L'Hôpital's rule*

In mathematics we often study a topic that is not immediately applicable because the knowledge will enhance our understanding of a broader concept. ***L'Hôpital's rule*** (lō-pĕ-tâls) falls into this category. This rule extends our knowledge of the limit of a quotient, and since calculus is based on the idea of the limit of a function, L'Hôpital's rule broadens our knowledge of calculus. This rule was discovered by a Swiss mathematician, Johann Bernoulli (1667–1748), but was named for his French student G. F. A. L'Hôpital (1661–1704).

L'Hôpital's rule can be used to find the limits of some quotients of polynomials. If the numerator and the denominator of a fraction of polynomials both approach zero as x approaches a, then $x - a$ must be a factor of both the numerator and the denominator. Both the numerator and the denominator of the following expression have a factor of $x - 2$, and the limit of the expression as x approaches 2 is 4.

$$\lim_{x \to 2} \frac{x^2 - 4}{x - 2} = \lim_{x \to 2} \frac{(x - 2)(x + 2)}{x - 2} = \lim_{x \to 2} x + 2 = 4$$

If we attempt to find the following limit, however, we get the indeterminate form zero over zero. We use the $[\neq]$ symbol because we do not wish to indicate that zero over zero is the limit. The substitution we have made results in an indeterminate form that is not the limit.

$$\lim_{x \to 0} \frac{\cos x - 1}{x} \ [\neq] \ \frac{1 - 1}{0} = \frac{0}{0}$$

In this example, the numerator and the denominator do not have a common factor, so an algebraic determination of the limit is not possible, but we can use L'Hôpital's rule instead. L'Hôpital's rule tells us to evaluate the limit of the derivative of the numerator divided by the limit of the derivative of the denominator.

$$\lim_{x \to 0} \frac{\cos x - 1}{x} = \lim_{x \to 0} \frac{\frac{d}{dx}(\cos x - 1)}{\frac{d}{dx} x} = \lim_{x \to 0} \frac{-\sin x}{1} = \frac{0}{1} = 0$$

Our first try at finding the limit resulted in zero over zero, which is an indeterminate form. By using L'Hôpital's rule, we get a limit of zero over 1, which is determinate because it equals zero. L'Hôpital's rule can be used to find the limit as x approaches a of $f(x)$ over $g(x)$ if both $f(a)$ and $g(a)$ equal 0 or "$\pm\infty$." **Thus L'Hôpital's rule cannot be used unless the quotient $f(a)$ over $g(a)$ has one of the following forms:**

$$\frac{0}{0} \qquad \frac{\infty}{\infty} \qquad \frac{-\infty}{\infty} \qquad \frac{\infty}{-\infty} \qquad \frac{-\infty}{-\infty}$$

If the first application of the rule again leads to one of these forms, the rule may be used again (and again). Of course, the first derivatives must exist for the first application, and the second derivatives must exist for the second application, etc.

L'HÔPITAL'S RULE

If $f(a)$ and $g(a)$ both equal zero or both equal $\pm\infty$, and if $\lim_{x \to a} \dfrac{f'(x)}{g'(x)}$ exists, then

$$\lim_{x \to a} \frac{f(x)}{g(x)} = \lim_{x \to a} \frac{f'(x)}{g'(x)}$$

Example 87.1 Find $\lim_{x \to 0} \dfrac{\cos x - 1}{x^2}$.

Solution If we let x equal zero, we get the indeterminate form 0 over 0.

$$\frac{\cos 0 - 1}{0^2} = \frac{1 - 1}{0} = \frac{0}{0}$$

The derivative of $\cos x$ exists, as does the derivative of x^2, so we try the ratio of the first derivatives.

$$\lim_{x \to 0} \frac{f'(x)}{g'(x)} = \lim_{x \to 0} \frac{-\sin x}{2x} \; [\neq] \; \frac{0}{0}$$

This result also has the form of zero over zero. Since the second derivatives also exist, we apply the rule again, and this time we find the limit.

$$\lim_{x \to 0} \frac{f''(x)}{g''(x)} = \lim_{x \to 0} \frac{-\cos x}{2} = \frac{-\cos 0}{2} = -\frac{1}{2}$$

Example 87.2 Find $\lim_{x \to 0} \dfrac{x^3 - 4x}{x^2 - 2x}$.

Solution If we let x equal 0, we get the indeterminate form 0 over 0.

$$\frac{(0)^3 - 4(0)}{(0)^2 - 2(0)} = \frac{0}{0}$$

Thus we use L'Hôpital's rule to find the limit.

$$\lim_{x \to 0} \frac{f'(x)}{g'(x)} = \lim_{x \to 0} \frac{3x^2 - 4}{2x - 2} = \frac{0 - 4}{0 - 2} = 2$$

Example 87.3 Find $\lim_{x \to 1} \dfrac{\ln x}{2 - 2x}$.

Solution The value of $e^0 = 1$, so $\ln 1$ is 0. Thus if we evaluate the expression at $x = 1$, we get

$$\lim_{x \to 1} \frac{\ln x}{2 - 2x} \; [\neq] \; \frac{\ln 1}{2 - 2} = \frac{0}{0}$$

Since $f(1)$ over $g(1)$ is indeterminate, we try the ratio of $f'(1)$ over $g'(1)$ and find that the limit is $-\frac{1}{2}$.

$$\lim_{x \to 1} \frac{f'(x)}{g'(x)} = \lim_{x \to 1} \frac{\dfrac{1}{x}}{-2} = -\frac{1}{2}$$

Example 87.4 Find $\lim_{x \to \infty} \dfrac{\cos x + 2x}{6x^2}$.

Solution First we evaluate the expression at ∞ and get an indeterminate result.

$$\frac{\cos \infty + 2(\infty)}{6(\infty)^2}$$

The value of $\cos x$ is never less than -1 or greater than $+1$, but $2(\infty)$ and $6(\infty)^2$ tell us that both the numerator and the denominator of this expression increase without bound as $x \to \infty$. Thus we apply L'Hôpital's rule to get

$$\lim_{x \to \infty} \frac{f'(x)}{g'(x)} = \lim_{x \to \infty} \frac{-\sin x + 2}{12x}$$

The value of $-\sin x$ is always between -1 and $+1$, so as x increases the numerator has a value between 1 and 3. The denominator increases without bound, however, so the limit is a number between 1 and 3 divided by a quantity that is increasing without bound. Thus the limit as x approaches ∞ is zero.

$$\lim_{x \to \infty} \frac{-\sin x + 2}{12x} = 0 \qquad \text{so} \qquad \lim_{x \to \infty} \frac{\cos x + 2x}{6x^2} = \mathbf{0}$$

87.B
Proof of L'Hôpital's rule

We want to prove that if $f(a)$ and $g(a)$ both equal zero the limit of the quotient as x approaches a is the limit of the derivative.

$$\lim_{x \to a} \frac{f(x)}{g(x)} = \lim_{x \to a} \frac{f'(x)}{g'(x)}$$

There are two forms of the proof. The form that permits repetitive use of the rule is called the *stronger form* and permits $g'(a)$ to have a value of zero. We will prove the weaker form, which requires that $g'(a)$ not equal zero. We will work backward and begin with $f'(a)$ over $g'(a)$ and show that this equals $\lim_{x \to a} f(x)/g(x)$. First we write the definition of $f'(a)$ over $g'(a)$.

$$\frac{f'(a)}{g'(a)} = \frac{\displaystyle\lim_{x \to a} \frac{f(x) - f(a)}{x - a}}{\displaystyle\lim_{x \to a} \frac{g(x) - g(a)}{x - a}}$$

The quotient of the limits equals the limit of the quotients. Thus we write the limit of the quotients and multiply above and below by $x - a$ to simplify.

$$\frac{f'(a)}{g'(a)} = \lim_{x \to a} \frac{\dfrac{f(x) - f(a)}{x - a}}{\dfrac{g(x) - g(a)}{x - a}} = \lim_{x \to a} \frac{f(x) - f(a)}{g(x) - g(a)}$$

But we began by noting that $f(a)$ and $g(a)$ both equal zero. If we substitute zero for $f(a)$ and $g(a)$, we can complete the proof.

$$\frac{f'(a)}{g'(a)} = \lim_{x \to a} \frac{f(x) - 0}{g(x) - 0} = \lim_{x \to a} \frac{f(x)}{g(x)}$$

Problem set 87

1. A particle moves along the x axis so that its acceleration at a given time t is given by

$$a(t) = 2 \cos t$$

If the velocity of the particle at $t = \frac{\pi}{2}$ is -4 and the position of the particle at $t = 0$ is $x = 8$, develop an equation which expresses the particle's velocity and position as a function of t.

2. A particle moves along the x axis so that its acceleration function is

$$a(t) = -6t$$

Furthermore, its velocity at $t = 1$ is -1 and its position at $t = 2$ is -3. Find the velocity of the particle at $t = 2$.

3. A rectangular tank whose depth is 2 meters, whose width is 4 meters, and whose length is 10 meters is completely filled with water. Find the work done in pumping out enough water to decrease the depth of the water to 1 meter.

4. A trough 6 meters long with cross section as shown is filled with a fluid whose weight density is 1000 newtons per cubic meter. Find the work done in pumping all the fluid out of the trough.

5. The side of a large tank filled with a fluid whose weight density is 2000 newtons per cubic meter contains a 1 by 1 meter square door at its base. Find the total force against the door if the top of the door lies 5 meters below the surface of the water.

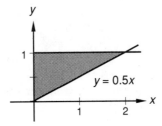

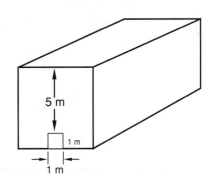

Evaluate the following limits:

6. $\lim\limits_{x \to 0} \dfrac{\sin x}{x}$

7. $\lim\limits_{x \to 0} \dfrac{2 - 2\cos x}{\sin x}$

8. $\lim\limits_{x \to \infty} \dfrac{x}{(\ln x)^2}$

9. $\lim\limits_{x \to \infty} \dfrac{x + \sin x}{x^2}$

10. $\lim\limits_{x \to 0} \dfrac{e^x - x}{\sin x}$

Integrate:

11. $\displaystyle\int \sin^3 x \, dx$

12. $\displaystyle\int \cos x \sin^3 x \, dx$

13. $\displaystyle\int (\log x + 43^x) \, dx$

14. The definite integral

$$\int_1^2 x\sqrt{2x - 1} \, dx$$

is equal to which of the following definite integrals?

(a) $\displaystyle\int_1^2 \frac{1}{2}(u^{3/2} + u^{1/2}) \, du$

(b) $\displaystyle\int_1^3 \frac{1}{2}(u^{3/2} + u^{1/2}) \, du$

(c) $\displaystyle\int_1^3 \frac{1}{2}(u^{3/2} - u^{1/2}) \, du$

(d) $\displaystyle\int_1^3 (u^{3/2} + u^{1/2}) \, du$

(e) None of the above

15. Suppose $f(x) = \tan x$, $g(x) = 3 \sin x$, and $h(x) = (fg)(x)$. Is the graph of h symmetric about the y axis, symmetric about the origin, or neither?

16. Find the equation of the tangent line which can be drawn to the graph of the function $y = x^3 + 6x^2 + 1$ at its point of inflection.

17. Suppose $f(x) = a \sin x + b \cos x$ and the slope of the graph of f at $(0, 2)$ is 2. Find $a + b$.

18. Write a definite integral whose value equals the area of the region between the graph of $y = x^2 + x - 2$ and the x axis over the interval $[-3, 2]$.

Differentiate:

19. $y = \dfrac{x + \sin x}{\cos x} + \arctan x^2 + e^x \csc 2x$

20. $h(x)$ if $h(x) = f(g(x))$, $f(x) = x^2$, and $g(x) = \sin x$

CONCEPT REVIEW   21. Suppose f is a function which is differentiable for all real values of x. Then

$$\lim_{h \to 0} \frac{f(a + h) - f(a)}{h}$$

equals which of the following?

(a) $f(a)$ (b) $\displaystyle\lim_{x \to a} \frac{f(x) - f(a)}{x - a}$ (c) 0 (d) undefined

---

LESSON 88 *Asymptotes of rational functions*

We have found that we can sketch the graph of a rational function quickly and easily if we first mark the locations of the poles and zeros of the function.

The poles are the zeros of the linear real factors of the denominator, and the zeros are the zeros of the linear real factors of the numerator. The functions that we have sketched have permitted us to study the behavior of rational functions, but since both polynomials must first be factored into a product of linear real factors and irreducible quadratic factors, the possible applications of this method are restricted. To use poles and zeros to graph the function

$$y = \frac{3x^{10} - 2x^5 + 7x^4 + x^3 - x + 5}{5x^8 - 4x^4 + 3x^3 - x^2 + x + 2}$$

would require that we first factor both polynomials. We are indebted to Gauss for proving that both of these polynomials can be factored, but unfortunately he did not come up with a method for doing the factoring. Modern computers, however, can be programmed to graph functions and to find zeros of functions to any degree of accuracy required.

It is possible to determine the asymptotes of a function for large positive and negative values of x even though the two polynomials have not been factored. If the degree of the numerator is less than the degree of the denominator, the x axis is the horizontal asymptote. If the degree of the numerator is equal to the degree of the denominator, the horizontal asymptote is a constant function whose value equals the coefficient of the highest-power term in the numerator divided by the coefficient of the highest-power term in the denominator. If the degree of the numerator is greater than the degree of the denominator, the first step is to divide the numerator by the denominator and consider the expression that results. We look at these cases in the following examples.

Example 88.1   Find the equation of the horizontal asymptote of $y = \dfrac{4x^4 + 3x^2 + 2x}{3x^5 + x^3 - 4}$.

Solution   The degree of the denominator is greater than the degree of the numerator, so the horizontal asymptote will be the x axis. To show this, we divide every term in the numerator and in the denominator by the highest power of x in the denominator, which is x^5.

$$y = \frac{\dfrac{4x^4}{x^5} + \dfrac{3x^2}{x^5} + \dfrac{2x}{x^5}}{\dfrac{3x^5}{x^5} + \dfrac{x^3}{x^5} + \dfrac{4}{x^5}} \longrightarrow y = \frac{\dfrac{4}{x} + \dfrac{3}{x^3} + \dfrac{2}{x^4}}{3 + \dfrac{1}{x^2} - \dfrac{4}{x^5}}$$

As x increases without limit positively or negatively, the value of each of the fractions approaches zero and the value of the function approaches 0/3, which equals zero. This means that the graph of the function approaches the x axis ($y = 0$) for both large positive values and large negative values of x.

Example 88.2   Graph the function $y = \dfrac{-5x + x^2}{2x^2 - 8}$.

Solution   In this example, the degree of the polynomial in the numerator equals the degree of the polynomial in the denominator, and the horizontal asymptote will be some constant that is not zero. To find the constant, we divide above and below by x^2, which is the highest power of x in the denominator.

$$\frac{\dfrac{-5x}{x^2} + \dfrac{x^2}{x^2}}{\dfrac{2x^2}{x^2} - \dfrac{8}{x^2}} \longrightarrow \frac{\dfrac{-5}{x} + 1}{2 - \dfrac{8}{x^2}}$$

As x increases without bound positively or negatively, the value of the fractions in the numerator and in the denominator approach zero and the value of the whole expressions approaches $\frac{1}{2}$. Thus **the horizontal asymptote is $y = \frac{1}{2}$.**

In the examples, we will concentrate on rational functions like this one that are easy to factor, so that the poles and zeros are easy to find. We write the factored form and show the graph here. **We note that the graph can cross the horizontal asymptote at values of x near the origin but cannot cross the horizontal asymptote far away from the origin.**

$$y = \frac{x(-5 + x)}{2(x + 2)(x - 2)}$$

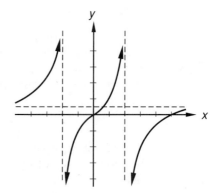

Example 88.3   Graph the function $y = \dfrac{x^2 + 1}{x}$.

Solution   The degree of the polynomial in the numerator is greater than the degree of the polynomial in the denominator. When this occurs, we will not have a horizontal asymptote because the graph will approach some nonconstant function of x.

The first step is to divide the numerator by the denominator.

$$y = \frac{x^2 + 1}{x} \longrightarrow y = x + \frac{1}{x}$$

For large values of x, the fraction $1/x$ has negligible value, so the value of y is approximately equal to the value of x.

$$y \approx x$$

This tells us that the line $y = x$ is the asymptote.

When we look at the original function, we see that it has a vertical asymptote when $x = 0$. Since no value of x will make $x^2 + 1$ equal zero, the function has no zeros and thus the graph of the function never touches the x axis.

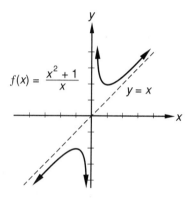

Example 88.4   Graph the function $y = \dfrac{x^2 - 1}{x - 2}$.

Solution   Since the degree of the numerator is greater than the degree of the denominator, the first step is to divide as indicated.

$$\begin{array}{r} x + 2 \\ x - 2\overline{\smash{\big)}\,x^2 \qquad\; - 1} \\ \underline{x^2 - 2x} \\ 2x - 1 \\ \underline{2x - 4} \\ 3 \end{array} \qquad y = \frac{x^2 - 1}{x - 2} = x + 2 + \frac{3}{x - 2}$$

For large values of x, the value of 3 divided by $x - 2$ becomes very small and the value of y approaches $x + 2$, so the asymptote for large values of x is

$$y = x + 2$$

To find the poles and the zeros of the function, we write the function in factored form and see that the function has a vertical asymptote at $x = 2$ and has zeros at x values of 1 and -1.

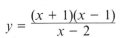

$$y = \frac{(x + 1)(x - 1)}{x - 2}$$

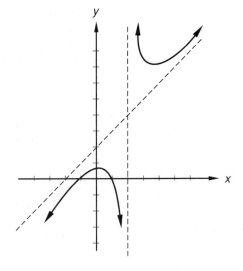

Problem set 88

1. A particle moves along the number line so that its acceleration at a given time t is given by $a(t) = 2t$. If the velocity of the particle is 10 at $t = 3$, find the time when the particle has a velocity of 17.

2. A rectangular tank is 4 meters high, 1 meter wide, and 3 meters long. The tank is half full of a fluid that has a weight density of 2000 newtons per cubic meter. Find the work done in pumping all the fluid out of the tank.

3. A ball is thrown straight upward from a height of 160 meters with an initial velocity of 50 meters per second. Write equations which express the height of the ball above the ground and its velocity as functions of the time t after the ball is thrown. How long after the ball is thrown will it reach its peak? How long after it is thrown will it hit the ground?

4. Find the equation of the horizontal asymptote of the graph of

$$y = \frac{3x^5 - 2x^3 + 1}{2x^5 - 1}$$

Sketch the graphs of the following functions, indicating clearly all asymptotes and x intercepts.

5. $y = \dfrac{x + 1}{x}$

6. $y = \dfrac{-24x + 6x^2}{3x^2 - 27}$

7. $y = \dfrac{x^2 - 1}{x}$

8. $y = \dfrac{x^2 - 1}{x - 3}$

Evaluate the following limits:

9. $\displaystyle\lim_{x \to 0} \frac{x}{\sin 45x}$

10. $\displaystyle\lim_{x \to \infty} \frac{x^2}{\ln x}$

11. $\displaystyle\lim_{x \to 0} \frac{\cos x - 1}{52 \sin x}$

12. $\displaystyle\lim_{x \to 1} \frac{x^2 - 3}{2x - 1}$

13. Let R be the region completely enclosed by the graph of $y = \sqrt{x}$, the x axis, and the line $x = 4$. Find the volume of the solid formed when R is revolved about the x axis.

14. Find the area of the region completely enclosed by the graphs of $y = x^3$ and $y = x$.

15.   Suppose $b > c > 1$ and f is continuous for all real numbers. If

$$\int_1^c f(x)\,dx = 3 \qquad \text{and} \qquad \int_1^b f(x)\,dx = 5 \qquad \text{evaluate} \qquad \int_c^b f(x)\,dx$$

16.   Differentiate: $y = \arctan(\sin x) + x^2 \ln|\sin x| + e^{\sec x}$

Integrate:

17. $\displaystyle\int \frac{3x^2 + e^x}{x^3 + e^x}\,dx$ 　　　　　　　　　　　　　**18.** $\displaystyle\int (\ln x + 43^x)\,dx$

CONCEPT REVIEW   **19.**   Let $f(x) = \sin(\arctan x)$. Compute the range of f.

20.   Suppose the function f is defined as follows:

$$f(x) = \begin{cases} 2x + 1 & \text{when } x < 1 \\ ax^2 + 1 & \text{when } x \geq 1 \end{cases}$$

Find the value of a which makes f continuous everywhere.

LESSON 89   *Balance points*

Every physical object has a "balance point" called the ***center of mass*** or the ***center of gravity.*** The body behaves as if all its mass were concentrated at this balance point. To begin our investigation of this concept, we note that if we place a fulcrum (support) at the balance point of a board, the board will balance in a horizontal position as we show on the left.

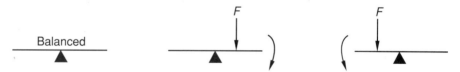

If a force is applied to the right of the fulcrum, the board will rotate as indicated in the center figure. If the force is applied to the left of the fulcrum, the board will rotate in the opposite direction as shown in the figure on the right. In a laboratory, if we use weights to apply forces on both sides of the support, we will make an unusual discovery. The board can be kept in balance by using weights of different sizes if the weights are placed at different distances from the fulcrum.

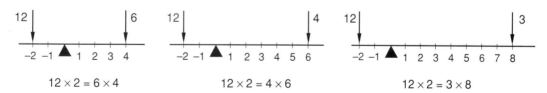

We find that a weight of 12 at a distance of 2 units from the fulcrum can be balanced by a weight of 4 at a distance of 6 units from the fulcrum or a weight of 3 at a distance of 8 units from the fulcrum. We note that 2 times 12 equals 24 and that both 4 times 6 and 3 times 8 also equal 24. If we investigate further, we will find that we can balance the board by using any size weight that we choose as long as the product of the weight and the distance from the fulcrum is 24. Any unit of length can be used as long as the same unit is used for both measurements, and likewise any unit of weight may be used.

The product of a force that tends to cause a rotation and its distance from a given point is so important that it had to be given a name. The name chosen for this product is *moment of force*. In this example, we note that the direction of each force is perpendicular to the board. If the force were applied at an angle, only the component of force perpendicular to the board would be used in computing the moment.

Moments can be used to find the balance point of a system. To develop this idea we will hypothesize a board that has no mass and thus has no weight. Thus, the weight of the board will not be considered. Forces are applied as shown.

We would like to find where to place the fulcrum so that the board would be in balance. Newton's laws of motion tell us that if an object is not accelerating in the vertical direction, then the sum of the vertical forces acting on the object must equal zero. Since the sum of the downward forces on the board equals 16, the upward force exerted by the fulcrum must also equal 16. But where should we place the fulcrum? **We must place the fulcrum at a point such that the sum of the moments about any point on the board equals zero.** Otherwise the unbalanced moments would cause the board to rotate about that point. Thus the location of the point chosen as the origin does not matter. We will call the distance from the origin to the unknown location of the fulcrum $\bar{x}$. To illustrate the fact that any point can be chosen as the origin, we will work the problem twice. On the left we decide to place the origin 2 units to the left of the 6-pound force. On the right we decide to place the origin 4 units to the right of the 6-pound force. In both figures we show a force of 16 acting upward at $\bar{x}$, a coordinate that has not yet been determined.

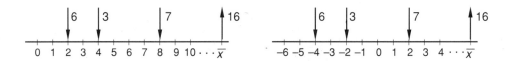

To help us keep track of the directions of the moments we will arbitrarily call downward forces *negative forces* and upward forces *positive forces*. We will use signed numbers to the left and the right of the origin to give us directed distances. The sum of the moments about the origin in both cases must equal zero. There are four moments in each case, so we have

$$F \cdot D + F \cdot D + F \cdot D + F \cdot D = 0 \qquad\qquad F \cdot D + F \cdot D + F \cdot D + F \cdot D = 0$$

$$(-6)(2) + (-3)(4) + (-7)(8) + (16)(\bar{x}) = 0 \qquad (-6)(-4) + (-3)(-2) + (-7)(2) + (16)(\bar{x}) = 0$$

$$-12 - 12 - 56 + 16\bar{x} = 0 \qquad\qquad\qquad 24 + 6 - 14 + 16\bar{x} = 0$$

$$16\bar{x} = 80 \qquad\qquad\qquad\qquad\qquad 16\bar{x} = -16$$

$$\bar{x} = 5 \qquad\qquad\qquad\qquad\qquad\qquad \bar{x} = -1$$

In the example on the left $\bar{x} = 5$, which says that the fulcrum should be placed 5 units to the right of the origin. In the example on the right $\bar{x} = -1$, so the fulcrum should be placed 1 unit to the left of the origin. Both answers tells us that the fulcrum should be placed 1 unit to the right of the 3-pound force.

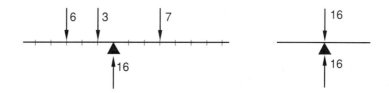

When we place the fulcrum as shown on the left, the board does not move up or down because the sum of the downward forces is 16 and the sum of the upward forces is 16. The board does not rotate because the sum of the moments that tend to rotate the board to the left is $(1 \times 3) + (3 \times 6) = 21$, and the sum of the moments that tend to rotate the board to the right is $7 \times 3 = 21$. The net effect is the same as we would have if all the weight were applied directly above the fulcrum, as we show in the figure on the right. **Thus we see that when the fulcrum is properly placed the sum of the moments about the fulcrum equals zero and that the upward force at the fulcrum does not cause an unbalanced moment.**

Consider the following system.

The **directed distance** from $\bar{x}$ to x_1 is $x_1 - \bar{x}$, and the **directed distance** from $\bar{x}$ to x_2 is $x_2 - \bar{x}$. If x_1 is less than $\bar{x}$, as in the figure above, then $x_1 - \bar{x}$ will be a negative number. If x_2 is greater than $\bar{x}$, as shown, then $x_2 - \bar{x}$ will be a positive number. The value of each downward force caused by a mass equals the product of the mass and the local acceleration of gravity. If we use $m_1 g$ as the downward force caused by mass 1 and $x_1 - \bar{x}$ as the directed distance from the balance point, the moment that mass 1 causes about the balance point is $m_1 g(x_1 - \bar{x})$.

Consider the following system of n masses that are suspended from a hypothetical linear support that has no mass.

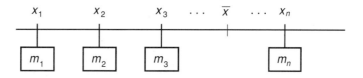

If we set equal to zero the sum of the moments about $\bar{x}$ caused by the masses and the pull of gravity, we get

$$m_1 g(x_1 - \bar{x}) + m_2 g(x_2 - \bar{x}) + \cdots + m_n g(x_n - \bar{x}) = 0$$

If we divide every term by g, we can eliminate the g's and get

$$m_1(x_1 - \bar{x}) + m_2(x_2 - \bar{x}) + \cdots + m_n(x_n - \bar{x}) = 0$$

If we multiply as indicated and rearrange the terms, we get

$$\bar{x}m_1 + \bar{x}m_2 + \cdots + \bar{x}m_n = x_1 m_1 + x_2 m_2 + \cdots + x_n m_n$$

If we factor $\bar{x}$ from the terms on the left-hand side, we get

$$\bar{x}(m_1 + m_2 + \cdots + m_n) = x_1 m_1 + x_2 m_2 + \cdots + x_n m_n \qquad \text{factored}$$

Now if we divide by the coefficient of $\bar{x}$, we get an expression for $\bar{x}$ that defines $\bar{x}$ as a function of masses and their positions.

$$\bar{x} = \frac{x_1 m_1 + x_2 m_2 + \cdots + x_n m_n}{m_1 + m_2 + \cdots + m_n} \quad \text{divided}$$

We began by defining a moment of force as the product of a force and a distance. In a system where all forces are caused by masses and gravity, we can define a **moment of mass** to be a force moment divided by the acceleration of gravity.

$$\text{Moment of mass} = \frac{\text{moment of force}}{\text{acceleration of gravity}} = \frac{mgx}{g} = mx$$

Thus the equation for $\bar{x}$ given above defines $\bar{x}$ for a gravitational system to be the sum of the individual moments of mass divided by the sum of the masses.

Example 89.1   Find the balance point for this system of masses suspended from a massless support as shown.

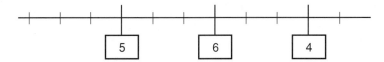

Solution   We can use any coordinate system we please, so we arbitrarily choose the leftmost mark as the origin.

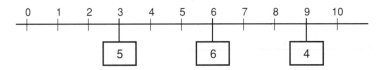

Now we find $\bar{x}$ by dividing the sum of the mass moments by the sum of the masses.

$$\bar{x} = \frac{(5)(3) + (6)(6) + (4)(9)}{5 + 6 + 4} = \frac{87}{15} = 5.8$$

Thus the balance point for this system is 5.8 units to the right of the origin. But everyone will not choose the same origin, so this answer is not satisfactory. Thus we will say that $\bar{x}$ **is located 0.2 unit to the left of the mass of 6,** a description that everyone will understand.

Problem set 89

1. A rectangle is inscribed in the region bounded by the x axis and the graph of $y = 4 - |x|$ as shown. Find the area of the rectangle of the greatest area which can be so inscribed.

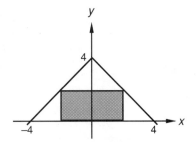

2. Determine the maximum value of the function f on the closed interval $[-4, 5]$ if $f(x) = -x^2 + 2x + 2$.

3. A rectangular tank 2 meters deep is completely filled with a fluid whose weight density is 2000 newtons per cubic meter. Find the total force exerted by the fluid against one face of the tank if its width is 1 meter.

4. A particle moves along the x axis so that its acceleration at any time t is given by $a(t) = 6t + 18$. At time $t = 0$, the velocity of the particle is $v(0) = 20$, and at

time $t = 1$, its position is $x(1) = 21$. Find the equations for the velocity, $v(t)$, and position, $x(t)$, of the particle.

Find the balance point for each of the following systems of masses to two decimal places.

5.    6.

7. Write the equations of the asymptotes of the graph of

$$y = \frac{2x^2 - 2x - 4}{x - 1}$$

Graph the following functions, indicating clearly the x intercepts and the asymptotes.

8. $y = \dfrac{x^2 + 1}{2x}$ 9. $y = \dfrac{x^2 + x - 2}{x + 1}$

Evaluate the following limits:

10. $\displaystyle\lim_{x\to 0} \frac{\sin 3x}{x}$ 11. $\displaystyle\lim_{x\to 2} \frac{x^3 - x^2 - x - 2}{x - 2}$

12. Approximate to two decimal places the slope of the tangent line which can be drawn to the graph of $y = 2^x$ at $x = 2$. Write the equation of the line.

13. If $\displaystyle\lim_{x\to 2} f(x) = 7$, then which of the following must be true?

    (a) f exists at $x = 2$ (b) $f(2) = 7$ (c) f is continuous at $x = 2$
    (d)   None of the above

14. Use y as the variable of integration to write a definite integral whose value is the area of the region bounded by $x = \sqrt{1 - y^2}$ and the y axis.

15. Differentiate: $y = e^{\sin x} + \ln |x^2 + 1| + \arcsin x - 3 \log_{14} x$

Integrate:

16. $\displaystyle\int \sin^3 x \, dx$ 17. $\displaystyle\int (x + 2)e^{x^2+4x} \, dx$ 18. $\displaystyle\int xe^{-x} \, dx$

19. If $f(x) = e^{3x}$, approximate to two decimal places the value of $f^{-1}(1)$ where f^{-1} is the inverse function of f.

CONCEPT REVIEW   20. Suppose the interval $[0, 10]$ along the x axis is partitioned into 20 equally long subintervals. Let x_1 be the leftmost point of the first subinterval, x_2 be the leftmost point of the second subinterval, and so forth. Which of the following must be true?

    (a) $\displaystyle\int_0^{10} x^2 \, dx > \sum_{i=1}^{20} \frac{1}{2}(x_i)^2$ (b) $\displaystyle\int_0^{10} x^2 \, dx < \sum_{i=1}^{20} \frac{1}{2}(x_i)^2$

    (c) $\displaystyle\int_0^{10} x^2 \, dx = \sum_{i=1}^{20} \frac{1}{2}(x_i)^2$ (d) $\displaystyle\int_0^{10} (1 - x^2) \, dx > \sum_{i=1}^{20} \frac{1}{2}(x_i)^2$

21. Suppose we are given the graph of a function f. Then we can obtain the graph of the inverse of f by doing which of the following?
    (a)   Reflecting the graph of the f in the line $y = x$
    (b)   Reflecting the graph of f in the x axis
    (c)   Reflecting the graph of f in the y axis
    (d)   Rotating the graph of f counterclockwise $90°$

LESSON 90 *Volume by washers*

Some solids of revolution have holes in them, and the volume can be computed as the difference of two volumes found by stacking disks. The volume can also be found by stacking washers. The volume of the solid formed by rotating the first-quadrant region shown about the y axis is the volume formed by revolving the region bounded by the graph of $y = x^2$ about the y axis reduced by the volume formed by revolving about the y axis the region bounded by the graph of $y = 2x^2$.

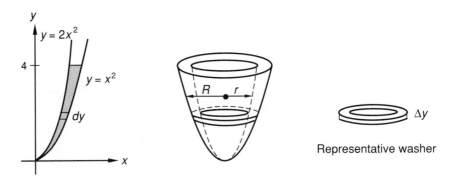

The solid formed is depicted in the center figure, and its volume can be approximated by a stack of circular washers similar to the representative washer shown. The volume of the representative washer is the product of the thickness (Δy) and the area of the whole disk, πR^2, reduced by the area of the hole in its center, πr^2.

$$\text{Volume} = (\pi R^2 - \pi r^2)\,\Delta y$$

Since this result is exactly the same as the difference in the volumes of two representative disks,

$$\text{Volume} = \pi R^2\,\Delta y - \pi r^2\,\Delta y$$

we see that volume-by-washer method is the difference-of-two-disks method in disguise. The washers allow us to visualize the problem.

Example 90.1 Find the volume of the solid formed by revolving the region shown about the y axis.

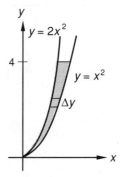

Solution The volume of the solid is the difference in two volumes. Since the larger solid is formed by the graph of $y = x^2$, its radius is $x = \sqrt{y}$. The smaller solid is formed by the graph of $y = 2x^2$, and its radius is $x = \sqrt{y/2}$. Thus the volume of the solid is

$$\text{Volume} = V_1 - V_2 = \int_0^4 \pi(\sqrt{y})^2\,dy - \int_0^4 \pi\left(\sqrt{\tfrac{y}{2}}\right)^2 dy$$

Now we integrate and evaluate.

$$\pi\left(\int_0^4 y\,dy - \int_0^4 \frac{y}{2}\,dy\right) = \pi\left[\frac{y^2}{2} - \frac{y^2}{4}\right]_0^4 = 8\pi - 4\pi = \mathbf{4\pi\ units^3}$$

Example 90.2   Find the volume of the solid formed by revolving about the x axis the region shown between the graphs of $y = \sqrt{x}$ and $y = x^2$.

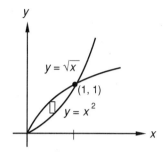

Solution   The width of the washer shown is Δx, the radius of the larger solid is $y = \sqrt{x}$, and the radius of the smaller solid is $y = x^2$. The difference of the values is

$$\text{Volume} = \int_0^1 \pi(\sqrt{x})^2\,dx - \int_0^1 \pi(x^2)^2\,dx$$

If we simplify, we get

$$\pi\int_0^1 x\,dx - \pi\int_0^1 x^4\,dx = \pi\left[\frac{x^2}{2} - \frac{x^5}{5}\right]_0^1 = \pi\left(\frac{1}{2} - \frac{1}{5}\right) = \frac{3}{10}\pi\ \text{unit}^3$$

Example 90.3   The region bounded by the graphs of $y = x^2 + 2$, $x = 0$, $x = 1$, and $y = \frac{1}{2}x + 1$ is revolved about the x axis. Find the volume of the solid of revolution generated.

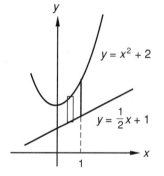

Solution   The rectangle is a profile of a section of a washer. The width of the washer is Δx, and we will stack these washers from $x = 0$ to $x = 1$. The radius of the inside of the washer is $y = \frac{1}{2}x + 1$, and the radius of the outside of the washer is $y = x^2 + 2$. These radii determine the two volumes whose difference we are computing.

$$\text{Volume} = V_1 - V_2 = \int_0^1 \pi(x^2 + 2)^2\,dx - \int_0^1 \pi\left(\frac{x}{2} + 1\right)^2 dx$$

We expand the integrands and integrate.

$$\pi\int_0^1 (x^4 + 4x^2 + 4)\,dx - \pi\int_0^1 \left(\frac{x^2}{4} + x + 1\right)dx \qquad \text{expanded}$$

$$= \pi\left[\frac{x^5}{5} + \frac{4x^3}{3} + 4x - \frac{x^3}{12} - \frac{x^2}{2} - x\right]_0^1 \qquad \text{integrated}$$

$$= \pi\left(\frac{1}{5} + \frac{4}{3} + 4 - \frac{1}{12} - \frac{1}{2} - 1\right) = \frac{79\pi}{20}\ \text{units}^3 \qquad \text{evaluated}$$

Problem set 90

1. A 10-meter-long trough with a right triangular cross section is partially filled with a fluid whose weight density is 9000 newtons per cubic meter. If the level of the fluid is 1 meter below the top rim of the trough, find the work done in pumping all the fluid out of the tank.

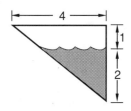

2. Suppose the function f is defined as follows:

$$f(x) = \begin{cases} x^3 + 2x & \text{when } x \leq 2 \\ 3x + b & \text{when } x > 2 \end{cases}$$

Find the value of b which makes f continuous everywhere.

3. Let f be a quadratic function. The slope of the tangent line which can be drawn to the graph of f at $x = 1$ is 1, and the slope of the tangent line which can be drawn to the graph of f at $x = 2$ is 5. If the graph of f passes through the point $(0, 1)$, find the equation of f.

4. Let R be the region in the first quadrant enclosed by the graphs of $y = x^2$, $y = \frac{1}{4}x^2$, and $y = 4$. Find the volume of the solid formed when R is rotated about the y axis.

5. Let R be the first-quadrant region completely bounded by the graph of $y = \sqrt{x}$ and $y = x^3$. Find the volume of the solid formed when region R is revolved about the x axis.

6. Let R be the region bounded by the graphs of $y = x^2 + 1$, $y = x$, $x = 0$, and $x = 2$. Find the volume of the solid formed when region R is rotated about the x axis.

7. Find the balance point for this system of masses.

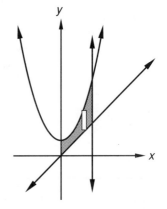

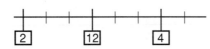

8. Make a rough sketch of $y = \dfrac{2(x - 1)(x + 2)}{x}$.

9. Write the equations of all the asymptotes of the graph of the function

$$y = \frac{x + 1}{x^3 - x^2 + x - 1}$$

Evaluate the following limits:

10. $\displaystyle\lim_{x \to \pi} \frac{\sin (x - \pi)}{2x - \dfrac{\pi}{2}}$

11. $\displaystyle\lim_{x \to \infty} \frac{x \ln x}{e^x}$

12. $\displaystyle\lim_{x \to 0^+} \left(1 - \frac{|x|}{x}\right)$

13. Find the slope of the line which can be drawn normal to the graph of

$$y = \arcsin \frac{x}{3} \qquad \text{at } x = 1$$

14. Differentiate: $y = x \ln |x^3 - x| + 2^{2x-3} + \arctan x$

15. Integrate: $\int \left(2^x + \dfrac{1}{1 + x^2}\right) dx$

16. Evaluate by using the change of variable method: $\displaystyle\int_0^\pi \dfrac{\cos x}{\sqrt{\sin x + 1}} \, dx$

17. The graph of which of the following functions is concave upward everywhere?
    (a) $y = x^3$ (b) $y = -x^2$ (c) $y = e^x$ (d) $y = \sin x$

18. If f is a function which is continuous and increasing for all real values of x, then which of the following must be true?
    (a) The graph of f is always concave up
    (b) The graph of f is always concave down
    (c) $f(x_1) < f(x_2)$ if $x_1 > x_2$
    (d) $f(x_2) > f(x_1)$ if $x_2 > x_1$

CONCEPT REVIEW   19. The graph of the function f is shown below.

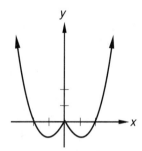

The graph of $g(x) = f(x + 2)$ most resembles which of the following graphs?

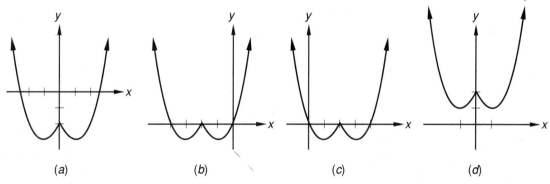

(a)   (b)   (c)   (d)

20. Determine the domain of $y = \sin (\sqrt{x - 1})$.

LESSON 91 *Limits and continuity · Differentiability*

91.A
Limits and continuity

We remember that the limit of a function as x approaches c is the number that the value of the function approaches as x approaches c. The definition of the limit of a function requires that both the right-hand and left-hand limits exist and requires that these limits be equal. If the limits exist and are equal at $x = c$ and if $f(c)$, the value of the function at c, exists and equals the limits, the function is continuous at c.

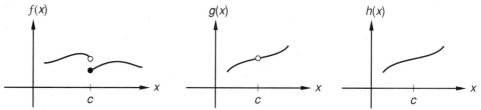

The function f, graphed on the left, has both a right-hand limit and a left-hand limit as x approaches c, but the limits are not equal, so the limit of the function as x approaches c does not exist. The function g has both limits and they are equal, so the function has a limit as x approaches c, but the function is not continuous because these limits do not equal $g(c)$ because $g(c)$ is not defined. The function h has a limit as x approaches c and this limit equals $h(c)$, so this function is a continuous function.

We also remember that the derivative of a function is a limit. We remember that the graphical interpretation of the derivative of $f(x)$ when $x = c$ is the limit of the slope of a secant line drawn through two points P_1 and P_2 on the graph of a function as P_2 approaches P_1 and as the horizontal distance $x - c$ between the points approaches zero. Point P_2 can be to the left of P_1 or to the right of P_1, as we show in the following figures.

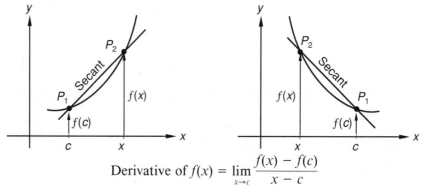

$$\text{Derivative of } f(x) = \lim_{x \to c} \frac{f(x) - f(c)}{x - c}$$

It is not obvious, but for a function to have a derivative at $x = c$ it is necessary that the function be continuous at $x = c$. We can see that this might be true if we look at an example of a function that is obviously discontinuous at $x = c$.

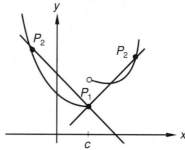

As the point P_2 to the left of P_1 moves down the curve and approaches P_1, the limit of the slope of the secant will approach the slope of the tangent to the curve at P_1. This is obviously not the same limit as the slope of the line through P_1 and the right-hand point P_2 as P_2 moves down the curve. An algebraic proof of the fact that the existence of the derivative implies continuity requires a trick. We want to show that if $f(c)$ exists and if the derivative of f at c exists (is some real number and thus is not infinite), then the limit of $f(x)$ as x approaches c is $f(c)$. We want to show that

$$\text{If } f'(c) \text{ exists} \quad \xrightarrow{\text{then}} \quad \lim_{x \to c} f(x) = f(c)$$

We begin by stating that $f'(c)$ exists and by noting that $f(x)$ equals $f(x)$.

$$f(x) = f(x)$$

Now we add and subtract $f(c)$ to the right side and get

$$f(x) = \boldsymbol{f(c)} + f(x) - \boldsymbol{f(c)}$$

Next we multiply and divide the last part of the sum on the right by $x - c$ and note that x must not equal c because we must rule out division by zero.

$$f(x) = f(c) + \frac{f(x) - f(c)}{\boldsymbol{x - c}} \boldsymbol{(x - c)} \quad x \neq c$$

Next we find the limit of both sides as x approaches c.

$$\lim_{x \to c} f(x) = \lim_{x \to c} \left[f(c) + \frac{f(x) - f(c)}{x - c} (x - c) \right]$$

We expand the limit on the right-hand side of the equals sign by remembering that, if all the individual limits exist, the limit of a sum is the sum of the individual limits and the limit of a product is the product of the individual limits.

$$\lim_{x \to c} f(x) = \lim_{x \to c} f(c) + \lim_{x \to c} \frac{f(x) - f(c)}{x - c} \cdot \lim_{x \to c} (x - c)$$

To the right of the equals sign, the limit of $f(c)$ as x approaches c is $f(c)$. The next limit is $f'(c)$, and the limit of $x - c$ as x approaches c is zero. Now we have

$$\lim_{x \to c} f(x) = f(c) + [f'(c)](0)$$

If $f'(c)$ exists, $f'(c)$ equals some real number, and the product of any real number and zero is zero. If $f'(c)$ had been infinite, we would have had a product on the right that could not have been evaluated.

$$f(c) + (\infty)(0) = ?$$

But since $f'(c)$ equals some real number, the product is zero, and finally we have

$$\lim_{x \to c} f(x) = f(c)$$

We began by assuming that $f'(c)$ exists and showed that with this assumption we can prove that the limit of the function as x approaches c exists and is equal to $f(c)$. **Thus the existence of the derivative at c tells us that the function is continuous at c.**

91.B
Differentiability

We remember that a continuous function is differentiable on an interval if the derivative exists at every point on the interval. For the derivative to exist at a point c, the derivative as x approaches c from the left must equal the derivative as x

approaches c from the right. A function is not differentiable at $x = c$ if the graph of the function comes to a sharp point when $x = c$ because the left-hand and right-hand derivatives will not be equal, so $f'(c)$ does not exist. A function is also not differentiable at $x = c$ if the graph has a vertical tangent line at c because, if it does, $f'(c)$ does not exist. We remember that the values of x for which the derivative does not exist are called **singular numbers.**

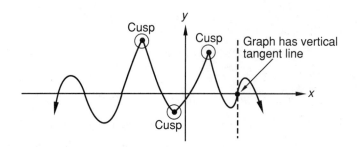

We define the limit on the left to be the left-hand derivative at $x = c$ and the limit on the right to be the right-hand derivative at $x = c$.

$$\lim_{x \to c^-} \frac{f(x) - f(c)}{x - c} \qquad \lim_{x \to c^+} \frac{f(x) - f(c)}{x - c}$$

If these limits exist and are equal, we say the derivative f exists at $x = c$ or that f is differentiable at $x = c$.

Example 91.1   Use left-hand and right-hand derivatives to determine if $f(x) = |x - 2|$ is differentiable at $x = 2$.

Solution   An absolute value function can be redefined as a piecewise function that does not use absolute value.

$$f(x) = \begin{cases} x - 2 & \text{when } x \geq 2 \\ -x + 2 & \text{when } x \leq 2 \end{cases}$$

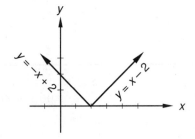

We find the derivatives of $y = x - 2$ and $y = -x + 2$.

$$\begin{array}{ll} f(x) = x - 2 & f(x) = -x + 2 \\ f'(x) = 1 & f'(x) = -1 \\ f'(2) = 1 & f'(2) = -1 \end{array}$$

The left-hand derivative does not equal the right-hand derivative when $x = 2$, so **the function does not have a derivative at $x = 2$.**

Example 91.2   For what values of x is the piecewise function shown at the top of the next page differentiable?

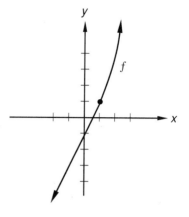

$$f(x) = \begin{cases} x^2 & \text{where } x \geq 1 \\ 2x - 1 & \text{where } x < 1 \end{cases}$$

Solution   First we look at the left-hand and right-hand derivatives.

LEFT-HAND DERIVATIVE	RIGHT-HAND DERIVATIVE
$f(x) = 2x - 1 \longrightarrow f'(x) = 2$	$f(x) = x^2 \longrightarrow f'(x) = 2x$

We see that the derivative of f for every value of x less than 1 is 2, and the derivative of f for every value of x greater than 1 is $2x$. Now we check the values of the left-hand and right-hand derivatives when $x = 1$.

LEFT-HAND DERIVATIVE	RIGHT-HAND DERIVATIVE
$f'(1) = 2$	$f'(1) = 2(1) = 2$

Since f has a derivative for all values of x greater than 1 and for all values of x less than 1, and since the left-hand and right-hand derivatives are equal when $x = 1$, $f(x)$ is differentiable **for all real values of x.**

Example 91.3   Let f be defined as follows:

$$f(x) = \begin{cases} |x| + 3 & \text{if } x < 1 \\ ax^2 + bx & \text{if } x \geq 1 \end{cases}$$

Find the values of a and b so that f is continuous and differentiable at $x = 1$.

Solution   This example is a continuation of Example 83.3 on continuity. At worst, f is discontinuous, as the graph below shows.

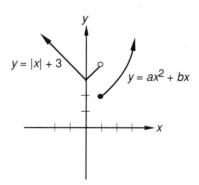

From the graph and from the equation of f, we see that

$$\lim_{x \to 1^-} f(x) = 4 \qquad \text{and} \qquad \lim_{x \to 1^+} f(x) = a + b$$

For f to be continuous at $x = 1$, these limits must be equal.

$$\lim_{x \to 1^-} f(x) = \lim_{x \to 1^+} f(x)$$

$$4 = a + b$$

We use this information to write the first equation in a and b that must be satisfied. Now for f to be differentiable at $x = 1$, we must choose a and b such that the left-hand derivative of f at $x = 1$ equals the right-hand derivative of f at $x = 1$. The equation of f just to the left of $x = 1$ is $y = x + 3$, and the equation of f just to the right of $x = 1$ is $y = ax^2 + bx$.

LEFT-HAND DERIVATIVE	RIGHT-HAND DERIVATIVE
$f(x) = x + 3$	$f(x) = ax^2 + bx$
$f'(x) = 1$	$f'(x) = 2ax + b$
$f'(1) = 1$	$f'(1) = 2a + b$

Equating these values of $f'(1)$ gives us our second equation in a and b, $1 = 2a + b$. Now we have

$$\begin{cases} 4 = a + b \\ 1 = 2a + b \end{cases}$$

The solution to this system is $a = -3$ and $b = 7$. Thus for the function to be differentiable and continuous at $x = 1$, the equation of the quadratic function must be

$$y = -3x^2 + 7x$$

Problem set 91

1. A 10-foot ladder leans against a vertical wall, and the bottom of the ladder is pulled away from the wall at a rate of 2 feet per second. At what rate is the angle between the ladder and the ground changing when the top of the ladder is 5 feet above the ground?

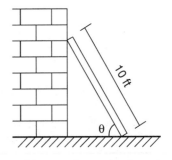

2. A particle moves along the x axis so that its position at time t is given by the equation

$$x(t) = t^2 - 6t + 5$$

Find the times for which the particle is momentarily at rest, the times for which it is moving to the right, and the times for which it is moving to the left.

3. A ball is thrown straight downward from the top of a 100-meter-high building with an initial velocity of 25 meters per second. Develop the velocity function and height function of the ball. How long will it take the ball to hit the ground?

4. A cylindrical tank 100 meters long whose radius is 2 meters is half-filled with a fluid whose weight density is 9000 newtons per cubic meter. Determine the total force exerted by the fluid against one end of the tank.

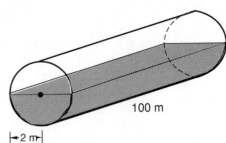

5. The function f is defined as follows:

$$f(x) = \begin{cases} x^2 + x + 1 & \text{when } x \le 1 \\ 2x + 1 & \text{when } x > 1 \end{cases}$$

Determine the left- and right-hand derivatives of f at $x = 1$.

6. For which values of x is the function f of Problem 5 not differentiable?

7. Let g be a function defined as follows:

$$g(x) = \begin{cases} 3x & \text{when } x \le 1 \\ ax^2 + b & \text{when } x > 1 \end{cases}$$

What must be the relationship between a and b for g to be continuous everywhere?

8. If g is as defined in Problem 7, find the numerical values of a and b which will make g both continuous and differentiable for all values of x.

9. Let R be the region completely bounded by the graphs of $y = x^2 + 1$ and $y = x + 1$. Write a definite integral whose value equals the volume of the solid formed when R is revolved about the x axis.

10. Let R be the region in the first quadrant completely enclosed by the graphs of $y = x$ and $y = x^2$. Compute the volume of the solid formed when R is revolved about the y axis.

11. Find the balance point for this system of masses suspended from a massless support as shown.

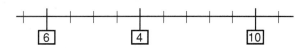

12. Write the equations of all the asymptotes of the graph of

$$f(x) = \frac{2(x^2 + x - 6)}{x - 1}$$

Sketch the graph of f.

Integrate:

13. $\displaystyle\int \cos^3 x \, dx$

14. $\displaystyle\int (\sin x \cos^3 x - \sin x \cos^5 x) \, dx$

15. $\displaystyle\int 2^x \, dx$

16. $\displaystyle\int xe^x \, dx$

17. $\displaystyle\int \frac{e^x + \cos x}{\sqrt{e^x + \sin x}} \, dx$

18. Find $\dfrac{dy}{dx}$ if $y = \dfrac{x}{\sin(1 + x^2)} + \arcsin \dfrac{x}{2} + \log_7 x - 14^x$.

CONCEPT REVIEW

19. Suppose f and g are functions such that $f(g(x)) = x$. Which of the following are possible choices for the functions f and g?

(a) $f(x) = \ln x,\ g(x) = \dfrac{1}{x}$ (b) $f(x) = 2x - 1,\ g(x) = \dfrac{1}{2}x + 1$

(c) $f(x) = \ln x,\ g(x) = e^x$ (d) $f(x) = x^3,\ g(x) = 3x^2$

20. Find the domain and range of $y = \sqrt{1 - \sin x}$.

LESSON 92 *Integration of even powers of sin x and cos x*

To integrate even powers of sin x and cos x, we use the identities

$$\sin^2 x = \frac{1}{2} - \frac{1}{2}\cos 2x \qquad \cos^2 x = \frac{1}{2} + \frac{1}{2}\cos 2x$$

A close look at the graphs of $y = \sin^2 x$ and $y = \cos^2 x$ will give us a better understanding of these identities. On the left we show the graph of $y = \sin x$. In the center, we see the effect of squaring. All negative values become positive. The curve still has a maximum value of 1, but the square of any number between 0 and 1 is less than the number, and this causes every other value of $\sin^2 x$ between 0 and π to be less than the value of sin x. The result is the curve shown.

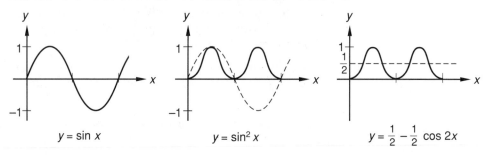

In the right-hand figure we draw a dotted centerline at $y = \frac{1}{2}$, and we see that the graph of $y = \sin^2 x$ looks like the graph of $y = \frac{1}{2} - \frac{1}{2}\cos 2x$. In the three figures below we show the corresponding graphs for the square of the cosine function.

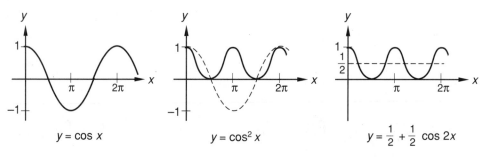

Example 92.1 Find $\int \cos^2 x \, dx$.

Solution We will substitute for $\cos^2 x$ and find that this leads to two integrals.

$$\int \left(\frac{1}{2} + \frac{1}{2}\cos 2x\right) dx = \frac{1}{2}\int dx + \frac{1}{2}\int \cos 2x \, dx$$

The second integral needs an additional factor of 2 to the right of the integral sign and an additional factor of $\frac{1}{2}$ in front, which we supply. Then we integrate.

$$\frac{1}{2}\int dx + \frac{1}{2}\cdot\frac{1}{2}\int \underbrace{(\cos 2x)}_{\cos u}\underbrace{(2\,dx)}_{du} = \frac{x}{2} + \frac{1}{4}\sin 2x + C$$

Example 92.2 Find $\int \sin^2 x \cos^2 x \, dx$.

Solution   Integration of expressions that contain only even powers of the sine and cosine are not difficult but are tedious because of the algebra involved. In this problem we must substitute for both $\sin^2 x$ and $\cos^2 x$ and multiply. Then, to our dismay, we will encounter a $\cos^2 2x$ which requires another substitution.

$$\int \left(\frac{1}{2} - \frac{1}{2}\cos 2x\right)\left(\frac{1}{2} + \frac{1}{2}\cos 2x\right) dx = \int \left(\frac{1}{4} - \frac{1}{4}\cos^2 2x\right) dx$$

For $\cos^2 2x$ we will substitute $\left(\frac{1}{2} + \frac{1}{2}\cos 4x\right)$, so we have

$$\int \left[\frac{1}{4} - \frac{1}{4}\left(\frac{1}{2} + \frac{1}{2}\cos 4x\right)\right] dx = \int \left(\frac{1}{4} - \frac{1}{8} - \frac{1}{8}\cos 4x\right) dx$$

Now we simplify and integrate. In the second integral we need additional factors of 4 and $\frac{1}{4}$, which we supply.

$$\int \left(\frac{1}{4} - \frac{1}{8}\right) dx - \frac{1}{8} \cdot \frac{1}{4} \int \underbrace{(\cos 4x)}_{\cos u}\underbrace{(4\,dx)}_{du} = \frac{x}{8} - \frac{1}{32}\sin 4x + C$$

Example 92.3   Find $\int \sin^4 x \, dx$.

Solution   First we will write $\sin^4 x$ as $(\sin^2 x)^2$. Next we will substitute for $\sin^2 x$ and expand the resulting expression.

$$\sin^4 x = (\sin^2 x)^2 = \left(\frac{1}{2} - \frac{1}{2}\cos 2x\right)^2 = \frac{1}{4} - \frac{1}{2}\cos 2x + \frac{1}{4}\cos^2 2x$$

Now for $\cos^2 2x$ we will substitute $\left(\frac{1}{2} + \frac{1}{2}\cos 4x\right)$.

$$= \frac{1}{4} - \frac{1}{2}\cos 2x + \frac{1}{4}\left(\frac{1}{2} + \frac{1}{2}\cos 4x\right) = \frac{3}{8} - \frac{1}{2}\cos 2x + \frac{1}{8}\cos 4x$$

We have reduced $\sin^4 x$ to an expression containing $\cos 2x$ and $\cos 4x$ which we can integrate if we insert the required constants.

$$\int \sin^4 x \, dx = \int \left(\frac{3}{8} - \frac{1}{2}\cos 2x + \frac{1}{8}\cos 4x\right) dx$$

$$= \frac{3}{8}\int dx - \frac{1}{2} \cdot \frac{1}{2}\int (\cos 2x)(2\,dx) + \frac{1}{8} \cdot \frac{1}{4}\int (\cos 4x)(4\,dx)$$

$$= \frac{3x}{8} - \frac{1}{4}\sin 2x + \frac{1}{32}\sin 4x + C$$

Problem set 92

1. A 3-meter-long trough whose cross section is that of an inverted isosceles triangle, as shown, is full of water. Determine the work done in pumping the water out of the trough. Dimensions are in meters. The density of water is 9800 newtons per cubic meter.

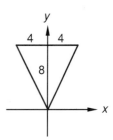

2. Suppose f is defined as follows:

$$f(x) = \begin{cases} ax^3 + b & x \le 1 \\ x^2 & x > 1 \end{cases}$$

What relationship between a and b will cause f to be continuous everywhere?

3. Determine the numerical values of a and b that will make f, as defined in Problem 2, continuous and differentiable everywhere.

4. Determine the maximum and minimum values of the function $f(x) = x^{2/3}$ on the closed interval $[-1, 8]$.

5. Let R be the region enclosed by the graphs of $y = \sqrt{x}$ and $y = x$ in the first quadrant. Find the volume of the solid formed when R is rotated about the x axis.

Use the appropriate double-angle identity to find the following integrals:

6. $\displaystyle\int \pi \sin^2 x \, dx$

7. $\displaystyle\int \frac{1}{4} \cos^2 x \, dx$

8. Assume the masses shown are suspended from a support that has no mass. Find the balance point for the system to two decimal places.

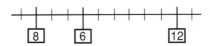

Evaluate the following limits:

9. $\displaystyle\lim_{x \to 0} \frac{3 \sin 2x}{4x}$

10. $\displaystyle\lim_{x \to \infty} \frac{x + \sin x}{\ln x}$

11. $\displaystyle\lim_{h \to 0} \frac{e^{x+h} - e^x}{h}$

12. Suppose f is a continuous function such that $-x^4 \le f(x) \le x^4$ for all values of x. Evaluate $\displaystyle\lim_{x \to 0} f(x)$.

Integrate:

13. $\displaystyle\int \sin^3 x \cos^2 x \, dx$

14. $\displaystyle\int \frac{x - 3}{x^2} \, dx$

15. $\displaystyle\int (\pi \cos x) e^{\sin x} \, dx$

16. $\displaystyle\int \frac{x}{x^2 - 1} \, dx$

17. Evaluate: $\displaystyle\int_1^{-3} f(x) \, dx$ if $\displaystyle\int_{-3}^0 f(x) \, dx = 4$ and $\displaystyle\int_0^1 f(x) \, dx = -1$

18. Find the area of the region between the graph of $y = xe^x$ and the x axis over the interval $[1, 3]$.

19. Find the equation of the line which can be drawn normal to the graph of f at $x = 3$ if

$$f(x) = \frac{x - 2}{x + 1}$$

CONCEPT REVIEW **20.** Suppose we are given the graph of the function $f(x) = x^2$. Then we divide the interval $[0, 3]$ into three equally long subintervals and draw rectangles over each of these subintervals. From left to right, the heights of the three rectangles are $f(0)$, $f(1)$, and $f(2)$. Which of the following must be true?

(*a*) The sum of the areas of the rectangles is less than $\int_0^3 x^2 \, dx$.

(*b*) The sum of the areas of the rectangles is greater than $\int_0^3 x^2 \, dx$.

(*c*) The sum of the areas of the rectangles is equal to $\int_0^3 x^2 \, dx$.

(*d*) The sum of the areas of the rectangles is equal to 27.

21. Let f be a function such that $f(1) = 2$, $f'(1) = 3$, $g(1) = -1$, and $g'(1) = 4$. Evaluate $(fg)'(1)$.

LESSON 93 *Centroids*

We can use the physical definition of the center of mass or center of gravity to help us define a purely mathematical concept called the ***centroid*** of a planar figure. If we cut a shape out of a thin sheet of metal of uniform density, we find that it is possible to balance the shape on the point of a cone as we show on the left below, and if the sheet is very, very thin, the balance point is almost exactly at the center of mass. To discuss this further, we need a coordinate system, and on the right we arbitrarily place the shape in the first quadrant of a rectangular coordinate system and draw vertical "rectangles" to represent the surfaces of "rectangular" solids whose thickness equals the thickness of the sheet of metal.

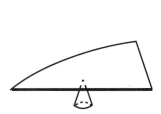 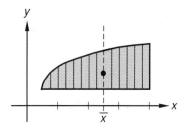

The mass of each rectangle equals the area of the rectangle times a constant k that equals the product of the thickness of the sheet and the density of the material.

Mass of each rectangle = $k \cdot$ area

Each of these rectangular masses causes a mass moment that tends to rotate the entire shape about a vertical line through the center of mass of the entire shape. But the sum of these mass moments must be zero because the shape is balanced and is not rotating.

If we extend our development of the concept of balance points from Lesson 89 to a second dimension, we can use the expression we developed to find $\bar{x}$ for a balance point for a linear system to finding $\bar{x}$ for this planar system. The value of $\bar{x}$ is the x coordinate of the center of mass and equals the sum of the mass moments about the y axis divided by the sum of the masses.

$$\bar{x} = \frac{x_1 m_1 + x_2 m_2 + \cdots + x_n m_n}{m_1 + m_2 + \cdots + m_n}$$

However, every mass equals a particular kA, where A is the area, so we can write

$$\bar{x} = \frac{x_1(kA_1) + x_2(kA_2) + \cdots + x_n(kA_n)}{kA_1 + kA_2 + \cdots + kA_n}$$

Every term in the numerator and in the denominator has k as a factor. If we divide every term by k, we get

$$\bar{x} = \frac{x_1 A_1 + x_2 A_2 + \cdots + x_n A_n}{A_1 + A_2 + \cdots + A_n} = \frac{\sum_{i=1}^{n} x_i A_i}{\text{area}}$$

This shows us that for a very, very thin sheet of uniform density, the x distance to the center of mass is the sum of the "area moments" divided by the total area. The same argument can be used to show that the y distance to the y coordinate of the center of mass is

$$\bar{y} = \frac{\sum y_i A_i}{\text{area}}$$

If we let the thickness of the sheet approach zero as a limit, the total mass will also approach zero, but the area remains and the area definitions of $\bar{x}$ and $\bar{y}$ remain. We call the point located by this area definition of $\bar{x}$ and $\bar{y}$ the **centroid** of the planar region.

Example 93.1   Find the x coordinate of the centroid of the plane figure bounded by the x axis, the graph of $y = \sqrt{x}$, and the line $x = 2$.

Solution   We graph the figure and show a typical "rectangle." The area moment about the y axis for this rectangle is its area, $y\,\Delta x$, times its distance from the y axis, which is x. The sum of all the area moments about the y axis is given by the integral in the numerator of the expression for $\bar{x}$ on the left. The total area is given by the integral in the denominator.

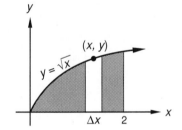

$$\bar{x} = \frac{\int_0^2 (y\,dx)(x)}{\int_0^2 y\,dx} = \frac{\int_0^2 (x^{1/2}\,dx)(x)}{\int_0^2 x^{1/2}\,dx}$$

In the expression on the right we replaced y with $x^{1/2}$. We finish by simplifying and evaluating the integrals.

$$\frac{\int_0^2 x^{3/2}\,dx}{\int_0^2 x^{1/2}\,dx} = \frac{\left[\frac{2}{5}x^{5/2}\right]_0^2}{\left[\frac{2}{3}x^{3/2}\right]_0^2} = \frac{\frac{2}{5}(2)^{5/2}}{\frac{2}{3}(2)^{3/2}} = \frac{\frac{8\sqrt{2}}{5}}{\frac{4\sqrt{2}}{3}} = \frac{3}{5}(2) = \frac{6}{5}$$

This result tells us that the x coordinate of the centroid of this planar region is $\frac{6}{5}$.

Example 93.2   Find the y coordinate of the centroid of the planar region defined in Example 93.1.

Solution   If a function can be solved explicitly for x, we can use horizontal "rectangles" and let y be the variable of integration. The area moment of this typical rectangle is the area, $(2 - x)(\Delta y)$, times its distance from the x axis, which is y, and $x = y^2$. Thus the area moment of this typical rectangle is $(2 - y^2)y\,\Delta y$. The sum of the area moments divided by the total area equals $\bar{y}$.

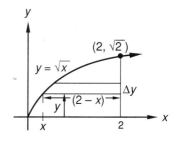

$$\bar{y} = \frac{\displaystyle\int_0^{\sqrt{2}} (2y - y^3)\,dy}{\displaystyle\int_0^{\sqrt{2}} (2 - y^2)\,dy} = \frac{2\displaystyle\int_0^{\sqrt{2}} y\,dy - \displaystyle\int_0^{\sqrt{2}} y^3\,dy}{2\displaystyle\int_0^{\sqrt{2}} dy - \displaystyle\int_0^{\sqrt{2}} y^2\,dy}$$

We finish by evaluating the integrals.

$$\bar{y} = \frac{\left[y^2 - \dfrac{y^4}{4}\right]_0^{\sqrt{2}}}{\left[2y - \dfrac{y^3}{3}\right]_0^{\sqrt{2}}} = \frac{2 - 1}{2\sqrt{2} - \dfrac{2\sqrt{2}}{3}} = \frac{1}{\dfrac{4\sqrt{2}}{3}} = \frac{3}{4\sqrt{2}} \approx \mathbf{0.53}$$

Example 93.3   Use vertical rectangles to find the y coordinate of the centroid of the region described in Example 93.1.

Solution   Vertical rectangles can be used to find $\bar{y}$ for planar regions bounded by functions that cannot be solved explicitly for x as well as for those that can be solved explicitly for x. To demonstrate this procedure, we remember that the definition of centroid came directly from the idea of center of mass and that in the development of the definitions of $\bar{x}$ and $\bar{y}$ we used the idea that the mass of an object can be considered to be concentrated at its center of mass.

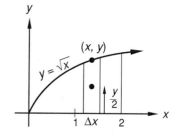

     If we use these definitions for the mass whose surface is represented by the rectangle shown, the area moment of the rectangle with respect to the y axis is the area of the rectangle, $y\,\Delta x$, times the distance from the x axis to the center of mass, which is $y/2$. This will lead to the integral in the numerator below, which equals the sum of the area moments. The integral for the area is in the denominator and is the same as the integral in the denominator in Example 93.1.

$$\bar{y} = \frac{\displaystyle\int_0^2 (y\,dx)\left(\dfrac{y}{2}\right)}{\displaystyle\int_0^2 y\,dx}$$

If we replace y with $x^{1/2}$, we get

$$\bar{y} = \frac{\displaystyle\int_0^2 (x^{1/2}\,dx)\left(\dfrac{x^{1/2}}{2}\right)}{\displaystyle\int_0^2 x^{1/2}\,dx}$$

In Example 93.1 we found that the value of the denominator is $4\sqrt{2}/3$. Now, if we evaluate the numerator, we get

$$\bar{y} = \frac{\dfrac{1}{2}\displaystyle\int_0^2 x\,dx}{\dfrac{4\sqrt{2}}{3}} = \frac{\dfrac{1}{2}\left[\dfrac{x^2}{2}\right]_0^2}{\dfrac{4\sqrt{2}}{3}} = \frac{\dfrac{4}{4}}{\dfrac{4\sqrt{2}}{3}} = \frac{3}{4\sqrt{2}} = \frac{3\sqrt{2}}{8} \approx 0.53$$

Problem set 93

1. Hunsinger has 120 m of fencing which is to be used for enclosing two separate fields. One of the fields is a square field, and the other field is a rectangular field whose length is 3 times its width. The square field must have an area of at least 100 m^2, and the rectangular field must have an area of at least 75 m^2. Let x be the width of the rectangular field. What are the maximum and minimum possible values of x? (No calculus is needed. Begin by expressing the areas of the rectangle and the square in terms of x. The minimum and maximum values of x are determined by the minimum area of the square and the minimum area of the rectangle.)

2. Express the sum of the areas of the two fields in Problem 1 in terms of x. Use the critical number theorem as a guide to find the value of x which maximizes the sum of the areas of the two fields.

3. Suppose $f(x) = ae^x + b\sin x$, $f'(0) = 4$, and $f'(\pi/2) = 1$. Approximate to two decimal places the values of a and b.

4. A rectangular tank is 3 meters deep and is filled with a fluid whose weight density is 2000 newtons per cubic meter. If the width of the tank is 4 meters, find the total force exerted by the fluid against one of the faces of the tank.

5. A particle moves along the x axis so that its acceleration function is $a(t) = -2$. The particle's velocity at $t = 1$ is 5, and its position at $t = 1$ is 7. Find the velocity function and the position function for the particle. Find the time(s) when the particle is moving to the right with a velocity of 3.

6. Let f be a function defined as follows:

$$f(x) = \begin{cases} 2x^2 - x & \text{when } x \le 1 \\ ax + b & \text{when } x > 1 \end{cases}$$

    What relationship between a and b is required for f to be continuous everywhere?

7. If f is as defined as in Problem 6, find the values of a and b which make f both continuous and differentiable everywhere.

8. Find the x coordinate of the centroid of the first-quadrant region bounded by the graphs of $y = x^2$, $y = 0$, and $x = 4$.

9. Use horizontal rectangles to find the y coordinate of the centroid of the region enclosed by the graphs of $x = y^2$, $y = 4$, and the y axis.

10. Use vertical rectangles to determine the y coordinate of the centroid of the region described in Problem 8.

Use double-angle identities to compute the following integrals:

11. $\displaystyle\int 2\sin^2 x\,dx$

12. $\displaystyle\int 4\sin^2 x \cos^2 x\,dx$

13. Integrate: $\displaystyle\int 2\sin^3 x\,dx$

14. Let R be the region bounded by the graphs of $y = 2x + 2$, $y = x$, the y axis, and $x = 2$. Find the volume of the solid formed when R is rotated about the x axis.

15. Let f be a continuous function for all real numbers whose graph lies above the x axis, and let R be the region between the graph of f and the x axis on the interval [1, 4]. Write a definite integral whose value equals the volume of the solid formed when R is rotated about the x axis.

16. Sketch the graph of $y = \dfrac{x^2 - 2x}{1 - x^2}$.

17. Suppose $f(x) = e^x$ and $g(x) = 5$. Determine whether $h(x) = g(f(x))$ is an odd function, an even function, or neither.

18. Differentiate: $y = \arcsin(\tan x) + 2^x - \dfrac{x}{1 + x}$

19. Integrate: $\displaystyle\int x^2\sqrt{x^3 - 1}\, dx$ 20. If $f(x) = x^3 + 1$, find $f^{-1}(2)$.

21. Evaluate: $\displaystyle\lim_{x \to \pi/2} \dfrac{\sin x - \sin \dfrac{\pi}{2}}{x - \dfrac{\pi}{2}}$

CONCEPT REVIEW 22. If $f(x) = x^{1/3}(x - 3)^{2/3}$, then what is the domain of f'?

LESSON 94 *Logarithmic differentiation*

If we use logarithms, we can simplify the process of finding the derivatives of rather complicated expressions. The process of logarithmic differentiation involves no new theory. Logarithmic differentiation is just a manipulative procedure that makes the process simpler because we can use the laws of logarithms to turn products into sums, quotients into differences, and exponents into coefficients.

Example 94.1 If $y = \dfrac{x^2}{(3x + 2)^4}$, find $\dfrac{dy}{dx}$.

Solution We could find the derivative by using the quotient rule, but we will use logarithmic differentiation to demonstrate the procedure. Then we will use the procedure on more complicated functions in the next four examples. We are going to take the logarithm of both y and x^2 divided by $(3x + 2)^4$. Negative numbers and zero do not have logarithms, so we first impose the condition that x be greater than zero. Then both x^2 and $3x + 2$ will always represent positive numbers. The first step is to take the logarithm of both sides. We remember that the logarithm of a quotient is the difference of the logarithms.

$$\ln y = \ln x^2 - \ln(3x + 2)^4 \qquad \text{ln of both sides}$$

$$\ln y = 2\ln x - 4\ln(3x + 2) \qquad \text{used power rule}$$

Next we find the differential of every term and then divide by dx.

$$\frac{dy}{y} = \frac{2\ dx}{x} - \frac{4(3\ dx)}{3x + 2} \qquad \text{differential}$$

$$\frac{1}{y}\frac{dy}{dx} = \frac{2}{x} - \frac{12}{3x + 2} \qquad \text{divided by } dx$$

Now we solve for dy/dx by multiplying both sides by y.

$$\frac{dy}{dx} = y\left(\frac{2}{x} - \frac{12}{3x + 2}\right) \qquad \text{solved for } \frac{dy}{dx}$$

As the final step we replace y with $\dfrac{x^2}{(3x + 2)^4}$ and get

$$\frac{dy}{dx} = \frac{x^2}{(3x + 2)^4}\left(\frac{2}{x} - \frac{12}{3x + 2}\right)$$

Whenever we use logarithmic differentiation to find the derivative of a quotient, we will get an answer that has this form:

$$\frac{dy}{dx} = f(x) \times \text{(a sum of fractions)}$$

We made the mental condition that x be greater than 0 so that $3x + 2$ and x would be positive so that $\ln(3x + 2)$ and $\ln x$ would be defined. **But the result we get is the same result we would have obtained if we had used the quotient rule for derivatives and is therefore valid for any value of x that does not cause a denominator of the final result to equal zero.**

Example 94.2   If $y = \dfrac{x^3\sqrt{x^2 + 1}}{(x + 2)^6}$, find $\dfrac{dy}{dx}$.

Solution   First we impose the condition that x be such that x^3, $x^2 + 1$, and $x + 2$ will always represent positive numbers. We also rewrite $\sqrt{x^2 + 1}$ by using $\frac{1}{2}$ as an exponent.

$$y = \frac{x^3(x^2 + 1)^{1/2}}{(x + 2)^6} \qquad x > -2,\ x \neq 0$$

Next we take the logarithm of both sides, remembering that the logarithm of a product is the sum of the logarithms and the logarithm of a quotient is the difference of the logarithms.

$$\ln y = 3\ln x + \frac{1}{2}\ln(x^2 + 1) - 6\ln(x + 2)$$

Now we take the differential of every term and divide by dx.

$$\frac{dy}{y} = \frac{3\ dx}{x} + \frac{\frac{1}{2}(2x)\ dx}{x^2 + 1} - \frac{6\ dx}{x + 2} \qquad \text{differentials}$$

$$\frac{1}{y}\frac{dy}{dx} = \frac{3}{x} + \frac{x}{x^2 + 1} - \frac{6}{x + 2} \qquad \text{divided by } dx$$

Next we solve for dy/dx and finish by replacing y with the original function.

$$\frac{dy}{dx} = y\left(\frac{3}{x} + \frac{x}{x^2 + 1} - \frac{6}{x + 2}\right) \qquad \text{solved for } \frac{dy}{dx}$$

$$\frac{dy}{dx} = \frac{x^3\sqrt{x^2 + 1}}{(x + 2)^6}\left(\frac{3}{x} + \frac{x}{x^2 + 1} - \frac{6}{x + 2}\right) \qquad \text{substituted}$$

Example 94.3 If $y = \dfrac{\sqrt{3x + 2}\,(x^3 + 1)^4(5x - 3)^2}{(x^3 - 2)^5}$, find $\dfrac{dy}{dx}$.

Solution This derivative would be very difficult to find if we did not use logarithmic differentiation. As the first step we rewrite $\sqrt{3x + 2}$ as $(3x + 2)^{1/2}$.

$$y = \frac{(3x + 2)^{1/2}(x^3 + 1)^4(5x - 3)^2}{(x^3 - 2)^5}$$

Now we mentally restrict x to values that cause $3x + 2$, $x^3 + 1$, $5x - 3$, and $x^3 - 2$ to represent positive numbers. Then we take the logarithm of both sides.

$$\ln y = \frac{1}{2}\ln(3x + 2) + 4\ln(x^3 + 1) + 2\ln(5x - 3) - 5\ln(x^3 - 2)$$

Next we find the differential of every term. Then we divide by dx and solve for dy/dx.

$$\frac{dy}{y} = \frac{\frac{3}{2}\,dx}{3x + 2} + \frac{12x^2\,dx}{x^3 + 1} + \frac{10\,dx}{5x - 3} - \frac{15x^2\,dx}{x^3 - 2} \qquad \text{ln of both sides}$$

$$\frac{1}{y}\frac{dy}{dx} = \frac{\frac{3}{2}}{3x + 2} + \frac{12x^2}{x^3 + 1} + \frac{10}{5x - 3} - \frac{15x^2}{x^3 - 2} \qquad \text{divided by } dx$$

$$\frac{dy}{dx} = y\left(\frac{\frac{3}{2}}{3x + 2} + \frac{12x^2}{x^3 + 1} + \frac{10}{5x - 3} - \frac{15x^2}{x^3 - 2}\right) \qquad \text{solved for } \frac{dy}{dx}$$

Now we complete the solution by replacing y with the original function.

$$\frac{dy}{dx} = \frac{\sqrt{3x + 2}\,(x^3 + 1)^4(5x - 3)^2}{(x^3 - 2)^5}\left(\frac{3}{6x + 4} + \frac{12x^2}{x^3 + 1} + \frac{10}{5x - 3} - \frac{15x^2}{x^3 - 2}\right)$$

Since this is the same derivative we would have found using the product and quotient rules, it is valid for every value of x that does not cause a denominator to equal zero.

Example 94.4 If $y = x^x$, find $\dfrac{dy}{dx}$.

Solution We have found derivatives of powers such as x^5 that have a variable base and a constant exponent. We have also found derivatives of exponentials such as 5^x that have a constant base and a variable exponent. This function has both a variable base and a variable exponent. The expression x^x has meaning for all positive values of x, so we restrict x to values greater than zero. We can turn the exponent into a coefficient if we take the logarithm of both sides.

$$\ln y = x \ln x$$

Next we take the differential of both sides and then divide by dx.

$$\frac{dy}{y} = x \cdot \frac{dx}{x} + \ln x\,dx \qquad \text{differential}$$

$$\frac{1}{y}\frac{dy}{dx} = 1 + \ln x \qquad \text{divided by } dx$$

Now we multiply both sides by y and finish by replacing y with x^x.

$$\frac{dy}{dx} = y(1 + \ln x) \qquad \text{solved for } \frac{dy}{dx}$$

$$\frac{dy}{dx} = x^x(1 + \ln x) \qquad \text{substituted}$$

This result is valid only for positive values of x because $\ln x$ is defined only for positive numbers.

Example 94.5   If $y = x^{x^3+4}$, find $\frac{dy}{dx}$.

Solution   If we take the logarithm of both sides, we can make a coefficient out of $x^3 + 4$. For this example we must restrict the domain of x to the positive numbers so that $\ln x$ will be defined.

$$\ln y = (x^3 + 4)(\ln x) = x^3 \ln x + 4 \ln x$$

Now we take the differential of both sides.

$$\frac{dy}{y} = (x^3 + 4) \cdot \frac{dx}{x} + (\ln x)(3x^2 \, dx)$$

Next we divide by dx and solve for $\frac{dy}{dx}$.

$$\frac{1}{y}\frac{dy}{dx} = x^2 + \frac{4}{x} + 3x^2 \ln x \qquad \text{divided by } dx$$

$$\frac{dy}{dx} = y\left(x^2 + \frac{4}{x} + 3x^2 \ln x\right) \qquad \text{solved for } \frac{dy}{dx}$$

We finish by replacing y with x^{x^3+4}.

$$\frac{dy}{dx} = x^{x^3+4}\left(x^2 + \frac{4}{x} + 3x^2 \ln x\right)$$

This result is valid only for values of x greater than zero.

Problem set 94

1. A spring whose spring constant is 2 newtons per meter is stretched from $x = 2$ meters to $x = 4$ meters. Find the work done to the spring.

2. A ball is thrown horizontally from the top of a 100-meter-tall building. The height of the ball above the ground at a given time t after the ball has been thrown is exactly the same as if it had been dropped. Find the equation that describes the height of the ball as a function of t. How long will it take the ball to reach the ground? If the horizontal velocity is 20 meters per second, what is the horizontal distance the ball will travel? (The horizontal distance the ball will travel equals the horizontal velocity times the time the ball is in the air.)

3. A cylindrical container 1 meter high with a circular base whose radius is 1 meter is filled with a fluid whose weight density is 100 newtons per cubic meter. Find the work performed in pumping the fluid out of the cylinder.

4. Let f be a function defined as follows:

$$f(x) = \begin{cases} x^3 & \text{when } x \le -1 \\ ax + b & \text{when } x > -1 \end{cases}$$

Determine the values of a and b that will make f both continuous and differentiable everywhere.

Use logarithmic differentiation to differentiate the following functions:

5. $y = \dfrac{x^2\sqrt{x^2 + 1}}{(x - 1)^4}$

6. $y = \dfrac{\sqrt{x - 1}(x^3 - 1)(\sin x)}{(x^2 + 1)(x^4 + 1)}$

7. $y = x^x$

8. $y = x^{\sin x}$

9. Let R be the region between the graph of $y = e^x$ and the x axis on the interval $[1, 4]$. Approximate to two decimal places the x coordinate of the centroid of R.

10. Let R be the region bounded by $x + y = 1$ and the coordinate axes. Use horizontal rectangles to determine the y coordinate of the centroid of R.

Integrate:

11. $\displaystyle\int 6 \cos^2 x \, dx$

12. $\displaystyle\int 2 \sin^2 x \cos^3 x \, dx$

Evaluate the following limits:

13. $\displaystyle\lim_{x \to 0} \dfrac{2 \sin 3x}{4x}$

14. $\displaystyle\lim_{x \to \infty} \dfrac{x^2}{1 - x^2}$

15. Determine the slope of the tangent line which can be drawn to the graph of $y = \log x$ at $x = 2$.

16. Determine the area between the graph of $y = xe^x$ and the x axis on the interval $[1, 2]$.

17. Determine the area of the region between the graph of $y = x^2 - x$ and the x axis on the interval $[-2, 1]$.

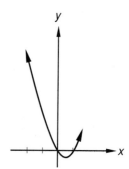

18. Determine the slope of the line which can be drawn tangent to the graph of the function $y = \sin(\cos x)$ at $x = \pi/2$.

19. Differentiate: $y = \dfrac{\sin(x^2 + 1)}{e^x - e^{-x}} - \arctan 2x$

20. Integrate: $\displaystyle\int (\cos x)\sqrt{1 - \sin x} \, dx$

CONCEPT REVIEW   **21.** The graph of the function $y = x^3 - 27x$ has
         (*a*)   No inflection points   (*b*)   One inflection point
         (*c*)   Two inflection points   (*d*)   Exactly two local maxima

LESSON 95 *The mean value theorem · Application of the mean value theorem · Proof of Rolle's theorem*

95.A
The mean value theorem

Existence theorems are crucial in mathematics, but the attention that they are given is often confusing to the beginner because the truth of the theorems is sometimes so obvious. It is hard to understand why theorems that are so obvious could be so important. Existence theorems are often used to prove other theorems. Two existence theorems that we have discussed thus far but have not proved are the **maximum-minimum value existence theorem** and the **intermediate value theorem.**

MAXIMUM-MINIMUM VALUE EXISTENCE THEOREM

If f is continuous on the closed interval $[a, b]$, then f has a maximum value M and a minimum value m on the interval $[a, b]$.

INTERMEDIATE VALUE THEOREM

If f is continuous on the closed interval $[a, b]$ and N is a number between f max and f min, then there is at least one number c between a and b inclusive for which $f(c) = N$.

The *mean value theorem* is another important existence theorem. This theorem is useful in other proofs. If $y = 2$, we know that $y' = 0$. If $y = 32$, we know that $y' = 0$. But if we are given that $y' = 0$, we need to use the mean value theorem to prove that y must equal some constant. The mean value theorem is also used to prove that if two functions have the same derivative, the functions differ by only a constant. For example,

$$\frac{d}{dx}(x^2 + 4x + 4) = 2x + 4 \qquad \frac{d}{dx}(x^2 + 4x + 32) = 2x + 4$$

Both of these derivatives are the same, but are we sure that if the derivative of some function is $2x + 4$, then the function must be $x^2 + 4x + c$, where c is some constant? This proof is possible in four short steps if we use the mean value theorem.

The graphical interpretation of the mean value theorem is as follows. If the graph of a function between x values of a and b inclusive is a smooth continuous curve that has no corners and is never vertical, a tangent line can be drawn to the graph somewhere between A and B that is parallel to the line through A and B. This means that a value of x between a and b **exists** such that the derivative of the function at this value of x equals the slope of the line through A and B, as we state algebraically on the right.

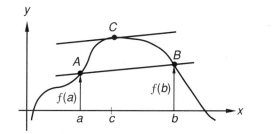

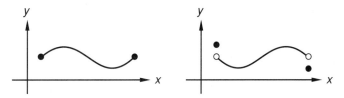

We must be careful in stating the conditions that are necessary for the mean value theorem to be applied. The function must be continuous and must have a defined slope (be differentiable) for every x value between a and b. **But if the function is differentiable on the open interval (a, b), it must also be continuous on the open interval (a, b) because differentiability requires continuity.** So we could just say that the function must be differentiable on the open interval (a, b). But the interval (a, b) is between a and b and does not include a and b, and we are trying to describe a function whose graph could be like the graph on the left that is also continuous at the endpoints.

We want to exclude functions that are discontinuous at one or both endpoints and whose graphs could resemble the one on the right. If we insist that the function be differentiable on the closed interval $[a, b]$, we must define what we mean by endpoint differentiability, and this is not necessary.

All we want to say is that the function is differentiable between a and b and is continuous at a and b. To say this it is customary to list two requirements that are somewhat redundant.

1. **The function must be defined and continuous on the closed interval $[a, b]$.** This requirement takes care of continuity at the endpoints.
2. **The function must be differentiable on the open interval (a, b).** This requirement prohibits sharp corners and vertical tangents on the graph and again requires that the function be defined and continuous between a and b.

THE MEAN VALUE THEOREM

If the function f is defined and continuous on the closed interval $[a, b]$ and is differentiable on the open interval (a, b), then there exists at least one number c in (a, b) such that

$$f'(c) = \frac{f(b) - f(a)}{b - a}$$

The mean value theorem states that the number c exists but does not tell us how to find it. Problems about the mean value theorem in calculus books are very straightforward. They are designed to determine whether the student knows what the mean value theorem is and whether the student knows the characteristics that a function must possess so that the use of the mean value theorem is permissible.

Example 95.1 Demonstrate an understanding of the mean value theorem by using the function $f(x) = x^2 - 2x - 8$ on the interval $[-2, 1]$.

Solution First we must see if the mean value theorem can be applied to this function.

1. Is the function continuous on the interval $[-2, 1]$? Yes. Polynomial functions are continuous for all values of x. Thus this function is continuous on the open interval $(-2, 1)$ and is also continuous at the endpoints.
2. Is the function differentiable everywhere between the endpoints? Yes. A polynomial function has a defined derivative for all real values of x. Thus the graph will have no sharp corners or places where the tangent is vertical.

To find the slope of the line that passes through the points whose x values are -2 and 1, we need to find $f(-2)$ and $f(1)$.

$$f(-2) = (-2)^2 - 2(-2) - 8 = 0$$
$$f(1) = (1)^2 - 2(1) - 8 = -9$$

Now we find the slope.

$$\frac{f(-2) - f(1)}{-2 - 1} = \frac{0 - (-9)}{-3} = -3$$

For this problem all the mean value theorem does is guarantee that for some value of x between -2 and 1 the value of the derivative (the slope of the graph) equals -3. We can find this value of c if we wish. First we find the derivative.

$$f'(x) = 2x - 2$$

Now we set $f'(x)$ equal to -3 and solve for x.

$$-3 = 2x - 2 \qquad f'(x) = -3$$
$$-1 = 2x \qquad \text{added } +2$$
$$x = -\frac{1}{2} \qquad \text{solved}$$

Thus the slope is -3 when $x = -\frac{1}{2}$.

Example 95.2 The value of the function

$$f(x) = \frac{1}{x^2} - 1$$

equals zero at $x = -1$ and $x = 1$. Thus the line connecting the points $(-1, 0)$ and $(1, 0)$ is a horizontal line and the slope of this line is zero. Use the mean value theorem to find a point between x values of -1 and $+1$ for which the tangent to the graph of the function (the value of the derivative) equals zero.

Solution The mean value theorem is an existence theorem and cannot be used to find anything. All it does is state that if certain requirements are met, a derivative of a particular value exists. Let's check the requirements.

1. The function must be continuous on the closed interval $[-1, +1]$. If we look at the function

$$f(x) = \frac{1}{x^2} - 1$$

we see that the function is not defined when $x = 0$.

$$\frac{1}{0^2} - 1 = ?$$

So the function is not continuous on the interval $[-1, 1]$ and the mean value theorem cannot be used.

Thus we do not need to check for requirement number 2, differentiability on the open interval (a, b).

Example 95.3   Demonstrate an understanding of the mean value theorem by using the function $f(x) = x^{2/3}$ and the interval $[-8, 27]$.

Solution   First we see if the function is continuous between x values of -8 and 27 inclusive. By inspection we can see that

$$x^{2/3}$$

equals a real number for any x value between -8 and 27 inclusive, so the requirement for continuity is met. Now we check for differentiability.

$$f'(x) = \frac{2}{3}x^{-1/3} = \frac{2}{3\sqrt{x}}$$

This derivative has no value when $x = 0$, so the function is not differentiable at $x = 0$ and thus is not differentiable everywhere on the interval $(-8, 27)$. Therefore, the mean value theorem cannot be used.

Example 95.4   The function $f(x) = |x| - 1$ is equal to 0 at $x = -1$ and $x = 1$. Does the mean value theorem imply that there exists some number c between $x = -1$ and $x = 1$ such that $f'(c) = 0$?

Solution   We check first to see if the requirements of the mean value theorem are met.

1. f is continuous on $[-1, 1]$. Yes.
2. f is differentiable on $(-1, 1)$. No.

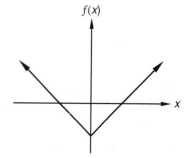

The derivative does not exist everywhere on the interval $(-1, 1)$ because the left-hand derivative does not equal the right-hand derivative at $x = 0$. Thus the mean value theorem is not applicable for this function on the interval $[-1, 1]$.

95.B
Application of the mean value theorem

> **THEOREM**
>
> If the derivative of a function equals zero for all real values of x, the function is constant function. A more formal statement of this is as follows.
>
> If $f'(x) = 0$ on an open interval I, then $f(x) = c$ on I.

PROOF. The mean value theorem makes the proof of this theorem almost trivial. We are given that the derivative of the function is zero for any real value of x, so the derivative exists everywhere for all x in any open interval (a, b) that we choose. The function is also defined and continuous at the endpoints a and b. Thus, if we choose any two distinct values of x for a and b, the mean value theorem guarantees that, for some c between a and b,

$$f'(c) = \frac{f(b) - f(a)}{b - a}$$

But the derivative equals zero everywhere, so we can write

$$0 = \frac{f(b) - f(a)}{b - a}$$

Now, if we multiply both sides by $b - a$, we get

$$0 = f(b) - f(a)$$

which can be rearranged as

$$f(b) = f(a)$$

This tells us that if we choose any two real numbers a and b, $f(a)$ will equal $f(b)$. This is another way of saying that the value of the function described is some constant, and thus the function must be a constant function.

$$f(x) = c$$

> **THEOREM**
>
> If two functions f and g have the same derivative for every real value of x, the functions differ by a constant.
>
> If $f'(x) = g'(x)$ on I, then $f(x) = g(x) + c$.

PROOF. To prove this theorem, we begin by defining a function $h(x)$.

$$h(x) = f(x) - g(x)$$

The derivative of a sum equals the sum of the derivatives, so if we find the derivative of both sides, we get

$$h'(x) = f'(x) - g'(x)$$

But we were given that the derivatives were equal, so their difference is zero. Thus

$$h'(x) = 0$$

In the preceding proof we showed that if the derivative of a function is zero, the function is a constant function. Thus we can substitute c for $h(x)$ and write

$$c = f(x) - g(x)$$

which can be rearranged as

$$f(x) = g(x) + c$$

This proves that if f and g have the same derivative, f and g differ by a constant.

95.C
Proof of Rolle's theorem

Rolle's theorem is a special case of the mean value theorem for which both $f(a)$ and $f(b)$ equal zero. This theorem is easier to prove than the mean value theorem. Rolle's theorem tells us that if we have a function f whose graph crosses the x axis at $x = a$ and $x = b$ and if f is continuous on $[a, b]$ and differentiable on (a, b), then some number c exists between a and b such that $f'(c) = 0$.

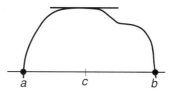

The proof of Rolle's theorem is an exercise in logic. The maximum-minimum value existence theorem tells us that somewhere on the interval $[a, b]$ a maximum value of f exists and a minimum value of f exists. If the maximum and minimum values are both zero, the graph of the function would be the graph of the constant function

$$f(x) = 0$$

whose slope is everywhere zero. Thus c could be any number between a and b and the proof is complete. If either the maximum value or the minimum value is not zero, then this extreme value must occur for some value c that is between a and b. The critical number theorem tells us that maximum and minimum values must occur at a critical number. These numbers are either

1. Endpoints
2. Values of x for which $f'(x)$ does not exist
3. Values of x for which $f'(x) = 0$

Since c is an interior number, it cannot be an endpoint and this excludes choice 1. We have defined the function to be a function that has a derivative everywhere on (a, b), so this excludes choice 2. Thus the maximum or minimum values must occur at one or more values of x where $f'(x) = 0$. The maximum-minimum value existence theorem told us that a maximum value and a minimum value of the function must exist on $[a, b]$. By a process of elimination we have proved that such value(s) must exist where $f'(x) = 0$, so we know that some number c must exist between a and b such that $f'(c) = 0$.

Problem set 95

1. The rate of increase of the bacteria was exponential. When $t = 0$, there were 30 bacteria, and when $t = 10$, there were 100 bacteria. How many bacteria were there when $t = 80$?

2. Punch flows into a crystal hemispherical punch bowl whose radius is 14 inches at a rate of 1 cubic inch per second. How fast is the punch rising when the

punch is halfway to the top? The equation that gives the volume of the bowl as a function of h is given on the right.

$$V = \pi r h^2 - \frac{1}{3}\pi h^3$$

3. Suppose $f(x) = \sin x + \cos x$ and f is defined only on the closed interval $[0, \pi]$. Use the critical number theorem to determine the maximum and minimum values of f. Find the x coordinate of any inflection points in the interval.

4. A particle moves along the x axis so that its velocity at time t is given by the equation $v(t) = a \sin t + b \cos t$, where a and b are real numbers. If the acceleration of the particle at time t is given by $a(t) = 2 \cos t - 4 \sin t$, determine the values of a and b.

The mean value theorem for derivatives states that if a function f is continuous on the closed interval $[a, b]$ and differentiable on the open interval (a, b), then there exists a number c in the interval (a, b) such that

$$f'(c) = \frac{f(b) - f(a)}{b - a}$$

Problems 5–7 consider the mean value theorem.

5. Illustrate the mean value theorem for derivatives by finding a number c, where $1 < c < 3$, and

$$f'(c) = \frac{f(3) - f(1)}{3 - 1} \qquad \text{if } f(x) = x^2 + 1$$

6. Illustrate the mean value theorem for derivatives by finding a number c, where $-2 < c < 1$, and

$$f'(c) = \frac{f(1) - f(-2)}{1 - (-2)} \qquad \text{if } f(x) = 2x^3 - x$$

7. The function $f(x) = |x| - 2$ equals 0 when $x = -2$ or when $x = 2$. There is no value of c between -2 and 2 where the slope of f equals 0, which is the slope of the line joining $(-2, 0)$ and $(2, 0)$. Why does this example not violate the mean value theorem?

Use logarithmic differentiation to find $\dfrac{dy}{dx}$:

8. $y = \dfrac{x^2\sqrt{x^3 - 1}}{\sin x \cos x}$

9. $y = x^x$

10. Find the x coordinate of the centroid of the region shown.

11. Find the y coordinate of the centroid of the region shown.

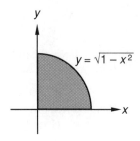

$y = \sqrt{1 - x^2}$

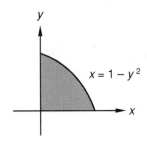

$x = 1 - y^2$

12. Integrate: $\int 3 \sin^2 x \, dx$

13. R is the region bounded by the graphs of $y = x^2 + 1$, $y = x$, $x = 3$, and the y axis. Use x as the variable of integration to write a definite integral that equals the volume of the solid formed when R is revolved about the x axis.

14. Sketch the graph of $f(x) = \dfrac{1 - x^2}{x}$.

Integrate:

15. $\int \sin^3 x \, dx$ 16. $\int \sin^3 x \cos x \, dx$ 17. $\int e^{\tan x}(\sec^2 x) \, dx$

18. Suppose f is a function defined for all real values of θ and $-\theta \le f(\theta) \le \theta$. Evaluate $\lim\limits_{\theta \to 0} f(\theta)$.

19. Differentiate: $\quad y = x \arcsin \dfrac{x}{3} + \dfrac{x}{\sqrt{1 + x}} + 3^x - 3 \log_{47} x$

CONCEPT REVIEW   20. Which of the following must be true?
    (*a*) If f is continuous on the interval $[1, 3]$ and both $f(1)$ and $f(3)$ equal zero, then there exists a number $c \in (1, 3)$ such that $f'(c) = 0$.
    (*b*) If f is continuous on the interval $[0, 3]$ and is differentiable on the interval $(0, 3)$, then there exists a number $c \in (0, 3)$ such that $f'(c) = 0$.
    (*c*) If f is continuous on the interval $[1, 3]$ and is differentiable on the interval $(0, 3)$ and if the graph of f touches the x axis at $x = 1$ and $x = 3$, then there exists some number $c \in (1, 3)$ such that $f(c) = 0$.
    (*d*) If a function f has a value of zero at $x = 1$ and $x = 3$, is continuous on the interval $[1, 3]$, and is differentiable in the interval $(1, 3)$, then there exists some number $c \in (1, 3)$ such that $f'(c) = 0$.

LESSON 96   *Rules for even and odd functions*

The zero function

$$f(x) = 0$$

is both an even function and an odd function because $f(x)$, $f(-x)$, and $-f(x)$ equal zero for all values of x. Thus

$$f(-x) = f(x) \qquad \text{and} \qquad f(-x) = -f(x)$$

If we exclude the zero function, the sum of an even function and an odd function is neither even nor odd.

    Sums of even functions are even functions, and sums of odd functions are odd functions. The product or quotient of two even functions is an even function, and the product or quotient of two odd functions is also an even function. These rules should sound familiar because they are almost exactly like the rules for signed numbers. They are easy to remember if we associate + signs with even functions and − signs with odd functions.

$$(+) + (+) = + \qquad (-) + (-) = -$$

$$(+)(-) = - \qquad \frac{(+)}{(-)} = - \qquad \frac{(-)}{(+)} = -$$

Example 96.1   If f is an odd function and g is an even function, show that fg is an odd function.

Solution   Proofs like this one are very straightforward. All we have to do is define our notations and substitute. First we note what we mean by $(fg)(x)$ and $(fg)(-x)$.

$$(fg)(x) = f(x)g(x) \qquad (fg)(-x) = f(-x)g(-x)$$

If f is odd, $f(-x) = -f(x)$, and if g is even, $g(-x) = g(x)$. We make these substitutions in the expression for $(fg)(-x)$.

$$\begin{aligned}
(fg)(-x) &= f(-x)g(-x) & \text{definition of } (fg)(x) \\
&= [-f(x)][g(x)] = -[f(x)g(x)] & \text{substituted} \\
&= -fg(x) & \text{simplified}
\end{aligned}$$

We have shown that if f is odd and g is even, $fg(-x) = -fg(x)$, so the function fg is an odd function.

Example 96.2   Show that the sum of two even functions f and g is an even function.

Solution   First we write the expressions for $(f + g)(x)$ and $(f + g)(-x)$.

$$(f + g)(x) = f(x) + g(x) \qquad (f + g)(-x) = f(-x) + g(-x)$$

Now, if f and g are even functions,

$$f(-x) = f(x) \qquad \text{and} \qquad g(-x) = g(x)$$

We make these substitutions in the expression for $(f + g)(-x)$ and get

$$\begin{aligned}
(f + g)(-x) &= f(-x) + g(-x) & \text{definition of } (f + g)(-x) \\
&= f(x) + g(x) & \text{even functions} \\
&= (f + g)(x) & \text{definition of } (f + g)(x)
\end{aligned}$$

We have shown that, if f and g are both even, the sum of $f(-x) + g(-x)$ equals the sum $f(x) + g(x)$, which is the same as $(f + g)(x)$. Thus the sum of two even functions is an even function.

Example 96.3   If f is an odd function and g is an even function, show that $f + g$ is neither even nor odd.

Solution   First we recall the definition of $(f + g)(x)$.

$$(f + g)(x) = f(x) + g(x)$$

Now we look at $(f + g)(-x)$.

$$(f + g)(-x) = f(-x) + g(-x)$$

But f is odd and g is even, so we can replace $f(-x)$ with $-f(x)$ and replace $g(-x)$ with $g(x)$ to get

$$(f + g)(-x) = -f(x) + g(x)$$

To be even, $(f + g)(-x)$ must equal $(f + g)(x)$, or $f(x) + g(x)$. It does not, so $(f + g)(x)$ is not even. To be odd, $(f + g)(-x)$ must equal $-[f(x) + g(x)]$, or $-f(x) - g(x)$. It does not, so $f + g$ is not odd. Thus, in this example, $f + g$ is neither even nor odd.

Example 96.4   Show that the quotient f/g is an odd function if f is an odd function and g is an even function.

Solution   First we recall the definitions of $(f/g)(x)$ and $(f/g)(-x)$.

$$\frac{f}{g}(x) = \frac{f(x)}{g(x)} \qquad \frac{f}{g}(-x) = \frac{f(-x)}{g(-x)}$$

Now if f is odd and g is even, the following is true.

$$f(-x) = -f(x) \qquad g(-x) = g(x)$$

Now we make these substitutions in the expression for $(f/g)(-x)$.

$$\frac{f}{g}(-x) = \frac{f(-x)}{g(-x)} \qquad \text{definition of } \frac{f}{g}$$

$$= \frac{-f(x)}{g(x)} \qquad \text{substituted}$$

$$= -\frac{f}{g}(x) \qquad \text{simplified}$$

We have shown that, if f is odd and g is even, $(f/g)(-x) = -(f/g)(x)$. Thus this quotient is an odd function.

Example 96.5   If f is an even function and if $\int_{2}^{4} f(x)\, dx = 7$, evaluate $\int_{-4}^{-2} f(x)\, dx$.

Solution   This is a trick problem to see if the reader knows the characteristics of an even function. Since the function is an even function, the graph on one side of the y axis is a mirror image in the y axis of the graph on the other side of the y axis. If the integral from 2 to 4 is 7, then the integral from -4 to -2 must also be **7**.

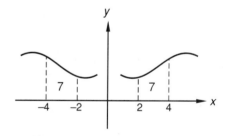

Example 96.6   If $\int_{-2}^{2} e^{x^2}\, dx = k$, then what is the value of $\int_{0}^{2} e^{x^2}\, dx$?

Solution   This problem is carefully contrived to see if the reader recognizes that e^{x^2} is an even function because $e^{(x)^2} = e^{(-x)^2}$. This integral cannot be evaluated using a technique of integration with which we are familiar. But since the value of the integral from -2 to 2 equals k, half of this integral is from 0 to 2 and must equal $k/2$.

$$\int_{0}^{2} e^{x^2}\, dx = \frac{k}{2}$$

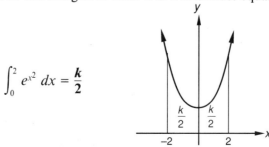

This trick question often appears on standardized tests.

Example 96.7   If $f(x)$ is an odd function and $\int_0^2 f(x)\,dx$ is 16, what is the value of $\int_{-2}^2 f(x)\,dx$?

Solution   If an odd function defines an area above the axis between 0 and 2, it defines an area of the same size below the axis between -2 and 0, and the definite integral from -2 to 2 must equal **zero**.

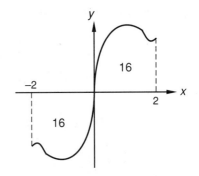

Problem set 96

1. A rectangular tank 8 meters deep is half-filled with a fluid whose weight density is 3000 newtons per cubic meter. Find the total force exerted by the fluid against one of the walls if the width of the wall is 2 meters.

2. Find the work performed in completely pumping out the tank of Problem 1 if the length of the tank is 6 meters.

The mean value theorem for derivatives states that if a function is continuous on the closed interval $[a, b]$ and differentiable on the open interval (a, b), then there exists a number c in the interval (a, b) such that

$$f'(c) = \frac{f(b) - f(a)}{b - a}$$

Problems 3 and 4 consider the mean value theorem.

3. Illustrate the mean value theorem by finding a number c, where $0 < c < 3$, such that

$$f'(c) = \frac{f(3) - f(0)}{3 - 0} \qquad \text{if } f(x) = x^2 + x + 1$$

4. Illustrate the mean value theorem by finding a number c, where $0 < c < \pi$, such that

$$f'(c) = \frac{f(\pi) - f(0)}{\pi - 0} \qquad \text{if } f(x) = \sin x$$

5. Prove that if f and g are both odd functions, then fg is an even function.

6. The function f is an odd function and

$$\int_0^4 f(x)\,dx = 7$$

Find the value of $\int_{-4}^4 f(x)\,dx$.

7. The function g is an even function and

$$\int_{-4}^4 g(x)\,dx = 4$$

Find the value of $\int_0^4 g(x)\,dx$.

8. Use logarithmic differentiation to compute

$$\frac{f'(x)}{f(x)} \qquad \text{if } f(x) = x \sin x \cos x$$

9. Let R be the region bounded by the graphs of $y = e^x$, $x = 0$, $x = 2$, and the x axis. Approximate to two decimal places the x coordinate of the centroid of region R.

Evaluate the following limits:

10. $\lim\limits_{x \to 0} (x \csc x)$ (Rewrite expression as a quotient.)

11. $\lim\limits_{x \to \infty} \dfrac{x + e^x}{x - e^x}$

12. Let R be the region between the graph of $y = e^{x^2}$ and the x axis on the interval $[1, 2]$. Use x as the variable of integration to write a definite integral whose value equals the volume of the solid formed when R is rotated about the x axis.

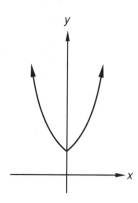

13. If $y = \arcsin \dfrac{x}{a}$, find y'.

14. Differentiate: $y = \arcsin (\cos x) + \dfrac{e^x - x}{\sin 2x + \cos x} - 2 \csc^2 x$

15. Use the result of Problem 13 to find $\displaystyle\int \dfrac{dx}{\sqrt{a^2 - x^2}}$.

Integrate:

16. $\displaystyle\int 2xe^x \, dx$ 17. $\displaystyle\int 2xe^{-x^2} \, dx$

18. Suppose f and g are both differentiable everywhere and $f(1) = 4$, $f'(1) = 2$, $g(1) = 1$, and $g'(1) = 2$. Use the quotient rule to compute $\left(\dfrac{f}{g}\right)'(1)$.

CONCEPT REVIEW   19. A function which is continuous and differentiable everywhere passes through the points $(1, 3)$ and $(6, 2)$. Which of the following must be true?
(a) There exists some c such that $1 < c < 6$ and $f'(c) = -\frac{1}{5}$.
(b) There exists some c such that $1 < c < 6$ and $f'(c) = -5$.
(c) There exists some c such that $1 < c < 6$ and $f'(c) = 0$.
(d) There exists some c such that $2 < c < 3$ and $f'(c) = -\frac{1}{5}$.

20. Let f be defined as follows:

$$f(x) = \begin{cases} x^2 + 1 & \text{if } x \geq 0 \\ ae^x + bx & \text{if } x < 0 \end{cases}$$

Find the numerical values of a and b which would make f differentiable everywhere.

LESSON 97 *Volume by shells*

The surface area of a right circular cylinder equals the circumference of the cylinder times its height. We can see this if we take a tin can, cut it vertically from top to bottom along the dotted line, and flatten it out as shown.

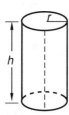
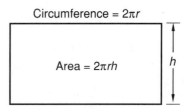

If the can has a thickness of Δx, we can find the volume of metal in the flat sheet by multiplying the area times the thickness Δx.

$$\text{Volume} = (2\pi rh)\, \Delta x$$

We can approximate the volume of a solid of revolution by summing the volumes of n concentric sheets or shells like the tin shell above. The center of every shell is the axis of revolution.

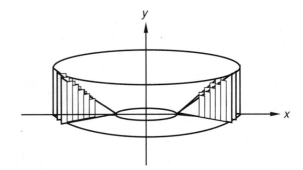

If the triangle in the figure on the left is revolved about the y axis, the solid represented on the right is generated. As we see on the left, the radius of the representative shell is x, the height is $f(x)$, and the thickness is Δx. The sum of the volumes of these shells as n increases without bound is the integral

$$\text{Volume} = \int_a^b 2\pi x[f(x)]\, dx$$

Example 97.1   The region bounded by $y = x - 1$, the x axis, and $x = 4$ is revolved about the y axis. Use the shell method to find the volume of the solid generated.

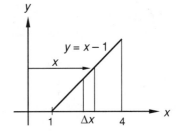

Solution   The volume of the representative shell is the circumference $2\pi r$ times the height times Δx. The radius in this problem is x, and the height of the shell is y. The thickness of the shell is Δx, and the shells cover the region between x values of 1 and 4. Thus

$$\text{Volume} = \int_1^4 2\pi xy \, dx$$

The dx reminds us that x is the variable of integration and that the only variable in the integrand should be x. Thus we replace y with $x - 1$.

$$\text{Volume} = \int_1^4 2\pi x(x - 1) \, dx$$

We simplify this expression, integrate, and evaluate.

$$\text{Volume} = 2\pi \int_1^4 (x^2 - x) \, dx \qquad \text{simplified}$$

$$= 2\pi \left[\frac{x^3}{3} - \frac{x^2}{2} \right]_1^4 \qquad \text{integrated}$$

$$= 2\pi \left[\left(\frac{64}{3} - \frac{16}{2} \right) - \left(\frac{1}{3} - \frac{1}{2} \right) \right] = \mathbf{27\pi \ units^3} \qquad \text{evaluated}$$

Example 97.2   Use the shell method to find the volume of the solid formed by revolving about the x axis the region in the first quadrant bounded by $x = 4 - y^2$ and the x and y axes.

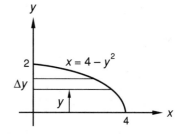

Solution   A representative shell is indicated in the figure. The radius of the shell is y, the height of the shell is x, and thickness is Δy.

$$\text{Volume} = \int_0^2 2\pi xy \, dy$$

The dy reminds us that the variable of integration is y and that the only variable in the integrand should be y. So we replace x with $4 - y^2$.

$$\text{Volume} = 2\pi \int_0^2 (4 - y^2) y \, dy$$

Now we simplify this expression, integrate, and evaluate.

$$\text{Volume} = 2\pi \int_0^2 (4y - y^3) \, dy = 2\pi \left[2y^2 - \frac{y^4}{4} \right]_0^2$$

$$= 2\pi(8 - 4) = \mathbf{8\pi \ units^3}$$

Example 97.3   Use the shell method to find the volume of the solid formed by revolving about the y axis the region bounded by the x axis and the graph of $y = -x^2 + 2x$.

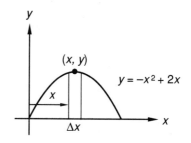

Solution   A representative shell is indicated in the figure. The radius of the shell is its distance from the axis of revolution. Thus the radius is x. The height of the shell is y, the thickness is Δx, and the shells cover the region from $x = 0$ to $x = 2$. Thus we have

$$\text{Volume} = \int_0^2 2\pi xy \, dx$$

The dx reminds us that x is the variable of integration and that the only variable in the integrand should be x. Thus we replace y with $-x^2 + 2x$.

$$\text{Volume} = 2\pi \int_0^2 x(-x^2 + 2x) \, dx$$

Next we multiply and integrate to get

$$\text{Volume} = 2\pi \int_0^2 (-x^3 + 2x^2) \, dx = 2\pi \left[\frac{-x^4}{4} + \frac{2x^3}{3} \right]_0^2$$

We finish by evaluating.

$$\text{Volume} = 2\pi \left(-4 + \frac{16}{3} \right) = \frac{8}{3}\pi \ \text{units}^3$$

Problem set 97

1. The money was compounded continuously, so the rate of increase of money was exponential. Initially there was $1000. After 100 days, there was $1050. Find the amount of money present after 200 days.

2. Let $f(x) = xe^{-x}$. Find all the critical numbers of f. Use the second derivative to determine where f attains local maximum and local minimum values, and find what those values are. Find the x coordinate of any points of inflection.

3. A particle moves along the x axis so that its acceleration function is $a(t) = -4t + \sin \pi t$. The velocity at $t = \frac{1}{2}$ is 4, and the position when $t = 1$ is 4. Find the velocity function and the position function of the particle. Find $v(0)$ and $x(0)$.

4. A ball thrown horizontally falls at the same rate it would fall if it were dropped. A ball is thrown horizontally from a height of 200 meters. How long will it take the ball to hit the ground? If the horizontal velocity is 40 meters per second, how far will it travel horizontally before it hits the ground? (The horizontal distance the ball travels equals the horizontal velocity times the time the ball is in the air.)

5. The slope of the tangent line to $y = x^3 + kx$ is 5 when $x = 1$. Find the value of k.

6. Let R be the region bounded by the graph of $y = \tan x$ and the x axis on the interval $[0, \pi/4]$. Use the method of shells to express as a definite integral, in the variable x, the volume of the solid formed when R is revolved about the y axis.

7. The region R is bounded by the x axis and the graph of $y = \sin x$ on the interval $I = [0, \pi]$. Find the volume of the solid formed when R is revolved about the y axis.

8. If $g(x) = \cos x$ and $\int_{-4}^{-1} g(x) \, dx = k$, evaluate $\int_1^4 g(x) \, dx$.

9. Find $\int_{-b}^{b} e^{x^2} \, dx$ if $\int_0^b e^{x^2} \, dx = L$.

10. Suppose $f(x) = x^3 + x$. Illustrate the mean value theorem by finding a number c, where $1 < c < 3$, such that

$$f'(c) = \frac{f(3) - f(1)}{3 - 1}$$

11. Use logarithmic differentiation to find $\dfrac{f'(x)}{f(x)}$ if $f(x) = \dfrac{\sqrt{x-1}\,\sin x}{(x^3+1)^{100}(x-1)^5}$. This problem asks for the result of an intermediate step in finding $f'(x)$ and is the kind of trick problem that is sometimes encountered on a standardized calculus test.

12. Integrate: $\displaystyle\int 4\sin^2 x\,dx$

13. Let R be the region bounded by the graphs of $x = y^2$, $x = \frac{1}{4}y^2$, and the line $x = 4$. Find the volume of the solid formed when R is rotated about x axis.

14. Sketch the graph of $y = \dfrac{x(3-x)(x+1)}{(x+1)(x^2+2)(x+3)}$.

15. Approximate to two decimal places the area between the graph of $y = 10^x$ and the x axis on the interval $[-1, 1]$.

16. Find the area between the graph of $y = x\sin x$ and the x axis on the interval $[0, \pi]$.

17. Suppose $f(x) = y = x^3 + x$. Write an equation which expresses the inverse of y implicitly. Evaluate $f^{-1}(2)$ by guessing the value of x for which $f(x) = 2$.

18. Differentiate: $y = \arctan\dfrac{x}{a} + \dfrac{1-e^x}{1+e^x} + \sin x\cot x$

19. Integrate: $\displaystyle\int \dfrac{a}{x^2+a^2}\,dx + \int \dfrac{2x}{x^2+a^2}\,dx$

CONCEPT REVIEW　　20. The point $(1, 3)$ lies on the graph of a function whose inverse is also a function. Which of the following must be true?
(*a*)　$(1, 3)$ lies on the graph of the inverse function.
(*b*)　$(1, 0)$ lies on the graph of the inverse function.
(*c*)　The graphs of both the function and its inverse pass through the origin.
(*d*)　The point $(3, 1)$ lies on the graph of the inverse function.

LESSON 98　*Separable differential equations*

The solution to an algebraic equation in x and y is the **set of all ordered pairs of numbers** (x, y) that satisfy the given equation. A **differential equation** is an equation that contains one or more derivatives or differentials. The solution to a differential equation is the set of all **functions** that satisfy the differential equation. We remember that we have rules for finding derivatives but our primary weapon for integrating is the ability to make a good guess. We then check our guess by differentiating. Making a good guess is also an excellent way to find the solution to a differential equation. Then we check our guess by seeing if our guess satisfies the given differential equation. If we guess a family of functions that satisfies the differential equation in question, we have our answer.

Mathematicians have developed procedures that can be used to find the solutions to certain types of differential equations. If it is possible to use the rules of algebra to put all terms involving x on one side of the equals sign and all terms involving y on the other side of the equals sign, we say that the differential equation is a ***separable differential equation.*** We can find the solution to a separable differential equation by integrating both sides of the equation. The differential equation (a) on the left is a separable differential equation because it can be written with the variables separated, as we show in (b).

$$(a)\ \ \frac{dy}{dx} = 4 \qquad (b)\ \ dy = 4\ dx$$

If we integrate both sides of equation (b), we can find a function that is a solution to the original differential equation. We can combine the constants of integration as we show.

$$\int dy = \int 4\ dx \ \longrightarrow\ y + C_1 = 4x + C_2 \ \longrightarrow\ y = 4x + C$$

The function $y = 4x + C$ is called the ***general solution*** to the problem because it contains an unspecified constant C and thus represents a **family of functions.** If we had been working a particular problem and information had been given to allow us to find that the value of C was 15, we could write

$$y = 4x + 15$$

In this case we would have the ***particular solution*** to the particular problem we were working. Some differential equations occur so often that we know just what we should guess to solve them. Many applied problems have the equation shown in (a) below, where Q represents a function whose value is always positive. If we take the differential of both sides, we get equation (b).

$$(a)\ \ Q = Ae^{kt} \qquad (b)\ \ dQ = Ake^{kt}\ dt \qquad (c)\ \ dQ = kQ\ dt$$

But in (a) we see that $Q = Ae^{kt}$. Thus, in (b), if we replace Ae^{kt} with Q, we get equation (c). Now, if the statement of the problem is that the rate of change of a quantity is proportional to the amount of the quantity, we could write

$$\frac{dQ}{dt} = kQ \qquad \text{or} \qquad dQ = kQ\ dt$$

The k is necessary because k is the constant of proportionality. To solve this differential equation, we guess that the function Q is

$$Q = Ae^{kt}$$

because if we take the differential of this function, we get

$$dQ = Ake^{kt}\ dt$$

so the **general solution** to this differential equation is

$$Q = Ae^{kt}$$

This is the familiar exponential increase or exponential decrease equation. If the necessary information is given in the problem to find that $k = -0.02$ and $A = 75$, we would have

$$Q = 75e^{-0.02t}$$

This would be the **particular solution** to this particular problem.

The discussion thus far permits us to find out that a particular statement about rate can be another way to state the exponential increase or decrease problem. The following statements imply the differential equation on the left whose general solution is the function on the right.

> The rate of change of volume at some time t is proportional to the volume at that time t.
>
> $$\frac{dV}{dt} = kV \longrightarrow V = Ae^{kt}$$

> The rate at which the population increases is proportional to the population.
>
> $$\frac{dP}{dt} = kP \longrightarrow P = Ae^{kt}$$

> The rate at which a radioactive substance decays is proportional to the amount present.
>
> $$\frac{dS}{dt} = kS \longrightarrow S = Ae^{kt}$$

Example 98.1 The rate at which a certain bacteria colony is growing at a given time is proportional to the number of bacteria present at that time. At time $t = 0$ there were 1000 bacteria. At time $t = 1$ there were 1050 bacteria. Write an equation which describes the number of bacteria present as a function of time, and determine the size of the bacteria colony at $t = 4$.

Solution On the left we write the differential equation indicated by the problem, and on the right we write the function that we know is the general solution to the differential equation. We use N_t to represent the number of bacteria present at time t.

$$\frac{dN}{dt} = kN \longrightarrow N_t = Ae^{kt}$$

First we find A by using zero for t and 1000 for N_t.

$$1000 = Ae^{k(0)} \longrightarrow A = 1000 \longrightarrow N_t = 1000e^{kt}$$

Now we use 1050 for N_1 and 1 for t and solve for k.

$$1050 = 1000e^{k(1)} \qquad \text{substituted}$$
$$1.05 = e^k \qquad \text{simplified}$$
$$0.049 = k \qquad \text{ln of both sides}$$

Thus the constant k in the differential equation and in the solution is approximately 0.049.

$$\frac{dN}{dt} = 0.049N \qquad \mathbf{N_t = 1000e^{0.049t}}$$

The particular solution on the right can be used to find N_t if t is given or to find t if N_t is given. The only difference in this problem and the exponential increase problem is that in this problem we began with a differential equation. Then we solved the differential equation by guessing the general solution and then used the general solution to find the particular solution, a process with which we are already familiar.

To find the number of bacteria when $t = 4$, we substitute 4 for t and evaluate.

$$N_4 = 1000e^{0.049(4)} = 1000e^{0.196} \approx \mathbf{1217}$$

Example 98.2 The slope of a curve everywhere is twice the value of the x coordinate. Find the equation of the curve if the curve passes through the point $(1, 2)$.

Solution First we write the implied differential equation.

$$\frac{dy}{dx} = 2x \qquad \text{differential equation}$$

We can look at this equation and see that y must equal $x^2 + C$. But let's pretend we don't see the answer and separate the variables by putting all y terms on the left and all x terms on the right.

$$dy = 2x \, dx$$

Now let's integrate both sides.

$$\int dy = \int 2x \, dx \quad \longrightarrow \quad y = x^2 + C$$

This family of functions is the general solution to the given differential equation because it satisfies the given differential equation since its derivative is $2x$. Separating the variables and integrating won't work on all differential equations because in some differential equations the variables are not separable. For this particular problem we can find the particular solution because we know the graph passes through $(1, 2)$. Thus we substitute.

$$2 = (1)^2 + C \quad \longrightarrow \quad C = 1$$

Thus the particular function that meets all the stated conditions is

$$y = x^2 + 1$$

Example 98.3   Find the general solution to the differential equation $x \, dx + y \, dy = 0$.

Solution   We don't know what to guess, but the variables are separable, so we put all the x's on one side and all the y's on the other side and integrate.

$$\int x \, dx = -\int y \, dy \quad \longrightarrow \quad \frac{x^2}{2} = \frac{-y^2}{2} + C \quad \longrightarrow \quad x^2 + y^2 = C$$

In the center equation C represents some number. If we multiply every term by 2, we get the right-hand equation, where C is again some number, which happens to be twice the value of the first C. If we find the differential of each term in $x^2 + y^2 = C$, we will get the original differential equation. Thus the equation $x^2 + y^2 = C$ is the general solution to the original differential equation since it defines implicitly the family of functions that satisfy the original differential equation.

Example 98.4   Find the general solution to the differential equation $f'(x) = 4x^2y^2$. Then find the particular solution if the point $(1, -1)$ lies on the graph of the curve.

Solution   When we write the equation, we find that the variables are separable.

$$\frac{dy}{dx} = 4x^2y^2 \quad \longrightarrow \quad y^{-2} \, dy = 4x^2 \, dx$$

We now integrate both sides.

$$\int y^{-2} \, dy = \int 4x^2 \, dx \quad \longrightarrow \quad \frac{-1}{y} = \frac{4x^3}{3} + C$$

If we multiply every term by $3y$ and solve for y, we get an expression that contains $3C$. Then we replace $3C$ with another C to get the general solution.

$$y = \frac{-3}{3C + 4x^3} \quad \longrightarrow \quad y = \frac{-3}{C + 4x^3}$$

To get the particular solution, we replace y with -1 and x with 1.

$$-1 = \frac{-3}{C + 4(1)^3} \longrightarrow C = -1$$

Now we have the particular solution.

$$y = \frac{-3}{-1 + 4x^3} \longrightarrow y = \frac{3}{1 - 4x^3}$$

We can show that this function is a solution to the original differential equation

$$\frac{dy}{dx} = 4x^2 y^2$$

We substitute for y on both sides of the equation and get

$$\frac{d}{dx}\left(\frac{3}{1 - 4x^3}\right) \overset{?}{=} 4x^2 \left(\frac{3}{1 - 4x^3}\right)^2$$

If we differentiate on the left-hand side and multiply on the right-hand side, we get

$$\frac{-(3)(-12x^2)}{(1 - 4x^2)^2} \overset{?}{=} \frac{4x^2(3)^2}{(1 - 4x^3)^2} \longrightarrow \frac{36x^2}{(1 - 4x^3)^2} = \frac{36x^2}{(1 - 4x^3)^2} \quad \text{check}$$

Since we get an identity as a result, we have shown that the quotient $y = 3$ over $1 - 4x^3$ is a solution to the differential equation $dy/dx = 4x^2y^2$.

Example 98.5 Use the method of separation of variables to find a general solution for the differential equation $y' = ky$, where y is a function of x and y is always positive.

Solution We pretend that we do not know what the answer is, so we separate the variables and integrate.

$$\frac{dy}{dx} = ky \longrightarrow \int \frac{dy}{y} = \int k \, dx \longrightarrow \ln|y| = kx + C$$

Since y is always positive, we can discard the absolute value sign. Now we have

$$\ln y = kx + C$$

which can be written as

$$y = e^{kx+C} \longrightarrow y = e^C e^{kx} \longrightarrow y = Ae^{kx}$$

In the final step we replaced e^c, where c is some unspecified constant, with another unspecified constant A. To check our solution, we differentiate.

$$\frac{d}{dx} Ae^{kx} = kAe^{kx}$$

But $y = Ae^{kx}$, and if we substitute, we get

$$\frac{d}{dx} Ae^{kx} = ky$$

Problem set 98 **1.** If money is compounded continuously, the rate of increase is proportional to the money present. This statement can be expressed as a differential equation: $dB/dt = kB$. The solution to this differential equation will be $B = Pe^{rt}$, where B is the balance in the account at some time t, P is the amount of the initial deposit, and r is the annual interest rate. If this equation is solved for P, we get $P = Be^{-rt}$, which can be used to find the amount P that should be invested to have a value of B in t years at a rate of r. If the annual interest rate is 8 percent, the rate *r* will be 0.08. How much money should be invested in an account now at 8 percent for the account to reach a value of $20,000 in 21 years?

2. The slope of the graph of a function *f* at a given point is 3 times the value of the *x* coordinate of that point. If the graph of the function *f* passes through the point (2, 3), write the equation of *f*.

3. The region *R* is bounded by the *x* axis and the graph of $y = e^x$ on the interval [1, 2]. Find the volume of the solid formed when *R* is revolved about the *y* axis.

4. The region *R* is bounded by the *x* axis and the graph of $y = \sec x$ on the interval $[0, \pi/4]$. Use *x* as the variable of integration to write a definite integral whose value equals the volume of the solid formed when *R* is revolved about the *y* axis.

5. A force, $F(x) = 3x^2 + 1$ newtons, is applied to an object to move it along the *x* axis. How much work is done between $x = 1$ meter and $x = 5$ meters?

Find a general solution to these differential equations:

6. $x\,dx - y\,dy = 0$

7. $\dfrac{dy}{dx} = 4x^3y^2$

8. Suppose $f(x) = \cos x$ and $g(x) = x^5 - x^3 + x$. Determine whether $(fg)(x)$ is odd, even, or neither.

9. Evaluate $\displaystyle\int_{-3}^{3} (fg)(x)\,dx$, where *f* and *g* are as defined in Problem 8.

10. The mean value theorem tells us that if a given function satisfies certain conditions, then there exists some $c \in (0, 1)$ such that

$$f'(c) = \frac{f(1) - f(0)}{1 - 0}$$

If the function $f(x) = e^{2x}$ satisfies the conditions, find a value of *c* for this function.

11. Let *R* be the first-quadrant region bounded by $x^2 + y^2 = 1$. Use horizontal rectangles to determine the *y* coordinate of the centroid of *R*.

12. Find the area of the region between $y = \sin^3 x$ and the *x* axis on the interval $[0, \pi/2]$.

Evaluate the following limits:

13. $\displaystyle\lim_{x \to 0} \frac{x^3 - 1}{x - 1}$

14. $\displaystyle\lim_{x \to 0} \frac{|x|}{x}$

15. $\displaystyle\lim_{h \to 0} \frac{\ln(x + h) - \ln x}{h}$

16. $\displaystyle\lim_{x \to 0} (x \csc 3x)$

17. Differentiate: $y = x \sec 2x - \dfrac{a - \sin x}{b + \cos x} - \arcsin \dfrac{x}{a}$

18. Integrate: $\displaystyle\int \left(\frac{1}{\sqrt{a^2 - x^2}} + \frac{x}{\sqrt{a^2 - x^2}} \right) dx$

CONCEPT REVIEW   19. Which of the following statements are true?
   (*a*) The axis of symmetry of a parabola always intersects the parabola at the vertex.

(*b*)   The vertex of a parabola is always the lowest point on the parabola.

(*c*)   The graph of the parabola will intersect the *x* axis at two different values of *x*.

(*d*)   Only one term in the equation of a parabola can have a degree less than 2.

20.   Suppose *f* is defined as follows:

$$f(x) = \begin{cases} ae^x + \sin x & \text{when } x \geq 0 \\ bx & \text{when } x < 0 \end{cases}$$

Write the equations involving *a* and *b* which must hold true for *f* to be continuous and differentiable everywhere. Then solve for *a* and *b*.

LESSON 99   *Average value of a function · Mean value theorem for integrals*

99.A
Average value of a function

The average value of a function can be explained graphically by using a side view of a tank made of glass that is sitting on the *x* axis and is partially filled with water.

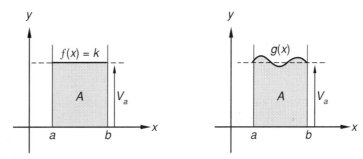

In the figure on the left the surface is smooth and the depth of the water is given by the constant function $f(x) = V_a$. The area *A* of the rectangle is the length $b - a$ times the height V_a.

$$\text{Area} = (b - a)V_a$$

In the figure on the right the water has been disturbed, and the depth of the water against the front glass of the tank is given by $g(x)$. If we assume that the depth of the water is $g(x)$ everywhere from the front of the tank to the back of the tank, the area *A* is unchanged because the amount of water in the tank is unchanged. This area can be described by the following integral.

$$\text{Area} = \int_a^b g(x)\, dx$$

Since the areas are equal, we can write the following equality and solve for V_a by dividing both sides by $b - a$.

$$(b - a)V_a = \int_a^b g(x)\, dx \quad \longrightarrow \quad V_a = \frac{1}{b - a}\int_a^b g(x)\, dx$$

This tells us that if we divide the area by the length of the tank, the result is V_a, a number that we call the ***average value*** of the depth of the water. This value is the same whether the surface is smooth or the surface is not smooth. We can extend this idea to define the **average value** of any continuous function on a closed interval $[a, b]$ where b is greater than a.

DEFINITION OF THE AVERAGE VALUE OF A FUNCTION

If f is continuous on the closed interval $I = [a, b]$, where $b > a$, then the average value of f is given by

$$V_a = \frac{1}{b - a} \int_a^b f(x)\, dx$$

If the average value computed for a given function on a particular closed interval I is negative, we know that more of the area between the x axis and the graph is below the x axis than above the x axis on the interval.

Example 99.1 Find the average value of the function $f(x) = x^2 - 10$ on the interval $I = [-1, 2]$.

Solution To find the average value between -1 and 2 inclusive, we divide the definite integral between -1 and 2 by the distance between the x values of -1 and $+2$, which is 3.

$$V_a = \frac{1}{2 - (-1)} \int_{-1}^2 (x^2 - 10)\, dx$$

Now we integrate and evaluate the integral at 2 and -1.

$$V_a = \frac{1}{3}\left[\frac{x^3}{3} - 10x\right]_{-1}^2 = \frac{1}{3}\left\{\left[\frac{2^3}{3} - 10(2)\right] - \left[\frac{(-1)^3}{3} - 10(-1)\right]\right\} = \frac{1}{3}(-27) = \mathbf{-9}$$

We remember that the definite integral assigns a $+$ sign to areas above the x axis and a $-$ sign to areas below the x axis. The average value of $\frac{1}{3}(-27)$ tells us that the algebraic sum of the areas above the x axis and the negative of the areas below the x axis is -27 and that the average value of the function is -9.

Example 99.2 Approximate to two decimal places the average value of the function $f(x) = 4e^{2x}$ on the interval $I = [0, 3]$.

Solution The average value of the function on $[0, 3]$ is the value of the definite integral from 0 to 3 divided by the length of the interval.

$$V_a = \frac{1}{3 - 0} \int_0^3 4e^{2x}\, dx$$

To integrate we need a constant factor of 2 to the right of the integral sign.

$$V_a = \frac{4}{3} \int_0^3 e^{2x}\, dx = \frac{4}{3}\left(\frac{1}{2}\right) \int_0^3 e^{2x}(2)\, dx = \frac{2}{3}[e^{2x}]_0^3 = \frac{2}{3}(e^6 - e^0)$$

We use a calculator to evaluate e^6 by finding the inverse natural logarithm of 6, and we remember that the value of e^0 is 1. So

$$V_a \approx \frac{2}{3}(403.43 - 1) = \mathbf{268.29}$$

99.B
Mean value theorem for integrals

The mean value theorem for integrals is an existence theorem that is used in the proof of other theorems. In a later lesson we will use the mean value theorem for integrals to prove that every continuous function has an integral. The mean value theorem for integrals tells us that if a function is continuous on the interval $[a, b]$, there exists at least one number c between a and b such that $f(c)$ is equal to the average value of the function on the interval $[a, b]$.

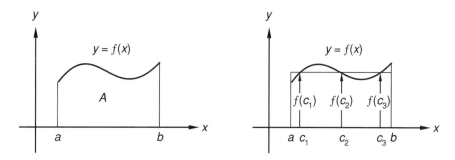

On the left we show the graph of $f(x)$ on the interval $[a, b]$. We know that the average value of the function, V_a, on this interval is the area A divided by $b - a$.

$$V_a = \frac{1}{b - a} \int_a^b f(x)\, dx$$

The mean value theorem says that there must be at least one number c between a and b such that $f(c)$ equals the average value of the function on $[a, b]$. For the function graphed above there are three such values of x, which we have labeled c_1, c_2, and c_3 in the figure on the right.

MEAN VALUE THEOREM FOR INTEGRALS

If f is continuous on the closed interval $I = [a, b]$, there exists at least one number c between a and b such that

$$f(c) = \frac{1}{b - a} \int_a^b f(x)\, dx$$

Example 99.3 Given that the average value of $f(x) = 2x^3$ on the interval $[0, 3]$ is $\frac{27}{2}$, use the mean value theorem to find some number c such that $f(c) = \frac{27}{2}$.

Solution The mean value theorem cannot be used to find anything. The mean value theorem simply states that such a c exists. We use algebra to find the value of c.

$$2c^3 = \frac{27}{2} \quad \longrightarrow \quad c^3 = \frac{27}{4} \quad \longrightarrow \quad c = \sqrt[3]{\frac{27}{4}} \approx 1.89$$

99.C
Proof (optional)

Some proofs are difficult to understand because we use the obvious to prove the obvious. The proof of the mean value theorem for integrals is one of these proofs. The proof is further complicated by the fact that it uses two existence theorems whose proofs are beyond the level of beginning calculus books. Nonetheless, a proof of the mean value theorem for integrals is usually presented in beginning calculus books.

We begin with a function that is continuous on the closed interval $[a, b]$.

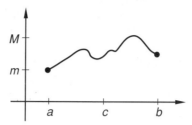

We want to show that for some c in (a, b), $f(c)$ equals the average value of the function. To do this we want to show that the average value of the function lies between the minimum value m and the maximum value M. The maximum-minimum value existence theorem assures us that such values exist. We want to prove that the average value lies between these extreme values. Thus we want to show that

$$m \le \frac{1}{b-a} \int_a^b f(x)\, dx \le M$$

If we can do this, we have our proof because the intermediate value theorem says that a continuous function **must** attain every value between m and M at least once on the interval $[a, b]$. We need to show that the value of $(b - a)m$ is less than $\int_a^b f$ and that the value of $(b - a)M$ is greater than $\int_a^b f$. Thus we want to show that

$$m(b - a) \le \int_a^b f(x)\, dx \le M(b - a)$$

Then we can divide all three terms by $b - a$ to get the desired result. We begin by partitioning the interval I into n subintervals. In the first subinterval we choose a point C_1, in the second subinterval we choose a point C_2, etc., until we get the point C_n in the nth subinterval. The value of the function at each of these chosen points, C_k, must be greater than or equal to the minimum value and less than or equal to the maximum value. We note that no matter what values of C_1, C_2, etc., we choose, the inequality

$$m \le f(C_k) \le M$$

must be true by definition of m and M. If we use Δx_k to represent the width of the kth subinterval, we can multiply each term by Δx_k and get

$$m\, \Delta x_k \le f(C_k)\, \Delta x_k \le M\, \Delta x_k$$

Thus for the first subinterval we could write

$$m\, \Delta x_1 \le f(C_1)\, \Delta x_1 \le M\, \Delta x_1$$

and for the second subinterval we could write

$$m\, \Delta x_2 \le f(C_2)\, \Delta x_2 \le M\, \Delta x_2$$

We could do this for every subinterval, and for the nth subinterval we would get

$$m\, \Delta x_n \le f(C_n)\, \Delta x_n \le M\, \Delta x_n$$

Now if we add the corresponding terms in all n inequalities, we get the sum

$$m(\Delta x_1 + \Delta x_2 + \Delta x_3 + \cdots + \Delta x_n) \le \sum_{k=1}^{n} f(C_k)\, \Delta x_k \le M(\Delta x_1 + \Delta x_2 + \Delta x_3 + \cdots + \Delta x_n)$$

But the sum of $\Delta x_1 + \Delta x_2 + \Delta x_3 + \cdots + \Delta x_n$ equals the length of the entire interval $b - a$, so we can substitute $b - a$ for both sums and get

$$m(b - a) \le \sum_{k=1}^{n} f(C_k)\, \Delta x_k \le M(b - a)$$

Now if we let n increase without bound as the width of the greatest subinterval $\|p\|$ approaches zero, the sum in the center can be represented as an integral, and we can write

$$m(b - a) \le \int_a^b f(x)\, dx \le M(b - a)$$

We finish by dividing every term by $b - a$, and we get

$$m \le \frac{1}{b - a} \int_a^b f(x)\, dx \le M$$

which completes the proof.

Problem set 99

1. Jan put \$1000 in the bank. The money is compounded continuously so that the amount in the account increases at a rate proportional to the amount. After 1 year, the account held \$1100. What annual interest rate did the bank pay? How much should Jan have deposited to have \$90,000 after 20 years?

2. The slope of a curve at any given point on the curve is twice its x coordinate. Find the equation of the curve if it passes through the point $(1, 1)$.

3. The end of a triangular trough is shown. The trough is filled to a depth of 2 meters with water whose weight density is 9800 newtons per cubic meter. Find the total force on the end of the trough.

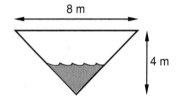

4. Find the work required to pump the water out of the trough in Problem 3 if the trough is 3 meters long.

5. The function $f(x) = 2x^{2/3}$ is defined on the closed interval $[-1, 8]$. Use the critical number theorem to find the maximum and minimum values of f on this interval.

6. The mean value theorem for integrals tells us that every function that is continuous on an interval attains its average value at some point on that interval. If $f(x) = x^3 + 4$, find a number $c \in [-2, 2]$ for which $f(c)$ equals the average value of the function f on this interval.

7. Approximate to two decimal places the average value of the function $f(x) = xe^x$ on the interval $[0, 2]$.

8. Let R be the region completely bounded by $y = x(1 - x)$ and the x axis. Use x as the variable of integration to write a definite integral whose value equals the volume of the solid formed when R is revolved about the y axis.

9. Let the functions f and g be defined for all values of x and let f be an odd function and g be an even function. Determine whether each of the following functions is odd, even, or neither.

   (a) $\dfrac{f}{g}$ (b) fg (c) f^2g

10. Use logarithmic differentiation to differentiate $f(x) = x^x$.

11. Find the area bounded by one arch of the graph of $y = \sin^2 x$ and the x axis.

12. Let R be the first-quadrant region bounded by $y = 1 - x^2$ and $x + y = 1$. Find the volume of the solid formed when R is rotated about the x axis.

13. Graph the function $y = \dfrac{x^2 + 1}{x}$.

14. Let R be the region bounded by the graph of $x + 2y = 3$ and the coordinate axes. Use y as the variable of integration to write a definite integral whose value equals the volume of the solid formed when R is rotated about the x axis.

Integrate:

15. $\displaystyle\int \cos 2x \; e^{\sin 2x} \, dx$

16. $\displaystyle\int \dfrac{x^2}{x^3 + 1} \, dx$

17. Differentiate: $y = \arctan x + \ln |\sin x| + 14^x - \dfrac{\sec x + e^x}{1 + x}$

18. Find $\dfrac{dy}{dx}$ if $x^3 + xy + y^2 = 0$.

CONCEPT REVIEW 19. Shown is the graph of the derivative f' of a function f:

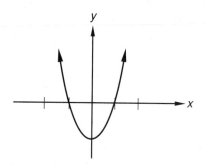

Which of the following graphs could be the graph of f?

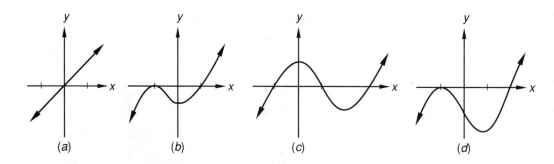

(a)   (b)   (c)   (d)

20. Given $f(x) = \sin(2x - \pi)$ and $g(x) = \cos(2x + \pi)$, which of the following statements are true?
    (a) The graphs of f and g are identical.
    (b) Both f and g are even functions.
    (c) The period of f equals the period of g.
    (d) The amplitude of g is greater than the amplitude of f.

LESSON 100   *Particle motion IV*

If the graph of a continuous function f is above the t axis between t_0 and t_1, the definite integral of the function from t_0 to t_1 will be a positive number that equals the area between the graph of f and the t axis between t_0 and t_1. If the graph of f is below the t axis between t_1 and t_2, the definite integral of the function from t_1 to t_2 will be a negative number that equals the negative of the area between the graph of f and the t axis between t_1 and t_2. The definite integral of f from t_0 to t_2 for the curve shown below will be the sum of the area above the t axis and the negative of the area below the t axis.

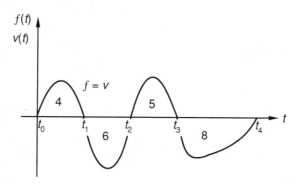

$$\int_{t_0}^{t_1} f(t)\, dt = 4 \qquad \int_{t_1}^{t_2} f(t)\, dt = -6 \qquad \int_{t_0}^{t_2} f(t)\, dt = -2$$

The definite integral of a **velocity function** of a particle moving left and right along the x axis represents the algebraic sum of the left ($-$) and right ($+$) distances traveled by the particle. For the velocity function graphed above the particle would travel 4 units to the right during the interval $[t_0, t_1]$ and would travel 6 units to the left during the interval $[t_1, t_2]$ for a net change of position of -2 during the interval $[t_0, t_2]$. The net change of position of the particle in the interval $[t_0, t_4]$ is 5 units to the left because the value of the definite integral for the velocity function between t_0 and t_4 is -5 since the algebraic sum of the areas between t_0 and t_4 is -5.

$$4 - 6 + 5 - 8 = -5$$

Example 100.1   The velocity function for a particle moving left and right along the x axis is $v(t)$. Given the following definite integrals:

$$\int_1^2 v(t)\, dt = -7 \qquad \int_2^3 v(t)\, dt = 3 \qquad \int_3^4 v(t)\, dt = -2 \qquad \int_4^5 v(t)\, dt = 6$$

(a)   How much did the position of the particle change during the interval $[1, 5]$?

(b)   If the particle was at $x = 7$ when t equaled 2, what was the position of the particle when t equaled 4?

Solution   (a)   The sum of the areas above the t axis between $t = 1$ and $t = 5$ is zero because $-7 + 3 - 2 + 6 = 0$. Thus the particle moved 7 units to the left, 3 units to the right, 2 units to the left, and 6 units to the right for a **net change of position of zero.**

(b)   Between $t = 2$ and $t = 4$ the particle moved 3 units to the right and 2 units to the left. Thus the particle moved from $x = 7$ to $x = 10$ and back to **$x = 8$ when t equaled 4.**

Example 100.2 A particle moves along the x axis so that its position function is

$$x(t) = 2t^3 - 9t^2 + 12t + 1$$

(a) What is the position of the particle when $t = 0$ and $t = 3$?
(b) What is the distance traveled between $t = 0$ and $t = 3$?

Solution (a) To find the position when $t = 0$ and when $t = 3$, we evaluate $x(0)$ and $x(3)$.

$$x(0) = 2(0)^3 - 9(0)^2 + 12(0) + 1 = \textbf{1}$$

$$x(3) = 2(3)^3 - 9(3)^2 + 12(3) + 1 = \textbf{10}$$

(b) The difference in position is 9 units, which is the sum of the areas above the t axis and the negative of the areas below the t axis on the graph of $v(t)$ between t values of 0 and 3. However, some of the areas might have been below the t axis and represent distances traveled to the left, so 9 is not necessarily the total distance traveled. Thus we begin by finding $v(t)$.

$$v(t) = \frac{d}{dx} x(t) = 6t^2 - 18t + 12 = 6(t^2 - 3t + 2)$$

It is not necessary to graph the function to find the areas. We just need to know when the graph is above the t axis and when the graph is below the t axis. Thus we need to know the zeros of the velocity function because its graph touches the t axis at these values of t. Thus we factor the equation for $v(t)$.

$$v(t) = 6(t - 2)(t - 1)$$

From the nonrepeating linear factors $t - 2$ and $t - 1$ we see that the zeros of the function are $+2$ and $+1$. If we use 0 as a test point, we see that $v(0) = +12$. We use this information to deduce that $v(t)$ is positive for t less than 1, is negative between 1 and 2, and is positive for t greater than 2.

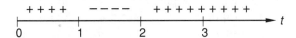

We are interested in the region between $t = 0$ and $t = 3$. We could add the areas above the graph to the negative of the areas below the graph by computing these integrals.

$$\int_0^1 v(t)\, dt - \int_1^2 v(t)\, dt + \int_2^3 v(t)\, dt$$

Rather than do this, we note that between $t = 0$ and $t = 1$ the particle moved to the right. Between $t = 1$ and $t = 2$, the particle moved to the left, and between $t = 2$ and $t = 3$ the particle moved to the right. If we evaluate $x(t)$ at $t = 0, 1, 2$, and 3, we get

$$x(0) = 1 \qquad x(1) = 6 \qquad x(2) = 5 \qquad x(3) = 10$$

During the interval $[0, 1]$ the particle moved from 1 to 6, a distance of 5. During the interval $[1, 2]$ the particle moved from 6 to 5, a distance of 1. During the interval $[2, 3]$ the particle moved from 5 to 10, a distance of 5. Thus the particle moved a total distance of

$$5 + 1 + 5 = \textbf{11 units}$$

The difference in the initial position and the final position was 9 units, but the total distance traveled was 11 units.

Example 100.3 The acceleration of a particle moving on the x axis is $4\pi \cos t$. If the velocity is 1 at $t = 0$, what is the average velocity of the particle over the interval $0 \le t \le \pi$?

Solution   Particles with an acceleration function of $4\pi \cos t$ exist only in calculus books. These problems are designed to let students play games with calculus. First we find the velocity function by integrating the acceleration function.

$$v(t) = \int a(t) = 4\pi \int \cos t \, dt = 4\pi \sin t + C$$

To find C we use the fact that $v(t) = 1$ when $t = 0$ and substitute.

$$1 = 4\pi \sin 0 + C \quad \longrightarrow \quad C = 1$$

Now we have the velocity function:

$$v(t) = 4\pi \sin t + 1$$

We can find the instantaneous velocity for any value of t by evaluating this function at t. **Average velocity is not the same thing as average speed. The average velocity between the two times t_1 and t_2 is defined to be the *directed distance* between the position of the particle at t_1 and the position of the particle at t_2 divided by the elapsed time $t_2 - t_1$.** The value of the definite integral of $v(t)$ between t_1 and t_2 equals the directed distance we need.

$$\text{Average velocity} = \frac{x(t_2) - x(t_1)}{t_2 - t_1} = \frac{\displaystyle\int_0^\pi (4\pi \sin t + 1)\, dt}{\pi - 0}$$

$$= \frac{[-4\pi \cos t + t]_0^\pi}{\pi} = \frac{4\pi + \pi}{\pi} - \left(\frac{-4\pi}{\pi}\right) = \frac{9\pi}{\pi}$$

$$= \textbf{9 units per second}$$

Example 100.4   The velocity function for a particle moving left and right along the x axis is given by $v(t) = 2\pi \cos \pi t$. For what values of t, $0 \le t \le 2$, is the particle not moving?

Solution   The particle is not moving when its velocity equals zero. The coefficient 2π is never zero since 2π always equals 2π. Thus the velocity equals zero when $\cos \pi t$ equals zero. This occurs when

$$\pi t = \frac{\pi}{2} \qquad \pi t = \frac{3\pi}{2} \qquad \pi t = \frac{5\pi}{2} \qquad \text{etc.}$$

which is when $t = \dfrac{1}{2} \qquad t = \dfrac{3}{2} \qquad t = \dfrac{5}{2} \qquad$ etc.

Only two of these values, $\dfrac{1}{2}$ and $\dfrac{3}{2}$, are between t values of 0 and 2.

Example 100.5   What is the total distance traveled to the left by the particle in Example 100.4?

Solution   The velocity is zero when $t = \frac{1}{2}$ and $\frac{3}{2}$.

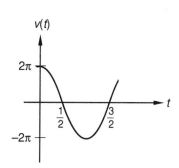

The particle is moving to the left when the velocity is negative. Thus we integrate from $t = \frac{1}{2}$ to $t = \frac{3}{2}$.

$$2 \int_{1/2}^{3/2} (\cos \pi t)(\pi \, dt) = 2[\sin \pi t]_{1/2}^{3/2} = 2\left(\sin \frac{3\pi}{2} - \sin \frac{\pi}{2}\right) = 2(-1 - 1) = -4$$

The negative sign on the definite integral indicates that the area is below the x axis and that the particle moved 4 units to the left between $t = \frac{1}{2}$ and $t = \frac{3}{2}$.

Problem set 100

1. A cone whose dimensions are shown contains water whose depth is h, and is dripping at a rate of $\frac{1}{2}$ cm³/sec. How fast is the depth of the water decreasing when the depth of the water is 2 cm?

    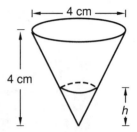

2. The velocity function for a particle moving along the x axis is $v(t)$. Suppose that

    $$\int_1^2 v(t) \, dt = -5 \qquad \int_2^3 v(t) \, dt = 6 \qquad \int_3^5 v(t) \, dt = -3$$

    If the particle's position at $t = 1$ was 5, find the particle's position at $t = 5$.

3. A particle moves along the x axis so that its position as a function of time t is given by $x(t) = t^2 - 3t + 2$. What is the position of the particle at $t = 0$ and at $t = 3$? What is the total distance traveled by the particle between $t = 0$ and $t = 3$?

4. The acceleration of a particle moving along a number line is given by the equation $a(t) = 4\pi \sin t$. If the velocity of the particle at $t = 0$ is π, find the average velocity of the particle over the interval $0 \le t \le \pi$.

5. The velocity function for a particle moving along the number line is the equation $v(t) = 2\pi \sin \pi t$. Find the times $t, \frac{1}{2} \le t \le \frac{3}{2}$, for which the particle is momentarily at rest.

6. Find the total distance traveled in the negative x direction by the particle of Problem 5.

7. The mean value theorem for integrals tells us that every continuous function attains its average value on an interval at some point in that interval. If $f(x) = x^2 + 1$, find a number $c \in [3, 4]$ for which $f(c)$ equals the average value of the function on this interval.

8. The slope at any given point on the graph of a certain function f is equal to the reciprocal of the x coordinate of the point. Find the equation of f if the graph of f passes through $(e, 3)$.

9. Suppose $f(x) = 2 \sin x$. Find the slope of the line joining the points $(0, f(0))$ and $(\pi, f(\pi))$. Illustrate the mean value theorem for derivatives for f on the interval $[0, \pi]$.

10. Let R be the region bounded by the graph of $y = 1/x$ and the x axis on the interval $[1, 2]$. Use x as the variable of integration to write a definite integral whose value equals the volume of the solid formed when R is revolved about the y axis. Evaluate this integral.

11. Let R be the region bounded by the graphs of $y = 0$, $y = \sqrt{x}$, and $x = 4$. Find the x coordinate of the centroid of R.

Integrate:

12. $\displaystyle\int 3^x \, dx$

13. $\displaystyle\int x \ln x \, dx$

14. $\displaystyle\int 3xe^{x^2} \, dx$

15. $\displaystyle\int \cot x \csc^2 x \, dx$

16. $\displaystyle\int \frac{5 \, dx}{1 + x^2}$

17. Find: $\dfrac{d}{dx}\left[\arctan(\sin x) + \ln(x^2 - 1) + \dfrac{1}{x + 1}\right]$

18. Given that

$$f(x) = \frac{4x^2 - 16}{x^2 - 9}$$

Determine whether f is an odd function, an even function, or neither. Then factor the numerator and denominator of f and use the factored form of the equation as an aid in sketching the graph of f.

CONCEPT REVIEW 19. Let f be defined as follows:

$$f(x) = \begin{cases} ax^2 + bx & x \geq 1 \\ 2x^2 & x < 1 \end{cases}$$

Find the values of a and b which make f continuous and differentiable everywhere.

20. If f is a function whose inverse is also a function, which of the following sets of points can lie on f?
(*a*) $\{(1, 3), (-1, 3), (2, 4)\}$ 　　 (*c*) $\{(1, 2), (2, 3), (3, 1)\}$
(*b*) $\{(3, 1), (3, 2), (2, 3)\}$ 　　 (*d*) $\{(\tfrac{1}{2}, 1), (-\tfrac{1}{2}, 1), (-1, 2)\}$

LESSON 101 *Derivatives of inverse functions*

We remember that a function is a one-to-one function if no two values of x have the same values of $f(x)$. Both of these graphs are graphs of functions because every value of x is paired with only one value of $f(x)$, or y.

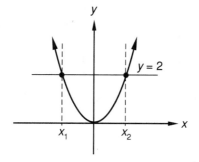
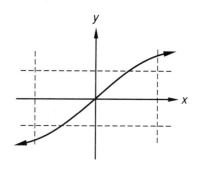

Any vertical line will touch either graph at only one point. But since the horizontal line $y = 2$ touches the graph on the left in two places, the function is not a one-to-one function because both x_1 and x_2 are paired with the y value of 2. The function graphed on the right is a one-to-one function, since no horizontal line touches the graph twice.

Every one-to-one function f has an inverse function whose graph is a mirror image of f in the line $y = x$. On the left we show the graph of a one-to-one function that we call f and the graph of its inverse function f^{-1}. The symbol f^{-1} is read as "f inverse." If the point (a, b) is on the graph of f, the point (b, a) will be on the graph of f^{-1}. The slope of f at (a, b) will be the reciprocal of the slope of f^{-1} at (b, a).

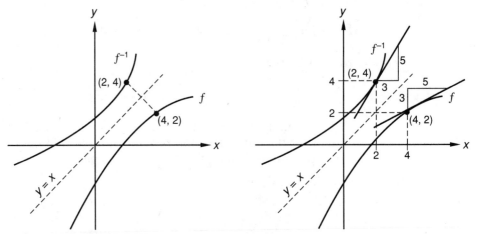

In the figure on the left above we show the point $(4, 2)$ on the graph of f and the point $(2, 4)$ on the graph of f^{-1}. For both functions, x is the independent (input) variable and y is the dependent (output) variable, as shown in the function machines below.

$$x \longrightarrow \boxed{f} \longrightarrow f(x) \qquad\qquad x \longrightarrow \boxed{f^{-1}} \longrightarrow f^{-1}(x)$$
$$4 \longrightarrow \phantom{\boxed{f}} \longrightarrow 2 \qquad\qquad 2 \longrightarrow \phantom{\boxed{f^{-1}}} \longrightarrow 4$$

From the graph on the right above we see that the slope of f^{-1} when $x = 2$ is $\frac{5}{3}$ and that the slope of the graph of f when $x = 4$ is $\frac{3}{5}$. But 4 is f^{-1} evaluated at 2, or $f^{-1}(2)$. Thus we can write for this example that the derivative of the inverse function evaluated at $x = 2$ equals the reciprocal of the derivative of the function evaluated at 4, which is $f^{-1}(2)$.

$$(f^{-1})'(2) = \frac{1}{f'(f^{-1}(2))} \qquad \text{because} \qquad \frac{5}{3} = \frac{1}{\dfrac{3}{5}}$$

This notation is very confusing, and the important thing to remember is that the slope of the inverse function at $x = c$ and $y = d$ equals the reciprocal of the slope of the original function evaluated at $x = d$ and $y = c$. We will investigate this in two steps. First we will use the function $y = x^3$ and its inverse function $x = y^3$.

FUNCTION	INVERSE FUNCTION
$y = x^3$	$x = y^3$

$$dy = 3x^2\, dx \longrightarrow \frac{dy}{dx} = 3x^2 \qquad\qquad dx = 3y^2\, dy \longrightarrow \frac{dy}{dx} = \frac{1}{3y^2}$$

$$f'(x) = \frac{dy}{dx} = 3x^2 \qquad\qquad (f^{-1})'(x) = \frac{dy}{dx} = \frac{1}{3y^2}$$

But what is y in the equation on the right? It is the output of the f^{-1} machine when the input is x, which we note by $f^{-1}(x)$. If we replace y^2 with $(f^{-1}(x))^2$, we get the following expression for the derivative of f inverse of x:

$$(f^{-1})'(x) = \frac{dy}{dx} = \frac{1}{3(f^{-1}(x))^2}$$

For a general proof we will use the one-to-one function $y = f(x)$.

FUNCTION	INVERSE FUNCTION
$y = f(x)$	$x = f(y)$
$dy = f'(x)\, dx$	$dx = f'(y)\, dy$
$\dfrac{dy}{dx} = f'(x)$	$(f^{-1})'(x) = \dfrac{dy}{dx} = \dfrac{1}{f'(y)}$

But again the inverse function y equals the output of the f^{-1} machine, which is $f^{-1}(x)$, so we can write

$$(f^{-1})'(x) = \frac{dy}{dx} = \frac{1}{f'(f^{-1}(x))}$$

Example 101.1   The function $f(x) = x^3 + x - 1$ is a one-to-one function. Find the slope of the graph of the inverse function at the point $(-1, 0)$.

Solution   We want to find the slope of the graph of the inverse function at the point $(-1, 0)$. Since we have an abundance of information, we can find the answer in two ways. The first is to find the equation of the inverse function, differentiate, and evaluate at $(-1, 0)$.

$$y = x^3 + x - 1 \qquad \text{function}$$
$$x = y^3 + y - 1 \qquad \text{inverse function}$$
$$dx = 3y^2\, dy + dy \qquad \text{differential}$$
$$(f^{-1})'(x) = \frac{dy}{dx} = \frac{1}{3y^2 + 1} \qquad \text{derivative}$$

Since we know that the y value of the point is 0 when $x = -1$, we let y equal zero and get

$$(f^{-1})'(-1) = \frac{1}{3(0)^2 + 1} = \mathbf{1}$$

The other way to arrive at this answer is to use the equation

$$(f^{-1})'(-1) = \frac{1}{f'(f^{-1}(-1))}$$

First we find $f'(x)$.

$$f'(x) = 3x^2 + 1$$

Now we remember that $f^{-1}(-1)$ is the value of $y = f^{-1}(x)$ when $x = -1$, which is 0. So

$$f^{-1}(-1) = \frac{1}{f'(f^{-1}(-1))} = \frac{1}{f'(0)} = \frac{1}{3(0)^2 + 1} = 1$$

Even when we know the answer we see that the notation leads to confusion!

Example 101.2   Let $f(x) = x^3 + x$. If h is the inverse function of f, find $h'(2)$.

Solution   We use h' instead of $(f^{-1})'$ because it is less confusing. We know the function is a one-to-one function because its inverse is a function, and only one-to-one functions have inverses that are functions. We begin by finding the equation for the slope of the inverse function.

$$y = x^3 + x \qquad \text{function}$$
$$x = y^3 + y \qquad \text{inverse function}$$
$$dx = 3y^2\, dy + dy \qquad \text{differential}$$
$$h'(x) = \frac{dy}{dx} = \frac{1}{3y^2 + 1} \qquad \text{derivative}$$

But what is y? We want to find $h'(2)$ and 2 is x, and our equation has $3y^2 + 1$ in the denominator. So we go back to the equation of the inverse function

$$x = y^3 + y$$

and find the value of y when $x = 2$.

$$2 = y^3 + y$$

Usually we would have to solve this cubic for y. Because the problem was carefully contrived, we can see that y has to equal 1.

$$2 = (1)^3 + 1$$

So our answer is

$$h'(2) = \frac{1}{3y^2 + 1} = \frac{1}{3(1)^2 + 1} = \frac{1}{4}$$

Had we been asked to find the value of $h'(12)$, we would have been in trouble because this would require that we find the roots of the cubic

$$12 = y^3 + y$$

Many standardized tests have these carefully contrived problems to see if the student understands the concept of the slope of the inverse function, so be forewarned.

Problem set 101

1. A particle traveling along the x axis begins at $x = 4$ when $t = 0$ and moves along the axis so that when $t > 0$, its velocity is given by

$$v(t) = \frac{4t}{1 + t^2}$$

Write the equations which describe the acceleration and position of the particle as a function of time. What velocity does the particle approach as t increases without bound?

2. Suppose $f(x) = xe^{-x^2}$. Find all the critical numbers of f and determine whether f attains a local maximum or minimum at each of the critical numbers found. Use the first derivative test to justify your answer.

3. A particle moves along the x axis so that its position function is given by the equation $x(t) = 2t^3 - 9t^2 + 12t + 9$. Determine the position of the particle

when $t = 0$ and $t = 2$. Now determine the total distance traveled by the particle between $t = 0$ and $t = 2$.

4. A particle moves along the x axis so that its acceleration at time t is given by $a(t) = 3 \sin t$. If the velocity of the particle is 3 at $t = 0$, find the average velocity of the particle on the interval $0 \le t \le \pi$.

5. A certain sum of money is deposited in an account where interest is compounded continuously at an annual rate of 9 percent. How much money should be deposited now so that the account will contain $50,000 in 30 years?

6. Suppose that $f(x) = x^3 - x - 1$. Find the slope of the graph of the inverse of f at the point $(-1, 0)$.

7. Suppose $f(x) = x^3 + 2x$ and h is the inverse function of f. Evaluate $h(3)$ and $h'(3)$. [Note that $h(3)$ can be evaluated by guessing.]

8. Suppose $f(x) = x^3 + x$ and h is the inverse function of f. Evaluate $h(0)$ and $h'(0)$.

9. The mean value theorem for integrals tells us that every continuous function attains its average value on an interval at some point in the interval. If the function $f(x) = 3x^2 + 2x + 1$, find some $c \in [-1, 2]$ for which $f(c)$ equals the average value of the f on this interval.

10. Use logarithmic differentiation to compute

$$\frac{f'(x)}{f(x)} \quad \text{if} \quad f(x) = \frac{\sin x}{(x^3 + 1)^3 (x^4 + 1)^4}$$

11. Let R be the region bounded by the graph of $y = \sin x$ and the x axis on the interval $[0, \pi]$. Find the volume of the solid formed when R is rotated about the x axis.

Evaluate the following limits:

12. $\lim\limits_{x \to 0} (4x \csc 2x)$

13. $\lim\limits_{x \to \infty} \dfrac{\ln x}{\sqrt{x}}$

14. The definite integral

$$\int_0^{\pi/2} (\cos x)[\cos (\sin x)] \, dx$$

is equal to which of the following definite integrals?

(a) $\displaystyle\int_{-1}^{1} \cos u \, du$ (b) $\displaystyle\int_0^{\pi/2} \cos u \, du$ (c) $\displaystyle\int_0^{\pi/2} \sin u \, du$

(d) $\displaystyle\int_0^{1} \cos u \, du$

15. Suppose $b > a$ and $\displaystyle\int_a^b e^{\cos x} \, dx = k$. Determine the values of

$$\int_b^a e^{\cos x} \, dx \quad \text{and} \quad \int_{-b}^{-a} e^{\cos x} \, dx$$

16. Find: $\dfrac{d}{dx} \arcsin \dfrac{x}{3} + \displaystyle\int \frac{1}{\sqrt{9 - x^2}} \, dx + \dfrac{d}{dx} \arctan \dfrac{x}{3} + \displaystyle\int \frac{3}{x^2 + 9} \, dx$

17. Differentiate: $y = \dfrac{1}{\sqrt{x}} + 2 \ln |\sin x + \cos x|$

18. Which of the following limits does not exist?

(a) $\lim\limits_{x\to 0} \dfrac{x}{\sin x}$ (b) $\lim\limits_{x\to 0} \sin \dfrac{x}{1}$ (c) $\lim\limits_{x\to 0} \sin \dfrac{1}{x}$ (d) $\lim\limits_{x\to 0} \dfrac{x^2 - 1}{x - 1}$

CONCEPT REVIEW   **19.** Suppose the points (4, 2), (3, 4), (5, 6) lie on the graph of the function f. Which of the following statements must be true?

(a)   The points $(-4, -2), (-3, -4), (-5, -6)$ lie on the graph of the inverse of f.

(b)   The points (4, 2), (3, 4), (5, 6) lie on the graph of f^{-1}.

(c)   The points $(\frac{1}{4}, \frac{1}{2}), (\frac{1}{3}, \frac{1}{4}), (\frac{1}{6}, \frac{1}{6})$ lie on the graph of f^{-1}.

(d)   The points (2, 4), (4, 3), (6, 5) lie on the graph of f^{-1}.

20. A right circular cone is inscribed inside a hemisphere so that its base is the same as the base of the hemisphere. If the radius of the hemisphere is r, find the surface area of the cone (including the base) and find the volume of the cone.

LESSON 102 *Solids of revolution IV*

Thus far we have considered solids of revolution formed by rotating regions about the y axis or the x axis. If the region is rotated about a line parallel to the x axis or the y axis, a different solid is formed.

Example 102.1   A region R is bounded by $y = x^3$, the x axis, and the line $x = 2$. Use the disk method to find an integral that can be evaluated to find the volume of the solid formed by rotating the region about the line $x = 2$. Evaluate this integral.

Solution   On the left we show the region described, and on the right we show the solid and a representative disk.

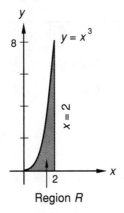

Region R

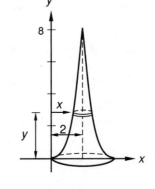

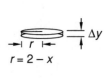

$r = 2 - x$

The volume of the representative disk is $\pi r^2 \, \Delta y$, and since r equals $2 - x$, the volume of the disk is $\pi (2 - x)^2 \, \Delta y$. The disks are stacked from $y = 0$ to $y = 8$, so the volume of the solid is

$$V = \int_0^8 \pi (2 - x)^2 \, dy$$

The *dy* tells us that *y* is the variable of integration, so the integrand should have no variable other than *y*. For this problem *x* and *y* are related by $y = x^3$, which tells us that $x = y^{1/3}$. Thus we replace *x* with $y^{1/3}$, expand, integrate, and evaluate.

$$V = \pi \int_0^8 (2 - y^{1/3})^2 \, dy \qquad\qquad \text{substituted}$$

$$= \pi \int_0^8 (4 - 4y^{1/3} + y^{2/3}) \, dy \qquad\qquad \text{expanded}$$

$$= \pi \left[4y - 3y^{4/3} + \frac{3y^{5/3}}{5} \right]_0^8 = \frac{16\pi}{5} \text{ units}^3 \qquad \text{evaluated}$$

Example 102.2   The region *R* is the region completely enclosed by the graphs of $x = y^2$, $y = 2$, and the *y* axis. The region is revolved about the line $y = 2$. Use the disk method to write an integral that defines the value of the solid generated in terms of *x*.

Solution   On the left we show the region defined, and on the right we show the solid formed and a representative disk.

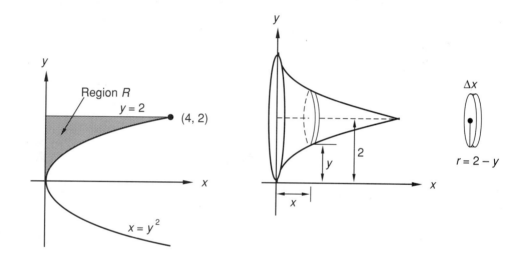

The volume of the disk is πr^2 times the thickness Δx. The radius *r* equals $2 - y$, so the volume of the disk is $\pi(2 - y)^2 \, \Delta x$. The disks are stacked from $x = 0$ to $x = 4$. Thus the volume of the whole solid is

$$V = \int_0^4 \pi(2 - y)^2 \, dx$$

The *dx* tells us that *x* is the variable of integration, so the integrand should have no variable other than *x*. In this problem $x = y^2$, so $y = x^{1/2}$. If we substitute $x^{1/2}$ for *y*, we have the desired integral.

$$V = \pi \int_0^4 (2 - x^{1/2})^2 \, dx$$

A numerical answer can be found by expanding, integrating, and evaluating the integral.

Example 102.3   Let *R* be the region bounded by $y = \sin x$ between $x = 0$ and $x = \pi$. This region is rotated about the line $y = -1$. Use the washer method to write an integral that expresses the volume entirely in terms of *x*.

Solution   On the left we show the region. On the right we show a sketch of the solid, as well as a representative washer.

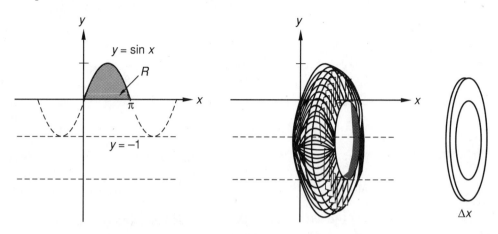

The width of the representative washer is Δx. The volume of the representative washer is the volume of the entire washer minus the volume of the hole in its center.

$$V_a = \pi r_W^2\, \Delta x - \pi r_h^2\, \Delta x = (\pi r_W^2 - \pi r_h^2)\, \Delta x = \pi(r_W^2 - r_h^2)\, \Delta x$$

The radius of the washer is $\sin x + 1$, and the radius of the hole is 1. The washers will be stacked from $x = 0$ to $x = \pi$. Thus the volume of the solid is defined by the integral

$$V = \pi \int_0^\pi [(\sin x + 1)^2 - (1)^2]\, dx \qquad \text{integral}$$

$$V = \pi \int_0^\pi (\sin^2 x + 2 \sin x)\, dx \qquad \text{expanded}$$

A numerical result can be obtained by integrating and evaluating, using 0 and π as the limits of integration.

Example 102.4   Let R be the region bounded by the graph of $y = e^x$, the x axis, and the lines $x = 1$ and $x = 2$. A solid of revolution is formed when this region is rotated about the line $x = 3$. Use the shell method to write an integral that could be evaluated to find the volume of this solid.

Solution   On the left we show the region R. On the right we show a sketch of the solid of revolution and a representative shell flattened out. Portions of the shell are represented by the nonshaded rectangles in the center figure.

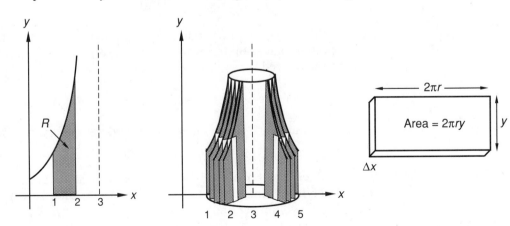

The volume of a representative shell is the area $(2\pi r)(y)$ times the thickness Δx.

$$V_{\text{shell}} = 2\pi ry\, \Delta x$$

The shells are stacked from $x = 1$ to $x = 2$. The radius of each shell is $3 - x$, the height is e^x, and the thickness is Δx. Thus the volume of the solid is

$$V = 2\pi \int_1^2 (3 - x)e^x\, dx$$

If we multiply, we get

$$V = 6\pi \int_1^2 e^x\, dx - 2\pi \int_1^2 xe^x\, dx$$

The value of the first integral is

$$[6\pi e^x]_1^2$$

and the value of the second integral can be found by using the same limits and the method of integration by parts.

Example 102.5   The region R is bounded by the graph of $\sqrt{x} + \sqrt{y} = 3$, the x and y axes, and the line $x = 3$. Use the shell method to write an integral that gives the value of the solid formed if R is revolved about the line $x = 6$.

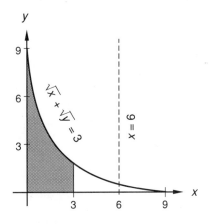

Solution   On the left we show a cross section of the solid of revolution that contains a representative shell. On the right we show the shell flattened out.

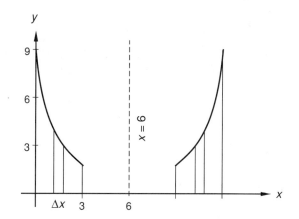

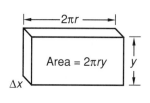

The volume of the representative shell is

$$V_{\text{shell}} = (2\pi r)(y)\, \Delta x$$

We must write y in terms of x. To do this it is necessary to rearrange the equation and square both sides.

$$\sqrt{x} + \sqrt{y} = 3 \quad \longrightarrow \quad y^{1/2} = 3 - x^{1/2} \quad \longrightarrow \quad y = (3 - x^{1/2})^2$$

The shells extend from $x = 0$ to $x = 3$, and the radius of each shell is $6 - x$. Thus the desired volume is

$$V = 2\pi \int_0^3 (6 - x)(3 - x^{1/2})^2 \, dx$$

To get a numerical answer, we would expand $(3 - x^{1/2})^2$, multiply by $6 - x$, integrate, and evaluate the integral from 0 to 3.

Problem set 102

1. A right circular cone is inscribed inside a hemisphere so that its base is the same as the base of the hemisphere. Suppose the surface area of the hemisphere, including its base, is increasing at a constant rate of 24 cm²/sec. Find the rate at which the radius of the sphere is increasing when $r = 4$ cm. Use that information to find the rate at which the volume of the cone is increasing when $r = 4$ cm.

2. The following integrals apply to the velocity of a particle moving along the x axis:

$$\int_0^2 v(t) \, dt = -5 \qquad \int_2^3 v(t) \, dt = 7 \qquad \int_3^6 v(t) \, dt = -2$$

    If the x coordinate of the particle is 5 when $t = 0$, what is the particle's position when $t = 6$?

3. A rectangular tank 4 meters wide, 5 meters long, and 4 meters deep is three-quarters full of a fluid whose weight density is 5000 newtons per cubic meter. Find the total force on the side of the wall whose width is 4 meters.

4. Find the total work done in pumping the fluid out of the tank described in Problem 3.

5. An object is suspended from an elastic spring whose spring constant is 2 newtons per meter. The object stretches the spring 6 meters from its rest position. What is the weight of the object? What is the total work the object does in stretching the spring?

6. The region R is bounded by the x axis and the graphs of $y = x^3$ and $x = 1$. Find the volume of the solid formed when R is revolved about the line $x = 1$.

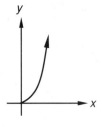

7. The region R is bounded by the y axis and the graph of $x = y^2 - 1$. Use y as the variable of integration to write a definite integral whose value equals the volume of the solid formed when R is revolved about the line $x = 1$.

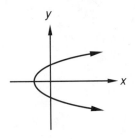

8. Let R be the region bounded by the x axis and the graph of $y = \tan x$ on the interval $[0, \pi/4]$. Express as an integral, in the variable x, the volume of the solid formed when R is rotated about the line $x = -1$.

9. Let R be the region bounded by the graphs of $y = e^x$, $x = 2$, $x = 3$, and $y = 0$. Use x as the variable of integration to write a definite integral whose value equals the volume of the solid formed when R is rotated about the line $x = 4$.

10. The function $f(x) = x^3 + x + 1$ is a one-to-one function, and thus its inverse f^{-1} is also a function. Find the equation of the tangent line that can be drawn to the graph of f^{-1} at the point $(1, 0)$.

11. If

$$f(x) = \sin x \qquad \text{where} \qquad -\frac{\pi}{2} \le x \le \frac{\pi}{2}$$

evaluate $(f^{-1})'$ at $x = \frac{1}{2}$.

12. The mean value theorem for integrals tells us that every continuous function attains its average value on an interval at some point in the interval. If the function $f(x) = x^3 + 2$, find some $c \in [0, 2]$ for which $f(c)$ equals the average value of the function on the interval.

13. Suppose $f(x) = x^2 + 1$. Find the slope of the line which passes through the points $(-1, f(-1))$ and $(1, f(1))$. Illustrate the mean value theorem for f on the interval $[-1, 1]$.

14. Sketch the graph of $y = \dfrac{x^2 + x}{x}$.

15. The region R is bounded by the graphs of $x = -y^2 - y + 2$ and $y = -x - 2$. Use y as the variable of integration to write an integral whose value equals the area of the region R.

16. Use horizontal rectangles to find the y coordinate of the centroid of the region R described in Problem 15

17. The region R is bounded by the graph of $y = \tan x$ and the x axis on the interval $[\pi/6, \pi/4]$. Estimate the area of R to two decimal places. (*Note:* The integral can be evaluated if $\tan x$ is rewritten as a quotient of two functions.)

18. The function $f(x) = e^x$, and the function $g(x) = \sin x$. We define h to be the composite function $h(x) = f(g(x))$. Evaluate $h'\left(\dfrac{\pi}{2}\right)$.

19. Find: $\dfrac{d}{dx}\left[\sin (x^2 - 1) + \dfrac{\sin x + 1}{e^x - 2}\right] + \displaystyle\int \dfrac{x^2}{x^3 - 1}\, dx$

CONCEPT REVIEW 20. The function f is defined as follows:

$$f(t) = \begin{cases} a \sin t - b \cos t & \text{when } t \ge \dfrac{\pi}{2} \\ \cos t & \text{when } t < \dfrac{\pi}{2} \end{cases}$$

Find the values of a and b which make f continuous everywhere.

21. Suppose f is a function and the inverse of f, f^{-1}, is also a function. Which of the following sets of points could lie on f?
(a) $\{(1, 2), (2, 3), (3, 4), (4, 5)\}$ (b) $\{(1, 2), (2, 3), (1, 3), (4, 5)\}$
(c) $\{(1, 1), (2, 2), (1, 2), (3, 3)\}$ (d) $\{(1, -1), (-1, 1), (2, -1), (3, 1)\}$

LESSON 103 *Absolute value*

In Lesson 81 we found that the derivative of $|f(x)|$ equals the derivative of $f(x)$ when $f(x)$ is positive and equals the negative of the derivative of $f(x)$ when $f(x)$ is negative. This rule can be recalled easily by visualizing the graph of $y = \sin x$ and the graph of $y = |\sin x|$.

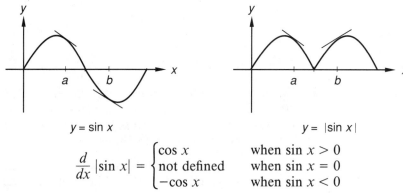

$$y = \sin x \qquad\qquad\qquad y = |\sin x|$$

$$\frac{d}{dx}|\sin x| = \begin{cases} \cos x & \text{when } \sin x > 0 \\ \text{not defined} & \text{when } \sin x = 0 \\ -\cos x & \text{when } \sin x < 0 \end{cases}$$

When $x = a$, the tangent lines to the two graphs have the same slopes because $\sin x$ is positive when x equals a. When $x = b$, the tangent lines to the graphs have different slopes because $\sin x$ is negative when x equals b.

Some books point out that the derivative of $|f(x)|$ can be written as

$$\frac{d}{dx}|f(x)| = \frac{f(x)}{|f(x)|}\frac{d}{dx}f(x)$$

The value of $f(x)$ divided by $|f(x)|$ equals 1 when $f(x)$ is positive, is -1 when $f(x)$ is negative, and is not defined when $f(x)$ equals zero. Thus

$$\frac{d}{dx}|\sin x| = \frac{\sin x}{|\sin x|}(\cos x)$$

makes exactly the same statement for this example as does the three-part piecewise definition above.

If the absolute value notation is used only with the variable

$$y = f(|x|)$$

the meaning is entirely different. This function is an even function because it has the same value for $-x$ that it has for $+x$. Thus the graph of the function to the left of the origin is a mirror image of the graph to the right of the origin. Graphing the function $y = f(|x|)$ requires that the graph of $y = f(x)$ to the left of the origin be replaced with the mirror image of the graph of $y = f(x)$ where $x \geq 0$, which is $y = f(-x)$ where $x \leq 0$. The graph of $y = f(x)$ is shown in the figure on the left.

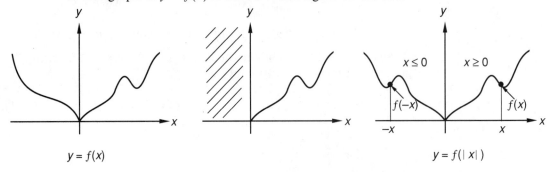

$$y = f(x) \qquad\qquad\qquad\qquad y = f(|x|)$$

In the center figure we discard the portion of the graph to the left of the origin, and in the figure on the right we replace the discarded portion with the graph of $y = f(-x)$ where $x \leq 0$. Since x is negative, every value of $f(-x)$ on the left is exactly the same as the corresponding value of $f(x)$ on the right.

To find the derivative of a function of the absolute value of x, we redefine the function as a piecewise function that does not use absolute value.

Example 103.1   If $y = e^{|x|}$, find $\dfrac{dy}{dx}$.

Solution   We begin by redefining the function without using the absolute value notation.

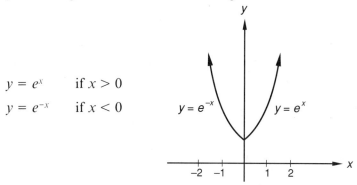

$$\begin{array}{ll} y = e^x & \text{if } x > 0 \\ y = e^{-x} & \text{if } x < 0 \end{array}$$

When x is greater than zero,

$$\frac{d}{dx} e^{|x|} = \frac{d}{dx} e^x = e^x$$

When x is less than zero, we use the chain rule to get

$$\frac{d}{dx} e^{|x|} = \frac{d}{dx} e^{-x} = e^{-x}(-1) = -e^{-x}$$

Because the left-hand derivative at $x = 0$ does not equal the right-hand derivative at $x = 0$, the derivative at $x = 0$ is not defined for this function.

Example 103.2   If $f(x) = \cos |2x|$, find $f'(x)$.

Solution   We begin by redefining the function as a piecewise function so that the absolute value notation is not required.

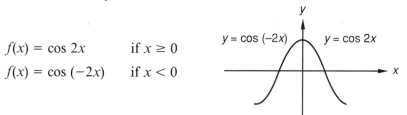

$$\begin{array}{ll} f(x) = \cos 2x & \text{if } x \geq 0 \\ f(x) = \cos (-2x) & \text{if } x < 0 \end{array}$$

The derivative to the right of the origin is

$$\frac{d}{dx} \cos 2x = -2 \sin 2x$$

To find the derivative to the left of the origin, we remember that $\cos x$ is an even function and that $\cos (-x) = \cos x$.

$$\frac{d}{dx} \cos (-2x) = \frac{d}{dx} \cos 2x = -2 \sin 2x$$

Since the derivative to the left of the origin equals the derivative to the right of the origin and the derivative at $x = 0$ exists, we can write

$$\frac{d}{dx} \cos |2x| = -2 \sin 2x$$

Example 103.3 Evaluate: $\displaystyle\int_{-3}^{3} |x + 1| \, dx$

Solution **We always begin with a graph of the function.** On the left we show the graph of the equation $y = x + 1$ between -3 and $+3$, and on the right we show the graph of the equation $y = |x + 1|$ between -3 and $+3$.

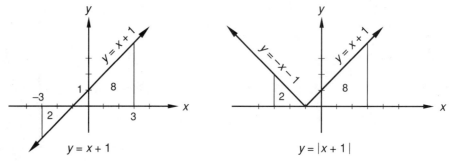

From the graphs we see that we have two choices. We have been asked to find the sum of the two triangular areas. By using $\frac{1}{2}bh$, we find that the area of the small triangle is 2 and the area of the large triangle is 8, as we show in both figures, so the answer is 10. To get this answer by using definite integrals, we can add the negative of the integral of $x + 1$ from -3 to -1 to the integral of $x + 1$ from -1 to 3, as we show on the left below.

$$-\int_{-3}^{-1} (x + 1) \, dx + \int_{-1}^{3} (x + 1) \, dx \quad \text{or} \quad \int_{-3}^{-1} (-x - 1) \, dx + \int_{-1}^{3} (x + 1) \, dx$$

$$= -(-2) + 8 = \mathbf{10} \qquad\qquad\qquad = 2 + 8 = \mathbf{10}$$

On the right we get the same result by adding the integral of $-x - 1$ from -3 to -1 to the integral of $x + 1$ from -1 to 3.

Example 103.4 Find $\displaystyle\int_{-\pi/2}^{0} \sin |2x|$.

Solution We begin by redefining $\sin |2x|$ without using the absolute value notation.

$$f(x) = \sin 2x \qquad \text{if } x \geq 0$$
$$f(x) = \sin (-2x) \qquad \text{if } x < 0$$

A graph of the function is always helpful. On the left we show the graph of $y = \sin 2x$ to the right of the origin. Then we show the graph of $y = \sin (-2x)$ to the left of the origin.

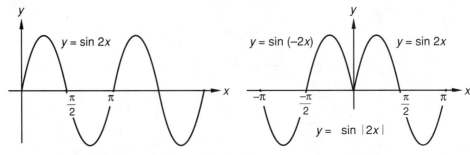

$$\int_{-\pi/2}^{0} \sin(-2x)\,dx = \frac{1}{2}\int_{-\pi/2}^{0} -\sin(-2x)(-2\,dx) = \frac{1}{2}[\cos(-2x)]_{-\pi/2}^{0}$$

$$= \frac{1}{2}\left\{\cos 0 - \cos\left[(-2)\left(-\frac{\pi}{2}\right)\right]\right\}$$

$$= \frac{1}{2}(1 - \cos \pi) = \frac{1}{2}(2) = \mathbf{1}$$

Example 103.5   Find $\displaystyle\int_{-\pi}^{\pi} |\sin x|\,dx$.

Solution   The graph of $y = |\sin x|$ shows us that the integral equals the area between the x axis and the graph from $x = -\pi$ to $x = \pi$. This is twice the area from $x = 0$ to $x = \pi$. Thus we will find the integral from 0 to π and multiply by 2.

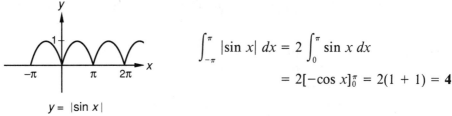

$$\int_{-\pi}^{\pi} |\sin x|\,dx = 2\int_{0}^{\pi} \sin x\,dx$$

$$= 2[-\cos x]_{0}^{\pi} = 2(1 + 1) = \mathbf{4}$$

$y = |\sin x|$

Example 103.6   If $f(x) = |\sin x - \frac{3}{4}|$, find the maximum value of f.

Solution   Since this is a calculus course, we would be tempted to try to take the derivative of f and find its value when $f' = 0$. But there is no simple algorithm for finding the derivative or the integral of the absolute value of a function. Thus we will investigate this function by drawing its graph. On the left we show the graph of $y = \sin x - \frac{3}{4}$.

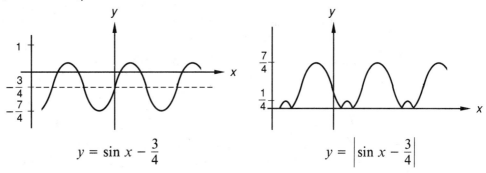

$$y = \sin x - \frac{3}{4} \qquad\qquad y = \left|\sin x - \frac{3}{4}\right|$$

On the right we show the graph of the absolute value of the function, and its maximum value is $\frac{7}{4}$. The graph on the right was really not necessary because the graph on the left went down to a y value of $-\frac{7}{4}$, and the absolute value of $-\frac{7}{4}$ is $\frac{7}{4}$. We used the graph to arrive at this conclusion.

Example 103.7   Given that f is a continuous function for all real numbers and given that the maximum value of f is 6 and the minimum value of f is -12, which of the following must be true?

     (*a*)   The maximum value of $|f(x)|$ is 6.
     (*b*)   The minimum value of $f(|x|)$ is 0.
     (*c*)   The maximum value of $|f(x)|$ is 12.

Solution   This question is typical of some of the questions that appear on multiple-choice calculus tests. Only one counterexample is necessary to eliminate a choice. We can eliminate (*a*) and (*b*) by using the graphs shown on page 508.

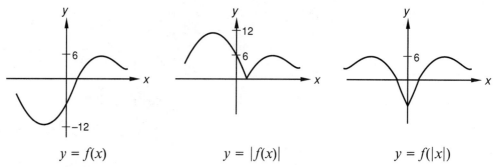

$$y = f(x) \qquad\qquad y = |f(x)| \qquad\qquad y = f(|x|)$$

The graph of f shows that f has a maximum value of 6 and a minimum value of -12. The next graph shows that $|f(x)|$ has a maximum value greater than 6, so this eliminates choice (a). The final graph shows a minimum value that is less than zero, so this eliminates choice (b). **Choice (c) is correct** because the maximum value of the absolute value of a function whose extreme values are 6 and -12 is 12.

Problem set 103

1. A particle moves along the x axis so that its position at time t ($t > 0$) is given by the equation $x(t) = 2t^3 - 9t^2 + 12t + 1$. Find the times when the particle is moving to the left.

2. Find the total distance traveled by the particle of Problem 1 between the times $t = 0$ and $t = 4$.

3. If the interest is compounded continuously, the rate of increase of money in an account is proportional to the amount of money present. If $500, deposited in an account at a particular interest rate, grows to $911 in 10 years, how much should have been deposited for the account to have a value of $20,000 in 20 years?

4. Suppose $f(x) = |x^2 - 1|$, where f is defined on the interval $I = [-1, \frac{1}{2}]$. Find all the critical numbers of f on I. Use the critical number theorem to determine the maximum and minimum values of f.

Evaluate the following definite integrals:

5. $\displaystyle\int_{-2}^{3} |x + 1|\, dx$

6. $\displaystyle\int_{-2}^{1} |x^2 + x|\, dx$

7. Suppose $f(x) = |\cos x - \frac{1}{2}|$. Determine the maximum value of f.

8. Consider a function f that is a continuous function for all real numbers. Furthermore, the maximum value of f is 7 and the minimum value of f is -10. Which of the following statements must be true?
   (a) The maximum value of $|f(x)|$ is 7.
   (b) The minimum value of $f(|x|)$ is 0.
   (c) The maximum value of $|f(x)|$ is 10.

9. Let R be the region bounded by the graph of $y = x^4$ and the x axis on the interval $[0, 1]$. Express as an integral, in the variable x, the volume of the solid formed when R is rotated about the line $x = 1$.

10. Let R be the region completely enclosed by the graph of $y = x^2$ and $y = x$. Use x as the variable of integration to write a definite integral whose value equals the volume of the solid formed when R is rotated about the line $y = -1$.

11. Let R be the region between the graph of $y = \sin x$ and the x axis when $0 \le x \le \pi$. Express as an integral, in the variable x, the volume of the solid formed when R is rotated about the line $x = 2\pi$.

12. The function $f(x) = x^3 + 2x$ is a one-to-one function, so its inverse is also a function. Evaluate $f^{-1}(3)$.

13. Suppose f is an odd function and g is an even function, and both functions are defined everywhere. Determine whether each of the following functions is odd, even, or neither.

   (a) fg (b) $\dfrac{f}{g}$ (c) f^2 (d) $f^2 g^3$

14. Use logarithmic differentiation to differentiate the function $y = x^{\sqrt{x}}$.

15. Find the area under one arch of the graph of $y = 2\sin^2 x$.

16. Suppose f is a function that is continuous at $x = 2$. Which of the following statements must be true?

   (a) $\lim\limits_{x \to 2} f(x) = f(2)$ (b) f is differentiable at $x = 2$

   (c) $\lim\limits_{x \to 2} \dfrac{f(x) - f(2)}{x - 2}$ exists (d) f attains a maximum value at $x = 2$

17. Find the intervals on which the graph of $y = x^3 - 6x^2 + 6x + 1$ is concave upward.

18. Evaluate: $\lim\limits_{x \to 3} \dfrac{e^x - e^3}{x - 3}$

19. Compute $\dfrac{d^3 y}{dx^3}$ if $y = (x - 4)^6 + \sin 2x$

20. Integrate: $\displaystyle\int \dfrac{e^x + \cos x}{e^x + \sin x}\, dx$

CONCEPT REVIEW 21. The inverse of $y = x$ is which of the following?
   (a) $y = x$ (b) $y = -x$ (c) $-\frac{1}{2}$ (d) $y = \sqrt{x}$

LESSON 104 *Integral of tan^n x · Integral of cot^n x*

104.A
Integral of tan^n x

We remember that we can find the integral of $\tan x\, dx$ because we can use $\sin x$ and $\cos x$ to write this integral in the form du over u.

$$\int \tan x\, dx = -\int \underbrace{\dfrac{\overbrace{-\sin x\, dx}^{du}}{\cos x}}_{u} = -\ln|\cos x| + C = \ln\left|\dfrac{1}{\cos x}\right| + C = \ln|\sec x| + C$$

Now we will consider the integral of $\tan^n x\, dx$, where n is an integer greater than 1. The key is to remember that the differential of $\tan x$ is $\sec^2 x\, dx$, so the integral of $\sec^2 x\, dx$ is $\tan x + C$. If n is equal to 2, we will use the Pythagorean identity

$$\tan^2 x + 1 = \sec^2 x$$

and replace $\tan^2 x$ with $\sec^2 x - 1$. If n is greater than 2, we will rewrite $\tan^n x$ as $\tan^{n-2} x \tan^2 x$ and again replace $\tan^2 x$ with $\sec^2 x - 1$.

Example 104.1   Find $\int \tan^2 x \, dx$.

Solution   If we replace $\tan^2 x$ with $\sec^2 x - 1$, we get two integrals which we can evaluate.

$$\int (\sec^2 x - 1) \, dx = \int \sec^2 x - \int dx = \mathbf{\tan x - x + C}$$

Example 104.2   Find $\int \tan^3 x \, dx$.

Solution   As the first step, we will separate a factor of $(\tan^2 x)$ and replace $\tan^2 x$ with $\sec^2 x - 1$.

$$\int \tan^3 x \, dx = \int (\tan x)(\tan^2 x) \, dx = \int (\tan x)(\sec^2 x - 1) \, dx$$

If we multiply, we get two integrals.

$$\int \underbrace{(\tan x)}_{u^n}\underbrace{(\sec^2 x \, dx)}_{du} - \int \tan x \, dx$$

We recognize the form of the first integral is $u^n \, du$ and know that the integral of $\tan x$ is $\ln |\sec x| + C$. Thus

$$\int \tan x \sec^2 x \, dx - \int \tan x = \frac{1}{2} \tan^2 x - \ln |\sec x| + C$$

Example 104.3   Find $\int \tan^4 x \, dx$.

Solution   We will separate a factor of $\tan^2 x$ and substitute.

$$\int \tan^4 x \, dx = \int (\tan^2 x)(\tan^2 x) \, dx = \int (\tan^2 x)(\sec^2 x - 1) \, dx$$

Now we multiply and get

$$\int \tan^2 x \sec^2 x \, dx - \int \tan^2 x \, dx$$

$\tan^2 x \sec^2 x \, dx$ has the form $u^n \, du$, so the first integral equals $\frac{1}{3} \tan^3 x$. From Example 104.1 we know that the integral of $\tan^2 x \, dx$ is $\tan x - x$, so we have finally

$$\frac{1}{3} \tan^3 x - \tan x + x + C$$

Although we will not consider them in this book, integrals of higher powers of $\tan x$ can be found by repeated use of the process shown in this example. Each step will result in an integral of the form of

$$u^n \, du + \int (\tan x)^{n-2} \, dx$$

To illustrate, the first step in the integration of $\tan^{11} x$ would be

$$\int \tan^{11} x \, dx = \int (\tan^9 x)(\sec^2 x - 1) \, dx = \int \underbrace{\tan^9 x}_{u^n} \underbrace{\sec^2 x \, dx}_{du} - \int \tan^9 x \, dx$$

The next step would reduce $\tan^9 x$ to $\tan^7 x$, and so forth.

104.B
Integral of cot^n x

We use a similar procedure to find integrals of $\cot^n x$. We remember that we can find the integral of $\cot x\, dx$ because we can use $\cos x$ and $\sin x$ to write this integral in the form of du over u.

$$\int \cot x\, dx = \int \frac{\overbrace{\cos x\, dx}^{du}}{\underbrace{\sin x}_{u}} = \ln |\sin x| + C$$

To find the integral of $\cot^n x\, dx$, we will use the identity

$$1 + \cot^2 x = \csc^2 x$$

and replace $\cot^2 x$ with $\csc^2 x - 1$. Since the derivative of $\cot x$ is $-\csc^2 x\, dx$, the integral of $-\csc^2 x\, dx$ is $\cot x + C$.

Example 104.4 Find $\int \cot^2 x\, dx$.

Solution We replace $\cot^2 x$ with $\csc^2 x - 1$.

$$\int \cot^2 x\, dx = \int (\csc^2 x - 1)\, dx = \int \csc^2 x\, dx - \int dx$$

We need a pair of negative signs in the first integral, which we provide.

$$-\int -\csc^2 x\, dx - \int dx = -\cot x - x + C$$

Example 104.5 Find $\int \cot^3 x\, dx$.

Solution We separate a factor of $\cot^2 x$ and replace it with $\csc^2 x - 1$.

$$\int \cot^3 x\, dx = \int (\cot x)(\cot^2 x)\, dx = \int (\cot x)(\csc^2 x - 1)\, dx$$

Next we multiply, insert two minus signs, and find the integral.

$$-\int \underbrace{(\cot x)}_{u^n}\underbrace{(-\csc^2 x\, dx)}_{du} - \int \cot x\, dx = -\frac{1}{2}\cot^2 x - \ln |\sin x| + C$$

Example 104.6 Find $\int \cot^4 x\, dx$.

Solution We separate a factor of $\cot^2 x$ and replace it with $\csc^2 x - 1$.

$$\int \cot^4 x\, dx = \int (\cot^2 x)(\cot^2 x)\, dx = \int (\cot^2 x)(\csc^2 x - 1)\, dx$$

Next we multiply, insert two minus signs, and get

$$-\int \underbrace{(\cot^2 x)}_{u^n}\underbrace{(-\csc^2 x\, dx)}_{du} - \int \cot^2 x\, dx$$

From Example 104.4 we know that $\int \cot^2 x\, dx$ is $-\cot x - x$, so we have

$$-\frac{1}{3}\cot^3 x + \cot x + x + C$$

Problem set 104

1. The base of a 4-meter ladder leaning against a vertical wall as shown is pulled away from the wall at $\frac{1}{2}$ meter per second. Find the rate at which the area of the triangle ABC is changing when C is 1 meter from the wall.

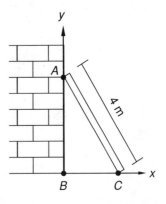

Use the appropriate trigonometric identity to find the following integrals:

2. $\displaystyle\int 2\tan^2 x \, dx$

3. $\displaystyle\int 3\cot^2 x \, dx$

4. $\displaystyle\int \tan x \tan^2 x \, dx$

5. $\displaystyle\int \cot^2 x \cot x \, dx$

6. Let f be a continuous function defined for all real numbers. The absolute maximum value of $f(x)$ is 7 and the absolute minimum value of $f(x)$ is -15. Which of the following statements must be true?
   (*a*) The maximum value of $f(|x|)$ is 7.
   (*b*) The maximum value of $|f(x)|$ is 7.
   (*c*) The minimum value of $f(|x|)$ is 0.
   (*d*) The minimum value of $|f(x)|$ is 0.

7. Use basic geometric formulas to evaluate $\displaystyle\int_{-3}^{4} |x-2| \, dx$.

8. Let R be the region enclosed by the graph of $y = e^{2x}$, $x = 2$, and the coordinate axes. Write an integral in one variable whose value equals the volume of the solid formed when R is revolved about the line $x = 3$.

9. Suppose R is as defined as in Problem 8. Write an integral in one variable whose value equals the volume of the solid formed when R is revolved about the x axis.

10. Let R be the region bounded by the graph of $y = x^2$ and the x axis on the interval $[0, 2]$. Write an integral in one variable whose value equals the volume of the solid formed when R is revolved about the line $y = -2$.

11. Let

$$f(x) = \tan x \qquad \text{where} \qquad -\frac{\pi}{2} < x < \frac{\pi}{2}$$

If f^{-1} is the inverse of f, find the value of $(f^{-1})(2)$ and $(f^{-1})'(2)$.

12. The function $f(x) = x^3 + x + 1$ is a one-to-one function, so $(f^{-1})'$ is also a function. Find the equation of $(f^{-1})'$.

13. The mean value theorem for integrals tells us that every continuous function attains its average value on an interval at some point in the interval. If the

function $f(x) = \tan x$, find some number $c \in [0, \pi/4]$ such that $f(c)$ equals the average value of the function on the interval.

14. Determine the slope of the line which joins the points $(1, f(1))$ and $(3, f(3))$ on the graph of f, where $f(x) = x^3 + 2x + 1$. Illustrate the mean value theorem for derivatives for f on the interval $[1, 3]$.

Integrate:

15. $\displaystyle\int \sin^3 x \, dx$

16. $\displaystyle\int \frac{\cos x \, dx}{\sqrt{a + \sin x}}$

17. Approximate to two decimal places the x coordinate of the centroid of the region bounded by $y = \sin x$ and the x axis on the interval $[0, 1]$.

18. If $y = \sin xy$, find $\dfrac{dy}{dx}$.

19. The definite integral $\displaystyle\int_0^\pi (\sin 5x)e^{\cos 5x} \, dx$ equals which of the following?

(a) $\displaystyle\int_{-1}^1 e^u \, du$ (b) $-\displaystyle\int_{-1}^1 e^u \, du$ (c) $-\dfrac{1}{5}\displaystyle\int_{-1}^1 e^u \, du$ (d) $\dfrac{1}{5}\displaystyle\int_{-1}^1 e^u \, du$

20. Differentiate: $y = \ln |\sin x - x^2| + \dfrac{e^x + x}{\arcsin x}$

CONCEPT REVIEW   21. If f is any continuous function, which of the following statements is always true?

(a) $\left| \displaystyle\int_1^5 f(x) \, dx \right| \geq \displaystyle\int_1^5 |f(x)| \, dx$

(b) $\displaystyle\int_1^5 |f(x)| \, dx = \displaystyle\int_1^3 |f(x)| \, dx + \displaystyle\int_3^5 |f(x)| \, dx$

(c) $\displaystyle\int_1^5 |f(x)| \, dx = -\displaystyle\int_1^5 |f(x)| \, dx$ (d) $\displaystyle\int_5^1 f(x) \, dx = \displaystyle\int_1^5 |f(x)| \, dx$

LESSON 105 *Second fundamental theorem of integral calculus · The natural logarithm function*

105.A
Second fundamental theorem of integral calculus

We have used the first fundamental theorem of integral calculus to evaluate the integral of a continuous function f on the interval $[a, b]$ by subtracting the value of some antiderivative F evaluated at a from the value of the same antiderivative evaluated at b.

$$\int_a^b f(x) \, dx = F(b) - F(a)$$

The *second fundamental theorem of calculus* guarantees us that every function that is continuous does have an antiderivative. We remember that a function is an input-output process that has exactly one output for every input value of x. With the function machine on the left, any input is squared. Thus, if the input is x, the output is x^2, and if the input is 3, the output is 3^2, or 9.

$$x \longrightarrow \boxed{(\ )^2} \longrightarrow \begin{matrix} x^2 \\ (3)^2 \end{matrix} \qquad x \longrightarrow \boxed{\int_a^x f(x)\, dx} \longrightarrow \ ?$$

$$3 \longrightarrow$$

The function machine on the right tells us to integrate the function f and evaluate it from $x = a$ to $x = x$. In this machine, x is the input, x is the upper limit, and x is also the variable of integration. We can clear up some of the confusion if we use t as a dummy variable as shown in the next machine. The output function F is some antiderivative of f. We note that F is a function of x even though we used the dummy variable t as the variable of integration.

$$x \longrightarrow \boxed{\int_a^x f(t)\, dt} \longrightarrow F(t)\Big|_a^x = F(x) - F(a)$$

We still have x as the input and as the upper limit, but x is no longer the variable of integration. To use this machine, we must first specify the function f and the lower limit a. To demonstrate, we will use the function $f(t) = t$ and a lower limit of 2. In the box we use t instead of x.

$$x \longrightarrow \boxed{\int_2^x t\, dt} \longrightarrow F(t)\Big|_2^x = F(x) - F(2)$$

For a graphical consideration of the integral as a function we will let x be a variable on the t axis.

$$\text{Shaded area} = \int_2^x f(x)\, dx$$

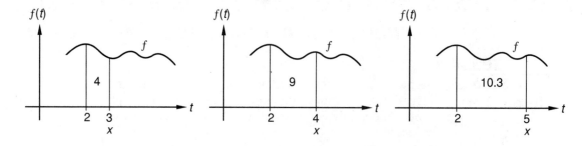

If the graph of a function is above the t axis on interval $[2, x]$ as shown, the area between the t axis and the graph equals the definite integral from 2 to x.

The leftmost figure shows that if x is 3, the area is 4. The second and third figures show us that if x is 4, the area is 9, and if x is 5, the area is 10.3. The left-hand boundary of each of the areas is fixed at 2, and thus each of the areas under the graph of f is a function of the position of the right-hand boundary x. This is the reason the area can be described by the definite integral

$$A(x) = \int_2^x f(t)\, dt$$

If we remove the restriction that the graph be above the t axis, we are no longer describing area but are still describing a definite integral,

$$F(x) = \int_a^x f(t)\, dt$$

The lower limit a does not have to be 2 but can be 0, -1, 5, or any real number that we choose. We do not know how to evaluate some definite integrals, but we can approximate their value between a and x to any desired degree of accuracy by using numerical methods. On the left we show a portion of the graph of $y = e^{-2x^2}$. We choose this function because it is famous for not having an antiderivative that can be expressed simply. The graph is not drawn to scale because the value of y where $x = 3$ is 1.5×10^{-8}, and the value of y where $x = 7$ is 2.7×10^{-43}.

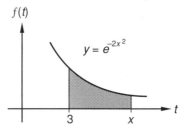 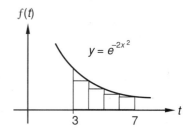

We can "see" in the figure on the left that the definite integral exists. This integral cannot be evaluated by using the fundamental theorem of Newton and Leibniz. But in the figure on the right we see that we can use the familiar method of summing the areas of rectangles to approximate $F(7)$, which is the value of the following integral when the upper limit is 7. Thus the following integral exists even though we can only find an approximation of its value.

$$F(x) = \int_3^x e^{-2t^2}\, dt \qquad F(7) = \int_3^7 e^{-2t^2}\, dt$$

If f is continuous on an interval I, the second fundamental theorem of calculus, which we will not prove, guarantees us that an antiderivative of f exists and describes the antiderivative.

SECOND FUNDAMENTAL THEOREM OF CALCULUS

If f is a function that is continuous on some open interval I and c is a number in the interval, then f has an antiderivative F on this interval which can be described as

$$F(x) = \int_c^x f(t)\, dt \qquad x \in I$$

Since F is an antiderivative of f, then the derivative of F equals f.

$$\frac{d}{dx} F(x) = \frac{d}{dx} \left(\int_c^x f(t)\, dt \right) = f(x)$$

Example 105.1   Find $\dfrac{d}{dx} \displaystyle\int_9^x t^2\, dt$.

Solution   First we find the integral.

$$\int_9^x t^2 \, dt = \left[\frac{t^3}{3}\right]_9^x = \frac{x^3}{3} - 243$$

Now we find the derivative and note that we eliminate the constant -243 when we differentiate. Thus the value of the lower limit of integration does not affect the derivative, as the contribution of this limit is eliminated when we differentiate.

$$\frac{d}{dx}\left(\frac{x^3}{3} - 243\right) = x^2$$

These two steps were unnecessary, as we could have used the second fundamental theorem to write the answer by inspection.

$$\frac{d}{dx}\int_9^x t^2 \, dt = x^2$$

Example 105.2   Find $\dfrac{d}{dx}\displaystyle\int_x^4 \dfrac{\sin t}{t}$.

Solution   We know that the integral from x to 4 is the negative of the integral from 4 to x, so we interchange the limits and insert a minus sign to get

$$\frac{d}{dx}\left(-\int_4^x \frac{\sin t}{t}\right) = -\frac{d}{dx}\int_4^x \frac{\sin t}{t}$$

We do not know how to evaluate the integral, but the second fundamental theorem of calculus assures us that the integral exists and that its derivative is $\sin x$ divided by x, so we get

$$-\frac{d}{dx}\int_4^x \frac{\sin t}{t} = -\left(\frac{\sin x}{x}\right) = -\frac{\sin x}{x}$$

Example 105.3   Find $\dfrac{d}{dx}\displaystyle\int_{17}^x e^{-t^2} \, dt$.

Solution   We do not know how to evaluate the integral, but we do know that it exists and that its derivative is e^{-x^2}.

$$\frac{d}{dx}\int_{17}^x e^{-t^2} \, dt = e^{-x^2}$$

105.B
The natural logarithm function

In precalculus mathematics we discussed the exponential function whose base is 10 and used this function to define the common logarithm function whose base is also 10. The common logarithm function is the implicit form of the exponential function whose base is 10.

$$y = 10^x \quad\longrightarrow\quad x = \log_{10} y$$

Then, when we got the idea of logarithms, we introduced the exponential function whose base is e and used this function to define the natural logarithm function whose base is also e. The natural logarithm function is the implicit form of the exponential function whose base is e.

$$y = e^x \quad\longrightarrow\quad x = \ln y$$

We have used the laws of exponents to develop the laws of logarithms, and we have assumed that these laws hold for all real values of x. These laws do hold and they do work. For the engineer this suffices. But the mathematician looks at all of this and sees a house of cards, for we have failed to prove everything that we have done. Mathematicians have found that we can use an integral to define a function that can be proved to have all the qualities that we have assigned to the function

$$y = \ln x$$

If this new function can be shown to have all the qualities of the natural logarithmic function whose base is *e*, then this function must be the same function. We do this because the integral definition will allow us to prove many things that we could not prove before. These proofs are a topic for courses above the level of this book. We can define the natural logarithmic function as follows.

$$\ln x = \int_1^x \frac{1}{t}\, dt$$

With this definition, we see in the figure above that ln *x* equals the area under the graph of $\frac{1}{t}$ between 1 and *x* if *x* is greater than 1. If *x* is between 0 and 1, then the expression that defines the integral will look the same but the integral will be the negative of the area.

$$\ln x = \int_1^x \frac{1}{t}\, dt = -\int_x^1 \frac{1}{t}\, dt$$

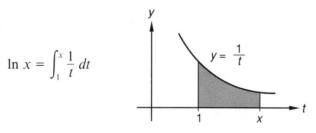

The value of this integral will be negative because the upper limit will be less than the lower limit, and we remember that

$$\int_a^b f = -\int_b^a f$$

Example 105.4   Show that using the new definition of the derivative of ln *x* results in the same derivative that $y = \log_e x$ has.

Solution   The second fundamental theorem allows us to write

$$\frac{d}{dx} \ln x = \frac{d}{dx} \int_1^x \frac{dt}{t} = \frac{1}{x}$$

Thus this function has the same derivative as the derivative of $y = \log_e x$. We will consider this fact further in Lesson 116.

Problem set 105   **1.**   The length of a rectangle is increasing at a rate of 2 centimeters per second, and the width of the rectangle is decreasing at a rate of 1 centimeter per second. Find the rate at which the area of the rectangle is changing when the length of the rectangle is 12 centimeters and the width of the rectangle is 10 centimeters.

2. The acceleration of a particle moving along the x axis at time t is given by the equation $a(t) = \pi \sin \pi t$. If the velocity at $t = 0$ is 0, approximate to two decimal places the average velocity of the particle over the interval $0 \le t \le 1$.

3. A trough 5 meters long whose cross section is shown is completely filled with a fluid whose weight density is 600 newtons per cubic meter. Find the force against one end of the trough. Dimensions shown in the figure are in meters.

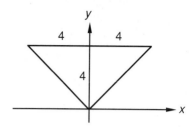

4. Find the work done in pumping all the fluid out of the trough described in Problem 3.

Simplify the following expressions by using two different methods: (1) evaluate the definite integral first and then differentiate, (2) apply the second fundamental theorem of calculus.

5. $\dfrac{d}{dx} \displaystyle\int_{1}^{x} t^2 \, dt$

6. $\dfrac{d}{dx} \displaystyle\int_{x}^{3} \sin t \, dt$

Use the second fundamental theorem of calculus to simplify the following expressions:

7. $\dfrac{d}{dx} \displaystyle\int_{18}^{x} e^{-t^2} \, dt$

8. $\dfrac{d}{dx} \displaystyle\int_{x}^{5} \dfrac{\cos t}{t} \, dt$

9. Which of the following equals ln 4?
   (a) ln 3 + ln 1
   (b) The area of the region between the graph of $y = \dfrac{1}{x}$ and the x axis on the interval [1, 4]
   (c) The area of the region between the graph of $y = \ln x$ and the x axis on the interval [1, ln 4]
   (d) The area of the region between the graph of $y = \ln x$ and the x axis on the interval [1, 4]

Use Pythagorean identities as necessary to find the following integrals:

10. $\displaystyle\int \tan^2 x \, dx$

11. $\displaystyle\int \tan^3 x \, dx$

12. If $f(x) = |2 \sin x - 1|$, find the maximum value of f.

13. Let R be the region in the first quadrant bounded by the graphs of $y = \sec x$ and $x = \pi/8$. Write a definite integral in one variable whose value equals the volume of the solid formed when R is revolved about the line $x = -1$.

14. Let R be the region bounded by the graphs of $y = \log x$ and the x axis on the interval [1, 10]. Use one variable to write a definite integral whose value equals the volume of the solid formed when R is revolved about the line $y = -1$.

15. Find the general solution to the differential equation $\dfrac{dy}{dx} = \sin 2x$.

16. Suppose $f(x) = \sin x$ and $g(x) = e^{x^2}$. Determine whether each of the following functions is odd, even, or neither.
   (a) $f + g$ (b) f^2 (c) $g \circ f$ (d) fg

17. Suppose $\log |f(x)| = \log |x^2 + 1| + \log |\sin x|$. Develop an expression that equals $f'(x)/f(x)$.

18. Given the functions f and g such that

$$\lim_{x \to 2} f(x) = 4 \quad \text{and} \quad \lim_{x \to 2} g(x) = -1 \quad \text{evaluate} \quad \lim_{x \to 2} [f(x)]^2 g(x)$$

19. Compute $\displaystyle\int_0^{\pi/4} \tan x \, dx$.

20. Find $\dfrac{d}{dx} [\tan (\sin x) + 3^{x^2}] + \displaystyle\int \dfrac{5}{1 + x^2} \, dx$

CONCEPT REVIEW **21.** Let f be defined as follows:

$$f(x) = \begin{cases} |x| + 2 & \text{if } x < 1 \\ ax^2 + bx & \text{if } x \geq 1 \end{cases}$$

Find the values of a and b which make f continuous and differentiable at $x = 1$.

22. Suppose f is a function f which exists for all real x and

$$\lim_{x \to a} f(x) = f(a) \quad \text{for any real number } a$$

Which of the following statements is true?
(*a*) The function f is differentiable at all real values of x.
(*b*) The function f is continuous at all real values of x.
(*c*) $f(0) = 0$.
(*d*) $f'(x) = f(x)$ for all real values of x.

LESSON 106 *Approximating with differentials*

Differentials can be used to get a quick approximation for the change in the value of a function that would be caused by a small change in the value of the independent variable. We remember that dy is an approximation for Δy and is defined as the product of the derivative and the change in x, which can be labeled either dx or Δx.

$$dy = f'(x) \, \Delta x$$

Suppose a farmer has a square field whose sides are 100 meters long and idly wonders how much the area of the field would increase if each side were $\frac{1}{4}$ meter longer. If he had his calculator, he could compute the new area and subtract the old area, and the difference would be the increase. But he can use a differential to get a quick approximation that is almost as good as the answer from a calculator. He knows that the area and the differential of the area are

$$\text{Area} = x^2 \qquad dA = 2x \, \Delta x$$

The change in area dA caused by a change of x of $\frac{1}{4}$ meter can be mentally computed.

$$dA = 2(100)\left(\frac{1}{4}\right) = 50 \text{ square meters}$$

If he had used his calculator, he would have found that the change in area would have been

$$(100.25)^2 - (100)^2 = 50.063 \text{ square meters}$$

As we can see, the use of the differential produces surprisingly accurate results with a minimum of effort. Differentials are often used by physicists and engineers to make quick estimates.

Example 106.1 Leena and Jenq had a solid brass ball whose radius was 20 cm. They wanted a quick estimate of the change in the volume if a coating of 0.02 cm was applied. What was their estimate?

Solution All they had to do was to write the equation of a sphere and find its differential.

$$V = \frac{4}{3}\pi r^3 \qquad dV = 4\pi r^2 \, dr$$

If they use 20 for r and 0.02 for dr, they get their estimate.

$$dV = 4\pi(20)^2(0.02) \approx \mathbf{100.53 \text{ cm}^3}$$

If they had computed the old volume and the new volume and found the difference, the result would have been 101.63 cm^3, a number very close to 100.53 cm^3.

Example 106.2 If a measurement is slightly in error and the measurement is used in a calculation, the error in the calculation caused by the faulty measurement is called a ***propagated error.*** When Kristin and Ferrell measured the radius of a ball, they found it to be 1.4 cm. If the error in measurement could be no greater than 0.01 cm, find the maximum value of the propagated error.

Solution We know the formula for the volume of a sphere, and we can find its differential.

$$V = \frac{4}{3}\pi r^3 \qquad dV = 4\pi r^2 \, dr$$

The propagated error in value is the differential dV whose maximum value is

$$dV = 4\pi(1.4)^2(0.01) = \mathbf{0.2463 \text{ cm}^3}$$

Example 106.3 If x represents the number of units produced in a given period, the profit p in dollars of a company for the period is given by the equation

$$p = (500x - x^2) - \left(\frac{1}{2}x^2 - 72x + 3000\right)$$

Estimate the change in profit if the production is increased from 115 to 120 units.

Solution All we have to do is find the differential and then use 115 for x and 5 for Δx.

$$dp = [(500 - 2x) - (x - 72)]\,\Delta x$$
$$dp = [(500 - 2(115)) - (115 - 72)]5 = 1135$$

Since dp is positive, the change in profit is positive and would be approximately **$1135.**

Problem set 106   **1.** Find the area of the largest rectangle that can be inscribed in the region bounded by $y = 9 - x^2$ and $y = x^2 - 1$.

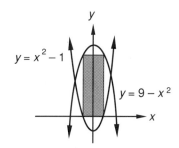

2. A metal ball 50 centimeters in diameter is coated with an 0.01-centimeter layer of gold. Use the method of differentials to estimate the increase in the volume of the ball.

3. If a measurement which is slightly in error is used in a calculation, we say that the original error in measurement is propagated. Franco and Davis wanted to calculate the surface area of a sphere, yet they felt that their measurement of 10 cm for the radius was in error by at most 0.001 cm. Use the method of differentials to determine by how much their figure for the surface area could be in error.

4. Suppose that the profit in dollars made from the sale of x items is given by

$$p(x) = -(x - 100)^2 + 200x$$

Use the method of differentials to estimate the change in profit if 101 items are sold instead of 100 items.

5. A particle moves along the x axis so that its velocity at time t ($t > 0$) is given by

$$v(t) = \frac{t + 1}{t}$$

If the particle's position at $t = 3$ was $x = 5$, write an equation for the position function $x(t)$.

6. An object is propelled along the x axis by the force $F(x) = \frac{1}{2}x^2$ newtons. Find the work done on the object as it is moved from the origin to $x = 6$ meters.

Use the second fundamental theorem of integral calculus to simplify the following expressions.

7. $\dfrac{d}{dx} \displaystyle\int_2^x e^{t^3} \, dt$

8. $\dfrac{d}{dx} \displaystyle\int_x^2 e^{1/t} \, dt$

Integrate:

9. $\displaystyle\int 2 \sin^2 x \, dx + \int \sin^3 x \, dx$

10. $\displaystyle\int 2 \tan^2 x \, dx$

11. $\displaystyle\int 2 \cot^2 x \, dx$

12. $\displaystyle\int \left(2^x + \frac{1}{\sqrt{x - 1}} \right) dx$

13. Suppose $f(x) = x^5 + x$ and f^{-1} is the inverse function of f. Evaluate $f^{-1}(2)$ and $(f^{-1})'(2)$.

14. Let R be the region bounded by the graph of $y = e^{-x^2}$ over the interval $[0, 1]$. Find the volume of the solid formed when R is revolved about the y axis.

15. If a function meets certain conditions on the interval $[1, 3]$, the mean value theorem tells us that there exists at least one number $c \in [1, 3]$ such that

$$f'(c) = \frac{f(3) - f(1)}{3 - 1}$$

If the function $f(x) = x^2 + x + 1$ satisfies the conditions, find such a number c.

16. Suppose $f(x) = 3x^2 + 2x + 1$. Verify the mean value theorem for integrals for f on the interval $[1, 3]$.

17. Let R be the region bounded by the graph of the hyperbola $xy = 1$, the y axis, and the lines $y = 1$ and $y = 2$. Express the area of R as an integral in the variable y.

18. Differentiate: $y = xe^{x^2} - \arcsin x^2 + \dfrac{\ln x + 1}{\cos x - x}$

CONCEPT REVIEW   **19.** The position of a particle moving along the x axis is defined by a continuous function $x(t)$. The value of $x(1)$ is 1 and the value of $x(3)$ is 5. Which of the following statements are true?
   (a) The velocity of the particle is always positive on the interval $[1, 3]$.
   (b) At some time on the interval $[1, 3]$ the velocity of the particle is $+2$.
   (c) The velocity of the particle is never zero on the interval $[1, 3]$.
   (d) The velocity is zero when $t = 3$.

20. If f is a function such that $f'(x) > 0$ for all real values of x, which of the following statements must be true?
   (a) $f(x) > 0$ for all values of x.
   (b) $f(x_1) > f(x_2)$ for every x_1 and x_2 where $x_1 > x_2$.
   (c) The graph of f is concave up everywhere.
   (d) The graph of f is concave down everywhere.

LESSON 107   *Limit of* $\dfrac{\sin x}{x}$ · *A note (optional)*

107.A

Limit of $\dfrac{\sin x}{x}$

In Lesson 37 we stated without proof that the derivative of $\sin \theta$ is $\cos \theta$. Then in Lesson 58 we used this fact to prove that the derivative of $\cos \theta$ is $-\sin \theta$ and showed how to use the derivatives of $\sin \theta$ and $\cos \theta$ to find the derivatives of other trigonometric functions. But we still have not proved that the derivative of $\sin \theta$ is $\cos \theta$. A crucial step in this proof requires that, if θ is measured in radians, we be able to evaluate the following limit.

$$\lim_{\theta \to 0} \frac{\sin \theta}{\theta}$$

This limit equals 1, because as θ gets closer to zero, $\sin \theta$ gets closer to the value of θ and the ratio gets closer to 1. If we use a calculator to find $\sin 0.087$, we get

$$\sin 0.087 = 0.08689 \quad \text{so} \quad \frac{\sin 0.087}{0.087} = \frac{0.08689}{0.087} \approx 0.998736$$

If we use even smaller values of θ, the ratio of $\sin \theta$ over θ will get even closer to 1. Thus it appears that in the limit this ratio is 1. A straightforward proof of this fact is a geometric proof. We will show that the following inequality is true and then complete the proof by letting θ approach zero.

$$\cos \theta < \frac{\sin \theta}{\theta} < 1$$

As θ approaches zero, $\cos \theta$ will approach 1. From this we see that $\sin \theta$ over θ is between 1 and a quantity that is approaching 1. Thus, by use of the pinching theorem for limits, the limit of $\sin \theta$ over θ as θ approaches zero is 1.

To prove this we shade different parts of the same figure as shown below. Point O is the center of a unit circle, so lengths OA and OC equal 1. We see that the area of the big triangle on the left is greater than the area of the sector of the circle shown in the center, which is greater than the area of the triangle shown on the right.

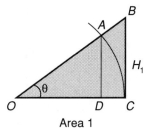 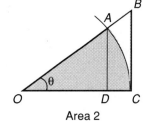 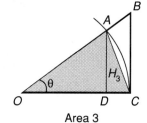

Area 1   Area 2   Area 3

Area 1 > area 2 > area 3

Area 1 is the area of the big triangle. Since the base of this triangle equals 1, $\tan \theta$ equals H_1 over 1, or H_1. So $\tan \theta = H_1$.

$$\text{Area 1} = \frac{1}{2} BH_1 = \frac{1}{2}(1)(\tan \theta) \quad \longrightarrow \quad \text{Area 1} = \frac{\tan \theta}{2}$$

Area 2 is the area of a sector of a circle whose central angle is θ and whose radius is 1.

$$\text{Area 2} = \frac{\theta}{2\pi}(\pi r^2) = \frac{\theta}{2\pi}\pi(1)^2 \quad \longrightarrow \quad \text{Area 2} = \frac{\theta}{2}$$

Area 3 is the area of a triangle whose height is H_3 and whose base, OC, has a length of 1. We can find H_3 because the hypotenuse of the right triangle it forms also equals 1. Thus $\sin \theta = H_3$ over 1. So $H_3 = \sin \theta$.

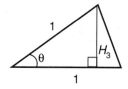

$$\text{Area 3} = \frac{1}{2} BH_3 = \frac{1}{2}(1)(\sin \theta)$$

$$= \frac{\sin \theta}{2}$$

Now we substitute the values found for the three areas and get

$$\frac{\tan \theta}{2} > \frac{\theta}{2} > \frac{\sin \theta}{2}$$

If we multiply every term by 2, we can write

$$\frac{\sin \theta}{\cos \theta} > \theta > \sin \theta$$

Now we divide every term by $\sin \theta$, where $\sin \theta > 0$, and get

$$\frac{1}{\cos \theta} > \frac{\theta}{\sin \theta} > 1$$

As the last step we invert each term and reverse the inequality symbols to get

$$\cos \theta < \frac{\sin \theta}{\theta} < 1$$

which "pinches" the middle term between $\cos \theta$ and 1. Since the drawing on which we relied shows θ to be positive and less than $\pi/2$, we know this inequality to be true when

$$0 < \theta < \frac{\pi}{2}$$

Thus, we must be careful to take the right-hand limit of $\frac{\sin \theta}{\theta}$ as θ approaches 0. By the pinching theorem

$$1 \le \lim_{\theta \to 0^+} \frac{\sin \theta}{\theta} \le 1 \qquad \text{or} \qquad \lim_{\theta \to 0^+} \frac{\sin \theta}{\theta} = 1$$

If θ is a negative angle, we get the same final result. To show this, we let θ equal $-x$, where x is a positive number. Then

$$\frac{\sin \theta}{\theta} = \frac{\sin (-x)}{-x} = \frac{-\sin x}{-x} = \frac{\sin x}{x}$$

Thus

$$\lim_{\theta \to 0^-} \frac{\sin \theta}{\theta} = \lim_{x \to 0^+} \frac{\sin x}{x} = 1$$

From the above we conclude that

$$\lim_{\theta \to 0} \frac{\sin \theta}{\theta} = 1$$

Example 107.1   Evaluate: $\lim_{x \to 0} \dfrac{\sin 4x}{x}$

Solution   L'Hôpital's rule can be used to find this limit, but the proof above gives us a way to find this special limit almost by inspection. The rule developed can be written as

$$\lim_{(\ ) \to 0} \frac{\sin (\ )}{(\ )} = 1$$

Since the limit of a constant times a function equals the constant times the limit of the function, we can get the form we need by multiplying in front by 4 and by multiplying x by 4. Since $4x$ approaches zero as x approaches zero, we can write

$$\lim_{x \to 0} \frac{\sin 4x}{x} = \lim_{4x \to 0} \frac{4 \sin 4x}{4x} = 4\left(\lim_{4x \to 0} \frac{\sin 4x}{4x} \right) = 4 \cdot 1 = \mathbf{4}$$

Example 107.2   Evaluate: $\lim_{x \to 0} \dfrac{x}{\sin 47x}$

Solution   The limit of the reciprocal of a function equals the reciprocal of the limit of the function. Thus

$$\lim_{x \to 0} \frac{x}{\sin 47x} = \frac{1}{\displaystyle\lim_{x \to 0} \frac{\sin 47x}{x}}$$

But we can evaluate $\lim_{x \to 0} \dfrac{\sin 47x}{x}$ by multiplying and dividing by 47.

$$\lim_{x \to 0} \frac{\sin 47x}{x} = 47\left(\lim_{47x \to 0} \frac{\sin 47x}{47x}\right) = 47(1)$$

Thus
$$\lim_{x \to 0} \frac{x}{\sin 47x} = \frac{1}{\displaystyle\lim_{x \to 0} \frac{\sin 47x}{x}} = \frac{1}{47}$$

107.B
A note (optional)

While proving

$$\lim_{x \to 0} \frac{\sin x}{x} = 1$$

we made use of the fact that

$$\lim_{x \to 0} \cos x = 1$$

This fact seems so obvious that it hardly warrants additional thought. However, some authors insist upon showing that $\lim_{x \to 0} \cos x = 1$, and other authors relegate its proof to the exercises.

Why do we even need to show anything? If we had desired, we could have begun this text with a close examination of polynomial functions. We could have shown that polynomial functions are everywhere continuous and hence for any polynomial P

$$\lim_{x \to c} P(x) = P(c)$$

The trigonometric functions are much more complicated than polynomial functions. Some may feel uneasy about making assertions about trigonometric functions without somehow basing these assertions on our knowledge of polynomials. Here we will prove that both $\sin \theta$ and $\cos \theta$ can be bounded by the first-degree polynomials $-\theta$ and θ and show that the limit of $\sin \theta$ as θ approaches zero is zero, and that the limit of $\cos \theta$ as θ approaches zero is 1.

Recall that we defined the radian measure of an angle to be the ratio of the arc s to the radius r.

$$\theta = \frac{s}{r}$$

We examine the unit circle centered at the origin and let $0 < \theta < \pi/2$. By definition of $\sin \theta$,

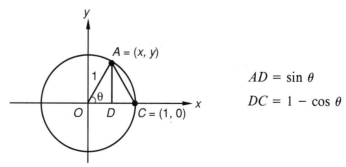

$$AD = \sin \theta$$
$$DC = 1 - \cos \theta$$

By using the Pythagorean theorem and triangle DAC, we can write

$$(AD)^2 + (DC)^2 = (AC)^2$$

Since $AD = \sin\theta$ and $DC = (1 - \cos\theta)$, we can substitute and get

$$\sin^2\theta + (1 - \cos\theta)^2 = (AC)^2$$

But the length of the segment $\overline{AC}$ is less than the length of the arc $\overset{\frown}{AC}$, which also equals θ, so we can substitute and get

$$\sin^2\theta + (1 - \cos\theta)^2 < (\overset{\frown}{AC})^2 \quad\longrightarrow\quad \sin^2\theta + (1 - \cos\theta)^2 < \theta^2$$

Any nonzero number squared is a positive number. Since θ is greater than zero, $\sin^2\theta$ and $(1 - \cos\theta)^2$ represent positive numbers. If the sum of two positive numbers is less than θ^2, then each of the positive numbers must be less than θ^2. This lets us write

$$\sin^2\theta < \theta^2 \qquad \text{and} \qquad (1 - \cos\theta)^2 < \theta^2$$

If $\sin^2\theta$ is less than θ^2, $\sin\theta$ must be between $-\theta$ and θ. If $(1 - \cos\theta)^2$ is less than θ^2, then $1 - \cos\theta$ must also be between θ and $-\theta$.

$$-\theta < \sin\theta < \theta \qquad -\theta < 1 - \cos\theta < \theta$$

Now θ is a polynomial function of degree 1, and we have shown that both $\sin\theta$ and $(1 - \cos\theta)$ can be bounded by θ. If we let θ approach zero, by the pinching theorem $\sin\theta$ must also approach zero because it is pinched between two quantities that are approaching zero.

$$\lim_{\theta\to 0} \sin\theta = 0$$

If we let θ approach zero, $1 - \cos\theta$ must also approach zero because this expression is pinched between two quantities that are both approaching zero.

$$\lim_{\theta\to 0} (1 - \cos\theta) = 0$$

If we write this limit as the difference of two limits, we can show that $\cos\theta$ must also approach 1 as θ approaches zero.

$$\lim_{\theta\to 0} (1 - \cos\theta) = 0 \quad\longrightarrow\quad \lim_{\theta\to 0} 1 - \lim_{\theta\to 0} \cos\theta = 0$$

The limit of 1 as θ approaches zero is 1, so we solve this last equation for the limit of $\cos\theta$ as θ approaches zero by adding -1 to both sides and find that this limit is 1.

$$1 - \lim_{\theta\to 0} \cos\theta = 0 \quad\longrightarrow\quad -\lim_{\theta\to 0}\cos\theta = -1 \quad\longrightarrow\quad \lim_{\theta\to 0}\cos\theta = 1$$

Problem set 107

1. The velocity of particle moving along a straight line at time t is given by the equation $v(t) = 2t^{1/2} + 4t^3$ meters per second. How many meters did the particle travel from $t = 0$ to $t = 9$?

2. A cube, each of whose sides is 5 centimeters long, is coated with a thin layer of brass. If the thickness of the coating is 0.01 centimeter, use the method of differentials to estimate the increase in volume of the cube.

3. The cost in dollars of producing x items is given by

$$c(x) = x(x - 150)^2 + 140$$

Use the method of differentials to estimate the cost of producing one more item if 151 have already been produced.

4. Suppose f is a function continuous on the interval $[1, 5]$. Suppose also that $f(1) = 6$, $f(2) = 2$, and $f(5) = 10$, and that other properties of f are as listed:

	$1 < x < 2$	$x = 2$	$2 < x < 5$
f'	negative	undefined	positive
f''	negative	undefined	negative

   Draw a rough sketch of f.

5. The rate of change in the number of bacteria is proportional to the number of bacteria present. Initially there were 1000 bacteria, and 10 minutes later there were 3000 bacteria. Write an equation which expresses the number of bacteria as a function of t.

Evaluate the following limits:

6. $\lim\limits_{x \to 0} \dfrac{\sin 2x}{x}$

7. $\lim\limits_{x \to 0} \dfrac{1 - \cos x}{x}$

8. $\lim\limits_{x \to \infty} \dfrac{2x^2 + x}{(\ln x)^2}$

9. $\lim\limits_{h \to 0} \dfrac{e^{2+h} - e^2}{h}$

10. If $f(x) = \dfrac{d}{dx} \displaystyle\int_3^x e^{t^2+4} \, dt$, find $f(0)$.

11. Let R be the region completely bounded by $y = x(1 - x)$ and the x axis. Use x as the variable of integration to write a definite integral whose value equals the volume of the solid formed when R is rotated about the line $x = -1$.

Integrate:

12. $\displaystyle\int \cot^2 x \, dx$

13. $\displaystyle\int (\pi \sec^2 x)(e^{\tan x}) \, dx$

14. Evaluate: $\displaystyle\int_{-3}^{1} 6|(x - 2)(x + 1)| \, dx$

15. Suppose $\displaystyle\int_0^k e^{x^2} \, dx = c$, where $k > 0$. Evaluate $\displaystyle\int_{-k}^k e^{x^2} \, dx$.

16. Let R be the region bounded by the graph of $y = \ln x$ and the x axis on the interval $[1, 3]$. Find the x coordinate of the centroid of R.

17. Let R be the region enclosed between the two graphs $y = \sin^2 x$ and $y = 2 \sin^2 x$, where $0 \le x \le \pi$. Express as a definite integral the volume of the solid formed when R is rotated about the x axis.

18. Find the equation of the tangent line which can be drawn to the graph of $y = 4^x$ at $(1, 4)$.

19. Differentiate: $y = \dfrac{2\sqrt{x^3 - 1}}{\sin x + \cos 2x} + e^{\sin x}$

CONCEPT REVIEW 20. Divide the interval $[0, 1]$ into n equal subintervals so the length of each subinterval is $1/n$. Let x_i be some point in the ith subinterval. If $f(x) = x^3 + 2x$, write a definite integral whose value equals

$$\lim_{n \to \infty} \frac{1}{n} \sum_{i=1}^{n} f(x_i)$$

LESSON 108　*Integrals of sec u and csc u · Trig substitution*

108.A
Integrals of sec *u* and csc *u*

Showing that a function f is the derivative of another function F tells us that the integral of $f(x)$ is $F(x) + C$. The fact that the differentials of the expressions to the right of the equals signs below equal the integrands to the left of the equals signs is a confirmation of the relationship stated. **These relationships should be memorized.**

$$\int \sin u \; du = -\cos u + C \qquad\qquad \int \cos u \; du = \sin u + C$$

$$\int \tan u \; du = \ln |\sec u| + C \qquad\qquad \int \cot u \; du = \ln |\sin u| + C$$

$$\int \sec u \; du = \ln |\sec u + \tan u| + C \qquad \int \csc u \; du = \ln |\csc u - \cot u| + C$$

$$\int \sec^2 u \; du = \tan u + C \qquad\qquad \int \csc^2 u \; du = -\cot u + C$$

$$\int \sec u \tan u \; du = \sec u + C \qquad\qquad \int \csc u \cot u \; du = -\csc u + C$$

We have developed all of these relationships except $\int \sec u \; du$ and $\int \csc u \; du$. To find the integral of sec u du, we guess that the integral is $\ln |\sec u + \tan u| + C$. To prove it, we find the derivative of our guess.

$$\frac{d}{du}(\ln |\sec u + \tan u| + C) = \left(\frac{1}{\sec u + \tan u}\right)(\sec u \tan u + \sec^2 u)$$

$$= \frac{(\sec u)(\tan u + \sec u)}{\sec u + \tan u} = \sec u$$

Since the derivative of $\ln |\sec u + \tan u| + C$ is sec u, we have our proof.

To find the integral of csc u du, we guess that the integral is $\ln |\csc u - \cot u| + C$. To prove it, we find the derivative of our guess.

$$\frac{d}{du}(\ln |\csc u - \cot u| + C) = \frac{1}{\csc u - \cot u} \cdot [-\csc u \cot u - (-\csc^2 u)]$$

$$= \frac{(\csc u)(-\cot u + \csc u)}{\csc u - \cot u} = \csc u$$

Since the derivative of $\ln |\csc u - \cot u| + C$ is csc u, we have our proof.

Guessing the answer might seem to be a poor technique, but it is the easiest way. In many books the authors guess that inserting a factor of $\frac{\sec x + \tan x}{\sec x + \tan x}$ would be a good idea.

$$\int \sec x \; dx = \int (\sec x)\left(\frac{\sec x + \tan x}{\sec x + \tan x}\right) dx$$

Then they expand this integrand and guess that the substitution $u = \tan x + \sec x$ and $du = (\sec^2 x + \sec x \tan x) \; dx$ would be a good idea. These two guesses will lead to the same result we obtained with a single guess.

108.B
Trig substitution

The three expressions shown here can be integrated if we recognize that one part of the expression is the differential of another part of the expression.

$$\int \frac{2x \; dx}{\sqrt{x^2 + 1}} \qquad\qquad \int \frac{-2x \; dx}{\sqrt{1 - x^2}} \qquad\qquad \int \frac{2x \; dx}{1 + x^2}$$

The differential of $x^2 + 1$ is $2x\,dx$, so the integrand on the left has the form $du/u^{1/2}$, or $u^{-1/2}\,du$, and can be integrated by inspection. In the integrand in the center the differential of $1 - x^2$ is $-2x\,dx$. Thus this expression also has the form $u^{-1/2}\,du$ and can be integrated by inspection. In the right-hand integrand the differential of $1 + x^2$ is $2x\,dx$, so this expression has the form du/u and can be integrated by inspection. The three integrals below look very similar.

$$\int \frac{dx}{\sqrt{x^2 + 1}} \qquad \int \frac{-dx}{\sqrt{1 - x^2}} \qquad \int \frac{dx}{1 + x^2}$$

These integrands do not have the x in the numerator, so they are not in the form $u^n\,du$ or du/u. If we look at the denominators, we see that the denominators remind us of right triangles and the Pythagorean theorem.

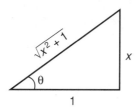 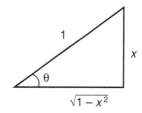 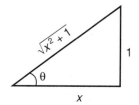

Then we think of the Pythagorean identities

$$\tan^2 \theta + 1 = \sec^2 \theta \qquad 1 - \sin^2 \theta = \cos^2 \theta \qquad \cot^2 \theta + 1 = \csc^2 \theta$$

Now consider the integral on the left above. If we let x equal $\tan \theta$, we could replace $x^2 + 1$ with $\tan^2 \theta + 1$ and replace dx with $\sec^2 \theta\,d\theta$. This substitution results in an expression that we can integrate.

$$\int \frac{dx}{\sqrt{x^2 + 1}} = \int \frac{\sec^2 \theta\,d\theta}{\sqrt{\tan^2 \theta + 1}} = \int \frac{\sec^2 \theta\,d\theta}{\sqrt{\sec^2 \theta}} = \int \sec \theta\,d\theta$$

Example 108.1   Find $\int \dfrac{dx}{\sqrt{1 - x^2}}$.

Solution   The differential of $1 - x^2$ is $-2x\,dx$. The numerator contains only dx, so this expression does not have the form $u^{-1/2}\,du$. The denominator does remind us of the length of a side of a right triangle. For an acute angle θ, we can get $\sqrt{1 - x^2}$ two different ways. The number 1 must be the hypotenuse and x must be either the side adjacent or the side opposite. Thus two triangles can be drawn, and each triangle suggests a possible substitution.

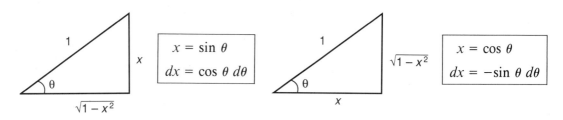

We decide to use the triangle on the left and make the substitutions suggested by it.

$$\int \frac{dx}{\sqrt{1 - x^2}} = \int \frac{\cos \theta\,d\theta}{\sqrt{1 - \sin^2 \theta}} = \int \frac{\cos \theta\,d\theta}{\sqrt{\cos^2 \theta}} = \int d\theta = \theta + C$$

In this example the integral has x as the variable, but our answer has θ as the variable. What is θ? **We can get the second substitution we need by looking at the**

triangle. Theta is the angle whose sine is x, whose cosine is $\sqrt{1 - x^2}$, and whose tangent is $x/\sqrt{1 - x^2}$. We could also say that θ is the angle whose cosecant is $1/x$, whose secant is $1/\sqrt{1 - x^2}$, or whose cotangent is $\sqrt{1 - x^2}/x$. Any of these forms would do, and we choose to use the form that is the least complicated.

$$\int \frac{dx}{\sqrt{1 - x^2}} = \sin^{-1} x + C$$

Example 108.2　　Find $\displaystyle\int \frac{dx}{\sqrt{x^2 - 5}}$.

Solution　　The differential of $x^2 - 5$ is $2x\, dx$. This numerator does not have a factor of x, so this expression is not in the form of $u^{-1/2}\, du$. We will try trigonometric substitution. The $\sqrt{x^2 - 5}$ suggests a right triangle with a hypotenuse of x and a side of length $\sqrt{5}$. There are two such triangles, and each triangle suggests a substitution.

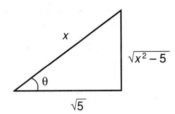

$$\frac{x}{\sqrt{5}} = \sec \theta \quad \longrightarrow \quad x = \sqrt{5} \sec \theta$$

$$dx = \sqrt{5} \sec \theta \tan \theta\, d\theta$$

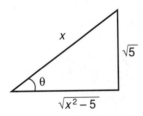

$$\frac{x}{\sqrt{5}} = \csc \theta \quad \longrightarrow \quad x = \sqrt{5} \csc \theta$$

$$dx = -\sqrt{5} \csc \theta \cot \theta$$

We decide to use the first triangle and the substitution it suggests.

$$\int \frac{dx}{\sqrt{x^2 - 5}} = \int \frac{\sqrt{5} \sec \theta \tan \theta\, d\theta}{\sqrt{5 \sec^2 \theta - 5}} \qquad \text{substituted}$$

Next we factor the denominator and then cancel the $\sqrt{5}$ with the $\sqrt{5}$ in the numerator.

$$\int \frac{\sqrt{5} \sec \theta \tan \theta\, d\theta}{\sqrt{5}\sqrt{\sec^2 \theta - 1}} \qquad \text{factored}$$

$$= \int \frac{\sec \theta \tan \theta\, d\theta}{\sqrt{\tan^2 \theta}} \qquad \text{canceled and used Pythagorean identity}$$

$$= \int \sec \theta\, d\theta \qquad \text{simplified}$$

The integral of $\sec \theta$ is $\ln |\sec \theta + \tan \theta| + C$. To write this answer in terms of x, we go back to the first triangle to find that $\sec \theta = \dfrac{x}{\sqrt{5}}$ and $\tan \theta = \dfrac{\sqrt{x^2 - 5}}{\sqrt{5}}$. So we have

$$\int \frac{dx}{\sqrt{x^2 - 5}} = \ln \left| \frac{x}{\sqrt{5}} + \frac{\sqrt{x^2 - 5}}{\sqrt{5}} \right| + C$$

Example 108.3   Find $\int \dfrac{dx}{\sqrt{x^2 + a^2}}$.

Solution   Again we do not have the form $u^{-1/2}\, du$. But the radical expression does make us think of a right triangle whose hypotenuse is $\sqrt{x^2 + a^2}$. There are two such triangles, and the triangles suggest the substitutions shown in the boxes.

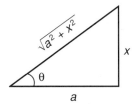

$$\frac{x}{a} = \tan\theta \longrightarrow x = a\tan\theta$$
$$dx = a\sec^2\theta\, d\theta$$

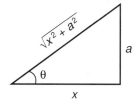

$$\frac{x}{a} = \cot\theta \longrightarrow x = a\cot\theta$$
$$dx = -a\csc^2\theta\, d\theta$$

We decide to use the first triangle and the substitution it suggests.

$$\int \frac{dx}{\sqrt{x^2 + a^2}} = \int \frac{a\sec^2\theta\, d\theta}{\sqrt{a^2\tan^2\theta + a^2}} = \int \frac{a\sec^2\theta\, d\theta}{a\sqrt{\tan^2\theta + 1}} = \int \frac{a\sec^2\theta\, d\theta}{a\sqrt{\sec^2\theta}}$$

$$= \int \frac{a\sec^2\theta\, d\theta}{a\sec\theta} = \int \sec\theta\, d\theta = \ln|\sec\theta + \tan\theta| + C$$

We can go back to the first triangle and find that $\tan\theta$ is x/a and $\sec\theta$ is $\sqrt{x^2 + a^2}/a$. Substituting, we get

$$\int \frac{dx}{\sqrt{x^2 + a^2}} = \ln\left|\frac{\sqrt{x^2 + a^2}}{a} + \frac{x}{a}\right| + C$$

Problem set 108   **1.**   Let R be the region between the graph of $y = 1/x$ and the x axis from $x = 1$ to $x = k$. First, determine the area of R. Then suppose that k is increasing at a rate of 1 unit per second. Find the rate the area of region R is increasing when $k = 10$.

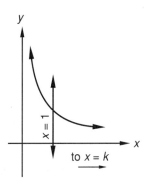

2.   Use the method of differentials to approximate the value of $\sqrt{10}$. (*Hint:* Use the equation $y = x^{1/2}$ to estimate Δy when $x = 9$ and $\Delta x = 1$.)

3. The end of a trough has two straight sides and one curved side as shown. The trough is 3 meters long and is filled with a fluid whose weight density is 3000 newtons per cubic meter. Express as a definite integral the work required to pump the fluid out of the trough.

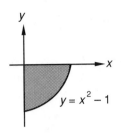

4. Suppose a particle moves along the x axis so that its velocity at time t is given by $v(t) = te^{-t}$. Approximate to two decimal places the acceleration of the particle at $t = 4$. If $x(0) = 0$, find $x(3)$.

Use trigonometric substitution to compute the following integrals. (*Note:* For Problem 6, refer to the lesson to find $\int \sec u \, du$.)

5. $\displaystyle \int \frac{dx}{\sqrt{1 - x^2}}$ 6. $\displaystyle \int \frac{dx}{\sqrt{x^2 - 9}}$ 7. $\displaystyle \int \frac{dx}{x^2 + 9}$

Evaluate the following limits:

8. $\displaystyle \lim_{x \to \infty} \frac{x \ln x}{x^2 + 1}$ 9. $\displaystyle \lim_{x \to 0} \frac{\sin 2x}{4x}$ 10. $\displaystyle \lim_{h \to 0} \frac{\sin \left(\frac{\pi}{2} + h \right) - \sin \frac{\pi}{2}}{h}$

11. Use the second fundamental theorem of calculus to simplify

$$\frac{d}{dx} \int_x^2 \frac{\ln t}{t} \, dt \qquad \text{where } x > 0$$

12. Suppose that f is a function which is defined for all real values of x. The graphs of $y = f(x)$ and $y = f(|x|)$ look identical when which of the following statements is true?
    (*a*) $f(x) > 0$ for all values of x (*b*) f is an odd function
    (*c*) f is an even function (*d*) f is a polynomial function

13. Let R be the region bounded by the graph of $y = 1/x$ and the x axis on the interval $[1, 2]$. Find the volume of the solid formed when R is revolved about the line $x = -1$.

Integrate:

14. $\displaystyle \int \frac{2x \, dx}{\sqrt{25 - x^2}}$

15. $\displaystyle \int \tan 2x \, dx$

16. Suppose f is a one-to-one function defined as follows:

$$f(x) = \sin x \qquad \text{for } -\frac{\pi}{2} \le x \le \frac{\pi}{2}$$

If f^{-1} is the inverse function of f, evaluate $f^{-1}(\frac{1}{2})$ and $(f^{-1})'(\frac{1}{2})$.

17. The mean value theorem for integrals tells us that a continuous function must attain its average value on an interval at some number c in the interval. If $f(x) = \sqrt{x}$, find some c in $[0, 1]$ where f equals its average value on this interval.

18. Write the equations of all the asymptotes of the graph of

$$f(x) = \frac{x^2 + x - 2}{x}$$

19.   The definite integral

$$\int_0^1 \sin \frac{\pi}{2} x \cos \frac{\pi}{2} x \, dx$$

equals which of the following definite integrals?

(a) $\dfrac{\pi}{2} \displaystyle\int_0^1 \sin u \, du$ (b) $\dfrac{2}{\pi} \displaystyle\int_0^1 \sin u \, du$ (c) $\dfrac{2}{\pi} \displaystyle\int_0^1 u \, du$

(d) $\displaystyle\int_0^{\pi/2} \sin u \, du$ (e) $\dfrac{2}{\pi} \displaystyle\int_0^{\pi/2} u \, du$

20.   Differentiate: $y = \arctan \dfrac{x}{2} + e^{\sin x + \cos x} - \dfrac{1 + x}{e^x - \sin x}$

CONCEPT REVIEW   **21.**   The mean value theorem tells us that if a function is differentiable on (a, b) and continuous on $[a, b]$, then at least one $c \in (a, b)$ exists such that

$$f'(c) = \frac{f(b) - f(a)}{b - a}$$

Rolle's theorem is a special case of the mean value theorem where $f(a) = f(b) = 0$. Geometrically, it tells us that if the graph touches the x axis at two points, the slope of the graph must be zero in a least one place between the two points. Rolle's theorem makes which of the following statements true?

(a)   If $f(x) = |x - 3| - 3$, then there must be some $c \in (0, 6)$ where $f'(c) = 0$.

(b)   If $f(x) = 2 - \dfrac{1}{x^2 - 1}$, then there must be a point $c \in (-1, 1)$ where $f'(c) = 0$.

(c)   If $f(x) = (x - 6)(x + 2)(x - 7)$, then there must be a point $c \in (-2, 6)$ such that $f'(c) = 0$.

(d)   The function $f(x) = x^2 + 1$ is never zero for any real value of x, so there is no real number such that $f'(c) = 0$.

LESSON 109   *Polar equations · Polar graphing*

109.A
Polar equations

We can describe the location of a point in a plane by using either rectangular or polar coordinates. When we do this, we are really using two different coordinate systems.

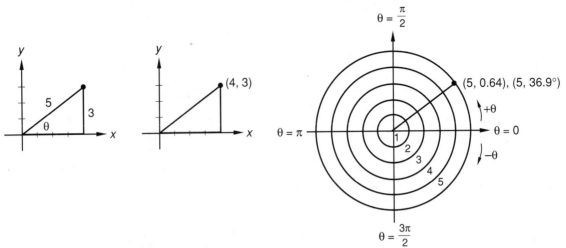

In the rectangular system the location of the point is designated by an ordered pair of x and y. The location of the point in the center figure is (4, 3). In the polar coordinate system the location of a point can be designated by an ordered pair of the radius r and the angle θ as (r, θ). The angle whose tangent is 3 over 4 is approximately 0.64 radian, or 36.9°, so we can designate this point by writing either (5, 0.64) or (5, 36.9°). An equation can be written in rectangular form by using x and y or in polar form by using r and θ. Sometimes the polar form of an equation is simpler or is easier to use. Sometimes the rectangular form is simpler or is easier to use.

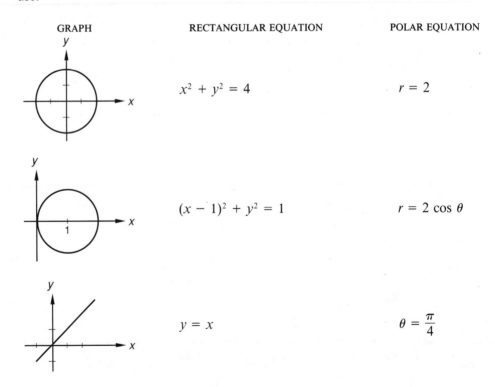

GRAPH	RECTANGULAR EQUATION	POLAR EQUATION
	$x^2 + y^2 = 4$	$r = 2$
	$(x - 1)^2 + y^2 = 1$	$r = 2\cos\theta$
	$y = x$	$\theta = \dfrac{\pi}{4}$
	$y = x + 1$	$r = \dfrac{1}{\sin\theta - \cos\theta}$

GRAPH	RECTANGULAR EQUATION	POLAR EQUATION
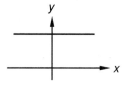	$y = 4$	$r = 4 \csc \theta$
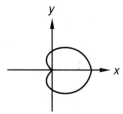	$x^2 + y^2 - 4x - 4\sqrt{x^2 + y^2} = 0$	$r = 4 + 4 \cos \theta$
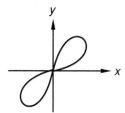	$x^4 + 2x^2y^2 - 2xy + y^4 = 0$	$r^2 = \sin 2\theta$

Converting equations from rectangular form to polar form and from polar form to rectangular form requires the use of the relationships designated by the two congruent triangles shown here.

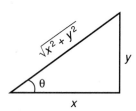   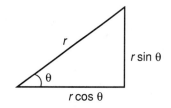

We see that $x = r \cos \theta$, $y = r \sin \theta$, and $r = \sqrt{x^2 + y^2}$. The sine, cosine, and tangent of θ can be written as follows.

$$\sin \theta = \frac{y}{\sqrt{x^2 + y^2}} \qquad \cos \theta = \frac{x}{\sqrt{x^2 + y^2}} \qquad \tan \theta = \frac{y}{x}$$

Example 109.1   Write the polar form of $y = x^2$.

Solution   We replace y with $r \sin \theta$ and replace x with $r \cos \theta$ to get

$$r \sin \theta = (r \cos \theta)^2 \qquad \text{substituted}$$
$$r \sin \theta = r^2 \cos^2 \theta \qquad \text{multiplied}$$
$$r = \frac{\sin \theta}{\cos^2 \theta} \qquad \text{rearranged}$$
$$\boldsymbol{r = \sec \theta \tan \theta} \qquad \text{substituted}$$

Example 109.2   Write the polar form of $y = \dfrac{x}{x + 1}$.

Solution We replace y with $r \sin \theta$, replace x with $r \cos \theta$, and simplify.

$$r \sin \theta = \frac{r \cos \theta}{r \cos \theta + 1} \qquad \text{substituted}$$

$$r^2 \sin \theta \cos \theta + r \sin \theta = r \cos \theta \qquad \text{multiplied}$$

$$\text{Now } r = 0 \text{ or } r \sin \theta \cos \theta + \sin \theta = \cos \theta \qquad \text{divided by } r, r \neq 0$$

$$r = \frac{\cos \theta - \sin \theta}{\sin \theta \cos \theta} \qquad \text{rearranged}$$

$$r = \frac{1}{\sin \theta} - \frac{1}{\cos \theta} \qquad \text{separated}$$

$$\boldsymbol{r = \csc \theta - \sec \theta} \qquad \text{reciprocals}$$

Example 109.3 Write the rectangular form of the equation $r = 1 - \cos \theta$.

Solution We replace r with $\sqrt{x^2 + y^2}$ and replace $\cos \theta$ with x over $\sqrt{x^2 + y^2}$.

$$\sqrt{x^2 + y^2} = 1 - \frac{x}{\sqrt{x^2 + y^2}}$$

Now we simplify and get

$$x^2 + y^2 = \sqrt{x^2 + y^2} - x \qquad \text{multiplied by } \sqrt{x^2 + y^2}$$

$$\boldsymbol{x^2 + y^2 - \sqrt{x^2 + y^2} + x = 0} \qquad \text{rearranged}$$

109.B
Polar graphing

Every point on the rectangular plane can be represented uniquely by an ordered pair of x and y. Thus, $(3, -2)$ represents the point whose x coordinate is 3 and whose y coordinate is -2. There is no other way to use rectangular coordinates to designate this point. Polar coordinates are different, as $(4, 20°)$, $(4, -340°)$, $(-4, 200°)$, and $(-4, -160°)$ are all ordered pairs of r and θ that designate the same point. This flexibility enhances the usefulness of polar coordinates while at the same time introduces an element of confusion. Polar coordinates can be used to write simple equations whose graphs are very interesting. Some of these figures are so unusual that they have names, as we show here.

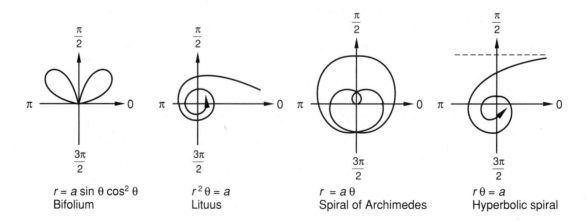

$r = a \sin \theta \cos^2 \theta$
Bifolium

$r^2 \theta = a$
Lituus

$r = a\theta$
Spiral of Archimedes

$r\theta = a$
Hyperbolic spiral

We will begin our investigation of graphs of polar equations by considering figures called ***rose curves.*** The equations of rose curves have the forms

$$r = a \sin n\theta \quad \text{and} \quad r = a \cos n\theta$$

The roses have n petals if n is odd and $2n$ petals if n is even. The figures can be graphed point by point, but after a little practice they can be graphed by inspection. Graphing by inspection can be tricky because of negative values of the sine and cosine.

Example 109.4 Graph $r = \sin 2\theta$.

Solution We must use all values of θ between 0 and 2π. For convenience we will use degree measure and a calculator to construct the table. First we will examine the behavior of the graph as θ goes from 0° to 180°. In our table we put values of θ, of 2θ, and of $\sin 2\theta$. **Since $\sin 2\theta$ has a maximum value when $\theta = 45°$, we are careful to include θ values of 45° and 135° in the table.**

θ	0°	30°	45°	60°	90°	120°	135°	150°	180°
2θ	0°	60°	90°	120°	180°	240°	270°	300°	360°
$r = \sin 2\theta$	0	0.87	1	0.87	0	−0.87	−1	−0.87	0

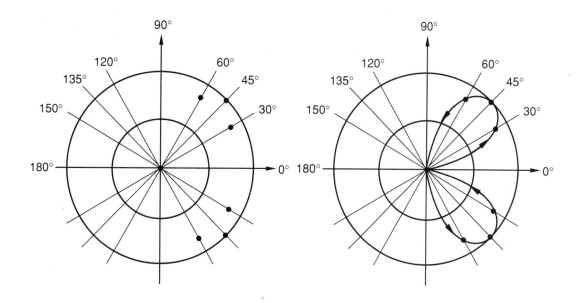

In the figure on the left we have graphed seven ordered pairs of (r, θ). In the figure on the right we see that as θ increases from 0° to 90°, the leaf in the first quadrant is traced. **As θ increases from 90° to 180°, the sine of 2θ is negative, so the angles are in the second quadrant but the graph is in the fourth quadrant.** Now we complete our task by finding the ordered pairs of (r, θ) as θ goes from 180° to 360°.

θ	180°	210°	225°	240°	270°	300°	315ᵈ	330°	360°
2θ	0°	60°	90°	120°	180°	240°	270°	300°	0°
$r = \sin 2\theta$	0	0.87	1	0.87	0	−0.87	−1	−0.87	0

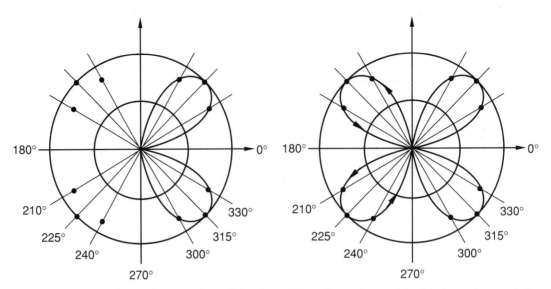

On the left we have graphed the points. Note than when θ is a third-quadrant angle, the graph is in the third quadrant because the sine of 2θ is positive for angles between $2(180°)$ and $2(270°)$. But when θ is a fourth-quadrant angle, the graph is in the second quadrant because the sine is negative for angles between $2(270°)$ and $2(360°)$.

Example 109.5   Graph $r = 2 \cos 3\theta$.

Solution   These equations can always be graphed by plotting points as we did in the preceding example. Plotting points is time-consuming, and we can graph such equations more quickly by plotting a few key points if we are very careful. The given equation is the equation of a rose that has three leaves because of the argument 3θ. The maximum and minimum values of the cosine are $+1$ and -1. Thus the maximum value of $2 \cos 3\theta$ will be $+2$ and will occur when 3θ equals $0°$ or $360°$, which occurs when θ equals $0°$ and $120°$. The minimum value of $2 \cos 3\theta$ is -2 and occurs when 3θ equals $180°$, which occurs when θ equals $60°$. On the left we graph the ordered polar pairs $(2, 0°)$, $(2, 120°)$, and $(-2, 60°)$.

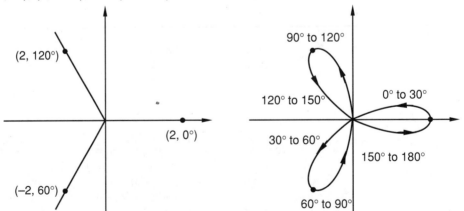

On the right, after a little more consideration, we draw the graph of the equation. First we consider the trace as θ goes from $0°$ to $180°$. The graph begins at $(2, 0°)$ and traces half a petal as θ increases from $0°$ to $30°$ and r decreases from 2 to 0. Then, as θ increases from $30°$ to $60°$, r goes from 0 to -2 and traces another half petal in the third quadrant. Four more half petals are traced between θ values of $60°$ and $90°$, between $90°$ and $120°$, between $120°$ and $150°$, and between $150°$ and $180°$. There are six half petals in all, so the entire figure is formed in 30° times 6, or 180°. As θ increases from 180° to 360°, the same patterns will be repeated and the three-leafed rose will be traced a second time.

Example 109.6   Graph $r = 4 \cos \theta$.

Solution   The maximum value of cos θ is +1, so the maximum value of 4 cos θ is 4 and occurs when θ = 0°. The minimum value of cos θ is −1, so the minimum value of 4 cos θ is −4 and occurs when θ = 180°. This is a one-leafed rose since $n = 1$, and a one-leafed rose turns out to be a circle.

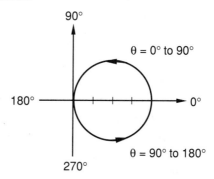

When θ = 0, $r = 4 \cos \theta = 4$ as shown. As θ increases from 0° to 90°, $r = 4 \cos \theta$ decreases from 4 to 0 and traces the top half of the circle. As θ goes from 90° to 180°, r is negative because cos θ is negative, and r goes from 0 to −4 to trace the bottom half of the circle. As θ goes from 180° to 360°, the pattern repeats and the circle is retraced.

Problem set 109

1. Use the method of differentials to approximate the value of $\sqrt{17}$. The equation is $y = x^{1/2}$. Take the differential and find its value when $x = 16$ and $\Delta x = 1$.

2. The position function of a particle that moves along the x axis is

$$x(t) = t^3 - 6t^2 + 9t + 1$$

Find the velocity function and the acceleration function for this particle. Determine $v(4)$ and $a(3)$.

3. For what values of t is the particle in Problem 2 moving to the left? For what values of t is the particle moving to the right? Find the total distance traveled by the particle between $t = 0$ and $t = 4$.

4. The slope of the tangent line which can be drawn to the graph of a function f at any point (x, y) on the graph is $1/x$. The graph of f passes through the point $(1, 1)$. Find the equation of f.

5. The figure shows the triangular end of a trough that is 20 meters long. The trough is filled to a depth of 3 meters with a fluid whose weight density is 3000 newtons per cubic meter. Find the force of the fluid on the end of the trough.

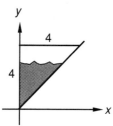

6. A ball is thrown upward from the top of a 60-meter-high building with a velocity of 30 meters per second. Develop the velocity function and the

position function for the ball. How long does it take the ball to reach its highest point? How long does it take the ball to hit the ground after reaching its highest point?

7. Consider the function $f(x) = ae^x + b \sin x$. If $f'(0) = 4$ and $f''(0) = 7$, what are the numerical values of a and b?

8. Write the polar form of $y = 2x^2$.

9. Write the rectangular form of the polar equation $r = \sin \theta$.

Graph the following functions on a polar coordinate system:

10. $r = 2 \sin \theta$ 11. $r = 2 \cos 2\theta$ 12. $r = \cos 3\theta$

Use trigonometric substitution to find the following integrals:

13. $\displaystyle\int \frac{dx}{\sqrt{4 - x^2}}$ 14. $\displaystyle\int \frac{dx}{\sqrt{x^2 - 4}}$ 15. $\displaystyle\int \frac{dx}{x^2 + 4}$

16. Find the area between the graph of $y = \tan^3 x$ and the x axis on the closed interval $[0, \frac{\pi}{4}]$.

Evaluate the following limits:

17. $\displaystyle\lim_{x \to 0} \frac{x - \sin x}{x}$ 18. $\displaystyle\lim_{x \to \infty} \frac{(\ln x)^2}{x}$

19. The mean value theorem tells us that if f is continuous on $I = [0, \frac{\pi}{4}]$ and differentiable on $(0, \frac{\pi}{4})$, then for some number c between 0 and $\frac{\pi}{4}$,

$$f'(c) = \frac{f\left(\frac{\pi}{4}\right) - f(0)}{\frac{\pi}{4} - 0}$$

Find the value of c for $f(x) = \tan x$ on the interval $(0, \frac{\pi}{4})$.

20. Suppose that f is a continuous function and

$$\int_1^7 f(x)\,dx = 4 \quad\quad \text{and} \quad\quad \int_3^7 f(x)\,dx = 5 \quad\quad \text{Find} \quad\quad \int_1^3 f(x)\,dx$$

21. Differentiate: $y = \tan^3 x - \dfrac{1 + \sin \pi x}{1 + cx}$

CONCEPT REVIEW   22. If

$$\int_c^x f(t)\,dt = 4x^4 - 4$$

find the equation of f. Then use the equation of f to find c. (*Hint*: Differentiate both sides of the equation.)

LESSON 110 *Partial fractions I*

If the numerator of a fraction is the differential of the denominator, the expression has the form du over u and the integral is $\ln |u| + C$.

$$\int \frac{du}{u} = \ln |u| + C \qquad \int \frac{dx}{x + 1} = \ln |x + 1| + C$$

A polynomial can be factored into a product of linear real factors and irreducible quadratic factors. In this lesson we will consider fractions of polynomials in which the denominator polynomial has only nonrepeating linear real factors and has no irreducible quadratic factors.

If the degree of the denominator of a fraction of polynomials is greater than the degree of the numerator, and if the denominator can be factored into nonrepeating linear real factors, it is possible to write the original fraction as the sum of simpler fractions. When we do this, we say we have **decomposed** the original fraction into a sum of **partial fractions.** The integral of the original fraction equals the sum of the integrals of the partial fractions, which are all in the form of du over u and thus all have integrals of the form $\ln |u|$. For example,

$$\frac{4x^2 + 13x - 9}{x(x + 3)(x - 1)} \qquad \text{equals} \qquad \frac{3}{x} + \frac{-1}{x + 3} + \frac{2}{x - 1}$$

Thus the integral of the original fraction will equal the sum of the integrals of the partial fractions.

$$\int \frac{4x^2 + 13x - 9}{x(x + 3)(x - 1)}\, dx = 3 \int \frac{dx}{x} - \int \frac{dx}{x + 3} + 2 \int \frac{dx}{x - 1}$$

All three of these integrals are of the form du over u, so the answer is

$$3 \ln |x| - \ln |x + 3| + 2 \ln |x - 1| + C$$

One procedure for finding the partial fractions is to use letters A, B, and C as the numerators and to use the linear factors of the denominator as the individual denominators, as we show here.

$$\frac{4x^2 + 13x - 9}{x(x + 3)(x - 1)} = \frac{A}{x} + \frac{B}{x + 3} + \frac{C}{x - 1}$$

The next step is to multiply every numerator on both sides by the denominator $x(x - 3)(x - 1)$ to get

$$(a) \quad 4x^2 + 13x - 9 = A(x + 3)(x - 1) + Bx(x - 1) + Cx(x + 3)$$

The unknown constants are A, B, and C. Since we have three unknowns, we need three independent equations. We can get the three equations by choosing three different values of x, say 5, 7, and 10. If we let x equal 5, we will get one equation in A, B, and C. If we let x equal 7, we will get another equation in A, B, and C. If we let x equal 10, we will get another equation in A, B, and C. Then we could solve this system of three equations in three unknowns for A, B, and C. But if we consider equation (a) carefully, we can see that there are choices of x that will allow us to find A, B, and C without solving a system of three equations. We note that x is a factor of the last two terms on the right in equation (a). If we let x equal zero, these terms will equal zero and we can solve for A.

$$4(0)^2 + 13(0) - 9 = A(0 + 3)(0 - 1) + B(0)(0 - 1) + C(0)(0 + 3)$$

$$-9 = A(3)(-1) \quad \longrightarrow \quad A = 3$$

Two of the terms on the right-hand side of the equals sign in equation (*a*) have $x - 1$ as a factor, and if we let x equal 1, these terms will equal zero, and we get

$$4(1) + 13(1) - 9 = A(0) + B(0) + C(1)(1 + 3) \quad \longrightarrow \quad C = 2$$

Two of the terms on the right side of the equals sign in equation (*a*) have $x + 3$ as a factor, and if we let x equal -3, these terms will equal zero, and we get

$$4(-3)^2 + 13(-3) - 9 = A(0) + B(-3)(-3 - 1) + C(0) \quad \longrightarrow \quad B = -1$$

But there is yet an easier way to find A, B, and C. We can write the values of A, B, and C almost by inspection if we use the original equation and use mental parentheses. We think of a set of parentheses as a factor of each fraction, as we show here.

$$\frac{4x^2 + 13x - 9}{x(x + 3)(x - 1)}(\ ) = \frac{A}{x}(\ ) + \frac{B}{x + 3}(\ ) + \frac{C}{x - 1}(\ )$$

Now to solve for A, we mentally insert x in each set of parentheses. The (x) factors we have inserted on the left of the equals sign and in the A term will cancel the x factors in the denominators of these terms, and we will get

$$\frac{4x^2 + 13x - 9}{\cancel{x}(x + 3)(x - 1)}(\cancel{x}) = \frac{A}{\cancel{x}}(\cancel{x}) + \frac{B}{x + 3}(x) + \frac{C}{x - 1}(x)$$

Now if we let x equal 0, we can solve for A because the B and C terms will equal zero.

$$\frac{-9}{3(-1)} = A + 0 + 0 \quad \longrightarrow \quad A = 3$$

We can refine this empty parentheses method and find the value of A quickly and accurately if we use two fingers. We use one finger to cover the x in the left-hand denominator, use another finger to cover the x in the A denominator, and ignore the B and C terms. It looks like this.

$$\frac{4x^2 + 13x - 9}{(\ \ )(x + 3)(x - 1)} = \frac{A}{(\ \ )}$$

Now we let x equal zero and solve for A.

$$\frac{-9}{3(-1)} = A \quad \longrightarrow \quad A = 3$$

We would repeat the process to solve for B and C.

Example 110.1   Find $\int \dfrac{dx}{x^2 - 1}$.

Solution   The denominator is factorable so we will use partial fractions.

$$\frac{1}{(x + 1)(x - 1)} = \frac{A}{x + 1} + \frac{B}{x - 1}$$

To find A, we use fingers to cover the $x + 1$ on the left and the $x + 1$ on the right, and ignore the B term. Then we let x equal -1, the number that would make $x + 1 = 0$.

$$\frac{1}{(\ \ )(x - 1)} = \frac{A}{(\ \ )} \quad \longrightarrow \quad \frac{1}{(-1) - 1} = A \quad \longrightarrow \quad -\frac{1}{2} = A$$

To find B, we use fingers to cover up $x - 1$ and $x - 1$, ignore the A term, and let x equal $+1$, the number that would make $x - 1 = 0$.

$$\frac{1}{(x+1)()} = \frac{B}{()} \quad \longrightarrow \quad \frac{1}{(1)+1} = B \quad \longrightarrow \quad \frac{1}{2} = B$$

Thus we have

$$\int \frac{dx}{x^2 - 1} = -\frac{1}{2}\int \frac{dx}{x+1} + \frac{1}{2}\int \frac{dx}{x-1}$$

Each of these integrals is in the form du over u, so we get

$$\int \frac{dx}{x^2 - 1} = -\frac{1}{2}\ln|x+1| + \frac{1}{2}\ln|x-1| + C$$

Example 110.2 Find $\displaystyle\int \frac{(2x+3)\,dx}{x(x+2)(x-1)}$.

Solution We begin by writing

$$\frac{2x+3}{x(x+2)(x-1)} = \frac{A}{x} + \frac{B}{x+2} + \frac{C}{x-1}$$

We use fingers to cover the x's, ignore the B and C terms, and then let x equal zero.

$$\frac{2(0)+3}{()[(0)+2][(0)-1]} = \frac{A}{()} \quad \longrightarrow \quad -\frac{3}{2} = A$$

Now we cover the $(x+2)$'s, ignore the A and C terms, and let $x = -2$.

$$\frac{2(-2)+3}{(-2)()(-2-1)} = \frac{B}{()} \quad \longrightarrow \quad -\frac{1}{6} = B$$

Now we cover the $(x-1)$'s, ignore the A and B terms, and let x equal $+1$.

$$\frac{2(1)+3}{(1)(1+2)()} = \frac{C}{()} \quad \longrightarrow \quad \frac{5}{3} = C$$

Now we finish by integrating the partial fractions

$$\int \frac{(2x+3)\,dx}{x(x+2)(x-1)} = -\frac{3}{2}\int \frac{dx}{x} - \frac{1}{6}\int \frac{dx}{x+2} + \frac{5}{3}\int \frac{dx}{x-1}$$

All the integrals have the form du over u, so the integrals equal

$$-\frac{3}{2}\ln|x| - \frac{1}{6}\ln|x+2| + \frac{5}{3}\ln|x-1| + C$$

The "cover-up" method is often called the **Heaviside cover-up method** after Oliver Heaviside (1850–1925), a pioneer in electrical engineering and vector analysis.

Problem set 110

1. The height of a right circular cone is increasing at a rate of 3 cm/sec, and the radius of the circular base of the cone is decreasing at a rate of 1 cm/sec. Find the rate at which the volume of the cone is changing when the height of the cone is 10 cm and the radius of the base is 4 cm.

2. Use the method of differentials to approximate the cube root of 9.

3. Determine the average value of $f(x) = \sin x$ on the interval $I = [0, \pi]$. Illustrate the mean value theorem for integrals for f on the interval I.

4. Find the x coordinate of the centroid of the region between the graph of $y = \sin x$ and the x axis on the interval $[0, \pi/2]$.

5. A variable force F is applied to an object to move it along a straight line such that $F(x) = xe^{x^2}$ newtons. Find the work done by the force on the object in moving it from $x = 0$ to $x = 3$ meters.

Use the method of partial fractions to find the following integrals:

6. $\displaystyle\int \frac{3x}{(x - 1)(x + 2)}\,dx$

7. $\displaystyle\int \frac{x^2 - 2}{x(x - 2)(x - 1)}\,dx$

8. $\displaystyle\int \frac{6x + 1}{x(x + 1)(x + 2)}\,dx$

9. Write the polar form of $x^2 + y^2 = 4$.

10. Write rectangular form of the polar equation $r = 2$.

Graph the following polar equations:

11. $r = \cos 4\theta$

12. $r = 2 \cos 2\theta$

Integrate by using trigonometric substitution:

13. $\displaystyle\int \frac{dx}{\sqrt{1 - 4x^2}}$

14. $\displaystyle\int \frac{dx}{1 + 9x^2}$

15. $\displaystyle\int \frac{2x}{4 + 9x^2}\,dx$

16. Evaluate: $\displaystyle\lim_{x \to 0} 27x \csc 4x$

17. Simplify: $\displaystyle\frac{d}{dx}\int_2^x \sqrt{1 + t^3}\,dt$

18. Suppose f is a function defined for all real values of x. Which of the following conditions guarantees that the graph of $y = |f(x)|$ and $y = f(x)$ will be identical?
    (a) f is an odd function   (b) f is an even function
    (c) $f(x) \geq 0$ for all x (d) f is continuous for all real x

19. If f is a function which is everywhere continuous and increasing, which of the following statements must be true?

    (a) The inverse of f is also a function
    (b) The inverse of f is everywhere increasing
    (c) f is everywhere differentiable
    (d) f^{-1} and f are the same function
    (e) $\dfrac{1}{f}$ and f^{-1} will have the same graph

20. Differentiate: $y = \dfrac{1}{\sqrt{x}} - x \ln |\sin x| + \arcsin \dfrac{x}{2}$

CONCEPT REVIEW 21. If f is a continuous function for all real values of x, $c > a$, and $b > 0$, which of the following integrals are equal?

$$(1)\ \int_a^c f(x)\,dx \qquad (2)\ \int_{a-b}^{c-b} f(x + b)\,dx \qquad (3)\ \int_0^{c-a} f(x + a)\,dx$$

    (a) (1) and (2) only   (b) (2) and (3) only
    (c) (1) and (3) only   (d) (1), (2), and (3)

LESSON *111* *Polar graphing II*

In this lesson we will extend our investigation of the graphs of polar equations to the graphs of limaçons and lemniscates. We remember that the equation of a rose curve can have one of the following two forms if n is a counting number.

$$r = b \sin n\theta \qquad r = b \cos n\theta$$

If we let n equal 1 and insert another constant, we get the equations of a limaçon.

$$r = a \pm b \sin \theta \qquad r = a \pm b \cos \theta$$

The letters a and b represent positive real numbers. The shape of the limaçon depends on the relative magnitudes of a and b. The values of $b \sin \theta$ and $b \cos \theta$ change from $+b$ to $-b$ as the values of the sine and cosine change from $+1$ to -1. If a is less than b, then $|b \sin \theta|$ and $|b \cos \theta|$ will be greater than a for some values of θ and the limaçon will have an inner loop as in the graph on the left.

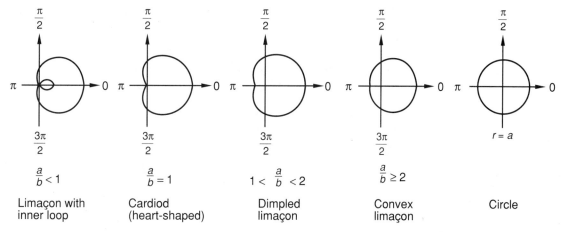

Limaçon with inner loop	Cardiod (heart-shaped)	Dimpled limaçon	Convex limaçon	Circle
$\frac{a}{b} < 1$	$\frac{a}{b} = 1$	$1 < \frac{a}{b} < 2$	$\frac{a}{b} \geq 2$	$r = a$

If a is equal to b, the graph is called a ***cardioid*** because it looks like a heart. If a over b is a number between 1 and 2, the graph is called a ***dimpled limaçon.*** If the ratio is greater than or equal to 2, the dimple disappears and we have a circle with one side flattened. As a gets greater and greater with respect to b, the contribution of $b \sin \theta$ or $b \cos \theta$ gets less and less and the graph will approach the graph of the **circle** $r = a$.

If n is a counting number, the graphs of the equations

$$r^2 = a \sin n\theta \qquad r^2 = a \cos n\theta$$

are called ***lemniscates.*** If $n = 2$, the graphs look like the graphs of the four-leafed roses whose equations are

$$r = a \sin 2\theta \qquad r = a \cos 2\theta$$

but will have two of the leaves missing. To understand why the leaves are missing, we will consider the equation

$$r^2 = -1$$

There are no real values of r that satisfy this equation because any real number squared is equal to or greater than zero. Thus the value of r^2 is always positive or zero in the following equations.

$$r^2 = a \sin 2\theta \qquad r^2 = a \cos 2\theta$$

Thus these equations have no solutions whenever $\sin 2\theta$ or $\cos 2\theta$ is negative. In the equations of the two four-leafed roses on the left below, r can be negative and the graphs will have leaves for all values of θ. In the equations of the two lemniscates on the right below, r^2 can never be negative, so there is no trace of the curve for values of θ that require r^2 to be negative. In the lemniscate equations we use a^2 for convenience so that the radius vector of the lemniscates will be a units long instead of $\sqrt{a}$ units long.

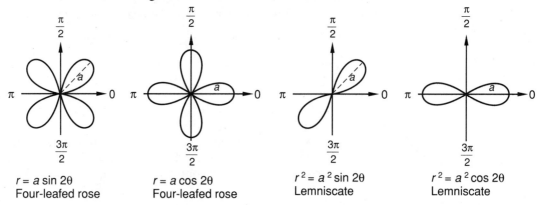

| $r = a \sin 2\theta$ | $r = a \cos 2\theta$ | $r^2 = a^2 \sin 2\theta$ | $r^2 = a^2 \cos 2\theta$ |
| Four-leafed rose | Four-leafed rose | Lemniscate | Lemniscate |

Example 111.1 Graph $r = 2 + 2 \sin \theta$.

Solution The graph of this function is neither a rose nor a lemniscate but is heart-shaped. To draw the graph, it is helpful to begin by visualizing the graph of the sine function.

$$y = 2 \sin \theta$$

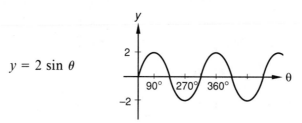

We see that $2 \sin \theta$ equals zero when $\theta = 0$ and equals 2 when $\theta = 90°$, so $2 + 2 \sin \theta$ goes from 2 to 4 as θ goes from $0°$ to $90°$. We show this in the figure on the left.

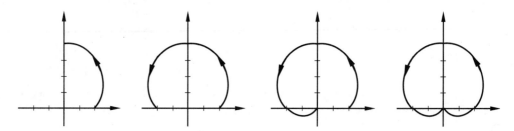

The value of $\sin \theta$ goes from 1 to 0 as θ goes from $90°$ to $180°$, so $2 + 2 \sin \theta$ goes from 4 to 2 between θ values of $90°$ and $180°$, as we show in the second figure. In the next $90°$, as shown in the third figure, $\sin \theta$ goes from 0 to -1, so $2 + 2 \sin \theta$ goes from 2 to 0. And in the fourth figure, we see that in the next $90°$, $2 + 2 \sin \theta$ goes from 0 to $+2$. Thus the graph is the graph of a cardioid whose axis of symmetry is the vertical axis.

Example 111.2 Graph $r = 3 - 3 \cos \theta$.

Solution We begin by visualizing the graph of $y = 3 \cos \theta$.

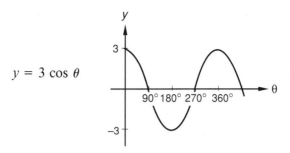

$$y = 3 \cos \theta$$

We note that 3 cos θ equals 3 when $\theta = 0$, so 3 − 3 cos θ equals zero when $\theta = 0°$. As θ increases from 0° to 90°, 3 cos θ goes from 3 to 0 and 3 − 3 cos θ goes from 0 to 3, as we show on the left below.

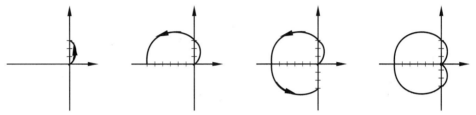

As θ increases from 90° to 180°, 3 cos θ goes from 0 to −3 and 3 − 3 cos θ goes from 3 to 6, as we show in the second figure. Between 180° and 270°, 3 cos θ goes from −3 to 0 and 3 − 3 cos θ goes from 6 to 3, as we show in the third figure. Finally, as θ goes from 270° to 360°, 3 cos θ goes from 0 to 3 and 3 − 3 cos θ goes from 3 to 0, as we show in the fourth figure.

Example 111.3   Graph $r = 2 + 4 \cos \theta$.

Solution   First we visualize the graph of $y = 4 \cos \theta$.

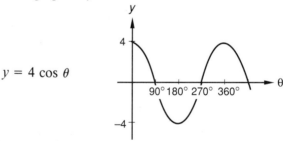

$$y = 4 \cos \theta$$

Graphing the given equation point by point can be tedious, so we will use the fact that the constant 2 in our equation is less than the coefficient 4 to deduce that the graph is a limaçon with an inner loop. We know that cos θ equals zero when θ equals 90° and 270°, so 2 + 4 cos θ equals 2 when θ equals 90° and 270°. A maximum value occurs when θ equals 0 because cos 0° = 1, and so 2 + 4 cos 0° = 6. We use this to guess the shape of the graph.

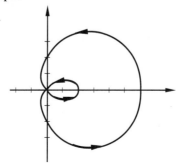

We check our guess by finding the crossing point of the inner loop. When θ equals 180°, cos θ equals -1 and $2 + 4 \cos \theta = 2 + 4(-1) = -2$. Thus, when θ equals 180°, $r = -2$, which gives us the crossing point shown. If we test other points, we will see that the inner loop is caused by the negative values of cosine between 90° and 270°, which causes r to be negative when θ has a value between 120° and 240°.

Example 111.4   Graph the equation $r^2 = 4 \cos 2\theta$.

Solution   First we visualize the graph of $y = 2 \cos 2\theta$.

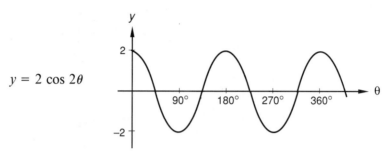

$y = 2 \cos 2\theta$

We use the graph above to help us graph the equation $r = 2 \cos 2\theta$, which is the four-leafed rose shown on the left.

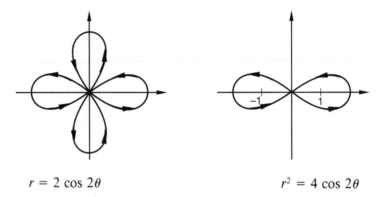

$r = 2 \cos 2\theta$ $r^2 = 4 \cos 2\theta$

The graph of $r^2 = 4 \cos 2\theta$ on the right is a similar graph with "blunter" ends and without the upper and lower leaves. These leaves are missing because cos 2θ can never be negative in this equation since r^2 can never be negative. In this book we will only consider graphs of the simplest of polar equations to acquaint ourselves with the idea of polar graphing. Computers can be used to get the graphs of more complicated equations. Plotting the graphs of more complicated equations can be a very time-consuming task.

Problem set 111   1.   A tank, all of whose faces are rectangular, is to be constructed so that the width of its base is 2 meters and so that the volume of the tank is 16 cubic meters. The material for the top and bottom of the tank costs $8 per square meter, and the material for each of the four sides costs $4 per square meter. Find the dimensions and cost of the tank which can be least expensively constructed.

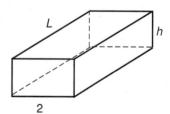

2. The acceleration at time t of a particle moving along the x axis is given by the equation $a(t) = 2\pi \sin t \cos t$. If the velocity of the particle at $t = 0$ is zero, what is the average velocity of the particle over the interval $0 \le t \le \pi$?

3. A solid spherical metal ball 1 meter in diameter is coated with a thin layer of gold 0.01 centimeter thick. Use differentials to approximate the increase in the surface area of the ball.

4. Suppose f is defined on the interval $I = [0, 2\pi]$, where $f(x) = \sin^2 x - 2 \sin x$. Find the critical numbers of f on I and then determine the maximum and minimum values of f on I.

5. Write the polar form of the equation $x = y^2$.

6. Write the rectangular form of the polar equation $r = \sin \theta \cos \theta$.

7. Graph $r = 2 \cos 3\theta$ on the polar coordinate plane.

Graph the following equations:

8. $r = 1 + \sin \theta$ **9.** $r = 1 - \cos \theta$

10. $r = 2 + 3 \cos \theta$ **11.** $r^2 = \cos 2\theta$

Use the method of partial fractions to compute the following integrals:

12. $\displaystyle\int \frac{dx}{x(x-1)}$ **13.** $\displaystyle\int \frac{3x^2 + 9x + 7}{x(x+1)(x+2)} \, dx$

Use trigonometric substitution to compute the following integrals:

14. $\displaystyle\int \frac{dx}{\sqrt{x^2 - 16}}$ **15.** $\displaystyle\int \frac{4 \, dx}{x^2 + 16}$

16. Let R be the region completely enclosed by the graphs of $y = 2^x$, $y = 3^x$, and the line $x = 3$. Write an integral in one variable whose value equals the volume of the solid formed when R is revolved about the x axis.

17. Sketch the graph of $y = \dfrac{(x-1)(x^2+1)}{(x-2)^2}$.

Integrate:

18. $\displaystyle\int \tan^2 x \, dx$ **19.** $\displaystyle\int \sin^3 x \, dx$ **20.** $\displaystyle\int \log_3 x \, dx$

21. Differentiate: $y = \arcsin \dfrac{x}{2} + e^x \sin x - \dfrac{\sin 2x}{x^2 + 1}$

CONCEPT REVIEW **22.** Given $f(2) = 3, f'(3) = 2, f'(2) = -4$. Then $(f \circ f)'(2)$ is equal to which of the following?
(*a*) -4 (*b*) -8 (*c*) -24 (*d*) -12

23. Let f be defined as follows:

$$f(x) = \begin{cases} a + bx^2 & \text{when } x \le 2 \\ x^3 & \text{when } x > 2 \end{cases}$$

Determine the values of a and b for which f is continuous and differentiable everywhere.

LESSON 112 *Partial fractions II*

Every polynomial can be factored into a product of linear real factors and irreducible quadratic factors. In this lesson we will consider fractions of polynomials whose denominators are of higher degree than the numerators and whose denominators do not have irreducible quadratic factors but do have linear real factors that are repeated. When a linear real factor of the denominator is repeated, additional terms are required in the decomposition of the fraction. If a factor appears twice, two terms are required for this factor in the decomposition.

$$\frac{1}{x(x+2)^2} = \frac{A}{x} + \frac{B}{x+2} + \frac{C}{(x+2)^2}$$

If a factor appears 3 times, three terms are required for this factor in the decomposition.

$$\frac{1}{x(x+2)^3} = \frac{A}{x} + \frac{B}{x+2} + \frac{C}{(x+2)^2} + \frac{D}{(x+2)^3}$$

If a factor appears n times, n terms are required for this factor. **The Heaviside cover-up method can be used to find the coefficients for the nonrepeated factors and for the highest power of the repeated factor.**

Example 112.1   Find $\displaystyle\int \frac{4}{x(x+1)^2}\, dx$.

Solution   First we will find a partial fraction expansion of the integrand.

$$\frac{4}{x(x+1)^2} = \frac{A}{x} + \frac{B}{x+1} + \frac{C}{(x+1)^2}$$

If we try to use the Heaviside cover-up method to find B, we will not succeed.

$$\frac{4}{x(x+1)^2}(x+1) = \frac{A}{x}(x+1) + \frac{B}{x+1}(x+1) + \frac{C}{(x+1)^2}(x+1)$$

After we cancel the $(x+1)$'s, we will still have an $x+1$ in the denominator of the original expression and also under C, and if we let $x = -1$, these denominators will equal zero.

But we can use the cover-up method to find A and C. First we will find A.

$$\frac{4}{(\;\underset{\equiv}{\bigcirc}\;)(x+1)^2} = \frac{A}{(\;\underset{\equiv}{\bigcirc}\;)} \qquad \text{if } x = 0,\ A = 4$$

$$\frac{4}{(x)(\;\underset{\equiv}{\bigcirc}\;)} = \frac{C}{(\;\underset{\equiv}{\bigcirc}\;)} \qquad \text{if } x = -1,\ C = -4$$

Now we have

$$\frac{4}{x(x+1)^2} = \frac{4}{x} + \frac{B}{x+1} + \frac{-4}{(x+1)^2}$$

This equation must be true for any x value that does not cause a denominator to equal zero, so we need to choose a convenient value for x and solve for B. We decide to let x equal 1.

$$\frac{4}{1(2)^2} = \frac{4}{1} + \frac{B}{1+1} + \frac{-4}{(1+1)^2} \quad \longrightarrow \quad B = -4$$

Now we can complete the solution.

$$\int \frac{4\,dx}{x(x+1)^2} = 4 \int \frac{dx}{x} - 4 \int \frac{dx}{x+1} - 4 \int \frac{dx}{(x+1)^2}$$

We note that the first two integrals have the form *du* over *u* but that the third has the form *u^n du*. So we can write

$$\int \frac{4\,dx}{(x+1)^2} = 4 \ln |x| - 4 \ln |x+1| - \frac{4(x+1)^{-1}}{-1} + C$$

$$= 4 \ln |x| - 4 \ln |x+1| + \frac{4}{x+1} + C$$

Example 112.2 Find $\int \dfrac{dx}{x^2(x+1)}$.

Solution First we find the partial fraction decomposition.

$$\frac{1}{x^2(x+1)} = \frac{A}{x} + \frac{B}{x^2} + \frac{C}{x+1}$$

We can use the cover-up method to find B and C.

$$\frac{1}{(\ \bigcirc\ )(x+1)} = \frac{B}{(\ \bigcirc\ )} \qquad \text{and if } x = 0 \qquad B = 1$$

$$\frac{1}{x^2(\ \bigcirc\ )} = \frac{C}{(\ \bigcirc\ )} \qquad \text{and if } x = -1 \qquad C = 1$$

Now we have

$$\frac{1}{x^2(x+1)} = \frac{A}{x} + \frac{1}{x^2} + \frac{1}{x+1}$$

It seems that 1 is a good choice for x since it causes no denominator to equal zero. Thus

$$\frac{1}{(1)^2(1+1)} = \frac{A}{(1)} + \frac{1}{(1)^2} + \frac{1}{(1+1)} \quad \longrightarrow \quad A = -1$$

Now we can substitute and get

$$\int \frac{dx}{x^2(x+1)} = -\int \frac{dx}{x} + \int \frac{dx}{x^2} + \int \frac{dx}{x+1}$$

The second integral is in the form $u^n\,du$, so the result is

$$-\ln |x| - \frac{1}{x} + \ln |x+1| + C$$

Problem set 112

1. The rate at which a rabbit colony is growing at a given time is proportional to the number of rabbits present at that time. Initially there were 2000 rabbits, and at $t = 1$ year, there were 3000 rabbits. Write an equation which expresses the number of rabbits present as a function of t.

2. A cubical tank, each of whose sides has a length of 5 meters, is filled with a fluid with a weight density of 5000 newtons per cubic meter. Find the work done in pumping the fluid out of the tank.

3. Use differentials to estimate the cube root of 28.

Integrate by using the method of partial fractions:

4. $\displaystyle\int \frac{5x - 9}{(x - 3)(x - 3)}$ **5.** $\displaystyle\int \frac{8}{x(x + 2)^2}\, dx$ **6.** $\displaystyle\int \frac{dx}{x^2(x - 1)}$

7. Write the following polar equation in rectangular form: $r = \sin\theta + \cos\theta$

Graph the following functions on a polar coordinate plane:

8. $r = 2\cos 2\theta$ **9.** $r = 3 + 3\sin\theta$

10. $r = 2 - 2\cos\theta$ **11.** $r = 1 + 2\cos\theta$

12. Find the area of the region between the graph of $y = \cos^2 x$ and the x axis on the interval $[0, \pi/4]$.

Integrate:

13. $\displaystyle\int \frac{2\, dx}{\sqrt{4 - x^2}}$ **14.** $\displaystyle\int \frac{3\, dx}{9 + x^2}$

15. $\displaystyle\int \frac{\cos^3 x \sin x}{\cos^4 x + 1}\, dx$ **16.** $\displaystyle\int 2x \cos x\, dx$

17. Evaluate: $\displaystyle\lim_{x \to 0} \frac{\cos x - 1}{3x}$ **18.** Simplify: $\displaystyle\frac{d}{dx}\int_1^x \sin t^2\, dt$

19. Suppose that $y = f(x)$ is a function which is everywhere continuous. Which of the following statements must be true about the function $y = f(|x|)$?
   (a) The graph of $y = f(|x|)$ lies above the x axis
   (b) $y = f(|x|)$ is an even function
   (c) $y = f(|x|)$ is an odd function
   (d) $\displaystyle\int_{-c}^{c} f(|x|)\, dx = 0$ for any real value of c

20. Let f be the one-to-one function $f(x) = x^3 + x - 1$. This means that the inverse of f, f^{-1}, is also a function. Evaluate $f^{-1}(1)$ and $(f^{-1})'(1)$.

21. Differentiate: $y = 3^{x^2} + \dfrac{2x - 1}{\sqrt{x - 2}} + \ln|1 + \sin x|$

22. Suppose $a < c < b$, and f is differentiable on (a, b) and is continuous on the interval $I = [a, b]$. Which of the following statements is not necessarily true?
   (a) There exists a c in I such that $f'(c) = \dfrac{f(b) - f(a)}{b - a}$

   (b) $\displaystyle\int_a^c f(x)\, dx + \int_c^b f(x)\, dx = \int_a^b f(x)\, dx$

   (c) $\displaystyle\int_a^b f(x)\, dx \geq 0$

   (d) There exists a c in I such that $f(c) = \dfrac{1}{b - a}\int_a^b f(x)\, dx$

LESSON *113* *Integration by parts II*

We remember that integration undoes differentiation and that our best weapon for integration is a guess. Then we check our guess. When a good guess does not come to mind, we fall back on methods such as substitution, integration by parts, and the method of partial fractions. These methods work for special types of integrands. We have found that we can use integration by parts to find the following integrals.

$$\int xe^x\,dx \qquad \int x\sin x\,dx \qquad \int x\cos x\,dx$$

We have learned to let x equal u and to let the rest of the expression equal dv. When we encounter integrals such as

$$\int x^2 e^x\,dx \qquad \int x^3 \sin x\,dx \qquad \int x^n \cos x\,dx$$

we can still use integration by parts, but we have to use it n times, where n is the exponent of the polynomial factor x^n. Each time we use integration by parts, the exponent of x will be 1 less than before.

When we encounter expressions in which one factor has the form e^{ax} and the other factor is $\sin bx$ or $\cos bx$, we can use integration by parts twice and then complete the solution by using algebra. For example, if the integrand is $e^x \cos x\,dx$ and we use integration by parts twice, we can get

$$\int e^x \cos x\,dx = e^x \sin x + e^x \cos x - \int e^x \cos x\,dx$$

This equation has $\int e^x \cos x\,dx$ on the left-hand side and on the right-hand side. If we add $\int e^x \cos x\,dx$ to both sides, we get

$$2\int e^x \cos x\,dx = e^x \sin x + e^x \cos x + C$$

Now if we divide both sides by 2, we have the indefinite integral we are looking for.

$$\int e^x \cos x\,dx = \frac{1}{2}(e^x \sin x + e^x \cos x) + C$$

Example 113.1 Find $\displaystyle\int x^2 \cos 3x\,dx$.

Solution We will use integration by parts twice. The first time we let u equal x^2.

$u = x^2$	
	$dv = \cos 3x$

$u = x^2$	$v = \dfrac{1}{3}\sin 3x$
$du = 2x\,dx$	$dv = \cos 3x$

$$\int u\,dv = uv - \int v\,du \quad \longrightarrow \quad (x^2)\left(\frac{1}{3}\sin 3x\right) - \frac{2}{3}\int x\sin 3x\,dx$$

Now we will use integration by parts again to find $\int x\sin 3x\,dx$. This time we will let $u = x$ and $dv = \sin 3x\,dx$.

$u = x$	
	$dv = \sin 3x\, dx$

$u = x$	$v = -\dfrac{1}{3}\cos 3x$
$du = dx$	$dv = \sin 3x\, dx$

$$\int u\, dv = uv - \int v\, du \longrightarrow (x)\left(-\frac{1}{3}\cos 3x\right) - \int\left(-\frac{1}{3}\cos 3x\right) dx$$

$$= -\frac{x}{3}\cos 3x - \frac{1}{3}\int\left(-\frac{1}{3}\cos 3x\right)(3\, dx)$$

$$= -\frac{x}{3}\cos 3x + \frac{1}{9}\sin 3x + C$$

Now we add the result of the first step to $-\frac{2}{3}$ of the result of the second step to get the final result.

$$\int x^2 \cos 3x\, dx = (x^2)\left(\frac{1}{3}\sin 3x\right) - \frac{2}{3}\left(-\frac{x}{3}\cos 3x + \frac{1}{9}\sin 3x\right) + C$$

$$= \frac{x^2}{3}\sin 3x + \frac{2x}{9}\cos 3x - \frac{2}{27}\sin 3x + C$$

Example 113.2   Find $\displaystyle\int e^x \sin x\, dx$.

Solution   The integrand is a product of the form $e^{ax}\sin bx$. We will have to integrate by parts twice and then use algebra to find the answer. We could use either e^x or $\sin x$ for u. We decide to let $u = e^x$.

$u = e^x$	
	$dv = \sin x\, dx$

$u = e^x$	$v = -\cos x$
$du = e^x\, dx$	$dv = \sin x\, dx$

$$\int u\, dv = uv - \int v\, du$$

so

$$\int e^x \sin x\, dx = -e^x \cos x - \int -e^x \cos x\, dx$$

$$= -e^x \cos x + \int e^x \cos x\, dx$$

We let $u = e^x$ in the first step. Now we need to find $\int e^x \cos x\, dx$. Experimenting with this problem will show us that it is also necessary to let $u = e^x$ in the second step if we are to be successful in our search for the original integral.

$u = e^x$	
	$dv = \cos x\, dx$

$u = e^x$	$v = \sin x$
$du = e^x\, dx$	$dv = \cos x\, dx$

$$\int u\, dv = uv - \int v\, du$$

$$\int e^x \cos x\, dx = e^x \sin x - \int e^x \sin x\, dx$$

Now, as the penultimate step, we combine the results of the first step and the second step to get

$$\int e^x \sin x \, dx = -e^x \cos x + e^x \sin x - \int e^x \sin x \, dx$$

If we add $\int e^x \sin x \, dx$ to both sides and then divide by 2, we get the final result.

$$2 \int e^x \sin x \, dx = -e^x \cos x + e^x \sin x + C$$

$$\longrightarrow \int e^x \sin x \, dx = -\frac{1}{2} e^x \cos x + \frac{1}{2} e^x \sin x + C$$

Example 113.3 Find $\int e^x \cos x \, dx$.

Solution In Example 113.2, we saw that a good choice for u in both steps is e^x. We will show that this choice for u is not necessary by letting $u = \cos x$ in the first step and letting $u = \sin x$ in the second step.

$u = \cos x$	
	$dv = e^x \, dx$

$u = \cos x$	$v = e^x$
$du = -\sin x \, dx$	$dv = e^x \, dx$

$$\int u \, dv = uv - \int v \, du$$

$$\int e^x \cos x \, dx = e^x \cos x - \int e^x(-\sin x) \, dx$$

$$= e^x \cos x + \int e^x \sin x \, dx$$

To get the expression we need, we must let $u = \sin x$ in the next step.

$u = \sin x$	
	$dv = e^x \, dx$

$u = \sin x$	$v = e^x$
$du = \cos x \, dx$	$dv = e^x \, dx$

Now we have

$$\int e^x \cos x \, dx = e^x \cos x + e^x \sin x - \int e^x \cos x \, dx$$

If we add $\int e^x \cos x \, dx$ to both sides and then divide by 2, we have the answer.

$$2 \int e^x \cos x \, dx = e^x \cos x + e^x \sin x + C \qquad \text{added}$$

$$\int e^x \cos x = \frac{1}{2} e^x \cos x + \frac{1}{2} e^x \sin x + C \qquad \text{divided}$$

Problem set 113   **1.** A point moves along the hyperbola

$$\frac{x^2}{4} - \frac{y^2}{9} = 1$$

so that its x coordinate is always increasing at a rate of 2 units per second. How fast is the y coordinate of the point changing the instant it is passing through the point $(2\sqrt{10}/3, 1)$?

2. When t is greater than zero, the acceleration function for a particle moving along the x axis is

$$a(t) = \frac{1}{t}$$

If $v(1) = 4$ and $x(1) = 5$, find the velocity function and the position function of the particle. Find $x(3)$ and $v(3)$.

3. A cubical tank, each of whose sides has a length of 5 meters, is filled with a fluid whose weight density is 5000 newtons per cubic meter. Find the total force against one of the vertical sides of the tank.

4. The acceleration due to gravity on planet X is 15 m/sec² toward the center of the planet. If a ball is thrown upward from the surface of the planet with an initial velocity of 40 m/sec, develop the velocity function and the position function for the ball. How long does it take after the ball is thrown for it to fall back to the surface of the planet?

Use integration by parts to find the following integrals:

5. $\int x^2 \cos 2x \, dx$ 6. $\int e^x \sin x \, dx$ 7. $\int x^2 e^x \, dx$

Integrate by using the method of partial fractions:

8. $\int \frac{2x + 1}{(x - 3)(x + 2)} \, dx$ 9. $\int \frac{2x}{(x - 1)(x + 1)^2} \, dx$ 10. $\int \frac{4 + 2x}{x^3(x - 1)} \, dx$

Graph the following equations on a polar coordinate plane:

11. $r = 3 + 2 \sin \theta$ 12. $r = 1 + 3 \cos \theta$

13. Use trigonometric substitution to find $\int \frac{dx}{\sqrt{9 - x^2}}$

14. Let R be the region between the graph of $y = \tan x$ and the x axis on the interval $[0, 1]$. Find the volume of the solid formed when R is revolved about the x axis.

15. Let R be as defined in Problem 14. Use one variable to write a definite integral whose value equals the volume of the solid formed when R is revolved about the line $x = -1$.

16. Which of the following integrals equals $\int_{\pi}^{2\pi} (\sin x)(e^{2 \cos x}) \, dx$?

(a) $-\int_{-1}^{1} e^u \, du$ (b) $-\int_{-1}^{1} e^{2u} \, du$ (c) $-\int_{-1}^{1} \frac{1}{2} e^u \, du$ (d) $\int_{\pi}^{2\pi} e^{2u} \, du$

17. Determine the average value of the function $f(x) = (\sin x)(e^{2 \cos x})$ on the interval $[\pi, 2\pi]$.

18. Suppose k is a positive real number such that

$$\int_{1}^{k} \frac{\sin x}{x} \, dx = 1 \qquad \text{Evaluate} \qquad \int_{-k}^{-1} \frac{\sin x}{x} \, dx$$

19. Express as the ratio of two definite integrals the x coordinate of the centroid of the region between the graph of $y = \sqrt{x^2 - 1}$ and the x axis on the interval $I = [1, 5]$.

20. Differentiate: $y = \arcsin (\tan x) + \dfrac{3 - x}{\sin x + \cos x}$

21. By inspection, tell which of the following definite integrals has a value of zero.

(a) $\displaystyle\int_0^\pi \sin^2 x \, dx$ (b) $\displaystyle\int_0^\pi \cos^2 x \, dx$ (c) $\displaystyle\int_{-\pi}^\pi \sin^3 x \, dx$

(d) $\displaystyle\int_0^\pi x^2 \sin^2 x \, dx$

LESSON 114 *Implicit differentiation II*

We remember from Lesson 45 that if an equation in x and y contains a description of one or more functions for an interval $[a, b]$, the derivative can be found by using the method of implicit differentiation. To this point we have used differentials to find the derivatives of implicit equations. To find dy/dx for the equation on the left below, we would first find the differential of each term as we show on the right.

$$2x^3 - y^2 = 7 \quad \longrightarrow \quad 6x^2 \, dx - 2y \, dy = 0$$

Since we want to find dy/dx, we divide every term by dx and then solve algebraically for dy/dx.

$$6x^2 - 2y \frac{dy}{dx} = 0 \qquad \text{divided by } dx$$

$$\frac{dy}{dx} = \frac{3x^2}{y} \qquad \text{solved for } \frac{dy}{dx}$$

We do not have to use differentials to differentiate implicit functions if we remember that y represents some function of x and that the derivative of a function of y, say $g(y)$, with respect to x is $g'(y) \, dy/dx$. To review, we let $g(y)$ be y^2 and remember that y is a function of x. Thus, using the chain rule to find the derivative of y^2 with respect to x, we get

$$g'(y) = \frac{d}{dx} g(y) = \frac{d}{dx} y^2 = 2y \frac{dy}{dx}$$

If we differentiate each term in the equation $2x^3 - y^2 = 7$ with respect to x, we get

$$\frac{d}{dx}(2x^3) - \frac{d}{dx}(y^2) = \frac{d}{dx}(7) \quad \longrightarrow \quad 6x^2 - 2y \frac{dy}{dx} = 0$$

If we solve this equation for dy/dx, we get the same result we got above by using differentials.

$$\frac{dy}{dx} = \frac{3x^2}{y}$$

Example 114.1 Find $\dfrac{dy}{dx}$ if $x^5 + 4xy^3 - 3y^5 = 2$.

Solution We will differentiate each term with respect to x.

$$\frac{d}{dx} x^5 + \frac{d}{dx} 4xy^3 - \frac{d}{dx} 3y^5 = \frac{d}{dx} 2$$

When we differentiate $4xy^3$ and $-3y^5$, we remember that y is a differentiable function of x, which requires that we use dy/dx as an additional factor. We get

$$5x^4 + 4\left[x(3y^2)\frac{dy}{dx} + y^3\right] - 15y^4\frac{dy}{dx} = 0$$

Now we simplify and then solve for $\frac{dy}{dx}$.

$$5x^4 + 12xy^2\frac{dy}{dx} + 4y^3 - 15y^4\frac{dy}{dx} = 0 \qquad \text{simplified}$$

$$\frac{dy}{dx}(12xy^2 - 15y^4) = -5x^4 - 4y^3 \qquad \text{rearranged}$$

$$\frac{dy}{dx} = \frac{-5x^4 - 4y^3}{12xy^2 - 15y^4} \qquad \text{solved}$$

Example 114.2 Find $\dfrac{d^2y}{dx^2}$ if $x^2 + y^2 = 100$.

Solution We begin by finding the first derivative, which we put in a box for later use.

$$2x + 2y\frac{dy}{dx} = 0 \qquad \text{differentiated}$$

$$\boxed{\frac{dy}{dx} = \frac{-x}{y}} \qquad \text{solved for } \frac{dy}{dx}$$

Now we use the quotient rule and differentiate again.

$$\frac{d^2y}{dx^2} = \frac{y(-1) - (-x)\dfrac{dy}{dx}}{y^2} \qquad \text{differentiated}$$

$$\frac{d^2y}{dx^2} = \frac{-y + x\dfrac{dy}{dx}}{y^2} \qquad \text{simplified}$$

But in the box we have an expression that we can substitute for dy/dx. We make this substitution and then simplify.

$$\frac{d^2y}{dx^2} = \frac{-y + x\left(\dfrac{-x}{y}\right)}{y^2} \qquad \text{substituted}$$

$$\frac{d^2y}{dx^2} = \frac{-1}{y} - \frac{x^2}{y^3} \qquad \text{simplified}$$

This answer is correct, but as the last step in one of these problems it is a good idea to write the answer as a single fraction and to look at the original equation to see if it can be used to make one more simplification. First we combine the terms in the numerator to get

$$\frac{d^2y}{dx^2} = \frac{-y^2 - x^2}{y^3} = \frac{-(y^2 + x^2)}{y^3}$$

The original equation tells us that $x^2 + y^2 = 100$, and if we make this substitution, we get

$$\frac{d^2y}{dx^2} = \frac{-100}{y^3}$$

Example 114.3 Find $\dfrac{d^2y}{dx^2}$ if $2x^3 - 3y^2 = 7$.

Solution First we differentiate implicitly and solve for dy/dx, which we put in a box for later use.

$$6x^2 - 6y\frac{dy}{dx} = 0 \qquad \text{differentiated}$$

$$\boxed{\frac{dy}{dx} = \frac{x^2}{y}} \qquad \text{solved for } \frac{dy}{dx}$$

Now we use the quotient rule to find the second derivative.

$$\frac{d^2y}{dx^2} = \frac{y(2x) - x^2\dfrac{dy}{dx}}{y^2}$$

But in the box we see that $dy/dx = x^2/y$, so we make this substitution and simplify.

$$\frac{d^2y}{dx^2} = \frac{2xy - x^2\left(\dfrac{x^2}{y}\right)}{y^2} \qquad \text{substituted}$$

$$= \frac{2xy - \dfrac{x^4}{y}}{y^2} \qquad \text{multiplied}$$

$$= \frac{2xy^2 - x^4}{y^3} \qquad \text{simplified}$$

Example 114.4 If $4y^2 = x^3$, use implicit differentiation to find $\dfrac{d^2y}{dx^2}$.

Solution To practice implicit differentiation, we often use simple problems like this one that could be solved explicitly and differentiated explicitly. We begin by finding the first derivative and putting it in a box for later use.

$$8y\frac{dy}{dx} = 3x^2 \qquad \text{differentiated}$$

$$\boxed{\frac{dy}{dx} = \frac{3x^2}{8y}} \qquad \text{solved for } \frac{dy}{dx}$$

Now we use the quotient rule to find the second derivative.

$$\frac{d^2y}{dx^2} = \frac{(8y)(6x) - (3x^2)\left(8\dfrac{dy}{dx}\right)}{64y^2}$$

Now we substitute for $\dfrac{dy}{dx}$ and simplify.

$$\frac{d^2y}{dx^2} = \frac{48xy - (3x^2)(8)\left(\frac{3x^2}{8y}\right)}{64y^2} \qquad \text{substituted}$$

$$= \frac{48xy - \frac{9x^4}{y}}{64y^2} \qquad \text{simplified}$$

$$= \frac{48xy^2 - 9x^4}{64y^3} \qquad \text{simplified}$$

This answer is correct, but because the original equation $4y^2 = x^3$ is a simple equation, it can be used to further simplify our answer. If we rearrange the answer, we can write the answer with factors of $4y^2$ and x^3.

$$\frac{(4y^2)(12x) - 9x(x^3)}{(4y^2)(16y)}$$

Now on the left we simplify by replacing $4y^2$ with x^3, and on the right we simplify by replacing x^3 with $4y^2$. Both substitutions lead to the same result.

$$= \frac{(x^3)(12x) - 9x(x^3)}{(x^3)(16y)} \qquad = \frac{48xy^2 - 9x(4y^2)}{(4y^2)(16y)}$$

$$= \frac{12x^4 - 9x^4}{16y^3} \qquad = \frac{48xy^2 - 36xy^2}{64y^3}$$

$$= \frac{3x^4}{16x^3y} \qquad = \frac{12xy^2}{64y^3}$$

$$= \frac{3x}{16y} \qquad = \frac{3x}{16y}$$

Had we tried to simplify the answer to Example 114.3, we could have worked for a long time and not come up with a simplification. The last step in problems like these is not calculus but is algebraic game playing. Sometimes the result can be simplified and sometimes it cannot.

Problem set 114

1. The acceleration function for a particle moving along the x axis is $a(t) = 20e^{4t}$. The velocity when $t = 0$ is 10 and the position when $t = 0$ is 4. Develop the velocity function and the position function of the particle. Find the total distance the particle travels during the time interval [5, 20].

2. Let f be the function defined on the closed interval $I = [-8, 8]$ by

$$f(x) = \frac{3}{4} x^{4/3} + 3x^{1/3}$$

Find f' and write the equation of f' as an expression with a single denominator. Determine the critical numbers of f in I. Find at which critical numbers the tangent to the graph of f is horizontal and at which critical numbers the tangent to the graph of f is vertical.

3. Let f be as defined in Problem 2. Find the x and y coordinates of all the relative maximum and minimum points of the graph of f. Determine the intervals on which f is concave upward and the intervals on which f is concave downward, and describe the x coordinate of all inflection points. Sketch the graph of f.

Differentiate implicitly to find $\dfrac{dy}{dx}$ and $\dfrac{d^2y}{dx^2}$ for the following equations:

4. $x^3 + y^3 = 100$ **5.** $y^3 + y = x^2$ **6.** $x^3 + y^2 + y = x$

Integrate by using integration by parts as many times as necessary:

7. $\displaystyle\int x^2 \sin x \, dx$ **8.** $\displaystyle\int e^{2x} \sin x \, dx$

Integrate by using the method of partial fractions:

9. $\displaystyle\int \dfrac{8x - 4}{(x - 1)^2 x} \, dx$ **10.** $\displaystyle\int \dfrac{x^2 + 4x + 1}{x^2(x + 2)} \, dx$

11. Write the equation of the hyperbola $x^2 - y^2 = 1$ in polar form.

12. Graph $r = 2 + 2 \sin \theta$ on the polar coordinate plane.

13. Evaluate: $\displaystyle\lim_{x \to 0} \dfrac{2 \cos x - 2}{3x}$

14. If $f(x) = \dfrac{d}{dx} \displaystyle\int_x^3 \dfrac{\cos t - 1}{t} \, dt$, find $f(\pi)$.

15. Evaluate: $\displaystyle\int_{-3}^4 |2x - 4| \, dx$

16. The region R is bounded by the y axis and the graph of $x = 1 - y^2$ on the interval $0 \le y \le 1$. Use y as the variable of integration to write a definite integral whose value equals the volume of the solid formed when R is revolved about the line $y = -1$.

17. Use logarithmic differentiation to compute $\dfrac{f'(x)}{f(x)}$ if $f(x) = x^{x^2}$.

18. Suppose $b > a$ and $\displaystyle\int_a^b f(x) \, dx > 0$. Which of the following must be true?

    (a) $f > 0$ for all values of x in the interval $[a, b]$ (b) $\displaystyle\int_b^a f(x) \, dx < 0$

    (c) f is an even function   (d)   If $a < c < b$, then $\displaystyle\int_a^c f(x) \, dx > 0$

19. Differentiate: $y = xe^{x^2} - \sqrt{x^3 + 1} - \dfrac{\cot x + x}{e^{-x} - 1}$

CONCEPT REVIEW   **20.** Let f be a function defined as follows:

$$f(x) = \begin{cases} ae^x + b & \text{when } x \ge 0 \\ \pi x & x < 0 \end{cases}$$

Find the values of a and b which make f continuous and differentiable everywhere.

21. Suppose f is differentiable for all real values of x and

$$f(x + h) - f(x) = x^2 h + 3h^3 \qquad \text{for all real values of } h$$

Evaluate $f'(3)$. *Hint*: Recall the definition of the derivative when you look at $f(x + h) - f(x)$:

$$f'(x) = \lim_{h \to 0} \dfrac{f(x + h) - f(x)}{h}$$

Then substitute $x^2 h + 3h^3$ in the numerator to find $f'(x)$. Then find $f'(3)$.

LESSON 115 *Partial fractions III*

If the denominator of a fraction of polynomials contains an irreducible quadratic factor, the numerator of the partial fraction decomposition must contain one term whose numerator is a linear term of the form $Ax + B$ and whose denominator is the irreducible quadratic factor. For example, the partial fraction decomposition shown here has a numerator $Ax + B$ for the quadratic denominator $x^2 + 1$ and a numerator of C for the linear denominator $x - 1$.

$$\int \frac{4x^2 - 2x + 2}{(x^2 + 1)(x - 1)} \, dx = \int \frac{Ax + B}{x^2 + 1} \, dx + \int \frac{C}{x - 1} \, dx$$

To find the constants A, B, and C, we will find three independent equations in A, B, and C and solve this system of equations for A, B, and C. To do this we will use the fact that a polynomial equals zero for every value of x if and only if every coefficient in the polynomial equals zero. For the polynomial

$$ax^2 + bx + c$$

to equal zero for all x values, a, b, and c would all have to equal zero. We can use this fact to argue that two polynomials are equal if every pair of corresponding coefficients are equal. For example, if these polynomials are equal,

$$5x^2 + 4x + 1 = ax^2 + bx + c$$

a must equal 5, b must equal 4, and c must equal 1. To show why this is so, we can add $-(ax^2 + bx + c)$ to both sides, combine like terms, and get

$$x^2(5 - a) + x(4 - b) + (1 - c) = 0$$

If $a = 5$, $b = 4$, and $c = 1$, then this polynomial equals zero for all values of x.

Now to find the values of A, B, and C in the expansion

$$\frac{4x^2 - 2x + 2}{(x^2 + 1)(x - 1)} = \frac{Ax + B}{x^2 + 1} + \frac{C}{x - 1}$$

we first find common denominators to add the two terms on the right of the equals sign.

$$\frac{4x^2 - 2x + 2}{(x^2 + 1)(x - 1)} = \frac{(Ax + B)(x - 1)}{(x^2 + 1)(x - 1)} + \frac{C(x^2 + 1)}{(x - 1)(x^2 + 1)}$$

If, in the numerator, we multiply $(Ax + B)$ by $(x - 1)$, and multiply C by $(x^2 + 1)$ and combine like terms, we get

$$\frac{4x^2 - 2x + 2}{(x^2 + 1)(x - 1)} = \frac{(A + C)x^2 + (B - A)x + (C - B)}{(x^2 + 1)(x - 1)}$$

For the numerator on the left-hand side to equal the numerator on the right-hand side, the coefficients of the x^2 terms must be equal, the coefficients of the x terms must be equal, and the constant terms must be equal.

$$\begin{cases} 4 = A + C & \text{coefficients of } x^2 \\ -2 = B - A & \text{coefficients of } x \\ 2 = C - B & \text{constant terms} \end{cases}$$

If we solve this system, we find

$$A = 2 \qquad B = 0 \qquad C = 2$$

Now we can write

$$\frac{4x^2 - 2x + 2}{(x^2 + 1)(x - 1)} = \frac{2x}{x^2 + 1} + \frac{2}{x - 1}$$

The integral of the expression on the left equals the sum of the integrals of the expressions on the right.

$$\int \frac{4x^2 - 2x + 2}{(x^2 + 1)(x - 1)} \, dx = \int \frac{2x \, dx}{x^2 + 1} + \int \frac{2 \, dx}{x - 1} = \ln |x^2 + 1| + 2 \ln |x - 1| + C$$

Example 115.1 Find $\int \frac{6x^2 - 3x + 1}{(4x + 1)(x^2 + 1)} \, dx$.

Solution The first step is to decompose the fraction into a sum of partial fractions.

$$\frac{6x^2 - 3x + 1}{(4x + 1)(x^2 + 1)} = \frac{Ax + B}{x^2 + 1} + \frac{C}{4x + 1}$$

Now we add the terms on the right-hand side of the equals sign and get

$$\frac{6x^2 - 3x + 1}{(4x + 1)(x^2 + 1)} = \frac{(Ax + B)(4x + 1) + C(x^2 + 1)}{(x^2 + 1)(4x + 1)}$$

If we multiply as indicated in the numerator, we get

$$\frac{6x^2 - 3x + 1}{(4x + 1)(x^2 + 1)} = \frac{4Ax^2 + Ax + 4Bx + B + Cx^2 + C}{(4x + 1)(x^2 + 1)}$$

Next we simplify and get

$$\frac{6x^2 - 3x + 1}{(4x + 1)(x^2 + 1)} = \frac{(4A + C)x^2 + (A + 4B)x + (B + C)}{(4x + 1)(x^2 + 1)}$$

If we equate coefficients, we get three equations in A, B, and C.

$$\begin{cases} 6 = 4A + C & \text{coefficients of } x^2 \\ -3 = A + 4B & \text{coefficients of } x \\ 1 = B + C & \text{constant terms} \end{cases}$$

We solve this system and find $A = 1$, $B = -1$, and $C = 2$. Thus we can write

$$\int \frac{6x^2 - 3x + 1}{(4x + 1)(x^2 + 1)} \, dx = \int \frac{x - 1}{x^2 + 1} \, dx + \int \frac{2 \, dx}{4x + 1}$$

The first integral can be written as the sum of two integrals, so we have

$$\int \frac{x \, dx}{x^2 + 1} - \int \frac{dx}{x^2 + 1} + \int \frac{2 \, dx}{4x + 1}$$

If we insert the required constants, we get

$$\frac{1}{2} \int \frac{2x \, dx}{x^2 + 1} - \int \frac{dx}{x^2 + 1} + \frac{1}{2} \int \frac{4 \, dx}{4x + 1}$$

$$= \frac{1}{2} \ln |x^2 + 1| - \tan^{-1} x + \frac{1}{2} \ln |4x + 1| + C$$

Problem set 115 1. A particle moves along the elliptical path defined by the equation

$$\frac{x^2}{9} + \frac{y^2}{8} = 1$$

Find the rate of change of the y coordinate of the particle the instant the particle passes through the point $(1, \frac{8}{3})$ if the x coordinate is increasing at a rate of 1 unit per second at that instant.

2.   Use differentials to approximate the cube root of 124.

3.   The region R is bounded by the graphs of $y = e^x$, $x = 0$, and $y = e^2$. Use one variable to write a definite integral whose value equals the volume of the solid formed when R is rotated about the line $x = -1$.

4.   The slope of the tangent line which can be drawn to the graph of a particular equation at any point (x, y) on its graph is x/y. Find the equation of the curve if the graph passes through the point $(1, 3)$.

5.   A variable force $F(x) = x\sqrt{x^2 - 1}$ newtons is used to propel an object along the x axis. Find the work done in moving the object from $x = 1$ to $x = 5$ meters.

Integrate using the method of partial fractions:

6. $\displaystyle \int \frac{3x^2 - x}{(x^2 + 1)(x - 1)} \, dx$

7. $\displaystyle \int \frac{-x^2 + 2x - 3}{(x^2 + 2)(x + 1)} \, dx$

8. $\displaystyle \int \frac{-x^2 + 2}{(x + 1)^2(x + 2)} \, dx$

9. $\displaystyle \int \frac{3x^2 + 7x + 6}{x^2(x + 2)} \, dx$

10.   Use implicit differentiation to find $\dfrac{d^2y}{dx^2}$ if $y^3 - x^2 = y$.

11.   Find the area between the graph of $y = \cot^2 x$ and the x axis on the interval $[\pi/4, 3\pi/4]$.

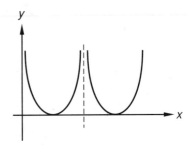

12.   Suppose f is a one-to-one function such that

$$f(x) = \frac{x + 1}{x}$$

Write the equation of f^{-1} and evaluate $f^{-1}(2)$ and $(f^{-1})'(2)$.

13.   The mean value theorem tells us that if f is continuous on $[a, b]$ and differentiable on (a, b), then there is some number $c \in (a, b)$ such that

$$f'(c) = \frac{f(b) - f(a)}{b - a}$$

If $f(x) = x^3 + 1$ meets the conditions, find such a number c in $(-1, 3)$.

Integrate:

14. $\displaystyle \int \sin^2 x \, dx$

15. $\displaystyle \int \sin^3 x \cos^2 x \, dx$

16. $\displaystyle \int 10^x \, dx$

17. $\displaystyle \int \frac{2x + 1}{\sqrt{x^2 + x + 1}} \, dx$

18. $\displaystyle \int x^2 e^x \, dx$

19. $\displaystyle \int \frac{4}{\sqrt{4 - x^2}} \, dx$

20. Write the equations of all the asymptotes of $f(x) = \dfrac{x}{1 - x^2}$ and sketch the graph of f.

21. Differentiate: $y = x \ln |x^3 - 1| - \sec 2x$

CONCEPT REVIEW   **22.** Let p be a cubic function whose equation is

$$p(x) = x^3 + bx^2 + cx + d$$

Suppose that p is an odd function and that p has local extreme points at $x = q$ and $x = -q$. Find b, c, and d. *Hint*: Every term in an odd polynomial function must have an odd exponent for x, so this tells us that the values of b and d must be 0. Then find dp/dx and find where $dp/dx = 0$. The coefficients must be chosen so that $dp/dx = 0$ at $x = q$ and $x = -q$.

LESSON 116 *Derivative of e^x and of ln x · Derivative of sin x*

116.A

Derivative of e^x and of ln x

In precalculus mathematics we defined the natural exponential function to be the exponential function whose base is e. Then we defined the natural logarithm function to be the inverse function of the natural exponential function. The base of the natural logarithm function is also e. We designate this function by writing either $\log_e x$ or $\ln x$.

FUNCTION		INVERSE FUNCTION
$y = e^x$	$\xrightarrow{\text{by definition}}$	$y = \log_e x$

We can use this defined relationship to prove that the derivative of e^x is e^x if we have already proved that the derivative of $\ln x$ is 1 over x. We remember that x is the symbol we usually use for the independent variable, but any other letter can be used.

$$\frac{d}{dx} \ln x = \frac{1}{x} \qquad \frac{d}{dz} \ln z = \frac{1}{z} \qquad \frac{d}{dy} \ln y = \frac{1}{y}$$

If we wish to find the derivative of e^x, we begin by writing

$$y = e^x$$

We want to find dy/dx. We begin by writing the implicit form of the same function as

$$x = \ln y$$

Now we take the differential of both sides and get

$$dx = \frac{1}{y} \, dy$$

Now if we divide both sides of the equation by dx and solve for dy/dx, we get

$$\frac{dy}{dx} = y$$

But we began by stating that y was equal to e^x, so if we replace y with e^x, we get

$$\frac{dy}{dx} = e^x$$

Thus the process of proving that the derivative of e^x is e^x is very straightforward if we have already proved that the derivative of $\ln y$ is 1 over y.

Calculus books usually use one of two different methods to prove that the derivative of $\ln x$ is 1 over x. Calculus books written before 1950 used a proof that was easy to understand but required that certain assumptions be made that authors of recent calculus books do not have to make because they use a different proof. The old way was to begin with the exponential function

$$y = e^x$$

where e is defined by either of the following limits:

$$(a) \quad e = \lim_{\Delta x \to 0} \left(1 + \frac{\Delta x}{x}\right)^{\frac{x}{\Delta x}} \quad \text{or} \quad (b) \quad e = \lim_{x \to \infty} \left(1 + \frac{1}{x}\right)^x$$

These limits are equal. In the left-hand expression x is some constant and Δx is a variable that is approaching zero. In the right-hand expression x is the variable and is increasing without bound. In both expressions the number inside the parentheses is a little greater than 1 and is approaching 1, and the exponent is increasing without bound. It would seem, at first glance, that the limit would be 1 because the number inside the parentheses is approaching 1 as a limit. However, because the exponent is increasing without bound, the value of the expression approaches an irrational number that is slightly greater than 2.718. To make a quick approximation of this number, we will use the expression on the right above, use the y^x key on a calculator, and let $x = 100$.

$$\left(1 + \frac{1}{100}\right)^{100} = (1.01)^{100} = 2.704813829$$

If we let x equal 1000, we get

$$\left(1 + \frac{1}{1000}\right)^{1000} = (1.001)^{1000} = 2.71692393$$

If we let x get larger and larger, the value of this expression will get closer and closer to the number we call e. This definition of e as a limit is necessary because the limit in the (a) definition of e above appears if we use the definition of a derivative to develop the derivative of $\log_e x$, as we will show.

$$\frac{d}{dx} \log_e x = \lim_{x \to 0} \frac{\log_e (x + \Delta x) - \log_e x}{\Delta x}$$

The next step is to write 1 over Δx as a factor of the difference of the two logarithms.

$$\frac{d}{dx} \log_e x = \lim_{\Delta x \to 0} \frac{1}{\Delta x} [\log_e (x + \Delta x) - \log_e x]$$

Since the difference of two logarithms can be written as the logarithm of a quotient, we can write

$$\frac{d}{dx} \log_e x = \lim_{\Delta x \to 0} \frac{1}{\Delta x} \log_e \left(\frac{x + \Delta x}{x}\right)$$

But the expression in parentheses does not have the exponent we want. We get the exponent by using a trick. We first insert a factor of x over x, which equals 1 as long as x is a nonzero real number, so the value of the expression is unchanged.

$$\frac{d}{dx} \log_e x = \lim_{\Delta x \to 0} \frac{1}{\Delta x} \cdot \frac{x}{x} \log_e \left(\frac{x + \Delta x}{x}\right)$$

Next we rearrange the two *x*'s and the Δx to get

$$\frac{d}{dx} \log_e x = \lim_{\Delta x \to 0} \frac{1}{x} \cdot \frac{x}{\Delta x} \log_e \left(\frac{x + \Delta x}{x}\right)$$

Now we can use the power rule for logarithms, which tells us that we can write the expression $x/\Delta x \, \log_e \, (\ )$ as $\log_e \, (\ )^{x/\Delta x}$. So now we have

$$\frac{d}{dx} \log_e x = \lim_{\Delta x \to 0} \frac{1}{x} \log_e \left(1 + \frac{\Delta x}{x}\right)^{x/\Delta x}$$

The variable in this expression is Δx and *x* is a constant. Thus we can write 1 over *x* in front of the limit notation.

$$\frac{d}{dx} \log_e x = \frac{1}{x} \lim_{\Delta x \to 0} \log_e \left(1 + \frac{\Delta x}{x}\right)^{x/\Delta x}$$

But, as Δx approaches zero, $(1 + \Delta x/x)^{x/\Delta x}$ approaches the number we call *e*. We assume that this limit exists, and now we have

$$\frac{d}{dx} \log_e x = \frac{1}{x} \cdot \log_e e$$

As the last step we note that the logarithm of *e* to the base *e* is 1, so

$$\frac{d}{dx} \log_e x = \frac{1}{x} \cdot 1 = \frac{1}{x}$$

This development was straightforward but required that we assume that e^x is continuous for all real values of *x*. This requirement does not bother beginning calculus students but causes mathematicians some concern, especially since it can be avoided. In Lesson 105 we discussed the second fundamental theorem of calculus, which assures us that every continuous function has an antiderivative and gives us a method of using an integral to define the antiderivative. The function

$$y = \frac{1}{x}$$

is continuous for all positive values of *x* and is the slope of the graph of the natural logarithm function $y = \log_e x$. If we use the second fundamental theorem of calculus to define the natural logarithm function to be the continuous function whose derivative is 1 over *x*, we take care of the continuity problem.

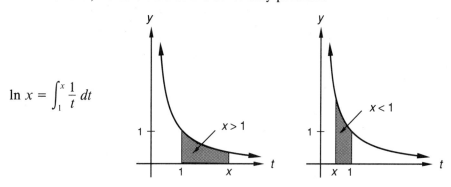

$$\ln x = \int_1^x \frac{1}{t} \, dt$$

This new definition of ln *x* equates the value of ln *x* to the area under the graph of $y = 1/t$ between 1 and *x* if *x* is greater than 1, as we show in the left-hand figure. If *x* is less than 1, as in the right-hand figure, the value of the integral will be negative, so ln x equals the negative of the area under the curve between 1 and x. For this development, instead of beginning with e^x and defining the inverse function to be ln x, we have begun with a definition of ln x, and now we define the inverse of this function to be **exp x.**

	FUNCTION		INVERSE FUNCTION
Old way	$y = e^x$	$\xrightarrow{\text{by definition}}$	$y = \log_e x$

	INVERSE FUNCTION		FUNCTION
New way	$y = \exp x$	$\xleftarrow{\text{by definition}}$	$y = \ln x$

We note that the old way used a base of e for both the natural exponential and the natural logarithm. The new way defines ln x as the function whose derivative is $1/x$ and makes no mention of a base. This is the reason that we designated the inverse of ln x with the notation exp x instead of e^x. We wanted to call attention to the fact that this function has a different development than e^x has and that exp x has no base.

At is possible to prove that $y = \exp x$ has all the properties of $y = e^x$ and thus is another way of writing the function $y = e^x$. Thus the new definition of ln x takes care of the continuity problem but really changes nothing, and it is still acceptable to think of the natural logarithm function and the natural exponential function as functions that have a base of e. In the following example we do one of these proofs that show that ln x has the same properties that $\log_e x$ has.

Example 116.1   Show that ln ab = ln a + ln b if a and b are any positive numbers.

Solution   We want to show that

$$\ln ab = \ln a + \ln b$$

But we need a variable, so we will replace b with x and will make the reverse substitution as the last step. Now we have

$$\ln ax \overset{?}{=} \ln a + \ln x$$

We do not know if this is a true statement of equality, but if it is a true statement, the derivative of the left-hand side must differ from the derivative of the right-hand side by a constant. We will show that the constant is zero. First we find the derivative of both sides.

$$\frac{d}{dx} \ln ax \overset{?}{=} \frac{d}{dx} \ln a + \frac{d}{dx} \ln x$$

We remember to use the chain rule to find the first derivative of ln ax, and we get

$$\frac{1}{ax}(a) \overset{?}{=} 0 + \frac{1}{x} \qquad \text{derivative}$$

$$\frac{1}{x} = \frac{1}{x} \qquad \text{simplified}$$

The derivatives are equal, so the functions differ by a constant. Thus we can write

$$\ln ax = \ln a + \ln x + C$$

This must be true for all positive values of x. If we let $x = 1$, we can find C in one step.

$$\ln a(1) = \ln a + \ln 1 + C \quad \longrightarrow \quad \ln a = \ln a + C \quad \longrightarrow \quad C = 0$$

Thus, because the derivatives differ by a constant and the constant is zero, the original statement is true. Thus

$$\ln ab = \ln a + \ln b$$

which is a property of the natural logarithm when defined by using e as the base.

116.B
Proof of the derivative of sin x (optional)

To prove that the derivative of sin x is cos x, we must first show that

$$\lim_{x \to 0} \frac{1 - \cos x}{x} = 0$$

To do this, we first multiply by $1 + \cos x$ over $1 + \cos x$ and mentally restrict x to values close to zero so that $1 + \cos x$ does not equal zero.

$$\lim_{x \to 0} \frac{1 - \cos x}{x} \left(\frac{1 + \cos x}{1 + \cos x} \right) \longrightarrow \lim_{x \to 0} \frac{1 - \cos^2 x}{x(1 + \cos x)}$$

But $1 - \cos^2 x = \sin^2 x$, and this substitution allows us to write the limit as a product.

$$\lim_{x \to 0} \frac{\sin^2 x}{x(1 + \cos x)} = \lim_{x \to 0} \frac{\sin x}{x} \cdot \frac{\sin x}{1 + \cos x}$$

Now we rewrite the limit of the product as a product of two limits and get

$$\lim_{x \to 0} \frac{\sin x}{x} \cdot \lim_{x \to 0} \frac{\sin x}{1 + \cos x}$$

In Lesson 107 we used a geometric proof to show that the limit of sin x over x as x approaches zero is 1. The limit of sin x over $1 + \cos x$ as x approaches zero is zero because sin x approaches zero and $1 + \cos x$ approaches 2. Thus

$$\lim_{x \to 0} \frac{\sin x}{x} = 1 \qquad \lim_{x \to 0} \frac{\sin x}{1 + \cos x} = \frac{0}{2} = 0$$

Thus the product of these limits is $1(0) = 0$. So we have shown that

$$\lim_{x \to 0} \frac{1 - \cos x}{x} = 0$$

The next step in the proof of the derivative of sin x requires that we use the definition of the derivative and the identity for sin $(A + B)$. The rest of the proof is just an application of the algebra of limits. First we use the definition of the derivative to write

$$\frac{d}{dx} \sin x = \lim_{\Delta x \to 0} \frac{\sin (x + \Delta x) - \sin x}{\Delta x}$$

Next we remember that sin $(A + B) = \sin A \cos B + \cos A \sin B$. If we let $A = x$ and let $B = \Delta x$, we can substitute for sin $(x + \Delta x)$ and get

$$\frac{d}{dx} \sin x = \lim_{\Delta x \to 0} \frac{\sin x \cos \Delta x + \sin \Delta x \cos x - \sin x}{\Delta x}$$

Then we rearrange the terms in the numerator.

$$\frac{d}{dx} \sin x = \lim_{\Delta x \to 0} \frac{\sin x \cos \Delta x - \sin x + \sin \Delta x \cos x}{\Delta x}$$

Now we factor the first two terms in the numerator.

$$\frac{d}{dx} \sin x = \lim_{\Delta x \to 0} \frac{(\sin x)(\cos \Delta x - 1) + \sin \Delta x \cos x}{\Delta x}$$

Since the limit of a sum equals the sum of the individual limits, we can write

$$\frac{d}{dx} \sin x = \lim_{\Delta x \to 0} (\sin x)\left(\frac{\cos \Delta x - 1}{\Delta x}\right) + \lim_{\Delta x \to 0} (\cos x)\left(\frac{\sin \Delta x}{\Delta x}\right)$$

In these limits the variable is Δx, so $\sin x$ and $\cos x$ can be treated as constants and can be written in front of the limit notations. Now we have

$$\frac{d}{dx} \sin x = (\sin x)\left(\lim_{\Delta x \to 0} \frac{\cos \Delta x - 1}{\Delta x}\right) + (\cos x)\left(\lim_{\Delta x \to 0} \frac{\sin \Delta x}{\Delta x}\right)$$

But the first of these limits equals zero and the second limit equals 1, so finally we have

$$\frac{d}{dx} \sin x = (\sin x)(0) + (\cos x)(1) = \mathbf{\cos x}$$

Problem set 116

1. Determine the absolute maximum and the absolute minimum values of the function $f(x) = xe^{-2x}$ on the interval $[0, 10]$.

2. A closed cylindrical barrel whose radius is 1 meter is positioned on its side. The barrel is half-filled with a fluid that has a weight density of 400 newtons per cubic meter. Find the force of the fluid against one circular end of the barrel.

Write the value of the following limits by inspection:

3. $\lim\limits_{x \to \infty} \left(1 + \dfrac{1}{x}\right)^x$

4. $\lim\limits_{\Delta x \to 0} \dfrac{\sin (x + \Delta x) - \sin x}{\Delta x}$

5. $\lim\limits_{\Delta x \to 0} \dfrac{1}{x} \log_e \left(1 + \dfrac{\Delta x}{x}\right)^{x/\Delta x}$

Integrate by using either integration by parts or the method of partial fractions:

6. $\displaystyle\int \frac{3x^2 - x + 4}{x(x^2 + 4)} \, dx$

7. $\displaystyle\int \frac{4x^2 - 3x + 5}{(x^2 + 1)(x - 1)} \, dx$

8. $\displaystyle\int x^2 \ln x \, dx$

9. $\displaystyle\int 2 \, e^x \sin x \, dx$

10. Use implicit differentiation to find $\dfrac{d^2y}{dx^2}$ if $x = \sin y + y$.

11. Graph $r = 2 - 2 \sin \theta$ on a polar coordinate plane.

12. Write the rectangular form of the polar equation $r^2 = \sin^2 \theta - 2 \cos^2 \theta$.

Evaluate the following limits:

13. $\lim\limits_{x \to 0} \dfrac{\tan 2x}{3x}$

14. $\lim\limits_{x \to \infty} \dfrac{x - x \ln x}{1 + x^2}$

15. If $\dfrac{d}{dx} \displaystyle\int_x^3 e^{\sin t} \, dt$, find the approximate value of $f(1)$.

16. The region R is bounded by the x axis and the graphs of $y = \sec x$, $x = -\pi/4$, and $x = \pi/4$. Write an integral in one variable whose value equals the volume of the solid formed when R is revolved about the line $x = \pi/2$.

17. Write a fraction of definite integrals whose value equals the x coordinate of the centroid of the region bounded by the x axis and the graph of $y = e^{x^3}$ on the interval $[0, 1]$.

18. The mean value theorem for integrals tells us that every continuous function attains its average value on an interval at some number c in the interval. If $v(t) = 3t^2 - 2t$, find such a number c in the interval $[0, 2]$.

19. Differentiate: $y = \arctan (\sin x) - \dfrac{2^x}{e^{2x} - \sin x}$

CONCEPT REVIEW 20. Let the closed interval $I = [1, 10]$ be subdivided into n equally long subintervals. Let x_i be the leftmost endpoint of the ith subinterval. Determine the value of

$$\lim_{n \to \infty} \frac{9}{n} \sum_{i=1}^{n} \frac{1}{x_i}$$

LESSON 117 *Proofs of the fundamental theorem ·*
Epsilon delta proofs

117.A
Proofs of the
fundamental
theorem

We will begin with a proof of the fundamental theorem that is typical of the proofs of this theorem in calculus books published in the first half of the twentieth century. We will prove that if we have a continuous function f whose graph is never below the x axis on the interval $[a, b]$, the area between the graph and the x axis on the same interval equals the value of any antiderivative F evaluated at b reduced by the value of the same antiderivative evaluated at a.

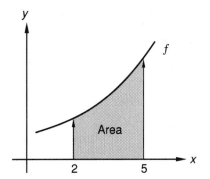
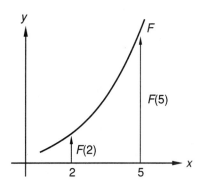

Thus, for the functions f and some antiderivative F, shown above, we would like to prove that the area under f between 2 and 5 equals $F(5) - F(2)$. To prove this we will introduce another function, $A(x)$, that we will call the *area function.* On the left on the next page we designate f as the ceiling function and consider that the area shown is "generated" or "swept out" by the left-to-right movement of the vertical segment that connects the x axis and the graph.

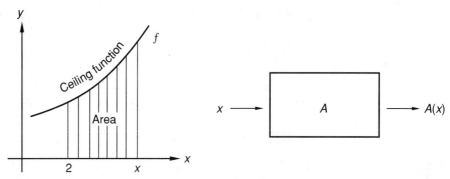

We hypothesize the existence of the area function machine shown on the right. The output $A(x)$ of this machine will equal the area under the curve to the left of x and to the right of 2. We note one characteristic that this function must possess. If $x = 2$, the segment that will sweep out the area has not yet moved, so the value of $A(2)$ must be zero.

$$A(2) = 0$$

The proof will consists of demonstrating that the derivative of $A(x)$ is $f(x)$. Since we already know that $F(x)$ is also an antiderivative of $f(x)$, then $F(x)$ and $A(x)$ must differ by a constant.

$$A(x) = F(x) + C$$

But we already know that $A(2) = 0$. If we let x equal 2, we get

$$A(2) = F(2) + C \qquad \text{let } x = 2$$
$$0 = F(2) + C \qquad A(2) = 0$$
$$C = -F(2) \qquad \text{solved for } C$$

Now that we have found the value of C, we can write a general expression for the area.

$$A(x) = F(x) - F(2)$$

Now, to find the area generated if the segment moves out to $x = 5$, we let x equal 5 and get

$$A(5) = F(5) - F(2)$$

But $A(5)$ equals the integral from 2 to 5 of $f(x)\, dx$, so finally we have

$$\int_2^5 f(x)\, dx = F(5) - F(2)$$

where F is some antiderivative of f. We now provide the missing step by showing that the derivative of the area function A is f. We can do this by looking at the following figures.

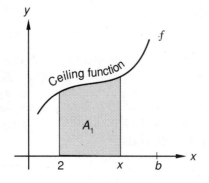

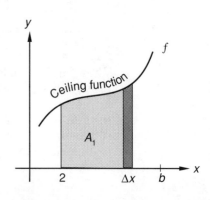

In the figure on the left the moving segment has swept out one area that we call A_1. Now if the segment moves a small distance Δx to the right, it will sweep out a small additional rectangular area ΔA. The height of the rectangle is $f(x)$ and the width is Δx, so we may write

$$\Delta A = f(x)\,\Delta x$$

If we divide both sides by Δx and find the limit as Δx approaches zero, we get

$$\lim_{\Delta x \to 0} \frac{\Delta A}{\Delta x} = f(x) \quad \longrightarrow \quad \frac{dA}{dx} = f(x)$$

This last step gives us the connection between the area under the curve and the derivative because it shows us that the instantaneous rate at which area is generated at a particular value of x is equal to the value of f at that instant.

The proof just presented is an informal proof that uses area as its justification. There are many proofs of the fundamental theorem that do not require that area be used. We will show two of them here. First we will restate the theorem.

FUNDAMENTAL THEOREM OF INTEGRAL CALCULUS

If f is continuous on $[a, b]$ and if F is an antiderivative of f on $[a, b]$, then

$$\int_a^b f(x)\,dx = F(b) - F(a)$$

Instead of using area, we will use the second fundamental theorem of integral calculus, which tells us that if a function f is continuous on $[a, b]$, then f must have an antiderivative G on $[a, b]$, and the antiderivative can be defined as

(1) $$G(x) = \int_a^x f(x)\,dx$$

Since both G and F are antiderivatives of f, the derivative of G equals f and the derivative of F equals f.

$$G' = f \quad \text{and} \quad F' = f$$

But a corollary of the mean value theorem tells us that any two functions that have the same derivative differ by a constant. Thus F and G differ by a constant, so we can write

(2) $$G(x) = F(x) + C$$

To find the value of the constant C, we let x equal a and get

$$G(a) = F(a) + C$$

This allows us to solve for C because $G(a)$ as defined by equation (1) is zero since in Lesson 66 we defined the integral of $f(x)$ from a to a to be zero. Thus we have

$$0 = F(a) + C \quad \longrightarrow \quad C = -F(a)$$

Now we substitute $-F(a)$ for C in equation (2) and get

(3) $$G(x) = F(x) - F(a)$$

The definition of G is given by equation (1), and we now have equation (3), which is another expression for G. If we equate (1) and (3), we get

$$\int_a^x f(x)\,dx = F(x) - F(a)$$

Now if we let the upper limit equal b, we can write

$$\int_a^b f(x)\,dx = F(b) - F(a)$$

We note that in the informal proof we used area to link the left side of the result to the right side and that in this proof we used the function G for the same purpose. We also note that neither of these proofs mentioned or even considered Riemann sums. Thus the definite integral, as can be defined by Riemann sums, can be entirely divorced from the definite integral of the fundamental theorem of integral calculus. But we can use the mean value theorem to connect these ideas. Again we want to show that

$$\int_a^b f(x)\,dx = F(b) - F(a)$$

where F is an antiderivative of the continuous function f. The integral is the limit of a Riemann sum that we can associate graphically with the area under F' between a and b, as we show on the left below, and we can picture $F(b) - F(a)$ as the difference in the distances from the x axis to the graph of F at b and at a, as we show on the right below.

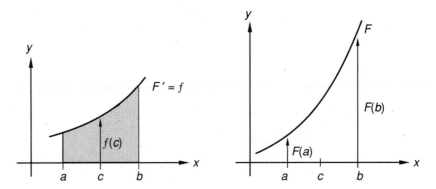

The mean value theorem tells us that for any continuous function F there exists some c on an interval $[a, b]$ such that

$$F'(c) = \frac{F(b) - F(a)}{b - a}$$

But $F'(c) = f(c)$, and if we make this substitution and then multiply both sides by $b - a$, we get

$$f(c)(b - a) = F(b) - F(a)$$

We see that the left-hand side is a gross approximation of the area which we want to represent by using a Riemann integral. To get a better approximation, we will partition $[a, b]$ into n subintervals and apply the above process to each subinterval.

The left-hand side of the first interval is x_0, which equals a, and the right-hand side of the nth subinterval is x_n, which equals b. We will use Δx_i as the width of the ith subinterval and use c_i as the number in the ith subinterval designated by the mean value theorem. We note that the right-hand side of the third subinterval is at x_3 and that the left-hand side is at x_2. Thus for the ith subinterval the right-hand side would be at x_i and the left-hand side would be at x_{i-1}. Thus $F(b) - F(a)$ for the ith subinterval would be written $F(x_i) - F(x_{i-1})$. To apply the mean value theorem to the ith subinterval, we would write

$$F'(c_i) = \frac{F(x_i) - F(x_{i-1})}{\Delta x_i}$$

We remember that $F'(c_i)$ is the same as $f(c_i)$, and if we make this substitution and multiply both sides by Δx_i, we get

$$f(c_i)\,\Delta x_i = F(x_i) - F(x_{i-1})$$

Now, if we sum the expressions on both sides of this equation for all n subintervals, we get

$$\sum_{i=1}^{n} f(c_i)\,\Delta x_i = \sum_{i=1}^{n} [F(x_i) - F(x_{i-1})]$$

The left-hand side of this expression is a Riemann sum, and if we increase the number of partitions as the length of the largest subinterval $\|p\|$ approaches zero, the left-hand side is the Riemann integral and becomes

$$\lim_{\|p\| \to 0} \sum_{i=1}^{n} f(c_i)\,\Delta x_i = \int_a^b f(x)\,dx$$

The right-hand side equals $F(b) - F(a)$. It is a series that is sometimes called a ***telescoping sum*** because all terms except the first and the last appear once with a plus sign and once with a minus sign and thus sum to zero. To see why we note that the right-hand side of the last subinterval is at b, which equals x_n, and the left-hand side is at x_{n-1}, so the last two terms in the series are

$$F(x_n) - F(x_{n-1})$$

The right side of the next to the last interval is at x_{n-1}, and the left side is at x_{n-2}. So the last four terms in the series are

$$F(x_n) - F(x_{n-1}) + F(x_{n-1}) - F(x_{n-2})$$

We see that the second to last and third to last terms have opposite signs and thus sum to zero. When the next interval is considered, the $F(x_{n-2})$ term will cancel, and, finally, the only terms that remain will be the first term and the last term.

$$F(x_n) + - + - + - + - \cdots - F(x_0)$$

But $F(x_n) = F(b)$ and $F(x_0) = F(a)$, so finally we have

$$\int_a^b f(x)\,dx = F(b) - F(a)$$

which completes the proof.

117.B
Epsilon delta proofs

Consider the function $y = \frac{1}{2}x - 1$. As the value of x gets closer and closer to 8, the value of y gets closer and closer to 3. This happens whether x approaches 8 from the left or from the right, and we say that the limit of y as x approaches 8 is 3.

$$\lim_{x \to 8} \left(\frac{1}{2}x - 1 \right) = 3$$

But how close is close? The student asked how far x could be from 8 for the value of y to be within ± 0.01 of 3. The teacher's answer was that x had to be within $\pm 2(0.01)$ of 8. The student asked how far x could be from 8 for the value of y to be within ± 0.007 of 3. The teacher's answer was that as long as x was within $\pm 2(0.007)$ of 8, the value of y would be within ± 0.007 of 3. The student asked how far x could be from 8 for the value of y to be within $\pm \varepsilon$ of 3. The teacher's answer was that as long as x was within $\pm 2\varepsilon$ of 8, the value of y would be within $\pm \varepsilon$ of 3, where ε is a positive number. The teacher had found a rule that could be used to select values of x that would yield values of y within the limits specified by the student's choice of acceptable error in y. We use the Greek letter ε (epsilon) to symbolize this error. The rule for this example is to multiply the student's choice of acceptable error by 2. The result is the acceptable deviation of x from 8 that will ensure y values that are within the prescribed limits of error. The rule defines acceptable deviations in x, symbolized by $\delta(\varepsilon)$, read "delta of epsilon." This symbol clearly indicates that $\delta(\varepsilon)$ is determined by the student's choice of ε. **Since the teacher has found the rule that can be used to define a range of acceptable values of x for any choice of error in y, no matter how small, we say that the teacher has proved that the limit of $\frac{1}{2}x - 1$ as x approaches 8 is 3.**

The process of determining the rule for finding $\delta(\varepsilon)$ is called an *epsilon delta proof.* If we can find such a rule, we say that we have proved that the limit we have tested is really the limit.

The following figure allows us to consider the problem graphically. It shows a function whose limit is L as x approaches a.

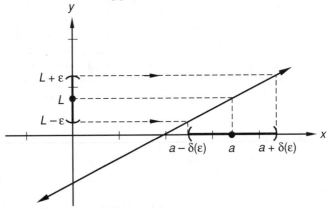

We are accustomed to entering on the x axis and reading out on the y axis. For these proofs the thought process requires that we enter on the y axis with epsilon and read out delta of epsilon on the x axis. We note in the figure that the acceptable y error ε determines $\delta(\varepsilon)$ and allows us to give a rigorous definition of the limit of a real function.

LIMIT OF A FUNCTION

Let f be a function which is defined on some open interval I that contains a, except possibly at the number a. The limit of $f(x)$ as x approaches a is L,

$$\lim_{x \to a} f(x) = L$$

if for any positive number ε, however small, there exists a positive number $\delta(\varepsilon)$ such that

$$L - \varepsilon < y < L + \varepsilon \qquad \text{whenever} \qquad a - \delta(\varepsilon) < x < a + \delta(\varepsilon)$$

Many books use absolute value notation to define the neighborhood bounded by $L - \varepsilon$ and $L + \varepsilon$ and the neighborhood bounded by $a - \delta(\varepsilon)$ and $a + \delta(\varepsilon)$. We remember that $|x - 1|$ can be interpreted geometrically as the distance from x to 1. Thus $|f(x) - L|$ is the distance from $f(x)$ to L. We want this distance to be less than ε. Also $|x - a|$ is the distance from x to a which is to be less than $\delta(\varepsilon)$. Thus we can use absolute value notation to write the last line in the box above as

$$|f(x) - L| < \varepsilon \qquad \text{whenever} \qquad |x - a| < \delta(\varepsilon)$$

The task of finding the delta of epsilon rule is not always an easy task. To illustrate the procedure, we will use linear functions in the next two examples.

Example 117.1   Prove that $\lim\limits_{x \to 2} (2x + 5) = 9$.

Solution   We are asked to find a rule for finding $\delta(\varepsilon)$ so that the distance between 9 and y will be less than ε, no matter how small a value of ε is chosen. Thus y must lie between $9 - \varepsilon$ and $9 + \varepsilon$.

$$9 - \varepsilon < y < 9 + \varepsilon$$

The value of y equals $2x + 5$, so we substitute and get

$$9 - \varepsilon < 2x + 5 < 9 + \varepsilon$$

Now we solve for x.

$$4 - \varepsilon < 2x < 4 + \varepsilon \qquad \text{added} -5$$

$$2 - \frac{\varepsilon}{2} < x < 2 + \frac{\varepsilon}{2} \qquad \text{divided by 2}$$

Thus $\delta(\varepsilon)$ equals $\varepsilon/2$. For any value of ε chosen, an x value between $2 - \varepsilon/2$ and $2 + \varepsilon/2$ will ensure a value of y that differs from 9 by less than ε.

Example 117.2   Prove the following limit by finding a $\delta(\varepsilon)$ greater than zero such that for any ε greater than zero $|f(x) - 4| < \varepsilon$ whenever $|x - 3| < \delta(\varepsilon)$.

$$\lim\limits_{x \to 3} (3x - 5) = 4$$

Solution   The value of y must be between $4 - \varepsilon$ and $4 + \varepsilon$.

$$4 - \varepsilon < y < 4 + \varepsilon$$

But $y = 3x - 5$, so we substitute and solve for x.

$$4 - \varepsilon < 3x - 5 < 4 + \varepsilon \qquad \text{substituted}$$

$$9 - \varepsilon < 3x < 9 + \varepsilon \qquad \text{added} +5$$

$$3 - \frac{\varepsilon}{3} < x < 3 + \frac{\varepsilon}{3} \qquad \text{divided by 3}$$

Thus we have found that $\delta(\varepsilon) = \varepsilon/3$. For any ε chosen, no matter how small, an x value between $3 - \varepsilon/3$ and $3 + \varepsilon/3$ will yield a value of y that differs from 4 by no more than ε.

Problem set 117

1. Suppose f is a function that is continuous for all real values of x, and F is an antiderivative of f. Which of the following statements must be true?

   (a) $F(x) = \int_a^x f(t)\, dt$ (b) $F'(x) = \int_a^x f(t)\, dt$ (c) $F(x) = \dfrac{d}{dx} \int_a^x f(t)\, dt$

   (d) $F(x)$ and $\int_a^x f(t)\, dt$ differ by at most a constant

2. Let R be the region bounded by the graph of $y = x(x - 3)$ in the fourth quadrant. Write a definite integral in one variable whose value equals the volume of the solid formed when R is revolved about the line $x = 4$.

3. Write a definite integral in one variable whose value equals the volume of the solid formed when region R of Problem 2 is revolved about the line $y = 1$.

4. Suppose a particle moves along the x axis so that its position at time t is given by

$$x(t) = \frac{1}{3} t^3 - \frac{3}{2} t^2 + 2t + 1$$

Over which time intervals is the particle moving to the right? What is the total distance traveled by the particle between $t = 0$ and $t = 3$?

5. Suppose f and g are functions which are continuous for all real values of x. On the interval $[1, 3]$, $f(x) \geq g(x)$, and on the interval $[3, 6]$, $f(x) \leq g(x)$. Which of the following definite integrals equals the area of the region between the graphs of f and g in the interval $[1, 6]$?

(a) $\int_1^3 [f(x) - g(x)]^2 \, dx + \int_3^6 [g(x) - f(x)]^2 \, dx$

(b) $\int_1^3 [f(x) - g(x)] \, dx + \int_3^6 [g(x) - f(x)] \, dx$

(c) $\int_1^3 [g(x) - f(x)] \, dx + \int_3^6 [f(x) - g(x)] \, dx$

(d) $\int_1^6 [f(x) - g(x)] \, dx$ (e) $\int_1^6 [g(x) - f(x)] \, dx$

Evaluate the following limits:

6. $\lim\limits_{h \to \infty} \left(1 + \frac{1}{h}\right)^h$

7. $\lim\limits_{h \to 0} \dfrac{\sin (x + h) - \sin x}{h}$

8. $\lim\limits_{x \to 0^+} \dfrac{|x|}{x}$

9. Use implicit differentiation to find $\dfrac{d^2 y}{dx^2}$ if $xy + y = x^2$.

10. Which of the following definite integrals equals $\int_1^2 \dfrac{e^{\sqrt{x}}}{\sqrt{x}} \, dx$?

(a) $\int_1^2 \dfrac{e^u}{u} \, du$ (b) $\int_1^{\sqrt{2}} \dfrac{e^u}{u} \, du$ (c) $\int_1^{\sqrt{2}} e^u \, du$ (d) $\int_1^{\sqrt{2}} 2e^u \, du$

Integrate:

11. $\displaystyle\int x^2 \cos x \, dx$

12. $\displaystyle\int \dfrac{-x^2 + x - 10}{(x^2 + 9)(x - 1)} \, dx$

13. $\displaystyle\int \dfrac{x^3 - x^2 + x - 2}{x^2(x^2 + 1)} \, dx$

14. $\displaystyle\int \dfrac{8 \, dx}{\sqrt{9 - 4x^2}}$

15. $\displaystyle\int \dfrac{8 \, dx}{9 + 4x^2}$

16. Find $\dfrac{dy}{dx}$ if $y = \arcsin (\tan x) - xe^{-x}$.

17. Find the equation of the line that is normal to the graph of $y = \ln |x|$ at $x = -\frac{1}{2}$.

18. Use logarithmic differentiation to compute y' if $y = (\sqrt{x})^x$.

CONCEPT REVIEW   We can prove that $\lim\limits_{x \to a} f(x) = L$ by demonstrating that for every $\varepsilon > 0$ that we choose, we can find a $\delta(\varepsilon)$ such that if x lies in the open interval $(x - \delta, x + \delta)$, then $f(x)$ lies in the open interval $(L - \varepsilon, L + \varepsilon)$. Prove that the following limits are true.

19. $\lim\limits_{x \to 1} (2x + 4) = 6$

20. $\lim\limits_{x \to 2} (3x - 1) = 5$

21. Use geometric formulas to find the area bounded by the graph of $f(x) = x$ and the x axis on the interval $I = [0, 1]$.

   (a) Divide the interval $[0, 1]$ into n equally long subintervals. Let x_i be the rightmost point of the ith subinterval. Express as a definite integral the sum

$$\lim_{n \to \infty} \sum_{i=1}^{n} \frac{1}{n} f(x_i)$$

   Evaluate this definite integral.

   (b) Describe the ith subinterval and find the value of $f(x_i)$.

   (c) Simplify

$$\sum_{i=1}^{n} \frac{1}{n} f(x_i) \quad \text{using the fact that} \quad \sum_{i=1}^{n} i = \frac{1}{2} n(n + 1)$$

   (d) Evaluate the limit of part (a).

Answers to odd-numbered problems

Problem set A   1. C 3. D 5. $R_1 = \dfrac{xyR_2}{mR_2 - axy}$ 7. $\dfrac{xm + 1}{a(xm + 1) + m}$ 9. $\dfrac{13 - 10\sqrt{2}}{31}$

11. $-3 + 4i$ 13. $x^{3a/2}y^{(a+1)}$ 15. $x^{7/6}y^{-1}$ 17. $8a^{2m+3}(2a^{2m} - 1)$

19. $(a^2 - 3bc)(a^4 + 3a^2bc + 9b^2c^2)$ 21. 495   23. $\dfrac{49}{4}$

Problem set B   1. $\sqrt{65}$ 3. $3y - 4x + 7 = 0$ 5. $x = \dfrac{3}{2} \pm \dfrac{\sqrt{21}}{2}$ 7. $\dfrac{1}{6} \pm \dfrac{\sqrt{83}}{6}i$

9. $(-1 + \sqrt{5}, -1 - \sqrt{5}), (-1 - \sqrt{5}, -1 + \sqrt{5})$ 11. $\dfrac{ax(dt + m)}{b(dt + m) + ct}$

13. $\dfrac{23}{5}\sqrt{10}$ 15. $x^{13/6}y^{11/6}$ 17. $7x^{2b}(2x^{2b-2} - 1)$ 19. 168   21. $\dfrac{-16}{3}$

23. $x = 30$ 25. $x = 25$

Problem set 1   1. Valid   3. If the switch is not on, then the light is not on.   5. 5

7. $\dfrac{y}{5} + \dfrac{x}{\frac{5}{2}} = 1$ 9. $\dfrac{3}{2} \pm \dfrac{\sqrt{19}}{2}i$ 11. $x^2 - 12x - 2 - \dfrac{10}{x - 1}$ 13. 2

15. $\dfrac{43\sqrt{21}}{21}$ 17. $\dfrac{5}{8}$ 19. $(ab - 2x^2y^3)(a^2b^2 + 2abx^2y^3 + 4x^4y^6)$ 21. $a - b$

23. 10,660   25. $x = 1$ 27. $x = 10$ and $y = 20$

Problem set 2   1. 120π ft/min   3. $-\dfrac{1}{4}$ 5. $\dfrac{-3\sqrt{3}}{2} + 1$ 7. $\cos \theta$

9. If a fangle is not a widgit, then two of its marks are equal.

11. $y + 3 = -\dfrac{1}{9}(x + 9) \rightarrow x + 9y + 36 = 0$ 13. $-\dfrac{1}{2} \pm \dfrac{\sqrt{3}}{2}i$ 15. $(2, -2), (-2, 2)$

17. $\dfrac{4}{7}$ 19. $-\dfrac{1}{10} - \dfrac{6}{5}i$ 21. $\dfrac{7}{2}$ 23. $x = 120$

Problem set 3   1. 4 hours   3. 10 days   5. 12:32 $\dfrac{8}{11}$ p.m.   7. $-2\sqrt{2}$ 9. $\dfrac{7}{4}$ 11. $\sin \alpha$

13. 1 and $\dfrac{1}{2}$ 15. $x = 1, y = 2$ 17. $x^2 + ax + a^2$ 19. $\dfrac{1}{5} + \dfrac{2}{5}i$ 21. 153

23. $x = 8$

Problem set 4   1. 12 minutes   3. Sharon = 32 years; Travis = 14 years   5. $\dfrac{130\pi}{3}$ radians/hour

7. (a) 3; (b) 0; (c) 1.2   9. $2x^2 + 4x \Delta x + 2(\Delta x)^2 - 1$

11.   Domain = $\{x \in \mathbb{R} \mid x \geq -1 \text{ and } x \neq 0\}$

13. $\dfrac{\sqrt{3}}{2}$ 15. $\csc x$ 17. Valid   19. $s = 9$ 21. $5 - 2\sqrt{6}$ 23. $x = 10$

Problem set 5   1. 4   3. 10 more days   5. $\dfrac{1}{5}$ m/sec   7. $\left(-\dfrac{1}{2}, -\dfrac{\sqrt{3}}{2}\right)$

9. $y = 2 + 3 \cos \left(x + \dfrac{\pi}{2}\right)$ 11. $f(x + h) = (x + h)^2 - (x + h)$ 13. $\dfrac{1}{4}$

15. $\cos^2 \theta$ 17. I, III   19. Not valid   21. $\dfrac{-1}{x(x + h)}$ 23. C

Problem set 6   **1.** Ignoramuses = 2; savants = 50   **3.** 14 years   **5.** $\dfrac{ad}{c}$

7. $x = 7.2$, $y = 5.4$, $z = 9.6$ **9.** 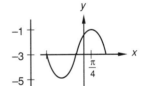   **11.** c **13.** $\sec^2 x$

15. 2   **17.** $x^2 + 2x + 1$

19. $\dfrac{mr^2 - pr^2y - my}{pr^2 + m}$

21. $x = 3$ **23.** $y = 2$

Problem set 7   **1.** $5\dfrac{5}{11}$ minutes   **3.** $6\dfrac{2}{13}$ hours   **5.** $2\left(x - \dfrac{1}{4} - \dfrac{\sqrt{23}}{4}i\right)\left(x - \dfrac{1}{4} + \dfrac{\sqrt{23}}{4}i\right)$

7. $y = 2x^2 - 2x - 4$ **9.** $AB = 6$ **11.**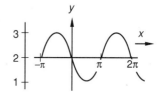

13. $f(x + \Delta x) = (2x + 2\,\Delta x - 1)^2$

15. 3   **17.** 1   **19.** $6\dfrac{1}{2}$

21. $\dfrac{\sqrt{x} + \sqrt{h}}{x - h}$

23. $x = 30$, $y = 10$

Problem set 8   **1.** $9\dfrac{4}{5}$ **3.** 8 days   **5.** $1 + \cot^2 \theta = \csc^2 \theta$; $\tan^2 \theta + 1 = \sec^2 \theta$ **7.** 0   **9.** $-\dfrac{4}{5}$

11. $\dfrac{1}{(-\csc x)^2} = \sin^2 x$ **13.** $\sin^2 x + \cos^2 x = 1$ **15.** $f(x) = 2x^2 + 10x + 12$

17. $x = 4.8$, $y = 3.6$, $z = 6.4$ **19.** $2 + 6 \sin\left(\theta + \dfrac{\pi}{2}\right)$ **21.** $-20i$ **23.** D

25. $x = 5$

Problem set 9   **1.** $\dfrac{rn}{n - r}$ **3.** x **5.** $140\pi r$ ft/hr   **7.** II or III   **9.** $-\dfrac{3}{4}$ **11.** $\dfrac{\cos^2 x}{\cos x} = \cos x$

13. $2x^2 - 2x - 4 = y$ **15.** $x = \dfrac{5}{2}$ **17.** $\left(-\dfrac{1}{2}, \dfrac{\sqrt{3}}{2}\right)$

19. b **21.** $a^2b^2 + abc + c^2$ **23.** D

Problem set 10   **1.** $\dfrac{2x + 3y}{5}$ mph   **3.** $\dfrac{100V}{V + W}$ **5.** b **7.**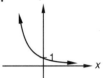

9. $\sin^2 \theta + \cos^2 \theta = 1$; $\tan^2 \theta + 1 = \sec^2 \theta$; $\cot^2 \theta + 1 = \csc^2 \theta$

11. $\cot^2 \theta$ **13.** $2x^2 - 2x - 4 = y$

15. $y = \dfrac{bx}{a}$

17. No; there are two different y values for the same x value of $x = 1$.   **19.** 13

21. h **23.** 50

Problem set 11   **1.** $\dfrac{40t}{t - 14}$ mph   **3.** z is multiplied by $\dfrac{3}{2}$ **5.** $5\underline{/126.87°}$ **7.** $6 \operatorname{cis} \dfrac{12}{35}\pi$

9.

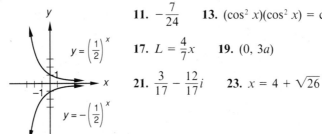

$y = \left(\frac{1}{2}\right)^x$

$y = -\left(\frac{1}{2}\right)^x$

11. $-\dfrac{7}{24}$ **13.** $(\cos^2 x)(\cos^2 x) = \cos^4 x$ **15.** 4

17. $L = \dfrac{4}{7}x$ **19.** $(0, 3a)$

21. $\dfrac{3}{17} - \dfrac{12}{17}i$ **23.** $x = 4 + \sqrt{26}$

Problem set 12   **1.** $\dfrac{wh}{w - y}$ **3.** Evelyn, $1200 - 15p$ ml; Jeannie, $15p - 600$ ml   **5.**

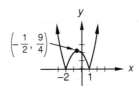

$-5 \qquad 0 \qquad 6$

7. $(x + 1)^2 + (y - 3)^2 = 9;\ x^2 + 2x + y^2 - 6y + 1 = 0$ **9.** $2\underline{/120°}$

11.

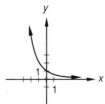

13. $-\sin\theta$ **15.** $-\dfrac{1}{9}$ **17.** $b = \dfrac{4x}{y}$

19. Domain $= \{x \mid x \in R\}$; range $= \{y \mid y \ge -1\}$

21. If the switch is not on, then the light is not on.   **23.** $x = \dfrac{z}{y}$.

Problem set 13   **1.** $\dfrac{g - x}{x}$ **3.** $\dfrac{4000}{x}$ people   **5.**

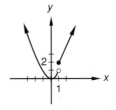

$\left(-\dfrac{1}{2}, \dfrac{9}{4}\right)$

7. $y = -2$ when $x < 0$; $y = x - 1$ when $0 \le x \le 3$; $y = 1$ when $x > 3$

9.

$-\dfrac{1}{2} \qquad 3\dfrac{1}{2}$

11. $(x + 2)^2 + (y - 3)^2 = 2$ **13.** $3 + 3\sqrt{3}\,i$ **15.** -1

17. $f(x) = 2x^2 - 2x - 4$ **19.** $2x + \Delta x$ **21.** D

Problem set 14   **1.** 20 cm $\times$ 25 cm   **3.** 3333.33 radians/min   **5.** $b = 1$

7. (*a*) 1; (*b*) -2

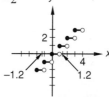

9.

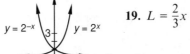

11. Circle with center $(0, 1)$ and radius 1   **13.** $2.999 < x < 3.001$

15.

$y = 2^{-x}$ $y = 2^x$

17. $(\cos^2 x + \sin^2 x)(\sin^2 x - \cos^2 x) = \sin^2 x - \cos^2 x$

19. $L = \dfrac{2}{3}x$

21. No; in some instances there are two different values of y for one value of x **23.** C

Problem set 15   **1.** Airplane's speed = 120 mph; wind speed = 20 mph

3. $(x + 2)^2 + (y - 3)^2 = 16$ **5.** $\pm 4, \pm 2, \pm 1$ **7.** (a) 0.60; (b) 1.39   **9.** $-\dfrac{3}{2}$

11.   **13.**   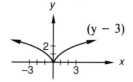   **15.**

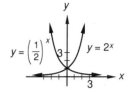

17. $\dfrac{3}{-3\tan\theta} = -\cot\theta$ **19.** $f(x) = x^2 + x - 6$ **21.** $x = 36°$

Problem set 16   **1.** 50 sophists   **3.** (a) 2; (b) 1; (c) 3; (d) 3   **5.** (a) -13; (b) 17; (c) -163

7. h is a zero if $x = 3, \dfrac{1}{2},$ or $-\dfrac{1}{3}$ **9.** $x = 2.30$ **11.** $(x - 1)^2 + (y - 2)^2 = 25$

13. $\dfrac{3}{2} + \dfrac{3\sqrt{3}}{2}i$ **15.** $\tan^2 x + 1 = \sec^2 x$ **17.** $(1, 3)$

19.   **21.** $6\sqrt{6}$

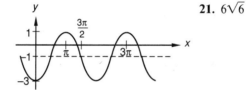

Problem set 17   **1.** Square: 2 by 2; rectangle: 8 by 4

3. See Lesson 17 for key identities: $\sin 2A = \sin A \cos A + \sin A \cos A = 2 \sin A \cos A$; $\cos 2A = \cos A \cos A - \sin A \sin A = \cos^2 A - \sin^2 A = 1 - 2 \sin^2 A = 2 \cos^2 A - 1$

5. $\sin^2 x + 2 \sin x \cos x + \cos^2 x = 1 + 2 \cos x \sin x = 1 + \sin 2x$

7. (a) 2; (b) 2   **9.** $4, -1, \dfrac{1}{2}$ **11.**

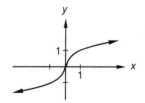

13.   **15.** $y = x^2 - x - 2$

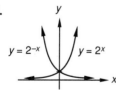

17.   **19.** $x \le 1$

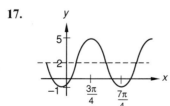

21. If the sides opposite two angles are not of equal length, then the two angles opposite those sides are not equal.

23. $2\sqrt{2}$

Problem set 18   **1.** $\dfrac{N}{2}\sqrt{17}$ **3.**

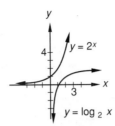

5. Amplitude = 2; period = 120°; phase angle = 15°

7. $\sin 2x = 2 \sin x \cos x$; $\cos 2x = \cos^2 x - \sin^2 x = 1 - 2 \sin^2 x = 2 \cos^2 x - 1$

9.

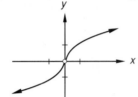

11. (*a*) 33; (*b*) 53; (*c*) 153   **13.** 4

15. $(x - 1)^2 + (y + 2)^2 = 4$ **17.** $4 + 4\sqrt{3}\,i$

19. Domain: entire set of real numbers; range: $1 \le y \le 3$ **21.** 2

Problem set 19   **1.** $\dfrac{7ks}{8(s + k)}$ **3.**

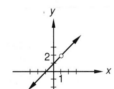

5. −1   **7.** −3   **9.** (*a*) 1; (*b*) 1; (*c*) 1

11.

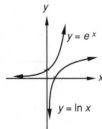

13. See Lesson 17; $\cos^2 x = \dfrac{1 + \cos 2x}{2}$ **15.** $-1, \dfrac{1}{2}, \dfrac{1}{3}$

17.

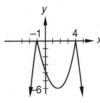

19. $\dfrac{14\sqrt{13}}{13}$ **21.** $1 - \sin^2 x = \cos^2 x$

23. $\dfrac{1}{\sqrt{x + h} + \sqrt{x}}$ **25.** $\dfrac{(m + s)(m + 2s) - 2y^2}{y}$

Problem set 20   **1.** $15a$ miles

3. Focus: (1, 0); directrix: $x = -1$; length of latus rectum = 4

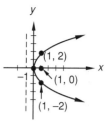

5. 2   **7.** $2a$ **9.**   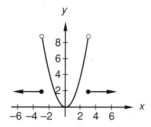   **11.**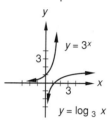

13. $y = -3 + 2 \sin \frac{5}{3}(\theta - 27°)$

15. $\dfrac{\sin(x + \Delta x) - \sin x}{\Delta x} = \dfrac{\sin x \cos \Delta x + \cos x \sin \Delta x - \sin x}{\Delta x}$

$= (\sin x)\left(\dfrac{\cos \Delta x - 1}{\Delta x}\right) + (\cos x)\left(\dfrac{\sin \Delta x}{\Delta x}\right)$

17. $\cos \dfrac{x}{2} = \pm\sqrt{\tfrac{1}{2}(1 + \cos x)}$; $\sin \dfrac{x}{2} = \pm\sqrt{\tfrac{1}{2}(1 - \cos x)}$

19. (0, 0), (1, 1)   **21.** 20°

Problem set 21   **1.** $S = \dfrac{360A}{M^2 P}$ **3.** $-45°$ **5.** $x = 210°, 330°$ **7.** $x = \dfrac{\pi}{2}$

9. Focus: (2, −1); directrix: $y = -3$; latus rectum = 4   **11.** 6

13.

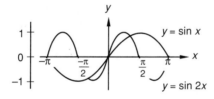

15. $\dfrac{\cos(x + \Delta x) - \cos x}{\Delta x} = \dfrac{\cos x \cos \Delta x - \sin x \sin \Delta x - \cos x}{\Delta x}$

$= \dfrac{(\cos x)(\cos \Delta x - 1)}{\Delta x} - \sin x \dfrac{\sin \Delta x}{\Delta x}$

17. $x = 2.77$ **19.** $\dfrac{2\sqrt{3}}{3} h$

21. $\cos 2A = \cos^2 A - \sin^2 A = 1 - 2 \sin^2 A = 2 \cos^2 A - 1$ **23.** 12

Problem set 22   **1.** $\dfrac{7mA}{m + A}$ **3.** (a) $(2, +\infty), (-\infty, -2)$ (b) $(-2, 2)$

5.

```
        0       0     0
--- ↓++++ ↓-- ↓++++
---+--+--+--+--+--+--+→ x
   -3      0    2
```

7. $\dfrac{\pi}{4}, \dfrac{5\pi}{4}, \dfrac{3\pi}{4}, \dfrac{7\pi}{4}$ **9.** $x = \sin y$ **11.** 0

13. 2   **15.** $\sin 2x = \sin(x + x) = \sin x \cos x + \cos x \sin x = 2 \sin x \cos x$

17. $\dfrac{5}{7}$ **19.** 1   **21.** 25

Problem set 23   **1.** 125 cars   **3.** $x = \dfrac{7}{4}$ **5.** $x = -\dfrac{1}{6}$ **7.** $x = -0.67$

9. Increasing on $(-1, 0)$ and $(1, \infty)$; decreasing on $(-\infty, -1)$ and $(0, 1)$

11.

```
+ + + + |— — |+ |— — — |+ + + +
        -2   0 1    3
```
$\longrightarrow x$

13. $(x + 1)^2 = -2\left(y - \dfrac{5}{2}\right)$ **15.** $2x$

17. $y = 35 + 40 \sin 4\left(\theta - \dfrac{\pi}{8}\right)$ **19.** Domain: $x < 0$; range: $-\infty < y < \infty$ **21.** *C*

Problem set 24   **1.** $\dfrac{40M + 60B}{M + B}$ **3.** $-\dfrac{3}{2}$ **5.** $2a$ **7.** $+\infty$ **9.** $+\infty$

11. Increasing: $-\infty < x < -1$; decreasing: $-1 < x < +\infty$, $x \neq 1$ **13.** No solution

15. $x = \sin y$ **17.** $\cos^2 A = \dfrac{1}{2}(1 + \cos 2A)$ **19.** $x = \dfrac{dc - ba}{b - d}$ **21.** -3.53 **23.** *C*

Problem set 25   **1.** $\dfrac{MABC}{BC + AC + AB}$ hours   **3.** $(f + g)(x) = x^2 + \sqrt{x - 1} + 1$; $(f + g)(5) = 28$

5. $\left(\dfrac{f}{g}\right)(x) = \dfrac{x^2 + 1}{\sqrt{x - 1}}$; $\left(\dfrac{f}{g}\right)(5) = 13$ **7.** $(f \circ g)(x) = x$, $(f \circ g)(3) = 3$

9. $(g \circ f)(x) = |x|$; domain: $-\infty < x < \infty$; range: $0 \leq y < \infty$ **11.** 0   **13.** $x = 1$

15. $g > 0$: $(-3, 0)$, $(2, \infty)$; $g < 0$: $(-\infty, -3)$, $(0, 2)$ **17.** $\left[0, \dfrac{\pi}{2}\right], \left[\pi, \dfrac{3\pi}{2}\right]$

19. $1, \pm\sqrt{3}$ **21.** $\dfrac{\tan^2 x \cos x}{\tan^2 x} = \cos x$ **23.** $\sin 2x$

Problem set 26   **1.** $\dfrac{13\pi}{528} r$ mph $= 0.077r$ mph

3. Center at $(1, -1)$; major axis: horizontal, length 6 units; minor axis, length 4 units

5. $\dfrac{x^2 - 1}{\ln x}$, $e^2 - 1$

7. Domain: $-\infty < x < -1$, $1 < x < \infty$; range: all real numbers; $(\ln x)^2 - 1$ **9.** 0

11. $-\dfrac{1}{4}$ **13.** $x = \ln y - 1$ **15.**

17. $(-\infty, -2), (-1, 3)$ **19.** $4 + 4\sqrt{3}\, i$ **21.** $f(x) = 2x$

23. -13.53 **25.** 71

Problem set 27   **1.** 32   **3.** $\dfrac{-2}{x^2}$ **5.**   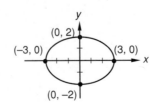   **7.** $(f \circ g)(x) = \ln \dfrac{1}{x}$ **9.** $+\infty$

11. ∞   **13.** [0, 2), [4, ∞)   **15.** $x = 3$ **17.** $\frac{1}{2}x^2$ **19.** $\frac{63}{65}$

21. $\sin^2 x = \frac{1}{2}(1 - \cos 2x)$ **23.** D

Problem set 28   **1.** $32\frac{8}{11}$ **3.** 1.95   **5.** $x > \frac{e + 3}{2}$ **7.** $6x$ **9.** $(0, \sqrt{7}), (0, -\sqrt{7})$

11. $f(g(x)) = \sin 2\left(x - \frac{\pi}{4}\right)$ **13.** Limit does not exist   **15.** 0   **17.** $x = 2 \sin y$

19. $k = 2$ **21.** $5 + 3\sqrt{3}$ **23.** C

Problem set 29   **1.** $L\left(\frac{100 - L}{2}\right)$ m^2 **3.**

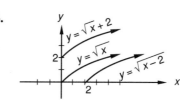

5. $\frac{\ln x}{\ln 10}$

7. $3 < x < 7$ **9.** $2x + 2$

11. Center $(1, -1)$; major axis: vertical length, 6 units;
minor axis, length 2 units;
foci: $(1, -1 + 2\sqrt{2}), (1, -1 - 2\sqrt{2})$

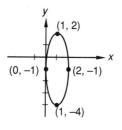

13. f: domain, all real numbers; range, $f(x) \geq 0$
g: domain, all real numbers; range, $g(x) > 0$
$f \circ g$: domain, all real numbers; range, $f \circ g \geq 1$

15. ∞   **17.** $x = -0.35$ or $-\frac{1}{2}\frac{\ln 5}{\ln 10}$ **19.** $(\sin x)(1 - \cos^2 x) = \sin^3 x$

21. $\cos^2 x = \frac{1}{2}(\cos 2x + 1)$ **23.** 8

Problem set 30   **1.** Trip out: 4 mph for 8 hr; trip back: 8 mph for 4 hr

3. Center $(-2, -1)$; vertices $(-2, 1), (-2, -3)$;
foci: $(-2, -1 + \sqrt{13}), (-2, -1 - \sqrt{13})$; asymptotes:
$y = \frac{2}{3}x + \frac{1}{3}, y = -\frac{2}{3}x - \frac{7}{3}$

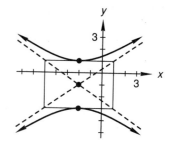

5.

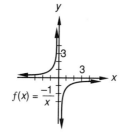

7. $x > \frac{2}{3}$ **9.** $2ax$

11. Domain of f: all real numbers, range of f: $0 \leq x < \infty$; domain of g: $0 < x < \infty$,
range of g: $-\infty < y < \infty$; domain of $g \circ f$: all real numbers except 0; range of
$g \circ f = -\infty < y < \infty$

13. -14 **15.** $x = -8$ **17.** $(x + 2)(x - 1)^2$ **19.** $\frac{1}{2}$ **21.** -1

23. $x = \dfrac{2a + ab - b}{4}$

Problem set 31

1. $4x^3 - 44x^2 + 120x \text{ in}^3$

3. $x^6 + 6x^5\,\Delta x + 15x^4(\Delta x)^2 + 20x^3(\Delta x)^3 + 15x^2(\Delta x)^4 + 6x(\Delta x)^5 + (\Delta x)^6$

5. Hyperbola whose equation is $\dfrac{(x - 1)^2}{1} - \dfrac{y^2}{1} = 1$

7. 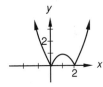   **9.** $\dfrac{\ln x}{\ln 3}$ **11.** 3

$f(x) = |x^2 - 1|$ $g(x) = |(x-1)^2 - 1|$

13. Domain of f: $0 < x < \infty$; domain of g: all real numbers   **15.** $\dfrac{1}{14}$

17. $240°$ **19.** $\dfrac{3 - \varepsilon}{2} < x < \dfrac{3 + \varepsilon}{2}$ **21.** $540°$

Problem set 32

1. The area of the circle is 27.32% greater than the area of the square.

3. $1, -1, i, -i$ **5.** $\dfrac{5\pi}{24}, \dfrac{11\pi}{24}, \dfrac{17\pi}{24}, \dfrac{23\pi}{24}, \dfrac{29\pi}{24}, \dfrac{35\pi}{24}, \dfrac{41\pi}{24}, \dfrac{47\pi}{24}$

7. Ellipse; center: $(0, 2)$; major axis: horizontal with length 4; minor axis: length 2; foci: $(-\sqrt{3}, 2)$, $(\sqrt{3}, 2)$

9. $g(x) = 2 + 3 \sin\left(x - \dfrac{\pi}{2}\right)$ 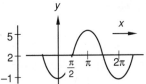   **11.** $x = \log_4 17$

13. -4 **15.** $(f \circ g)(x) = \sin(x^2)$ **17.** $x \geq -\dfrac{1}{2}$ **19.** $1 - \sin^2 x = \cos^2 x$

21. $\cos^2 x = \dfrac{1}{2}(1 + \cos 2x)$ **23.** $x = 5$

Problem set 33

1. Capacity $= 20(x)(1 - 2x) \text{ m}^3$ **3.** $f'(x) = \dfrac{1}{3}x^{-2/3}$ **5.** $D_x y = \dfrac{3}{4}x^{-1/4}$

7. cis $20°$, cis $140°$, cis $260°$

9. Parabola with vertex $(1, -1)$, focus $\left(\dfrac{17}{16}, -1\right)$, and directrix $x = \dfrac{15}{16}$

11. 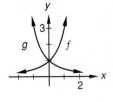   **13.**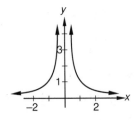

15. $f'(x) = 4x$

17. f: domain $-\infty < x < \infty$, range $0 \le y < \infty$; g: domain $4 \le x < \infty$, range $0 \le y < \infty$; $(g \circ f)$: domain $2 \le x < \infty \cup -\infty < x \le -2$, range: $0 \le y < \infty$

19. $4x + 6y - 15 = 0$ **21.** $1 + \tan^2 x = \sec^2 x$ **23.** b

Problem set 34 **1.** $\dfrac{250NL}{K}$ newtons/m^2 **3.** $2 + \sqrt{3}$ **5.** $\dfrac{16}{3}\pi$ cm^3 **7.** $\dfrac{dy}{dx} = \dfrac{-3}{x^4}$

9. $\dfrac{ds}{dt} = \dfrac{-1}{2\sqrt{t^3}}$ **11.** cis 75°, cis 165°, cis 255°, cis 345°

13. Circle: $(x - 1)^2 + (y + 2)^2 = 9$; radius 3; center $(1, -2)$ **15.** 40 **17.** $\dfrac{1}{2}$

19. $f(1.2) = 1; f(-1.5) = -2; f\left(-2\dfrac{1}{2}\right) = -3$ **21.** 5

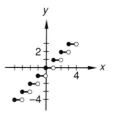

$f(x) = [x]$

Problem set 35 **1.** $d = \sqrt{(x - 3)^2 + (x^2 - 4)^2}$ **3.** $\dfrac{dy}{du} = \dfrac{-8}{u^3} - \dfrac{3}{2\sqrt{u}}$ **5.** $f'(x) = \dfrac{1}{2\sqrt{x}}$

7. $2(hw + hL + wL)$ **9.** $1, -\dfrac{1}{2} + \dfrac{\sqrt{3}}{2}i, -\dfrac{1}{2} - \dfrac{\sqrt{3}}{2}i$

11. $\dfrac{(x - 2)^2}{4} - \dfrac{y^2}{4} = 1$; hyperbola: center $(2, 0)$; vertices $(0, 0)$, $(4, 0)$; foci $(2 + 2\sqrt{2}, 0)$, $(2 - 2\sqrt{2}, 0)$: asymptotes $y = x - 2$, $y = -x + 2$

13. **15.** $x > 5$ **17.**

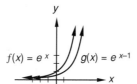

$f(x) = e^x$ $\quad g(x) = e^{x-1}$

19. $k = \dfrac{\ln 2}{9}$ **21.** $\dfrac{ac}{a + b}$

Problem set 36 **1.** $\dfrac{3200}{9}$ or $355\dfrac{5}{9}$ grams **3.** $f'(t) = \dfrac{-2\sqrt{2}}{t^3} - \dfrac{9}{t^4}$ **5.** $D_u y = 4u - \dfrac{1}{9}u^{-2/3}$

7. $2 - \sqrt{3}$ **9.** $\dfrac{1}{2} + \dfrac{\sqrt{3}}{2}i, -1, \dfrac{1}{2} - \dfrac{\sqrt{3}}{2}i$

11. $\dfrac{y^2}{16} - \dfrac{x^2}{4} = 1$; hyperbola: center $(0, 0)$; vertices $(0, 4)$, $(0, -4)$; foci $(0, 2\sqrt{5})$, $(0, -2\sqrt{5})$; asymptotes $y = 2x$, $y = -2x$

13. $y = \dfrac{\ln x}{\ln 2}$ **15.** $x = \dfrac{\sqrt{2}}{3}$ **17.** $\sin^2 A = \dfrac{1}{3}$

19. **21.** 9

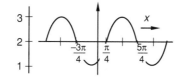

Problem set 37   **1.** Approx. 3:31 p.m.   **3.** $\dfrac{dy}{du} = \dfrac{1}{u} - 2e^u + \dfrac{1}{2\sqrt{u}}$ **5.** $s'(t) = v_0 + at$

7. $\cos A = \dfrac{4}{5}$, $\cos B = \dfrac{3}{5}$ **9.** 24π cm^2

11. $y = 2 + \sin\left(x - \dfrac{\pi}{4}\right)$ **13.** $-\dfrac{3}{2}$

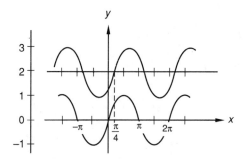

15. 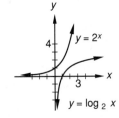   **17.**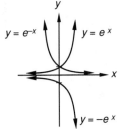

19. If a function f is continuous at $x = a$, then the function has a derivative at $x = a$; no

21. Midpoint from (b, c) to $(a, 0)$ is $\left(\dfrac{a + b}{2}, \dfrac{c}{2}\right)$; midpoint from $(0, 0)$ to $(a + b, c)$ is $\left(\dfrac{a + b}{2}, \dfrac{c}{2}\right)$; the midpoints of the two line segments (diagonals of the parallelogram) are the same, so the diagonals of the parallelogram bisect each other

Problem set 38   **1.** \$11,534,025   **3.** $\dfrac{-1}{x^2} + \dfrac{2}{x} - 3 \cos x$ **5.** $-3 \sin t - \dfrac{1}{t^2}$ **7.** 0.24

9. $\tan 2A = \dfrac{2 \tan A}{1 - \tan^2 A}$ **11.** cis 54°, cis 126°, cis 198°, cis 270°, cis 342°

13. $\dfrac{(y - 1)^2}{9} - \dfrac{x^2}{4} = 1$; hyperbola: center $(0, 1)$; vertices $(0, 4)$, $(0, -2)$; foci $(0, 1 + \sqrt{13})$, $(0, 1 - \sqrt{13})$; asymptotes $y = \dfrac{3}{2}x + 1$, $y = -\dfrac{3}{2}x + 1$

15. 1.46

17. $(f \circ g)(x) = \sqrt{x^2 - 1}$; domain of $f \circ g$, $-\infty < x \le -1$, $1 \le x < \infty$; range, $(f \circ g)(x) \ge 0$

19. (a)   (b) 2   **21.** $2x^2 + 2x - 4 = y$ **23.** 22

Problem set 39   **1.** The fourth day of the month

3.

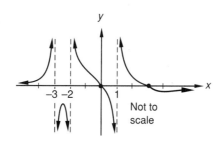

Not to scale

5. $y = -x + 2$ **7.** $\frac{1}{4}$

9. 0   **11.** $x + \sqrt{2}i$ and $x - \sqrt{2}i$

13. $\frac{x^2}{9} + \frac{y^2}{25} = 1$

15. $(y - 1)^2 = 6\left(x - \frac{1}{2}\right)$

17. -5 **19.** $\frac{2 \sin x \cos x}{-2 \sin x} = -\cos x$

21. $\left(\frac{c}{2}, \frac{d}{2}\right), \left(\frac{a + c}{2}, \frac{d}{2}\right)$; $y = \frac{d}{2}$; the line that bisects two sides of a triangle is parallel to the third side

Problem set 40   **1.** $5\frac{5}{11}$ minutes   **3.** $dy = \frac{-6}{x^3} dx + 2 \cos u \, du + 2e^t \, dt$ **5.** $dy = \frac{1}{3\sqrt[3]{t^2}} dt$

7. $y = \frac{1}{4}x + 1$ **9.** -2.89 **11.** $\frac{LE^2\sqrt{3}}{4}$

13. $\frac{7\pi}{24}, \frac{11\pi}{24}, \frac{19\pi}{24}, \frac{23\pi}{24}, \frac{31\pi}{24}, \frac{35\pi}{24}, \frac{43\pi}{24}, \frac{47\pi}{24}$

15. $\frac{1}{x}$ **17.**

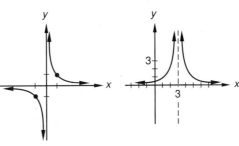

19. $\cos 2A = \cos (A + A) = \cos^2 A - \sin^2 A = 2 \cos^2 A - 1 = 1 - 2 \sin^2 A$

21. Domain: all real numbers; range: $-1 \le y \le 3$

23. Hypotenuse $= \sqrt{a^2 + b^2}$, median $= \frac{1}{2}\sqrt{a^2 + b^2}$; the length of the hypotenuse is twice the length of the median drawn to it

Problem set 41   **1.** $\frac{MH}{H - 2}$ mph   **3.**

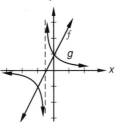

5. $dy = 3 \cos u \, du - \sqrt{2} \, e^t \, dt + \frac{1}{3x} dx$

7. $y = -0.66x + 3.22$ **9.** $\frac{dy}{du} = -14 \sin u + \frac{e^u}{2} - \frac{1}{u}$ **11.** e^2 or 7.39 **13.** $x > 6$

15. $\cos \frac{x}{2} = \pm\sqrt{\frac{1}{2}(1 + \cos x)}$ **17.**

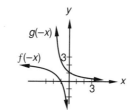

19. $0.23i - 1.60j$ **21.** $x = \dfrac{5 + \sqrt{13}}{2}$

Problem set 42   **1.** $v(x) = 4x^3 - 40x^2 + 100x \text{ in}^3$ **3.** $y' = x^3 e^x + 3x^2 e^x$ **5.** $f'(-2) = -4.77$

7. $s'' = \dfrac{-3}{4x^2\sqrt{x}} - 2\cos x$ **9.**

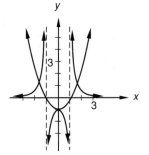

11. 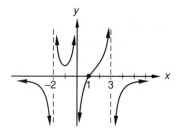   **13.**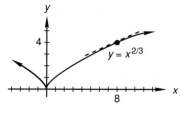

15. $3\pi \text{ cm}^3$ **17.** 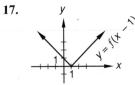   **19.** $1 + \sqrt{2}$ **21.** $1, i\sqrt{2}, -i\sqrt{2}$

23. $3\sqrt{3}$

Problem set 43   **1.** Surface area increases by a factor of $\sqrt[3]{4}$ **3.** x^5 **5.** $\sin x + C$

7. $\cos x + C$ **9.** $du = x^2\,dy + 2xy\,dx$ **11.** 1.92

13.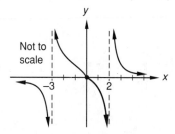

15. Center $(0, 1)$; vertices $(2, 1)$, $(-2, 1)$;
foci $(2\sqrt{2}, 1)$, $(-2\sqrt{2}, 1)$;
asymptotes $y = x + 1$, $y = -x + 1$

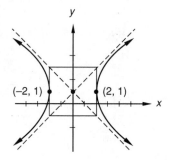

17. $-\infty$ **19.** $\lim\limits_{x\to 0^+} f(x) = 1$; $\lim\limits_{x\to 0^-} f(x) = 0$

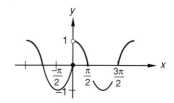

21. $\cos A = \dfrac{2\sqrt{2}}{3}$

23. m_1 = slope of diagonal from $(0, 0)$ to $(a, a) = 1$; m_2 = slope of diagonal from $(a, 0)$ to $(0, a) = -1$; slopes indicate that the diagonals of a square are perpendicular

Problem set 44

1. Area of $\triangle = y$ **3.**   **5.** c

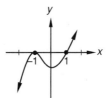

7. $y = e^x + C$, where C is any number   **9.** $f'(6) = 1500.25$

11. $dy = 2e^x\, dx - \dfrac{1}{u}\, du + 4\cos t\, dt$

13. $f'(x) = 2\cos x$; $f''(x) = -2\sin x$; $f'''(x) = -2\cos x$

15. Ellipse; center $(0, 2)$; major axis vertical, length = 6; minor axis length = 2

17. $\dfrac{2\tan A}{1 - \tan^2 A}$ **19.**   **21.** $6! = 720$

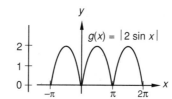

Problem set 45

1. $6{:}32\dfrac{8}{11}$ p.m.   **3.** $\dfrac{dx}{dt} = \dfrac{2y}{2x - \sin x}\dfrac{dy}{dt}$ **5.**

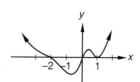

7. $F(x) = x^3$ or $F(x) = x^3 + $ any number   **9.** $e^t + C$

11. $y' = 3x^2\cos x - x^3\sin x$ **13.** $\dfrac{dy}{dx} = \dfrac{2}{x} + \dfrac{8}{3\sqrt[3]{x}} - \dfrac{e^x}{3}$

15.   **17.** 2 cis $11°$, 2 cis $131°$, 2 cis $251°$

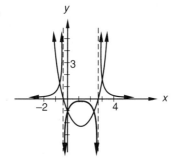

19. The locus of points described is an ellipse with foci at F and G and a major axis of length C

21. -1 **23.** $m \angle D = \dfrac{x}{2}$; $m \angle B = \dfrac{y}{2}$; $m \angle CED = m \angle B + m \angle D$; $m \angle CED = \dfrac{x}{2} + \dfrac{y}{2}$

Problem set 46   **1.** $V(L) = 25L - \dfrac{L^3}{2}$ cm^3 **3.** $-3 \cos x + C$ **5.** $\dfrac{3}{8}\sqrt[3]{u^4} + C$

7. $\dfrac{dy}{dx} = -\dfrac{4xy + \sin x}{2x^2 + 2y}$ **9.** $y = 1$ **11.**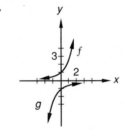

13. e^x **15.** 1   **17.** $x = \dfrac{5}{6}$ **19.** 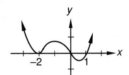   **21.** $\dfrac{\pi}{6}, \dfrac{\pi}{2}, \dfrac{5\pi}{6}$ **23.** 25

Problem set 47   **1.** Circumference of base $= \dfrac{360 - x}{18}\,\pi$ cm; radius of base $= \dfrac{360 - x}{36}$ cm

3. Critical numbers at $x = 1, 2$; local minimum: $(2, 5)$; local maximum: $\left(1, \dfrac{11}{2}\right)$

5. $2 \sin t + C$ **7.** $\dfrac{dy}{dx} = \dfrac{e^x - y}{3y^2 + x}$ **9.** $\dfrac{dx}{dt} = \dfrac{2xy}{2x - 1}\dfrac{dy}{dt}$

11. $\dfrac{dy}{dx} = 4x + 3 \cos x + 4 \sin x + \dfrac{1}{x}$ **13.**

15.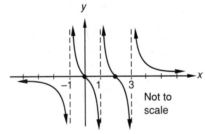

17. Parabola: vertex $(1, 2)$; focus $\left(1, \dfrac{33}{16}\right)$; directrix $y = \dfrac{31}{16}$

19. $-\dfrac{2}{5}$ **21.** $\sqrt{7}$ cis $49.1°$ **23.** $\dfrac{5\sqrt{2}}{2}$

Problem set 48   **1.** $(200P - 16{,}000)$ liters   **3.** $\dfrac{dy}{dt} = 3t^2 \cos(t^3 + 1)$ **5.** $\dfrac{dy}{dx} = \dfrac{2x}{x^2 + 1}$

7. $\dfrac{-x}{\sqrt{(x^2 - 1)^3}}$ **9.** $6\sqrt{u} + C$ **11.** $\dfrac{2}{5}x^{5/2} + C$ **13.** $y = -2x + 10$

15.    **17.** $(f \circ g)(x) = \ln \sqrt{x - 1}$; domain: $1 < x < \infty$

19. 2 cis $10°$, 2 cis $100°$, 2 cis $190°$, 2 cis $280°$ **21.** $y = x^2 - x - 2$ **23.** $d = \dfrac{1}{2}$

Problem set 49   **1.** 325 minutes   **3.** $\frac{2}{3}x^3 - 6\sqrt{x} + 3x + C$

5. $\frac{dy}{dx} = -(3x^2 + 2) \sin (x^3 + 2x + 1)$ **7.** $\frac{-x}{\sqrt{(x^2 + 1)^3}}$

9. Critical numbers: -1, 1, 2; local minimum points: $(-1, -20)$, $(2, 7)$; local maximum point: $(1, 12)$

11. $f'(x) = \frac{e^x + 2f(x)}{2[f(x) - x]}$ **13.**

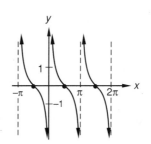

15.

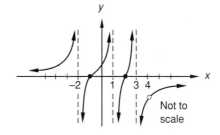

Not to scale

17. Hyperbola: vertices $(1, 1)$, $(-1, 1)$; center $(0, 1)$; foci $(\sqrt{5}, 1)$, $(-\sqrt{5}, 1)$; asymptotes: $y = 2x + 1$, $y = -2x + 1$

19.

$+ + + + \;|- \;| + \;| - - - - \;| + + +$

$\qquad -2\ -1\ \ 0 \qquad\quad 3$

21. $\sin^2 x + \cos^2 x = 1$ **23.** C

Problem set 50   **1.** p is divided by 18   **3.** $s'(1) = -1$ unit/sec

5. Critical points: $x = -2$, local maximum of 12; $x = 1$, local minimum of -1.5

7. $\sqrt{2} \ln |t| + 3 \sin t + t + C$ **9.** $4e^x - 2\sqrt{x} + 6x + C$ **11.** $\cot t$

13. $\frac{dy}{dx} = \frac{\cos x - y}{\sin y + x}$ **15.** $-\frac{1}{2}$ **17.**

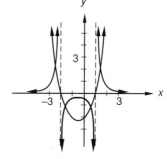

19. 1.46   **21.** $x = -2, -1, 1$

23. $9\sqrt{3}$

Problem set 51   **1.** 1.37×10^{-3} liter   **3.**   **5.** $4\pi r^2 \frac{dr}{dt}$

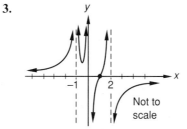

Not to scale

7. Local maximum point: $\left(-1, \frac{73}{12}\right)$; local minimum points: $\left(-2, \frac{17}{3}\right)$, $\left(1, \frac{41}{12}\right)$

9. $-3 \ln t + C$ **11.** $f'(x) = -x(x^2 + 1)^{-3/2}$ **13.** $y' = \cot x$ **15.** $1 + \ln |x|$

17. $(fg)(x) = \frac{\ln x}{x}$; domain: $0 < x < \infty$ **19.** $\lim\limits_{x \to 1^-} f(x) = 0$; $\lim\limits_{x \to 1^+} f(x) = 1$ **21.** $\frac{s^2 \sqrt{3}}{4}$

Problem set 52   **1.** $\frac{2kH}{P}$ hours   **3.** $f'(x) = \dfrac{(\cos x)(\cos x) - (\sin x)(-\sin x)}{\cos^2 x} = \dfrac{1}{\cos^2 x} = \sec^2 x$

5.

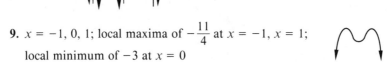

7. $\dfrac{\pi}{3}\left(r^2 \dfrac{dh}{dt} + 2rh \dfrac{dr}{dt}\right)$

9. $x = -1, 0, 1$; local maxima of $-\dfrac{11}{4}$ at $x = -1$, $x = 1$;
local minimum of -3 at $x = 0$

11. $-\dfrac{8}{3}u^{3/2} + C$ **13.** $\dfrac{2x + \cos x}{x^2 + \sin x}$ **15.** $s'(t) = \dfrac{-1}{\sqrt{t^3}} + \dfrac{1}{t}$

17. $0 \le x \le \dfrac{\pi}{4}, \dfrac{3\pi}{4} \le x \le \dfrac{5\pi}{4}, \dfrac{7\pi}{4} \le x \le 2\pi$

19. $\cos \dfrac{x}{2} = \pm\sqrt{\dfrac{1 + \cos x}{2}}$; $\sin \dfrac{x}{2} = \pm\sqrt{\dfrac{1 - \cos x}{2}}$ **21.** $a = 2, b = -2, c = -4$

23. B

Problem set 53   **1.** $h = \dfrac{20 - \pi r - 2r}{2}$; $A = 20r - 2r^2 - \dfrac{\pi r^2}{2}$ **3.** 1.93 units²

5. $D_x\left(\dfrac{e^x + x}{\cos x}\right) = \dfrac{(e^x + 1)(\cos x) + (e^x + x)(\sin x)}{\cos^2 x}$ **7.** $d\left(\dfrac{u}{v}\right) = \dfrac{v\, du - u\, dv}{v^2}$

9. $6000e^{12}$

11. Critical numbers: $x = 2$, relative minimum, $y = 4$; $x = 1$, relative maximum, $y = \dfrac{9}{2}$

13. $f'(x) = \dfrac{-2x}{3}(x^2 - 1)^{-4/3}$ **15.** $3 \ln |x| + \dfrac{3\sqrt{2}}{7}\sqrt[3]{x^7} + \sin x - 4e^x + C$

17.

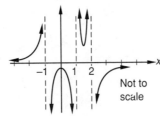

19. $\lim\limits_{x \to 0^+} f(x) = -\infty$ **21.** $\dfrac{5}{2}$

Problem set 54   **1.** 98,304 troubles   **3.** $15x^2 \cos 5x^3$ **5.** $\dfrac{3x^2 + 2}{2\sqrt{x^3 + 2x + 1}}$ **7.** Upper sum: $\dfrac{25}{32}$

9. $\dfrac{(\sin x + \cos x)\dfrac{1}{x} - (\ln x)(\cos x - \sin x)}{1 + 2 \sin x \cos x}$ **11.** $-\dfrac{2}{3}$ unit/sec

13. $6t^{1/2} + 4 \sin t + 2t^3 + 6t + C$ **15.** $12e^x \sin x + 12e^x \cos x$ **17.** $-\dfrac{x}{\sqrt{(x^2-4)^3}}$

19. 0   **21.** 2 cis 4°, 2 cis 76°, 2 cis 148°, 2 cis 220°, 2 cis 292°   **23.** $x = y$

Problem set 55   **1.** $\sqrt{100 - x^2}$ feet   **3.**   **5.** $\dfrac{\cos \sqrt{x}}{2\sqrt{x}}$ **7.** $\dfrac{e^x}{1 + e^x}$

9. 1.11   **11.** $\dfrac{e^x(1 - 2x + x^2)}{(1 + x^2)^2}$ **13.** $\dfrac{dy}{dx} = \dfrac{-3}{2}x^2(x^3 + 5)^{-3/2}$ **15.** $s'(t) = v_0 + gt$

17. $4 \ln |u| - \dfrac{3}{14}u^{-14} + C$ **19.** $(f \circ g)(x) = \sqrt{x^2 - 1}$ **21.** 3   **23.** 530

Problem set 56   **1.** $\dfrac{-2\sqrt{21}}{21}$ m/sec   **3.**   **5.** $\dfrac{x}{\sqrt{x^2 + 1}}$ **7.** $\dfrac{1}{2}$

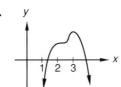

9. $f'(x) = \dfrac{1}{1 + \sin 2x}$ **11.** $\dfrac{dy}{dx} = \dfrac{x}{\sqrt{x^2 + 1}}$ **13.** 2.74

15. $\dfrac{3}{2}x^2 + e^x - 2\sqrt{x} + \dfrac{x}{3} + C$ **17.**

19. $\dfrac{2 \tan A}{1 - \tan^2 A}$ **21.** 13 cm

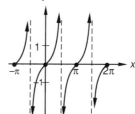

Problem set 57   **1.** $-\dfrac{5}{6}$ m/sec   **3.** 3   **5.** ln 3 = 1.10

7. $x = 0$, local maximum, $y = -4$; $x = -1$, local minimum, $y = -5$

9. $(1 + \cos x)e^{x + \sin x}$ **11.** 4   **13.** $4t^2(1 + 3 \ln t)$

15. $\dfrac{(x^2 + 1)(\cos x) - 2x \sin x}{(x^2 + 1)^2}$ **17.**

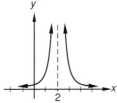

19. Domain, $-1 \le x \le 1$; range, $0 \le y \le \pi$ **21.** $\dfrac{\pi}{6}, \dfrac{5\pi}{6}, \dfrac{3\pi}{2}$

23. $\dfrac{14}{11}$

Problem set 58   **1.** 160π cm³/sec   **3.** Use the fact that $y = \cos x = \sin\left(\dfrac{\pi}{2} - x\right)$ and chain rule; $-\sin x$

5. $-\cot x \csc x$ **7.** $x^2 \sec x \tan x + 2x \sec x$ **9.** 2.57   **11.** 2

13. Local minimum   **15.** $\dfrac{e^x}{2\sqrt{(e^x - 1)^3}}$

17. $-2u^{1/2} + \dfrac{2}{3}u^3 - u + 2u^{3/2} - \sin u - 2 \cos u - \dfrac{1}{4}u^{-4} - 4e^u + C$ **19.** 1.25

21.   **23.** $f(x) = 2x^2 - 2x - 4$ **25.** C

Problem set 59   **1.** $\dfrac{-4}{25\pi}$ cm/sec

3. Critical numbers: 0, 1, −1;
local minimum points: (1, −1), (−1, −1);
local maximum point: (0, 0)

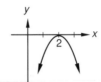

5. $2\sqrt{3}$ **7.** $8\dfrac{1}{4}$ **9.** 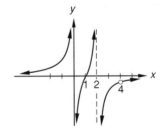   **11.** $\ln x + 1 - \tan x - x \sec^2 x$

13. $\dfrac{dy}{dx} = 24 \cos 2x \,(1 + \sin 2x)$ **15.**

17. Define $y = \cos x$ in terms of the sine function and use the chain rule

19. 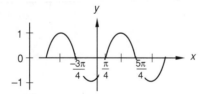   **21.** $3x$ **23.** Use quotient rule   **25.** $\dfrac{-\sqrt{2}}{4}$

Problem set 60   **1.** $\dfrac{\sqrt{2}}{2}$ units/sec

3. Critical numbers: $\dfrac{1}{8} - \dfrac{\sqrt{33}}{8}$, 0, $\dfrac{1}{8} + \dfrac{\sqrt{33}}{8}$; relative maximum at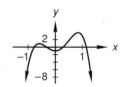
$x = \dfrac{1 - \sqrt{33}}{8}, \dfrac{1 + \sqrt{33}}{8}$; relative minimum at $x = 0$

5. $f'(x) = (6x - 4) \sec^2 (3x^2 - 4x + 1)$ **7.** $h'(x) = 100x(x^2 - 4)^{49}$

9. $g'(t) = 2 \sec^2 t$ **11.** $e^{1.5} - e^{0.5} - 1 \approx 1.83$ **13.** $\dfrac{2}{5}\sqrt{x^5} - \dfrac{4}{3}\sqrt{x^3} + C$

15. $y = -2\sqrt{2}x + 9$ **17.** e^x **19.**

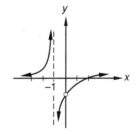

21. $g(x) = \sqrt{x^2 + 1}$ **23.** A

Problem set 61

1. $\dfrac{dr}{dt} = -\dfrac{3}{100\pi}$ cm/sec

3. Critical numbers: $x = -1$ and $x = 2$; extreme values: $y = -19$ at $x = 2$ (local minimum); $y = 8$ at $x = -1$ (local maximum)

5. $(x^2 + 4)^6 + C$ **7.** $\sqrt{x^2 + 4} + C$ **9.** $\ln |3x^2 + x| + C$

11. $60x(x^2 + 1)^{29}$ **13.** $\dfrac{(\cos x)(x^2 + 1) - 20x \sin x}{(x^2 + 1)^{11}}$ **15.** $e^1 - e^{-2}$

17. Undefined   **19.** $y = \dfrac{x + 1}{x}$ **21.** c

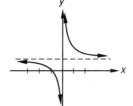

Problem set 62

1. Relative maximum: $x = 1$, $y = 0$; relative minimum: $x = -1$, $y = -4$; $f''(x) = -6x$; $f''(-1) = 6 > 0$, and therefore the graph is concave upward, which implies a relative minimum; $f''(1) = -6 < 0$, and therefore the graph is concave downward, which implies a relative maximum; point of inflection: $(0, -2)$

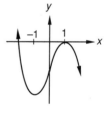

3. Length = 100 yards, width = 50 yards   **5.** $\sin^5 x + C$

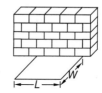

7. $e^{x^2} + C$ **9.** $\dfrac{2}{5}x^{5/2} - \dfrac{2}{3}x^{3/2} + C$ **11.** $\dfrac{1}{2(x - 1)^{1/2}(x + 1)^{1/2}} - \dfrac{(x + 1)^{1/2}}{2(x - 1)^{3/2}}$

13. $e^{x^2+1}(1 + 2x^2)$ **15.** $e - e^{-1} + 2$ **17.** 3   **19.** $\{x: x \geq 0; x \neq 1\}$ **21.** a

Problem set 63

1. $40\sqrt{2}$ yards   **3.** $\dfrac{dA}{dt} = 24$ cm^2/sec; $\dfrac{dp}{dt} = 8$ cm/sec

5. $20 - e^3 + e$ **7.** $\displaystyle\int_0^2 x \, dx = 2$ **9.** $\sin^8 x + C$ **11.** $e^{4x^2} + C$

13. $2 \ln (x^2 + 1) + \left(\dfrac{4x^2}{x^2 + 1}\right) + 4 \sec^2 x$ **15.** a

17. Left and right limits may be equal, yet function may not be defined at point in question; that is, $\lim\limits_{x \to 1^+} f(x) = \lim\limits_{x \to 1^-} f(x)$, where $f(x) = \dfrac{x^2 - 1}{x - 1}$, yet f is not defined at $x = 1$. Hence f is not continuous at $x = 1$.

19. c

Problem set 64   **1.** 240 m   **3.** Never at rest; always accelerating   **5.** $\dfrac{16}{3}$ **7.** $\dfrac{1}{2}$

9. $(x^2 + 1)^{3/2} + C$

11. $(\ln x)^4 + C$ **13.** $\dfrac{dy}{dx} = \dfrac{-2x + \cos y}{x \sin y + 3y^2}$

15. $y - (1 - \ln 3) = \dfrac{1}{e}(x - e) \rightarrow y = \dfrac{x}{e} - \ln 3$ **17.** 0

19. $\dfrac{\pi}{2}$

Problem set 65   **1.** 40 cm $\times$ 40 cm $\times$ 40 cm   **3.** $t = 1$; moving right: $t > 1$; moving left: $0 \leq t < 1$

5. 2   **7.** $2e^{x^2} + C$ **9.** $\dfrac{1}{4} \ln |2x^2 + 1| + C$ **11.** $\dfrac{4}{9} \sin^3 3t + C$

13. $\dfrac{(x^2 + 2)\cos(2x + 1)(2) - [\sin(2x + 1)](2x)}{(x^2 + 2)^2} + 2\sec^2 x$ **15.** Concave upward

17. $\dfrac{2\sqrt{5}}{5}$ **19.**

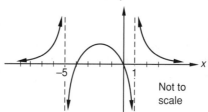

Not to scale

21. $\dfrac{\ln x}{\ln 3}$

Problem set 66   **1.** $(2, 3)$ **3.** $t = 2$ **5.** 14   **7.** 4   **9.** $\dfrac{1}{2} \ln |3x^2 + 2x| + C$

11. $2\sqrt{x^2 + x + 1} + C$ **13.**

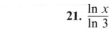

15. d **17.** $y = \dfrac{8}{3}x - \dfrac{13}{3}$

19. 1   **21.** 5

Problem set 67   **1.** $x\sqrt{16 - x^2}$ **3.** 240π cm^2/sec

5. $f^{-1}(x) = \dfrac{x + 3}{4}$; $(f \circ f^{-1})(x) = (f^{-1} \circ f)(x) = x$ **7.** $x = \sin y \cos x$

9. a **11.** $y = 1$ **13.** $\dfrac{dy}{dx} = \dfrac{(x^3 + 1)(2e^{2x} - 2xe^{-x^2}) - (e^{2x} + e^{-x^2})(3x^2)}{(x^3 + 1)^2} + 3\csc^2 x$

15. $\dfrac{1}{5a} \sin^5 ax + C$ **17.** $-\dfrac{1}{5}$ **19.** $c = \dfrac{2\pi}{5}$ **21.** $\tan \theta = \dfrac{h}{6} \rightarrow \sec^2 \theta \dfrac{d\theta}{dt} = \dfrac{1}{6}\dfrac{dh}{dt}$

Problem set 68   **1.** $V = x(4 - 2x)(4 - x)$; V is maximum when $x = 2 - \dfrac{2}{3}\sqrt{3}$ **3.** 4 units^2

5. $f^{-1}(x) = \dfrac{x-2}{3}$; $f^{-1}(4) = \dfrac{2}{3}$; $(f \circ f^{-1})(x) = (f^{-1} \circ f)(x) = x$

7. $x = \tan y$ **9.** $\dfrac{1}{4}(x^2 + 2)^4 + C$ **11.** $-\dfrac{\pi}{6}\cos^3 2x + C$ **13.** e^2

15. $\dfrac{-3(x^2 + 2)\sin 3x - 2x \cos 3x}{(x^2 + 2)^2} + 2\sec^2 2x$ **17.** $\dfrac{dy}{dx} = \dfrac{\sec xy - y}{x}$

19.

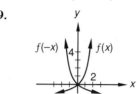

Problem set 69

1. 10 in. × 10 in. × 10 in.   **3.** $\dfrac{1}{8}(\sin^4 2x) + C$ **5.** $x + \ln|x| + C$ **7.** $2\dfrac{2}{3}$ units²

9. $6\dfrac{3}{4}$ units²   **11.** $y = \arcsin x$ **13.** $\dfrac{(\cot x)(x^2 - 1) - 2x \ln|\sin x|}{(x^2 - 1)^2}$ **15.** 1

17. C **19.**

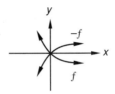

Problem set 70

1. $\dfrac{1}{40\pi}$ in/sec   **3.** $f(x) = x^2 + 3x + 1$ **5.** $f = 3x^2 - 2x + 3$

7. $-(\sin x)^{-1} + C$ **9.** 9 units²   **11.** $k = \dfrac{15}{4}$ **13.** $k = e$

15. The graph of f is an upside down parabola   **17.** $\dfrac{-1}{x^2}$ **19.** $-1 \le x \le 1$

21. $\dfrac{b}{a}\sqrt{a^2 - x^2}$

Problem set 71

1. 32 units²   **3.** $\dfrac{117}{8}$ J   **5.** $34\dfrac{1}{2}$ units   **7.** $f(x) = x^2$ **9.** $\dfrac{2}{3}x^{3/2} - 2x^{1/2} + C$

11. $\dfrac{1}{4}\tan^4 x + C$ **13.** $\dfrac{8}{3}$ units²   **15.** e^1 **17.** $\dfrac{e^{\sin x}\cos x}{\sqrt{2x - 1}} + \dfrac{-e^{\sin x}}{(\sqrt{2x - 1})^3} + \dfrac{1}{x}$

19. $\dfrac{1}{2}$ **21.** $\dfrac{4\sqrt{3}\,h^2}{3}$ ft³

Problem set 72

1. $\dfrac{dh}{dt} = \dfrac{1}{8}$ ft/min   **3.** Minimum is 0 at $x = 0$; maximum is 4 at $x = 8$ **5.** 8 J

7. $a = 3, b = 0$ **9.** 2   **11.** $-\dfrac{1}{2}e^{-2x} + C$ **13.** $\dfrac{1}{2}$ unit²

15. $(2e^{2x}\tan x)(\sec^2 x + \tan x)$ **17.** d **19.** $\cos y = \dfrac{\sqrt{a^2 - x^2}}{a}$

21. $R = 11{,}000p - 50p^2$

Problem set 73

1. \$28   **3.** Maximum point: $(2, 2\sqrt{2} - 2)$; minimum point: $\left(\dfrac{4}{9}, -\dfrac{4}{27}\right)$

5. $\dfrac{1}{\sqrt{9-x^2}}$ **7.** $\dfrac{2}{4+x^2}$ **9.** 12 J   **11.** 1 unit^2 **13.** $-\dfrac{1}{4}$

15. $\dfrac{1}{3}(\sin 2x + x)^{-2/3}(2\cos 2x + 1) + \dfrac{-3\csc 3x \cot 3x}{x^3 + 1} - \dfrac{3x^2 \csc 3x}{(x^3 + 1)^2}$ **17.** 0

19. $y = \dfrac{b}{a}\sqrt{a^2 - x^2}$ where $0 \le x \le a$

Problem set 74   **1.** $\dfrac{1}{50}$ rad/sec

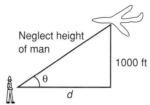
Neglect height of man
1000 ft
θ
d

3. $h(t) = 100 + 30t - 4.9t^2$; maximum height 145.9 m   **5.** $\dfrac{\sqrt{5}}{5}$

7. Minimum value of 0 at $x = 1$; maximum value of 2 at $x = -1, 3$

9. 3 J   **11.** $\sqrt{1 + \sin 2x} + C$ **13.** $\dfrac{1}{6}$ unit^2 **15.** 1

17. $-\dfrac{1}{2}\dfrac{\cos x}{\sqrt{1 - \sin x}} + \dfrac{2e^{2x}(\sec x + 1) - e^{2x}\sec x \tan x}{(\sec x + 1)^2} + \dfrac{\csc x}{x} - (\ln x)(\csc x \cot x)$

19. 0   **21.** b

Problem set 75   **1.** $\dfrac{16}{3}$ J

3. $h(t) = 160 + 20t - 4.9t^2$; $h(2) = 180.4$ m; $v(2) = 0.4$ m/sec; $a(2) = -9.8$ m/sec^2

5. $\dfrac{e - e^{-1}}{5}$ **7.** $\dfrac{2\sqrt{3}}{9}$

9. Minimum is -1 at $x = 1$; maximum is 0 at $x = 0$ and $x = 2$

11. $a = -2, b = -4$ **13.** $\dfrac{1}{4}(x + \sin x)^4 + C$

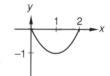

15. $\dfrac{1}{2}\ln(x^2 + 1) + C$

17. $\dfrac{dy}{dx} = (e^{2x}\sec \pi x)(\pi \tan \pi x + 2)$ **19.** c **21.** $\cos^2 \theta = \dfrac{100}{100 + x^2}$

Problem set 76   **1.** $\dfrac{5}{169}$ rad/sec   **3.** $\dfrac{125}{6}$ units^2 **5.** $\displaystyle\int_0^3 \left(\dfrac{3-y}{2}\right) dy$ **7.** b **9.** $\dfrac{4}{7}$

11. $\dfrac{1}{4}\sin^4 x + C$ **13.** $2(x + \sin x)^{1/2} + C$ **15.** b

17. $\dfrac{(2\sqrt{x} + 1)(-e^{-x} - \sin x\, e^{\cos x}) - (e^{-x} + e^{\cos x})(x^{-1/2})}{(2\sqrt{x} + 1)^2}$

19. $w = L$; $h = \dfrac{300}{L^2}$; $C = 12L^2 + \dfrac{18,000}{L}$

Problem set 77   **1.** $5\sqrt[3]{6}$ m $\times$ $5\sqrt[3]{6}$ m $\times$ $2\sqrt[3]{6}$ m   **3.** Even   **5.** Neither

7. Odd   **9.** $\dfrac{1}{(x^2 + \sin^3 2x)\sqrt{x + 1}} - \dfrac{2\sqrt{x + 1}\,(2x + 6\sin^2 2x \cos 2x)}{(x^2 + \sin^3 2x)^2}$

11. $\dfrac{1}{12}\sin^4 3x + C$ **13.** $4\dfrac{1}{2}$ units^2 **15.** Maximum at $x = 0.88$; minimum at $x = -1$

17. $A = 10;\ B = -5$ **19.** 1   **21.** $y = e^{x \ln 2}$

Problem set 78   **1.** $L = 100$ m   **3.** $(x - 1)e^x + C$ **5.** $\dfrac{x^2 \ln x}{2} - \dfrac{x^2}{4} + C$

7. $\sin x - x \cos x + C$ **9.** y axis   **11.** $\dfrac{2x}{\sqrt{1 - x^4}}$ **13.** $\dfrac{e - 1}{2}$ **15.** $4\dfrac{1}{2}$ units^2

17. $3\dfrac{3}{4}$ **19.** a

Problem set 79   **1.** $h(t) = 100 + 10t - 4.9t^2$; $h(3) = 85.9$ m; 5.65 sec   **3.** $f(x) = \dfrac{3}{2}x^2 + 2x + 2$

5. 1   **7.** $+\infty$ **9.** $2\pi^2$ **11.** 1   **13.** $-3x \cos x + 3 \sin x + C$

15. $x \ln x - x + C$ **17.** $\dfrac{1}{6}$ unit^2

19. $\dfrac{-\sin^2 x\, e^{\cos x} + \cos x\, e^{\cos x}}{\ln 2x} - \dfrac{e^{\cos x} \sin x}{x(\ln 2x)^2} - \dfrac{2}{1 + 4x^2}$

21. $-\dfrac{1}{2}\cos(x^2 + \pi) + C$ **23.** $\dfrac{\ln x}{\ln 3}$

Problem set 80   **1.** $w = 4\sqrt{3}$ **3.** $\dfrac{1}{6}\pi$ units^3 **5.** $\displaystyle\int_0^2 \pi(4 - y^2)\, dy$ **7.** 4π **9.** 0

11. $3(-x \cos x + \sin x) + C$ **13.** $\displaystyle\int_0^1 \sqrt{1 - y^2}\, dy$ **15.** $-\dfrac{4}{x\sqrt{x^2 - 16}}$

17. $\dfrac{1}{3}e^{x^3} + C$ **19.** $f^{-1}(x) = \dfrac{x + 5}{4}$ **21.** d

Problem set 81   **1.** $\dfrac{128}{3}\pi$ cm^3/sec   **3.** -73.77 m/sec or 73.77 m/sec toward the ground

5. $\dfrac{1}{\ln 2}\displaystyle\int_2^8 \ln x\, dx$ **7.** 43.28 units^2 **9.** $\dfrac{3}{5}\pi$ units^3 **11.** $\pi \displaystyle\int_0^1 (1 - y)\, dy$

13. $-\cos \pi x + C$ **15.** $\dfrac{1}{3\pi}$

17. $-4(\cos x)(\sin x) + \dfrac{2}{1 + 4x^2} + \dfrac{2}{(\sqrt{2x + 1})(x^2 + 1)} - \dfrac{4x\sqrt{2x + 1}}{(x^2 + 1)^2}$

19. $\dfrac{1}{2}\ln |x^2 + 1| + C$

Problem set 82   **1.** -2.5 m^3/sec   **3.** 27,000 N

5. $\left[2000 \displaystyle\int_{-3}^0 (\sqrt{9 - y^2})(-y)\, dy\right]$ N or $\left(2000 \displaystyle\int_0^3 y\sqrt{9 - y^2}\, dy\right)$ N   **7.** $\dfrac{32}{5}\pi$

9. $(\ln 3.5)(3.5^x) - \dfrac{2}{(\ln 3)x}$ **11.** $2xe^{2x} - e^{2x} + C$ **13.** $-\dfrac{1}{3}(1 + 2 \cos x)^{3/2} + C$

15. $\dfrac{a}{x\sqrt{x^2 - a^2}}$ **17.** c **19.** $Q(p) = 1500 - 5p$; $R(p) = p(1500 - 5p)$

Problem set 83   **1.** $p = \$1.50$

3. False, since *f* could be discontinuous and could look as shown

5. $b = 0$

7. $25{,}000 \int_0^4 y\, dy$; or $25{,}000 \int_0^4 (4 - y)\, dy$ newtons

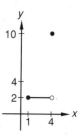

9. Minimum: 0 at $x = 0, 2$; maximum: 8 at $x = -2$

11. $(2x)(\ln 5)5^{x^2+1} + \dfrac{2}{\sqrt{x+1}} - \dfrac{x}{(x+1)^{3/2}}$ **13.** $xe^{-x} + e^{-x} + C$ **15.** *h* is even

17. $\left(y - \dfrac{\pi}{6}\right) = \dfrac{4\sqrt{3}}{3}\left(x - \dfrac{1}{4}\right) \rightarrow y = \dfrac{4\sqrt{3}}{3}x + \left(\dfrac{\pi}{6} - \dfrac{\sqrt{3}}{3}\right)$ **19.** *d*

Problem set 84

1. $\$20{,}289.21$ **3.** $-\cos x + \dfrac{1}{3}\cos^3 x + C$ **5.** $-\dfrac{1}{3}\cos^3 x + \dfrac{1}{5}\cos^5 x + C$

7. $b = 1$ **9.** $a = 2, b = 0, c = 1 \rightarrow f(x) = x^3 + 2x^2 + 1$ **11.** $\pi \int_0^1 (1 - x)\, dx$

13. $(2x)(\ln 5)5^{x^2+1} + \arctan \dfrac{x}{2} + \dfrac{2x}{4 + x^2} + \dfrac{1}{(\ln 24)x}$

15. $\dfrac{1}{\sqrt{1 - x^2}} + \arcsin x + C$ **17.** $y = 1$ **19.** $\dfrac{32}{3}\pi$ cm^3

Problem set 85

1. $\dfrac{3}{16\pi}$ cm/sec   **3.** $\left[180{,}000 \int_0^2 y\left(\dfrac{5}{\sqrt{2}} - y\right) dy\right]$ J   **5.** $\dfrac{1}{3}\sin^3 x - \dfrac{1}{5}\sin^5 x + C$

7. $a = -1$ **9.** $y = -x + \dfrac{1}{\ln 3} - \dfrac{\ln (\ln 3)}{\ln 3}$ **11.** 0   **13.** $\dfrac{1}{12}$ unit^2

15. $\dfrac{2}{1 + 4x^2} + \dfrac{2\cos x}{\sqrt{\cos x + 1}} + \dfrac{\sin^2 x}{(\cos x + 1)^{3/2}} + \sec x \tan^2 x + \sec^3 x \tan x$

17. $\dfrac{1}{2}x^2 + \ln |x| + C$ **19.** *c*

Problem set 86

1. $\dfrac{\sqrt{2}}{2}$ **3.** $v(t) = 3t^2 - 4t; \; x(t) = t^3 - 2t^2 - 4$

5. $240{,}000 \int_{-5}^{-3} (-y)\sqrt{25 - y^2}\, dy = 5.12 \times 10^6$ J

7. False; *f* need not even be defined at $x = 0$ **9.** $\dfrac{1}{2}xe^{2x} - \dfrac{1}{4}e^{2x} + C$

11. $2\ln |x^2 + 1| + C$ **13.** $\int_0^4 \sqrt{y}\, dy$ **15.** $x = e^y + y$

17. $\dfrac{2}{\sqrt{1 - 4x^2}} + \arcsin 2x + C$ **19.**   **21.** *b*

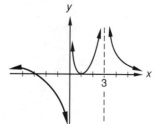

Problem set 87   **1.** $v(t) = 2 \sin t - 6$; $x(t) = -2 \cos t - 6t + 10$ **3.** 196,000 J   **5.** 11,000 N

     7. 0   **9.** 0   **11.** $-\cos x + \frac{1}{3} \cos^3 x + C$ **13.** $\frac{1}{\ln 10}(x \ln x - x) + \frac{1}{\ln 43} 43^x + C$

     15. Symmetric about y axis   **17.** $a = 2, b = 2 \to a + b = 4$

     19. $\dfrac{1 + \cos x}{\cos x} + \dfrac{(\sin x)(x + \sin x)}{(\cos x)^2} + \dfrac{2x}{1 + x^4} + e^x \csc 2x - 2e^x \csc 2x \cot 2x$ **21.** b

Problem set 88   **1.** 4 sec   **3.** $h(t) = 160 + 50t - 4.9t^2$ m; $v(t) = 50 - 9.8t$ m/sec; 5.1 sec; 12.76 sec

     5. $y = 1 + \dfrac{1}{x}$; asymptotes: $y = 1, x = 0$

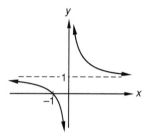

     7. $y = \dfrac{(x - 1)(x + 1)}{x}$; asymptotes: $x = 0, y = x$

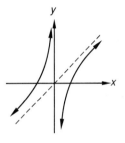

     9. $\dfrac{1}{45}$ **11.** 0   **13.** 8π units^3 **15.** 2   **17.** $\ln |x^3 + e^x| + C$

     19. Range $= \{y: -1 < y < 1\}$

Problem set 89   **1.** 8 units^2 **3.** 4000 N   **5.** 1 unit to the right of the middle 4 mass

     7. Vertical asymptote: $x = 1$; oblique asymptote: $y = 2x$

     9. $y = \dfrac{(x - 1)(x + 2)}{x + 1}$; asymptotes: $y = x, x = -1$;

       x intercepts: $x = 1, x = -2$

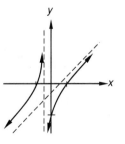

     11. 7   **13.** d

     15. $(\cos x)(e^{\sin x}) + \dfrac{2x}{x^2 + 1} + \dfrac{1}{\sqrt{1 - x^2}} - \dfrac{3}{x \ln 14}$

     17. $\dfrac{1}{2} e^{x^2 + 4x} + C$ **19.** 0   **21.** a

Problem set 90   **1.** 400,000 J   **3.** $y = 2x^2 - 3x + 1$ **5.** $\dfrac{5}{14}\pi$ units^3

     7. $\dfrac{1}{3}$ unit to the right of 12 mass   **9.** $x = 1, y = 0$ **11.** 0   **13.** $-2\sqrt{2}$

     15. $\dfrac{1}{\ln 2} 2^x + \arctan x + C$ **17.** c **19.** b

Problem set 91   **1.** $\dfrac{d\theta}{dt} = -\dfrac{2}{5}$ rad/sec   **3.** $v(t) = -25 - 9.8t$ m/sec; $h(t) = 100 - 25t - 4.9t^2$ m; 2.64 sec

     5. Left-hand derivative at $x = 1$:3; right-hand derivative at $x = 1$:2   **7.** $a + b = 3$

9. $\pi \int_0^1 (-x^4 - x^2 + 2x)\, dx$ units^3 **11.** $1\frac{3}{10}$ units to the right of 4 mass

13. $\sin x - \frac{1}{3} \sin^3 x + C$ **15.** $\frac{1}{\ln 2} 2^x + C$ **17.** $2(e^x + \sin x)^{1/2} + C$ **19.** c

Problem set 92

1. 2,508,800 J   **3.** $a = \frac{2}{3}, b = \frac{1}{3}$ **5.** $\frac{\pi}{6}$ units^3 **7.** $\frac{1}{4}\left(\frac{1}{2}x + \frac{1}{4}\sin 2x\right) + C$

9. $\frac{3}{2}$ **11.** e^x **13.** $-\frac{1}{3}\cos^3 x + \frac{1}{5}\cos^5 x + C$ **15.** $\pi e^{\sin x} + C$ **17.** -3

19. $\left(y - \frac{1}{4}\right) = -\frac{16}{3}(x - 3) \rightarrow y = -\frac{16}{3}x + \frac{65}{4}$ **21.** 5

Problem set 93

1. Minimum value of x: 5; maximum value of x: 10   **3.** $a = 0.21, b = 3.79$

5. $v(t) = -2t + 7$; $x(t) = -t^2 + 7t + 1$; $t = 2$ **7.** $a = 3, b = -2$ **9.** $\bar{y} = 3$

11. $x - \frac{1}{2}\sin 2x + C$ **13.** $-2\cos x + \frac{2}{3}\cos^3 x + C$ **15.** $\pi \int_1^4 [f(x)]^2\, dx$

17. Even function   **19.** $\frac{2}{9}(x^3 - 1)^{3/2} + C$ **21.** 0

Problem set 94

1. 12 J   **3.** 50π J   **5.** $\frac{x^2\sqrt{x^2 + 1}}{(x - 1)^4}\left(\frac{2}{x} + \frac{x}{x^2 + 1} - \frac{4}{x - 1}\right)$ **7.** $(\ln x + 1)x^x$

9. $\bar{x} = 3.16$ **11.** $3x + \frac{3}{2}\sin 2x + C$ **13.** $\frac{3}{2}$ **15.** $\frac{1}{2\ln 10}$ **17.** $\frac{29}{6}$ units^2

19. $\frac{2x\cos (x^2 + 1)}{e^x - e^{-x}} - \frac{(e^x + e^{-x})\sin (x^2 + 1)}{(e^x - e^{-x})^2} - \frac{2}{1 + 4x^2}$ **21.** b

Problem set 95

1. k is approximately 0.12, which gives us 442,943 bacteria

3. Minimum value: -1 at $x = \pi$; maximum value: $\sqrt{2}$ at $x = \frac{\pi}{4}$; inflection point at $x = \frac{3\pi}{4}$

5. $c = 2$

7. f is not differentiable on $[-2, 2]$, so the mean value theorem is not applicable

9. $x^x(\ln x + 1)$ **11.** $\frac{3}{8}$ **13.** $\pi \int_0^3 (x^4 + x^2 + 1)\, dx$ **15.** $-\cos x + \frac{1}{3}\cos^3 x + C$

17. $e^{\tan x} + C$ **19.** $\arcsin\frac{x}{3} + \frac{x}{\sqrt{9 - x^2}} + \frac{1}{\sqrt{1 + x}} - \frac{x}{2(1 + x)^{3/2}} + (\ln 3)3^x - \frac{3}{(\ln 47)x}$

Problem set 96

1. 48,000 N   **3.** $c = \frac{3}{2}$

5. Suppose f and g are odd; then $f(-x) = -f(x)$ and $g(-x) = -g(x) \rightarrow$
$(fg)(-x) = f(-x)g(-x) = [-f(x)][-g(x)] = f(x)g(x) = (fg)(x) \rightarrow$
fg is even since $(fg)(-x) = (fg)(x)$

7. 2   **9.** 1.31   **11.** -1 **13.** $\frac{1}{\sqrt{a^2 - x^2}}$ **15.** $\arcsin\frac{x}{a} + C$

17. $-e^{-x^2} + C$ **19.** a

Problem set 97

1. \$1102.50

3. $v(t) = -2t^2 - \frac{1}{\pi}\cos \pi t + \frac{9}{2}$; $x(t) = -\frac{2}{3}t^3 - \frac{1}{\pi^2}\sin \pi t + \frac{9}{2}t + \frac{1}{6}$; $v(0) = \frac{9}{2} - \frac{1}{\pi}$;

$x(0) = \frac{1}{6}$

5. 2   **7.** $2\pi^2$ units^3 **9.** $2L$ **11.** $\dfrac{1}{2(x-1)} + \cot x - \dfrac{300x^2}{x^3+1} - \dfrac{5}{x-1}$

13. 24π units^3 **15.** 4.30   **17.** $x = y^3 + y$; $f^{-1}(2) = 1$

19. $\arctan \dfrac{x}{a} + \ln |x^2 + a^2| + C$

Problem set 98   **1.** \$3727.48   **3.** $2\pi e^2$ units^3 **5.** 128 J   **7.** $y = -\dfrac{1}{x^4 + C}$ **9.** 0   **11.** $y = \dfrac{4}{3\pi}$

13. 1   **15.** $\dfrac{1}{x}$

17. $\sec 2x + 2x \sec 2x \tan 2x + \dfrac{\cos x}{b + \cos x} - \dfrac{(\sin x)(a - \sin x)}{(b + \cos x)^2} - \dfrac{1}{\sqrt{a^2 - x^2}}$ **19.** a

Problem set 99   **1.** 9.53%; \$13,377.93   **3.** $\dfrac{78,400}{3}$ N   **5.** Minimum: 0 at $x = 0$; maximum: 8 at $x = 8$

7. 4.19   **9.** (a) odd; (b) odd; (c) even   **11.** $\dfrac{1}{2}\pi$ units^2

13. Asymptotes: $y = x$, $x = 0$ **15.** $\dfrac{1}{2}e^{\sin 2x} + C$

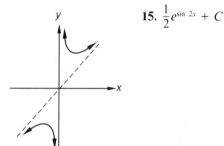

17. $\dfrac{1}{1 + x^2} + \cot x + (\ln 14)14^x - \dfrac{\sec x \tan x + e^x}{1 + x} + \dfrac{\sec x + e^x}{(1 + x)^2}$ **19.** d

Problem set 100   **1.** Dropping at rate of $\dfrac{1}{2\pi}$ cm/sec   **3.** $x(0) = 2$; $x(3) = 2$; 4.5   **5.** $t = 1$

7. $\dfrac{\sqrt{111}}{3}$ **9.** $c = \dfrac{\pi}{2}$ **11.** $\bar{x} = \dfrac{12}{5}$ **13.** $\dfrac{x^2}{2}\ln x - \dfrac{x^2}{4} + C$

15. $-\dfrac{1}{2}\csc^2 x + C$ or $-\dfrac{1}{2}\cot^2 x + C$ **17.** $\dfrac{\cos x}{1 + \sin^2 x} + \dfrac{2x}{x^2 - 1} - \dfrac{1}{(x + 1)^2}$

19. $a = 2$, $b = 0$

Problem set 101   **1.** $a(t) = \dfrac{4}{1 + t^2} - \dfrac{8t^2}{(1 + t^2)^2}$; $x(t) = 2 \ln (1 + t^2) + 4$; 0

3. $x(0) = 9$, $x(2) = 13$; 6   **5.** \$3360.28   **7.** $h(3) = 1$; $h'(3) = \dfrac{1}{5}$

9. $-\dfrac{1}{3} + \dfrac{\sqrt{13}}{3}$ **11.** $\dfrac{1}{2}\pi^2$ units^3 **13.** 0   **15.** $-k$; k

17. $y' = -\dfrac{1}{2x^{3/2}} + \dfrac{2(\cos x - \sin x)}{\sin x + \cos x}$ **19.** d

Problem set 102   **1.** $\dfrac{dr}{dt} = \dfrac{1}{\pi}$ cm/sec; 16 cm^3/sec   **3.** 90,000 N

5. 12 N; 36 J   **7.** $\pi \displaystyle\int_{-1}^{1} (y^4 - 4y^2 + 3)\, dy$ **9.** $2\pi \displaystyle\int_{2}^{3} (4 - x)e^x\, dx$ **11.** $\dfrac{2\sqrt{3}}{3}$

13. $m = 0$; $c = 0$ **15.** $\displaystyle\int_{-2}^{2} (4 - y^2)\, dy$ **17.** $[-\ln |\cos x|]_{\pi/6}^{\pi/4} \approx 0.20$ unit^2

19. $2x \cos (x^2 - 1) + \dfrac{\cos x}{e^x - 2} - \dfrac{e^x(\sin x + 1)}{(e^x - 2)^2} + \dfrac{1}{3} \ln |x^3 - 1| + C$ **21.** *a*

Problem set 103   **1.** Particle is moving to the left when $1 < t < 2$ **3.** \$6023.88   **5.** $\dfrac{17}{2}$ **7.** $\dfrac{3}{2}$

9. $2\pi \displaystyle\int_0^1 x^4(1 - x)\, dx$ **11.** $2\pi \displaystyle\int_0^\pi (2\pi - x)(\sin x)\, dx$

13. (*a*) odd; (*b*) odd; (*c*) even; (*d*) even   **15.** π units^2 **17.** $(2, \infty)$

19. $120(x - 4)^3 - 8 \cos 2x$ **21.** *a*

Problem set 104   **1.** $\dfrac{7\sqrt{15}}{30}$ m^2/sec   **3.** $-3 \cot x - 3x + C$

5. $-\dfrac{1}{2} \cot^2 x + \ln |\sin x| + C$ or $-\dfrac{1}{2} \csc^2 x - \ln |\sin x| + C$ **7.** $\dfrac{29}{2}$

9. $\pi \displaystyle\int_0^2 e^{4x}\, dx$ **11.** 1.107 rad; $\dfrac{1}{5}$ **13.** $\tan^{-1} \left(\dfrac{4 \ln \sqrt{2}}{\pi} \right)$ **15.** $-\cos x + \dfrac{1}{3} \cos^3 x + C$

17. 0.66   **19.** *d*   **21.** *b*

Problem set 105   **1.** 8 cm^2/sec   **3.** 12,800 N   **5.** $\dfrac{d}{dx}\left(\dfrac{x^3}{3} - \dfrac{1}{3} \right) = x^2; \dfrac{d}{dx} \displaystyle\int_1^x t^2\, dt = x^2$ **7.** e^{-x^2}

9. *b*   **11.** $\ln |\cos x| + \dfrac{1}{2} \tan^2 x + C$ or $\ln |\cos x| + \dfrac{1}{2} \sec^2 x + C$

13. $2\pi \displaystyle\int_0^{\pi/8} (1 + x) \sec x\, dx$ **15.** $y = -\dfrac{1}{2} \cos 2x + C$ **17.** $\dfrac{2x}{x^2 + 1} + \cot x$

19. $\ln \sqrt{2}$ **21.** $a = -2, b = 5$

Problem set 106   **1.** $\dfrac{40\sqrt{15}}{9}$ **3.** 0.25 cm^2 **5.** $x(t) = t + \ln t + (2 - \ln 3)$ **7.** e^{x^3}

9. $x - \dfrac{1}{2} \sin 2x - \cos x + \dfrac{1}{3} \cos^3 x + C$ **11.** $-2 \cot x - 2x + C$

13. $f^{-1}(2) = 1; (f^{-1})'(2) = \dfrac{1}{6}$ **15.** $c = 2$ **17.** $\displaystyle\int_1^2 \dfrac{dy}{y}$ **19.** *b*

Problem set 107   **1.** 6597 m   **3.** 303   **5.** $N(t) = 1000e^{0.1099t}$ **7.** 0   **9.** e^2

11. $2\pi \displaystyle\int_0^1 (x - x^3)\, dx$ **13.** $\pi e^{\tan x} + C$ **15.** $2c$ **17.** $3\pi \displaystyle\int_0^\pi \sin^4 x\, dx$

19. $y = \dfrac{3x^2}{\sqrt{x^3 - 1}(\sin x + \cos 2x)} - \dfrac{2\sqrt{x^3 - 1}(\cos x - 2 \sin 2x)}{(\sin x + \cos 2x)^2} + (\cos x)(e^{\sin x})$

Problem set 108   **1.** $\dfrac{1}{10}$ unit^2/sec   **3.** $-9000 \displaystyle\int_{-1}^0 y\sqrt{y + 1}\, dy$ **5.** $\arcsin x + C$

7. $\dfrac{1}{3} \arctan \dfrac{x}{3} + C$ **9.** $\dfrac{1}{2}$ **11.** $-\dfrac{\ln x}{x}$ **13.** $2\pi(\ln 2 + 1)$ units^3

15. $-\dfrac{1}{2} \ln |\cos 2x| + C$ or $\dfrac{1}{2} \ln |\sec 2x| + C$ **17.** $\dfrac{4}{9}$ **19.** *c*   **21.** *c*

Problem set 109   **1.** $4\dfrac{1}{8}$ **3.** Left when $1 < t < 3$; right when $0 \leq t < 1$ or $t > 3$; 12   **5.** 13,500 N

7. $a = 7, b = -3$ **9.** $x^2 + y^2 = y$ **11.**

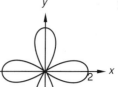

13. $\arcsin \frac{x}{2} + C$

15. $\frac{1}{2} \arctan \frac{x}{2} + C$ **17.** 0   **19.** $c = \text{arcsec} \ \frac{2}{\sqrt{\pi}}$

21. $3 \tan^2 x \sec^2 x - \dfrac{\pi \cos \pi x}{1 + cx} + \dfrac{c(1 + \sin \pi x)}{(1 + cx)^2}$

Problem set 110   **1.** $-\frac{32}{3} \pi \ \text{cm}^3/\text{sec}$ **3.** $\frac{2}{\pi}$; $c = \arcsin \frac{2}{\pi} \approx 0.69$ radian   **5.** $\frac{1}{2}(e^9 - 1)$ J

7. $-\ln |x| + \ln |x - 2| + \ln |x - 1| + C$ **9.** $r = 2$

11. $r = \cos 4\theta$

13. $\frac{1}{2} \arcsin 2x + C$ **15.** $\frac{1}{9} \ln (4 + 9x^2) + C$

17. $\sqrt{1 + x^3}$ **19.** a, b **21.** d

Problem set 111   **1.** 2 m × 4 m × 2 m; \$192   **3.** 12.57 cm²   **5.** $r = \cot \theta \csc \theta$

7. $r = 2 \cos 3\theta$

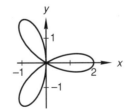

9. $r = 1 - \cos \theta$

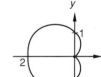

11. $r^2 = \cos 2\theta$

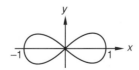

13. $\frac{7}{2} \ln |x| - \ln |x + 1| + \frac{1}{2} \ln |x + 2| + C$ **15.** $\arctan \frac{x}{4} + C$

17. Asymptotes: $y = x + 3$, $x = 2$

19. $-\cos x + \dfrac{1}{3} \cos^3 x + C$

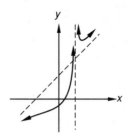

21. $\dfrac{1}{\sqrt{4 - x^2}} + e^x \cos x + e^x \sin x - \dfrac{2 \cos 2x}{x^2 + 1} + \dfrac{2x \sin 2x}{(x^2 + 1)^2}$ **23.** $a = -4$, $b = 3$

Problem set 112   **1.** $N(t) = 2000e^{0.4055t}$ **3.** $3\dfrac{1}{27}$ **5.** $2 \ln |x| - 2 \ln |x + 2| + 4(x + 2)^{-1} + C$

7. $y^2 + x^2 = y + x$ **9.** $r = 3 + 3 \sin \theta$

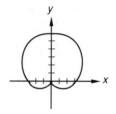

11. $r = 1 + 2 \cos \theta$ **13.** $2 \arcsin \dfrac{x}{2} + C$

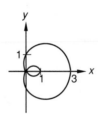

15. $-\dfrac{1}{4} \ln |\cos^4 x + 1| + C$ **17.** 0 **19.** b

21. $2x(\ln 3)3^{x^2} + \dfrac{2}{\sqrt{x - 2}} - \dfrac{2x - 1}{2(x - 2)^{3/2}} + \dfrac{\cos x}{1 + \sin x}$

Problem set 113   **1.** $3\sqrt{10}$ units/sec   **3.** $312{,}500$ N   **5.** $\dfrac{1}{2}x^2 \sin 2x + \dfrac{1}{2}x \cos 2x - \dfrac{1}{4} \sin 2x + C$

7. $x^2 e^x - 2xe^x + 2e^x + C$ **9.** $\dfrac{1}{2} \ln |x - 1| - \dfrac{1}{2} \ln |x + 1| - \dfrac{1}{x + 1} + C$

11. $r = 3 + 2 \sin \theta$ **13.** $\arcsin \dfrac{x}{3} + C$

15. $2\pi \displaystyle\int_0^1 (1 + x) \tan x \, dx$ **17.** $\dfrac{-(e^2 - e^{-2})}{2\pi}$ **19.** $\dfrac{\displaystyle\int_1^5 x\sqrt{x^2 - 1} \, dx}{\displaystyle\int_1^5 \sqrt{x^2 - 1} \, dx}$ **21.** c

Problem set 114   1. $v(t) = 5e^{4t} + 5$; $x(t) = \frac{5}{4}e^{4t} + 5t + \frac{11}{4}$; v is positive for all t, so total distance

$$= x(20) - x(5) = \frac{5}{4}(e^{80} - e^{20}) + 75$$

3. Local maximum: 6 at $x = -8$; local minimum: $-2\frac{1}{4}$ at

$x = -1$; local maximum: 18 at $x = 8$;
concave downward: $(0, 2)$;
concave upward: $(-8, 0) \cup (2, 8)$;
inflection points at $x = 0$, $x = 2$

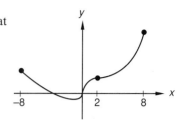

5. $\frac{dy}{dx} = \frac{2x}{3y^2 + 1}$; $\frac{d^2y}{dx^2} = \frac{2}{3y^2 + 1} - \frac{24x^2y}{(3y^2 + 1)^3}$

7. $-x^2 \cos x + 2x \sin x + 2 \cos x + C$ 9. $4 \ln |x - 1| - \frac{4}{x - 1} - 4 \ln |x| + C$

11. $r^2 = \frac{1}{\cos^2 \theta - \sin^2 \theta}$ 13. 0   15. 29   17. $2x \ln x + x$

19. $\frac{dy}{dx} = e^{x^2} + 2x^2e^{x^2} - \frac{3x^2}{2\sqrt{x^3 + 1}} - \frac{1 - \csc^2 x}{e^{-x} - 1} - \frac{e^{-x}(\cot x + x)}{(e^{-x} - 1)^2}$ 21. 9

Problem set 115   1. $-\frac{1}{3}$ unit/sec   3. $\pi \int_1^{e^2} [(\ln y)^2 + 2 \ln y] \, dy$ 5. $16\sqrt{6}$ J

7. $\frac{1}{2} \ln |x^2 + 2| + \frac{1}{\sqrt{2}} \arctan \frac{x}{\sqrt{2}} - 2 \ln |x + 1| + C$

9. $2 \ln |x| - \frac{3}{x} + \ln |x + 2| + C$ 11. $2 - \frac{\pi}{2}$ 13. $c = \frac{\sqrt{21}}{3}$

15. $-\frac{1}{3} \cos^3 x + \frac{1}{5} \cos^5 x + C$ 17. $2\sqrt{x^2 + x + 1} + C$ 19. $4 \arcsin \frac{x}{2} + C$

21. $y = \frac{3x^3}{x^3 - 1} + \ln |x^3 - 1| - 2 \sec 2x \tan 2x$

Problem set 116   1. Minimum: 0 at $x = 0$; maximum: $\frac{1}{2e}$ at $x = \frac{1}{2}$ 3. e 5. $\frac{1}{x}$

7. $\frac{1}{2} \ln |x^2 + 1| - 2 \arctan x + 3 \ln |x - 1| + C$ 9. $-e^x \cos x + e^x \sin x + C$

11.

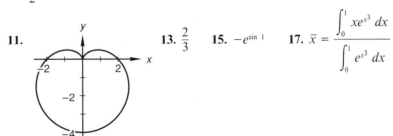

13. $\frac{2}{3}$ 15. $-e^{\sin 1}$ 17. $\bar{x} = \dfrac{\displaystyle\int_0^1 xe^{x^3} \, dx}{\displaystyle\int_0^1 e^{x^3} \, dx}$

19. $\frac{\cos x}{1 + \sin^2 x} - \frac{(\ln 2)2^x}{e^{2x} - \sin x} + \frac{2^x(2e^{2x} - \cos x)}{(e^{2x} - \sin x)^2}$

Problem set 117   1. D 3. $\pi \int_0^3 \{[1 - x(x - 3)]^2 - 1\} \, dx$ 5. b 7. $\cos x$

9. $\frac{2 + 2y - 2x}{(x + 1)^2}$ 11. $x^2 \sin x + 2x \cos x - 2 \sin x + C$

13. $\ln |x| + \dfrac{2}{x} + \arctan x + C$ **15.** $\dfrac{4}{3} \arctan \dfrac{2x}{3} + C$ **17.** $y = \dfrac{1}{2}x + \dfrac{1}{4} - \ln 2$

19. Given ε; choose $\delta = \dfrac{\varepsilon}{2}$. Then $1 - \delta < x < 1 + \delta$ implies $6 - \varepsilon < 2x + 4 < 6 + \varepsilon$

21. (a) $\displaystyle\int_0^1 x \, dx = \dfrac{1}{2}$;

(b) ith subinterval: $\left[\dfrac{i-1}{n}, \dfrac{i}{n}\right]$; $f(x_i) = f\left(\dfrac{i}{n}\right) = \dfrac{i}{n}$;

(c) $\displaystyle\sum_{i=1}^{n} \dfrac{1}{n} f(x_i) = \sum_{i=1}^{n} \dfrac{1}{n}\dfrac{i}{n} = \dfrac{1}{n^2}\sum_{i=1}^{n} i = \dfrac{1}{n^2}\left[\dfrac{1}{2}n(n+1)\right] = \dfrac{n+1}{2n}$;

(d) $\displaystyle\lim_{n\to\infty} \sum_{i=1}^{n} \dfrac{1}{n} f(x_i) = \lim_{n\to\infty} \dfrac{n+1}{2n} = \dfrac{1}{2}$

APPENDIX *Important formulas, facts, and rules*

Formulas from solid and plane geometry

CIRCLE Area $= \pi r^2$

Circumference $= 2\pi r$

SECTOR OF A CIRCLE Area of sector $= \dfrac{\theta r^2}{2}$

$s = r\theta$

TRIANGLE Area $= \dfrac{1}{2}bh = \dfrac{1}{2}ab \sin \theta$

$= \dfrac{1}{2}bc \sin x$

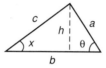

Area (Heron's formula) $= \sqrt{s(s - a)(s - b)(s - c)}$ where $s = \dfrac{1}{2}(a + b + c)$

Law of cosines: $c^2 = a^2 + b^2 - 2ab \cos \theta$

RIGHT TRIANGLE Pythagorean theorem: $a^2 + b^2 = c^2$

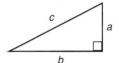

PARALLELOGRAM Area $= bh$

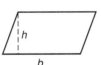

TRAPEZOID Area $= \dfrac{h}{2}(b_1 + b_2)$

RIGHT CIRCULAR CONE Volume $= \dfrac{\pi r^2 h}{3}$

Lateral surface area $= \pi r \sqrt{r^2 + h^2}$

RIGHT CIRCULAR CYLINDER Volume $= \pi r^2 h$

Lateral surface area $= 2\pi rh$

SPHERE   Volume $= \dfrac{4}{3} \pi r^3$

Surface area $= 4\pi r^2$

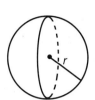

Important formulas and identities from trigonometry

$$\csc x = \frac{1}{\sin x} \qquad \sec x = \frac{1}{\cos x} \qquad \cot x = \frac{1}{\tan x} \qquad \tan x = \frac{\sin x}{\cos x} \qquad \cot x = \frac{\cos x}{\sin x}$$

$$\sin(-x) = -\sin x \qquad \cos(-x) = \cos x \qquad \tan(-x) = -\tan x$$

$$\csc(-x) = -\csc x \qquad \sec(-x) = \sec x \qquad \cot(-x) = -\cot x$$

$$\sin^2 x + \cos^2 x = 1 \qquad \tan^2 x + 1 = \sec^2 x \qquad 1 + \cot^2 x = \csc^2 x$$

$$\sin(A + B) = \sin A \cos B + \cos A \sin B \qquad \sin(A - B) = \sin A \cos B - \cos A \sin B$$

$$\cos(A + B) = \cos A \cos B - \sin A \sin B \qquad \cos(A - B) = \cos A \cos B + \sin A \sin B$$

$$\tan(A + B) = \frac{\tan A + \tan B}{1 - \tan A \tan B} \qquad \tan(A - B) = \frac{\tan A - \tan B}{1 + \tan A \tan B}$$

$$\cos 2A = \cos^2 A - \sin^2 A \qquad \cos 2A = 1 - 2\sin^2 A \qquad \cos 2A = 2\cos^2 A - 1$$

$$\sin 2A = 2 \sin A \cos A \qquad \cos^2 A = \frac{1}{2} + \frac{1}{2}\cos 2A \qquad \sin^2 A = \frac{1}{2} - \frac{1}{2}\cos 2A$$

$$\sin A \cos B = \frac{1}{2}[\sin(A + B) + \sin(A - B)] \qquad \cos A \sin B = \frac{1}{2}[\sin(A + B) - \sin(A - B)]$$

$$\sin A \sin B = \frac{1}{2}[\cos(A - B) - \cos(A + B)] \qquad \cos A \cos B = \frac{1}{2}[\cos(A - B) + \cos(A + B)]$$

$$\sin x + \sin y = 2 \sin \frac{x + y}{2} \cos \frac{x - y}{2} \qquad \sin x - \sin y = 2 \cos \frac{x + y}{2} \sin \frac{x - y}{2}$$

$$\cos x + \cos y = 2 \sin \frac{x + y}{2} \cos \frac{x - y}{2} \qquad \cos x - \cos y = -2 \sin \frac{x + y}{2} \sin \frac{x - y}{2}$$

Differentiation facts and rules

DERIVATIVE FORM   DIFFERENTIAL FORM

SUM AND DIFFERENCE RULES

$$\frac{d}{dx}(u \pm v) = \frac{du}{dx} \pm \frac{dv}{dx} \qquad\qquad d(u \pm v) = du \pm dv$$

CONSTANT-MULTIPLE RULE

$$\frac{d}{dx}(cu) = c\frac{du}{dx} \qquad\qquad d(cu) = c\, du$$

PRODUCT RULE

$$\frac{d}{dx}(uv) = u\frac{dv}{dx} + v\frac{du}{dx} \qquad\qquad d(uv) = u\, dv + v\, du$$

QUOTIENT RULE

$$\frac{d}{dx}\left(\frac{u}{v}\right) = \frac{v\dfrac{du}{dx} - u\dfrac{dv}{dx}}{v^2} \qquad\qquad d\left(\frac{u}{v}\right) = \frac{v\, du - u\, dv}{v^2}$$

POWER FUNCTIONS	$\dfrac{d}{dx}\,u^n = nu^{n-1}\,\dfrac{du}{dx}$	$d(u^n) = nu^{n-1}\,du$
EXPONENTIAL FUNCTIONS	$\dfrac{d}{dx}\,e^u = e^u\,\dfrac{du}{dx}$	$d(e^u) = e^u\,du$
	$\dfrac{d}{dx}\,a^u = (\ln a)(a^u)\,\dfrac{du}{dx}$	$d(a^u) = (\ln a)(a^u)\,du$
LOGARITHMIC FUNCTIONS	$\dfrac{d}{dx}\,\ln u = \dfrac{1}{u}\,\dfrac{du}{dx} \quad (u > 0)$	$d(\ln u) = \dfrac{1}{u}\,du \quad (u > 0)$
	$\dfrac{d}{dx}\,\ln |u| = \dfrac{1}{u}\,\dfrac{du}{dx} \quad (u \neq 0)$	$d(\ln |u|) = \dfrac{1}{u}\,du \quad (u \neq 0)$
	$\dfrac{d}{dx}\,\log_a u = \dfrac{1}{\ln a}\,\dfrac{1}{u}\,\dfrac{du}{dx}$	$d(\log_a u) = \dfrac{1}{\ln a}\,\dfrac{1}{u}\,\dfrac{du}{dx}$
SINE FUNCTION	$\dfrac{d}{dx}\,\sin u = \cos u\,\dfrac{du}{dx}$	$d(\sin u) = \cos u\,du$
COSINE FUNCTION	$\dfrac{d}{dx}\,\cos u = -\sin u\,\dfrac{du}{dx}$	$d(\cos u) = -\sin u\,du$
TANGENT FUNCTION	$\dfrac{d}{dx}\,\tan u = \sec^2 u\,\dfrac{du}{dx}$	$d(\tan u) = \sec^2 u\,du$
COTANGENT FUNCTION	$\dfrac{d}{dx}\,\cot u = -\csc^2 u\,\dfrac{du}{dx}$	$d(\cot u) = -\csc^2 u\,du$
SECANT FUNCTION	$\dfrac{d}{dx}\,\sec u = \sec u \tan u\,\dfrac{du}{dx}$	$d(\sec u) = \sec u \tan u\,du$
COSECANT FUNCTION	$\dfrac{d}{dx}\,\csc u = -\csc u \cot u\,\dfrac{du}{dx}$	$d(\csc u) = -\csc u \cot u\,du$
ARCSINE FUNCTION	$\dfrac{d}{dx}\,\arcsin\dfrac{u}{a} = \dfrac{1}{\sqrt{a^2 - u^2}}\,\dfrac{du}{dx}$	$d\left(\arcsin\dfrac{u}{a}\right) du = \dfrac{1}{\sqrt{a^2 - u^2}}\,du$
ARCCOSINE FUNCTION	$\dfrac{d}{dx}\,\arccos\dfrac{u}{a} = -\dfrac{1}{\sqrt{a^2 - u^2}}\,\dfrac{du}{dx}$	$d\left(\arccos\dfrac{u}{a}\right) = -\dfrac{1}{\sqrt{a^2 - u^2}}\,du$
ARCTANGENT FUNCTION	$\dfrac{d}{dx}\,\arctan\dfrac{u}{a} = \dfrac{a}{a^2 + u^2}\,\dfrac{du}{dx}$	$d\left(\arctan\dfrac{u}{a}\right) = \dfrac{a}{a^2 + u^2}\,du$
ARCCOTANGENT FUNCTION	$\dfrac{d}{dx}\,\text{arccot}\dfrac{u}{a} = -\dfrac{a}{a^2 + u^2}\,\dfrac{du}{dx}$	$d\left(\text{arccot}\dfrac{u}{a}\right) = -\dfrac{a}{a^2 + u^2}\,du$
ARCSECANT FUNCTION $\left(\dfrac{u}{a} > 0\right)$	$\dfrac{d}{dx}\,\text{arcsec}\dfrac{u}{a} = \dfrac{a}{u\sqrt{u^2 - a^2}}\,\dfrac{du}{dx}$	$d\left(\text{arcsec}\dfrac{u}{a}\right) = \dfrac{a}{u\sqrt{u^2 - a^2}}\,du$
ARCCOSECANT FUNCTION $\left(\dfrac{u}{a} > 0\right)$	$\dfrac{d}{dx}\,\text{arccsc}\dfrac{u}{a} = -\dfrac{a}{u\sqrt{u^2 - a^2}}\,\dfrac{du}{dx}$	$d\left(\text{arccsc}\dfrac{u}{a}\right) = -\dfrac{a}{u\sqrt{u^2 - a^2}}\,du$
ABSOLUTE VALUE FUNCTION	$\dfrac{d}{dx}\,|u| = \dfrac{|u|}{u}$	$d(|u|) = \dfrac{|u|}{u}\,du$

Integration techniques and facts

INTEGRATION BY PARTS

$$\int u \, dv = uv - \int v \, du$$

POWER FUNCTIONS

$$\int u^n \, du = \frac{1}{n+1} u^{n+1} + C \quad (n \neq -1)$$

$$\int \frac{1}{u} \, du = \ln |u| + C$$

EXPONENTIAL FUNCTIONS

$$\int e^u \, du = e^u + C \qquad \int a^u \, du = \frac{1}{\ln a} a^u + C$$

SINE FUNCTION

$$\int \sin u \, du = -\cos u + C$$

COSINE FUNCTION

$$\int \cos u \, du = \sin u + C$$

TANGENT FUNCTION

$$\int \tan u \, du = \ln |\sec u| + C$$

COTANGENT FUNCTION

$$\int \cot u \, du = \ln |\sin u| + C$$

SECANT FUNCTION

$$\int \sec u \, du = \ln |\sec u + \tan u| + C$$

COSECANT FUNCTION

$$\int \csc u \, du = \ln |\csc u - \cot u| + C$$

ARCSINE FUNCTION

$$\int \arcsin u \, du = u \arcsin u + \frac{1}{a} \sqrt{1 - u^2} + C$$

ARCTANGENT FUNCTION

$$\int \arctan u \, du = u \arctan u - \frac{1}{2} \ln (1 + u^2) + C$$

OTHER IMPORTANT INTEGRALS

$$\int \sec^2 x \, dx = \tan x + C$$

$$\int \sec x \tan x \, dx = \sec x + C$$

$$\int \csc^2 x \, dx = -\cot x + C$$

$$\int \csc x \cot x \, dx = -\csc x + C$$

$$\int \frac{dx}{\sqrt{a^2 - x^2}} = \arcsin \frac{x}{a} + C$$

$$\int \frac{dx}{x^2 + a^2} = \frac{1}{a} \arctan \frac{x}{a} + C$$

$$\int \sin^n x \, dx = -\frac{\sin^{n-1} x \cos x}{n} + \frac{n-1}{n} \int \sin^{n-2} x \, dx$$

$$\int \cos^n x \, dx = \frac{\cos^{n-1} x \sin x}{n} + \frac{n-1}{n} \int \cos^{n-2} x \, dx$$

**LESS FREQUENTLY
ENCOUNTERED
INTEGRALS**

$$\int \frac{dx}{\sqrt{a^2 + x^2}} = \ln(x + \sqrt{x^2 + a^2}) + C \qquad (x > a \text{ or } x < -a)$$

$$\int \frac{dx}{\sqrt{x^2 - a^2}} = \ln|x + \sqrt{x^2 - a^2}| + C \qquad (x > a \text{ or } x < -a)$$

$$\int \frac{dx}{x\sqrt{a^2 - x^2}} = \frac{1}{a} \ln\left|\frac{a - \sqrt{a^2 + x^2}}{x}\right| + C$$

$$\int \frac{dx}{x\sqrt{x^2 - a^2}} = \frac{1}{a} \operatorname{arcsec} \frac{x}{a} + C$$

$$\int \sqrt{a^2 - x^2}\, dx = \frac{x}{2}\sqrt{a^2 - x^2} + \frac{a^2}{2} \arcsin \frac{x}{a} + C$$

$$\int \sqrt{a^2 + x^2}\, dx = \frac{x}{2}\sqrt{a^2 + x^2} + \frac{a^2}{2} \ln(x + \sqrt{x^2 + a^2}) + C$$

$$\int \sqrt{x^2 - a^2}\, dx = \frac{x}{2}\sqrt{x^2 - a^2} - \frac{a^2}{2} \ln|x + \sqrt{x^2 - a^2}| + C$$

$$\int \sin ax \cos bx\, dx = -\frac{\cos(a + b)x}{2(a + b)} - \frac{\cos(a - b)x}{2(a - b)} + C \qquad a^2 \neq b^2$$

$$\int \sin ax \sin bx\, dx = \frac{\sin(a - b)x}{2(a - b)} - \frac{\sin(a + b)x}{2(a + b)} + C \qquad a^2 \neq b^2$$

$$\int \cos ax \cos bx\, dx = \frac{\sin(a - b)x}{2(a - b)} + \frac{\sin(a + b)x}{2(a + b)} + C \qquad a^2 \neq b^2$$

$$\int \sin^n ax \cos^m ax\, dx = -\frac{\sin^{n-1} ax \cos^{m+1} ax}{a(m + n)} + \frac{n - 1}{m + n} \int \sin^{n-2} ax \cos^m ax\, dx \qquad n \neq -m$$

$$\int \sin^n ax \cos^m ax\, dx = \frac{\sin^{n+1} ax \cos^{m-1} ax}{a(m + n)} + \frac{m - 1}{m + n} \int \sin^n ax \cos^{m-2} ax\, dx \qquad m \neq -n$$

$$\int \tan^n ax\, dx = \frac{\tan^{n-1} ax}{a(n - 1)} - \int \tan^{n-2} ax\, dx \qquad n \neq 1$$

$$\int \cot^n ax\, dx = -\frac{\cot^{n-1} ax}{a(n - 1)} - \int \cot^{n-2} ax\, dx \qquad n \neq 1$$

$$\int \sec^n ax\, dx = \frac{\sec^{n-2} ax \tan ax}{a(n - 1)} + \frac{n - 2}{n - 1} \int \sec^{n-2} ax\, dx \qquad n \neq 1$$

$$\int \csc^n ax\, dx = -\frac{\csc^{n-2} ax \cot ax}{a(n - 1)} + \frac{n - 2}{n - 1} \int \csc^{n-2} ax\, dx \qquad n \neq 1$$

Index